THE NEGOTIATION

SOURCEBOOK

Second Edition

edited by

IRA ASHERMAN
and
SANDRA ASHERMAN

HRD PRESS

Published by:
HRD Press
22 Amherst Road
Amherst, MA 01002
1-800-822-2801 (U.S. and Canada)
413-253-3488
413-253-3490 (FAX)
www.hrdpress.com

ISBN 0-87425-604-6

Cover design by Eileen Klockars
Editorial services by Suzanne Bay
Production services by CompuDesign

TABLE OF CONTENTS

www.asherman.com

Introduction ix

Section I.   **Negotiation: A Framework**

Chapter One   Approaches To Negotiation 3

   Understanding Competing Theories of Negotiation . . . . 5 *
      John S. Murray   *collaborative of accomodating backup style*

   Negotiating: A Conceptual Model . . . . 15 *
      Willem F. G. Mastenbroek

   Negotiation Today: Everyone Wins. 29
      Beverly Byrum-Robinson

Chapter Two   Conflict Resolution 41

   Use of the Collaborative Ethic and Contingency Theories
      in Conflict Management 43
      Susan Hoefflinger Taft

   Managing Conflict and Disagreement Constructively 53
      Herbert S. Kindler

Chapter Three   Power 59

   The Bases of Social Power . . . . 61 *
      John R.P. French, Jr. and Bertram Raven

   Negotiating Power: Getting and Using Influence 75
      Roger Fisher

Section II.   **Persuasion**

Chapter Four   Trust and Negotiation 89

Trust and Managerial Problem-Solving 91*
Dale E. Zand

The Parking Space Theory Sheet. 105
Fred E. Jandt

The Paradox of Trust and Mistrust 109*
David S. Weiss

Chapter Five   The Influence Process 119

How to Increase Your Influence. 121
David E. Berlew

The Tactics and Ethics of Persuasion 125*
Philip G. Zimbardo

The Language of Persuasion. 139*
David Kipnis and Stuart Schmidt

Section III.   **Negotiator Competencies**

Chapter Six   Negotiator Skills 147

Style and Effectiveness in Negotiation. 149*
Gerald R. Williams

Today's Negotiator 167
Ira G. Asherman and Sandy Asherman

The Art of Negotiation: An Essential Management Skill 171*
David Kuechle

Achieving Integrative Agreements. 187
Dean G. Pruitt

Chapter Seven   Planning and Preparation. 197

Before You Negotiate: Get Your Act Together. 199*
Gary G. Whitney

Teamwork. 211*
Bill Scott

team negotiations

How to organize your team

Chapter Eight   Negotiation Failure 217

       Why Negotiations Go Wrong 219
       Max H. Bazerman

       How to Avoid the Eight Biggest Negotiating Traps 225
       Bob Busch and Phil Faris

Section IV.   **Gender Issues in Negotiation**

Chapter Nine   Women at the Bargaining Table 233

       Our Game, Your Rules: Developing Effective Negotiating
       Approaches. 235
       Leonard Greenhaigh and Roderick W. Gilkey

       The Power of Talk: Who Gets Heard and Why. 245
       Deborah Tannen

       Her Place at the Table: A Consideration of Gender
       Issues in Negotiation 259
       Deborah M. Kolb and Gloria G. Coolidge

Section V.   **Cross-Cultural Negotiation**

Chapter Ten   International Negotiations 279

       The Nuances of Negotiating Overseas 281
       David N. Burt

       Hofstede's Dimensions: A High-Level Analytical Tool for
       Working Internationally 291
       John W. Bing

       Negotiating Across Cultures. 297
       Gary P. Ferraro

       The Basics of Intercultural Communication 309
       The American Society for Training and Development

Chapter Eleven   Negotiating with Americans 317

       Welcome To America: Watch Out for Culture Shock 319
       David Stamps

[handwritten note:] Hofstede's Book "Culture and Organizations"

· · · · ·

Negotiators Abroad: Don't Shoot from the Hip! 329
    John L. Graham and Roy A. Herberger, Jr.

American Values and Assumptions 341
    Gary Althen

Section VI.   **Individual Differences**

Chapter Twelve   Dealing with Difficult People 353

When the Boss Is a Bully 355
    Hara Estroff Marano

Taking the Bull Out of the Bully 359*
    Len Leritz

How to Negotiate with Really Tough Guys 367
    An Interview with Bill Richardson

Chapter Thirteen   Dealing with Stakeholders 371

Stakeholder Negotiations: Building Bridges with
    Corporate Constituents 373
    Ram Charan and R. Edward Freeman

How to Negotiate with Employee Objectors. 381
    David W. Ewing

Section VII.   **Team-Based Negotiation**

Chapter Fourteen   Negotiating in Groups 393

Negotiating Group Decisions 395
    Jeanne M. Brett

The Group and What Happens On the Way To "Yes" 413
    Deborah G. Ancona, Raymond A. Friedman,
    and Deborah M. Kolb

*Newsletter
Jay Cherny*

Section VIII.   **Individual Negotiations**

Chapter Fifteen   Career Negotiations. 433

How to Ask for a Raise 435
Jeff B. Copeland and Peter McKillop

How to Negotiate a Job Transfer 437
William C. Banks

Don't Just Sit There—Negotiate 441
*Nkiru Asika, Kevin J. Delaney, Brooke Deterline,
and Vera Gibbons*

Chapter Sixteen   Personal Negotiations 451

How Much Will You Pay for This Hotel Room? Too Much 453
Everett Potter

Dealer Tactics and How to Counter Them. 461
Burke Leon and Stephanie Leon

Bargain for That House Like a Pro. 469
*from Kiplinger/Changing Times:
Guide to Buying and Selling a Home*

INTRODUCTION

Welcome to the second edition of *The Negotiation Sourcebook*. As in the first edition, our primary concern is to address the needs of active negotiators—the men and women who negotiate with vendors, government officials, and co-workers. The articles were selected to cover a cross section of the negotiations that you are likely to encounter. There are also a number of articles that provide different theoretical frameworks for the negotiation process, since it is our strong belief that to be an effective negotiator, you must have much more than technique.

In approaching this first revision of *The Negotiation Sourcebook*, we paid particular attention to the comments we received from readers of the first edition and from participants in our *Successful Negotiator* workshops. With these comments in mind, we added seven new chapters and altered a number of others. The new chapters are:

- Conflict Resolution (Chapter 2)
- Trust and Negotiation (Chapter 4)
- Women at the Bargaining Table (Chapter 9)
- International Negotiations (Chapter 10)
- Negotiating with Americans (Chapter 11)
- Dealing with Difficult People (Chapter 12)
- Negotiating in Groups (Chapter 14)

- Career Negotiations (Chapter 15)
- Personal Negotiations (Chapter 16)

OUR PHILOSOPHY

We do not negotiate in a vacuum, but rather within the context of a relationship, the nature of which directly impacts the outcome of the negotiation. Since we first began conducting negotiating seminars for corporate executives more than twenty years ago, we have become more convinced than ever that the best approach to the negotiating process is through problem-solving and collaboration. The collaborative methodology supports our strong belief that the relationship of the parties involved is every bit as important as the outcome of a particular deal. This is most true in large corporations, where relationships are ongoing and where one cannot easily walk away to find another supplier.

Not everyone readily accepts the collaborative approach we find most helpful. Accordingly, we have included several articles on how to deal with people who use different styles of negotiation.

HOW TO USE THIS BOOK

The Sourcebook is divided into eight sections, each covering a particular area. The areas are divided into consecutive chapters, from 1–16. The easiest way to use it is to look for those chapters that directly address issues that concern you today. If you are new to the field of negotiations, we suggest that you read the articles in the first section (Approaches to Negotiation) before moving on to the sections and chapters that examine specific situations.

Many of the chapters in this book were included in the previous edition. They proved to be particularly useful, so we are including them again. The newer ones address current issues or take a more detailed look at an important topic. The book is organized into the following sections and chapters:

SECTION 1—NEGOTIATION: A FRAMEWORK

The initial section of the book is designed to provide a conceptual framework and overview of the negotiation process.

Chapter 1—Approaches To Negotiation

"Negotiating Today—Everyone Wins" by Beverly Byrum-Robinson is the one new article in this chapter; the remaining two are from the first edition. The first article, by John S. Murray, reviews the differences between the competitive and collaborative approaches to negotiation. He discusses the basic assumptions, the behavioral patterns, and the downside risks associated with each approach. The second article, by Dutch consultant Willem Mastenbroek, offers a conceptual model based on two distinct perspectives. Ms. Robinson's article provides a broad overview of the negotiating process, but breaks it down into six major elements common to all negotiations.

Chapter 2—Conflict Resolution

So much of what happens in negotiation involves or is caused by some type of conflict between the parties. Sometimes, the conflict is clear and on the surface but it is often hidden and not quite so obvious. Resolving the conflict is critical, however, if the negotiation is to be successfully concluded. Both of the articles in this chapter, new to this edition, provide a framework for looking at conflict within a collaborative process.

The first article, "Use of the Collaborative Ethic and Contingency Theories in Conflict Management" by Susan Hoefflinger Taft, explores the relationship between collaborative and contingency theories and their impact on conflict management.

In "Managing Conflict and Disagreement Constructively," Herbert S. Kindler identifies three core principles he believes ought to be used in conflict management. He outlines nine strategies that derive from these core principles and decisions and provides a clear process for managing conflict. Chapters one and two provide an in-depth look at the collaborative framework in which we believe most negotiation should take place.

Chapter 3—Power

Negotiations are frequently affected by how much power we have—or perceive that we have. These articles explore the sources of power available to us, as well as ways to effectively use them. In the first article, John French and Bertram Raven discuss five types of power that we all bring to relationships, in varying degrees. While not directly addressing issues specific to negotiation, their analysis applies to the negotiation process, as well.

In the second article, Roger Fisher discusses six elements of negotiating power and provides the would-be negotiator with a checklist of what can be done before entering any negotiation in order to enhance one's negotiating position. Taken together, the two articles give today's negotiator an integrated view of power and its sources.

Section 2—PERSUASION

The two chapters in this section explore various issues critical to the influence process.

Chapter 4—Trust and Negotiation

We believe strongly that all negotiations take place within the context of a relationship, and that *the most important aspect of that relationship is the degree of trust that exists between the parties.* Without sufficient trust, negotiation is severely compromised and much more difficult. All the articles in this chapter are new, chosen to provide a look at the research as well as the application of trust to the negotiation process.

The initial article by Dale Zand does not directly address the issue of negotiation, but rather looks at the impact of trust on group problem-solving effectiveness. However, we believe Zand's findings have strong implications for the process of negotiation.

"The Parking Space Theory Sheet" by Fred Jandt looks directly at the impact of trust on the negotiation process. It is brief and to-the-point.

In the third selection, David Weiss talks about the importance of trust and discusses the steps we can take to be more trustworthy. It was taken from his book *Beyond the Walls of Conflict.*

Chapter 5—The Influence Process

Negotiation is really an attempt to influence the other party to accept your point of view—to say *yes.* This chapter examines the issues involved in accomplishing that objective. The articles are all from the first edition, as relevant today as they were when we first presented them. In the first article, David E. Berlew suggests that the use of logical arguments is not always effective in gaining commitment. The option he recommends is one called "exchange strategy." As Berlew describes it, "There are three critical elements: Know what you want. Ask for it. And then be

prepared to pay for it." Phillip Zimbardo's article draws upon the research of social psychologists and identifies several approaches that can be used to bring about attitude change. The paper was originally prepared to help students persuade adults to use their voting power to promote peace, but the techniques Zimbardo explains can be easily applied to all areas of influence.

In the third article, David Kipnis and Stuart Schmidt report on their research with dating couples and business managers. The article explores the approaches used by these two groups to influence others, and the factors that affect an individual's choice of negotiating style.

Section 3—NEGOTIATOR COMPETENCIES

This section presents several different approaches to examining the skills of the effective negotiator. You will no doubt see yourself in some or all of these descriptions.

Chapter 6—Negotiator Skills

This chapter includes two of the articles in the first edition, as well as two new ones that we feel add more depth and a greater understanding of the skills required of successful negotiators.

In the first new article, "Style and Effectiveness in Negotiation," Gerald Williams reports on a study conducted at Brigham Young University that examined the negotiating patterns of experienced lawyers. While the study is a narrow one, the results are instructive for all of us.

Sandy and Ira Asherman, the editors of this Sourcebook, contributed the second new article, entitled "Today's Negotiator." In it they detail the steps negotiators need to take during the three key phases of the negotiation process: 1) the planning phase, 2) when the parties meet, and 3) during the follow-up or implementation phase. The third article, David Kuechle's "The

Art of Negotiation: An Essential Management Skill," examines the skills of the effective negotiator through several case studies—two involving companies in the U.S. and Canada, and a third involving an Iranian hostage crisis. In Kuechle's own words, "We will identify the ingredients of success and judge whether these ingredients have transfer value to other settings."

The last article, "Achieving Integrative Agreements" by Dean Pruitt, stresses the importance of integrative or collaborative solutions, and presents several approaches to achieving them.

Chapter 7—Planning and Preparation

Critical to any negotiator's success is the effectiveness of his/her planning. Too many of us leave planning to the last minute, sometimes failing to understand all of the issues or implications or even failing to clarify what our settlement options are.

Gary Whitney's "Before You Negotiate—Get Your Act Together" describes the critical issues we must consider when preparing for a negotiation. Gary provides a checklist to aid the planning process.

Because of their complexity, many negotiations involve teams of negotiators, but negotiating in a team requires some very specific skills. Bill Scott's "Teamwork" looks directly at this issue in terms of planning: In it he answers the question of how to organize your team, and describes the different roles people must take on if the negotiating team is to be effective.

Chapter 8—Negotiation Failure

Not all negotiations go as we expect; unfortunately, we do not always realize what went wrong. The two articles in this chapter should provide you with some answers. Max Bazerman's article "Why Negotiations Go Wrong" appeared in our first edition. In it, he explains many of the psychological traps we get ourselves into that tend to complicate or undermine our work. Bob

Busch and Phil Faris take a somewhat different perspective in what they see as "The Eight Most Common Negotiation Traps," and provide a solution for each one and a checklist for your specific situation.

When we began looking at the issues that interest and even perplex today's organizational leaders, we knew immediately that we needed to explore the particular challenges women face in negotiations. Section IV is devoted exclusively to this important topic.

Chapter 9—Women at the Bargaining Table

Of the three articles in this chapter, one is from the first edition—Leonard Greenhaigh's and Roderick W. Gilkey's article, "Our Game, Your Rules: Developing Effective Negotiating Approaches."

Greenhaigh and Gilkey describe their research that explored the differences in how men and women approach negotiation. They also examine the implications of their research for individual skill development, as well as for future research.

While not directly related to negotiation, the second article, Deborah Tannen's "The Power of Talk: Who Gets Heard and Why," looks at the different ways men and women communicate. Understanding those differences can be of significant value when we negotiate with members of the opposite sex.

The Kolb and Coolidge article, "Her Place at the Table," takes a much broader look at gender differences at the bargaining table. The article explores four themes that the authors believe are unique to understanding how women "frame" and conduct negotiations.

Section 5—CROSS-CULTURAL NEGOTIATION

So many of the negotiations we conduct today are with people from other nations or from different cultures, proving once again that we do not have to leave our own country to be involved with cross-cultural negotiations. This new section provides a broader framework for looking at cultural issues and the potential impact of these issues on the negotiation process.

Chapter 10—International Negotiations

This new chapter explores the subject of cultural differences and the way our knowledge of them can affect our negotiation success. David Burt's important article appeared also in the first edition; the remaining selections are all new.

Burt's article, "The Nuances of Negotiating Overseas," looks at individual countries and at specific issues we need to concern ourselves with when negotiating in those countries. He focuses on communication within a cross-cultural framework.

John Bing's article, "Hofstede's Dimensions," provides us with a look at the pioneering work of Geert Hofstede, the first person to use quantitative approaches to look at the influence of culture in the workplace. "Negotiating Across Cultures" by Gary P. Ferraro provides us with a list of useful strategies and approaches for increasing our success when working in another culture. The last article, "The Basics of Intercultural Communication," explores the communication process and explains the basics of this important area.

Chapter 11—Negotiating with Americans

We are working with an increasing number of non-American clients who find themselves confused and perplexed when dealing with Americans. The articles in this chapter are designed to make it easier for others to work with Americans, but the articles should be read by Americans and non-Americans alike. Davis Stamp's "Welcome to America: Watch Out for Culture Shock" provides the non-American with some very direct advice on dealing with Americans, and Graham and Herberger's "Negotiators Abroad: Don't Shoot

from the Hip!" (from our first book) provides an overview of the different negotiating styles Americans assume, as well as some of the problems they create at the international bargaining table. "American Values and Assumptions," taken from Gary Althen's *American Ways*, considers the values and assumptions that Americans live by. As a group, these three articles give non-Americans a solid perspective concerning U.S. culture.

Section 6—INDIVIDUAL DIFFERENCES

The two chapters in this section discuss how to deal with the people in our lives—particularly those who sometimes put pressure on us to act in ways with which we don't necessarily agree. This section provides some real help in dealing with them.

Chapter 12—Dealing with Difficult People

We have all worked with at least one difficult person, either on the job or in our personal lives. Questions about how to deal with difficult people, in fact, are the most frequently asked questions in our workshops, so we know it is a problem many of you are struggling with. The articles in this chapter are new to this edition and are designed to help the reader to deal with difficult individuals. Hara Marano's article looks at the difficult boss and provides suggestions about how to survive in the environment they create.

In the second article, a chapter from Len Leritz's *No Fault Negotiating*, the author takes us from our difficult boss to the difficult person in general, and explores how we can understand and deal with them.

The third article, first published in Fortune Magazine, is a brief interview with Bill Richardson, a seven-term U.S. Congressman who, at the time of the interview, had been representing the United States in some very critical and difficult international negotiations. In this article he shares his insights on negotiating with difficult people.

Chapter 13—Dealing with Stakeholders

Teams as well as individuals negotiate with outsiders, be they co-workers, politicians, or activist groups. These people or groups present negotiators with some very unique problems. We found all the articles, taken from the first edition, equally relevant today, providing insight into how these challenging issues can be addressed. The initial article, by Ram Charan and R. Edward Freeman, discusses the importance of stakeholder negotiations and provides a framework for conducting them. David Ewing's article focuses on a very specific stakeholder group—employee objectors—and discusses how to effectively negotiate with them.

The challenges facing teams of people who are expected to explore broad topics and then come together on decisions that have far-reaching implications are vastly different from the challenges facing a single negotiator. We chose to present this timely information in a separate section devoted exclusively to the challenges of this dynamic.

Chapter 14—Negotiating in Groups

Increasing numbers of us are working in matrix teams, and a constant in all of these teams is the tendency to negotiate everything, from agendas to priorities to resource allocation. As one workshop participant recently said, *"Every item on the agenda is a negotiation."* The articles in this chapter address the unique issues associated with intra-group negotiations, and both are new to this edition.

Jeanne M. Brett's "Negotiating Group Decisions" and "The Group and What Happens on the Way to *Yes*" by Deborah G. Ancona, David A. Friedman, and Deborah Kolb provide information on group negotiations and ways to handle

group dynamics, and explain their impact on the negotiation process.

Section 9—INDIVIDUAL NEGOTIATIONS

The following two chapters relate to the personal negotiations we all face at one time or another.

Chapter 15—Career Negotiations

At some point in our careers, each of us faces a time when we must talk with our supervisor or someone in Human Resources about our professional future. Two of the articles in this unit, both from the first edition, look at negotiating for job transfers and for a raise—two of the more difficult negotiations we are likely to face at least once.

"How to Ask for a Raise" by Jeff B. Copeland and Peter McKillop provides some helpful advice on how to go about asking for a raise, and looks at how we can determine what we are worth before entering any salary negotiation. This article will no doubt be extremely helpful as you prepare for a salary negotiation.

William C. Banks' article "How to Negotiate a Job Transfer" raises some very interesting points to consider when you have been asked to take on an assignment in a new location.

In the third article in this chapter (originally published by Smart Money Magazine), "Just Don't Sit There—Negotiate," Asika, Delaney, Deterline, and Gibbons put forth the argument that today's worker can negotiate for much more than he or she is used to getting—and get it.

All three articles provide you with surprising insights in how to negotiate with your boss and your organization's Human Resources department on these critical issues.

Chapter 16—Personal Negotiations

Many of our day-to-day negotiations relate to non-work issues. Two negotiations most significant from a dollar perspective—buying a home and buying a car—are examined in separate articles. The third article looks at a negotiation that many of us do not think of as negotiable—negotiating for a hotel room. With so many of us traveling for business purposes, this can represent substantial savings.

In the first article, "How Much Will You Pay for this Hotel Room?" Everett Potter contends that most of us never question the price of a hotel room, but that there are many different prices usually available, at far below what we ordinarily pay.

"Dealer Tactics and How to Counter Them" outlines various tactics used by salespeople, and discusses how we should respond to each of them.

"Bargain for That House Like a Pro," the third article, provides the necessary know-how for the potential homeowner. The article, taken from *Changing Times: The Kiplinger Guide to Buying a Home,* identifies the critical issues involved when negotiating for a new home.

All three articles should provide you with some fascinating new insights!

SUMMARY

In preparing this book of readings on negotiations, we attempted to select articles that address a wide range of issues the active negotiator is asked to face on a regular basis, but with which they may have only limited experience in addressing. These articles are designed to fill that gap. Since the field is in constant change and new articles appear daily, we suggest that you visit our Web site **asherman.com**, updated quarterly with an ever-expanding bibliography. We hope that you find this book to be informative and stimulating, and a useful resource as you go about conducting negotiations in your professional as well as personal life.

We would like to dedicate the 2000 edition of **The Negotiation Sourcebook** to the loving memory of our parents, Beatrice and George Asherman and Vivian and Walter Vance.

Section I

Negotiation: A Framework

Chapter One   *Approaches to Negotiation*
Chapter Two   *Conflict Resolution*
Chapter Three   *Power*

Chapter One

APPROACHES TO NEGOTIATION

UNDERSTANDING COMPETING THEORIES OF NEGOTIATION

John S. Murray

A theory is like a map describing a limited geographic area from a specific, functional perspective. Such a map helps the user understand at a glance the full dimension of the area being described, as well as determine the best plan or strategy for completing a stated project.

By defining comprehensive issues in a meaningful way and identifying the right questions to ask in support of a particular objective, a theory provides the same benefits for its user. Again similar to a map, theory is best evaluated by a set of realistic standards. I believe there are three standards that are appropriate: a reasonably accurate description of the reality for which it is being presented; a useful description of the factors important to the person needing to take action; and a consistently good outcome achieved by the competent user.

Negotiation theorists appear to be deeply divided between proponents of competitive and of problem-solving theories. Competitive theorists claim both a close approximation to the

actual experience of negotiators and a general superiority of outcomes. Problem-solving theorists assert the prescriptive superiority of their mode of conflict resolution in terms of outcomes, although some profess that competitive theory describes reality more accurately.

Many teachers—and most students—of negotiation are confused by the often polemical dialogue between opposing theorists. Adding to this confusion is the lack of precision with which theorists and practitioners use the terms *theory, strategy, and style*. Commentors representing separate disciplines have referred to many different negotiation theories and models: competitive and coordinative (Pruitt, 1981); competitive and cooperative (Williams, 1983); adversarial and problem-solving (Menkel-Meadow, 1984); hard, soft, and principled (Fisher and Ury, 1981); disruptive and integrative (Raiffa, 1982); and functional and developmental models of negotiating behavior (Gulliver, 1979).

Although these multiple references appear to sift naturally into the two competing camps that I am calling *competitive* and *problem-solving*, the confusion remains. Are there really two competing theories that explain realities in the negotiation setting? Should there be just one? If there are two, do the strategies that each favors necessarily conflict? What behavioral characteristics does each explain, and what are the downside risks that are hidden within each?

The following is an attempt to sketch a theoretical map that is both accurate for purposes of understanding the negotiating situation and descriptive in a way that is useful to the practicing negotiator. For purposes of evaluating possible outcomes, I have assumed a high level of negotiator competence, whether competitive or problem-solving (Williams, 1983, p. 41).

RECOGNIZED PATTERNS

Most negotiators, particularly lawyers, exhibit two distinct behavioral patterns. Table 1 lists some of the more obvious characteristics attached to each of these patterns.

An effective and dramatic way to appreciate the differences between the two patterns is to see them reflected in the writings of their respective proponents. In support of the competitive pattern, James J. White, commenting on a draft of the new Model Rules of Professional Conduct for lawyers, wrote:

> A final complication in drafting rules about truthfulness arises out of the paradoxical nature of the negotiator's responsibility. On the one hand the negotiator must be fair and truthful; on the other he must mislead his opponent. . . . The critical difference between those who are successful negotia-

---

TABLE 1
Recognized Patterns of Negotiators

Competitive	*Problem-Solving*
The negotiator:	The negotiator:
Tries to maximize tangible resource gains for own client within limits of the current dispute-problem.	Tries to maximize returns for own client, including any joint gains available.
Makes high opening demands and is slow to concede.	Focuses on common interests of parties.
Uses threats, confrontation, argumentation.	Tries to understand the merits as objectively as possible.
Manipulates people and the process.	Uses nonconfrontational debating techniques.
Is not open to persuasion on substance.	Is open to persuasion on substance.
Is oriented to quantitative and competitive goals.	Is oriented to qualitative goals: a fair/wise/durable agreement, efficiently negotiated.

tors and those who are not lies in this capacity both to mislead and not to be misled.

Some experienced negotiators will deny the accuracy of this assertion, but they will be wrong. . . . To conceal one's true position, to mislead an opponent about one's true settling point, is the essence of negotiation (White, 1980, p. 927).

In support of problem-solving, Roger Fisher and William L. Ury conclude their book *Getting to YES* by stating:

In most instances to ask a negotiator, "Who's winning?" is as inappropriate as to ask who's winning a marriage. If you ask that question about your marriage, you have already lost the more important negotiation—the one about what kind of game to play, about the way you deal with each other and your shared and differing interests.

This book is about how to "win" the important game—how to achieve a better process for dealing with your differences (Fisher and Ury, 1981, p. 154).

The patterns are easily recognizable. The stereotypical competitive negotiator is a zealous advocate: tough, clever, thorough, articulate, unemotional, demanding, aggressive, and unapproachable—a Sylvester Stallone "Rambo" type who achieves victory by defeating the opponent. The problem-solver is also thorough and articulate, but in addition: personable, cooperative, firm, principled, concerned about the other side's interests, and committed to fairness and efficiency—a Jimmy Stewart—Mr. Smith Goes to Washington approach to resolving disputes amicably. Even terminology reflects the distance between the patterns. A competitive bargainer, for instance, negotiates *against* an opponent; a problem-solver negotiates *with* the other side.

BASIC ASSUMPTIONS

The gap between these recognized patterns suggests that negotiators who exhibit either type of behavior are operating under sets of different assumptions about the nature of the negotiating world. Table 2 lists some of the principal assumptions.

The competitive negotiator views the negotiating world as one controlled by an egocentric self-interest. This world is made up of limited resources that are divided by highly competitive people in a succession of independent transactions. The distribution system for these limited resources is fundamentally distributive in nature, presenting each person with an either-or choice. The competition is for the resource dollar. There is no sharing the last dollar; either one negotiator or the other gets it. The goal is victory—to win as much as possible, and especially more than the opponent. The negotiating atmosphere in such a world is divisive, tense, game-like, and transactional.

To the problem-solver, the negotiating world is controlled by an enlightened self-interest. The negotiator values the common interests that bind parties together within an interdependent system. Although self-interest is reflected in the recognition of limited resources, the problem-solver sees an unlimited variation in individual preferences among the resources. The dollar may be a scarce resource desired by both negotiators, but each values that dollar differently. The distribution system, therefore, is fundamentally integrative in nature, with each party maximizing joint gains based upon their individual value preferences. The goal is a mutually agreeable solution to the dispute or problem, a solution that balances fairness for all parties and that is efficient for the community.

EXPLANATION OF NEGOTIATING BEHAVIOR

Each of these views has a significant and distinct impact on the behavior of negotiators who accept it.

The competitive negotiator appears to have a narrow perspective on the negotiation as a whole, but broad and flexible standards for selecting strategies and manipulating the process. Competitive theory is reflected in behavior when the negotiator:

1. Maximizes his or her own return in the present transaction.

2. Considers the needs/interests/attitudes of opponent as not legitimate, and only relevant when usable to achieve #1 above.

3. Views all disputing processes and strategies as equally valuable and useful if they are helpful in achieving #1 above.

4. Behaves cooperatively only if it helps achieve #1 above.

5. Chooses processes and strategies similar to military maneuvers. The focus is on the process of winning, not on the resolution of disputes.

6. Presents a strong defense against the opponent's tactics.

7. Must control the negotiating process for proper manipulation.

The problem-solving negotiator, on the other hand, holds a broad perspective on the negotiation as a whole, combined with more rigid limits on acceptable strategies and conduct. Some of the key behavioral elements for the problem-solver are:

1. Maximizes his or her own return within the larger time and community context.

2. Considers needs/interests/attitudes of the

TABLE 2
Basic Assumptions

Competitive	Problem-Solving
Negotiating world is controlled by egocentric self-interest. • Underlying motivation is competitive/antagonistic. • There are limited resources. • There are independent choices: tomorrow's decision is unaffected materially by today's.	Negotiating world is controlled by enlightened self-interest. • Common interests are valued. • Interdependence is recognized. • There are limited resources with unlimited variation in personal preferences.
Resource distribution system is distributive in nature (either-or).	Resource distribution system is integrative in nature (joint).
Goal: To win as much as you can—and especially more than the other side	Goal: A mutually agreeable solution that is fair to all parties and efficient for the community.

other side as both relevant and legitimate to resolving the dispute.

3. Is competitive but not antagonistic.

4. Tries to discover and share any joint gains available.

5. Concentrates on the substance of the dispute or decision.

6. Considers negotiation and other voluntary processes as superior to nonvoluntary methods (adjudication).

These separate behavioral characteristics contain significant strengths within the bargaining situation. The competitive negotiator can be focused and single-minded, with no details being materially relevant other than the present dispute and the party/client. This concentration allows the competitive negotiator to prepare fully for a specific settlement conference. He or she can come armed with a solid offer and fixed negotiation strategies. The opponent's perspective and tactics will not affect the opening position or strategies; they are important only for the manner and rate of concessions, should the negotiator decide to make any at all. Such knowledge gives the negotiator a reassuring sense of control that translates into confidence that is impressive in the negotiation setting.

Another strength follows directly from this disregard for the opponent's position and tactics. The competitive negotiator has analyzed the facts, determined the position, and made the case. The opponent cannot dislodge or defeat this preparation by any means of persuasion based on the merits. Having such an unbreachable defensive position permits the competitive negotiator to stress an aggressive offense aimed at persuading, coercing, deceiving, or otherwise manipulating the opponent to an acceptable agreement.

There is also strength in the competitive negotiator's flexibility in selecting strategies. Everything is acceptable, including the alternative of not negotiating, with the only limit being the express violation of ethical obligations. The ultimate selection is based directly on which strategy yields the maximum expected gain for the party/client. A significant element of bargaining power is the attractiveness of a good alternative to negotiating with the opponent. The competitive negotiator does not hesitate to choose that alternative when it is perceived as yielding a bigger gain, even if that choice places the party/client in a psychologically costly court trial. The relevant standards are quantitative: the size of gain expected from the alternative, discounted to reflect any time delay, compared to what appears possible in settlement. The competitive negotiator thereby avoids the confusion and indecision fostered by the impact of intangible or psychological factors and the normative arguments of fairness, wisdom, durability, and efficiency.

Finally, there is psychological strength in the excitement of doing battle. Like a military general, the competitive negotiator concentrates full attention on manipulating the tools and processes available within the negotiation setting. The goal is victory over the opponent on the field of battle. Resolving the underlying disagreements between parties/clients is left to others. With no responsibility for resolving these underlying problems, the negotiator can savor the excitement and challenge of the negotiation chase as if it were only a game, like baseball, chess, or poker.

On the other side, the problem-solving negotiator also brings strengths to the bargaining table. Concentration on the merits of the dispute gives the problem-solver a sense of legitimacy, centrality, and purpose. The problem-solver is responsible not only for tactical decisions within the negotiation setting but also for helping resolve the underlying problems of the party/client. Such a central role to the life of the party/client makes the negotiator's efforts less like a game and more like a serious human responsibility. In addition, using the merits as the central negotiating focus establishes a more objective and predictable control mechanism than can be achieved by relying on manipulation of the personal strategy and style decisions of the negotiators.

The problem-solving negotiator also generates strength by recognizing the importance of common interests and joint gains. Such objectives can be shared among negotiators and parties/clients in a mutually positive and reinforcing way; quite different than the competitive effect that the goal of victory has.

Finally, successful problem-solving is a satisfying experience on a human level. Since the intended outcome of the negotiation is a win-win result, the accomplishment of creating an innovative solution that maximizes joint as well as individual gains can be shared with the other side. The process of reaching this goal is psychologically unifying, rather than divisive. Negotiating is thus an enjoyable and challenging personal experience, rather than a highly stressful battle of wits and words.

DOWNSIDE RISKS

Each behavioral pattern exhibits weaknesses as well as strengths. Table 3 lists the downside risks that negotiators accepting each theory meet. The significance of recognizing these risks lies in understanding negotiator vulnerabilities, identifying possible threats to consistently good outcomes, and developing appropriate responses or changes to improve the result.

It is especially enlightening to analyze the downside risks with the objective of devising actions that might decrease or eliminate them. For the competitive negotiator, adopting actions intended to lessen the risks appears to change negotiating behavior from a competitive to a problem-solving mode.

For example, actions aimed at reducing the harmful effects of frustration, anger, mistrust,

misinformation, and misjudgment must of necessity include building a better working relationship between the negotiators. The objective would be to identify and eliminate possible breakdowns that are based on emotional and communication problems and not due to the inability to find an outcome that maximizes the party/client gain. The result of adopting such actions would be to improve the amount and credibility of information exchanged, increase the grounds for trust, and lessen the use of manipulation based on process rather than substance.

The success of misrepresentation and deceit as a strategy to elicit information leading to joint gains depends largely on an inequality in the relative level of negotiator competence, which is not a solid base for generating consistently good outcomes. Therefore, actions intended by the competitive negotiator to uncover joint gains would need to include improvement in active listening and acceptance of the opponent's legitimacy.

Reducing brinkmanship would help eliminate impasses where settlement at the party/client's maximum is possible but is frustrated by the psychological impact of the frequent use of threats. Pulling back from the brink requires fewer threats of impasse, less psychological tension, and more recognition of substantive fairness.

The competitive negotiator who tries to counter these downside risks becomes more problem-solving than competitive in orientation, thereby exhibiting more of the characteristics and strengths associated with problem-solving theory.

On the other side, analysis of the downside risks of problem-solving theory suggests that corrective actions will lead to a strengthening of problem-solving skills, not to a change in basic negotiating behavior. The theories are in this way asymmetrical.

For example, the tendency toward unwarranted compromise and accommodation is countered not by confrontation and stubbornness but by more thorough preparation on the merits and a stronger commitment to an identifiable substantive standard (Pruitt and Lewis, 1977, p. 183). Indefinite aspiration levels and bottom lines pose serious problems for the problem-solving negotiator at all stages of negotiation, from the initial planning to post-agreement evaluation. Corrective steps include the development and use of more accurate analysis of the subject

TABLE 3
Downside Risks

Competitive:

1. Strong bias toward confrontation, encouraging the use of coercion and emotional pressure as persuasive means; hard on relationships, breeding mistrust, feelings of separateness, frustration and anger, resulting in more frequent breakdowns in negotiations; and distorts communication, producing misinformation and misjudgment.

2. Guards against responsiveness and openness to opponent (defensive), thereby restricting access to joint gains.

3. Encourages brinkmanship by creating many opportunities for impasse.

4. Increases difficulty in predicting responses of opponent because reliance is on manipulation and confrontation to control process.

5. Contributes to overestimation of return possible through alternatives (court) because focus is not on a relatively objective analysis of substantive merits as the standard for resolution.

Problem-Solving:

1. Strong bias toward cooperation, creating internal pressures to compromise and accommodate.

2. Avoids strategies that are confrontational because they risk impasse, which is viewed as failure.

3. Focuses on being sensitive to other's perceived interests; this increases vulnerability to deception and manipulation by a competitive opponent, and increases the possibility that settlement might be more favorable to the other side than fairness would warrant.

4. Increases difficulty of establishing definite aspiration levels and bottom lines because of reliance on qualitative (value-laden) goals.

5. Requires substantial skill and knowledge of process in order to do well.

6. Requires strong confidence in own assessment powers (perception) regarding interests/needs of other side and other's payoff schedule.

matter, not a shift to process manipulation and positional bargaining.

Viewing impasse not as failure but as a better alternative than agreeing to an unfair settlement does not force a negotiator to be confrontational in a competitive sense. Rather, it causes the problem-solver to be even more committed to a recognized standard of fairness and more flexible in strategy selection.

One of the most feared downside risks for the problem-solver is vulnerability to deception and manipulation by a competitive opponent. The result can be not only an inequitable outcome but also a residual sense of personal and professional embarrassment. Reciprocating with equally deceptive and competitive behavior may be the easiest response, but such reciprocity is defensive in nature, not corrective. Actions to detect and counter deception and manipulation must focus on ways to build confidence in the truthfulness of information exchanged and in the identification of various negotiating tactics.

Personal confidence in the negotiator's own ability and judgment is a prerequisite for effective problem-solving. The negotiator builds such confidence by acquiring up-to-date knowledge of both substance and process, preparing rigorously for each case, and seeking practical negotiating experiences.

Negotiation for the problem-solver who tries to correct for downside risks does not shift to a more competitive and confrontational mode but rather retains and enhances problem-solving characteristics.

CONCLUSION

Current thought accepts the notion that there are two exclusive and competing theories that explain negotiation behavior: the competitive theory and the problem-solving theory. Each theory has certain basic assumptions that appeal to

establish it as unique. The resulting behavior of negotiators who accept each set of assumptions has characteristics that are identifiable and important within the negotiation setting.

An analysis of the downside risks of each of these theories, however, raises some question about their uniqueness. As attempts are made to improve negotiator performance within each, the problem-solving theory becomes dominant. This result appears incompatible with the conclusion of some empirical studies of negotiator effectiveness (Williams, 1983), but the difficulty of defining and measuring effectiveness is widely recognized. The analysis in this article suggests that the more proficient a negotiator becomes under either theory, the more his or her behavior will reflect the elements of problem-solving theory.

The conclusion might be unavoidable: that only the problem-solving theory satisfies all three quality standards for a general theory. It describes negotiation realities with reasonable accuracy, is useful in developing strategies, and provides consistently good outcomes for the competent negotiator. The recognizable competitive variant might just reflect different negotiator personality and style characteristics, and the quality and consistency of outcomes might depend partly on the relative levels of negotiator competence.

REFERENCES

Fisher, R. and Ury, W.L. *Getting to YES: Negotiating agreement without giving in.* Boston: Houghton Mifflin, 1981.

Gulliver, P.H. *Disputes and negotiations: A cross-cultural perspective.* New York: Academic Press, 1979.

Menkel-Meadow, C. Toward another view of negotiation: The structure of legal problem-solving. *UCLA Law Review* 31 (1984):754.

Pruitt, D.G. *Negotiating behavior.* New York: Academic Press, 1981.

Pruitt, D.G. and Lewis, S.A. In *Negotiations: Social-psychological perspectives,* D. Druckman (ed.). Beverly Hills, Calif.: Sage, 1977.

Raiffa, H. *The art and science of negotiation.* Cambridge, Mass.: Harvard University Press, 1982.

Williams, G.R. *Legal negotiation and settlement.* St. Paul: West, 1983.

White, J.J. Machiavelli and the Bar: Ethical limitations on lying in negotiation. *American Bar Foundation Research Journal* (Fall 1980):926.

NEGOTIATING: A CONCEPTUAL MODEL

Willem F. G. Mastenbroek

The ability to negotiate is vital to cope with conflicting interests. Knowledge—handed down by practitioners and behavioral scientists—is very fragmented regarding specific social skills and precise insights used in negotiating. This article offers a conceptual model based on two encompassing perspectives: (1) negotiating as a set of dilemmas that are derived from the "cooperation-fighting" polarity and (2) negotiating as a composition of four kinds of activities, each connected to a different intention.

INTRODUCTION

People are increasingly confronted with the question of how to cope with conflicting interests. Councils and boards representing various interests are increasing in numbers and importance in government and business. Discord within organizations, conflicts of interest between departments in industry, tensions and conflicts within departments of an organization, difficult relations with external interest groups, etc., are making ever-increasing demands on people's ability to handle pronounced differences and clearly opposed viewpoints.

One way of dealing with conflicting interests is to negotiate. Capable negotiators know how to reach compromises that satisfy both parties. Sometimes they are able to find solutions that have clear benefits for both parties. They can generally prevent escalations and lasting deadlocks.

The model developed in this article is an instrument that can aid constructive negotiations. Although the target is a wide variety of negotiations, a great deal of feedback on the model was received from experienced Dutch international negotiators who represent the Dutch government abroad. In a series of three workshops with international negotiators, the model was explained and negotiators commented on it. Simulations of real-life negotiations were evaluated in terms of the model as summarized at the end of this article (Figure 4). Delegations scored each other's behavior in terms of the model. At the end of the workshops, participants were asked to write down their comments and suggest improvements. These suggestions resulted in a more experience-based and easily recognizable comprehensive model. Another series of workshops is planned, and further refinements and improvements are probable.

In answer to questions on the type of ability needed, the way people negotiate constructively, and the definition of *negotiating*, experienced negotiators for centuries have given certain rules of thumb (Karrass, 1974). Some examples are listed below:

1. Do not be tough unless necessary.
2. Be flexible and firm.
3. Do not be afraid to adjourn.
4. Never do your thinking aloud in front of the other side.
5. Decide on your opening tactic carefully.
6. Do not pull a fast one; remember continuing relationships.
7. Remember the importance of time.
8. Recognize that some questions do not deserve answers.
9. Study the opponent's agenda for what it deliberately leaves out.

These rules of thumb give useful hunches but no real understanding of the process. There simply are too many, and they lack order or system. Karrass assembled over two hundred strategies and tactics, and the classification system he used was in alphabetical order!

Negotiating has become an important topic of research in the social sciences. Rubin and Brown (1975) wrote an outstanding review and summary of several hundred studies. Still, findings are too numerous and too isolated. Comprehensive frameworks that offer insights into the negotiating process as a whole are missed.

Peterson (1978), in his review of another excellent summary of the major literature on negotiations by Morely and Stephenson (1977), has some reservations about the general state of our findings. He says that much of the literature is overly concerned with narrow constructs rather than broader conceptual models, and that although the review of theoretical and experimental research by psychologists is beneficial, it offers neither a theoretical model of negotiations to academicians nor particular help to the labor or management negotiators who wish to better understand the negotiation process.

This present article elaborates on a theoretical model of negotiating, which is seen as a specific social skill characterized by a range of dilemmas. These dilemmas fit into an overarching model of negotiating as a set of four basic processes. Each process has its own strategies and tactics, and at least one of these processes is structured in a specific way over time.

NEGOTIATING AS A RANGE OF DILEMMAS

The ways in which people can deal with each other around the conference table can be represented on a continuum that runs from cooperation via negotiation to "fighting" (Peabody, 1971), without clearcut borders.

Cooperation is appropriate if interests and goals are similar. It is the obvious method if the benefits for those concerned are directly dependent on the degree to which they can pool their resources.

Negotiation is the correct strategy when interests are different or if there is so much mutual dependence that an agreement has advantages for both parties. In this case, parties disagree but are willing to come to an agreement because letting things drift or fighting would be disadvantageous for both parties.

Fighting is the most likely strategy when either party thinks it can win more by fighting than by negotiating. Sometimes it is used from a powerless position to build up a strong negotiating position. A fighting strategy is concerned with obtaining mastery. One tries to reduce the opponent to submission.

On this continuum further distinctions are possible. For example, persuasion and debate fit between cooperation and negotiation. Negotiations can be further differentiated, as Walton and McKersie (1965) show, into integrative, mixed, and distributive negotiations. Gradations can also be distinguished in fighting. For our purposes here, the threefold division is sufficient. Figure 1 further clarifies the differences among these three basic strategies.

A negotiator is faced with a number of dilemmas between cooperation and fighting: "Am I pressing too hard, or was my concession too early or too big?" "Am I revealing too much of my position, or do I give too few clues of my interests?" "To what extent can I trust the other party?" "Would too much distrust destroy our relationship?" "Should I side with my rank and file and play it as tough as they would like?" These and other dilemmas sometimes manifest themselves vaguely as uncertainty and doubt, and sometimes explicitly in the realization that one is between two fires. They make negotiating, especially for the inexperienced, stressful and frustrating. The temptation to tip the scales to one of the extremes can be great. The inclination to follow the all-or-nothing, win-lose model can be very strong.

Processes whereby parties maneuver so clumsily that they end up in fights that seriously weaken them both are repeatedly noted in the research on negotiation (Rubin and Brown, 1975). This possibility is the reason that capable negotiators do not like to deal with inexperienced opponents, whose toleration for the stress and ambiguity connected with the dilemmas is generally too low. They become emotionally upset, start fighting, or naively get themselves into a predicament before the attainable limits have been explored. Negotiating is the subtle handling of the delicate balance between cooperation and fighting.

NEGOTIATING AS FOUR PROCESSES

Negotiating—a very complex process—is a combination of different processes. A model that separates negotiating into the following four kinds of activities will be presented:

1. Activities directed at dividing, which are directly concerned with the distribution of benefits and burdens.

2. Activities that influence personal relations and the negotiating climate between parties.

3. Activities that a negotiator uses to influence his rank and file.

4. Activities that are directed at influencing the balance of power between the parties.

The outstanding work conceptualizing negotiating as different kinds of activities is still that of Walton and McKersie (1965). They distinguish the processes of (1) *distributive bargaining*, directed toward maximizing one's share of the benefits; (2) *integrative bargaining*, attempting to solve problems and increase mutual benefits; (3) *attitudinal structuring*, oriented toward obtaining and maintaining a good working relationship; and (4) *intra-organizational bargaining*, attempting to influence teammates and constituents.

The separation of distributive and integrative bargaining clouds one of the most essential characteristics of negotiating: negotiating is *both* distributive *and* integrative. Walton and McKersie are entangled in this problem. They try to find a solution by introducing a fifth process—*mixed bargaining* that incorporates elements of both. To

Figure 1.
Examples of Corresponding Tactics Used in Cooperation, Negotiation, and Fighting

Cooperation	Negotiation	Fighting
Conflict is seen as a common problem.	Conflict is seen as a clash between different but mutually dependent interests.	Conflict is seen as a question of winning or losing, "over or under," or "we or they."
People present their own goals as accurately as possible.	People exaggerate their own interests but pay attention to possible areas of agreement.	People emphasize the superiority of their own objectives.
Each other's weak points and personal problems can be openly discussed.	Personal problems are disguised or very circumspectly presented.	Personal problems are treated as though they did not exist.
The information provided is honest.	The information given is not false, but one sided. The facts favorable to one's own party are deliberately emphasized.	If it can help to make the opponent submit, false information is deliberately spread.
Discussion subjects are presented in terms of underlying problems.	Agendas are formulated in terms of alternative solutions.	Points of disagreement are formulated in terms of one's own solution.
Possible solutions are tested against their practical consequences.	Occasionally the linking of solutions to principles is used to put some pressure on the other side.	One's own solutions are rigidly tied to higher principles.
Speaking out for one particular solution is deliberately delayed as long as possible.	Strong preference for a particular solution is shown, but a scope for concessions is self-evident.	An absolute and unconditional preference for one's own solution is expressed at every opportunity.
Threatening, creating confusion, and taking advantage of the mistakes of others are seen as detrimental.	Occasionally a modest and carefully calculated use is made of threats, confusion, and surprise.	Threats, confusion, shock effects, etc., are welcome at any time to reduce the opponent to submission.

minimize the dilemmas, Walton (1972) recommends separation of the distributive and integrative elements as much as possible (e.g., by agenda, by people, by time, and by space). Given the mixed character of most negotiations, this solution would be awkward at times or even impossible. This delicate process of balancing is a separate skill, not an alternation between two different sets of behaviors.

Activities Directed at Dividing

The activities directed at dividing usually attract the greatest attention. They are explicitly directed toward the end result. The most important subactivities in this category are (1) exchanging information about aims, expectations, and acceptable solutions; (2) exercising pressure to influence each other's perception of what is attainable; and (3) working step by step toward a compromise with mutual concessions.

Figure 1. (continued)
Examples of Corresponding Tactics Used in Cooperation, Negotiation, and Fighting

Cooperation	Negotiation	Fighting
Active participation of all concerned is encouraged.	Contacts between parties are limited to only a few spokesmen.	Contacts between the parties take place indirectly via "declarations."
An attempt is made to spread power as much as possible and to let it play no further role.	Occasionally each other's power is tested, or attempts are made to influence the balance of power in one's own favor.	Both parties engage in a permanent power struggle by strengthening their own organizations, increasing independence, and dividing and isolating the opponent.
People try to understand each other and share each other's personal concerns.	Understanding the views of the other side is seen as a tactical instrument.	No one bothers to understand the opponent.
Personal irritations are expressed to clear the air of tensions that could hamper future cooperation.	Personal irritations are suppressed or ventilated indirectly (e.g., with humor).	Irritations confirm negative and hostile images. Hostility is expressed to break down the other side.
Both parties find it easy to call in outside expertise to help in decision-making.	Third parties are brought in only if there is a complete deadlock.	Outsiders are welcome only if they are "blind" supporters.

The strategic and tactical choices that the negotiators must continually make can be understood best in the framework of the information dilemma and the pressure dilemma.

The Information Dilemma

To obtain results, the parties must have information about each other's aims. The side that has a start in that respect is in an advantageous position. It is easier for that side to choose a good strategy and a favorable starting position. It knows better what is attainable and, therefore, how far it can go with its own demands. There is an increased likelihood that it will not have to make all the concessions that it is prepared to make. Both parties know this and are therefore cautious about releasing information. Both parties also realize that too much reticence makes effective negotiation impossible. Therefore the skill lies in carefully bringing about a step-by-step exchange of information that gradually gives shape to realistic expectations on both sides. The tactical use of information is meant to control this dilemma. Specific tactics that negotiators use in this dilemma and the following dilemma are more elaborately described elsewhere (Mastenbroek, 1979).

The Pressure Dilemma

The process of building up information about the aims of both sides can become complicated, because a negotiator often is not sure which objectives are attainable and realistic. To decide this, the negotiator must know more about the priorities and possibilities of the other side and realize that the opponent is faced with the same problem. To keep the opponent's expectations low, the negotiator's requirements must appear as self-evident and unassailable as possible. Both know that margins for concessions are built in. Some indication of this must also be shown; otherwise, one can forget about results. A subtle tournament often develops on this flexible/firm

axis. After each side has given the other side sufficient peeps between its firm positions and strong arguments, possible solutions can begin to be outlined.

Firmness on both sides can result in a deadlock, which is often used as pressure to test each other's strength. Deadlocks also can be used to gather information about possible concessions. Often they are unavoidable and become constructive—as a last test of each other's position—in making concessions.

The Structure of the Activities Directed at Dividing

The activities directed at dividing usually go through a number of phases. For many years Douglas (1962) studied the structure of the negotiating process between employers and employees in the United States. Karrass (1970), who is more concerned with commercial negotiations, took over and slightly adapted her findings. Albeda (1975) arrived at a similar picture in his study of collective labor negotiations in the Netherlands. In the light of their work, the following phases can be deduced:

Preparation. Experienced negotiators emphasize the importance of the preparation stage. It is concerned with determining not only one's own standpoint, but also the strategy to be followed. A complete scenario can be composed of the consecutive steps to be followed, with adaptations for the alternatives. Such a guide can then be tested and adapted by trial negotiations in one's own group. A thorough preparation will harden one's own standpoint and thereby reduce the chances of agreement. This result can be avoided by introducing informal consultations.

Representatives of the parties do not then negotiate, but they make each other aware of their points of departure. The more informal exchange of thoughts, the more likely the success during the actual negotiations.

Verbal Fireworks. This forerunner of the actual negotiations often begins even before the parties sit down at the negotiating table. Both parties make firm statements in which they present their demands and conditions as completely fixed and unassailable. At the negotiating table this often takes the form of speeches in which a statement of principle is coupled with the great righteousness of the demands. Thoroughly bolstered with facts, the proposals are presented as reasonable and fair. Vicious criticism of the other side is no exception. Outsiders often fear the worst and wonder how there could ever be a compromise. Meanwhile the parties remain laconic. The function of this phase is clear: the rank and file are shown that their interests are being taken to heart, and signals are sent out about what the important issues will be. This information is important for both sides.

Psychological Warfare. In the discussions that follow the verbal fireworks, repeated attempts are made to find out how definite the opponent's demands are, while one's own proposals continue to be presented as unassailable and obviously justified. Arguments, bluffs, or threats might be used to obtain a concession. Although this tactic sounds harsh, it has a clear information-gathering function. When the limits of what is attainable are explored, sometimes a hard-and-fast contention can be weakened. A sounding may be made to discover the first reaction to a certain proposal. Sometimes all the consequences of particular points are thoroughly investigated. Carefully created misunderstandings can again cause confusion: The parties are enveloped in mists of vagueness with nothing important settled. However, gradually the contours of a possible agreement become clear. The reactions of the rank and file may also tell the negotiators how far they can still go.

Crisis and Settlement. Pressure and confusion lead to a crisis atmosphere. At a certain point—sometimes under the pressure of a time limit—it becomes apparent that no progress is being made. Often there must be intense discussions with the rank and file. Further crises might be necessary to crystallize a compromise. Sometimes final negotiations can be amazingly fast—the time is ripe, point after point is dealt with, and a committee arranges the details.

This crisis atmosphere with high feelings of tension is necessary as the final test of the firmness of the different standpoints. The crisis, sometimes reinforced by binding time limits, finally forces the parties to make decisions and come to an agreement.

Himmelmann (1971) has developed this picture still further. He sees, after various preliminary phases, the following main phases: (1) confrontation of the standpoints, (2) consideration of detail (involving much use of pressure tactics), (3) a maturing phase, (4) cooperative searches, (5) a crisis, and (6) compromise and agreement. Many negotiations do not have such a fully developed form. However, every negotiation probably has a probing phase, during which the parties try to keep as many options open as possible while trying each other's tenacity.

Influencing Relationships and Climate

It is important to keep personal relationships between negotiators on a reasonable footing. A poisoned atmosphere in which the negotiators have a negative approach to each other as individuals hampers the division-oriented activities. In this matter of bringing out the mutual dependence of the parties and of building up sufficient trust, acceptance, and credibility, the dependency dilemma and the credibility dilemma are manifest.

The Dependency Dilemma

The dependency dilemma is the strain between "We both want an agreement" and "I want a result as favorable as possible for myself." Each negotiator tries to achieve certain interests for his own party, but this can only be done by agreement with the other party. If one tries too hard to get the best result, this can be so unsatisfactory for the other party that it breaks off the negotiations. If one lets the mutual dependence weigh heavily, one might agree to less than could be obtained. Thus there is continual doubt as to whether all the margins have been well utilized. Yet competent negotiators consciously reject getting everything possible out of the situation. They have good reasons for this. Fulfillment of an agreement often depends on the good will of the opponent, who might afterward feel very uncomfortable with the results, and seek revenge indirectly. Moreover, it is likely that the parties will meet again at the negotiating table. Continuity of good relations is then more important than incidental advantage. A good mutual relationship can, paradoxically, exist very well together with a strong presentation of one's own interest.

If somebody puts up strong opposition, there is a great temptation to react to that person rather than to concentrate on the issue. A way out is to regard the opponent's strong action as typical role behavior for anyone in that position. Douglas (1962, p. 17) comments on distinguishing role behavior from personal relationships: "While the parties are busily engaged in depreciating each other, at the level of interpersonal relationships there flow warm currents of personal good will and friendly respect."

Experienced negotiators no longer have too much difficulty with this distinction. On the contrary, there is often a clear respect for a firm position well supported by facts and arguments. In this connection the distinction made by Pruitt and Lewis (1977) between a firm statement of demands and a flexible strategic position is important. Capable negotiators sometimes search persistently for possibilities that are relatively satisfactory for both parties.

The Credibility Dilemma

A negotiator who trusts the opponent without reservations runs the risk of ending up with a result favorable to the opponent. The negotiator who mistrusts the opponent seriously undermines the likelihood of an agreement. Negotiation could be defined as gradually and carefully building up sufficient mutual trust to make an agreement possible.

This balance is very fine. If a negotiator abuses the trust (for example, by lying) and is caught, his or her credibility is lost, and the relationship between the parties is considerably worsened.

In any negotiation, certain factors may contribute to a climate of trust. Examples include the following:

1. Consideration of the personal needs of others.

2. Attention to what others say and respect for their arguments even if one is not in agreement with them.

3. A sense of humor and the ability to see one's behavior in perspective.

4. Informal discussions that are concerned with personal things and incidental matters.

Activities Oriented toward the Rank and File

According to Walton and McKersie (1965), taking care of the rank-and-file relationship, which has a negotiation aspect, is a core variable in the negotiating process. In fact, without involving this dimension, much of what happens at the negotiating table would be inexplicable. Sometimes a "gentleman's agreement" is made between the negotiators. For example, they might help each other to save face, form a stronger coalition, or make possible the emergence of alternatives to the present dependency relationship. It is sometimes possible to demonstrate the changing power relationships by carefully planned and timed action that clarifies the potential sources of power (Deutsch, 1973).

Dominating the negotiation discussion. This strategy is more subtle and more dependent on the personalities of the negotiators. It is a question of using *special* kinds of pressure methods, because they are aimed at a person's feelings of self-esteem. It involves a person's identity, values, norms, relations with the rank and file, personal characteristics, and behavior at the negotiating table. The risks of this strategy are not small. One must, in fact, manipulate in the true sense of the word, which means making the other submit without realizing it. Otherwise one slips into a fighting situation. This strategy is perhaps possible with a naive opponent, but it can create a vague grudge that might hinder future negotiations. However, this strategy is often attempted.

This strategy can be used so slyly and covertly that even the victim will not clearly understand the reason for this resentment or irritation. Quickly recognizing precisely what is happening can help a person to counteract and put the negotiations on a healthier footing.

With five examples, Figure 2 parallels emotional manipulations, the intended effect on the opponent, and the possibilities of defending oneself by counteraction (Delden, 1977).

The manipulations in Figure 2 are intended to disparage the opponent. Figure 3 illustrates manipulations that are more subtle and more difficult to ward off, because they appeal to the so-called "general norms of correct behavior."

If manipulations of this kind are made with sufficient conviction, the opponent can hardly escape them. The opponent begins to feel involuntarily guilty, ashamed, inferior, and insecure and then hesitates and makes mistakes.

Such manipulations are really "fighting" techniques. One disparages the other with the tem-

porary advantage of obtaining a leading position in the discussion. Ultimately one increases the likelihood of escalation, because the effect on the other is irritation about that person's own powerless position. If that feeling of powerlessness cannot be converted, one should keep each other's prestige intact, give each other scope for considerable showmanship at certain times, or refuse to make concessions quickly so that the opponent's rank and file will not develop unrealistic expectations.

The Representation Dilemma

The dilemma that exists in this situation can be called the "representation" dilemma. Yielding to pressure of the rank and file often means that the chance of the negotiators to achieve results is reduced. Constituents tend to be more radical than their representatives. They not only want a larger share of the benefits, but they also see their adversaries in more negative and stereotyped ways. If a representative goes along with these tendencies, his or her position as a representative is often strengthened. Members approve a tough stand. It gives them confidence in the credibility and leadership of the representative. Emotionally it is more satisfying to unite with the constituents than to work through the inevitable frustrations of concessions and compromise.

Being a "good" representative often means being trapped in a fighting situation. A negotiator has to find ways to resist the pressure of the constituents to reach an agreement with the opponent.

It can be difficult for negotiators to resist this kind of pressure from the rank and file, especially when yielding to it strengthens their own positions. Negotiating in front of the rank and file reduces the chance of an agreement (Iklé, 1964; Schelling, 1960; Stevens, 1963).

Sometimes it is possible to remove the negotiations from the eye of the onlookers by communiqués that say nothing, an isolated place for negotiations, etc. Even then the negotiator feels obliged to establish a good impression as a negotiator, because he is judged afterward by the results. The desire for prestige, the fear of being regarded as weak, and the fear of losing one's position are important factors. Strangely enough, negotiators who do not consider themselves too strongly tied by their rank and file often obtain the best results (Hornstein and Johnson, 1966; Lamm and Kogan, 1970; Vidmar, 1971).

The same dilemmas exist in principle when negotiating with the rank and file as with the opponent. Walton and McKersie (1965) distinguish some tactics specifically for this process. The most important are the following:

1. Avoid a strict mandate or precise terms of reference by allowing only a short time for preparation or by keeping the subject unclear.

2. Moderate the demands of the rank and file by giving tactical information about what is attainable.

FIGURE 2.
Examples of Manipulation, Intended Effect, and Counteraction During Negotiations

Manipulation	Intended Effect on Opponent	Counteraction
Indication that opponent's rank and file or the public may be critical.	Feelings of insecurity or of being threatened.	Indication or amazement at such pedestrian considerations.
Demonstration of immovability and unassailable self-confidence.	Conclusion that a request for a favor is mandatory because no results are evident.	Skepticism about the position of the other and gradual demonstration of the same posture.
Explicit statements that opponent's arguments are not valid.	Feeling of powerlessness.	Polite statement that the other has not understood.
Rhetorical questions about the behavior or arguments of opponent.	Inclination either to answer the questions in the intended way or to say nothing and feel powerless.	No answer to questions, but statements that the other is not posing the problem fairly.
"Pleasant and mean" behavior—alternatively friendly and indignant.	Uncertainty, disorientation, and intimidation.	Mild reaction to both friendly and indignant behavior.

· · · · ·

3. Do not appoint people whose expectations are too high to the actual negotiating team.

4. Report the results of the negotiations in vague or complicated terms, so that immediate criticism has little firm basis.

5. Exaggerate the concessions of the opponent.

Influencing the Balance of Power

The result of negotiations is connected with power and dependency relationships, but negotiation assumes a certain degree of equality between the parties. A survey of the experimental research in the field leads to the conclusion that effective negotiation is related to a certain balance of power (Rubin and Brown, 1975). When there are obvious differences in power, different behavior occurs: manipulative and exploiting versus submissive and accommodating. Although attempting to make fundamental changes in the existing balance of power is generally the signal for fighting, some space for movement will still exist.

The Power Dilemma

Maintaining and strengthening one's own power involves strengthening one's own organization and consideration of coalition partners. The rank and file must also be kept informed and influenced so that they can be mobilized.

The boundary between activities of this kind and actively influencing the balance of power is not clearly defined. A careful and restrained strategy is desirable, because otherwise one is triggered into a fighting situation. Broadly speaking, there are two kinds of strategies:

Making it clear that the starting situation has changed. With this strategy a party can try to change the balance of power while minimizing the possibility of a fighting situation. The "new facts" that directly affect the power relationship must be manifest and credible. Examples of new facts are the formation of a stronger coalition and the emergence of alternatives to the present dependency relationship. It is sometimes possible to demonstrate the changing power relationships by carefully planned and timed action that clarifies the potential sources of power (Deutsch, 1973).

Dominating the negotiation discussion. This strategy is more subtle and more dependent on the personalities of the negotiators. It is a question of using special kinds of pressure methods, because they are aimed at a person's feelings of self-esteem. It involves a person's identity, values, norms, relations with the rank and file, personal characteristics, and behavior at the negotiating table. The risks of this strategy are not small. One must, in fact, manipulate in the true sense of the word, which means making the other submit without realizing it. Otherwise one slips into a fighting situation. This strategy is perhaps possible with a naive opponent, but it may nevertheless create a vague grudge that hinders future negotiations. However, this strategy is often attempted.

This strategy can be used so slyly and covertly that even the victim will not clearly understand the reason for this resentment or irritation. Quickly recognizing precisely what is happening can help a person to counteract and put the negotiations on a healthier footing.

With five examples, Figure 2 parallels emotional manipulations, the intended effect on the opponent, and the possibilities of defending oneself by counteraction (Delden, 1977).

The manipulations in Figure 2 are intended to disparage the opponent. Figure 3 illustrates manipulations that are more subtle and more difficult to ward off, because they appeal to the so-called "general norms of correct behavior."

If manipulations of this kind are made with sufficient conviction, the opponent can hardly escape them. The opponent begins to feel involuntarily guilty, ashamed, inferior, and insecure and then hesitates and makes mistakes.

Such manipulations are really "fighting" techniques. One disparages the other with the temporary advantage of obtaining a leading position in the discussion. Ultimately one increases the likelihood of escalation, because the effect on the other is irritation about that person's own powerless position. If that feeling of powerlessness cannot be converted into purposeful counteraction, it can lead to a blind and obstinate retention of one's own position.

CONCLUSION

Negotiation has been presented as a combination of four kinds of activities. Each of these activities is connected with a different intention: obtaining results, promoting a respectful relationship, establishing a favorable balance of

---

FIGURE 3

Additional (and More Subtle) Examples of Manipulation, Intended Effect, and Counteraction During Negotiations

Manipulation	Intended Effect on Opponent	Counteraction
Friendly behavior and respect for opponent.	Friendly (and therefore lenient) reaction.	Friendly (not lenient) or aggressive behavior.
"Pathetic" requests for understanding of own position.	Inclination to grant "generous" and disinterested favor.	Rejection of responsibility.
Semblance of incompetence to understand "complicated" position of other side.	An awareness for a need to explain things, thereby giving new information.	Specific questions on what is not understood and why it is not clear.
Businesslike orientation, treating problems as incidental questions.	A feeling of "old boys," who should not make difficulties for each other.	Serious indications that there are some important obstacles.
Rational-serious attitude— with great gravity and authority, producing long arguments about problems.	Fear of seeming unintelligent, difficult, or nonconstructive.	Serious assertions that there are also other aspects.

power, and consolidating one's position as a representative. To choose and develop the right behavior to fulfill these intentions is a stressful job for a negotiator.

The difficulties experienced can be conceptualized as a set of dilemmas derived from the cooperation-fighting polarity. Experienced negotiators probably sense precisely the meaning of certain activities and the intentions of their negotiating partners. This perception prevents disorientation and misunderstandings, and it reduces stress and insecurity. The model of negotiating presented here is intended to aid orientation and to make the activities at the negotiating table easier to understand. Figure 4 summarizes the model for

FIGURE 4

Summary Chart of Negotiating as Four Processes Connected with Intents and as a Range of Dilemmas

Intent of Process	Type of Dilemma		
Obtaining results by dividing scarce resources and receiving a favorable deal.	The Information Dilemma open	_____ 1 2 3 4 5	closed
	The Pressure Dilemma flexible, compliant	_____ 1 2 3 4 5	firm, rigid
Promoting respectful personal relations and a constructive climate.	The Credibility Dilemma inspiring confidence	_____ 1 2 3 4 5	threatening, confusing
	The Dependency Dilemma stressing mutual dependence	_____ 1 2 3 4 5	stressing own interests
Establishing a favorable balance of power.	The Power Dilemma maintaining the balance of power	_____ 1 2 3 4 5	trying to dominate
Consolidating one's position as a representative.	The Representation Dilemma trying to enlarge the integrative space	_____ 1 2 3 4 5	maintaining partisan-like behavior; dependency toward one's constituency

use as an instrument for scoring and discussing specific negotiating behavior. There are no right or wrong scores for the dilemmas in Figure 4. In some instances "positive" behavior at the left side of each scale can produce very bad or even destructive results. Generally in negotiations there are strong behavioral tendencies toward the right side of the scale. The challenge is to move gradually and reciprocally toward the left, but certainly not to the extreme.

NOTES

1. The Dutch workshops were organized by Peter Hoogendorp, who provided many useful suggestions for the model, under the auspices of the Rijiks Opleidings Instituut of the Netherlands Ministry of Internal Affairs.

REFERENCES

Albeda, W. *Arbeidsverhoudingen in Nederland.* Alphen a/d Rijn, Netherlands: Samsom, *1975.*

Delden, P.J. van, *Het onderhandelingsgesprek.* Amsterdam, Netherlands: Organisatieadviesgroep Van Son, 1977.

Deutsch, M. *The resolution of conflict.* New Haven, CT: Yale University Press, 1973.

Douglas, A. *Industrial peacemaking.* New York: Columbia University Press, 1962.

Himmelmann, G. *Lohn bildung durch Kollektivverhandlungen.* Berlin, Federal Republic of Germany: Duncker and Humblot, 1971.

Hornstein, H.A. and Johnson, D.W. The effects of process analysis and ties to his group upon the negotiator's attitudes toward the outcomes of negotiations. *Journal of Applied Behavioral Science,* 1966, 2,449–463.

Iklé, F.C. *How nations negotiate.* New York: Harper & Row, 1964.

Karrass, C.L. *The negotiating game.* New York: Thomas Y. Crowell, 1970.

Karrass, C.L. *Give and take: The complete guide to negotiating strategies and tactics.* New York, Thomas Y. Crowell, 1974.

Lamm, H. and Kogan, N. Risk-taking in the context of intergroup negotiation. *Journal of Experimental Social Psychology,* 1970, 6, 351–363.

Mastenbroek, W.F.G. *[Negotiating as a social skill].* Leren en leven met groepen Alphen a.d. Rijn, Netherlands: Samsom, 1979. (Available in English from Free University of Amsterdam, Department of Social Psychology.)

Morley, J. and Stephenson, G. *The social psychology of bargaining.* London: Allen & Unwin, 1977.

Peabody, G.L. Power, Alinsky and other thoughts. In H.A. Hornstein and B.B. Bunker (eds.), *Social intervention.* New York: Free Press, 1971.

Pruitt, D.G. and Lewis, S.A. The psychology of integrative bargaining. In D. Druckman (ed.), *Negotiations, social psychological perspectives.* London: Sage, 1977.

Rubin, J.Z. and Brown, B.R. *The social psychology of bargaining and negotiation.* New York: Academic Press, 1975.

Schelling, T.C. *The strategy of conflict.* Cambridge, Mass.: Harvard University Press, 1960.

Stevens, C.M. *Strategy and collective bargaining negotiation.* New York: McGraw-Hill, 1963.

Vidmar, N. Effects of representational roles and mediation on negotiation effectiveness. *Journal of Personality and Social Psychology, 1971,14,* 48–49.

Walton, R.E. Interorganizational decision making and identity conflict. In M. Tuite, R. Chisholm and M. Radnor (eds.), *Interorganizational decision-making.* Chicago: Aldine, 1972.

Walton, R.E. and McKersie, R.B. *A behavioral theory of labor negotiations.* New York: McGraw-Hill, 1965.

NEGOTIATION TODAY: EVERYONE WINS

Beverly Byrum-Robinson

The large number of books, journals, articles, tapes, seminars, and workshops on negotiation attests to the growing popularity of the subject. Three major factors contribute to the increasing recognition of the importance of negotiation: (1) negotiation "stars," (2) a shift in power, and (3) negotiation as an alternative to conflict.

1. *Negotiation Stars.* High-powered negotiators admired for making "megadeals" have thrust the process and skill of negotiation into the limelight. People like Gerard Nierenberg—himself a successful negotiator—are making money by teaching and sharing their experiences with others.

2. *Shift in Power.* As organizational power continues to shift from dictatorial to democratic, more and more people have been seeing a need for effective negotiation skills. Consequently, negotiation courses, seminars, and workshops have sprung up for virtually every need, including those for buyers, sellers, managers, health professionals, school administrators, and women, as well as the more traditionally addressed courses for labor and international negotiators. Even computers are being used to effect more equitable conflict resolution.

3. *Alternative to Conflict.* Negotiation, in its broadest implication, is seen as an alternative to conflict and strife at interpersonal, organizational, and international levels. Because of the importance of negotiation—in some cases, a life-or-death matter—we should consider the meaning of "winning." Waitley (1985) gave a new view of winning:

> Our former basis for defining winning, according to external standards set by a hedonistic, egocentric, highly impressionable society, is being transformed. The new view of winning is based on internal standards which, while different for each individual, are consistent in that they take into account moral and spiritual values and principles that affect all of humankind and the natural world. (p. 30)

This article addresses the need to understand and practice negotiation skills. It defines negotiation, distinguishes it from other responses to conflict situation, and discusses the critical negotiation elements. The conclusion explores cur-

From *The 1991 Annual: Developing Human Resources*, Jossey-Bass/Pfeiffer. Reprinted by permission.

rent trends and implications for HRD (human resource development) professionals.

DEFINITION

Minimally, **negotiation** is a process by which two or more parties, each with its own goals and perspectives, coordinate areas of interest through concession and compromise to reach agreement and take jointly decided action about areas of common concern in a situation in which neither side has or wants to use complete power. Ideally, negotiation will produce a wise agreement and will improve—or, at least, not damage—the relationship of the parties.

To define negotiation properly, one needs to distinguish it from arbitration and mediation. *Arbitration* uses a third party to intervene. When the parties submit a dispute to an arbitrator, they agree to comply with the arbitrator's decision. *Mediation* also uses a third party, but the mediator has no authority to make a binding decision. The mediator facilitates a decision by listening, guiding, suggesting, and persuading the parties. Although multilateral negotiation might require a third party, this article focuses on negotiation between two parties.

CRITICAL ELEMENTS

Six major elements are common to all negotiations: the approach and outcome, the issues at stake, the negotiators, their relationship, the communication process, and the context.

Approach and Outcome

The outcomes of negotiation depend on the approach taken and the options that have been generated, considered, and synthesized in arriving at a final agreement. Four possible approaches are win-lose, lose-win, win-win, and mixed.

Win-Lose

Win-lose negotiation is characterized by each party's seeking its own advantage, usually to the detriment of the other party. This is the win-at-all-costs approach.

Lose-Win

A party may go into the negotiation with plans to yield to pressure. In the lose-win approach, one party seeks the acceptance of the other side regardless of the costs to itself. This is the peace-at-any-price approach.

Win-Win

Win-win negotiation is characterized by each party's seeking an agreement that provides joint gain. This is the everyone-a-winner approach.

Mixed

In a mixed approach, each party tries to be realistic. Both parties realize that usually one party wins more than does the other.

Issues

The issues include the interests that are at stake, the real or perceived conflicting positions that each negotiator takes, the best alternative to a negotiated agreement (BATNA), and the bottom line (the point at which the negotiator will walk away).

Interests and Positions

Each party enters the negotiation with the belief that its interest cannot be achieved without some cooperation from the other party. The negotiators take explicit positions, but their interests are often implicit. While the surface conflict in negotiation stems from the stated positions, a more serious conflict may stem from differences in interests. However, if interests are carefully discussed and explored, they may not be as far apart as the stated positions.

Needs

Essential human needs, such as security, affiliation, self-esteem, and recognition are at the base of all negotiation. Needs (that is, what is essential in the outcome) can be distinguished from wants (what is desirable but not necessary in the outcome). The combination of needs and wants contribute to the strategy and tactics that each negotiator uses.

Bottom Lines and Alternatives

Issues involve each party's bottom line (that is, its walk-away point). An alternative to a bottom line that saves the negotiator both from accepting unfavorable terms and from rejecting terms that would be beneficial is the BATNA—Best Alternative to a Negotiated Agreement. A way to discover a BATNA is to ask, "What will I do if I cannot get what I want?" For example, if purchasing a new personal computer is not possible, the alternative could be upgrading an old computer, leasing a new one, using someone else's, or delaying the purchase until a specified time. To arrive at the BATNA, one must identify one of the alternatives as being the best.

THE NEGOTIATORS

This section examines the negotiator profile—that is, the attributes that are necessary for a successful negotiator. These include personality, knowledge, mental and communication skills, and negotiation style.

Personality

Negotiators need moral and intellectual attributes. Necessary moral attributes include patience and self-restraint, objectivity, dedication or commitment, courage, honesty, integrity, perseverance, courtesy, and the ability to harmonize.

Intellectual attributes include wisdom, a clear and analytical mind, creativity, general intelligence, and leadership ability. Also, high self-esteem supports a negotiator's sense of confidence and competence.

Knowledge and Skills

Natural abilities need to be supplemented by several skills, including an understanding of human behavior. The negotiator also needs knowledge in the areas that are being negotiated and the ability to identify the issues, to perceive power, and to prepare and plan strategy and tactics.

Also required are excellent communication skills in the areas of argument and persuasion. Important interpersonal skills include the ability to express strong feelings appropriately and rationally, to be assertive rather than aggressive, and to listen attentively and actively.

Style

Although negotiators' styles stem primarily from personality predilection, various styles can be learned and adapted to expand their repertoire. The style used depends a great deal on the approach a negotiator takes. For example, if the negotiator has a win-lose approach, he or she is likely to be confident, impatient, and/or competitive.

RELATIONSHIP

When two negotiators come together, they form a relationship that comprises power, duration, and relationship style.

Power

The power in the relationship is not constant. Both parties can increase power, and an increase on one side does not necessarily mean a decrease for the other party. The following power paradoxes have been seen in the negotiation relationship (Bacharach and Lawler, 1986):

1. *Power is based on giving.* Providing the other party with benefits makes that party dependent on the one who is making the concessions, because a better deal might not be available outside this negotiation.

2. *To use power is to lose it.* Coercive action leads to reciprocal threats and/or compliance with resentment. If the "victim" holds a grudge, he or she might either "get back" or terminate the relationship. Neither of those actions is a favorable consequence for the negotiator who used the coercive tactics.

3. *The manipulation of power might have integrative effects.* If power is gained by giving, the other negotiator might reciprocate the giving or concession making, thus moving the negotiation toward a mutual, joint gain.

4. *An inferior power position can provide a tactical advantage.* If commitment to the negotiation is low, the more highly committed will yield to the lower committed, because there is more for the highly committed party to lose by walking away from the negotiation.

These paradoxes imply that short-term gains can lead to long-term losses. In fact, it has been suggested that an ongoing relationship should be the second most desirable outcome in a negotiation (Wall, 1985; Fisher and Ury, 1981). The most desirable outcome is, of course, a substantive agreement.

Duration

Trust is a rich concept in practical negotiations: the longer the relationship, the more opportunity to build trust; and the higher the trust, the easier it is to negotiate openly, flexibly, and creatively. Fisher and Ury's (1981, p. 55) negotiation dictum, "Be hard on the problem, soft on the people," points to the importance of the working relationship between the negotiators.

Style

The perception of trust and the perception of agreement are important dimensions of relationship style. Block (in Copeland, 1990) developed the following five styles from these two dimensions:

1. *High Agreement, High Trust.* With these two dimensions, the negotiating parties are *allies.* They will find it most effective to affirm the agreement and the quality of the relationship, to acknowledge any doubts, and to consult each other for advice and support.

2. *High Agreement, Low Trust.* In this case the parties are *bedfellows.* They find it most effective to reaffirm the agreement, to determine what each party wants, to acknowledge cautiousness, and to establish procedures for working together.

3. *Low Agreement, Low Trust.* These parties are obviously *adversaries.* With them, it is most effective for each party to establish its own position without making demands, to understand the other's position, to acknowledge its own responsibility in the problem, and to conclude by detailing its plans of action.

4. *Somewhere between High Agreement, Low Trust and Low Agreement, Low Trust.* These are *fence sitters.* It is most effective for them to determine where each stands and to urge each other to think about the issues.

5. *Low Agreement, High Trust.* These negotiators are *opponents,* and their most effective move is to affirm the quality of the relationship, to determine each side's position, and to use creative problem-solving to reach an outcome .

These styles are illustrated in Figure 1.

Figure 1
Negotiation Relationship Styles

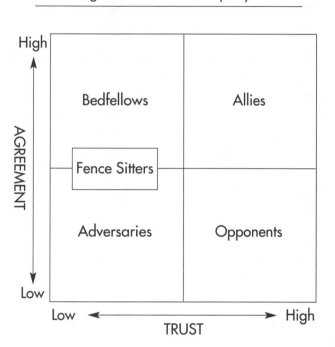

THE PROCESS

Negotiation stages, strategies, and tactics constitute the negotiation process.

Stages

Although negotiation is a moment-by-moment process, the stages through which it proceeds are identifiable: pre-negotiation, negotiation, and post-negotiation—each of which is divided into substages.

Pre-Negotiation

The subphases of this stage are pre-conference negotiation and preparation. Pre-conference negotiation involves setting the requirements of the negotiation and selecting the site. The parties must agree on the general issue or purpose and the initial negotiation objectives for each party. Site selection can be critical because of the advantages and disadvantages of particular sites.

For example, "your place" means unfamiliarity with surroundings for one party, but it also gives that party the ability to delay action because of lack of access to superiors. "My place" makes it difficult for the host to walk out, but it provides easy access to experts, superiors, and information. A neutral "some place" might complicate the picture with a third party, but it could ease tension regarding territorial problems. "No place" is also possible; that is, teleconferencing and other types of technological forms of communication. The no-place site might allow time to respond but it eliminates the ability to read nonverbal language.

Preparation can be a year-round process. It includes self-preparation for the negotiator, establishing one's objectives, and attempting to determine the other party's objectives.

Negotiation

This stage begins when the parties actually meet together to do business or at least to discuss the issues at hand. The subphases are climate-setting, orientation, opening, conflict, bargaining, and agreement.

Although the *climate* depends on the approach the negotiators take, it should be polite and cooperative, because this is the most effective climate. The negotiator's *orientation* should be flexible, and neither party should reveal its BATNA. The *opening* can begin with a statement of position or a statement of interests.

Conflict will occur regardless of how the other subphases are positioned, because negotiation always involves some real or perceived conflict. To avoid a stalemate, the negotiators will begin *bargaining*. Generally the negotiators will bargain a number of times before *agreement*, or the closing, is reached. In the agreement subphase, the parties move from a crisis point to cohesion.

Post-Negotiation

The final stage ensures implementation of the agreement. The formal contract is written, approved, and administered. In some cases, closure might be episodic and renegotiating will be needed.

Strategy and Tactics

The distinctions between *strategy* and *tactics* are blurred. However, the strategy can be seen as the overall game plan that the negotiator follows in achieving his or her goals, whereas tactics are the specific actions used to effect the strategy (Calero and Oskam, 1983). In other words, strategy is the use of tactics to achieve an end.

The broadest categories of tactics are *rational* and *irrational*. Rational tactics (see Figure 2) are those designed by the negotiator to provide a positive outcome, and include debate and bargaining. There are three types of debate tactics: structural, competitive, and joint problem-solving.

The largest category of rational tactics (bargaining) is used to alter the other party's behavior. It can be divided into aggressive, nonaggressive, and posturing tactics. The hostile, aggressive tactics are generally *threat* and *coercion*. Non-aggressive bargaining allows the parties to use conciliatory and reward tactics. Posturing tactics are used to alter the perception of the negotiator and the behavior that was probably planned. Tough posturing is used to give the appearance of strength; soft posturing, to influence cooperation and respect; and neutral posturing, to allow the negotiator to be inscrutable.

Figure 2
Rational Tactics

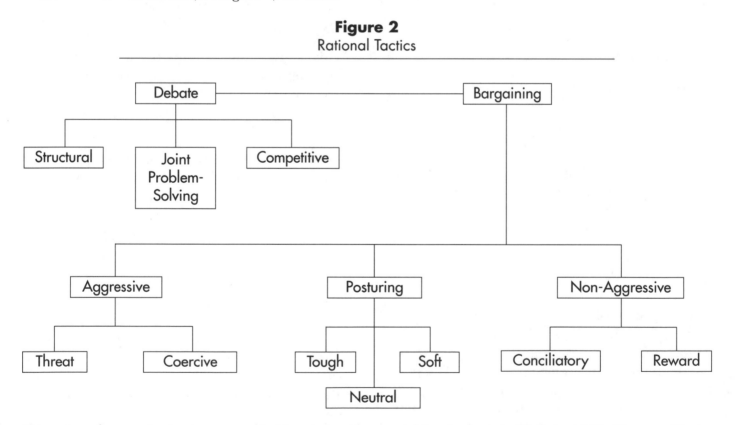

This system of categorization is presented in Negotiation: Theory and Practice by J. A. Wall, Jr., 1985, Glenview, Illinois: Scott, Foresman.

NEGOTIATION CONTEXT

Because the negotiation context refers to the immediate environment, the site selection is very important in the preparation phase of negotiation. However, there will be external environmental influences that are beyond the negotiator's immediate control. These include legal, social, economic, and political influences. The negotiators must be aware of these influences and the impact that they might make on the negotiation process and outcome.

TRENDS

A review of experimental and theoretical research and of the basic negotiation elements indicates a movement toward win-win negotiation. Roth and Schoumaker (1983) contend that fostering common outcome expectations between negotiators encourages reaching agreement. In replying to an experiment of noncooperative strategies in which buyers met the demands of sellers, Neelin, Sonnenschein, and Spiegel (1988) and Binmore, Shaked, and Sutton (1988) explain that if the proper environment is established, *games* people can be replaced by *fair* people.

In reviewing experimental, computer-simulation, and international studies about useful strategies for gaining cooperation, Patchen (1987, p. 182) discovered a "remarkable convergence of findings." While unconditional cooperation drew exploitation and coercion drew fighting, reciprocity strategies were most effective in gaining cooperation. In linking theory to field research, Tracy and Peterson (1986) discovered that integrative bargaining (win-win) tactics were also useful for distributive (win-lose) bargaining, but the reverse was not true. Furthermore, integrative bargaining tactics were recommended because they have the potential to expand alternatives and increase outcomes for both parties. This study reinforced the importance of a trusting and respectful relationship built on clarity, open-

ness, and the suspension of commitment while options are being explored.

HRD IMPLICATIONS

The trend toward accepting the win-win approach as superior has some implications for HRD professionals. They would benefit in several dimensions from knowing and practicing this negotiation orientation.

1. As the call for empowerment grows stronger, more and more people in organizations are profiting from negotiation-skills training. Because HRD professionals often act as instructors, they need to know how to explain to others that negotiation is not only an interpersonal process but a learnable skill. Although all organizational levels can benefit from negotiation-skills training, management is particularly in need of these skills. Negotiation is becoming a way of life for managers, and a good percentage of the manager's time is spent in negotiating—with superiors, subordinates, colleagues, customers, competitors, and vendors. Brooks and Odiorne (1984) herald negotiation as the "new nineties management style."

2. Since HRD professionals are expected to be proficient in all interpersonal skills, they obviously need to have negotiation skills. However, these competencies can also help the HRD professional in taking his or her rightful place at the executive level and in becoming involved in the organization's strategic planning. The HRD professional needs to know how to negotiate for his or her own special interest, for the long-term human needs of the organization, and for the overall business objectives.

3. Strong corporate cultures practice more win-win than win-lose negotiating. Because the creation and maintenance of a healthy

corporate culture comes under the auspices of organizational development and value-based strategic planning, HRD professionals need to promote and practice cooperative organizational behavior. They must model a win-win attitude, which consists of openness, receptivity, integrity, flexibility, and creativity.

4. A background in negotiation can lead to new organizational roles for the HRD professional. Organizational mediators and corporate ombudspeople are emerging in organizations, with more new roles likely to follow.

5. Effective negotiation can facilitate the establishment of partnerships and networks, both of which are important to the HRD professional's need to move ideas through the organization and to pave the way for change.

6. On a personal level, the HRD professional's ability to negotiate from a win-win stance can improve relationships both on the job and away from work. Human resource development emphasizes a balanced life, and improvement of one's personal relationships can only benefit all other areas of an HRD professional's life.

CONCLUSION

The time for cooperation has arrived. The win-win approach to negotiation, requiring a repertoire of practical skills, is gaining wide acceptance. Because win-win negotiation is more time consuming than unilateral decision making, some believe that it is a weak approach. However, it allows negotiators—who traditionally regard each other as adversaries—to share and understand interests, to build a relationship, and to explore options and make commitments that produce joint mutual gain. Win-win negotiation might not be a perfect process; it is, however, better than the alternatives.

REFERENCES

Bacharach, S. B., and Lawler, E. J. (1986). Power dependence and power paradoxes in bargaining. *Negotiation Journal*, 167–174.

Binmore, K., Shaked, A., and Sutton, J. (1988, September). A further test of noncooperative bargaining theory: Reply. *American Economic Review*, pp. 837–839.

Brooks, E., and Odiome, G. S. (1984). *Managing by negotiations.* New York: Van Nostrand Reinhold.

Calero, H. H., and Oskam, B. (1983). *Negotiate the deal you want.* New York: Dodd, Mead.

Copeland, G. (1990, July). Increasing group productivity: A practical guide for health professionals. *The IHS Primary Care Provider*, pp. 1–9.

Fisher, R., and Ury, W. (1981). *Getting to YES: Negotiating agreement without giving in.* Boston: Houghton Mifflin.

Neelin, J., Sonnenschein, H., and Spiegel, M. (1988, September). A further test of noncooperative bargaining theory: Comment. *American Economic Review*, pp. 824–836.

Patchen, M. (1987). Strategies for eliciting cooperation from an adversary. *Journal of Conflict Resolution*, 31(1), 164–185.

Roth, A. E., and Schoumaker, F. (1983, June). Expectations and reputations in bargaining: An experimental study. *American Economic Review*, pp. 362–372.

Tracy, L., and Peterson, R. B. (1986). A behavioral theory of labor negotiations—How well has it aged? *Negotiation Journal*, Z 93–108.

Waitley, D. (1985). *The double win: Success is a two-way street.* Old Tappen, N.J.: Fleming H. Revell.

Wall, J. A., Jr. (1985). *Negotiation: Theory and practice.* Glenview, Ill.: Scott, Foresman.

ANNOTATED BIBLIOGRAPHY[1]

Anderson, H. J. (ed.). (1976). *New techniques in labor dispute resolution.* Washington, D.C.: Bureau of National Affairs.

 Compilation of two professional conferences. Focuses on resolution of union-management disputes. Recommends mediation as a positive problem-solving alternative to the more common collective bargaining/ arbitration processes used in labor-dispute resolution.

Bacharach, S. B., and Lawler, E. J. (1981). *Bargaining power, tactics, and outcomes.* San Francisco: Jossey-Bass.

Describes bargaining theory in detail. Emphasizes that bargaining power is the essence of the process, context, and outcomes of bargaining. Focuses on labor-management disputes.

Beckmann, N. W. (1977). *Negotiations.* Lexington, Mass.: Lexington Books.

 Focuses on the buyer-seller relationship. States that concepts can be applied to all negotiating relationships. Outlines the characteristics of a negotiator along with many details of cost-pricing data.

Brooks, E., and Odiorne, G. S. (1984). *Managing by negotiations.* New York: Van Nostrand Reinhold.

 Suggests that negotiation is part of a new 1990s management style. Helps readers to assess their personal strategies, then provides exercises and checklists to help readers learn practical tactics. Recommends the use of win-win techniques. Discusses ways that negotiation can ease the depersonalization of bureaucracy and how principles of transactional analysis (recognizing parent, child, and adult ego states) can help the negotiation process.

Burrows, S. J. (1984). *Win/win outcomes: A physician's negotiating guide.* Chicago: Pluribus Press.

 Hypothesizes that physicians tend to have negative attitudes about negotiating because of their inability to negotiate in their daily lives. Provides a format for learning better negotiation skills. Emphasizes protection of the physician and proper training in win/win negotiation skills.

Calero, H. H., and Oskam, B. (1983). *Negotiate the deal you want.* New York: Dodd, Mead.

 Includes an extensive problem-solving key that summarizes the core material. Focuses on business people, but emphasizes that good negotiation skills enhance any interaction. Stresses win-win negotiation and cooperation in order to meet both parties' needs.

Casse, P., and Deol, S. (1985). *Managing intercultural negotiations: Guidelines for trainers and negotiators.* Washington, D.C.: SIETAR International.

 Consists of a self-help workbook structured as ten mini-workshops. Includes many definitions of negotiation and a discussion of the implications of intercultural negotiations. Includes psychological concepts, such as cognitive dissonance, individuation, and Group Planning Technique (GPT).

Cohen, H. (1980). *You can negotiate anything.* Secaucus, N.J.: Lyle Stuart.

 Serves as a practical guide to negotiation skills. Relates negotiation to roles as consumers, parents, spouses, and co-workers. Emphasizes a win/win philosophy in a how-to format. Includes one chapter on the use of the win-lose negotiation strategy.

Coulson, R. (1979). *Labor arbitration—What you need to know.* New York: American Arbitration Association.

 Describes the labor grievance process as set out by the American Arbitration Association.

Dunlop, J. T. (1984). *Dispute resolution: Negotiation and consensus building.* Dover, Mass.: Auburn House Publishing Company.

 Analyzes in detail the negotiation process in United States labor and management organizations and in public and private management. Focuses on long-term negotiations. Stresses consensus building as an effective negotiation tool.

Ebener, P.A., and Betancourt, D. R.. (1985). *Court-annexed arbitration: The national picture.* Santa Monica, Calif.: Institute for Civil Justice, The Rand Corporation.

 Reveals the findings of a national survey of the status of court-annexed arbitration among state and federal trial courts. This alternative means of dispute resolution has grown in popularity

The author would like to thank Connie Robertson for researching the Annotated Bibliography.

since 1980, especially because it can reduce court delays and the expense of civil cases.

Elkin, R. D., and Hewitt, T. L. (1980). *Successful arbitration: An experiential approach.* Reston, Va.: Reston Publishing.

> Includes four simulations of major labor-management arbitration cases, with tips on successful arbitration. Written in a win-lose negotiation style.

Fisher, R., and Brown, S. (1988). *Getting together.* Boston: Houghton Mifflin.

> Emphasizes relationships, how they affect negotiation, and how people can get what they want.

Fisher, R., and Ury, W. (1981). *Getting to YES: Negotiating agreement without giving in.* Boston: Houghton Mifflin.

> Provides new ideas on negotiation based on the Harvard Negotiation Project. Suggests creative alternatives to situational bargaining and competitive tactics, with an emphasis on interests (the win/win strategy) rather than on positions (the win/lose strategy).

Folberg, J., and Taylor, A. (1986). *Mediation: A comprehensive guide to resolving conflicts without litigation.* San Francisco: Jossey-Bass.

> Stresses mediation as an alternative conflict-resolution process. Presents mediation as cooperative, as opposed to litigation, which is adversarial. Written for therapists, counselors, social workers, lawyers, and others in the helping professions. Illustrates uses of mediation in different settings—families, communities, labor, and so on.

Guder, R. F. (ed.). (1985). *Negotiating techniques: How to work toward a constructive agreement.* Fairfield, N.J.: Economics Press.

> Written for managers rather than formal labor/management negotiators. Endorses the we of win-win strategies, with special emphasis on relationships.

Henry, J. F., and Kieberman, J. K. (1985). *The manager's guide to resolving legal disputes: Better results without litigation.* New York: Harper & Row.

> Explains why resolving conflict outside of court is good and what processes can be used to resolve conflicts. Includes a chapter on negoti-

ating settlements that explains both the adversarial, zero-sum approach and the problem-solving, interest-based approach.

Hensler, D. R. (1986). *What we know and don't know about court-administered arbitration.* Santa Monica. Calif.: Institute for Civil Justice, The Rand Corporation.

> Reports what has been learned from court-administered arbitration and what questions remain concerning the process. Uses win/lose language in a courtroom style.

Hoffman, E. B. (1973). *Resolving labor-management disputes: Nine-country comparison.* New York: The Conference Board.

> Discusses the dispute-resolution methods of conciliation and mediation, inquiry and investigation, arbitration, and judicial settlement, all of which are used to resolve deadlocked labor-management negotiations. Compares the effectiveness of negotiations in the United States and other countries. Suggests that employee involvement in management could alleviate labor-management disputes.

Jandt, F. E., and Gillette, P. (1985). *Win-win negotiating: Turning conflict into agreement.* New York: John Wiley.

> Discusses organizational and on-the-job conflict. Suggests the use of interest (win-win) bargaining rather than positional (win-lose) bargaining.

Kagel, S., and Kelly, K. (1989). *The anatomy of mediation.* Washington, D.C.: Bureau of National Affairs

> Illustrates how mediation works, with the use of a case study. Points out that the use of mediation is rising because of problems with litigation (such as time, money, and frustration).

Karrass, C. L. (1970). *The negotiating game.* New York: Thomas Y. Crowell.

> Combines modern analytical thinking with bargaining-table practice. Uses research findings to show that negotiation is a consciously undertaken process that anyone can learn. Discusses many theories and models. Includes a chapter on negotiation in marriage.

• • • • •

Karrass, C. L. (1974). *Give and take: The complete guide to negotiating strategies and tactics.* New York: Thomas Y. Crowell.
> Includes an alphabetical list of strategies and countermeasures in practical negotiation. Written for business executives, but many of the techniques discussed are directed toward sellers.

Karrass, G. (1985). *Negotiate to close: How to make more successful deals.* New York: Simon & Schuster.
> Emphasizes sales negotiation. Written from the seller's point of view. Stresses the importance of long-term relationships and keeping customers happy, especially in industrial sales.

Kennedy, M. M.. (1982). *Salary strategies: Everything you need to know to get the salary you want.* New York: Rawson, Wade.
> Includes models of recommended strategies in a chapter on negotiating for money. Written to help employees get what they want. Does not emphasize the needs of the organization.

Laborde, G. Z. (1987). *Influencing with integrity: Management skills for communication and negotiation.* Palo Alto, Calif.: Syntony Publishing.
> Uses the Syntonics model, a model of communications theory based on neurolinguistic programming (NLP) . Written for management and business. Emphasizes the use of syntonic skills rather than manipulation. Presents negotiation tactics that utilize the Syntonics model.

Lax, D. A., and Sebenius, J. K. (1986). *The manager as negotiator: Bargaining for cooperation and competitive gain.* New York: Free Press.
> Uses the terms "value creators" (win-win) and "value claimers" (win-lose). Written specifically for managers.

Lazarus, S., Bray, J. J., Jr., Carter, L. L., Collins, K. H., Giedt, B. A., Holton, R. V. Jr., Matthews, P. D., and Willard, G. C. (1965). *Resolving business disputes: The potential of commercial arbitration.* New York: American Management Association.
> Supports commercial arbitration and advocates its use in business disputes. Suggests use of commercial arbitration by businesspeople, lawyers, and arbitrators. States that commercial arbitration, using a knowledgeable third party, is the best method of keeping buyer-seller relationships running smoothly. Discusses the international business arena as well.

Lemmon, J. A. (1985). *Family mediation practice.* New York: Free Press.
> Written for families with conflicts who might want to use mediation, and for professionals who wish to acquire mediation skills. States that mediation is a better alternative to conflict resolution than court litigation because of costs and time involved with the latter.

Lewicki, R. J., and Litterer, J. A. (1985). *Negotiation.* Homewood, Ill.: Richard D. Irwin.
> Includes theory, models, and how-to material. Stresses a cooperative, win/win approach in a chapter on integrative bargaining. Discusses the win/lose strategy and the problems stemming from this competitive approach. Includes research results and consequences of ethical and unethical behaviors.

Mackay, H. (1988). *Swim with the sharks without being eaten alive.* New York: Ivy Books.
> Outlines a how-to approach to winning and negotiating sales. Includes a chapter on the "Buyer/Seller Battle." Discusses the importance of creating loyalty and long-term relationships between sellers and customers.

Moore, C. W. (1986). *The mediation process: Practical strategies for resolving conflict.* San Francisco: Jossey-Bass.
> Written for mediators, lawyers, therapists, teachers, and any other professionals who use negotiation. Details the mediation process and the appropriateness and effectiveness of mediation in dispute resolution. Suggests that mediation can teach negotiators to be cooperative (win/win) rather than competitive (win/lose).

Nierenberg, G. I. (1986). *The complete negotiator.* New York: Nierenberg and Zeif.
> Emphasizes that negotiation is part of all aspects of life—personal, social, and work. States that negotiation is not a competitive game. Stresses cooperative agreement (a win/win strategy).

Nierenberg, J., and Ross, I. S.. (1985). *Women and the art of negotiating.* New York: Simon & Schuster.
> Written to teach women negotiation skills in various settings. Based on the "everyone wins'

philosophy of negotiation.

Prasow, P., and Peters, F. (1983). *Arbitration and collective bargaining: Conflict resolution in labor relations.* New York: McGraw-Hill.
> Provides a history of arbitration; includes discussions of arbitrators' authority, written contracts, legal developments, and case studies.

Raiffa, H. (1982). *The art and science of negotiation.* Cambridge, Mass.: Harvard University Press.
> Based on discussions in the Harvard Negotiation Workshop. Includes mathematical models of negotiation theory and case studies of applied knowledge.

Reck, R. R., and Long, B. C. (1985). *The win-win negotiator.* Kalamazoo, Mich.: Spartan Publications.
> Outlines an easy-to-use negotiation method.

Scott, B. (1988). *Negotiating constructive and competitive negotiations.* London: Paradigm Publishing.
> Used as a textbook in business and management courses, with emphasis on commercial and allied negotiations. Presents two negotiating styles: constructive and competitive, without judgments of the methods' merits.

Sloss, L., and Davis, M. S.. (eds.). (1986). *A game for high stakes: Lessons learned in negotiating with the Soviet Union.* Cambridge, Mass.: Ballinger.
> Based on seminars presented on Soviet Union and American negotiations. Includes main findings of discussions, papers submitted, and edited oral presentations. Focuses on arms control negotiation (the topic of most of the seminars).

Sparks, D. B. (1982). *The dynamics of effective negotiation.* Houston, Texas: Gulf Publishing.
> Focuses on long-term relationships. Stresses the importance of balancing a competitive approach with present objectives. Outlines techniques for acquiring negotiation skills.

Spitz, J. A. (ed.). (1976). *Grievance handling and preparing for arbitration in the public sector.* Los Angeles: UCLA Institute of Industrial Relations.
> Used as a training manual for state and local public managers and employees in labor-relations conduct.

Waitley, D. (1985). *The double win: Success is a two-way street.* Old Tappan, N.J.: Fleming H. Revell.
> Presents the author's belief that the double win is possible and that it works. States that cooperation with and concern for others is the way to success.

Wall, J. A., Jr. (1985). *Negotiation: Theory and practice.* Glenview, Ill.: Scott, Foresman.
> Provides the pros and cons of different negotiation strategies.

Warschaw, T. A. (1980) *Winning by negotiation.* New York: McGraw-Hill.
> Outlines winning strategies used in business that can be used in everyday life. Describes in detail several different negotiating styles, with exercises provided to determine the reader's own negotiating profile.

Zack, A. M. (ed.). (1984). *Arbitration in practice.* Ithaca, New York: ILR Press.
> Includes insights and philosophies of experienced arbitrators. States that labor arbitration is a voluntary judicial process and an alternative to the court system.

Beverly Byrum-Robinson, Ph.D., is a professor of communication at Wright State University, Ohio, and the president of her own company, The Communication Connection. Dr. Byrum-Robinson conducts seminars on topics such as conflict management, team building, stress and time management, and assertiveness. As a consultant, she facilitates team-building sessions in organizations. She has written one book and co-authored three others, and has published articles on interpersonal and group communication and training.

• • • • •

Chapter Two

CONFLICT RESOLUTION

USE OF THE COLLABORATIVE ETHIC AND CONTINGENCY THEORIES IN CONFLICT MANAGEMENT

Susan Hoefflinger Taft

As American organizations change, social forces from within and international pressures from without are causing managers to re-examine the basic principles of management practice. In an era of rapid change and high uncertainty, the management of conflict and differences assumes an important role in assuring organizational viability.

The appreciation of differences is a central tenet of conflict management. Organizations are becoming increasingly diverse and are grappling with ways and means to capitalize on the diversity. At the same time, the open-system nature of organizations requires a receptivity to the inputs and forces of the environment. Openness requires a respect for and understanding of differences.

In the absence of important stakes—resources, opportunities, power, and control—differences between people are rarely a cause of conflict. In the presence of these stakes, however, and usually in direct proportion to them, conflict arises and escalates. The form of the conflict can be as

simple as a difference of opinion between two colleagues, a supervisor and a subordinate, or two groups with differing core tasks; or it can be as complex as differences among U.S. senators who are trying to formulate international policy and pass legislation. The management of conflict in widely varying contexts requires a complex set of interpersonal and cognitive skills to locate and manipulate the key stakes.

Only recently has research in conflict management taken full account of the complex nature of conflict and the wide range of stakes to which incumbents might be attached. The call in the literature for more contingency theories (Filley, 1978; Robbins, 1978; Thomas, 1978; Thomas, Jamieson, and Moore, 1978) reflects our developing interest in finding comprehensive and flexible tools. This article reviews some of the theoretical heritage of conflict management. Based on the ideas of this heritage, a conflict-intervention process will be described.

Two schools of thought in conflict management are useful for the intervention process described later. These are the "collaboration ethic" (Thomas, 1977, 1978) and "contingency" approaches. The intervention process draws on the creative

From *The 1987 Annual: Developing Human Resources,* Jossey-Bass/Pfeiffer. Reprinted by permission.

usefulness of working with several different frames of reference—collaboration as a value position and contingency approaches as tools of flexibility.

According to K. W. Thomas, collaboration has been "variously called 'confrontation,' 'problem solving,' 'integrating,' and 'integrative bargaining.' This behavioral mode seeks joint optimization of the concerns of two or more parties, with an emphasis on openness and trust. Advocates for this mode have often lapsed into absolutism" (Thomas, 1977, p. 485). This reference to absolutism implies that collaboration has been taken as a single-value stance without an acknowledgment of the benefits and efficacy of multi-value stances. The second school, contingency theory, addresses this limitation.

Contingency theories acknowledge complexity. They direct the manager to an appreciation of the multiple factors—the contingencies—involved in a conflict, because a suitable strategy can often be derived by considering these contingencies. The strategy might be collaborative, it might involve accommodation, or it might alter power relationships or adjust resources.

THE COLLABORATION ETHIC

Collaboration as an approach to conflict management was first elaborated by Mary Parker Follett in the early years of the twentieth century. Because her classic work influenced many subsequent theorists and became the underpinning of the collaborative ethic, a closer look at some of her ideas is appropriate. In the collection of her papers by Metcalf and Urwick (1940, p. 30), her simple definition of conflict—"the appearance of difference, difference of opinions, of interest"— suggests that conflict results from the richness of diverse human interaction. She delineates three primary methods for dealing with conflict.

The first of these methods is *domination*, synonymous with the current-day term "competition,"

which provides for the victory of one side over the other. This method is easiest in the short run, requiring relatively little expenditure of time or energy, but it is often unsuccessful in the long run. The issues leading to the original conflict will often resurface later under the domination mode.

The second method is *compromise*, which is a common way to settle controversy. In compromise, each side gives something up for the sake of peace or resolution. Since some degree of sacrifice is involved, unsatisfied needs and wants are likely to resurface again later, as with domination.

Follett's third method of resolving conflict is *integration*, which is synonymous with "collaboration." Integration is a dialectical process: both parties speak to their needs, desires, and visions. As clarity emerges around the issues of both sides, inventiveness is used to seek an original, higher-order synthesis. The integration process supports and encourages diversity. Follett asserts the need for both sides to be highly self-interested; for without this characteristic, the data supplied will be insufficient to enable both parties to find a creative solution. Integration eliminates a win-lose attitude. Follett believes that "there are always more than two alternatives in a situation, and our job is to analyze the situation carefully enough for as many as possible to appear" (Metcalf and Urwick, 1940, pp. 219–220). Diversity is united, the integrity of both parties is protected, and creative problem-solving is advanced; these benefits accrue to the parties in conflict as well as, in a ripple effect, to society in general (Metcalf and Urwick, 1940). Follett considers integration a qualitative adjustment and compromise a quantitative one. An integrative experience is a progressive experience, because it moves both parties forward.

Integration as a method for conflict resolution is not always possible. Follett (1951, p. 163) admits that "not all differences. . . can be integrated. That we must face fully, but it is certain that there are fewer irreconcilable activities than we at present think, although it often takes ingenuity, a 'creative intelligence,' to find the integration." Other writers agree that integration is not always possible, but it might be useful more often than most people realize (Deutsch, 1969; Katz and Kahn, 1966). Many people find it easier to fight than to work constructively toward mutually satisfying conflict solutions.

Follett emphasized examining the conflict process as part of integrative resolutions. Messages between parties in conflict can include subtle or nonverbal cues, and a look at only the content of the message can lead one on a convoluted chase. Process cues can, at times, help to locate key issues quickly. Attending to both the content and the process enhances the likelihood of a collaborative solution.

Intellectually analytic activities are necessary in the pursuit of successful collaborative outcomes. Eiseman (1977, 1978) uses the development of a conceptual framework for looking at the parties' desires, beliefs, experiences, and behavior. The issue in contention is *reframed* intellectually so that opposing sides locate a perspective compatible to both. Reframing can involve moving toward more *abstract* ideals (e.g., "What is our common vision of what is best for the organization as a whole?") or toward more *concrete* concerns (e.g., "If we implement this policy, how are employees likely to respond?"). Moving between the abstract and concrete poles will assist in seeing the total situation. True to the spirit of collaboration, Eiseman (1978, p. 134) considers a conflict resolved "only when each party is convinced that his or her final way of thinking about the conflict embodies not only his initial position, but also those of his adversaries."

The manner in which individuals engage in conflict tends to draw on a few preferred behaviors. One model for identifying conflict style is oriented along two axes representing self-interest and concern for others (Thomas, 1976). Col-

laborative problem-solving requires both a high degree of concern for self and a great amount of empathy for the other party. This view incorporates and synthesizes potentially opposing desires: the desire to win and the need to cooperate. Five conflict-handling orientations are plotted on the model, with collaborative behaviors initially representing the ideal orientation (high self-interest and high concern for others).

Subsequently, Thomas began to question the ideal status of collaboration, and his views illustrate the rising popularity of contingency theory. Differing values and situations often call for the functionally useful application of modes other than collaborating: competing, compromising, avoiding, and accommodating (Thomas, 1977). Although collaborating can be an idealized and valued strategy, it is not always possible or efficacious. A simplistic normative prescription for collaboration denies the inherent variability and complexity of life in modern-day organizations .

The foregoing views were selected to illustrate some of the history and ideas on the collaborative ethic. Although collaboration is a rich and provocative heritage and useful in managing many forms of conflict, it has limitations, which include the following:

1. An assumption basic to collaboration theory is the existence of two clearly defined sides or camps. In reality, the network of allies can take the form of a meandering chain with various degrees of wants and needs centered around multiple foci.

2. The collaborative ethic fails to address power inequities that are frequently present in conflict situations . For example, it is naive to believe that a collaborative spirit is all that is necessary to solve every conflict between a supervisor and subordinate.

3. The collaborative ethic assumes that both parties have good will and a desire to achieve the best possible outcome. However,

conflict—by definition—assumes the presence of stakes; therefore, even the most honorable intentions may be derailed as parties examine their differences.

CONTINGENCY APPROACHES

The complexity of society—local, national, and international—is paralleled in organizations. It is a rare organization that does not need to cope with extensive social diversity and worldwide economic forces while pursuing its mission. Contingency theory takes into account variation, diversity, and complexity. Instead of advancing a normative prescription, it assists in the analysis of situations based on a range of intervening factors.

A contingency view of the collaborative ethic suggests that collaboration might well be the best alternative when certain conditions are present: power equalization between parties; present and future interdependence; mutual interest in solving the problem; openness; organizational support and procedures for collaboration; and a desire to defeat the problem rather than the opponent (Derr, 1978; Phillips and Cheston, 1979). When sufficient conditions are not present for collaboration, other modes might be more useful. The absence of motivation to resolve a conflict can lead logically and functionally to an avoidance posture. Sharply differing value systems within an organization might be best coaxed into peaceful coexistence through compromise. The need for quick action might call for, at least temporarily, competing behaviors. Social credits and debits can be tallied through accommodation maneuvers, to be drawn on in the next conflict. Varying demands of a situation influence the choice of conflict strategy (Derr, 1978; Filley, 1978; Phillips and Cheston, 1979; Robbins, 1978; Thomas, 1977, 1978). Choices are contingent on a range of relevant factors, and managers are denied a quick and simple prescription for conflict interventions.

Power inequities make a major impact on conflict situations, and contingency theorists recognize this dynamic influence. Successful collaborative outcomes in the absence of power parity are difficult, and yet power differentials between conflicting parties are quite prevalent. Power is associated with a host of factors: significant resources (money, information, connections to important people), legitimate authority, social demographic characteristics, alliances and positioning, facility with language, knowledge, and more.

Fisher and Ury (1981) explicitly address power inequities in negotiation. Much of their work is based on collaboration theory: for example, working to surface basic interests of parties rather than taking positions (which tend to become hardened and entrenched during negotiations). They propose using the following strategies when the opponent wields power:

1. Develop your best alternative to a negotiated agreement. Protect yourself from making an agreement that is not in your best interest.

2. Focus on the merits (i.e., the principles you and they wish to obtain in the outcome) rather than on positions.

3. Avoid defensiveness and counterattacking. Invite their criticism and advice. Ask questions.

4. Consider bringing in a third party.

Their book is rich with techniques and methods for conflict management. Although their philosophy is consistent with the collaborative ethic, it extends one's options for dealing with a variety of common contingencies. A limitation to the theory is the continued exploration of conflict between two parties without addressing the phenomenon as a disparate, multifocused, ubiquitous resident of organizations.

Locating and defining the most germane conflict in an organization is a first and difficult task confronting the conflict manager. Behind every conflict there may lurk a small army of disparate employees, each with individual beliefs, perceptions, and stakes. Choosing the pertinent issue and addressing the most relevant interests are not simple tasks; frequently managers are caught in this bog and try to solve the wrong problem. What looks on the surface like a classic case of conflict between two stakeholders, and therefore between two parties, might take on subtle and varied nuances as the manager digs deeper to find the real sources of tension experienced by organizational members. Elusiveness of clearly definable sides in a conflict is common in real organizations.

The complex nature of conflict in organizations and the need for analytic tools are addressed in Brown's (1983) comprehensive theory. An extensive contingency framework is developed to assist managers and organizational theorists in the management of conflict. Focusing on a conflict interface, Brown conducts an in-depth examination of the fields or clusters of people grouped around the conflict. His most significant contribution is to tackle, ambitiously, the complexity of organizational conflict and to suggest "countervening" strategies tailored to the situation. Because of the extent of detail, Brown's theory is difficult to summarize; yet a few words on the framework are necessary for any review of contingency theories.

A central tenet of Brown's theory is that conflict can exist in different quantities in organizations: too much, too little, or a productive amount. The dynamics of conflict may lead to problem-solving or bargaining (productive), escalation (too much), or suppression or withdrawal (too little). An initial diagnosis by the manager should determine if conflict is at the right level. Too often conflict is attended to only when in abundance. It is, however, unhealthy for an organization to have too little conflict, because this condition means that the natural and creative

diversity of the entity is not being expressed. Brown also addresses in-depth intervention strategies relevant to the diagnosis at hand: redirecting behavior, reallocating resources, reframing perspectives, and realigning underlying forces.

Brown's theory is an important and long-awaited addition to the conflict-management literature. It helps in understanding why the use of limited tools in conflict management may lead to frustration, at worst, or incomplete success, at best. His theory views organizations as multifaceted and multifocused; he recommends a fully-equipped tool chest when searching for optimum outcomes. A criticism of his work, however, is that practicing managers find the complex theory difficult to comprehend and use.

Although contingency theories address some of the limitations of the collaborative ethic, they still have shortcomings, including the following:

1. Guiding values, although present, are less apparent in contingency approaches than in the collaborative ethic. Approaches to conflict management may become driven by pragmatics rather than by values, leading to a "whatever works" attitude.

2. Many contingency theories are complex and difficult to remember, making them less accessible and less useful than are simple frameworks.

3. Little has been done to integrate contingency theories, leaving students of conflict resolution with confusing choices. The respective strengths and weaknesses of the theories have not been examined in any comprehensive way, and no guidelines exist to direct the choices. Often the theories seem to say only "it depends."

A CONFLICT-INTERVENTION PROCESS

A set of approaches—based on the theories that have been reviewed—have been designed to assist managers in conflict management. The approaches suggest a process that supports both collaborative outcomes and the use of choices based on relevant contingencies. The process includes analyzing, diagnosing, and intervening.

Four Approaches to Conflict Inquiry

Most conflict phenomena in organizations are complex, with multiple stakeholders, goals, group interests, and personal motivations behind any significant conflict. Resolving a conflict without having a broad information base on which to make decisions almost ensures that some form of the same conflict will emerge again. The process described in this article helps to expand the information available to managers by surfacing needs, wishes, goals, role issues, and the nature of the interactive process between conflicting parties. It is also useful for extending one's conceptualization of the dimensions of a conflict process and the range of access points for intervention. The process is simple enough to be remembered and used with ease.

This conflict-intervention process relies on the use of two dimensions in analyzing a situation: the *conflict-content/conflict-process* dimension, and the *abstract/concrete reframing* dimension.

1. *Conflict content* refers to the nature of the disagreement, the stakes involved, and what is being kept or given up.

2. *Conflict process* refers to the nature of the interaction over the content and to the way the parties conduct themselves with each other, vis-a-vis the content, both verbally and nonverbally.

3. *Reframing toward the abstract (up)* refers to the use of cognitive processes to search for higher principles or more generalized ways of conceptualizing the issues than are currently being exhibited.

4. *Reframing toward the concrete (down)* refers to the use of cognitive processes to bring the conflict "home" (i.e., to the parties' own felt needs and motivations), to review practical implications, and to increase ownership of the problem.

These dimensions provide direction for diagnosing conflict and intervening in it. They can be illustrated with a matrix, as shown in Figure 1, in which four approaches emerge.

Figure 2 illustrates how each of the four approaches can be used in reframing a conflict between two departments of an organization. This situation involves interdependencies.

Figure 3 illustrates how each of the approaches can be used when the conflict involves two employees of equal rank.

Figure 4 illustrates the approaches when the conflict is between a supervisor and subordinate.

Figure 1
Approaches Emerging from Content/Process and Reframing Dimension

	Conflict Content	Conflict Process
Reframing toward Abstract (Up)	Content Reframing (Up)	Process Reframing Up
Reframing toward Concrete (Down)	Content Reframing (Down)	Process Reframing Down

◆   ◆   ◆   ◆   ◆

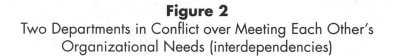

Figure 2
Two Departments in Conflict over Meeting Each Other's
Organizational Needs (interdependencies)

SALES

PRODUCTION

"Production won't manufacture our widgets fast enough to meet customer orders!"

"The Sales Department does not understand our pressures. We cannot respond to the whims of every customer!"

Content reframing up:	"What do you think is best for the organization as a whole?"
Content reframing down:	"What would be the best possible situation for sales? For production?"
Process reframing up:	"What is a better way for your two departments to manage your demands on each other?"
Process reframing down:	"How do you communicate your needs to each other?"

The examples in Figures 2 through 4 illustrate the flexibility one can enjoy by using a reframing approach along the process/content and abstract/concrete dimensions. The use of new dimensions in a conflict situation can help the conflicting parties view and respond to the conflict with fresh and potentially creative perspectives. The conflicting parties would then be able to provide more accurate answers to the following questions: Is collaboration possible and desirable? What contingencies influence the situation? Is this a focused conflict or a multifocused, elusive conflict? Are major changes needed to resolve the issues? Can the perspectives be altered through reframing activities? Such an inquiry process, which draws on both collaborative and contingency-based methods, would help

to clarify the parameters of the conflict and the extent of the intervention needed to manage the situation.

Guidelines for Choosing an Approach

The following guiding principles are helpful in choosing a reframing approach:

1. Try reframing the content when:

   ▪ The inherent stakes are unknown.

   ▪ The social context is relevant but incompletely acknowledged.

   ▪ Differences in goals or roles have not been examined.

   ▪ A win-lose or we-they battle line has been drawn.

Figure 3
Two Managers in Conflict over a Performance-Appraisal System

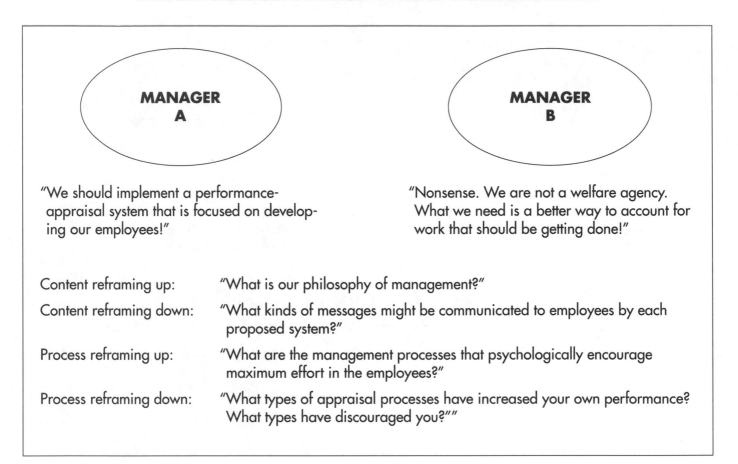

MANAGER
A

MANAGER
B

"We should implement a performance-appraisal system that is focused on developing our employees!"

"Nonsense. We are not a welfare agency. What we need is a better way to account for work that should be getting done!"

Content reframing up:	"What is our philosophy of management?"
Content reframing down:	"What kinds of messages might be communicated to employees by each proposed system?"
Process reframing up:	"What are the management processes that psychologically encourage maximum effort in the employees?"
Process reframing down:	"What types of appraisal processes have increased your own performance? What types have discouraged you?""

- Relevant reference groups influence the thinking of the parties.

2. Try reframing the process when:

   - Power inequities exist.

   - Parties exhibit exaggerated posturing toward one another.

   - Behavior seems to be occurring without much reflective thought; responsibility for personal behavior and experience is missing from the interchanges.

   - Ongoing interdependence is necessary.

3. Try reframing toward the abstract (up) when:

   - Disagreement is at a personal or parochial level.

   - Narrow values are being served, and/or

   - Personal feelings have served to paralyze progress.

4. Try reframing toward the concrete (down) when:

   - Arguing over principles is creating a stalemate.

   - Sweeping generalizations or stereotypes serve to separate personal experience from the discussion.

   - The dilemmas of the parties' own feelings have not been explored.

Figure 4
Conflict between Supervisor and Subordinate Manager over Organizational Priorities

SUPERVISOR

SUBORDINATE MANAGER

"Our production figures need to increase dramatically in the next six months!"

"If we don't improve some of our management systems—like promotion policies, equipment maintenance, and fringe benefits—we will soon have a very demoralized group of employees."

Content reframing up:	"What kind of climate and incentives do you envision as necessary for meeting organizational goals?"
Content reframing down:	"Each of you seems to have different perspectives and different goals. Describe the sources of your respective concerns."
Process reframing up:	"Is it possible to devote effort and resources to the pursuit of both goals? What would need to happen for that to occur?"
Process reframing down:	"What do you need from each other in order to realize your own goals?"

The conflict-intervention process that has been described is most easily implemented when conflict is focused, as in dyadic conflict. It can also be useful in multifocal conflicts as a method by which information is surfaced and the problem elaborated, enabling parties to improve comprehension of the phenomenon and choose strategies based on full information. The simplicity of the framework makes it easy to remember and makes it readily useful to managers.

The reframing process helps to facilitate conflict management, regardless of whether collaborative or contingency approaches are subsequently pursued. It is rooted in the values and processes of collaboration (i.e., attention to both process and content, the seeking of a higher-order synthesis, creative outcome, and attention to both personal and social values), which discourage a "whatever works" mentality. At the same time, contingency thinking is a natural outcome of the reframing process, because complex intervening factors are surfaced and examined.

A search for new and more refined uses of contingency strategies should not disregard the values, principles, and ideals behind the collaborative ethic. In fact, collaboration is more than an ethic; it is a fundamental human drive and is critically needed in complex social forms of organizations. As an ideological orientation, collaboration actualizes many preferred values: mutualism, acceptance of diversity, common vision, and dialectical creativity. Nevertheless, more comprehensive tools for conflict management are still needed. Much remains to be done in the way of testing, altering, and expanding theories that have recently appeared. Differing theories might be needed for different contexts. Questions still remain, for example, about the differences in conflict-management strategies among various types of organizations (e.g., manufacturing plants, high-technology service organizations, and government agencies).

In the meantime, the author hopes that this discussion will assist the reader in recognizing different schools of thought concerning conflict management, and that the information will provide useful tools for diagnosing conflict and making appropriate interventions.

REFERENCES

Brown. L.D. (1983). *Managing conflict at organizational interfaces*. Reading, Mass.: Addison-Wesley.

Derr, C.B. (1978, Summer). Managing organizational conflict. *California Management Review*, pp. 76–83.

Deutsch, M. (1969, January). Productive and destructive conflict. *Journal of Social Issues*, pp. 7–42.

Eiseman, J.W. (1977). A third-party consultation model for resolving recurring conflicts collaboratively. *Journal of Applied Behavioral Science*, 13(3), 303–314.

Eiseman, J.W. (1978). Reconciling incompatible positions. *Journal of Applied Behavioral Science, 14(2)*. 133–150.

Filley, A.C. (1978, Winter). Some normative issues in conflict management. *California Management Review*, pp. 61–66.

Fisher, R., and Ury, W. (1981). *Getting to YES*. Boston, Mass.: Houghton Mifflin.

Follett, M.P. (1951). *Creative experience*. New York: Peter Smith.

Katz, D., and Kahn, R.L. (1966). *The social psychology of organizations* (2nd ed.). New York: John Wiley.

Metcalf, H.C., and Urwick, L. (eds.). (1940). *Dynamic administration: The collected papers of Mary Parker Follett*. New York: Harper Brothers.

Phillips, E., and Cheston, R. (1979, Summer). Conflict resolution: What works? *California Management Review*, pp. 7643.

Robbins, S.P. (1978, Winter). "Conflict management" and "conflict resolution" are not synonymous terms. *California Management Review*, pp. 67–75.

Thomas, K. (1976). Conflict and conflict management. In M.D. Dunnette (ed.), *Handbook of industrial and organizational psychology*. Chicago: Rand McNally.

Thomas, K.W. (1977, July). Toward multi-dimensional values in teaching: The example conflict behaviors. *Academy of Management Review*, pp. 484–490.

Thomas, K.W. (1978, Winter). Introduction to special section: Conflict and the collaborative ethic. *California Management Review*, pp. 56–60.

Thomas, K.W., Jamieson, D.W., and Moore, R.K. (1978, Winter). Conflict and collaboration: Some concluding observations. *California Management Review*, pp. 91–95.

Susan H. Taft is a doctoral candidate in the Department of Organizational Behavior, Weatherhead School of Management, Case Western Reserve University. Prior to doing doctoral work, she held various managerial positions in health-care organizations, and taught in the Frances Payne Bolton School of Nursing at Case Western Reserve University. She is currently doing research, teaching, and consulting with a variety of organizations.

MANAGING CONFLICT AND DISAGREEMENT CONSTRUCTIVELY

Herbert S. Kindler

A vital part of a trainer's or consultant's repertoire is being able to manage—and teach others to manage—conflict and disagreements. The five-mode model for managing conflict, introduced in 1964 by Blake and Mouton, was useful in stable organizational environments. However, today's rapid changes in organizational systems and technologies require more skills and more options.

This article introduces three core principles to apply when engaging in conflict management and nine strategies—with varying degrees of flexibility and intensity—that can be selected or combined when dealing with others in a conflict situation. It also presents a systematic process for diagnosing, planning, implementing, and following up any attempt to manage conflict and disagreement constructively.

It is common to hear people in organizations say something like the following about disagreement:

■ "I hate the endless arguing—and feeling trapped by having to listen to someone's stored-up anger."

■ "Nothing is less productive than dancing around our differences. People don't really change their minds."

Unskillfully or insensitively managed conflict results in bickering, bruised feelings, wasted time, and unproductive rivalry. In contrast, when disagreement is handled well, opportunities arise for learning, cooperative work, and creative ideas. Teamwork improves, stress is reduced, trust is built, and people feel more committed to agreed-on decisions.

THE CONCEPTS

Managing conflict well requires conceptual tools, sensitivity, and practice. To facilitate the constructive resolution of conflict, a five-mode model (Blake and Mouton, 1964) was introduced. This model is still used by many consultants because it is easy to teach and learn. It was

From *The 1995 Annual: Volume1, Training,* Jossey-Bass/Pfeiffer. Reprinted by permission.

adequate when technology and the competitive environment were more stable. Nevertheless, contemporary managers need all the help they can get to improve productivity and maintain staff commitment. A research-based, comprehensive, nine-strategies model for managing conflict and disagreement (Kindler, 1994) is better suited for use in flatter organizations that experience more fluid relationships.

The following sections contain three core principles, nine strategies, and a four-step process (Figure 1) that can help any consultant's success rate in dealing with conflict.

Principles for Managing Conflict and Disagreement Constructively

1. *Maintain mutual respect.* Ask yourself, "How can I discuss our differences in ways that allow the other person to retain his or her dignity? How can I avoid having the other person feel denigrated or 'put down'?"

2. *Seek common ground.* Explore your overarching goals, values, and shared purpose. Try to see things through the other person's eyes (e.g., his or her culture, race, gender, age, or life experiences). Don't lock yourself into adversarial or polarized positions.

3. Deal with disagreement after choosing an appropriate level of *flexibility and involvement.* The more you can learn from the other person, the more you can gain from a flexible stance. The more a good working relationship is desired, the more personal should be your interaction.

Strategies for Managing Conflict and Disagreement Constructively

Conflict and disagreement can be handled most effectively by employing a wide range of approaches. In a research study to understand actual behavior (Kindler, 1983), people were asked the following: "When your views on a work-related issue differ from the views of others who are also importantly involved, how do you prepare for such situations?" From the responses, two behaviors emerged as themes:

- Deciding how firm or flexible to be when asserting one's viewpoint, and
- Choosing how intensely involved to be with others who hold divergent views.

After these two dimensions—viewpoint flexibility and interaction intensity—were identified, a study of the literature on conflict revealed the following nine strategies, which are depicted in Figure 1.

Dominate.

Using power and pressure when speed or confidentiality are important or when the situation is too minor to warrant time-consuming involvement of others. Also for self-protection against people who would use their power abusively.

Smooth.

Gaining acceptance of one's views by accentuating the benefits and smoothing over disadvantages that would fuel opposition.

Maintain.

Holding onto the status quo by deferring action on views that differ from one's own. Useful as an interim strategy when time is needed to collect information or to let emotions cool down.

Bargain.

Offering something the other party wants in exchange for something one wants. Expedient when time pressures preclude collaboration. A mediator can facilitate for this strategy.

Coexist.

Determining jointly to follow separate paths for an agreed-on period of time. Use when both par-

Figure 1
Nine Strategies for Managing Conflict and Disagreement Constructively[1]

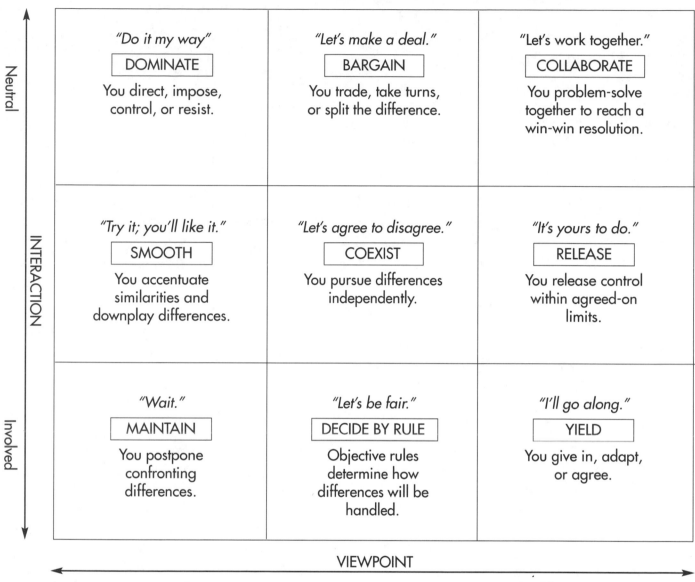

ties are firm, and pilot testing will determine which path has greater merit.

Decide by Rule.

Agreeing jointly to use an objective rule such as a vote, lottery, seniority system, or arbitration. Helpful when one wants to be seen as impartial but when decisive action is needed.

Collaborate.

Joint exploration to develop a creative solution that satisfies the important concerns of all parties. Useful when the issues are too important to be compromised, or when commitment is vital to successful implementation of the solution.

Release.

Let go when the issue doesn't warrant your time or energy, or when you want others to resolve a non-critical issue to foster their initiative and provide a learning opportunity.

Yield.

Support the other person's views when you become convinced it is more appropriate, or when the issue is much more important to them than to you.

It is a good idea to avoid overusing one or two habitual approaches. Rather, one should consciously choose the strategy—or a blend of strategies—appropriate to the situation.

Process for Managing Conflict and Disagreement Constructively

As important as guiding principles are and as helpful as a repertoire of strategies can be, a systematic process for dealing with conflict and disagreement is vital to producing desirable outcomes. The process consists of the following four steps:

Diagnosis. Monitoring where differences simmer in order to be able to handle the situation before it boils over into overt conflict. Potential sources of conflict are:

▪ Information is interpreted differently.

▪ Goals appear to be incompatible.

▪ Boundaries are violated.

▪ Old wounds have not healed.

▪ Symptoms are confused with underlying causes.

Planning

Develop a strategy and action plan.

▪ Choose one of the nine available strategies or a blend of strategies that are congruent with the situation, along with a backup plan.

▪ Mutually agree with the other party on a time and place to explore differences and a time frame in which to do it.

▪ Decide how to monitor the process and what the consequences will be of failure to live up to any agreement.

Implementation

Carry out the plan.

▪ Maintain a tone of mutual respect and goodwill.

▪ Monitor results to verify that the agreement is being honored.

▪ If the agreement is not being honored, learn why and then take corrective action.

▪ Reinforce behavior that supports the agreement.

▪ Learn from each experience with conflict and disagreement.

USES OF THE CONCEPTS

Organizational change—whether a program of continuous improvement, total quality management, process reengineering, empowerment, or simply a change in a bookkeeping system—creates personal vulnerability. Change threatens existing competence, control, status, and privilege. Therefore, it is not unusual for people to have different views of a proposed change or of how to implement changes. One key to implementing change successfully is dealing constructively with people who hold different views. Therefore, the concepts presented here are of value to organizational consultants and managers.

When consultants and trainers introduce the nine-strategies model to clients and seminar participants in a conflict-management context, their presentations are more relevant. As trainees practice using the principles, strategies, and process for managing conflict and disagreement constructively, results will manifest as better teamwork, improved communication, and more creative solutions.

References

Blake, R. R. and Mouton, J. S. (1964). *The managerial grid.* Houston, Texas: Gulf.

Kindler, H. S. (1983). The art of managing differences. *Training and Development Journal, 37(1),* 27–32.

Kindler, H. S. (1994). *Management of differences inventory* (rev. ed.). Pacific Palisades, Calif.: Center for Management Effectiveness.

Herbert S. Kindler, Ph.D., is the director of the Center for Management Effectiveness, Pacific Palisades, California, and is professor emeritus of management and organization at Loyola Marymount University. He is the author or co-author of five books and the author of several workbooks, and is the director of educational films and the developer of the Management of Differences Inventory. *Dr. Kindler's past experience as the CEO of an engineering firm enriches his international training and consulting activities.*

Chapter Three

POWER

THE BASES OF SOCIAL POWER

John R.P. French, Jr. and Bertram Raven

The processes of power are pervasive and complex, and often disguised in our society. Accordingly, one finds in political science, in sociology, and in social psychology a variety of distinctions among different types of social power or among qualitatively different processes of social influence. Our main purpose is to identify the major types of power and to define them systematically so that we can compare them according to the changes that they produce and the other effects that accompany the use of power. The phenomena of power and influence involve a dyadic relation between two agents that can be viewed from two points of view: (a) What determines the behavior of the agent who exerts power? (b) What determines the reactions of the recipient of this behavior? We take this second point of view and formulate our theory in terms of the life space of P, the person upon whom the power is exerted. In this way we hope to define basic concepts of power which will be adequate to explain many of the phenomena of social influence, including some that have been

Reprinted by permission of The Institute for Social Research from *Studies in Social Power,* "The Bases of Social Power," by John R.P. French, Jr. and Bertram Raven. Copyright © 1959 , Ann Arbor, Mich.: Institute for Social Research, University of Michigan, pp. 150–167.

described in other less genotypic terms.

Recent empirical work, especially on small groups, has demonstrated the necessity of distinguishing different types of power in order to account for the different effects found in studies of social influence. Yet there is no doubt that more empirical knowledge will be needed to make final decisions concerning the necessary differentiations, but this knowledge will be obtained only by research based on some preliminary theoretical distinctions. We present such preliminary concepts and some of the hypotheses they suggest.

POWER, INFLUENCE, AND CHANGE

Psychological Change

Since we shall define power in terms of influence, and influence in terms of psychological change, we begin with a discussion of change. We want to define change at a level of generality that includes changes in behavior, opinions, attitudes, goals, needs, values, and all other aspects of the person's psychological field. We shall use the word "system" to refer to any such part of the life space.[1] Following Lewin (1951, p. 305) the state of a system at time 1 will be denoted $s1(a)$.

Psychological change is defined as any alteration of the state of some system a over time. The amount of change is measured by the size of the difference between the states of the system a at time 1 and at time[2]: $ch(a) = s2(a) - s1(a)$.

Change in any psychological system can be conceptualized in terms of psychological forces. But it is important to note that the change must be coordinated to the resultant force of all the forces operating at the moment. Change in an opinion, for example, might be determined jointly by a driving force induced by another person, a restraining force corresponding to anchorage in a group opinion, and an own force stemming from the person's needs.

Social Influence

Our theory of social influence and power is limited to influence on the person, P, produced by a social agent, O, where O can be either another person, a role, a norm, a group or a part of a group. We do not consider social influence exerted on a group.

The influence of O on system a in the life space of P is defined as the resultant force on system a that has its source in an act of O. This resultant force induced by O consists of two components: a force to change the system in the direction induced by O and an opposing resistance set up by the same act of O.

By this definition the influence of O does not include P's own forces nor the forces induced by other social agents. Accordingly, the "influence" of O must be clearly distinguished from O's "control" of P (Chapter 11). O might be able to induce strong forces on P to carry out an activity (i.e., O exerts strong influence on P); but if the opposing forces induced by another person or by P's own needs are stronger, then P will locomote in an opposite direction (i.e., O does not have control over P). Thus psychological change in P can be taken as an operational definition of the social influence of O on P only when the effects of other forces have been eliminated.

It is assumed that any system is interdependent with other parts of the life space so that a change in one can produce changes in others. However, this theory focuses on the primary changes in a system that are produced directly by social influence; it is less concerned with secondary changes that are indirectly effected in the other systems or with primary changes produced by nonsocial influences.

Commonly social influence takes place through an intentional act on the part of O. However, we do not want to limit our definition of "act" to such conscious behavior. Indeed, influence might result from the passive presence of O, with no evidence of speech or overt movement. A policeman's standing on a corner may be considered an act of an agent for the speeding motorist. Such acts of the inducting agent will vary in strength, for O might not always utilize all of his power. The policeman, for example, can merely stand and watch or act more strongly by blowing his whistle at the motorist.

The influence exerted by an act need not be in the direction intended by O. The direction of the resultant force on P will depend on the relative magnitude of the induced force set up by the act of O and the resisting force in the opposite direction which is generated by that same act. In cases where O intends to influence P in a given direction, a resultant force in the same direction may be termed positive influence whereas a resultant force in the opposite direction may be termed negative influence.

If O produces the intended change, he has exerted positive control; but if he produces a change in the opposite direction, as for example in the negativism of young children or in the phenomena of negative reference groups, he has exerted negative control.

Social Power

The *strength of power* of O/P in some system a is defined as the maximum potential ability of O to influence P in a.

By this definition influence is kinetic power, just as power is potential influence. It is assumed that O is capable of various acts which, because of some more or less enduring relation to P, are able to exert influence on P.2. O's power is measured by his maximum possible influence, though he may often choose to exert less than his full power.

An equivalent definition of power can be stated in terms of the resultant of two forces set up by the act of O: one in the direction of O's influence attempt and another resisting force in the opposite direction. Power is the maximum resultant of these two forces:

$$\text{Power of O/P(a)} = \text{fa,x} - \text{f}\bar{\text{a}}\text{,x}) \text{ max}$$

where the source of both forces is an act of O.

Thus the power of O with respect to system a of P is equal to the maximum resultant force of two forces set up by any possible act of O: (a) the force that O can set upon the system a to change in the direction x, (b) the resisting force[3] in the opposite direction. Whenever the first component force is greater than the second, positive power exists; but if the second component force is greater than the first, then O has negative power over P.

It is necessary to define power with respect to a specified system because the power of O/P can vary greatly from one system to another. O can have great power to control the behavior of P but little power to control his opinions. Of course a high power of O/P does not imply a low power of PLO; the two variable s are conceptually independent (Chapter 11).

For certain purposes it is convenient to define the range of power as the set of all systems within which O has power of strength greater than zero. A husband might have a broad range of power over his wife, but a narrow range of power over his employer. We shall use the term "magnitude of power" to denote the summation of O's power over P in all systems of his range.

The Dependence of s(a) on O.

Several investigators have been concerned with differences between superficial conformity and "deeper" changes produced by social influence. The kinds of systems that are changed and the stability of these changes have been handled by distinctions such as "public vs. private attitudes," "overt vs. covert behavior," "compliance vs. internalization," and "own vs. induced forces." Though stated as dichotomies, all of these distinctions suggest an underlying dimension of the degree of dependency of the state of a system on O.

We assume that any change in the state of a system is produced by a change in some factor upon which it is functionally dependent. The state of an opinion, for example, can change because of a change either in some internal factor such as a need or in some external factor such as the arguments of O. Likewise the maintenance of the same state of a system is produced by the stability or lack of change in the internal and external factors. In general, then, psychological change and stability can be conceptualized in terms of dynamic dependence. Our interest is focused on the special case of dependence on an external agent, O.

In many cases the initial state of the system has the character of a quasi-stationary equilibrium with a central force field around 21(a) (Lewin, p. 106). In such cases we might derive a tendency toward retrogression to the original state as soon as the force induced by O is removed.[4] Let us suppose that O exerts influence producing a new state of the system, s2(a). Is s2(a) now dependent on the continued presence of O? In principle we could answer this question by removing any traces of O from the life space of P and by observing the consequent state of the system at time 3. If $s3(a)$ retrogresses completely back to $s1(a)$, then we can conclude that maintenance of $s2(a)$ was completely dependent on O; but if $s3(a)$ equals $s2(a)$, this lack of change shows that $s2(a)$ has become completely independent of O.

In general the degree of dependence of $s2(a)$ on O, following O's influence, can be defined as equal to the amount of retrogression following the removal of O from the life space of P:

$$\text{Degree of dependence of } s2(a) \text{ on O} = s2(a) - s3(a).$$

A given degree of dependence at time 2 can later change, for example, through the gradual weakening of O's influence. At this later time, the degree of dependence of $s4(a)$ on O would still be equal to the amount of retrogression toward the initial state of equilibrium $s1(a)$. Operational measures of the degree of dependence on O will, of course, have to be taken under conditions where all other factors are held constant.

Consider the example of three separated employees who have been working at the same steady level of production despite normal, small fluctuations in the work environment. The supervisor orders each to increase his production, and the level of each goes up from 100 to 115 pieces per day. After a week of producing at the new rate of 115 pieces per day, the supervisor is removed for a week. The production of employee A immediately returns to 100 but B and C return to only 110 pieces per day. Other things being equal, we can infer that A's new rate was completely dependent on his supervisor whereas the new rate of B and C was dependent on the supervisor only to the extent of 5 pieces. Let us further assume that when the supervisor returned, the production of B and of C returned to 115 without further orders from the supervisor. Now another month

goes by during which B and C maintain a steady 115 pieces per day. However, there is a difference between them: B's level of production still depends on O to the extent of 5 pieces whereas C has come to rely on his own sense of obligation to obey the order of his legitimate supervisor rather than on the supervisor's external pressure for the maintenance of his 115 pieces per day. Accordingly, the next time the supervisor departs, B's production again drops to 110 but C's remains at 115 pieces per day. In cases like employee B's, the degree of dependence is contingent on the perceived probability that O will observe the state of the system and not P's conformity. The level of observability will in turn depend on both the nature of the system (e.g., the difference between a covert opinion and overt behavior) and on the environmental barriers to observation (e.g., O is too far away from P). In other cases, for example that of employee C, the new behavior pattern is highly dependent on his supervisor, but the degree of dependence of the new state will be related not to the level of observability but rather to factors inside P, in this case a sense of duty to perform an act legitimately prescribed by O. The internalization of social norms is a related process of decreasing degree of dependence of behavior on an external O and increasing dependence on an internal value; it is usually assumed that internalization is accompanied by a decrease in the effects of level of observability (37).

The concepts "dependence of a system on O" and "observability as a basis for dependence" will be useful in understanding the stability of conformity. In the next section we shall discuss various types of power and the types of conformity that they are likely to produce.

THE BASES OF POWER

By the basis of power we mean the relationship between O and P, which is the source of that power. It is rare that we can say with certainty that a given empirical case of power is limited to one source. Normally, the relation between O and P will be characterized by several qualitatively different variables that are bases of power (30, Chapter 11). Although there are undoubtedly many possible bases of power that can be distinguished, we shall here define five that seem especially common and important. These five bases of O's power are: (1) reward power, based on P's perception that O has the ability to mediate rewards for him; (2) coercive power, based on P's perception that O has the ability to mediate punishments for him; (3) legitimate power, based on the perception by P that O has a legitimate right to prescribe behavior for him; (4) referent power, based on P's identification with O; (5) expert power, based on the perception that O has some special knowledge or expertness.

Our first concern is to define the bases that give rise to a given type of power. Next, we describe each type of power according to its strength, range, and the degree of dependence of the new state of the system that is most likely to occur with each type of power. We shall also examine the other effects which the exercise of a given type of power can have upon P and his relationship to O. Finally, we shall point out the interrelationships between different types of power, and the effects of use of one type of power by O upon other bases of power that he might have over P. Thus we shall both define a set of concepts and propose a series of hypotheses. Most of these hypotheses have not been systematically tested, although there is a good deal of evidence in favor of several. No attempt will be made to summarize that evidence here.

Reward Power

Reward power is defined as power whose basis is the ability to reward. The strength of the reward power of O/P increases with the magnitude of the rewards that P perceives that O can mediate

for him. Reward power depends on O's ability to administer positive valences and to remove or decrease negative valences. The strength of reward power also depends upon the probability that O can mediate the reward, as perceived by P. A common example of reward power is the addition of a piecework rate in the factory as an incentive to increase production.

The new state of the system induced by a promise of reward (for example the factory worker's increased level of production) will be highly dependent on O. Since O mediates the reward, he controls the probability that P will receive it. Thus P's new rate of production will be dependent on his subjective probability that O will reward him for conformity minus his subjective probability that O will reward him even if he returns to his old level. Both probabilities will be greatly affected by the level of observability of P's behavior. Incidentally, a piece rate often seems to have more effect on production than a merit rating system because it yields a higher probability of reward for conformity and a much lower probability of reward for nonconformity.

The utilization of actual rewards (instead of promises) by O will tend over time to increase the attraction of P toward O and therefore the referent power of O over P. As we shall note later, such referent power will permit O to induce changes that are relatively independent. Neither rewards nor promises will arouse resistance in P, provided P considers it legitimate for O to offer rewards.

The range of reward power is specific to those regions within which O can reward P for conforming. The use of rewards to change systems within the range of reward power tends to increase reward power by increasing the probability attached to future promises. However, unsuccessful attempts to exert reward power outside the range of power would tend to decrease the power; for example, if O offers to reward P for performing an impossible act, this will reduce for P the probability of receiving future rewards promised by O.

Coercive Power

Coercive power is similar to reward power in that it also involves O's ability to manipulate the attainment of valences. Coercive power of O/P stems from the expectation on the part of P that he will be punished by O if he fails to conform to the influence attempt. Thus negative valences will exist in given regions of P's life space, corresponding to the threatened punishment by O. The strength of coercive power depends on the magnitude of the negative valence of the threatened punishment multiplied by the perceived probability that P can avoid the punishment by conformity: i.e., the probability of punishment for nonconformity minus the probability of punishment for conformity (11). Just as an offer of a piece-rate bonus in a factory can serve as a basis for reward power, so the ability to fire a worker if he falls below a given level of production will result in coercive power.

Coercive power leads to dependent change also; and the degree of dependence varies with the level of observability of P's conformity. An excellent illustration of coercive power leading to dependent change is provided by a clothes presser in a factory observed by Coch and French (3). As her efficiency rating climbed above average for the group, the other workers began to "scapegoat" her. That the resulting plateau in higher production was not independent of the group was evident once she was removed from the presence of the other workers. Her production immediately climbed to new heights.[5]

At times, there is some difficulty in distinguishing between reward power and coercive power. Is the withholding of a reward really equivalent to a punishment? Is the withdrawal of punishment equivalent to a reward? The answer must be a psychological one—it depends upon the situation as it exists for P. But ordinarily we would answer these questions in the affirmative; for P, receiving a reward is a positive valence as is the relief of suffering. There is some evidence that conformity to group norms in order to gain acceptance (reward power) should be distinguished from conformity as a means of forestalling rejection (coercive power).

The distinction between these two types of power is important because the dynamics are different. The concept of "sanctions" sometimes lumps the two together despite their opposite effects. While reward power might eventually result in an independent system, the effects of coercive power will continue to be dependent. Reward power will tend to increase the attraction of P toward O; coercive power will decrease this attraction. The valence of the region of behavior will become more negative, acquiring some negative valence from the threatened punishment. The negative valence of punishment would also spread to other regions of the life space. Lewin (1935) has pointed out this distinction between the effects of rewards and punishment. In the case of threatened punishment, there will be a resultant force on P to leave the field entirely. Thus, to achieve conformity, O must not only place a strong negative valence in certain regions through threat of punishment, but O must also introduce restraining forces, or other strong valences, so as to prevent P from withdrawing completely from O's range of coercive power. Otherwise the probability of receiving the punishment, if P does not conform, will be too low to be effective.

Legitimate Power

Legitimate power is probably the most complex of those kinds treated here, embodying notions from the structural sociologist, the group-norm and role-oriented social psychologist, and the clinical psychologist.

There has been considerable investigation and speculation about socially prescribed behavior, particularly that which is specific to a given role or position. Linton (1945) distinguishes group norms according to whether they are universals for everyone in the culture, alternatives (the individual having a choice as to whether or not to accept them), or specialties (specific to given positions). Whether we speak of internalized norms, role prescriptions and expectations, or internalized pressures, the fact remains that each individual sees certain regions toward which he should locomote, some regions toward which he should not locomote, and some regions toward which he can locomote if they are generally attractive for him. This applies to specific behaviors in which he may, should, or should not engage; it applies to certain attitudes or beliefs which he may, should, or should not hold. The feeling of "oughtness" might be an internalization from his parents, from his teachers, or from his religion, or might have been logically developed from some idiosyncratic system of ethics. He will speak of such behaviors with expressions like "should," "ought to," or "has a right to." In many cases, the original source of the requirement is not recalled.

Though we have oversimplified such evaluations of behavior with a positive-neutral-negative trichotomy, the evaluation of behaviors by the person is really more one of degree. This dimension of evaluation, we shall call "legitimacy." Conceptually, we might think of legitimacy as a valence in a region that is induced by some internalized norm or value. This value has the same conceptual property as power, namely an ability to induce force fields (Lewin 1951, p. 40–41). It might or might not be correct that values (or the superego) are internalized parents, but at least they can set up force fields that have a phenomenal "oughtness" similar to a parent's prescription. Like a value, a need can also induce valences (i.e., force fields) in P's psychological environment, but these valences have more the phenomenal character of noxious or attractive properties of the object or activity. When a need induces a valence in P, for example, when a need makes an objective attractive to P, this attraction applies to P but not to other persons. When a value induces a valence, on the other hand, it not only sets up forces on P to engage in the activity, but P might feel that all others ought to behave in the same way. Among other things, this evaluation applies to the legitimate right of some other individual or group to prescribe behavior or beliefs for a person even through the other cannot apply sanctions.

Legitimate power of O/P is here defined as that power that stems from internalized values in P that dictate that O has a legitimate right to influence P and that P has an obligation to accept this influence. We note that legitimate power is very similar to the notion of legitimacy of authority, which has long been explored by sociologists, particularly by Wever, and more recently by Goldhammer and Shils. However, legitimate power is not always a role relation: P might accept an induction from O simply because he had previously promised to help O and he values his word too much to break the promise. In all cases, the notion of legitimacy involves some sort of code or standard, accepted by the individual, by virtue of which the external agent can assert his power. We shall attempt to describe a few of these values here.

Bases for legitimate power

Cultural values constitute one common basis for the legitimate power of one individual over another. O has characteristics that are specified by the culture as giving him the right to prescribe behavior for P, who may not have these characteristics. These bases, which Weber has called the authority of the "external yesterday," include such things as age, intelligence, caste, and physical characteristics. In some cultures, the aged are granted the right to prescribe behavior for others in practically all behavior areas. In most cultures, there are certain areas of behavior in which a person of one sex is granted the right to prescribe behavior for the other sex.

Acceptance of the social structure is another basis for legitimate power. If P accepts as right the social structure of his group, organization, or society, especially the social structure involving a hierarchy of authority, P will accept the legitimate authority of O who occupies a superior office in the hierarchy. Thus legitimate power in a formal organization is largely a relationship between offices rather than between persons. And the acceptance of an office as *right* is a basis for legitimate power—a judge has a right to levy fines, a foreman should assign work, a priest is justified in prescribing religious beliefs, and it is the management's prerogative to make certain decisions. However, legitimate power also involves the perceived right of the person to hold the office.

Designation by a legitimizing agent is a third basis for legitimate power. An influencer O may be seen as legitimate in prescribing behavior for P because he has been granted such power by a legitimizing agent whom P accepts. Thus a department head accepts the authority of his vice-president in a certain area because that authority has been specifically delegated by the president. An election is perhaps the most common example of a group's serving to legitimize the authority of one individual or office of other individuals in the group. The success of such legitimizing depends upon the acceptance of the legitimizing agent and procedure. In this case it depends ultimately on certain democratic values concerning election procedures. The election process is one of legitimizing a person's right to an office that already has a legitimate range of power associated with it.

Range of legitimate power of O/P

The areas in which legitimate power are exercised are generally specified along with the designation of that power. A job description, for example, usually specifies supervisory activities and also designates the person to whom the job-holder is responsible for the duties described. Some bases for legitimate authority carry with them a very broad range. Culturally derived bases for legitimate power are often especially broad. It is not uncommon to find cultures in which a member of a given caste can legitimately prescribe behavior for all members of lower castes in practically all regions. More common, however, are instances of legitimate power where the range is specifically and narrowly prescribed. A sergeant in the army is given a specific set of regions within which he can legitimately prescribe behavior for his men.

The attempted use of legitimate power that is outside of the range of legitimate power will decrease the legitimate power of the authority figure. Such use of power that is not legitimate will also decrease the attractiveness of O.

Legitimate power and influence

The new state of the system that results from legitimate power usually has high dependence on O though it can become independent. Here, however, the degree of dependence is not related to the level of observability. Since legitimate power is based on P's values, the source of the forces induced by O include both these internal values and O. O's induction serves to activate the values and to relate them to the system that is influenced, but thereafter the new state of the system might become directly dependent on the values with no mediation by O. Accordingly this new state will be relatively stable and consistent across varying environmental situations since P's values are more stable than his psychological environment.

We have used the term "legitimate" not only as a basis for the power of an agent, but also to describe the general behaviors of a person. Thus, the individual P might also consider the legitimacy of the attempts to use other types of power by O. In certain cases, P will consider that O has a legitimate right to threaten punishment for nonconformity; in other cases, such use of coercion would not be seen a legitimate. P might change in response to coercive power of O, but it will make a considerable difference in his attitude and conformity if O is not seen as having a legitimate right to use such coercion. In such cases, the attraction of P for O will be particularly diminished, and the influence attempt will arouse more resistance (11). Similarly the utilization of reward power varies in legitimacy; the word "bribe," for example, denotes an illegitimate reward.

Referent Power

The referent power of O/P has its basis in the identification of P with O. By identification, we mean a feeling of oneness of P with O, or a desire for such an identity. If O is a person toward whom P is highly attracted, P will have a desire to become closely associated with O. If O is an attractive group, P will have a feeling of membership or a desire to join. If P is already closely associated with O he will want to maintain this relationship. P's classification with O can be established or maintained if P behaves, believes, and perceives as O does. Accordingly O has the ability to influence P, even though P might be unaware of this referent power. A verbalization of such power by P might be, "I am like O, and therefore I shall behave or believe as O does," or "I want to be like O, and I will be more like O if I behave or believe as O does." The stronger the identification of P with O the greater the referent power of O/P.

Similar types of power have already been investigated under a number of different formulations. Festinger points out that in an ambiguous situation, the individual seeks some sort of "social reality" and might adopt the cognitive structure of the individual or group with which he identifies. In such a case, the lack of clear structure can be threatening to the individual and the agreement of his beliefs with those of a reference group will both satisfy his need for structure and give him added security through increased identification with his group.

We must try to distinguish between *referent* power and other types of power that might be operative at the same time. If a member is attracted to a group and he conforms to its norms only because he fears ridicule or expulsion from the group for nonconformity, we would call this *coercive* power. On the other hand if he conforms in order to obtain praise for conformity, it is a case of *reward* power. The basic criterion for distinguishing referent power from both coercive and reward power is the mediation of the punishment and the reward by O: to the extent that O mediates the sanctions (i.e., has means control over P) we are dealing with coercive and reward power; but to the extent that P avoids discomfort or gains satisfaction by conformity based on identification, regardless of O's responses, we are dealing with referent power. Conformity with majority opinion is sometimes based on a respect for the collective wisdom of the group, in which case it is expert power. It is important to distinguish these phenomena, all grouped together elsewhere as "pressures toward uniformity," since the type of change that occurs will be different for different bases of power.

The concepts of "reference group" and "prestige suggestion" can be treated as instances of referent power. In this case, O, the prestigeful person or group, is valued by P; because P desires to be associated or identified with O, he will assume attitudes or beliefs held by O. Similarly a negative reference group that O dislikes and evaluates negatively can exert negative influence on P as a result of negative referent power.

It has been demonstrated that the power that we designate as referent power is especially great when P is attracted to O. In our terms, this would mean that the greater the attraction, the greater the identification, and consequently the greater the referent power. In some cases, attraction or prestige has a specific basis, and the range of referent power will be limited accordingly: a group of campers might have great referent power over a member regarding campcraft, but considerably less effect on other regions. However, we hypothesize that the greater the attraction of P toward O, the broader the range of referent power of O/P.

The new state of a system produced by referent power can be dependent on or independent of O; but the degree of dependence is not affected by the level of observability to O. In fact, P is often not consciously aware of the referent power that O exerts over him. There is probably a tendency for some of these dependent changes to become independent of O quite rapidly.

Expert Power

The strength of the expert power of O/P varies with the extent of the knowledge of perception that P attributes to O within a given area. Probably P evaluates O's expertness in relation to his own knowledge as well as against an absolute standard. In any case, expert power results in primary social influence on P's cognitive structure and probably not on other types of systems. Of course, changes in the cognitive structure can change the direction of forces and hence locomotion, but such a change of behavior is secondary social influence. Expert power has been demonstrated experimentally. Accepting an attorney's advice in legal matters is a common example of expert influence; but there are many instances based on much less knowledge, such as the acceptance by a stranger of directions given by a native villager.

Expert power, where O need not be a member of P's group, is called "informational power" by Deutsch and Gerard. This type of expert power must be distinguished from influence based on the content of communication as described by Hovland et al. The influence of the content of a communication upon an opinion is presumably a secondary influence produced after the *primary* influence (i.e., the acceptance of the information). Since power is here defined in terms of the primary changes, the influence of the content on a related opinion is not a case of expert power as we have defined it, but the initial acceptance of the validity of the content does seem to be based on expert power or referent power. In other cases, however, so-called facts might be accepted as self-evident because they fit into P's cognitive structure; if this impersonal acceptance of the truth of the fact is independent of the more less enduring relationship between O and P, then P's acceptance of the fact is not an actualization of expert power. Thus we distinguish between expert power based on the credibility of O and informational influence, which is based on characteristics of the stimulus such as the logic of the argument or the "self-evident facts."

Wherever expert influence occurs, it seems to be necessary for P to think that O knows, and for P to trust that O is telling the truth (rather than trying to deceive him).

Expert power will produce a new cognitive structure that is initially relatively dependent on O, but informational influence will produce a more independent structure. The former is likely to become more independent with the passage of time. In both cases the degree of dependence on O is not affected by the level of observability.

The "sleeper effect" is an interesting case of a change in the degree of dependence of an opinion on O. An unreliable O (who probably had negative referent power but some positive expert power) presented "facts" that were accepted by the subjects and that would normally produce secondary influence on their opinions and beliefs. However, the negative referent power aroused resistance and resulted in negative social influence on their beliefs (i.e., set up a force in the direction opposite to the influence attempt), so that there was little change in the subjects' opinions. With the passage of time, however, the subjects tended to forget the identity of the negative communicator faster than they forgot the contents of his communication, so there was a weakening of the negative referent influence and a consequent delayed positive change in the subjects' beliefs in the direction of the influence attempt ("sleeper effect"). Later, when the identity of the negative communicator was experimentally reinstated, these resisting forces were reinstated, and there was another negative change in belief in a direction opposite to the influence attempt.

The range of expert power, we assume, is more delimited than that of referent power. Not only is it restricted to cognitive systems, but the expert is seen as having superior knowledge or ability in very specific areas, and his power will be limited to these areas, though some "halo effect" might occur. Some of our renowned physical scientists have found quite painfully that their expert power in physical sciences does not extend to regions involving international politics. Indeed, there is some evidence that the attempted exertion of expert power outside of the range of expert power will reduce that expert power. An undermining of confidence seems to take place.

SUMMARY

We have distinguished five types of power: referent power, expert power, reward power, coercive power, and legitimate power. These distinctions led to the following hypotheses:

1. For all five types, the stronger the basis of power, the greater the power.

2. For any type of power, the size of the range varies greatly, but in general referent power will have the broadest range.

3. Any attempt to use power outside the range of power will tend to reduce the power.

4. A new state of a system produced by reward power or coercive power will be highly dependent on O, and the more observable P's conformity the more dependent the state. For the other three types of power, the new state is usually dependent, at least in the beginning, but in any case the level of observability has no effect on the degree of dependence.

5. Coercion results in decreased attraction of P toward O and high resistance; reward power results in increased attraction and low resistance.

6. The more legitimate the coercion, the less it will produce resistance and decreased attraction.

NOTES

1. The word "system" is here used to refer to a whole or to a part of the whole.

2. The concept of power has the conceptual property of *potentiality*; but it seems useful to restrict this potential influence to more or less enduring power relations between O and P by excluding from the definition of power those cases where the potential influence is so momentary or so changing that it cannot be predicted from the existing relationship. Power is a useful concept for describing social structure only if it has a certain stability over time; it is useless if every momentary social stimulus is viewed as actualizing social power.

3. We define resistance to an attempted induction as a force in the opposite direction that is set up by the same act of 0. It must be distinguished from opposition, which is defined as existing opposing forces that do not have their source in the same act of 0. For example, a boy might resist his mother's order to eat spinach because of the manner of the induction attempt, and at the same time he might oppose it because he didn't like spinach.

4. Miller assumes that all living systems have this character. However, it might be that some systems in the life space do not have this elasticity.

5. Though the primary influence of coercive power is dependent, it often produces secondary changes that are independent. Brainwashing, for example, utilizes coercive power to produce many primary changes in the life space of the prisoner, but these dependent changes can lead to identification with the aggressor and hence to secondary changes in ideology, that are independent.

REFERENCES

Asch, S.E. *Social psychology*. New York: Prentice-Hall, 1952.

Back, K.W. Influence through social communication. *Journal of Abnormal Social Psychology*, 1951, 46, 9–23.

Coch, L., and French, J.R.P., Jr. Overcoming resistance to change. *Hum. Relat.*, 1948, 1, 512–32.

Deutsch, M. and Gerard, H.B. A study of normative and informational influences upon individual judgment. *Journal of Abnormal Social Psychology*, 155, 51, 629–36.

Dittes, J. E. and Kelley, H.H. Effects of different conditions of acceptance upon conformity to group norms. *Journal of Abnormal Social Psychology, 156,53*, 100–107.

Festinger, L. An analysis of compliant behavior. In Sherif, M. and Wilson, M.O., (eds.). *Group relations at the crossroads*. New York: Harper, 1953, 232-56.

Festinger, L. Informal social communication. *Psychol. Rev.*, 1950, 57, 271–82.

Festinger, L., Gerard, H.B., Hymovitch, B., Kelley, H.H. and Raven, B.H. The influence process in the presence of extreme deviates. *Hum. Relat.*, 1952, 5. 327–346.

Festinger L., Schachter, S. and Back, K. The operation of group standards. In Cartwright, D. and Zander, A. *Group Dynamics: Research and Theory*. Evanston: Row, Peterson, 1953, 204–23.

French, J.R.P., Jr., Israel, Joachim and As, Dagfinn. "Arbeidernes medvirkining i industribedriften. En eksperimentell undersøkelse." Institute for Social Research, Oslo, Norway, 1957.

French, J.R.P., Jr., Levinger, G. and Morrison, H.W. The legitimacy of coercive power. (In preparation.)

French, J.R.P., Jr. and Raven, B.H. An experiment in legitimate and coercive power. (In preparation.)

Gerard, H.B. The anchorage of opinions in face-to-face groups. *Hum. Relat.*, 1954, 7, 313–325.

Goldhammer, H. and Shils, E.A. Types of power and status. *Amer. J. Sociol.*, 1939, 45, 171–178.

Herbst, P.G. Analysis and measurement of a situation. *Hum.Relat.*, 1953, 2,113–140.

Hochbaum, G.M. Self-confidence and reactions to group pressures. *Amer. Soc. Rev.*, 1954, 19, 678–687.

Hovland, C.I., Lumsdaine, A.A. and Sheffield, F.D. *Experiments on mass communication*. Princeton: Princeton University Press, 1949.

Hovland, C.I. and Weiss, W. The influence of source credibility on communication effectiveness. *Publ. Opn. Quart.*, 1951, 15, 635–650.

Jackson, J.M. and Saltzstein, H.D. The effect of person-group relationships on conformity processes. *Journal of Abnormal Social Psychology*, 1958, 57, 17–24.

Jahoda, M. Psychological issues in civil liberties. *American Psychologist*, 1956, 11, 234–240.

Katz, D. and Schank, R.L. *Social psychology*. New York: Wiley, 1938.

Kelley, H.H. and Volkart, E.H. The resistance to change of group-anchored attitudes. *Amer. Soc. Rev.*, 1952, 17, 453–465.

Kelman, H. Three processes of acceptance of social influence: Compliance, identification and internalization. Paper read at the meetings of the American Psychological Association, August 1956.

Kelman, H. and Hovland, C.I. "'Reinstatement'" of the communicator in delayed measurement of opinion change. *Journal of Abnormal Social Psychology*, 1953, 48, 327–335.

Lewin, K. *Dynamic theory of personality.* New York: McGraw-Hill, 1935, 114–170.

Lewin, K. *Field theory in social science.* New York: Harper, 1951.

Lewin, K., Lippitt, R. and White, R.K. Patterns of aggressive behavior in experimentally created social climates. *J. Soc. Psychol.*, 1939, 10, 271–301.

Lasswell, H.D. and Kaplan, A. *Power and society: A framework for political inquiry.* New Haven: Yale University Press, 1950.

Linton, R. *The cultural background of personality.* New York: Appleton-Century-Crofts, 1945.

Lippitt, R., Polansky, N., Redl, F., and Rosen, S. The dynamics of power. *Hum. Relat.*, 1952, 5, 37–64.

March, J.G. An introduction to the theory and measurement of influence. *Amer. Polit. Sci. Rev.*, 1955, 49, 431–451.

Miller, J.G. Toward a general theory for the behavioral sciences. *Amer. Psychologist*, 1955, 10, 513–531.

Moore, H.T. The comparative influence of majority and expert opinion. *Amer. J. Psychol.*, 1921, 32, 16–20.

Newcomb, T.M. *Social psychology.* New York: Dryden, 1950.

Raven, B.H. The effect of group pressures on opinion, perception, and communication. Unpublished doctoral dissertation, University of Michigan, 1953.

Raven, B.H. and French, J.R.P., Jr. Group support, legitimate power, and social influence. *J. Person.*, 1958, 26, 400–409.

Rommetveit, R. *Social norms and roles.* Minneapolis: University of Minnesota Press, 1953.

Russell, B. Power: *A new social analysis.* New York: Norton, 1938.

Stotland, E., Zander, A., Burnstein, E., Wolfe, D. and Natsoulas, T. Studies on the effects of identification. University of Michigan, Institute for Social Research (forthcoming).

Swanson, G.E., Newcomb, T.M. and Hartley, E.L. *Readings in social psychology.* New York: Henry Holt, 1952.

Torrance, E.P. and Mason, R. Instructor effort to influence: An experimental evaluation of six approaches. Paper presented at USAF-NRC Symposium on Personnel, Training, and Human Engineering. Washington, D.C., 1956.

Weber, M. *The theory of social and economic organization.* Oxford: Oxford University Press, 1947.

NEGOTIATING POWER: GETTING AND USING INFLUENCE

Roger Fisher

Getting to Yes (Fisher and Ury, 1981) has been justly criticized as devoting insufficient attention to the issue of power. It is all very well, it is said, to tell people how they might jointly produce wise outcomes efficiently and amicably, but in the real world people don't behave that way; results are determined by power—by who is holding the cards, by who has more clout.

At the international level, negotiating power is typically equated with military power. The United States is urged to develop and deploy more nuclear missiles so that it can negotiate from a position of strength. Threats and warnings also play an important role in the popular concept of power, as do resolve and commitment. In the game of chicken, victory goes to the side that more successfully demonstrates that it will not yield.

There is obviously some merit in the notion that physical force, and an apparent willingness to use it, can affect the outcome of a negotiation. How does that square with the suggestion that negotiators ought to focus on the interests of the parties, on the generating of alternatives, and on objective standards to which both sides might defer?

Roger Fisher, Negotiating Power, *American Behavioral Scientist*, Vol. 27, no. 2, Dec. 1983. pp. 149–166. Copyright © 1983 by Sage Publications. Reprinted by permission of Sage Publications, Inc.

This article is a brief report on the present status of some thinking about negotiating power. It represents work in progress. After briefly suggesting a definition of negotiating power, and the kind of theory for which we should be looking, I set up two "straw" men that are perhaps not made wholly of straw: (1) the basic way to acquire real power in a negotiation is to acquire the capacity to impose unpleasant physical results on the other side; and (2) an effective way to exercise negotiating power is to start off by letting the other side know of your capacity to hurt them and of your willingness to do so. Both propositions seem wrong. In the central body of the paper, I discuss six elements of negotiating power that can be acquired before and during negotiation, only one of which is the capacity to make a credible threat. Finally, I consider the sequence in which those different elements of power are best used to maximize their cumulative impact, and explore the debilitating effect of making threats at an early stage.

HOW SHOULD WE DEFINE NEGOTIATING POWER?

It seems best to define *negotiation* as including all cases in which two or more parties are communicating, each for the purpose of influencing the other's decision. Nothing seems to be gained by limiting the concept to formal negotiations taking place at a table, and much to be gained by defining the subject broadly. Many actions taken away from a table—ranging from making political speeches to building nuclear missiles—are taken for the purpose of "sending a message" to affect decisions of the other side.

The concept of *negotiating power* is more difficult. If I have negotiating power, I have the ability to affect favorably someone else's decision. This being so, one can argue that my power depends upon someone else's perception of my strength, so it is what they *think* that matters, not what I actually have. The other side might be as much influenced by a row of cardboard tanks as by a battalion of real tanks. One can then say that negotiating power is all a matter of perception.

A general who commands a real tank battalion, however, is in a far stronger position than one in charge of a row of cardboard tanks. A false impression of power is extremely vulnerable, capable of being destroyed by a word. In order to avoid focusing our attention on how to deceive other people, it seems best at the outset to identify what constitutes "real" negotiating power—an ability to influence the decisions of others, assuming they know the truth. We can then go on to recognize that, in addition, it will be possible at times to influence others through deception, through creating an illusion of power. Even for that purpose, we will need to know what illusion we wish to create. If we are bluffing, what are we bluffing about?

WHAT KIND OF THEORY ARE WE LOOKING FOR?

An infinite number of truths exist about the negotiation process, just as an infinite number of maps can be drawn of a city. It is easy to conclude that negotiators who are more powerful fare better in negotiations. By and large, negotiators who have more wealth, more friends and connections, good jobs, and more time will fare better in negotiations than will those who are penniless, friendless, unemployed, and in a hurry. Such statements, like the statement that women live longer than men, are true—but they are of little help to someone who wants to negotiate, or to someone who wants to live longer. Similarly, the statement that power plays an important role in negotiation is true—but irrelevant.

As negotiators we want to understand power in some way that helps us. We want diagnostic truths that point toward prescriptive action. The statement that women live longer than men points toward no remedial action. I am unable to live longer by choosing to become a woman. On the other hand, the statement that people who don't smoke live longer than people who do smoke is just as true, but it is far more helpful since I can decide not to smoke.

Thus a lively interplay exists between descriptive and prescriptive theory. The pure scientist might not care whether his truths have any relevance to the world of action; he leaves that to others. But those of us who are primarily concerned with change (one hopes, for the better) are searching for descriptive categories that have prescriptive significance.

We are looking for ideas that will help us make better choices. We are not simply trying to describe accurately what happens in a negotiation: We are trying to produce advice of use to negotiators, advice that will help them negotiate better. We need to say something other than that powerful princes tend to dominate less powerful princes, as true as that might be. We are looking for the kind of theory that will help a prince. He, presumably, has two key questions with respect to negotiating power: how to enhance negotiating power and how to use the power he has.

MISTAKEN VIEWS OF NEGOTIATING POWER

(1) "Physical Force = Negotiating Power"

It is widely believed that in order to enhance our negotiating power, we should acquire those assets like a strike-fund, a band of terrorists, or 100 MX missiles, which convey an implicit or explicit threat to harm the other side physically if it fails to agree with us. This belief is based on the assumption that since threats of physical force undoubtedly exert influence, the ability to make such threats is the essence of negotiating power. Force is seen as the necessary and sufficient element of negotiating power.

Negotiating power is the ability to influence others. The pain that we threaten to inflict if the other side does not decide as we like is simply one factor among many. And as I have written elsewhere, making threats is a particularly expensive and dangerous way of trying to exert influence.[1]

Total negotiating power depends upon many factors. Enhancing negotiating power means building up the combined potential of them all. Exercising negotiating power effectively means orchestrating them in a way that maximizes their cumulative impact. And this is where a second, widely held assumption about negotiating power appears to be mistaken and dangerous.

(2) "Start Tough; You Can Always Get Soft Later."

There is a widespread belief that the best way to start a negotiation is by taking a hard line. "Let them know early who's in charge." The thought is that since, in the last analysis, physical power might be the decisive factor, the entire negotiation should take place governed by its shadow. Conventional wisdom insists that it is easier to soften one's position than to harden it. A negotiator is encouraged to start off flexing his muscles.

Alan Berger, reviewing Seymour Hersh's *Kissinger in the White House*, emphasizes this feature of Nixon's foreign policy. "Nixon's first impulse was to attempt to intimidate his adversaries." He was anxious to "get tough," to "seem tough," to "be tough." "The nuclear option was not an ultimate recourse to be considered only *in extremis*; it was, as Hersh persuasively demonstrates, the point of departure . . . " (Boston Globe 1983).

President Reagan appeared to be operating on a similar assumption with respect to negotiating power: We begin with a threat. We seek to influence the Soviet Union with respect to intermediate-range nuclear missiles in Europe by starting off with a public commitment that U.S. Pershing II missiles will be deployed in Europe before the end of 1983 unless by that time the Soviet Union has agreed to withdraw all its missiles from Europe, on terms acceptable to us.

The notion that is it best to start off a negotiation with a warning or threat of the consequences of nonagreement might result from a false analogy. Other things being equal, it is true that in purely positional bargaining, the more extreme one's initial position (the higher a price one demands or the lower a price one offers), the more favorable an agreed result is likely to be. But opening with a very low substantive offer is quite different from opening with a threat of painful consequences if that offer is not accepted. The more firmly one is committed at an early stage to carrying out a threat, the more damaging that threat is to one's negotiating power.

If these two propositions are wrong, how should someone enhance and exercise negotiating power?

CATEGORIES OF POWER

My ability to exert influence depends upon the combined total of a number of different factors. As a first approximation, the following six kinds of power appear to provide useful categories for generating prescriptive advice:

1. The power of skill and knowledge
2. The power of a good relationship
3. The power of a good alternative to negotiating
4. The power of an elegant solution
5. The power of legitimacy
6. The power of commitment

Here is a checklist for would-be negotiators of what they can do in advance of any particular negotiation to enhance their negotiating power. The sequence in which these elements of power are listed is also important.

1. The Power of Skill and Knowledge

All things being equal, a skilled negotiator is better able to influence the decisions of others than is an unskilled negotiator. Strong evidence suggests that negotiating skills can be both learned and taught. One way to become a more powerful negotiator is to become a more skillful one. Some of these skills are those of dealing with people: the ability to listen, to become aware of the emotions and psychological concerns of others, to empathize, to be sensitive to their feelings and one's own, to speak different languages, to communicate clearly and effectively, to become integrated so that one's words and nonverbal behavior are congruent and reinforce each other, and so forth.

Other skills are those of analysis, logic, quantitative assessment, and the organization of ideas. The more skill one acquires, the more power one will have as a negotiator. These skills can be acquired at any time, often far in advance of any particular negotiation.

Knowledge also is power. Some knowledge is general and of use in many negotiations, such as familiarity with a wide range of procedural options, and awareness of national negotiating

styles and cultural differences. A repertoire of examples, precedents, and illustrations can also add to one's persuasive abilities.

Knowledge relevant to a particular negotiation in which one is about to engage is even more powerful. The more information one can gather about the parties and issues in an upcoming negotiation, the stronger one's entering posture. The following categories of knowledge, for example, are likely to strengthen one's ability to exert influence: Knowledge *about the people involved*. What are the other negotiators' personal concerns, backgrounds, interests, prejudices, values, habits, career hopes, and so forth? How would we answer the same questions with respect to those on our side?

Knowledge about the interests involved

In addition to the personal concerns of the negotiators, what additional interests are involved on the other side? What are their hopes, their fears, their needs? And what are the interests on our side?

Knowledge about the facts

It is impossible to appreciate the importance of unknown facts. Time permitting, it is usually worthwhile to gather a great deal of unnecessary information about the subject under negotiation in order to gather a few highly relevant facts. The more one knows about the history, geography, economics, and scientific background of a problem, as well as its legal, social, and political implications, the more likely it is that one can invent creative solutions.

It takes time and resources to acquire skill and knowledge; it also takes initiative and hard work. Lawyers who would never think of walking into a trial without weeks of preparation will walk into a negotiation with almost none: "Let's see what they have to say." Yet the lawyer would help his client more by persuading the other side next week rather than in trying to persuade a judge next year. The first way to enhance one's negotiating power is to acquire in advance all the skill and knowledge that one reasonably can.

2. The Power of a Good Relationship

The better a working relationship I establish in advance with those with whom I will be negotiating, the more powerful I am. A good working relationship does not necessarily imply approval of each other's conduct, though mutual respect and even mutual affection—when it exists—can help. The two most critical elements of a working relationship are, first, *trust*, and second, the *ability to communicate easily and effectively*.

Trust

Although I am likely to focus my attention in a given negotiation on the question of whether or not I can trust those on the other side, my power depends upon whether they can trust me. If over time I have been able to establish a well-deserved reputation for candor, honesty, integrity, and commitment to any promise I make, my capacity to exert influence is significantly enhanced.

Communication

The negotiation process is one of communication. If I am trying to persuade some people to change their minds, I want to know where their minds are; otherwise, I am shooting in the dark. If my messages are going to have their intended impact, they need to be understood as I would have them understood. At best, interpersonal communication is difficult and often generates misunderstanding. When the parties see each other as adversaries, the risk of miscommunication and misunderstanding is greatly increased. The longer two people have known each other, and the more broadly and deeply each understands the point of view and context from which the other is operating, the more likely they can communicate with each other easily and with a minimum of misunderstanding.

Each side benefits from this ability to communicate. We might have interests that conflict, but our ability to deal with those conflicting interests at minimum risk and minimum cost is enhanced by a good working relationship. Two men in a lifeboat at sea quarreling over limited rations have sharply conflicting interests. But the longer they have known each other, the more dealings they have had, and the more they speak the same language, the more likely they are to be able to divide the rations without tipping over the boat. The ability of each to affect favorably the other's decision is enhanced by an ability to communicate. More power for one is consistent with more power for the other.

A good working relationship is so helpful to the negotiation of satisfactory outcomes that it is often more important than any particular outcome itself. A banker, for example, is often like a person courting. The prospect of a satisfactory relationship is far more important than the terms of a particular loan or a particular date. A relationship that provides a means for happily resolving one transaction after another becomes an end in itself. Particular substantive negotiations become opportunities for cooperative activity that builds the relationship.

The same is true internationally. A better working relationship between the world's superpowers and the United States will facilitate the negotiation of arms-control agreements. Even more important, having a better working relationship would enhance the security of each nation more than would the outcome of any particular treaty. The better the working relationship we develop with other nations, the more likely they are to heed what we have to say.

3. The Power of a Good Alternative to Negotiation

To a significant extent, my power in a negotiation depends upon how well I can do for myself if I walk away. In *Getting to YES*, we urge a negotiator to develop and improve his "BATNA"—his Best Alternative To a Negotiated Agreement. One kind of preparation for negotiation that enhances one's negotiating power is to consider the alternatives to reaching agreement with this particular negotiating partner, to select the most promising, and to improve it to the extent possible. This alternative sets a floor. If I follow this practice, every negotiation will lead to a successful outcome in the sense that any result I accept is bound to be better than anything else I could do.

In the case of buying or selling, my best alternative is likely to result from dealing with a competitor. Obtaining a firm offer from such a competitor in advance of a proposed negotiation strengthens my hand in that negotiation. The better the competing offer, the more my hand is strengthened.

In other cases, my best alternative might well be self-help. What is the best I can do on my own? If the two boys offering to shovel the snow off the front walk are asking an exorbitant price, my best alternative might be to shovel the walk myself. Thinking about that option and having a snow shovel in the basement strengthens my hand in trying to negotiate a fair price with the boys.

The less attractive the other side's BATNA is to them, the stronger my negotiating position. In negotiating with my son to cut the lawn, I might discover that he lacks interest in earning a little pocket money: "Dad," he says, "you leave your wallet on your bureau and if I need a little money I always borrow some." My son's best alternative to a negotiated agreement to cut the lawn is to get the same amount or even more for doing nothing. To enhance my negotiating power, I will want to make his BATNA less attractive by removing that alternative. With my wallet elsewhere, he can be induced to earn some money by cutting the lawn.

Conventional military weapons typically enhance a country's negotiating power by making a non-negotiated solution less attractive to a hostile neighbor. With adequate defense forces, Country A can say to Country B: "Let's settle our boundary dispute by negotiation; if you try to settle it by military force, you will fail." With sufficient military force, Country A might be able to improve its alternative to negotiation enough that it will be in an extremely strong negotiating position: "We hope you will agree through negotiation to withdraw your forces to the boundary that has been recommended by impartial experts; if you do not agree to withdraw your forces voluntarily, we can force them to withdraw."

The better an alternative one can develop outside the negotiation, the greater one's power to favorably affect a negotiated outcome.

4. The Power of an Elegant Solution

In any negotiation, there is a melange of shared and conflicting interests. The parties face a problem. One way to influence the other side in a negotiation is to invent a good solution to that problem. The more complex the problem, the more influential an elegant answer. Too often, negotiators battle like litigators in court. Each side advances arguments for a result that would take care of its interests but would do nothing for the other side. The power of a mediator often comes from working out an ingenious solution that reconciles reasonably well the legitimate interests of both sides. Either negotiator has similar power to effect an agreement that takes care of his or her interests by generating an option that also takes care of some or most of the interests on the other side.

A wise negotiator includes in his or her preparatory work the generation of many options designed to meet as well as possible the legitimate interests of both sides. Brainstorming enhances my negotiating power by enhancing the chance that I will be able to devise a solution that amply satisfies my interests and also meets enough of your interests to be acceptable to you.

In complicated negotiations, and even in some fairly simple ones, there is usually a shortage of options on the table. The United States and the Soviet Union would presumably welcome a plan that left them at the same level of insecurity at substantially less cost, but no one has yet been able to devise one. In any negotiation, generating a range of options in advance, some of which might later be put on the table, is another way to increase the chance that I will affect the outcome favorably.

5. The Power of Legitimacy

Each of us is subject to being persuaded by becoming convinced that a particular result *ought* to be accepted because it is fair; because the law requires it; because it is consistent with precedent, industry practice, or sound policy considerations; or because it is legitimate as measured by some other objective standard. I can substantially enhance my negotiating power by searching for and developing various objective criteria and potential standards of legitimacy, and by shaping proposed solutions so that they are legitimate in the eyes of the other side.

Every negotiator is a partisan as well as someone who must be persuaded if any agreement is to be reached. To be persuasive, a good negotiator should speak like an advocate who is seeking to convince an able and honest arbitrator, and should listen like such an arbitrator, always open to being persuaded by reason. Being open to persuasion is itself persuasive.

Like a lawyer preparing a case, a negotiator will discover quite a few different principles of fairness for which plausible arguments can be advanced, and often quite a few different ways of interpreting or applying each principle. A tension exists between advancing a highly favorable principle that appears less legitimate to the other side and a less favorable principle that appears more legitimate. Typically, there is a range within which reasonable people could differ. To retain

his power, a wise negotiator avoids advancing a proposition that is so extreme that it damages his credibility. He also avoids so locking himself into the first principle he advances that he will lose face in disentangling himself from that principle and moving on to one that has a greater chance of persuading the other side. In advance of this process, a negotiator will want to have researched precedents, expert opinion, and other objective criteria, and to have worked on various theories of what ought to be done, so as to harness the power of legitimacy—a power to which each of us is vulnerable.

6. The Power of Commitment

The five kinds of power previously mentioned can each be enhanced by work undertaken in advance of formal negotiations. The planning of commitments and making arrangements for them can also be undertaken in advance, but making commitments takes place only during what everyone thinks of as negotiation itself.

There are two quite different kinds of commitments—affirmative and negative:

A. Affirmative commitments

1. An offer of what I am willing to agree to.

2. An offer of what, failing agreement, I am willing to do under certain conditions.

B. Negative commitments

1. A commitment that I am unwilling to make certain agreements (even though they would be better for me than no agreement).

2. A commitment or threat that, failing agreement, I will engage in certain negative conduct (even though to do so would be worse for me than a simple absence of agreement).

Every commitment involves a decision. Let's first look at affirmative commitments. An *affirmative commitment* is a decision about what one is willing to do. It is an offer. Every offer ties the negotiator's hands to some extent. It says, "'This, I am willing to do.'" The offer might expire or later be withdrawn, but while open it carries some persuasive power. It is no longer just an idea or a possibility that the parties are discussing. Like a proposal of marriage or a job offer, it is operational. It says, "I am willing to do this. If you agree, we have a deal.'"

We have all felt the power of a positive commitment—the power of an invitation. (We are not here concerned with the degree of commitment, or with various techniques for making a constraint more binding, but only with the content of the commitment itself. Advance planning can enhance my power by enabling me to demonstrate convincingly that a commitment is unbreakable. This subject, like all of those concerned with the difference between appearance and reality, is left for another day.) The one who makes the offer takes a risk. If he had waited, he might have gotten better terms. But in exchange for taking that risk, he has increased his chance of affecting the outcome.

A wise negotiator will formulate an offer in ways that maximize the cumulative impact of the different categories of negotiating power. The terms of an affirmative commitment will benefit from all the skill and knowledge that has been developed; the commitment benefits from the relationship and is consistent with it; it takes into account the walk-away alternatives each side has; the offer will constitute a reasonably elegant solution to the problem of reconciling conflicting interests; and the offer will be legitimate—it will take into account considerations of legitimacy.

With all this power in its favor, there is a chance the offer will be accepted. No other form of negotiating power may be needed. But as a last resort the negotiator has one other form of power: that of a negative commitment, or threat.

A *negative commitment* is the most controversial and troublesome element of negotiating power.

No doubt, by tying my own hands I might be able to influence you to accept something more favorable to me than you otherwise would. The theory is simple. For almost every potential agreement, there is a range within which each of us is better off having an agreement than walking away. Suppose that you would be willing to pay $135,000 for my house if you had to; but for a price above that figure, you would rather buy a different house. The best offer I have received from someone else is $122,000, and I will accept that offer unless you give me a better one. At any price between $122,000 and $135,000 we are both better off than if no agreement is reached. If you offer me $122,100, and so tie your hands by a negative commitment that you cannot raise your offer, presumably, I will accept it since it is better than $122,000. On the other hand, if I can commit myself not to drop the price below $135,000, you presumably will buy the house at that price. This logic might lead us to engage in a battle of negative commitments. Logic suggests that "'victory" goes to the one who first and most convincingly ties his own hands at an appropriate figure. Other things being equal, an early and rigid negative commitment at the right point should prove persuasive.

Other things, however, are not likely to be equal. The earlier I make a negative commitment—the earlier I announce a take-it-or-leave-it position—the less likely I am to have maximized the cumulative total of the various elements of my negotiating power.

The power of knowledge

I probably acted before learning as much as I could have learned. The longer I postpone making a negative commitment, the more likely I am to know the best proposition to which to commit myself.

The power of a good relationship

Being quick to advance a take-it-or-leave-it position is likely to prejudice a good working relationship and to damage the trust you might otherwise place in what I say. The more quickly I confront you with a rigid position on my part, the more likely I am to make you so angry that you will refuse an agreement you might otherwise accept.

The power of a good alternative

There is a subtle but significant difference between communicating a warning of the course of action that I believe it will be in my interest to take should we fail to reach agreement (my BATNA), and locking myself in to precise terms that you must accept in order to avoid my taking that course of action. Extending a warning is not the same as making a negative commitment. If the United States honestly believed in the 1980s that deploying one hundred MX missiles was a vital part of national security, then letting the Soviet Union know that in the absence of a negotiated agreement it intended to deploy them appeared to be a sound way to exert influence. In these circumstances, the United States remained open to considering any negotiated agreement that would be better for us than the MX deployment. The U.S. was not trying to influence the Soviet Union by committing itself to refuse to accept an agreement that was in its interest (in hopes of getting one even more favorable). The U.S. was simply trying to influence the Soviets with the objective reality that deployment seemed to be our best option in the absence of agreement.

Two kinds of negative commitments are illustrated by the MX case. One is the example of Mr. Adelman's letter, which apparently described the only possible agreement that the United States was willing to accept. His letter appeared to commit the United States to refusing to agree to any treaty that did not commit the Soviet Union "to forego their heavy and medium ICBM's" (New York Times, 1983). This was an apparent attempt to influence the Soviet Union by making a public commitment about what the United States

would not do—we would not take anything less than a Soviet agreement that it would dismantle all its heavy and medium missiles in exchange for a United States promise not to add one hundred MX missiles to its arsenal. The second kind of negative commitment is illustrated by the MX case if one assumes, as many citizens believed, that deploying one hundred MX missiles would not really enhance U.S. security, but rather damage it. The proposed deployment would be bad for us; perhaps worse for the Soviet Union. On this assumption, the threat to deploy the MX missiles is like my trying to influence a fellow passenger by threatening to tip over a boat, whether or not I am the better swimmer. Tipping over the boat will be bad for both of us, perhaps worse for him. I am committing myself to do something negative to both of us in the hope of exerting influence. If I make such a commitment, it is because I hope that by precluding myself from acting in some ways that would be in my interest, I will be able to achieve a result that is even more favorable.

To make either kind of negative commitment at an early stage of the negotiation is likely to reduce the negotiating power of a good BATNA. It shifts the other side's attention from the objective reality of my most attractive alternative to a subjective statement that I won't do things that (except for my having made the commitment) would be in my interest to do. Such negative commitments invite the other side to engage in a contest of will by making commitments that are even more negative, and even more difficult to get out of. Whatever negotiating impact my BATNA has, it is likely to be lessened by clouding it with negative commitments. This is demonstrated by Deputy Secretary of State Kenneth Dam's insistence (following Mr. Adelman's ill-fated letter) that the MX "is not a bargaining chip in the sense that we are just deploying it for purposes of negotiation. It is a vital part of our national security." That statement implicitly recognizes that a statement made for negotiating reasons is likely to exert less influence at the negotiating table than would a good alternative away from the table. Mr. Dam's statement also reflects recognition on the part of the United States that a premature negative commitment weakens rather than strengthens our negotiating power.

The power of an elegant solution

The early use of a negative commitment reduces the likelihood that the choice being considered by the other side is one that best meets its interests consistent with any given degree of meeting our interests. If we announce early in the negotiation process that we will accept no agreement other than Plan X, Plan X probably takes care of most of our interests. But it is quite likely that Plan X could be improved. With further study and time, it might be possible to modify Plan X so that it serves our interests even better at little or no cost to the interests of the other side.

Second, it might be possible to modify Plan X in ways that make it more attractive to the other side without in any way making it less attractive to us. To do so would not serve merely the other side but would serve us also by making it more likely that the other side will accept a plan that so well serves our interests.

Third, it might be possible to modify Plan X in ways that make it much more attractive to the other side at a cost of making it only slightly less attractive to us. The increase in total benefits and the increased likelihood of quickly reaching agreement might outweigh the modest cost involved.

Premature closure on an option is almost certain to reduce our ability to exert the influence that comes from having an option well crafted to reconcile, to the extent possible, the conflicting interests of the two sides. In multilateral negotiations it is even less likely that an early option will be well designed to take into account the plurality of divergent interests involved.

The Power of Legitimacy

The most serious damage to negotiating power that results from an early negative commitment is likely to result from its damage to the influence that comes from legitimacy. Legitimacy depends upon both process and substance. As with an arbitrator, the legitimacy of a negotiator's decision depends upon having accorded the other side "due process." The persuasive power of my decision depends in part on my having fully heard your views, your suggestions, and your notions of what is fair before committing myself. And my decision will have increased persuasiveness for you to the extent that I am able to justify it by reference to objective standards of fairness that you have indicated you consider appropriate. That factor, again, urges me to withhold making any negative commitment until I fully understand your views on fairness.

The power of an affirmative commitment

Negative commitments are often made when no affirmative commitment is on the table. The Iranian holders of the hostages in Tehran said for months that they would not release the hostages until the United States had adequately atoned for its sins and had met an ambiguous set of additional demands. No clear offer was given by Iran, and the United States, accordingly, was under no great pressure to do any particular thing. During the Vietnam War, the United States similarly failed to offer those on the other side any clear proposition. We would not leave, we said, until North Vietnam agreed "to leave its neighbors alone"—but no terms were on the table; no offer, no affirmative commitment was given.

Once an affirmative commitment is on the table, the negotiator must make sure that the varied elements of the communication are consistent with each other. No matter what the magnitude of a threat, it will have little effect unless it is constructed so that the sum total of the consequences of acceptance are more beneficial to the other side than is the sum total of the consequences of rejection. While negotiators frequently try to increase power by increasing the magnitude of a threat, they often overlook the fact that increasing the favorable consequences of acceptance can be equally important.

But no matter how favorable the consequences of acceptance are to the other side, and how distasteful the consequences of rejection, the proposition will carry little impact if the various implications of timing have not been thought through as well. Just as my son will look at me askance if I tell him that unless he behaves next week he will not be permitted to watch television tonight, so the North Vietnamese were unable to comply when the United States said, in effect, "If over the next few weeks you haven't reduced support for opponents of South Vietnam, we will bomb you tomorrow." The grammar must parse. (See *International Conflict for Beginners*.)

To make a negative commitment either as to what we will not do or to impose harsh consequences unless the other side reaches agreement with us, without having previously made a firm and clear offer, substantially lessens our ability to exert influence. An offer might not be enough, but a threat is almost certainly not enough unless there is a "YES-ABLE" proposition on the table— a clear statement of the action desired and a commitment as to the favorable consequences that would follow.

This analysis of negotiating power suggests that in most cases it is a mistake to attempt to influence the other side by making a negative commitment of any kind at the outset of the negotiations, and that it is a mistake to do so until one has first made the most of every other element of negotiating power.[2]

This analysis also suggests that when as a last resort threats or other negative commitments are used, they should be so formulated as to complement and reinforce other elements of negotiating power, not undercut them. In particular, any statement to the effect that we have finally reached a take-it-or-leave-it position should be made in a way that is consistent with maintaining a good working relationship, and consistent with the concepts of legitimacy with which we are trying to persuade the other side. For example, I might say:

Bill, I appreciate your patience. We have been a long time discussing the sale of my house, and I believe that we each fully understand the other's concerns. We have devised a draft contract that elegantly reconciles my interest in a firm deal, adequate security, and reasonable restrictions to protect the neighbors with your interest in being able to move in early, to stretch out the payments, and to have your professional office in the house. The only open issue is price. On that, we have discussed various criteria, such as market value based on recent sales, providing me a fair return on my investment, and value based on professional estimates of replacement cost depreciated for wear and tear. These criteria produced figures ranging from $135,000 down to $130,000. I have offered to sell you the house for $132,000.

Your response, as I understand it, is to say that you will pay no more than $100 above the best written offer I have from another potential buyer, now $122,000. Knowing that you would pay $135,000 if you had to, I am unable to understand why you should get all but $100 of the advantage of our shared interest in my selling and your buying the house. Nor, as we have discussed, do I think it a wise practice for me to defer to what looks to me like an arbitrary commitment.

The transaction costs of further discussion would appear to outweigh any potential advantage. Unless you have something further you would like to say now, or unless you would like to try to convince me that this procedure is unfair, I hereby make a final offer of $130,000, the lowest figure I believe justified by objective criteria. Let me confirm that offer now in writing and commit myself to leaving that offer open for three days. Unless something wholly unexpected comes up, I will not sell the house to you for less. Please think it over.

In any event, let's plan to play golf on Saturday afternoon if you are free.

A great deal of work remains to be done toward formulating the best general advice that can be given to help a negotiator increase his or her ability to influence others. Some of that work relates to what can be done to acquire power in advance of a negotiation; much relates to how best to use such power as one has. No attempt has been made to advance propositions that will be true in every case—only to advance rules of thumb that should be helpful in many cases. So far, I have been unable to come up with any better rules of thumb covering the same ground.

As indicated at the outset, this article does not cover the kind of negotiating power that comes from creating in the mind of others an impression that is false—from bluffing, deceit, misrepresentation, or other such act or omission. For the moment, I remain unconvinced that the best advice for a negotiator would include suggestions of how to create a false impression in the mind of the other side, any more than I would advise young lawyers on how best to create a false impression in the mind of a judge or arbitrator. But that is a subject for another day.

NOTES

1. See "Making Threats Is Not Enough", Chapter Three in *International Conflict for Beginners* (Fisher, 1969).

2. On reading this article, Douglas Stone of the Harvard Law School suggested that there might be one kind of negative commitment that could be made at the outset of negotiations without damage to the relationship, to legitimacy, or to other elements of one's total power. This might be done by establishing an early commitment never to yield to unprincipled threats. I might, for example, make a negative commitment that I would not respond to negative commitments but only to facts, objective criteria, offers, and reasoned argument. Like an advance commitment not to pay blackmail, such a negative commitment is consistent with legitimacy. In fact, one might propose that both sides make mutual commitments not to respond to threats. An early commitment not to respond to threats might, if convincingly made, preemptively foreclose threats from the other side.

REFERENCES

Fisher, R. (1969). *International conflict for beginners.* New York: Harper & Row.

Fisher, R. and W. Ury. (1981). *Getting to YES.* Boston: Houghton-Mifflin.

Berger, A. (1983). Hersch probes Nixon years relentlessly. *Boston Globe* (June 19): B-10, B-12.

Freudenheim, M. and H. Giniger (1983). Adelman gets a lesson in letter writing. *New York Times* (June 26): 2E.

Section II

Persuasion

Chapter Four   *Trust and Negotiation*
Chapter Five   *The Influence Process*

Chapter Four

TRUST AND NEGOTIATION

TRUST AND MANAGERIAL PROBLEM- SOLVING

Dale E. Zand

This article presents a model of trust and its interaction with information flow, influence, and control, and reports on an experiment based on the model to test several hypotheses about problem-solving effectiveness. The subjects were managers and the independent variable was the individual manager's initial level of trust. Groups of business executives were given identical factual information about a difficult manufacturing–marketing policy problem: Half the groups were briefed to expect trusting behavior, the other half to expect untrusting behavior. There were highly significant differences in effectiveness between the high-trust groups and the low-trust groups in the clarification of goals, the reality of information exchanged, the scope of the search for solutions, and the commitment of managers to implement solutions. The findings indicate that shared trust or lack of trust apparently are significant determinants of managerial problem-solving effectiveness.*

There is increasing research evidence that trust is a salient factor in determining the effectiveness of many relationships, such as those between parent and child (Baldwin *et al.*, 1945), psychotherapist and client (Fiedler, 1953; Seeman, 1954), and members of problem-solving groups (Parloff and Handlon, 1966). Trust facilitates interpersonal acceptance and openness of expression,

* Dale E. Zand, "Trust and Managerial Problem Solving", *Administrative Science Quarterly*, Vol. 17, No. 2 (June 1972), pp. 229–239. Reprinted by permission.

whereas mistrust evokes interpersonal rejection and arouses defensive behavior (Gibb, 1961).

During the past fifteen years many managers have been introduced to programs, variously called sensitivity training (Bradford *et al.*, 1964), grid laboratories (Blake and Mouton, 1964), or group workshops (Sehein and Bennis, 1965), in order to improve their skills in developing trust and thus, presumably, their managerial effectiveness. It has been difficult, however, to show a direct correlation between trust and managerial effectiveness in a working organization (Dunnette and Campbell,

1968; House, 1967), so that there is a need to clarify the theoretical basis for assertions about trust and managerial effectiveness and to devise experiments to test them.

INTRODUCTION

Rogers (1961) found that in an effective helping relationship, one participant (counselor, therapist, helper) behaved in ways that developed trust and the other experienced an increase in trust, and concluded that the development of trust is a crucial initial factor and a necessary continuing element in such a relationship. He summarized extensive research in which an increase in trust appeared to be causally related to more rapid intellectual development, increased originality, increased emotional stability, increased self-control, and decreased physiological arousal to defend against threat.

The level of trust in a relationship affects the degree of defensiveness. Gibb (1961) found that members of small groups that developed a "defensive climate" had difficulty concentrating on messages, perceived the motives, values, and emotions of others less accurately, and increased the distortion of messages. Other studies suggest that some interpersonal trust is required for effective problem-solving in a group. Parloff and Handlon (1966) found that intensive, persistent criticism increased defensiveness and mistrust among members of a group and decreased their ability to recognize and accept good ideas. Meadow *et al.* (1959) reported that defensiveness induced a lasting decrease in problem-solving effectiveness. They found that groups penalized for poor ideas and admonished to produce only good ideas while working on early problems produced poorer solutions to later problems when these restrictions were removed than groups that were not penalized and admonished during their early problem assignments.

This article: (1) analyzes the concept of trust, (2) presents a model of the interaction of trust and problem-solving behavior, and (3) reports the results of an experiment that attempted to test several hypotheses derived from the model.

ANALYSIS OF CONCEPT

Trusting behavior, following Deutsch (1962), is defined here as consisting of actions that (a) increase one's vulnerability, (b) are directed toward another whose behavior is not under one's control, (c) take place in a situation in which the penalty (disutility) one suffers if the other abuses that vulnerability is greater than the benefit (utility) one gains if the other does not abuse that vulnerability. For example, a parent is exhibiting trusting behavior in hiring a babysitter so he can see a movie. The action significantly increases his vulnerability, since he cannot control the babysitter's behavior after leaving the house. If the baby sitter abuses that vulnerability, the penalty might be a tragedy that adversely affects the rest of his life; if the babysitter does not abuse that vulnerability, the benefit will be the pleasure of seeing a movie. Thus trust, as the term will be used in this article, is not a global feeling of warmth or affection, but the conscious regulation of one's dependence on another that will vary with the task, the situation, and the other person.

MODEL

The following model, based on Gibb (1964), conceptualizes the transforming of one's inner state of trust (or mistrust) into behavior that is trusting (or mistrusting) through (1) information, (2) influence, and (3) control.

One who does not trust others will conceal or distort relevant information, and avoid stating or will disguise facts, ideas, conclusions, and feelings that he believes will increase his exposure to others, so that the information he provides will be low in accuracy, comprehensiveness, and timeliness; and therefore have low congruence with reality. He will also resist or deflect the attempts of others to exert influence. He will be suspicious of their views, and not receptive to their proposals of goals, their suggestions for reaching goals, and their definition of criteria and methods for evaluating progress. Although he rejects the influence of others, he will expect them to accept his views. Finally, one who does not trust will try to minimize his dependence on others. He will feel he cannot rely on them to abide by agreements and will try to impose controls on their behavior when coordination is necessary to attain common goals, but will resist and be alarmed at their attempts to control his behavior.

When others encounter low-trust behavior, initially they will hesitate to reveal information, reject influence, and evade control. This short cycle feedback will reinforce the originator's low trust, and unless there are changes in behavior, the relationship will stabilize at a low level of trust.

All of this behavior, following from a lack of trust, will be deleterious to information exchange, to reciprocity of influence, and to the exercise of self-control, and will diminish the effectiveness of joint problem-solving efforts.

To the objective uncertainty inherent in a problem (unavailable facts and unknown causal relationships between actions and results, for example), low trust will add social uncertainty: that is, uncertainty introduced by individuals withholding or distorting relevant information and concepts.

Persons lacking trust but attempting to solve a problem jointly will try to minimize their vulnerability. There will be an increase in the likelihood of misunderstanding or misinterpretation. The social uncertainty induced by their low trust will increase the probability that underlying problems will go undetected or be avoided, and that inappropriate solutions will be more difficult to identify. If the group is incapable of breaking out of this ineffective pattern of problem solving, it might seize an expedient solution as a device to

end its work and dissolve itself.

Persons who trust one another will provide relevant, comprehensive, accurate, and timely information, and thereby contribute realistic data for problem-solving efforts. They will have less fear that their exposure will be abused, and will therefore be receptive to influence from others. They will also accept interdependence because of confidence that others will control their behavior in accordance with agreements, and therefore will have less need to impose controls on others (see Figure 1). Consequently, they will contribute to a decrease in social uncertainty, and be less likely to misinterpret the intentions and the behavior of others. As a result, underlying problems are more likely to be identified and examined, and solutions more likely to be appropriate, creative, and long-range.

Hypotheses

It is not assumed here that trust alone will solve a technical problem; it is assumed that group members collectively have adequate knowledge, experience, and creativity to define and solve a complex problem. It is also assumed that it is possible to increase or decrease trust in members of a problem-solving group.

On the basis of the model described, the following differences can be predicted in the problem-solving behavior of groups with high and low trust.

An increase in trust will increase the exchange of accurate, comprehensive, and timely information. Problem-solving groups with high trust will:

Hypothesis 1. Exchange relevant ideas and feelings more openly.

Hypothesis 2. Develop greater clarification of goals and problems.

An increase in trust will increase one's willingness to influence others and to be receptive to the influence of others. Hence, problem-solving groups with high trust will:

Figure 1
A Model of the Relationship of Trust to Information, Influence, and Control

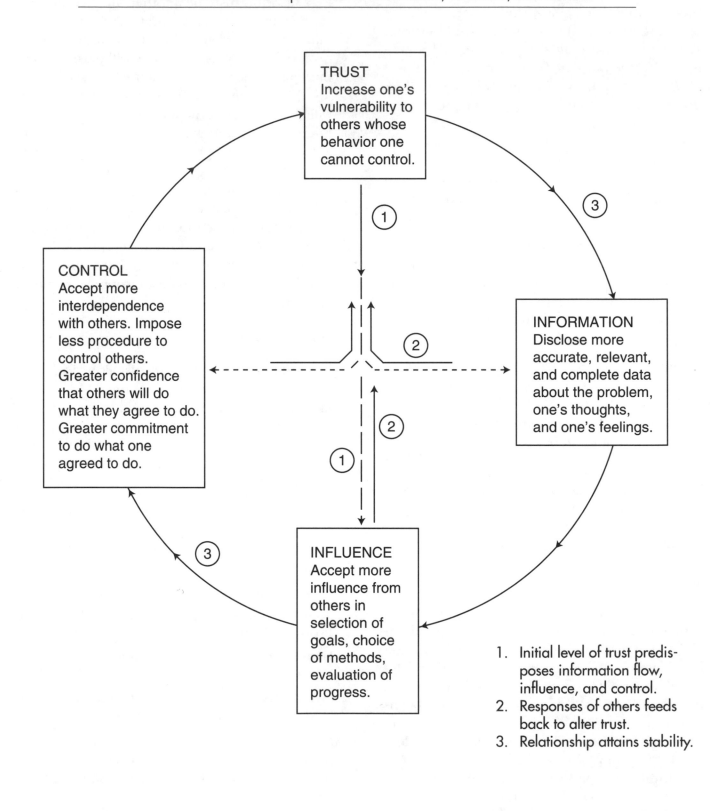

TRUST
Increase one's vulnerability to others whose behavior one cannot control.

CONTROL
Accept more interdependence with others. Impose less procedure to control others. Greater confidence that others will do what they agree to do. Greater commitment to do what one agreed to do.

INFORMATION
Disclose more accurate, relevant, and complete data about the problem, one's thoughts, and one's feelings.

INFLUENCE
Accept more influence from others in selection of goals, choice of methods, evaluation of progress.

1. Initial level of trust predisposes information flow, influence, and control.
2. Responses of others feeds back to alter trust.
3. Relationship attains stability.

Hypothesis 3. Search more extensively for alternative courses of action.

Hypothesis 4. Have greater influence on solutions.

Finally, an increase in trust will increase the willingness to control one's own behavior and will increase confidence in the reliability of others, and will decrease efforts to control the behavior of others, all of which will contribute to increased satisfaction and motivation. Hence, problem-solving groups with high trust will:

Hypothesis 5. Be more satisfied with their problem-solving efforts.

Hypothesis 6. Have greater motivation to implement conclusions.

Hypothesis 7. See themselves as closer and more of a team.

Hypothesis 8. Have less desire to leave their group to join another.

Dynamics of Trust

Trust takes form in the interaction of two (or more) people, and the dynamics of this interaction are illustrated in Figure 2.

Let P denote one person and O the other. If (1) P lacks trust, (2) he will disclose little relevant or accurate information, be unwilling to share influence, and will attempt to control O. (3) Assume that O also lacks trust, (4) perceives P's initial behavior as actually untrusting, and (5) concludes that he was right to expect P to be untrustworthy; then (6) he will feel justified in his mistrust of P. Since (7) P sees O's behavior as untrusting, he (8) will be confirmed in his initial expectation that O would not be trustworthy and P will behave with less trust than when he entered (back to 2).

The interaction will continue around the loop, inducing O and P to behave with less and less trust until they arrive at an equilibrium level of low trust, each attempting to minimize his vulnerability and to maximize his control of the other. In the process, the effectiveness of problem-solving will decrease. After interaction has continued, each will tend to hold more firmly to his entering beliefs. They will not have a reliable basis for accepting or sharing influence, and the mutual resistance to influence will arouse feelings of frustration in both. If they have a deadline, each will attempt to impose controls on the other. If P is O's organizational superior, he might command O's compliance, which will reinforce O's mistrust. Usually, by the middle of the meeting the level of trust will be lower than the initial level.

Gibb (1964) offers support for the dynamics of this interaction. In observing small group behavior, he noted that the defensive behavior of a listener generated cues that subsequently increased the defensiveness of the communicator, resulting, if unchecked, in a circular pattern of escalating defensiveness.

The pattern of spiral reinforcement illustrated in Figure 2 would operate constructively if it is assumed that both P and O entered the relationship with trust in the other. Gibb (1964) observed that when defensiveness was reduced, members were better able to concentrate on the content and meaning of a message, became more problem-oriented, and were less concerned about imposing controls on each other's behavior.

METHOD

The spiral reinforcement model of the dynamics of trust (Figure 2) has been presented to establish a theoretical rationale for the methods used to induce different levels of trust, but this study did not focus on a test of the spiral reinforcement model. The aim of this study was to examine the relation between trust and problem-solving effectiveness as formulated in the eight hypotheses.

To test the hypotheses derived from the model, the research was designed so that half of the experimental groups started work on a business-

Figure 2
A Model of the Interaction of Two Persons With Similar Intentions and Expectations Regarding Trust

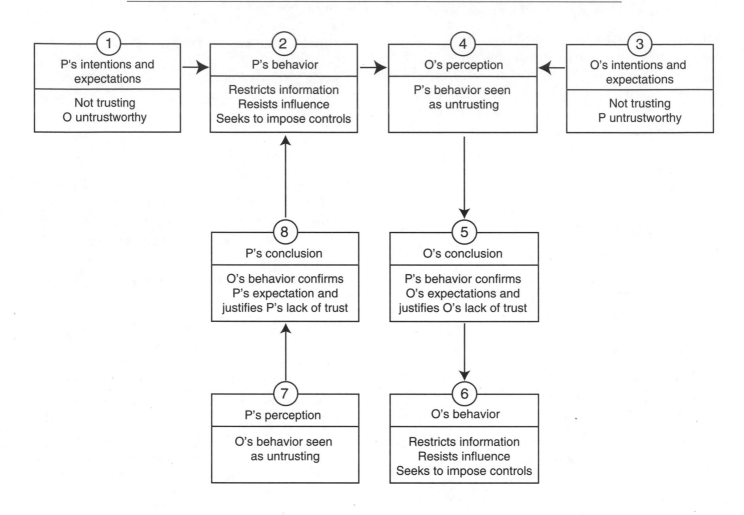

management problem with a mental set toward low trust and half with a mental set toward high trust. Mental set, as used here, includes intentions as to one's behavior, expectations as to the behavior of others, feelings such as anxiety or discomfort, and a cognitive frame used to interpret events and form perceptions. In this research, trust was not examined as a personality variable (that is, an element of individual character), but instead as an induced attitude, one that the individual could alter in a situation in which he was led to intend and to expect trust (or mistrust) from others as he attempted to solve a problem. Because trust as a personality trait was not relevant, and to avoid alerting the subjects to the issue of trust, no prior measures were taken of the subjects' attitude toward trust.

Subjects. Because of their high candidate potential for top management, upper-middle managers from all functions and product divisions of a large, international electronics company were periodically selected by their superiors, after discussion with the corporate personnel staff, to attend an off-site, four week, in-residence program in management development given several times a year that accepted only sixteen managers at a time. Eight managers in each program were randomly chosen to be subjects and distributed into two problem-solving groups, each with four members. The remaining eight managers were observers; each was randomly assigned to a group with four members, and each group observed one problem-solving group. Data were gathered in eight programs, providing a total of sixty-four subjects in sixteen problem-solving groups and fifty-nine observers (five programs were short one manager) in sixteen observing groups. There were no subordinates, superiors, or peers from the same department or division in any program. Interviews confirmed that the subjects and the observers did not know about the experiment, which was designed as a learning event embedded in the program.

Problem. The central problems involved (1) developing a strategy to increase short-term profits without undermining long-term growth of a medium-sized electronics company with very low return on investment, outdated manufacturing facilities, and a labor force that had been cut 25 percent (and whose top management personnel had been changed and reorganized two years before), and (2) obtaining commitment to implement such a program despite strong managerial disappointment because expectations of immediate investment for expansion and modernization would not be met. The situation, a variation of one described by Maier *et al.* (1959), involved four executive roles: the president and the vice presidents for marketing, manufacturing, and personnel. Subjects were randomly assigned to the roles.

Procedure. All subjects and observers were given a written description of the production, marketing, financial, and personnel difficulties of the company.

In the presence of the observers, subjects were told they were to conduct a meeting lasting thirty minutes in the president's office in order to make appropriate management decisions. Ostensibly, they were to demonstrate their deci-sion-making competence to their fellow managers, the observers.

Each subject was then given an additional written statement with factual and attitudinal information relevant to his/her function. Each subject had no knowledge of the role information given to other subjects. The subjects privately read and absorbed this problem information for twenty-five minutes so there would be minimal need to refer to it during the meeting.

Treatments. Subjects were randomly assigned to one of two group conditions: an entering mental set toward high or toward low trust.

The factual data about production, marketing, finance, and so on was identical in both conditions, and all vice presidents were led to expect that the president would announce approval of a long-studied plant expansion.

In both conditions, the president stated that on the preceding day he had received an ultimatum from the board of directors demanding an increase in profits within one year or else he would be forced to resign. Furthermore, he was told that expansion was not feasible because it would reduce short-term profits and take more than a year to build and start up a new plant, and that the board was not likely to approve the financing. As a first step toward increasing profits, he would have to announce his decision against expansion. The vice presidents had no knowledge of the president's dilemma when they started their thirty-minute problem-solving meeting.

Induction of conditions of trust. The induction of the two levels of trust was accomplished by operating on the following entering beliefs of subjects: (1) the task competence of others, (2) norms on introducing information and new ideas, (3) norms on attempts to influence managers outside of one's primary responsibility, (4) likelihood that others would abuse trusting behavior, and (5) competitiveness or collaborativeness for rewards.

In a high-trust group, a manager's entering mental set toward trust was shaped by the following paragraph, which followed the factual information in the role statement:

> You have learned from your experiences during the past two years that you can trust the other members of top management. You and the other top managers openly express your differences and your feelings of encouragement or of disappointment. You and the others share all relevant information and freely explore ideas and feelings that are in or out of your defined responsibility. The result has been a high level of give and take and mutual confidence in each other's support and ability.

Subjects in low-trust groups had a similar paragraph in their role information, worded to induce a *decrease* in trust.

The reward system was operated on by information placed only in the president's statement. In the high-trust condition, the president was led to see his relation to his vice presidents as collaborative. His role statement said that "although the Board's decision considered you specifically, since you appointed the current top management team it is likely that the Board will go outside for a successor and possibly other vice presidents."

In the low-trust condition, the president was led to see his relation to his vice presidents as potentially competitive. His role statement said that since the board's ultimatum pertained to him, it was possible that they might appoint one of the vice presidents as his successor. The vice presidents in both conditions were given no information about whether their relation to the president was potentially competitive or collaborative.

All subjects were told that "whenever information is incomplete, introduce whatever facts and experiences seem reasonable under the circumstances."

Observers. In addition to reading the written general description of the company's problems before observing the problem-solving meeting, the observers were told of the vice presidents' factual basis for seeking and expecting to get final approval for plant expansion, and that the president had received a one-year ultimatum from the board the preceding day, but they were given no information about the attitudinal parts of the statements.

Measures. After thirty minutes, group discussion was stopped and each subject and observer completed a questionnaire with eight or nine items. The respondent was to indicate whether in his group or the group he observed there was "much" or "little" of the property described in each item.

The items were: (1) trust, (2) openness about feelings, (3) clarification of the group's basic problems and goals, (4) search for alternative courses of action, (5) mutual influence on outcomes, (6) satisfaction with the meeting, (7) motivation to implement decisions, and (8) closeness as a management team as a result of the meeting. The subjects' questionnaire had a ninth item: "As a result of this meeting, would you give little, or much serious consideration to a position with another company?" The written statement could only suggest to each subject an entering mental set toward high or low trust. By the end of the meeting, each subject's level of trust would depend on the extent to which his entering beliefs were confirmed by the behavior of the other managers.

RESULTS

Measures of Trust. The responses of subjects and of observers are reported separately in Table 1, with the chi-square value for each item.

The subjects' rating of level of trust confirms that the induction of high and low trust was successful ($p < .001$) after one-half hour of problem discussion. This result, although not a direct test of the spiral reinforcement model, does offer support for it.

Since the observers used only their personal standards for their ratings, it is noteworthy that they had little difficulty recognizing the behavior indicative of low or high trust (P < .001).

The hypotheses about differences between groups with high or low trust were confirmed by the responses of the subjects (items 2–9, P <.001) and observers (items 3–9, P <.001; item 2, p < .05).

Qualitative Differences. There were also observable qualitative differences in the comprehensiveness and creativity of the problem-solving of the two groups.

High-Trust Groups. In the high-trust groups the president consistently and voluntarily disclosed the board's demand for better short-term performance. These teams, after initial frustration with the disapproval of immediate expansion, dealt with the short-range plans to increase profitability, and then began to design long-range plans for modernization and expansion that they would present to the board.

Short-range plans emerging from the discussion among the vice presidents included straightforward proposals to review the product line, to identify and promote sales of high-profit items, and to cut back output of low-profit items. Their more creative proposals, flowing from substantial changes in their perceptions, included, for example, leasing space in a nearby vacant plant, rearranging work flow, selectively modernizing equipment that would provide greatest cost-benefits and require minimal capital, subcontracting standard components, and rapidly converting two new products from research to production. In one group, the managers agreed to invest their personal savings to help finance modernization in order to show the board their strong commitment to the company's future.

Low-Trust Groups. In low-trust groups, the vice presidents had difficulty understanding the basis for the president's decision against expansion and his desire for short-range profits. Several groups asked him if there were reasons behind his decision other than those he had disclosed, but he steadfastly refused to reveal information about the board's demands. As a result, the vice presidents in low-trust groups could not sense how close the company might be to reorganization and possibly dissolution. They spent most of the meeting disagreeing with the president by repeating their basic arguments for immediate expansion. Finally, after prolonged frustration, the president would impose directives on the group. Usually he would demand review of the product line to eliminate low-profit items. If there was any creativity, it came from the president, who was desperately seeking a solution in spite of the resistance of his vice presidents. Occasionally, the president would propose that it might be possible to lease space in a nearby vacant plant, but his idea would be discarded as unworkable by the belligerent vice presidents. In several groups, the president threatened to dismiss a vice president.

Conversations among subjects of the low-trust groups after they had answered the questionnaire showed the high defensiveness and antagonism they had induced in each other. For example, half the vice presidents said that they were so discouraged, they were thinking about looking for another job in the middle of the meeting, and several said they hoped the president's plane would be hijacked, or even crash. The president usually retorted that he had decided to dismiss them before the next meeting.

Discussion. One might contend that the managers were attempting to rigidly follow the attitude toward trust suggested in their briefing, but in the debriefing interviews, the managers said that after their meeting had started, their level of trust varied in response to the behavior of the other managers. In low-trust groups, for example, about half of the vice presidents said that by the end of the meeting, they found themselves trusting one or another vice president more than they expected to, and trusting the president much less than when they had started.

That the pattern of spiral reinforcement requires all members of a group to hold similar intentions to trust (or not trust) may be too stringent a condition. The following anecdotal evidence suggests that having several members with similar intentions can be sufficient. An unanticipated incident illustrates how difficult it sometimes is for one person acting alone to break the reinforcement pattern, even though he has formal power. In one low-trust group, in an effort to

Table 1
Frequency of Response to Each Item by Subjects and Observers under High Trust and Low Trust, with Chi-Square Values for Differences

| Item | Response | Subjects Condition | | | Observers Condition | | |
		High trust	Low trust	χ^2	High trust	Low trust	χ^2
1. Trust	Much	30	9	28.1	19	7	16.7
	Little	2	23		6	26	
2. Openness about feelings	Much	31	15	26.4	15	12	4.2
	Little	1	17		7	21	
3. Clarification of problems and goals	Much	24	10	10.8	18	7	12.9
	Little	8	22		8	26	
4. Search	Much	21	6	13.8	11	5	14.7
	Little	11	26		11	28	
5. Influence	Much	29	6	30.8	19	2	32.0
	Little	3	26		6	31	
6. Satisfaction	Much	28	7	25.6	20	2	32.7
	Little	4	25		6	31	
7. Motivation to implement conclusions	Much	30	10	26.6	19	4	22.2
	Little	2	22		7	29	
8. Closeness as a team	Much	27	9	19.1	17	5	16.6
	Little	5	23		9	28	
9. Desire to take a job in another company	Much	8	22	10.8			
	Little	24	10				

*   P < .001 for all χ^2 values in this column.
** P < .001 for all χ^2 values in this column except item 2, for which P < .05.

behave with trust toward his vice presidents, the president early in the meeting disclosed that the board wanted better profit performance in one year or else might ask for his resignation, but this attempt to show trust did not alter the emergence of low-trust behavior among the vice presidents. Indeed, in interviews after the meeting, the vice presidents said they interpreted the president's statement as a means of shifting blame to the board for his decision not to approve expansion, so that instead of increasing their trust, his behavior confirmed their mistrust. Also, they interpreted the president's comment that he might be forced to resign as evidence that the board did not trust him, so they should not either. Two vice presidents in this group said that by the middle of the meeting, they were thinking about how they might hasten the president's resignation. It seems that behaving with high trust toward others who are not trusting *will not* necessarily induce trust, and if one does so it is wise to limit one's increase in vulnerability.

Another illustration of the difficulty of interrupting the spiral reinforcement pattern occurred in a high-trust group, when the president did not reveal the board's demand for short-term profits. The vice presidents said that the president seemed troubled, and asked him if he was explaining all the reasons behind his decision not to expand. In the debriefing interviews, after they learned about the president's predicament, one vice president turned to the president and said, "Why didn't you tell us? We could have done so much more to help you and ourselves." The group's level of trust had remained high, but the creativity and comprehensiveness of its solutions had suffered in comparison with other high-trust groups.

Because of the many limitations of the experiment—that is, the small number of subjects, data gathered over several years, the study conducted within the context of a management-development program—the study was restricted to con-

ditions in which all managers in a group had the same initial level of trust. The condition of mixed trust, in which some members would tend to trust and others would tend to mistrust, was not included; one could, however, predict that the effects on creativity and comprehensiveness of solutions (and on motivations to implement solutions) might be intermediate between those of the high-trust and low-trust groups. The two incidents described above are consistent with such a prediction.

Furthermore, the problem used in this study was quite complex; it required that the participants generate the alternatives; and it had no unique, optimal solution. There might be less of a difference in the output of high-trust and low-trust groups working on highly structured problems— problems with clear, tangible goals, with well-defined information, with alternatives provided, and with a unique solution. Theoretically, the structure inherent in the problem might reduce a group's susceptibility to the social uncertainty generated by low-trust behavior. On the basis of the data in Table 1, however, it would seem that, given similar member competence, groups that develop high trust would solve problems more effectively than low trust groups; they would do better in locating relevant information, in using their members' skills to generate alternatives, and in eliciting commitment.

The data also indicate that patterns of low-trust and high-trust group behavior are recognizable by untrained observers. Possibly the consistency between the responses of subjects and observers was increased by the fact that they were all managers in one company and presumably exposed to a common organizational culture, but any such effect was probably offset by the fact that they came from widely separated divisions, and some people were foreign nationals who had worked in overseas subsidiaries.

Finally, this study revealed that theory and research on group forces have had only a minor impact on the thinking of managers. The managers in this study were among the best educated and the most sophisticated to be found in corporate organizations. After completing the questionnaires (but without any information about the trust model), they were brought together and asked for their explanations of what had happened in the two groups. They consistently responded that the outcomes were the result of the personalities of the subjects (who had been randomly assigned to the different roles) or the president's style (which they interpreted as autocratic or democratic), or even the time he stated his decision not to expand (either early or late in the meeting). The possibility that a shared level of trust—a group force or a belief held by several or all members of a group—might have constituted a social reality that could significantly affect problem-solving effectiveness was not mentioned.

CONCLUSIONS

The findings of this study confirm the hypotheses derived from the model. The results indicate that it is useful to conceptualize trust as behavior that conveys appropriate information, permits mutuality of influence, encourages self-control, and avoids taking advantage of the vulnerability of others.

It appears that when a group works on a problem, there are two concerns: one is the problem itself, and the second is how the members relate to each other to work on the problem. Apparently interpersonal relationships in low-trust groups interfere with and distort perceptions of the problem. Energy and creativity are diverted from finding comprehensive, realistic solutions, and members use the problem as an instrument to minimize their vulnerability. In contrast, in high-trust groups there is less socially-generated uncertainty, and problems are solved more effectively.

This study also offers qualitative support for the spiral-reinforcement model. It suggests that mutual trust or mistrust among members of a

group is likely to be reinforced, unless there is marked or prolonged disconfirming behavior. Exactly what disconfirmation is needed and how much requires further investigation.

Finally, this research offers evidence that a social phenomenon—trust—can significantly alter managerial problem-solving effectiveness.

REFERENCES

Baldwin, Alfred L., Joan Kalhorn, and Fay Hoffman Breese. (1945). *Patterns of parent behavior.* Psychological monograph, 58, 268, pp. 1–75.

Blake, Robert R., and Jane S. Mouton. (1964). *The managerial grid.* Houston: Gulf Publishing.

Bradford, Leland P., Jack R. Gibb, and Kenneth D. Benne. (1964). *T-Group theory and laboratory method.* New York: John Wiley.

Deutsch, Morton. (1962). *Cooperation and trust: Some theoretical notes.* In Marshall R. Jones (ed.) Nebraska Symposium on Motivation. Lincoln, Nebraska: University of Nebraska Press, pp. 275– 319.

Dunnette, Marvin D., and John P. Campbell. (1968). Laboratory education: Impact on people and organizations. *Industrial Relations,* 8, 1, pp. 1–27.

Fiedler, Fred E. (1953). Quantitative studies on the role of therapists' feelings toward their patients. In Orval H. Mowrer (ed.), *Psychotherapy: Theory and Research.* New York: Ronald Press, Ch. 12.

Gibb, Jack R. (1961). Defense level and influence potential in small groups. In Luigi Petrillo and Bernard M. Bass (eds.), *Leadership and Interpersonal Behavior.* New York: Holt, Rinehart, and Winston, pp. 66–81.

Gibb, Jack R. (1964). Climate for trust formation. In Leland P. Bradford, Jack R. Gibb, and Kenneth D. Benne (eds.), *T-Group Theory and Laboratory Method.* New York: John Wiley, pp. 279–301.

House, R. J. (1967). T-group education and leadership effectiveness: A review of the empiric literature and a critical evaluation. *Personnel Psychology*, 20, 1, pp. 1–32.

Maier, Norman R. F., Allen R. Solem, and Ayesha A. Maier. (1959). *Supervisory and executive development.* New York: John Wiley, pp. 308–315.

Meadow, Arnold S., Sidney J. Parnes, and Hayne Reese. (1959). Influence of brainstorming instructions and problem sequence on creative problem-solving tests. *Journal of Applied Psychology*, 43, pp. 413–416.

Parloff, Morris B., and Joseph H. Handlon. (1966). The influence of criticalness on creative problem-solving dyads. *Psychiatry*, 29, pp. 17–27.

Rogers, Carl R. (1961). *On becoming a person.* Boston: Houghton Mifflin. 39–58.

Seeman, Julius. (1954). Counselor judgments of therapeutic process and outcome. In Carl R. Rogers and Rosalind F. Dymond (eds.), *Psychotherapy and personality change.* Chicago: University of Chicago Press, chapter 7.

Schein, Edgar H., and Warren G. Bennis. (1965). *Personal and organizational change through group methods.* New York: John Wiley.

Dale F. Zand is a professor of management in the Graduate School of Business Administration at New York University.

THE PARKING SPACE THEORY SHEET

Fred E. Jandt

Attempts to resolve conflict involve assessing the relative power of the people involved and the relationship between them. Negotiation and mediation are most effective when—indeed, are effective *only* when—the people involved in the conflict perceive themselves to be of relatively equal power. Relative power is directly related to the relationship between people.

In conflicts between people with greatly discrepant power, the person with more power can at any time exercise that power in an attempt to gain his or her objectives. By agreeing to negotiation or mediation, two people agree to put power aside; however, one or the other often resorts to power advantages if the resulting agreement is not to his or her liking. In situations of greatly discrepant relative power, to use negotiation and mediation effectively, the lower-power person must first equalize the perception of power.

The sociologist Lewis Coser (1956) provided an important, early definition of *conflict*. The first part of his definition refers to struggles over val-

From *The 1991 Annual: Developing Human Resources,* Jossey-Bass/Pfeiffer. Reprinted by permission.

ues and scarce resources, including status and power. Conflict over *values* refers to differing beliefs of "right" or "wrong." People in the contemporary United States experience value conflicts over abortion, animal rights, the death penalty, and smoking in public places, among other issues. Conflicts over *scarce status, power, and resources* are the kinds of conflict likely to be present in organizations. Scarce resources might be thought of in terms of limited dollars and budgets; in organizations, individuals and departments compete for adequate resources to fund their legitimate activities. However, organization members compete over a host of other resources: the office with the best view, the newest computer, access to upper levels of management, the most productive territory and employees, preferential scheduling of days off, and even parking places.

Why are these things sources of conflict? Because people believe them to be limited. In fact, one can observe that as desired resources become more limited, the conflict over them becomes more intense. This suggests a first step to resolving such conflicts: to determine whether or not the resources are as limited as the parties believe them to be. Is there another office with an

Figure 1
Issue/Relationship Matrix

	What Happens When an Issue Is Not Critical	What Happens When an Issue Is Critical
Good Relationship	■ People accept differences. ■ Problem-solving is easy. ■ Differences are expressed and understood. ■ The issue is not worth resolving.	■ People are more concerned with truth than with their own positions. ■ Differences are expressed and understood. ■ Issues are considered worth raising and worth working toward agreement. ■ Problem-solving negotiation is win-win. ■ The relationship can be strengthened. ■ If the relationship ends, the ending is painful but "clean."
Poor Relationship	■ Differences present problems. ■ Little things easily become big things. ■ Situations can escalate.	■ Differences present almost insurmountable problems. ■ Situations have the potential to polarize parties. ■ People have little willingness to work toward agreement. ■ Situations can become win-lose. ■ Escalation or suppression is likely. ■ People can break off the relationship. ■ Ending will be painful and "dirty" (blame, attack, defense, and so on).

approximately equal view? Can access to the new computer be shared by scheduling time slots?

It is important to recognize how competition can turn into conflict. The second part of Coser's definition says that in conflict situations, opponents strive to neutralize, injure, or eliminate rivals. Runners in a foot race compete for the limited resource of first prize. There is only one first prize and there is intense competition for it—but runners do not attempt to harm one another in their attempts to secure the limited resource. If the runners sought to sabotage one another's efforts, conflict would exist. Similarly, employees in organizations might not attempt to kill their rivals, but they often look for ways to neutralize their power and influence.

In reality, the best possible resolution of conflict is not an all-or-nothing proposition. When either party wins all, it either kills the relationship or sets the stage for future conflicts. Negotiation involves creating a solution that satisfies both parties and enables the relationship to continue. In the vast majority of conflicts, the relationship is more important than the conflict. Often a person's interests are best served by thinking of the *relationship* with the other person rather than thinking of winning the conflict.

The Issue/Relationship Matrix (Figure 1) clarifies this point by listing what happens when noncritical issues are dealt with in a "good" relationship versus what happens when the same kinds of issues are dealt with in a "poor" relationship. It is extremely important to deal with issues. In a good relationship, if an issue is repeatedly ignored—regardless of whether that issue is critical—people's responses start resembling those in the bottom half of the matrix; in fact, over time the relationship can change to a poor one.

A focus on maintaining relationships encourages people to use win-win negotiation skills. Win-win outcomes support and reinforce the relationship and make it possible for both parties to achieve their goals. Major win-win negotiating skills include the following:

1. *Unpacking.* To unpack a single-issue conflict, determine all the components of the issue. This changes single-issue conflicts into multiple-issue conflicts that are more likely to result in win-win outcomes. For example, the demand for a raise can result in a negotiation over how large the raise might be. But to unpack that demand is to negotiate over the raise, its date of implementation, other benefits, and so on.

2. *Looking for the reasons that led to the demands.* It is often a mistake to believe that problems that lead to an adversary's demands can only be solved by agreeing to the demands. Frequently, an adversary's problem can be mitigated to the adversary's satisfaction in other ways that are easier to meet. For example, an employee's demand for a salary increase might have resulted from a need to buy another car because work hours have created problems. Rather than negotiate a raise, it might be easier to change the work hours.

3. *Being the first to make a concession, to link issues, and to suggest trade-offs.* Take the lead in making the negotiation work. An early concession in areas important to an adversary usually results in his or her reciprocating in other areas. Take the lead in suggesting trade-offs by giving something another person wants in return for something you want.

References

Coser, L. (1956). *The functions of social conflict.* New York: Free Press.

Jandt, F. E. (1985). *Win-win negotiating: Turning conflict into agreement.* New York: John Wiley.

THE PARADOX OF TRUST AND MISTRUST

David S. Weiss

If you make vacation arrangements at a luxurious resort and arrive at your destination only to be told by the airline that your luggage is lost, you will probably be:

1. Disappointed.

2. Furious.

3. Disappointed and furious.

Because of the airline's mistake, you might have to spend valuable vacation time communicating with the airline about when your luggage will arrive and then washing out the clothes you have on and shopping for new items. What happens if the airline does not respond to your predicament? Will you tell the airline how you feel? Usually, dissatisfied customers tell approximately 20 people about their frustration with a company but often do not discuss it with the company itself. Frequently, the company doesn't know the customer is making negative comments about them.

Trust can be very fragile in a business context. After a shareholder takeover, for example, the displaced party often waits for the opportunity to retaliate. If a time comes when power is redistributed, the disadvantaged party will engage in "terrorist" activities to inflict pain on the perpetrator of the crime.

From Weiss, David S. *Beyond the Walls of Conflict: Mutual Gains Negotiating for Unions and Management,* copyright © (1996), McGraw-Hill. Reprinted by permission.

"Terrorism" is often viewed as an activity that needs to be obliterated. In union-management disputes, terrorist acts can be aggressive responses to the other side's overuse of power. The only recourse for the powerless is to find an alternative "terrorist" method to even the power base. A well-known principle in negotiating is that one should never "win too big" or the opposition will focus on getting even by any method it can find.

Powerless countries also find ways to strike back at their adversaries. During the Gulf War, Iraq recognized that it could not beat the United States-led alliance. Instead, it conducted a brilliant military maneuver; it chose *not* to fight back—to become defenseless. The U.S.-led alliance had no choice but to stop the aggression before it completed its unstated mission of changing the Baghdad leadership.

Shortly after a cease-fire agreement was reached, Iraq demonstrated that it was fully capable of fighting, by attacking the Kurds. Iraq's nonviolent response to the U.S.-led alliance was strictly a military ploy that worked exceedingly well. We can only imagine the extent to which non-Democratic countries like Iraq direct terrorist activities against countries that humiliate them.

A union leader pointed out that Iraq's use of this strategy was proof that it understood the "wolfpack syndrome." When wolves are totally help-less, they lie on their backs with their paws in the air, placing themselves at the mercy of others. The wolves in power usually refrain from destroy-ing them. Wolves that have displayed weakness once are not necessarily weak forever. If nego-tiators trust once and are abused, they might not be willing to trust again.

Winning Isn't Final; Losing Isn't Fatal

If you hurt someone while you are in a position of strength, do not forget that that person will probably find an opportunity to hurt you in return. It is very possible that you will not be strong forever, and that the person you hurt will reciprocate. People rarely forget feeling betrayed or being hurt when they are weak. As one nego-tiator said, "What goes around, comes around." When an opponent has a moment of weakness, the *strong* negotiator recognizes the opportunity to work out a fair deal—*not* one that takes advan-tage of the counterpart's weaknesses.

Dissatisfied parties who have been given no choice often find ways of retaliating through terrorism. In one negotiation, the union demanded a $4 per hour wage increase. The company responded by saying that it would accept a strike over the issue. The strike lasted for six months, and in the interim, the market share and the customer base of the company eroded dramatically. The union returned to work without the $4 increase. However, the company found that costs rose by the equivalent of $4 per hour per per-son anyway as a result of inefficiencies the angry employees intentionally introduced.

The Paradox of Trust and Mistrust

Think of trust as a precious jewel. You keep it inside a beautiful case, polish it frequently, and treasure it. The tiniest scratch on this jewel can destroy its value, and it will be very difficult to regain that value once it has been lost. Just as you would care for a precious jewel that is your most treasured possession, you must nurture your rela-

tionships so that you develop trust. It is a para-dox that trust is vulnerable even to the slightest betrayal. A lie, a break of confidence, a bit of withheld information, or a personal attack—any of these can result in an immediate break of trust.

Ironically, the mistrust that is created from a brief moment persists. A party's attempts to regain that trust often look suspect to the other party and are identified as manipulative behav-ior. The result? The person is still not considered worthy of trust.

> **The Paradox of Trust and Mistrust**
> Trust takes forever to build and a moment to destroy, while Mistrust takes forever to destroy and a moment to build.

Trust and Mutual Gains Negotiations

The foundation of mutual gains negotiations is the extent to which trust is built between the negotiating parties. All relationships are built on some level of trust. To develop that trust, parties must deliver what is expected of them and max-imize the relationship. Unfortunately, mistrust takes only a moment of indiscretion to create and is very difficult to eliminate.

The level of trust between parties is usually reflected in the text of the collective bargaining agreement. It is evident by the number of letters of understanding that follow a signature page and the attention to exceptions within the agree-ment. As indicated earlier, you never make a peace treaty between friends. You have a collec-tive agreement because parties often have lim-ited trust between them. The collective agreement creates boundaries. The greater the opportunity to maximize that trust during the life of the agreement, the greater the ability to negotiate wise solutions that are simple enough to live by and that enhance the quality of the relationships.

Trust does not occur by accident. It results from building assumptions and expectations that are supported by actual behavior. The behaviors are continually reinforced so that all parties' needs are met.

Assumption of Mistrust or Trust

The assumption of trust or mistrust is based on relationships. People believe they can trust you during and after the negotiation process based on factors such as what people are saying, what they know about you from previous experiences, and what rumors they have heard about you.

People also have very important personal characteristics that determine whether they are by nature trusting. Some people become more trusting as soon as that trust is deserved, while others remain mistrustful. And there are those who trust even when situations are not worthy of trust.

The adversarial negotiating process, by virtue of its hostile environment and relationships, engenders mistrust. In addition, people selected to negotiate often have personal characteristics that make them cynical and mistrustful. These characteristics are useful in adversarial negations, but are a hurdle in the process of mutual gains negotiations. To break out of that mistrust, both parties in a negotiation must be willing to see the potential of union-management peace and make the effort to create it.

Expectations of Trust or Mistrust

A person's level of trust or mistrust causes them to set up specific expectations of future behaviors. Most people perform to expectations rather than to potential. While some individuals are driven to fulfill their potential, expectations are more likely to be the driving force for performance. The idea of creating objectives as a stimulus to help people increase their performance is built on this concept.

Here's an exercise that demonstrates the power of expectations: A flipchart is placed eight feet off the ground. With both feet on the ground, participants reach as high as they can and draw a line across the chart page. Most people are able to do this reasonably well. Next, the same people are asked to try the exercise again. This time they are requested to draw the line at least two inches above the first line they drew. In most cases, the participants can do this.

This exercise is intriguing because the participants have two inches to spare the first time, even though they are asked to draw the line as high as they can. The first time they draw a line, they are exploring their potential. But when they are asked to draw a line two inches above the first line, they are responding to expectations. Performance attributed to meeting expectations often exceeds performance based on fulfilling potential.

The message of this exercise is the power of expectations. Expectations govern much of our lives and shape the way we approach situations, and they have tremendous impact on trust.

The expectations we set up of trust or mistrust contribute to a person's willingness to participate in mutual gains negotiations. Specific strategies are needed to maximize the negotiators' potential to trust one another, and great care should be taken to make sure the trust is not betrayed.

Behavior That Is Trustworthy or Not Trustworthy

Behaviors do not occur until someone forms expectations of trust or mistrust. An individual's behaviors toward another are often reciprocated. Negotiators can assume that their counterparts will probably respond to their displays of trust or mistrust in like manner.

During the process of negotiating, a roller coaster of trust or mistrust emerges. If the process is one of continual mistrust between participants and their behaviors support that mistrust, the participants begin to expect each other to be untrustworthy. The negotiation process breaks down, collaborative work becomes nonexistent, and the ability to reach mutual gains solutions is limited. Both parties lose in this case. If one of the parties emerges as an apparent winner—even in the short term—the loser usually retaliates with a "terrorist" attack at the winner if the opportunity presents itself.

The Three Levels of Trust

Let's consider an example of trust in a totally different environment. Say you are having Sunday brunch and need to purchase some bagels. At the bagel store, you ask for a dozen bagels, but the salesperson gives you only 11. You gently explain that you asked for 12 and received 11. The salesperson insists that she gave you 12 and suggests that you must have eaten one. You begin to get angry and ask for the manager. Unfortunately, the salesperson says she is the manager and the owner of the store.

Later, another bagel store opens down the block. You begin purchasing bagels there and tell everyone you meet about the terrible customer service at the first bagel store. The owner at that store failed to understand a basic principle about building trust: Meet your customer's expectations to achieve a basic level of satisfaction—or the customer will go elsewhere.

Now, let's say more and more bagel stores open on the same street and it becomes known as "bagel street." The store where you buy your bagels begins to throw in one extra with each dozen purchased—a baker's dozen of 13 bagels. You are delighted with the bonus you are receiving and continue to give that store your business.

The owner of the store decides to shock her customers into permanent customer loyalty. When you order a dozen bagels, she gives you three dozen. Since you don't need that many bagels

and your freezer is too small to store them, the bagels will be wasted. You don't understand why the store owner gave you so many. You even wonder whether they were meant for someone else— maybe the store owner will accuse you of stealing the bagels. Because you had such an uncomfortable experience when you questioned the owner of the first bagel store, you decide not to question the second one. Your concern convinces you to try a third bagel store down the street.

The second store owner tried to build trust by exceeding your expectations. But by surpassing your expectations excessively, the strategy backfired and actually reduced your loyalty and satisfaction. The moral of the second store owner is: If you are one step ahead, you are a genius, but if you are two steps ahead, you are a quack. Exceed expectations to build trust, but don't exceed them by so much that the other party does not understand what happened.

Now, back to your bagel adventure. You still need bagels for your Sunday brunches, so you start purchasing your bagels at a third bagel store. They are also giving a baker's dozen when you order 12 bagels. You are delighted that they exceed your expectations in a way that you can comprehend. One Saturday afternoon, you are very busy and realize you may not get the bagel store before it closes at 7:00 p.m.—one hour after all the other bagel stores close. You race to the store and arrive just five minutes before closing time. However, you find that all the bagel shelves have been cleaned out. With your head down, you slowly walk out the door. As you reach your car, the store owner runs after you and says, "Hello! It's good to see you. I knew you would come, so I put aside a dozen bagels just for you."

You are in shock! At the precise moment of your vulnerability, you are rescued. The store owner not only exceeds your expectations for the delivery of good-quality bagels, but actually surpasses expectations on the trust side as well. The store is there for you when you need it. Even if other stores start undercutting this store on price, your loyalty will not be shaken—they will have a customer as long as the trust continues to exist.

The bagel story is a simple way of illustrating the levels of trust that can be reached in negotiations as well. The two essential variables of building trust or mistrust are:

▪ Expectations

▪ Behavior

Mistrust is created when your behavior does not meet the other party's expectations.

Behavior that does not meet expectations
= MISTRUST

An acceptable level of trust exists when you behave in a way that is consistent with the other party's expectations of you.

Behavior that meets expectations
= ACCEPTABLE LEVEL OF TRUST

Behavior consistent with the other party's expectations might allow you to achieve an acceptable level of trust, but if you exceed expectations, the trust has greater sustaining power.

Behavior that exceeds expectations
= SUSTAINED TRUST

Let's add something to expectations and behavior: the highest level of trust, which includes the supportive relationship between the parties. If parties have established a supportive relationship, they will be able to help each other in time of need. They are loyal to their counterparts and make sure that they do not do anything that will hurt their credibility with their constituencies. They are also able to recover more quickly if they ever need to resort to power as a last resort.

They engage in mutual gains negotiations at a level of "loyal trust," which helps them achieve union-management peace.

Behavior that exceeds expectations +
a supportive relationship = LOYAL TRUST

The Three Stages Involved in Building a Supportive Relationship

A supportive relationship essential for loyal trust is characterized by three stages of development. In each stage, a trusting relationship is created that is deeper and more lasting than the previous. The stages are:

Stage 1: Trust in your competence.

Stage 2: Trust in your honesty.

Stage 3: Trust that when I am vulnerable, you will not hurt me and will be there for me.

Imagine that you are asked by two colleagues to participate in an experiment in which you will have to demonstrate a significant amount of trust. They ask you to allow them to take care of you when they take you to a restaurant—blindfolded. To participate in this exercise, you need a loyal trust relationship with your colleagues (behavior that exceeds expectations, and a supportive relationship). The minimum standards for a supportive relationship are Stages 1 and 2. You must trust their competence and honesty.

You first assess your colleagues' competence to care for you through lunch. You consider whether they are able to perform the task and whether they will tell you if a particular task is beyond their capability. You decide that you can trust that they will fulfill the first stage of a supportive relationship: the basic competence to do the task.

You then consider the second stage of a supportive relationship. Your colleagues might have the competence, but will they do what they say they will do? Will they not only "walk the talk," but also "walk the talk of quality thought"? Do you trust their honesty when they say they will take you to lunch? You feel sufficiently reassured that your colleagues will do as they promised, so you proceed with the exercise.

Now, let's say your colleagues take you to a restaurant with stairs to the entrance. Instead of instructing you about the stairs and carefully leading you up them, they don't say anything. You stumble on the first step. They catch you, but then they take you up the stairs very quickly, without any regard for the fact that you are blindfolded. You have no idea how many steps are remaining and you are nervous because you have just recovered from a slip on one of the steps. You begin to doubt your colleagues' level of competence and honesty. They are not doing what they said they would do. You decide to take off the blindfold and stop the exercise.

Instead, imagine that your colleagues instruct you adequately about the stairs and lead you carefully and slowly up them so that you do not stumble. They have maintained Stage 1 (competence) and Stage 2 (honesty) trust. While you are still very anxious, you have a basic level of trust in them and are looking forward to relaxing and enjoying your food. You begin to ask yourself whether you can extend trust to the third stage of a supportive relationship.

Your colleagues lead you to your table and give you very explicit instructions about where you are and how to seat yourself, and then they make certain you are seated without any problems. After you are seated, you overhear someone laughing and talking about your blindfold. Your colleagues come to your defense and explain what you are doing. As a result, the other people express amazement at your courage in participating in the exercise. Next, your colleagues talk to you about how the table is set so that you know exactly where your plate, silverware, and glass are positioned. They suggest that you order something that will be easy for you to eat blindfolded.

You begin to realize that your colleagues might be trustworthy when you are at the third stage of a supportive relationship. They are serious about being there for you at every turn. You feel that you can trust your colleagues completely because they have demonstrated their loyalty to you. You relax and enjoy the meal.

How to Become More Trustworthy in Negotiations

Parties in mutual gains negotiations should at least strive to build a trust relationship by meeting expectations and by achieving the first two stages of a supportive relationship. They need to know their areas of competence, and need to communicate honestly. This means that each party will trust the other to deliver the expectations that have been created. Trust allows the negotiating parties to communicate honestly about their problems and to jointly explore mutual gains solutions. Trust allows you to understand alternatives and make effective choices.

Most people find that Stage 3 of a supportive relationship applies only to a love relationship. Many people who are divorced find the relationship has ended because Stage 3 was broken. Somehow, at the moment of greatest need, one of the two parties breaks the trust and is not there for the other partner when he or she is needed the most.

If negotiating parties are able to develop a Stage 3 supportive relationship, they will probably achieve magnificent results—far beyond their expectations. In Stage 3, parties have a joint understanding that they will use the *interests* approach for the mutual gains negotiations process, and that they will apply *rights* and *power* approaches only as a last resort.

How to Move from Mistrust to Trust

When you lose the trust of the other party, you must immediately try to regain it. Mistrust that lingers grows in strength and becomes much more difficult to overcome. As soon as you see mistrust emerging, respond immediately.

You can "fall out of trust" when the other person begins to mistrust you based on:

1. Expectations: a perception that is incorrect because of a misunderstanding, or

2. Behavior: an inappropriate action on your part.

When other parties mistrust you based on a misunderstanding, your chances of persuading them to trust you are directly related to your relationship with them. If the trust relationship is strong and loyal, they will probably believe you, give you a chance to explain your interpretation of events, and then consider rebuilding the trust. If you do not have a strong, loyal trust relationship, they might see your attempts to defend yourself as a defensive reaction. This will only enhance any feelings of mistrust they already have of you.

If you have a strong relationship with your counterpart and find you have been misjudged, it might have happened for one of two reasons:

■ **The behaviors the other party believed you showed are less than what you know you actually delivered.** You will then need to clarify that you actually did what was expected of you.

■ **You and your counterpart differ in your assessments of what is expected of you.** In this case, if you have a strong relationship, you might be able to clarify the expectations, renegotiate them, and show that you are doing what your counterpart expects of you. In a situation like this, the problems often are communication-based. If you act quickly, you probably will be able

to reduce the mistrust and regain the trust. If you let the mistrust linger and allow your counterpart to believe that you are not delivering the agreed-upon expectations, your good relationship can be destroyed.

Of course, sometimes you deserve to fall out of trust. This is because you either do not behave in a manner consistent with what is expected of you, or you agree to expectations that are beyond your ability to deliver. In these situations, the following actions are essential:

■ Respond quickly.

■ Help the other party understand that your behavior will match expectations in the future.

■ Establish an agreement about expectations you believe you can fulfill.

■ Maximize your strong relations if it exists. The better the trust relationship, the more likely you will recover from the mistrust.

Give a Free Stage-3 Trust: Be There for Them When They Are Vulnerable

The quickest way to recover from mistrust is to be there for your counterparts at the moment of their greatest need—to give them a free "Stage 3" level of trust. If you help rather than hurt your counterparts when they are vulnerable, you can improve their trust significantly, and they are likely to believe that you are willing to change. The gift of trust becomes a dividend that will be available to you in any future negotiation.

One poignant example of this occurred in a recent negotiation. In a premeeting between the chief spokespeople for the company and union, the union representative accidentally left behind the folder that included his demands for the upcoming round of negotiations. After the meeting, the company spokesperson found the folder, looked inside at the first page, and identified it as the union demands.

The company spokesperson saw this as a no-lose, trust-building opportunity. He chose not to read the contents of the folder, but instead phoned the union spokesperson. He told him that he had found the folder, looked at the first page, noticed what it was, closed the folder, and called him immediately.

If the company spokesperson had looked at the contents of the folder or photocopied them, he would have been in a vulnerable position. He might later slip and reveal something he saw in the document, proving that he was lying about not having looked at the material. In addition the union spokesperson was supposed to present the demands the next week, so there was little advantage in knowing the explicit demands early. Finally, leaving the folder might have been a setup—a way to see if the company spokesperson could be trusted enough to engage in mutual gains negotiations.

The union negotiator's response was very astute. He recognized an opportunity to clean the slate on the trust extended to him. Instead of saying that the company person should send the material to him, the union negotiator told him to shred it! It was a brilliant move in the chess game of escalating trust. Clearly, if the trust account was not balanced right away, the union representative would "owe him" one measure of trust sometime during the negotiation. So the union representative paid it back by trusting him to shred the material.

The company person told the union representative to hold the line while he shredded the folder. He put the phone down, shredded the material, and returned to the phone to tell him it was finished. They thanked each other and hung up the phone.

Later, the company spokesperson said he wished he had saved the shredded paper. He thought it might have been beneficial sometime later in the negotiations as a symbolic statement of trust.

Nevertheless, the actions he took earned the trust of the union representative sufficiently so that he was willing to start exploring some level of mutual gains negotiations with the company.

Be Consistent Over the Long Run

The best way to build trust, although it takes much longer, is to change your behavior and start exceeding expectations. Changing mistrust to trust by just promising to be better and by trying to fight your counterpart's expectations with your expectations usually results in disbelief. The other party assumes you are lying. He or she might not believe you, assuming that since you did not deliver before, you will not deliver now. If you change your behavior, however, and sustain it over an extended period of time, your counterpart might begin to believe you. Once your actions show that you have made a change, then you can explain your new expectations.

Think of trust levels as the floors in a 10-story building, with the 10th floor being the highest level of trust. You can proceed with mutual gains negations if you are on the second floor; however, you will have to work slowly and focus more on the problems that are in the common interest. By doing this, you can demonstrate mutual gains and begin to climb to higher floors.

It is extremely rare that any two parties will reach the highest floor. That extent of trust is reserved for parties who have very few or no separate interests. The parties in a negotiation will always have separate interests, focusing on how to represent their constituencies' interests fairly. The two negotiating parties never really become one team. They are two teams with some common interests on which to build mutual gains solutions. But if they can climb the seventh floor, or even the fifth, they will have a significant opportunity to reshape the way the company and the union work together for the betterment of all.

· · · · ·

Trust and Agreement

Empirical evidence indicates that the stronger the trust between negotiating parties, the greater the probability the parties will discover solutions that will result in mutual gains agreements. Nevertheless, low trust doesn't guarantee disagreement, just as high trust doesn't guarantee agreement.

When trust is low, disagreement often results because of the destructive nature of the interactions in which the parties treat one another with personal contempt. The negations show a focus on self-interest, a low level of innovation and risk-taking, and an inadequate resolution of problems. A disagreement on one issue probably will affect the way the next issue will be resolved. It might be difficult for these negotiating parties to reach agreement. However, low-trust relationships can still generate agreements for a variety of reasons. These include:

- The solution is obvious, and even though trust is low, the parties can agree on a common direction.

- The parties have a common enemy that unites them. (For example, trust might be low between a company and union, but the two parties will work together to resist a common problem, such as a shut-down.)

- An unequal distribution of power requires one of the parties to agree passively to a solution. This party will "get even" when the opportunity arises.

When trust is high, disagreements are often constructive and issue-based. There might be conflict, but it will be without contempt. If the parties cannot agree on an issue, it does not mean that they will be unable to agree on the next issue.

When negotiating parties agree on a common direction and have a high-trust relationship, they often are willing to engage in innovative problem-solving and some risk-taking. The parties consider the common interests and discover creative solutions they can put into operation. High-trust agreements are longer lasting and create momentum for resolving more complex problems.

The return on investment for building trust between union and management is substantial. The collective agreements developed when trust is high are designed to achieve mutual gains. The trust relationship contributes to meaningful continuous dialogue between the parties, even after contract negotiations. The climate necessary to get beyond the walls of conflict is in place.

Summary

- In union-management disputes, terrorist acts can be aggressive responses to the overuse of power by the other side.

- A well-known principle in negotiating is that one should never "win too big" or the opposition will focus on getting even by any method it can find.

- Trust takes a long time to build and only a moment to destroy, while mistrust takes a moment to build and what seems like forever to erase.

- The foundation of mutual gains negotiations is the extent to which trust is built between the negotiating parties.

- The adversarial negotiating process, by virtue of its hostile environment and relationships, engenders mistrust.

- The trust or mistrust individuals possess leads them to specific expectations of future behaviors.

- Most people perform to expectations, rather than to potential.

- The expectation of trust or mistrust contributes to a person's willingness to participate in mutual gains negotiations. Specific strategies are necessary to maximize negotiators' potential to trust each other, and great care should be taken to make sure the trust is not betrayed.

■ Negotiators can assume that their counterparts will probably respond to their displays of trust or mistrust in like manner.

■ The two essential variables of building trust or mistrust are behavior and expectations.

— Behavior that does not meet expectations = MISTRUST.

— Behavior that meets expectations = ACCEPTABLE LEVEL OF TRUST.

— Behavior that exceeds expectations = SUSTAINED TRUST.

— Behavior that exceeds expectations and a supportive relationship = LOYAL TRUST.

■ A supportive relationship, essential for loyal trust, is characterized by three stages. Each stage creates a trusting relationship that is deeper and more lasting than the previous. The stages are:

—Stage 1: Trust in your competence.

—Stage 2: Trust in your honesty.

—Stage 3: Trust that when I am vulnerable you will not hurt me, and that you will be there for me.

■ At a minimum, parties in mutual gains negotiations should strive to build a trust relationship by meeting expectations and by achieving the first two stages (competence and honesty) of a supportive relationship.

■ When you lose the trust of the other party, you must try to regain it very quickly.

■ You can fall out of trust when the other person begins to mistrust you based on:

1. Expectation: a perception that is incorrect because of a misunderstanding, or

2. Behavior: an inappropriate action on your part.

■ When other parties mistrust you based on a misunderstanding, your chances of persuading them to trust you are directly related to your relationship with them.

■ The quickest way to recover from mistrust is to be there for your counterparts at the moment of their greatest need—to give them a free "Stage 3" level of trust.

■ Empirical evidence indicates that the stronger the trust between negotiating parties, the greater the probability that they will discover solutions to their problems that will result in mutual gains agreements.

■ High-trust agreements are longer lasting, and create the momentum for resolving more complex problems.

Chapter Five

THE INFLUENCE PROCESS

HOW TO INCREASE YOUR INFLUENCE

David E. Berlew

Negotiation is nothing more than a process for reaching agreement when there are conflicting interests. The basis of negotiation is exchange: every party gains and gives concessions until they reach agreement. Negotiation appears to be the most effective process for this purpose, but unfortunately it is complex and difficult to do well. In every negotiation course I have taught, an over-dependence on logical persuasion has been the biggest obstacle to effective negotiating. To understand why, it is necessary to examine what I will call the "logical persuasion influence strategy."

To pursue a logical persuasion strategy, the influencer makes a proposal or suggestion and supports it with facts or reasons. If the "influence target" is inclined to resist, he or she will challenge the weakest of the influencer's supporting arguments by offering counter-arguments. The influencer refutes the target's weakest counter-argument. And so it goes, back and forth, until one party concedes or both become weary. With each round of argument and counter-argument is the danger of getting farther and farther away from the influencer's objective.

Logical persuasion works best when one party is acknowledged as having more expertise than the other, and when neither party has a vested interest in the position. By this I mean that they have something to gain if their own proposal is accepted, and something to lose by accepting the other party's proposal.

Logical persuasion is least effective as a strategy for reaching agreement when expertise is balanced or unrecognized, and when each party has a vested interest in his or her position.

Let us examine a typical line-staff interaction. A training manager proposes to a senior line manager that the latter identify the training and development needs of his management and professional staff using a new needs assessment methodology just developed by the training department. To support her proposal, the training manager gives three reasons: it will give the line manager more detailed information about the development needs of his staff than the informal method used previously; the new needs assessment methodology is state of the art; and a standardized methodology will provide comparable data regarding development needs across the entire organization.

The senior line manager rejects the training manager's proposal, giving the following reasons:

the informal method he used in the past is quite adequate; new state-of-the-art systems are never reliable until they have been field-tested for at least one year; and comparable data arc unnccessary because the work his unit does and his staff's development needs are unique in the organization.

The training manager probably will challenge the weakest of the line manager's three reasons, beginning an argument/counter-argument spiral. Given this start, reaching a mutually satisfactory agreement quickly, if at all, is unlikely. To get her needs assessment study done, the training manager will have to get support from a higher level. This is not surprising, since we can assume that each party has a vested interest in the position he or she has taken. If the line manager will not adopt the new technology, the training manager will experience a severe setback in her new program. If the line manager agrees to use the new methodology, time and resources he would prefer to use elsewhere will be required. The training manager's technical expertise will have little impact on the line manager.

Another dynamic at work here can reduce further the effectiveness of a logical persuasion strategy. To paraphrase an Eastern saying: "An idea that has to be defended is least likely to change." When the training manager pushes against the line manager with logical arguments, the line manager almost instinctively mobilizes his energy, in the form of counter-arguments, to push back. Every argument elicits a counter-argument, every force an equal and opposite force. This dynamic increases the probability that the logical persuasion strategy will lead to an extended debate or argument.

So what can you do when persuasion doesn't work? One alternative is to use an exchange strategy of influence: a simplified form of the negotiation process. At the most basic level it involves three elements: know what you want, ask for it, and be prepared to pay for it.

In behavioral terms, using an exchange strategy requires that you state exactly what you want or need (expectation), ask about and then listen carefully to any problems your request causes for the other person (active listening), and find ways to resolve those problems or satisfy additional needs the other person has in order to gain his or her cooperation (offering incentives).

In our example, the training manager might use an exchange strategy this way:

- *Training Manager:* I would like you to use this new needs assessment technology in your division this year. (expectation) What kind of problems would that cause you? (active listening)

- *Line Manager:* Well, it sounds like extra work. We know how to do the informal needs assessment and it takes very little of our time.

- *Training Manager:* So it would take extra resources, which are limited. I know that your division is very busy. Would it cause you any other problems? (active listening)

- *Line Manager:* (Beginning to trust the training manager who is "pulling" rather than "pushing") Well . . . frankly, I am somewhat intimidated by the complexity of the new method. I know we can turn out a good report the old way, but if we use the new methodology we might produce a poor report, especially if we don't have enough manpower to put on it. It is a risk I would prefer not to take if I can avoid it.

- *Training Manager:* Since you haven't had any experience with the new methodology, you are concerned that you might not turn out a first class report, and that your division's reputation might be damaged. Is that it? (active listening)

- *Line Manager:* Yes, that's right. I can't think of anything else. But as you can see, it would be quite inconvenient for me to do what you ask right now.

- *Training Manager:* Yes, I know what I am asking is inconvenient for you. But I would really like you to do it. (expectation) Let me propose an exchange that might work for both of us. If you will agree to help me by being the first division to use the new needs assessment methodology, I will spend whatever time necessary working with you and your staff to collect the data and prepare the report. That way, you will have an extra pair of hands, and I can guarantee that your division's report will be first class. (offering incentives) Is that agreeable with you?

- *Line Manager:* That takes care of my problems. Under those conditions I think I can cooperate with you.

The training manager simply told the line manager what she wanted, acknowledged that it might be inconvenient for the line manager to comply, and indicated her willingness to give something to get what she wanted. By doing so, she successfully avoided a time-consuming discussion about the relative advantages of the old and new methodologies.

The power of the exchange strategy of influence stems from several sources. First, the way the training manager opened the conversation discouraged a debate on the merits of the new technology. Second, by accepting rather than questioning or refuting the problems raised by the line manager, the training manager avoided "pushing back" and thereby creating resistance. This also encouraged the line manager to be more open about his real concern. Finally, because the training manager acknowledged that what she wanted might inconvenience the line manager, he was able to let his guard down in anticipation of a balanced agreement.

Used skillfully, the exchange strategy usually results in an agreement that is fair and acceptable to both parties. The line manager did not have to accept the training manager's offer: he could have asked for more, or even refused if the training manager could not or would not offer him enough to compensate him for his inconvenience. The training manager would have to decide how important the line manager's cooperation was to her, and what she was willing to give in order to get it.

This third basic element of the exchange strategy of influence—being prepared to pay for what you want—deserves special attention. Thinking of incentives (things you can give to get what you want) as currencies of exchange is useful. In our example, the line manager had the prime currency: his agreement to cooperate. The training manager used two alternative currencies of exchange to obtain the line manager's agreement to use the new technology: her time and the guarantee of a first class report.

But what if the training manager had no time that she could give to the line manager to gain his agreement? What other incentives or currencies might she exchange? "I do not have much to offer," is a common lament of staff personnel, as well as managers trying to exert influence laterally and upward. Is that true in the training manger's case?

Let us begin with the problems the training manager is creating for the line manager by requesting his cooperation: extra work and extra risk. Type 1 currencies are anything the influencer can do that will help alleviate any problems or inconvenience that his or her request will cause the other person. If we brainstormed we might come up with several viable currencies our training manager might offer, such as:

- the assistance of one of her subordinates
- a training session for the line manager's staff members who will prepare the report

- a "fool-proof" report format (just fill in the numbers)

- the training manager's gratitude (an intangible currency).

Although we can identify potential currencies in advance, we cannot accurately assess their value until we find out from the influence target exactly how they expect to be inconvenienced by our request.

The influencer can offer Type 2 currencies to satisfy other needs the influence target may have—needs or problems other than those the influencer has caused by his or her request or expectation. In our example, possible Type 2 currencies are:

- special training for the line manager's staff (unrelated to needs assessment)

- rescheduling standard training sessions to the convenience of the line manager

- informal publicity that the line manager is enlightened and avant-garde with respect to training and development

- extra counseling for the line manager's problem employees

- consultation for the line manager on a specific problem, by the training manager or one of her colleagues from personnel.

Again, we can anticipate potential Type 2 currencies, but their exchange value is determined by the influence target's needs.

For most of us, the exchange strategy of influence is less natural and more difficult to use than a logical persuasion strategy. Logical persuasion is tolerant of imprecision; it never hurts to modify a proposal. To use the exchange strategy successfully, the influencer must be clear about their basic need, and know how much they are willing to give up to satisfy it. If they ask for too little and the other party agrees, they are stuck with an unsatisfactory agreement. This would have been the case if our training manager, in her opening statement, had asked the line manager to *consider* using the new technology, and he had replied, "I would be happy to consider it," and walked away. Conversely, if the influencer asks for too much, he or she is perceived as unreasonable and loses credibility.

The exchange strategy can have negative results if it is not carried out thoughtfully and with skill.

Badly implemented, it sounds like attempted bribery. Skillfully executed, it produces an agreement that both parties can accept and carry out. It leaves the impression that the influencer is a person who knows what he or she wants, and who is also sensitive to the needs of the other person.

THE TACTICS AND ETHICS OF PERSUASION

Philip G. Zimbardo

The police interrogator is recognized by society as an agent of change whose job it is to persuade witnesses and suspects to give evidence, admissions, and confessions of guilt. When he is successful, the individual might lose his freedom or his life, but society is presumed to be the beneficiary of this loss. The salesman's effective persuasion may or may not benefit either the "target" of his sales attempt or the society, but it certainly brings personal gain to the salesman and those he represents. What is similar about both is that they are "formal" persuasive communicators insofar as their goal to effect a specified change is explicitly formulated and their tactics often are laid down in training manuals used in their initiation. Examination of their tactics reveals a further basis of similarity—a willingness to employ virtually any means to achieve their goals. Indeed, for one, it has been necessary to establish Supreme Court rulings to limit the use of third-degree physical brutality and excessive psychological coercion; for the other, the Better Business Bureaus and Ralph Nader are needed to limit the excessive exploitation of the consumer.

Reprinted with permission from *Attitudes, Conflicts, and Social Change*, by King and McGuinnes (ed.). Orlando, Fla.: Academic Press, 1972.

Every social interaction, however, carries the burden of being a potential attitude-change encounter. The ethical issues raised by deceptive business practices or police coercion are often ignored in other equally compelling influence situations. Parents, educators, priests, and psychotherapists, for example, represent some of the most powerful "behavioral engineers" in this society. It is rare that the appropriateness of evaluating what they do in ethical terms is even considered. This is largely because they are not perceived as formal agents of attitude and behavior change. They function with the benefits of socially sanctioned labels that conceal persuasive intent: parents "socialize," teachers "educate," priests "save souls," and therapists "cure the mentally ill."

There are two other characteristics of the influence situations in which they operate that minimize any issue of unethical, deceptive, or coercive persuasion. First, there is an illusion that the goal of the situation is defined in terms of the best interests of the target person: the child, student, sinner, sick patient. Second, an attribution error process typically occurs by which we judge that the individual could have resisted the pressures brought to bear upon him. One wants to believe that people change only when they want to or when they are subjected to overwhelming *physical* forces. The extent to which behavior is controlled by external social and psychological forces is denied in favor of the presumed strength of individual will power to resist. Given these three characteristics, then, the most persuasive communicators are not acknowledged as such, or are not recognized as exerting a potentially negative effect on the individuals with whom they interact.

Upon closer analysis, however, these underpinnings of this naive view of such attitude-change agents lose some of their foundation. For example, all of them can be viewed as "salesmen" for the established *status quo* with the best interest of society placed before the best interest of the individual. "Socialization" to be a Hitler *Jungn,* "socialization" to repress impulses, to be a good child, to do what one is told, to be seen and not heard, to be patriotic, to be polite, not to question elders, and so forth are goals of the adults in the society, which may be at odds with the child's personal growth. "Education" can mean to bias, to present prejudiced opinion as scientific or accepted fact, to perpetuate preferred ways of thinking. For example, the Russians teach the doctrine of Lysenko, some U.S. schools reject Darwinism, teachers can be models of racial prejudice, and the like. To save sinners may involve making people feel guilt, shame, anxiety—deny the pleasure of physical contact; accept the poverty and *status quo* of this world for a pie in the sky when you die. To cure the mentally ill sometimes involves communicating what the person must do in order that society does not label him a "deviant" and cast him out into a madhouse. Psychotherapy can be seen as conformity training in which there is a unilateral influence attempt to make the patient's "abnormal" behavior "normal" (like everyone else's) again.

Such a predisposition to make the attribution error of overestimating internal relative to external causality is seen repeatedly in those phenomena that most intrigue and fascinate us. Hypnosis, voodoo deaths, brainwashing, placebo effects, Asch's conformity, and Milgram's obedience findings all share this property. Dramatic changes in behavior occur in others, which we believe we personally could resist. The strength of the situational forces are not appreciated, while our own ability not to be tender-minded, or weak-willed, or suggestible, or controlled by words is magnified.

Research from many disparate areas clearly reveals how easy it is to bring behavior under situational control. Hovland (1954) has noted that it is almost impossible *not* to get positive attitude change in a laboratory study of attitude change. Orne (1962) despairs at being able to find a task so repulsive and demeaning that "experimental subjects" will *not* perform it readily upon request. Milgram (1963) shows that the majority of his subjects engage in extremely aggressive behavior in a situation psychiatrists had believed would only have a weak effect in inducing blind obedience. We comply, conform, become committed, are persuaded daily in the endless procession of influence situations that we enter, yet each of us continues to maintain an illusion of personal invulnerability. It is only when the situational forces become so obviously unfair—so physically suppressive or psychologically repressive—that we question the ethics of the change situation.

In this sense, then, one talks about the politics of persuasion, since an influence attempt backed by society is persuasion sanctioned by established policy. If a *communicator* advocates change that is not acceptable to the power structure controlling the resources of the society, then pressure is applied to change the communicator. Attempts are made to bring him back in line or, failing this, to reject him by relabeling him as a "revolutionary," "radical," or "traitor."

Society in the United States is now in a state of confusion because agents of change whose persuasive influence once was sanctioned by society are no longer granted dispensation to use the approved labels "educator," "pediatrician," and so forth, or to be immune from persuasion attempts themselves. It then becomes obvious to former "targets" that there was previously an implicit contract of complicity and that there still is with other agents. When people become aware of this duplicity and are cognizant of the hidden situational forces, they lose trust in parents, educators, politicians, and all those who now reveal themselves as undercover agents of change. They become cynical toward a system that professes to function for the people when, in fact, it functions for the communicator and his powerful backers, the "Society." Finally, when the illusion of individual assertiveness, resistance, and willpower disintegrates under the realization of the overwhelming forces operating to keep even their "personal" communicators in line, then feelings of hopelessness come to the surface.

If a society, through its political power base, wants to make war and not peace and most of its traditional communicators support this view (or do not openly oppose it), how can the society ever be changed? The two alternatives are revolution (which destroys the established base of power) or persuasion, which redirects available knowledge and tactics and utilizes former "targets" as new agents of communication.

The remainder of this chapter presents one attempt to apply the research findings of social psychology and the salesman's intuition to just this problem. Can "students" and young people effectively persuade adults, who collectively have the power to change the system, to use their voting power in an effort to promote peace?

Tactics and strategies designed to achieve this goal will be formulated explicitly, and then, for purposes of comparison, the tactics of the police interrogator will be outlined. The ethical issues involved in attempting to turn a society around

by working through its system will not be discussed, but the question of using "Machiavellian" techniques on an individual in order to do so will be raised.

PERSUADING FOR NEW POLITICS

Preparing for the Initial Contact

A. Be informed.

Get as much accurate, up-to-date, reliable evidence as you can. Commit important facts, arguments, statistics, and quotations to memory so they are "natural" when you need them. You should see yourself as more expert on the particular issue of concern than the people you will try to persuade. Your perceived competence is a very important source trait. However, *do not use information as a put-down.* Do not overkill. Hold your storehouse in reserve and select only the facts you need.

B. Learn as much as you can about those you will engage.

Be familiar with their neighborhood, local issues, basic values, language style (use of diction, clichés, homilies), source of local pride and discontent, the nature of usual influence media, attitudes on the issue in question, and the like. You can obtain this information from local businessmen (barbers, cab drivers, grocery store employees, bartenders, and others), salesmen, letters to the newspaper, and distinguishing characteristics of the neighborhood or the individual home. You can also encourage people to state their opinions on preliminary telephone surveys. When you are in this learning phase, do not try to exert influence.

C. Actively role-play the anticipated situation with a friend.

Imagine and then work through as realistically as possible the persuasion situation in which you will operate. If available, tape-record or video-tape such dress rehearsals and then critically analyze your performance. Switch roles and try to be the target person in the situation where someone is experiencing pressure to comply with a request for some commitment.

D. Do a critical self-appraisal.

Analyze your own personal strengths and weaknesses and your appearance, and discuss any source of fear, anxiety, anticipated embarrassment, and so forth with one or more persons with whom you feel comfortable before you actually start out.

E. Be confident.

Expect that you will be effective more often than not. You must expect some setbacks, but you must be dedicated to winning, to making the "sale." If you do not handle the situation carefully, you might produce the undesirable effect of increasing the person's resistance to any further influence attempts by others, or you may generate a backlash effect yourself. If you blow it once or twice, or if you get doors slammed in your face before you even start talking (this will surely happen in some neighborhoods), keep trying. If you lose your confidence, however, or you get negative results in a variety of neighborhoods with a variety of techniques, then perhaps you are not suited for face-to-face confrontations and your talents could be put to better use elsewhere.

F. Be sensitive to the varied reasons underlying the attitude(s) in question.

Attitudes are formed and maintained because of needs for information, for social acceptance by other people, or for ego protection from unacceptable impulses and ideas. Deeply held attitudes probably have all three of these motivational bases. Information *per se* is probably the least effective way of *changing* attitudes and behavior.

Its effectiveness is maximum at the attitude formation stage when the person has not yet taken a stand and put his ego on the dotted line. Your general approach must acknowledge that the individual is more than a rational, information processor—sometimes he is irrational, inconsistent, unresponsive to social rewards, or primarily concerned about how he appears to himself and to others.

G. Even as a stranger you can exert considerable influence.

You can be an effective agent for change by serving as a model for some behavior by publicly engaging in it, selectively reinforcing some opinions rather than others, and providing a new source of social contact, recognition, and reward for many people.

Gaining Access to and Establishing the Contact

A. Before you can persuade, you must get the person to acknowledge your presence, to attend to you, and to follow your presentation. People are wary of an assault on their privacy and "life space" by an unknown person on their doorstep. You might want to consider an initial phone call or letter instead of initial contacts face-to-face.

B. If you are making a home contact, be aware of the particular situation you have encountered. Be sure that the person is willing to give you the required time. You might be interrupting dinner, a phone call, a family quarrel, a visit with guests, or some bad news. You do not want the dominant motivation of the homeowner to be to get rid of you as soon as possible.

C. Although strangers can influence everyday behavior, persuasion is enhanced when the target perceives some basic similarity with the source. This "strategy of identification" (practiced by all good entertainers and politicians) involves finding something in common between you. Physical similarity is the most obvious: age, sex, race, ethnic features, dress (distribution of hair). In addition, similarity is inferred from voice dialect, regionalisms, and appropriate slang, jargon, or group-membership-identifying phrases (for example, "such a lot of *chutzpah* he's got, that vice president," or "People like us who work for a living have callouses on their hands; a politician like X who talks about working for the people, probably has them only on his mouth"). Canvassing should be arranged to optimize this perceived similarity by selecting neighborhoods and locations that are approximately matched to the available canvassers. The canvasser should try to uncover as many points of similarity as possible because similarity breeds familiarity, which breeds liking and enhances credibility and greater acceptance of the message.

D. Students are not seen as credible sources on most issues that concern them directly; to be effective, it is important that they increase their source credibility. This can be accomplished in a number of ways:

1. Impress the audience with your expertise, concern, and dedication, being forceful but not overbearing.

2. Make some points that are against your own best interest: indicate the sacrifices you have made and would be willing to make.

3. Have a respected person introduce you, or make the contact for you.

4. Begin by agreeing with what the audience wants to hear, or with whatever they say first.

5. Minimize your manipulative intent until you ask for the commitment.

E. Avoid group situations where the majority of people are known to be or expected to be against you, since they will provide support for each other and their cohesion might make salient the group norm that you appear to be attacking (which they never cherished so much before your attack).

Maintaining, Intensifying, and Directing the Interpersonal Relationship

Once you have managed to get the person to receive you, then you must hold this attention, while trying to get your message (and yourself) accepted.

A. You have the power to reinforce many behaviors of the target person, a power you should use judiciously but with conscious awareness of what and how you are reinforcing.

1. Listen attentively to what the other person has to say about anything of personal interest. This not only "opens up" the person for a dialogue and helps in establishing what are the primary values, beliefs, and organization of his (or her) thinking, but establishes you as someone open to what others have to say. (The opportunity to tell a college student where to get off is very rewarding for many people.)

2. Maintain eye contact with the person and as close physical proximity as seems acceptable to the person.

3. Individuate the person by using names (with Mr. or Mrs. or titles where there is an age or status discrepancy). Make the person feel you are reacting to his uniqueness and individuality—which *you should be*—and are not reacting in a programmed way to your stereotyped conception of a housewife, blue-collar worker, etc. Similarly, help the other person to individuate you, to break through the categorization and pigeonholing process that makes you just an anonymous canvasser. At some point, describe something personal or unique about your feelings, background, interests, and so forth (which you expect will be acceptable). However, once

accomplished, then do not allow yourself to be the exception to the stereotype—say, "most other students are like me in how we feel about X."

4. Reinforce specific behaviors explicitly and immediately, by nodding, saying "good," "that's an interesting point," and the like. Reinforce more general classes of behavior by smiling, and by making it obvious you enjoy the interaction and by being impressed with the person's openness, sensitivity, intelligence, or articulateness. As a student with a lot of book learning, you can still learn a lot from people who have gone to the "school of hard knocks," who have real-life learning and street savvy to offer you. Let them know that this is how you feel when talking to someone who has not had the benefit of your degree of education.

5. The person must perceive that you personally care about and are enthusiastic about the item(s) under discussion; moreover he/she must perceive that *you* as a person really care at a personal level and not merely as part of your role.

6. Your reinforcement rate should increase over the course of the interaction, so that ideally, at the end of the time, the person is sorry to see you leave.

B. Be aware of resentment for what you represent because of such things as your physical appearance or group membership (as a student). Work first to separate those biased and often unfounded feelings and reactions from those reactions you want to elicit by your influence attempt.

Working class people in particular will resent you for having an easy life. They have worked with their hands, strained their backs and calloused their knees scrubbing, lifting, sweating, struggling, eking out a measly subsistence, while you (as they see it) sit on your butt and have every need catered to. You can blunt this resentment in at least two ways: (1) by showing respect and even awe for how hard they work, acknowledging that you found it really tough that summer you worked as a hod-carrier, and so forth; (2) by offhandedly noting how exhausting it was studying for that last calculus exam or that while other students may have a lot of money, *you* don't and you don't know whether you can afford to make it through college—whatever you can honestly say to undercut the perception that you are privileged and spoiled.

In contrast, middle-class office workers are likely to resent you for a different set of reasons: that (according to the stereotype) you do not show respect for your elders; that you are an uncouth, dirty, disruptive, pot-smoking libertine; and so forth. A neat appearance and a considerate, respectful manner will do much to combat this stereotype.

C. Plan the organization of your approach well enough so that it seems natural and unplanned, and be flexible enough to modify it as necessary.

1. Do not surround your best arguments with tangential side arguments or a lot of details. Arguments that come in the middle of a presentation are remembered least well. Put your stronger arguments first if you want to motivate or interest uninvolved people.

2. Draw your conclusions explicitly. Implying that you have come to a conclusion should be left for only very intelligent audiences.

3. Repeat the main points in your argument, and the major points of agreement between you and the target person.

D. Tailor your approach to the target person.

1. Do not put him on the defensive, or even encourage or force a public defense of (and thus commitment to) any position against you. Expressions of opposing beliefs

are seen as opportunities for open discussion, and starting points in an effort to find areas of common agreement. If the person is for you, then get a public commitment early, and try to make that commitment more stable and more extreme than it was originally.

2. If possible, have the person restate your ideas and conclusions for himself, in his own words (encourage active participation).

3. If the person appears to be very authoritarian in manner and thinking, then he will probably be more impressed by status sources, decisiveness, and one-sided generalizations than by informational appeals, expert testimony, unbiased presentation of both sides of the issue, and so forth. Make any approach responsive to the dominant personality and social characteristics of the person to whom you are talking.

4. Work in pairs. Although a more personal relationship can be established in a two-person interaction, there is much to be gained from teamwork. Working in pairs provides each student with social support, lowers apprehension about initiating each new contact, and allows one of you to be "off the firing line" appraising the situation, to come in when help is needed, to refocus the direction, or respond to some specific trait detected in the target person. There are several ways in which teams can be composed to produce interesting effects. There is a general principle covering them all: *the two members of the team should differ in some obvious characteristic, such as temperament, age, or sex.* There are two reasons behind this principle: First, it maximizes the chances that either one or the other member will be similar to the target person and therefore can gain a persuasive advantage at the appropriate

moment; second, it promotes that subtle idea that even when people differ in outward characteristics, they can still agree on the important issue of peace—therefore, the target person, who may differ from both persuaders, can be encouraged to agree also. The obverse of this "team difference" principle is also important: *it is very inefficient for similar canvassers to accompany each other.*

Getting the Commitment and Terminating the Contact

Do not insist that the person accept and believe what you have said before he makes a behavioral commitment. Get the behavioral commitment anyway, and attitude change will follow. The ideal conclusion of the contact will also leave the person feeling that the time spent was worthwhile, and his self-esteem will be greater than it was before you arrived.

A. Do not overstay your welcome or be forced to stay longer than is worthwhile according to your time schedule. Timing is essential both in knowing when to ask for the commitment and in knowing when to quit with an intractable person. For a person who needs more time to think, encourage him if you get a promise to allow you to come back.

B. Provide several levels of possible behavioral alternatives for the person: pushing the most extreme is likely to get a greater level of compliance even if the extreme is rejected.

C. Be clear as to what actions are requested or what has been agreed upon or concluded.

D. Use a "bandwagon" effect, if called for, to indicate prestigious others who have joined in the action.

E. When you believe the target person is about to make the commitment (or after a verbal agreement is made), stress the fact that the decision is his own; it involves free choice, no pressure. This maximizes the dissonance experienced by the decision made and forces the individual to make his behavior internally consistent by generating his own intrinsic justification for his behavior. Each person is his own best persuader. After the final commitment, honestly and openly thank the person and reinforce his behavior.

F. Broaden the contact in two ways. First, get the names of one or more neighbors who would agree with that person's position—you will talk to each person and use the person's name in other discussions if that is O.K. with him. Second, honestly react to something about this person that is irrelevant to the main social/political issue at hand—the house, decor, hair, clothes, and avocation mentioned, or a favor that you can do related to something mentioned.

G. Extend your influence if you can get the target person also to be an agent of influence. Try to enlist his aid in getting at least one other person to agree to do what he has just done. He should be motivated to proselytize at this time, especially if he is an outgoing person good at persuading others. If he convinces others, that will reduce his own doubts about whether he has done the right thing.

MACHIAVELLIAN STRATEGIES

Just how far should you go to make the "sale," to get the commitment? The answer to such a question depends ultimately on a complex interplay of ethical, ideological, and pragmatic issues. Each individual must establish his own set of weighting coefficients to determine how much pressure he is willing to exert. Assuming that your approach will achieve your purpose, is it "right," "proper," "decent," "humane," "moral" for you to deceive someone, to hit him below his unconscious, to arouse strong negative feelings of guilt, anxiety, or shame, or even positive feel-

ings of false pride? Behaving unethically for whatever reason pollutes the psychological environment by replacing trust, understanding, and mutual respect with deceit, lies, and cynicism.

Police interrogation manuals state: "When you break a man by torture, he will always hate you. If you break him by your intelligence, he will always fear and respect you" (Kidd, 1940, p. 49). This generalization might only hold when he does not realize that you, in fact, have broken him by intention. When deception techniques are employed by a sophisticated, trained practitioner, the "victim"—be he a criminal subject, a collegiate experimental subject, or "mark" in a pool-hall hustle—does not realize he has been conned. But *you* always know what your intention was and that you "broke a man" thus. What effect does such knowledge have upon you? Do you respect yourself more because of it? Do you begin to depersonalize other human beings as they become notches on your gun handle, "hits/misses," "easy cases/tough customers"? Thus, you must reflect upon the psychological effects of behaving unethically, both upon the target person and upon yourself. If you are so ideologically committed to your cause or goal that any ends justify the means, then ethical issues will get a zero weighting coefficient. But that alone should give you pause.

A. Will it be possible to restore ethical precepts after your ends have been achieved?

B. If you have been converted to such an extreme view, can others be similarly moved without recourse to deception?

C. Have you not been duped into the extreme position you now hold?

D. Are you being honest with yourself in recognizing that you are about to be dishonest with others, and are you sure that you are not covering up the fact with rationalizations about "the other side did it first" (if that's true, then the poor victim gets it from both ends)?

Finally, if you cast ethics to the wind, yet proceed firmly convinced that Goodness, Justice, and Truth are what you stand for, then ask one more practical question: "Is it likely to work?" How much effort, training, staging, and time will it take to carry off the caper? Are you the type of person who can be effective at this game? What happens if the person discovers the gimmick? Will each "miss" turn into a "boomerang" or a backlash that will actively work against your cause? Will you then get only the immediate, small behavioral compliance, but blow the hoped-for bigger subsequent commitment and attitude change? Have you "ruined" the person for further persuasion attempts (or experiments) by your colleagues?

Having posed and answered such questions to your own satisfaction, if you still want to go for broke, then the time has come to go Machiavellian. Once such a decision has been made, your only concern is to find the weak points of the target person, and learn what conditions to manipulate and how best to exploit the unsuspecting victim.

Before describing several concrete examples of how Machiavellian tactics can be used in even such an incongruous situation as a "peace campaign," let us see how they are already effectively being used.

The Police Interrogator Misrepresents a Little Bit

Confessions are often obtained by either minimizing the seriousness of the offense and allowing the suspect a "face-saving" out, or by doing the opposite: misrepresenting and exaggerating the seriousness of the crime.

The first approach can be accomplished through "extenuation"—in which the investigator reports that he does not take too seriously a view of the subject's indiscretion, since he has seen thousands of others in the same situation. Or he may "shift the blame" to circumstances, the environment, or a subject's weaknesses, any of which might lead anyone to do what the suspect did. A more morally acceptable motive might be suggested for the crime, such as self-defense, an accident, a mistake, heat of passion, and so forth. In order to "open up" a suspect, it is recommended that good "bait" is to blame anyone who might be associated with the crime other than the suspect; for example, an accomplice, a fence, a company, loan sharks, or even the victim.

Here are some provocative examples of the way in which experts use this approach in order to misrepresent the nature of the crime to the suspect in order to get him to talk about it:

1. A 50-year old man accused of having taken "indecent liberties" with a 10-year-old girl was told:

   "This girl is well developed for her age. She probably learned a lot about sex from the boys in the neighborhood and from the movies and TV; and knowing what she did about it, she may have deliberately tried to excite you to see what you would do" (Inbau and Reid, 1962, p.45).

2. Or, in forcible rape cases, "where circumstances permit, the suggestion might be offered that the rape victim acted like she might be a prostitute . . . that the police knew she had been engaged in acts of prostitution on other occasions" (Inbau and Reid, 1962, p. 46).

3. "During the interrogation of a married rape suspect, blame might be cast on the subject's wife for not providing him with the necessary sexual gratification. 'When a fellow like you doesn't get it at home, he seeks it elsewhere'" (Inbau and Reid, 1962, p. 51).

Once the suspect is in a state of emotional confusion, then "he is unable to think logically and clearly, since his sense of values has been disturbed and his imagination is distorting his perspective. It is possible for the investigator to obtain admissions or even a confession from the suspect by further misrepresenting the picture" (O'Hara, 1956, p. 105).

This misrepresentation can take the form of a "knowledge bluff"—revealing a few known items and pretending to know more, or lying to the suspect that his fingerprints, blood, etc. were found at the scene of the crime (even show him falsified samples and records). In some cases of murder, it might be stated that the victim is not dead or, as happened in Minneapolis, a youthful offender, John Biron, might be told that he will be tried as a juvenile when it was known that he is legally an adult (see *Time Magazine*, December 3, 1965, p. 52; April 29, 1966, p. 65).

Since modern interrogation involves establishing "rapport" or a meaningful interpersonal relationship between the suspect and the interrogator, it must involve a distortion of the social-psychological situation. Even before the questioning begins, the interrogator is urged to role-play the position of the subject in order to be able to respond to him—"man to man, not as policeman to prisoner" (Inbau and Reid, 1962, p. 19).

Under this category would fall all the appeals that depend upon the interrogator being friendly, kind, sympathetic, understanding, "a Dutch uncle," or an older brother. He is the one who provides social approval and recognition, who accords the suspect status, and who is aware of and able to manipulate the suspect because of his social values, feelings of pride, and class or group membership.

The police manuals recognize that "It is a basic human trait to seek and enjoy the approval of other persons." Therefore, it is wise to flatter some subjects, for example, by complimenting an accused driver of a getaway car for his maneuvering and "cornering," or by comparing a juvenile with his movie idol, or a member of a racial group with a respectable, outstanding member of that group. This approach apparently works best with "the uneducated and underprivileged," since they "are more vulnerable to flattery than the educated person or the person in favorable financial circumstances."

A slightly different approach is needed for the white-collar first offender, a group that includes clerks, managers, cashiers, office workers, professionals, and teachers—in short, most of the audience of this book. Since these people traditionally subscribe to orthodox ethical principles and conventional moral standards, the calm, dignified approach of the physician is respected and effective. One police manual author states rather boldly: "The character of a person in this category is weak and must be exploited fully" (O'Hara, 1956).

To create rapport, the interrogator could pat the suspect on the shoulder, grip his hand, or offer to do a favor for him—get water, talk to his wife or his employer, etc. O'Hara says (1956): "Gestures of this type produce a very desirable effect. They impart an attitude of understanding and sympathy better than words."

For a suspect who has pride in his or her family, if an attempt to get the parents to cooperate fails, their attention is called to a (faked) circular being prepared for broadcast and distribution throughout the country. It not only describes the fugitive, but lists all of his known relatives' names and addresses as possible leads for approaching him. Cooperation quite often is obtained in this way.

The reader might recall that in the famous case of George Whitmore, Jr. (who confessed to the slaying of two society girls in New York in 1963), he gave a 61-page typed confession after 20 hours of interrogation. He virtually sentenced himself to death or life imprisonment with this confession—which later was proved coerced false when the true murderer was subsequently exposed.

MAKING MACHIAVELLI WORK FOR PEACE

The following hypothetical examples do not have the time-tested validity of those reported in the police interrogator's literature; rather, they merely illustrate how such tactics can be adapted to suit virtually any cause. The content of our cause will be related to "canvassing for peace," but one can imagine an adversary who would use them to canvass for war.

A. Mutt and Jeff

The so-called Mutt and Jeff technique of police interrogation involves a sneaky one-two punch in grilling suspects. A rough analogue of this tactic in political persuasion can be devised. One persuader is militant in style and extreme in his position; the second persuader is moderate and reasonable as if to save the listener from the excess of the first, but in fact exacts a considerable concession by virtue of his soothing performance.

A very skilled and aggressive antiwar debater, who is dying to be turned loose but who may sometimes turn people off, can be paired with a sympathetic gentlemanly type who can gently chide him in the presence of the listener with remarks such as, "My friend might be overdoing it a little because he feels so strongly about the war, but what I would say on this point is that the war is much too expensive. I think that this is a position with which most hard-headed Americans can agree." Thus, the "moderate" brings the listener over to his side by using the "militant" as a foil.

This technique at best must be used very delicately and sparingly. It is double-edged. Too much "Mutt" militance on the doorstep will drive the listener up the wall, and both might get thrown out before Jeff can intervene. Furthermore, it takes a couple of good ham actors to carry it off, and too much "con" in the canvassing operation would be unfortunate, especially if neighbors compare notes.

B. The Stigmatized Persuader

Recent research has found that a person with a visible stigma (someone, say, who is blind or crippled) elicits a mixed reaction. There is sympathy and a tendency to want to help in some way, but also considerable tension from guilt, revulsion, and resentment (the disabled person has intruded on the complacent life-space of the individual). These basic motives to help and to ignore can be elicited by having a person with a real or faked stigma appear on the doorstep (for example, a pretty girl with a scar, a boy on crutches, a team where one member is apparently blind). After the general introduction, the person with the stigma clearly states the level of commitment desired and then suggests that if the person does not want to act on it now, they could perhaps spend some time together talking it over. Embarrassed sympathy will make it difficult to terminate the interaction brusquely, but if an easy way out is provided by the canvasser, it will be the preferred way of resolving the conflict. They might sign now to avoid facing the stigmatized of the world any more than is necessary.

C. The "Overheard" Communication

It is a well-known result of studies of persuasive communication that a message accidentally overheard can be more effective than when the speaker is aware of the listener's presence. In the "accidental" case, the listener has no reason to be suspicious that the speaker is trying to manipulate him.

The following setup tries to make use of this advantage of overhearing. Since it is an artifice, it is not recommended for widespread use.

In a possible one-person version, a coed enters a busy laundromat with a basket of laundry, puts the clothes in the machine, and asks another customer for change for a quarter to make a phone call to her mother. While pretending to call

Mom she describes the chores she is doing and checks on the groceries she is to buy at the supermarket. "A daughter like that, I should only have," is the kind of thought running through the heads of the women there. "Good Daughter" then proceeds to talk to her mother briefly about the war and agree with her mother that it is awfully important to end this terrible war very soon and that she is happy that the mother has written to her congressman, and hopes she will also vote for Candidate X. She talks loudly enough to let the target audience hear, but then goes about her business unless someone in the audience initiates a conversation. The point of the artifice was to advance arguments opposing a war in a non-confrontational subtle way.

Variations on this idea can be adapted for use in bus stations, drugstores, barber shops, and other such places, although this technique suffers from the general difficulty that the same person cannot wash the same bundle repeatedly, call the same Mom over and over, or get more than a few hair cuts a day without seeming very peculiar indeed.

The two-person version is more practical. This can be enacted when riding back and forth on crowded subways or buses, never traveling the same line at the same hour of a weekday. A student and an older person (his uncle or Dad, presumably) make the ideal team. The two get into a spirited argument about today's mood of campus protest. Even though they argue, it is obvious that they have a great deal of affection for each other, and the student (or son) slips in references to good behaviors ("When I was fixing our sink last night with that rusty drainpipe, I was thinking, "down the drain, down the drain, boy, all the money we're spending in Vietnam is just going right down the drain, totally wasted"). Their voices are raised just enough so that people can hear, but not enough to be obnoxious. The Dad complains that students aren't working hard like he did in his day (avoid references to riots, drugs, and the like—the most intense anti-student issues). The son agrees that this may be true, but the reason is that they are disillusioned because America is fighting an expensive, far-away war when there are all these problems that need working on at home. The Dad tentatively offers a few lukewarm arguments in favor of present war policy, but soon changes his mind when the student confidently (but not arrogantly) cites facts and arguments for quick withdrawal. The Dad agrees to write against the war to his congressman, but counterattacks with gusto on the issue of student laziness. The son now concedes this point (it would not leave a good taste with the listeners if the cocky son triumphed completely over the wishy-washy Dad). The son resolves to get back to his campus and get all his buddies more involved in their own education and in constructive action. He compliments his Dad on his understanding and on all he has done all these years for his son. They now chat amiably about other things. Again, the arguments were advanced, but the "advance" was not aware that it was all for their benefits.

POSTSCRIPT

The fundamental thesis of this paper is reflected in Bandura's (1969) perceptive concern for the potential misuse of the therapist's influence in his one-way power relationship with those labeled "patients":

> As behavioral science makes further progress toward the development of efficacious principles of change, man's capacity to create the type of social environment he wants will be substantially increased. The decision process by which cultural priorities are established must, therefore, be made more explicit to ensure that "social engineering" is utilized to produce living conditions that enrich life and behavioral freedom rather than aversive human effects. (p. 112.)

REFERENCES

Bandura, A. *Principles of behavior modification.* New York: Holt, 1969.

Hovland, C. I. Reconciling conflicts results derived from experimental and survey studies of attitude change. *American Psychologist,* 1954. 14; 8–17.

Inbau, F. E., and Reid, J. E. *Criminal interrogation and confessions.* Baltimore: Williams and Wilkins, 1962.

Kidd, W. R. Police interrogation. *The Police Journal.* New York, 1940.

Milgram, S. Behavioral study of obedience. *Journal of Abnormal and Social Psychology,* 1963. 67; 371–378.

Mulbar, H. *Interrogation.* Springfield, Ill.: Charles C. Thomas, 1951.

O'Hara, C. E. *Fundamentals of criminal investigation.* Springfield, Illinois: Thomas, 1956.

Orne, M. On the social psychology of the psychological experiment: With special reference to demand characteristics of their implications. *American Psychologist,* 1962. 17; 776–785.

Time Magazine, December 3, 1965, p. 52.

Time Magazine, April 29, 1966, p. 65.

THE LANGUAGE OF PERSUASION

David Kipnis and Stuart Schmidt

"I had all the facts and figures ready before I made my suggestions to my boss." (manager)

"I kept insisting that we do it my way. She finally caved in." (husband)

"I think it's about time that you stop thinking these negative things about yourself." (psychotherapist)

"Send out more horses, skirr the country round. Hang those that talk of fear. Give me mine armour." (Macbeth, Act 5)

These diverse statements—rational, insistent, emotional—have one thing in common. They all show people trying to persuade others, a skill we all treasure. Books about power and influence are read by young executives eager for promotion, by politicians anxious to sway their constituents, by lonely people looking to win and hold a mate, and by harried parents trying to make their children see the light.

Despite this interest in persuasion, most people are not really aware of how they go about it. They spend more time choosing their clothes than they do their influence styles. Even fewer are aware of how their styles affect others or themselves. Although shouts and demands might make people dance to our tune, we will probably lose their goodwill. Beyond that, our opinion of others can change for the worse when we use hard or abusive tactics (see "The View from the Top," *Psychology Today*, December 1984).

Popular books on influencing others give contradictory advice. Some advocate assertiveness, others stealth, and still others reason and logic. Could they all *be* right? We decided to see for ourselves what kinds of influence people actually use in personal and work situations and why they choose the tactics they do.

We conducted studies of dating couples and business managers in which the couples described how they attempted to influence their partners and the managers told how they attempted to influence their subordinates, peers, and superiors at work. We then used these descriptions as the basis for separate questionnaires in which we asked other couples and managers how frequently they employed each tactic. Using factor analysis and other statistical techniques, we found that the tactics could be classified into three basic strategies—hard, soft and rational (see the "Influence Strategies" box).

These labels describe the tactics from the standpoint of the person using them. Since influencing someone is a social act, its meaning depends upon the observer's vantage point. For example, a wife might ask her husband, "I wonder what we should do about the newspapers in the garage?" The husband could consider this remark nagging to get him to clean up the garage. The wife might say her remark was simply a friendly suggestion that he consider the state of the garage. An outside observer might feel that the wife's remark was just conversation, not a real attempt to influence.

As the box illustrates, hard tactics involve demanding, shouting, and assertiveness. With soft tactics, people act nice and flatter others to get their way. Rational tactics involve the use of logic and bargaining to demonstrate why compliance or compromise is the best solution.

Why do people shout and demand in one instance, flatter in a second, and offer to compromise in a third? One common explanation is that the choice of tactics is based upon what "feels right" in each case. A more pragmatic answer is that the choice of tactics is based strictly on what works.

Our studies show that the reasons are more complex. When we examine how people actually use influence, we find that they use many different strategies, depending on the situation and the

INFLUENCE STRATEGIES

Strategy	Couples	Managers
Hard	I get angry and demand that he/she give in.	I simply order the person to do what I ask.
	As the first step, I make him/her feel stupid and worthless.	I threaten to give an unsatisfactory performance evaluation.
	I say I'll leave my spouse if he/she does not agree.	I get higher management to back up my request.
Soft	I act warm and charming before bringing up the subject.	I act very humble while making my request.
	I am so nice that he/she cannot refuse.	I make the person feel important by saying that she/he has the brains and experience to do what I want.
Rational	I offer to compromise; I'll give up a little if she/he gives up a little.	I offer to exchange favors: You do this for me, and I'll do something for you.
	We talk, discussing our views objectively without arguments.	I explain the reason for my request.

• • • • •

WHY PEOPLE CHOOSE EACH STRATEGY

Hard tactics are normally used when:
- Influencer has the advantage.
- Resistance is anticipated.
- Target's behavior violates social or organizational norms.

Soft tactics are normally used when:
- Influencer is at a disadvantage.
- Resistance is anticipated.
- The goal is to get benefits for one's self.

Rational tactics are normally used when:
- Neither party has a real power advantage.
- Resistance is not anticipated.
- The goal is to get benefits for one's self and one's organization.

BYSTANDERS, TACTICIANS, AND SHOTGUN MANAGERS

When we analyzed data from our study of managers, three distinct types emerged:

Shotgun managers use any and all means to get their way. Compared with the others we studied, they have the least managerial experience, hold staff rather than line positions, and express the greatest number of personal needs (to receive benefits) and organizational needs (to sell their ideas) that require them to exercise influence. Shotgun managers are young, ambitious, and unwilling to take no for an answer.

Tacticians rely heavily on reason to influence others. They usually have considerable power in an organization, direct units that do technologically complex work, and feel that they influence company policy. Bystanders are the timid souls of the sample. They seldom use their managerial power to persuade others. Bystanders usually direct units that do routine work and have been in the same job for more years, on the average, than the other managers. Our impression is that they are marking time and feel it is futile even to try to influence others.

person being influenced. We gathered information from 195 dating and married couples, and from 360 first- and second-line managers in the United States, Australia, and Great Britain. We asked which influence tactics they used, how frequently, and in what conditions.

The choice of strategies varied predictably for both managers (see the "Bystanders" box) and couples. It depends on their particular objectives, relative power position, and expectations about the willingness of others to do what they want. These expectations are often based on individual traits and biases rather than facts.

Objectives

One of our grandmothers always advised sweetly, "Act nice if you want a favor." We found that people do, indeed, vary their tactics according to what they want.

At work, for instance, managers frequently rely on such soft tactics as flattery, praise, or acting humble when they want something from a boss, such as time off or better assignments. However, when managers want to persuade the boss to accept ideas, such as a new work procedure, they're more likely to use reason and logic. Occasionally, they will even try hard tactics, such as going over the boss's head, if he or she can't be moved any other way.

Couples also vary their choice of tactics, depending upon what they want from each other. Personal benefits such as choosing a movie or restaurant for the night call for a soft, loving approach. When they want to change a spouse's unacceptable behavior, anger, threats and other hard tactics come into play.

Power Positions

People who control resources, emotions, or finances valued by others clearly have the advantage in a relationship, whether it is commercial or personal. In our research with couples, we discovered which partner was dominant by asking who made the final decision about issues such as spending money, choosing friends, and other family matters. We found that people who say they control the relationship ("I have the final say") often rely on hard tactics to get their way. Those who share decision power ("We decide together") bargain rationally and often compromise. Partners who admit that they have little power ("My partner has the final say") usually favor soft tactics.

We found the same patterns among managers. The more one-sided the power relationship at work, the more likely managers are to demand, get angry, and insist with people who work for them, and the more likely they are to act humble and flatter when they are persuading their bosses.

The fact that people change influence tactics depending on their power over the other person is hardly surprising. What is surprising is how universal the link is between power and tactics. Our surveys and those conducted by others have found this relationship among children trying to influence younger children or older children, and among executives dealing with executives at other companies more or less powerful than

their own, as well as among spouses and business managers dealing with their own subordinates and bosses.

There seems to be an "Iron Law of Power": The greater the discrepancy in clout between the influencer and the target, the greater the likelihood that hard tactics will be used. People with power don't always use hard tactics as their first choice. At first, most simply request and explain. They turn to demands and threats (the iron fist lurking under the velvet glove of reason) only when someone seems reluctant or refuses to comply with their request.

In contrast, people with little power are likely to stop trying or immediately shift to soft tactics when they encounter resistance. They feel the costs associated with the use of hard or even rational tactics are unacceptable. They are unwilling to take the chance of angering a boss, a spouse, or an older child by using anything but soft methods.

Expectations and Biases

We have found that people also vary their strategies according to how successful they expect to be in influencing their targets. When they believe that someone is likely to do what is asked, they make simple requests. When they anticipate resistance and have the power, they use hard tactics.

This anticipation may be realistic. Just as a robber knows that without a gun, a polite request for money is unlikely to persuade, a boss knows that a request for work on Saturday needs more than a smile to back it up. But less realistic personal and situational factors sometimes make us expect resistance where none exists. People who are low in self-esteem and self-confidence, for instance, have difficulty believing that others will comply with simple requests.

We found that lack of confidence and low self-esteem are characteristic of managers who bark orders and refuse to discuss the issues involved; of couples who constantly shout and scream at each other; and of parents who rely on harsh discipline. These hard tactics result from the self-defeating assumption that others will not listen unless they are treated roughly.

Social situations and biases can also distort expectations of cooperation. Misunderstandings based on differences in attitudes, race, or sex can lead to hard tactics. Our research and that of others shows that orders, shouts, and threats are more likely to be used between blacks and whites or men and women. The simple perception that "these people are different than I am" leads to the idea that "they are not as reasonable as I am" and must be ordered about.

The reasons shown in the "Why People Choose" box are generalizations. They don't necessarily describe how a particular person will act in a particular situation. People tend to choose influence tactics because of habit, lack of forethought, or lack of social sensitivity. Most of us would be more effective persuaders if we analyzed why we act as we do. Simply writing a short description of a recent incident in which we tried to persuade someone can help us understand better our own tactics, why we use them, and, perhaps, why a rational approach might be better.

People who know we have studied the matter sometimes ask, "Which tactics work best?" The answer is that they all work if they are used at the right time with the right person. But both hard and soft tactics involve costs to the user even when they succeed. Hard tactics often alienate the people being influenced and create a climate of hostility and resistance. Soft tactics—acting nice, being humble—might lessen self-respect and self-esteem. In contrast, we found that people who rely chiefly on logic, reason, and compromise to get their way are the most satisfied both with their business lives and with their personal relationships.

Section III

Negotiator Competencies

Chapter Six   *Negotiator Skills*
Chapter Seven   *Planning and Preparation*
Chapter Eight   *Negotiation Failure*

Chapter Six

NEGOTIATOR SKILLS

STYLE AND EFFECTIVENESS IN NEGOTIATION

Gerald R. Williams

Should alternative dispute resolution be taught in a prescriptive, or a descriptive, manner? A prescriptive approach says, "This is how it ought to be done." A descriptive approach says, "I have examined large numbers of experienced dispute resolvers and this is how they do it; here are the characteristics and patterns of highly effective negotiators."

Roger Fisher is one of the best examples of a negotiator who takes the prescriptive approach; I am at the opposite end of the spectrum. I have always believed that the most important information a negotiator should have is an accurate description of how experienced negotiators operate. What are the patterns, the traits, the characteristics of effective and of ineffective negotiators? If you have an understanding of the patterns of behavior of effective as well as ineffective negotiators, then your own experience, intuition, judgment, and instincts come into play and help you adjust to particular negotiating situations.

My message is that I can't give you a prescription; I won't presume to tell you what you ought to do, but I can give you a detailed report on the negotiating patterns of highly effective negotiators,

and also the patterns of ineffective negotiators. Then I hope you will go out and apply that knowledge in your own individual ways.

To my mind, the prescriptive and descriptive approaches are highly complementary. I believe we benefit most by using a combination of the two. It seems to me that any course in negotiation ought to include them both, and should perhaps begin with a description of negotiating patterns and end with our best prescription for improving on the state of the art.

THE BRIGHAM YOUNG UNIVERSITY STUDY OF LAWYERS' NEGOTIATING BEHAVIOR

Let us focus on describing the negotiating patterns of experienced lawyers. The first two chapters of my book *Legal Negotiation and Settlement* (Williams, 1983) give a formal description of our findings. An appendix at the back my book describes the research methodology of the Brigham Young University study. Very briefly, in 1972 I joined with three behavioral scientists to study the negotiating characteristics of lawyers. We were fortunate to receive a grant from the Law and Social Sciences Division of the National Science Foundation. Over a period of three years, we used a variety of methods to learn as much as possible about lawyers and negotiators. We studied about 350 to 400 lawyer/negotiators in Denver and a comparable number in Phoenix. I will describe the results of this research below, but before doing so, there is a threshold question that deserves our attention: Do negotiating patterns or skills really make a difference in the outcome of particular cases? The best way to answer this question is to find a group of experienced negotiators, pair them up one on one, and have them negotiate the same case to a conclusion, and then compare the outcomes.

And that is exactly what we did. In cooperation with the Drake Law School and the bar association in Des Moines, Iowa, we asked experienced lawyers if they would volunteer to participate in this experiment. We were not sure whether lawyers would agree to this because we informed them that if they volunteered, they were giving us permission to publish the results with their names attached. In other words, their reputation was on the line.

Remarkably, 40 lawyers agreed to participate. We assigned half of them the role of plaintiff and half the role of defendants; we then provided them with the facts, and gave them two weeks to prepare. Then we had them come together on a Saturday morning to negotiate a solution, if they could. Of the 20 pairs of attorneys, only 14 pairs were willing to give us the results with their names, so I can only report what happened with them. I assume, although it is pure conjecture, that the other six outcomes might have been more extreme.

Table 11.1 lists the plaintiff's opening demand, the defendant's opening offer, and the agreed

settlement (if any) for each of the 14 pairs of negotiators. They went out and negotiated, and when they returned, each pair of attorneys handed me a piece of paper and I wrote their names and outcome on the board. As indicated by the table, the first pair settled for $18,000. The second pair could not agree; they are going to trial. The third pair settled at $56,875. As I recorded these outcomes on the chalkboard, tension in the room began to mount. People were looking at each other, and they were wondering about their own competence. The next pair settled at $25,120; the next for $95,000; the next for $25,000. Out of 14 pairs of experienced attorneys, working with identical facts, we had a low of $15,000; a high of $95,000; and an average of about $47,000. Everyone else was scattered somewhat randomly between the extremes.

I was feeling very nervous, and I began wondering if we could make sense of this apparent chaos. You can imagine what happened. Up went the hand of the plaintiff's lawyer who settled for $15,000, the lowest outcome of any negotiator in the room. He explained that this was a case of doubtful liability, and that to get $1,000 or $2,000 would be a victory and $10,000 to $12,000 would be stealing, and he had gotten $15,000. "That," he said, "is the most that you can get on these facts." Up went another hand. We know whose hand it was. It was the defense lawyer who had just paid $95,000 to settle this case. The lawyer explained that this case has a potential $0.5-million liability and to negotiate it down to $400,000 or $300,000 would be a moral victory; he had gotten it down to $95,000. That was the true bottom-value of this case. We all chuckled sort of nervously, believing as a matter of etiquette that we ought to let the two worst negotiators in the room defend themselves. But that was not the whole story. Other hands went up— the person who got $56,000 or $25,000 or $80,000—every lawyer in the room wanted to tell us about their outcome.

TABLE 11.1
Des Moines Personal Injury Case: Outcomes by Experienced Attorneys on Identical Facts

Pair Number	Defendant's Opening Demand (dollars)	Agreed Opening Offer (dollars)	Agreed Settlement (dollars)
1	32,000	10,000	18,000
2	50,000	25,000	no agreement
3	100,000		56,875
4	110,000	3,000	25,120
5	657,000	32,150	95,000
6	100,000	5,000	25,000
7	475,000	15,000	no agreement
8	210,000	17,000	57,000
9	180,000	40,000	80,000
10			15,000
11	350,000	48,500	61,000
12	87,500	15,000	30,000
13	175,000	50,000	no agreement
14	97,000	10,000	57,000

Average settlement: $47,318

It was one of those times when there is mass confusion and hysteria and you are afraid of the situation because you cannot learn from it. It slowly began to dawn on us what was happening: Every lawyer in that room believed he or she had wondered what God would have done in similar circumstances. They each believed their outcome was the single best outcome. Since that day, I have felt much more humble about my ability to tell what a case is worth. This experience, and many others like it, suggests that negotiating skills really do make a difference, and that it is well worth our time to learn as much as we can about the patterns and characteristics of highly effective negotiators.

THE PROCESS

Outcomes are concrete, specific, measurable, and quantifiable, but experiences like the one in Des Moines convince me that they do not teach us very much about negotiation, because they are too variable. Rather than worry too much about outcomes, it is better to focus our attention on the process. After all, once you have your outcome, it is too late to do anything about it. So I recommend becoming an expert not on outcomes, but rather on the *process* by which they are arrived at.

Initially, most people assume that negotiating behavior is too unpredictable. In my experience, that is not true. Negotiating behavior tends to fall into patterns that can be recognized and responded to by astute observers. Process is more important to pay attention to than outcome. The predictive power of knowing what experienced negotiators do is not to be underestimated.

CHARACTERISTICS OF EFFECTIVE AND INEFFECTIVE NEGOTIATORS

The most important goal of our negotiation research project was to learn the characteristics of highly effective negotiators. We selected attorneys as our subjects not only because three of the researchers were law school professors, but because attorneys as a whole are experienced negotiators since they regularly negotiate in their daily work.

But not everyone agrees on the definition of *effective*. In working with lawyers around the country, we found that the most frequent definition was this: Effective negotiators are *the ones who get the most money for their clients.* But immediately someone else would chime in and say *no*, effective negotiators are *the ones whose clients are most satisfied*, on the theory that you might obtain a very high dollar outcome, but if your client is not satisfied, what good have you done? Then the next person would interrupt and say *no*, effective negotiators are *the ones where both sides are the most satisfied*, in the belief that agreements in which both sides are satisfied will be self-enforcing; they will not come unraveled over time. Finally, there were a few lawyers who thought the most effective negotiators were *the ones who came closest to totally destroying the other side.*

Obviously, in studying the characteristics of effective negotiators, it would make a lot of difference which one of these definitions was being used. Rather than impose our own definition or pref-

erences, we were determined to keep these possibilities open, so we could learn from experienced negotiators how they themselves define *effectiveness.*

Our solution was to keep all of these possibilities open, and see what we could learn from the experience of many hundreds of experienced legal negotiators. We mailed a questionnaire to a random sample of 1,000 attorneys in the metropolitan Denver area, asking this question: Think of an attorney against whom you have negotiated, who was so effective as a negotiator that you would hire that person to represent you if you were involved in a similar case in the future. The questionnaire then asked them to describe briefly the case or transaction, and then to describe that person by answering the items in the questionnaire (which contained about 130 different items relating to negotiator traits, behavior, strategy, and motivation). We also asked for descriptions of "average" and "ineffective" negotiators.

We received a total of 351 completed questionnaires, giving us 351 very richly detailed descriptions of negotiators who were considered effective by their peers. In our review of the literature, we had hypothesized that the results would show that cooperative approaches to negotiation were more effective than "tough" or combative approaches. Our initial analysis of the completed questionnaires seemed to confirm this hypothesis; then we ran the usual descriptive statistics of the lawyer responses, and the resulting profile of effective negotiators was overwhelmingly "cooperative" in its makeup. We reported this outcome at a conference on law and the behavioral sciences in 1974, where several respected behavioral scientists took issue with our general conclusion. Prompted by their critique, we realized that standard statistical analysis focuses on characteristics of the group as a whole; it does not attempt to differentiate among subgroups that might exist within the data. With the help of consulting statisticians, we discovered a method, called Q-Analysis, that allowed us to search for statistically significant subgroups among effective negotiators.

This resulted in a major breakthrough that proved our critics right: Effective negotiators were not *all* cooperative in their approach. Rather, they represented three distinct approaches to negotiation, each with a different set of negotiating characteristics. When we performed this analysis on the average and ineffective negotiators, we found that they each contained three significantly different subgroups. The results are shown in Figure 11.1. When we studied their characteristics, it was apparent that attorneys in Group 1 were basically *cooperative* in their approach to negotiation, and that attorneys in Group 2 were basically *aggressive* in their approach. Attorneys in Group 3 did not represent a discernible pattern.[2]

When readily identifable patterns emerge from questionnaire data like this, there are two possibilities. Either you are very lucky, or there is a flaw in your research design. My three social-scientist colleagues felt that it was better to be

cautious about this, so we did what any of you would do in similar circumstances: We went back to the federal government, we got more money, and we replicated the study in a different metropolitan area, this time in Phoenix, Arizona. We restructured the language and location of the questions on effectiveness, so that the same patterns could not be produced unless they were actually present among attorneys in Phoenix. Remarkably, the replication produced the same patterns as in Denver. My colleagues tell me that from a (social) scientific point of view, these patterns are very solid. Our methodology in Phoenix also gave us information on the numbers of attorneys that fall into each category, as you can see in Figure 11.2.

Aggressive and Cooperative Patterns of Effective and Ineffective Negotiators

In my opinion, the discovery of these two patterns among effective, average, and ineffective negotiators is the single most important product of our research. Among other things, it sheds new light on the perennial question among

Figure 11.1
Patterns of Negotiation among Attorneys in Denver

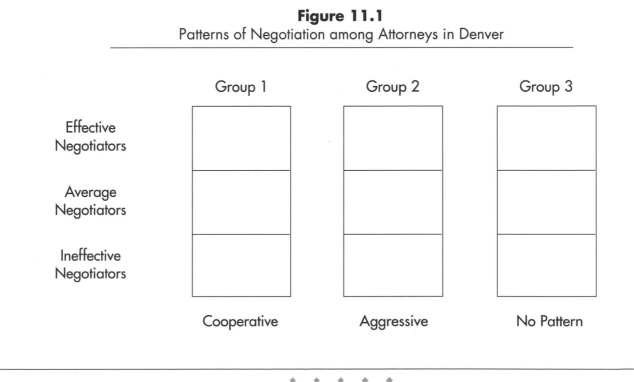

Figure 11.2
Negotiating Patterns of Experienced Attorneys

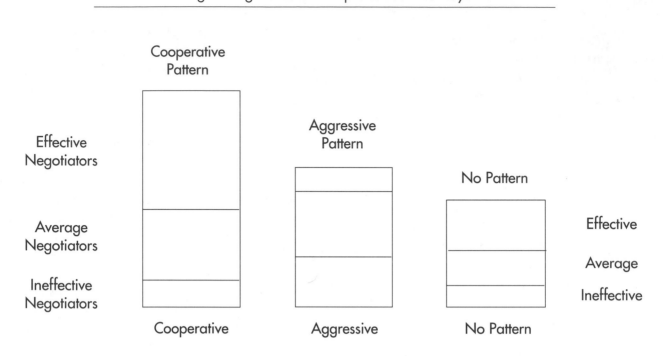

negotiation theorists: Which is the most effective strategy, toughness or cooperation? As you can see from Figure 11.2, neither approach can claim a monopoly on effectiveness. A cooperative negotiator might be effective, or average, or ineffective; likewise for the aggressive negotiator. So it is a mistake to assume that if you are cooperative (or if you are aggressive), you will be effective. Effectiveness as a negotiator depends not on which approach you adopt but on *what you do within that particular strategy*. Both have the potential to be used effectively.

At this point, the most important task is to learn as much as we can about the qualities or characteristics of the negotiators in each pattern, as shown in Figures 11.3 and 11.4.

Let us begin by looking at Figure 11.3, which shows descriptions of effective negotiators of both types. Each individual item is important, and I do not know any other single exercise that would be more beneficial to you in terms of

developing as a negotiator than to learn the characteristics so well that they become second nature to you.

One set of comparisons is too important to skip, and that has to do with the *objectives* of the negotiators in each pattern. In the questionnaire, we asked attorneys to tell us what their opponents' *objectives* or motives were, what their goals were, and what they were trying to accomplish. The results are very instructive.

Look in the upper left-hand corner of Figure 11.3 (Cooperative Objectives). The highest-rated objective of negotiators who fell in the effective cooperative category is to "Conduct themselves ethically." The second-highest objective was "Maximize the settlement for their clients," which is, after all, an ethical duty of lawyers. But for effective cooperative attorneys, the word *maximize is* modified by item number three, "Get a fair settlement." We find that cooperative attorneys want to get a good outcome, but they are

Figure 11.3
Effective Legal Negotiators.

Cooperative Objectives

1. Conduct self ethically
2. Maximize settlement
3. Get a fair settlement

Aggressive Objectives

1. Maximize settlement for client
2. Obtain profitable fee for self
3. Out-do or out-maneuver opponent

Cooperative Traits

1. Trustworthy
   Ethical
   Fair
2. Courteous
   Personable
   Tactful
   Sincere
3. Fair-minded
4. Realistic opening position
5. Does not use threats
6. Willing to share information
7. Probes opponent's position

Aggressive Traits

1. Dominating
   Forceful
   Attacking
2. Plans timing and sequence of
      actions (strategy)
   Rigid
   Uncooperative
3. Carefully observes opponent
4. Unrealistic opening position
5. Uses threats
6. Reveals information gradually
7. Willing to stretch the facts

Traits Shared by Both Types of Effective Negotiators

1. Prepared on the facts
2. Prepared on the law
3. Observes the customs and courtesies of the bar
4. Takes satisfaction in using legal skills
5. Effective as a trial attorney
6. Self-controlled

also concerned with fairness. They are *self-monitors* who do not want to go beyond what would be fair to both sides.

By comparison, look at the upper right-hand corner of Figure 11.3, which shows the objectives of the effective aggressive negotiators: Their highest-rated motive is to "Maximize the settlement for the client," and then to "obtain a profitable fee" for themselves. This interests me, because another part of the questionnaire asked if they were greedy. They rated themselves as *not* greedy but very interested in making a lot of money for themselves. Now, there is a thin line between greed and a thirst for riches, and somehow effective aggressive negotiators manage to stay on the high side of that line.

Figure 11.4
Ineffective Legal Negotiators

COOPERATIVE STYLE
Cooperative Objectives

Same as Effective Cooperatives

Cooperative Traits
1. Trustworthy
   Ethical
   Fair
2. Trustful
3. Courteous
   Personable
   Sociable
   Friendly
4. Gentle
   Obliging
   Patient
   Forgiving
5. Intelligent
6. Dignifed
7. Self-controlled

AGGRESSIVE STYLE
Aggressive Objectives

Same as Effective Aggressives

Aggressive Traits
1. Irritating
2. Unreasonable opening position
   Bluffs
   Uses "take it or leave it"
   Withholds information
   Attacking
   Argumentative
   Quarrelsome
   Demanding
   Aggressive
3. Rigid
   Egotistical
   Headstrong
4. Arrogant
   Disinterested in others' needs
   Intolerant
   Hostile

Traits shared by both types of ineffective negotiators: None

But the most telling objective for effective aggressives is item number three: "Outdo or outmaneuver the opponent." Do you see the patterns emerging here? If you think about the terms *win-win* and *win-lose* negotiating, it seems that effective cooperatives epitomize the spirit of win-win negotiating; they want to get a good outcome for their client, but they want the other side to also feel that it got a good outcome as well. Cooperatives are quintessential win-win negotiators.

On the other hand, effective aggressive negotiators see it completely differently. Their attitude is this: "If all you want me to do is go around making everybody feel good about themselves, you don't need me. . . . It's not worth getting up in the morning for; it's not a serious objective." So they are win-lose negotiators: They want a clear winner and a clear loser. If the score is still tied, then the game's not over yet; you have to go into overtime.

• • • • •

Let me ask this question: Which is the better approach? In my opinion, they both have a place in the world of negotiation. As our study shows, experienced negotiators value both; both can be effective. So in general, our task is to accept the reality that both approaches are valid and both have their place. Of course, there is one more nagging issue, and it is this: Are they both equally effective in every situation? Or are there situations in which one of them will be less effective (or even crushingly so) and times when the reverse would be true? All of my experience tells me that there are differences in this respect, and that an important task for every negotiator is to learn to recognize these patterns, to understand how they operate, to know when they are likely to be productive and when counterproductive, and (most important) perhaps how to deal with opponents in each of the patterns.

Turning to Figure 11.4, a couple of things bear mentioning. One is that the objectives of ineffective negotiators as rated by their opponents are identical to the objectives of their effective counterparts, so they are trying to accomplish the same thing. The only variable is how they go about it. *It is what you do, not what you are trying to do, that becomes important.*

The second point is to *look for the defects in the ineffective cooperative negotiator's approach,* because people who are interested in dispute resolution tend to be cooperative, although this is not universally so. I suppose all of us wake up in a cold sweat occasionally, thinking, "I'm a marshmallow." Let us look at what makes marshmallows.

Look at cluster number one: Ineffective cooperatives are trustworthy, ethical, and fair. There is no weakness in any of these characteristics because they are true for effective cooperatives as well. If you, like me, aspire always to be ethical, trustworthy, and fair, we ought to stand up and shout "hurrah!" We can be these things and still be effective, although they cannot protect us against being ineffective.

Cluster two, ineffective cooperatives, are trustful. Therein lies a key to the overwhelming defect in ineffective cooperative negotiators. It is one thing to be trustworthy and to have people take you at your word no matter what, but it is quite another thing to be as trustful of the other side as you would like them to be of you. In every videotape we have made that has a cooperative versus an aggressive negotiator, trustfulness is the fatal weakness of the ineffective cooperative. In the dictionary, synonyms for *trustful* include words like *gullible, naive, easily exploited,* and so on.

Cluster three, ineffective cooperatives, are courteous, personable, sociable, and friendly. There is nothing wrong with these traits. They are also true of effective cooperatives.

Cluster four gives us another handle on ineffective cooperatives: They are gentle, obliging, patient, and forgiving. They never can be stirred up. It seems that no matter what happens, they are going to be polite and courteous and forgive you for what you do, and will try to get along with you.

Number five, they are intelligent. It is not out of brute stupidity that they do what they do.

Number six, they are dignified, as they give it all away. Number seven, they are self-controlled. Self-control also turns out to be a very important quality for effective negotiators of both types, so we will return to it.

Ineffective cooperatives are, in a manner of speaking, marshmallows. They are Casper or Casperina Milquetoast. I will admit that I was born and raised a Milquetoast. My mother would tear her hair out and say, "Gerry, I don't know the key to success in life, but I know the key to failure. And that is trying to please all of the people all of the time." It is the need to be loved and the belief that you have to be "nice" in order to be loved. No one can resist you if you are nice. This is the internal logic and personality dilemma of cooperatives.

•   •   •   •   •

The need-to-be-loved problem has never entered the consciousness of ineffective aggressives. Lawyers have a phrase for them: insufferably obnoxious. If you have dealt with somebody who is insufferably obnoxious, you know what it means. If you are normally a calm person who never raises your voice and 30 seconds into a telephone conversation you are screaming into the mouthpiece, you know you are dealing with an aggressive, ineffective person. You do not know what to do except shout back, because they are so outrageously irrational. They bring that out in a person.

One reason that ineffective aggressive negotiators are so obnoxious or irritating (the highest-rated characteristic laid out in cluster two) is that they make unreasonable opening demands or offers, even more extreme than their effective counterparts, and it is a pure bluff. They are affirmatively unprepared on the law and unprepared on the facts. With this in mind, it is easy to see why they are so irritating. As you see in cluster two, they adopt an unreasonable opening position and it is a bluff.

They use a take-it-or-leave-it strategy. When you ask them, "What have you got that makes this worth $5 million?" they will withhold information rather than tell you. Instead of giving you information, they will attack you for being stupid enough to ask. They are attacking, argumentative, quarrelsome, demanding, and aggressive.

In the third cluster, they are seen as rigid, egotistical, and headstrong. Now you begin to appreciate why effective negotiators get such a high rating on self-control. It requires a lot of self-control to deal with obnoxious opponents without losing your head.

Finally, the fourth cluster. Someone suggested that these symptoms border on a clinical condition; they are arrogant, disinterested in the needs of others, intolerant, and affirmatively hostile.

How many negotiators fit this description? According to our numbers, 8% of the practicing bar are insufferably obnoxious, at least when it comes to negotiating strategy. Judging from reactions of groups of businesspeople to these results, it appears that the 8% figure is not too far off for other occupational groups as well.

This is a snapshot of the characteristics of cooperative and aggressive negotiators. Of course snapshots are static; they freeze the action into a single moment in time. The best way to expand on our understanding of these patterns is to watch them in action, see how they unfold over time, and correlate the static descriptions with particular sequences of action in actual negotiations.

Based on the percentages of cooperative and aggressive negotiators we found in our research, there are three possible combinations of patterns in one-on-one negotiation:

1. Cooperative negotiator versus cooperative negotiator
2. Cooperative negotiator versus aggressive negotiator
3. Aggressive negotiator versus aggressive negotiator

It is possible to predict some general tendencies for each combination. The first combination, cooperative versus cooperative, is the most stable; if the problem can be solved, they will solve it. This is their common goal. The third combination, aggressive versus aggressive, is intriguing. In a way, you might expect a brawl. But this often is not the case; although there is a higher risk of breakdown and the negotiation will take longer and consume more resources, the negotiators do speak the same language and do understand one another. They are also perfectly capable of cooperating with one another if they are convinced that is the better way to proceed. So this is not a bad combination either. Now what about the second combination, cooperative versus aggressive? In my opinion, this combination is at the root of the majority of problems in negotiation, because these two negotiators do not speak the same language; they do not understand one another. They are operating on contrary assumptions.

Let us pursue this one step farther. As you can see from the empirical descriptions in Figure 11.3, cooperative negotiators are trustworthy, ethical, and fair; they want a fair outcome; they adopt realistic positions; they avoid the use of threats; they disclose the facts early; and they value the prospect of agreement. In other words, cooperatives are problem solvers. How do they solve problems? On the merits; their instincts are to lay the facts out on the table. If I am a cooperative negotiator and I lay out my facts, and if you are cooperative and you lay out your facts, then the two of us, as objective, fair-minded adults, can solve any problem. That is how cooperatives see their task. Against other cooperatives, this works very well. And since 65% of the negotiators in our study are basically cooperative, a cooperative will face another cooperative about 66% of the time.

But aggressive negotiators do not see themselves primarily as problem-solvers, at least not in the same sense as cooperatives. They are warriors. Their strategy assumes that the other side is an enemy to be attacked and defeated, and their strategy is well adapted to that end. They are dominating, forceful, and attacking; they adopt more extreme positions; they use threats; they are reluctant to reveal information; and they seek a victory over the other side.

Which is the better strategy? Of course, we all prefer our own. Cooperatives feel that their way is better; aggressives have no doubt it is their own. In my opinion, they are both wrong, because when you need a problem-solver or a healer, nothing else will quite do, and when you really need a warrior, it is also true that nothing

else will do. We cannot escape the reality that they are *both* legitimate and, in their time, indispensable. The question is not: Which strategy should I invariably use? but rather: *How can I develop sufficiently as a negotiator so that I can appropriately invoke one or the other, depending on the requirements of the situation?* I have come to believe that a fully developed negotiator should be capable of appropriately adopting either one in the proper circumstances.

In Figures 11.5 and 11.6, I have taken the descriptions of effective cooperative and effective aggressive negotiators and made lists showing how the patterns look when both sides remain true to their pattern in a negotiation against their opposite type. Surprising as it may seem, these two lists are good predictors of what will happen in initial encounters between cooperative and aggressive negotiators. The quality of the process and the outcome will depend on the ability of the two negotiators to diagnose the problem and appropriately adjust to compensate for it.

Highlighting some of the items in the figures, we see that the typical pattern that occurs when an aggressive attorney and a cooperative attorney negotiate against each other is that the aggressive negotiator looks more capable, and makes the negotiation a lot more interesting to watch. As you can see at the top of Figure 11.5, aggressives make high opening demands. Why doesn't it undermine their credibility? Of course, in many instances it does, but effective aggressives are smarter than that; they tend to be more subtle. They do not make all their demands at once. Instead, they test the waters and see how much they can get away with. Their demands often begin reasonably, then escalate over time. If they made those outrageous demands up front, they would be laughed at because they have not yet learned how much they can get away with. It would expose their hand.

Figure 11.5
The Aggressive Negotiator

A. Typical pattern against a trustful cooperative
   1. Made high demands (escalating over time)
   2. Stretch the facts (increasing over time)
   3. Outmaneuver the opponent (to look foolish, to lose)
   4. Use intimidation
   5. Make no concessions

B. Typical objectives of aggressive negotiators
   1. Intimidate the opponent
   Question: Why intimidate?
      Answer #1: Against cooperative opponent, maximize own gain and maximize opponent's losses
      Answer #2: Against aggressive opponent, reduce likelihood of exploitation and attack

C. Weaknesses or risks of the aggressive approach
   1. Creates tension, mistrust, and misunderstanding
   2. Fewer settlements (more cases go to trial)
   3. Lower joint outcome (lower joint gains)
   4. If taken too far, often provokes costly retaliation

Aggressive negotiators tend to move slowly and cautiously and they are outrageous only in proportion to how much trust is placed in them. Stretching the facts is a real dilemma. Most people, all cooperatives included, feel it is unethical to stretch the facts. In my experience, effective aggressives feel the same way, but they define their terms much differently, which gives them far more leeway than cooperatives feel is appropriate.

Aggressives seem to find satisfaction or meaning in outmaneuvering their opponents. Even though the aggressive in the *Cottonburger* videotape[3] does not crack a smile, he enjoys or takes satisfaction in his ability to take unanswered swipes against his opponent, and he systematically and repeatedly does this. To win by forcing the other party to look foolish and to get a miserable outcome or no outcome at all is often part of their agenda. They use intimidation, which comes in many varieties.

They try not to make any concessions. In this negotiation, the aggressive makes none at all.

Why do aggressives do what they do? Why do they operate in this way, and why do they continue their attack against opponents who are clearly being cooperative? I can imagine two objectives. One, against a cooperative opponent, an aggressive believes it serves his or her purposes in two ways: It maximizes their own gains, and it minimizes their opponents' gains. Axelrod's book *Evolution of Cooperations* really repudiates their belief in all except pure zero-sum situations. But it appears that something in the aggressive's worldview leads them to a contrary opinion. Second, and especially evident in foreign policy, aggressives recognize that one way to avoid being too soft is always to be hard negotiators; that way, they are never in danger of being too trusting. This saves them from the more difficult task of figuring out when and whom to trust.

The following characteristics held true for all cooperatives negotiating against aggressive opponents. The first was that they tend to make a fair, objective statement of the facts. Cooperatives do not build in a fudge factor; they do not start at one position and then move toward another one just for the effect. They think that

Figure 11.6
The Cooperative Negotiator

A. Typical pattern of cooperatives (against strong aggressives)
  1. Make fair, objective statement of facts
  2. Make reasonable demands
  3. Make repeated unilateral concessions
  4. Ignore intimidation and bluffing by opponent
  5. Accept opponent's factual representations without question

B. Objectives of cooperative negotiators
  1. Establish cooperative, trusting atmosphere
  2. Induce aggressive attorney to reciprocate, based on what I call the cooperative assumption:
     ▪ If I am fair and trustworthy and
     ▪ If I make unilateral concessions,
     ▪ Then the other side will feel an irresistible moral obligation to reciprocate

C. Weaknesses or risks of the cooperative approach
  1. Risk of exploitation (if aggressive fails to reciprocate)
  2. Risk of later overreacting to aggressive's unfairness

the facts. They tend to stay very close to what they really hope to get or to what their client is expecting.

Third, cooperatives tend to make repeated unilateral concessions—not reciprocated concessions, but unilateral concessions. They seem to want to rely on the principle of reciprocity. I'll come back to that in a moment.

Continuing down the list, cooperatives tend to ignore the intimidation and bluffing and huffing and puffing of their opponent. To a cooperative, smoke tactics are irrelevant: "So what if the other side doesn't trust my client. . . . We are mature objective adults. That doesn't get in our way." But to the aggressive opponent, this is a sign of weakness and vulnerability in their opponent, and they feel emboldened to increase their attack, to go for the jugular.

Fifth, cooperatives tend to accept their opponents' factual representations as the unquestionable truth.

The cooperative's underlying goal and their number one objective (based on the data) is to establish a cooperative, trusting atmosphere in which common interest and values are shared: "If there is a problem to solve, we can solve it. I trust you, you can trust me."

Putting these several items together, it is easy to see why you would negotiate this way against a cooperative opponent, but why would you behave this way against an aggressive opponent? Psychologists tell us that a very effective way to influence another's behavior is to *model* it; and it seems that cooperative negotiators in this situation are modeling the very behavior they wish to see in their opponents. Sociologists and anthropologists would probably say that cooperatives are invoking the principle of reciprocity, or mutual exchange, which is found in every human society. Cast in this light, the cooperative who follows this pattern of behavior against an aggressive opponent is relying on an unwritten,

the way to solve a problem is on the merits. They are eager to lay out all the facts as soon as they are given the opportunity. This gives an enormous advantage to aggressives who play the opposite strategy.

Second, cooperatives tend to make very reasonable demands, consistent with a fair statement of unspoken, and perhaps unconscious assumption along these lines:

> If I am fair and trustworthy, and if I make repeated unilateral concessions, then at some point in the negotiation process, the other side will recognize my good faith and will feel an irresistible moral obligation to reciprocate with concessions of comparable value.

This assumption is what makes cooperative negotiators so vulnerable to exploitation. And it shows why I feel the tit-for-tat strategy is an important step in the right direction. It is not, by any means, a complete solution, but it teaches cooperatives to be alert for aggressiveness and the need to do something about it.

VIDEOTAPE OF THE COTTONBURGER NEGOTIATION

According to an old proverb, what we hear, we forget; what we see, we remember; what we do, we master. Applied to the study of negotiation, it is not enough merely to hear about the patterns of cooperative and aggressive negotiators. To arrive at a common understanding of the vocabulary of cooperation and aggressiveness, and to gain an appreciation of how visible these patterns are when you watch for them, we need to see and discuss these patterns as they occur naturally among experienced negotiators.

As part of our research effort, we asked attorneys for the names of people they considered to be effective negotiators; then we contacted them and asked if they would be willing to come to Provo, Utah, and let us videotape them as they negotiated a case or transaction. We prepared the fact situations for use in these negotiations. Our goal was to learn what experienced negotiators actually do, and we gave them no instructions about how to negotiate. We said nothing about cooperation or aggressiveness or any other strategy. Our only instruction was this: Negotiate

on these facts just as you would if a real client were involved. In our first attempt, we videotaped six negotiations. By random chance, two of the six involved a cooperative negotiator against an aggressive opponent. The facts involved a new technology that allowed a high protein meat substitute to be made from cotton seed. Although it might sound farfetched, it is based on an actual technology.

We also wanted to avoid a situation I have seen many times before, where the two negotiators get together and decide in advance what they are going to do: We did not permit them to talk with one another until they were brought to the negotiating table and the cameras were running. Because they had no opportunity to feel each other out beforehand, they were forced to rely on their own assumptions. As a result, the negotiating dynamics are more dramatic than they would be in real life, because in real life the negotiators would not proceed until they had learned more about each other.

I say this because the two negotiators in the *Cottonburger* tape have solid reputations as exceptionally effective negotiators in their respective communities; I am certain they fully deserve those reputations. In the appropriate situation, I would be honored to be represented by either one. If negotiators of this high caliber can have a temporary blind spot in a spontaneous negotiation on videotape, so can you and I. So my advice is this: If anyone ever asks you to negotiate on videotape in a situation like this, you should absolutely refuse, because it is impossible to show your full abilities in this distorted setting. You cannot learn enough about one another in front of a camera to do justice to the situation.

To appreciate what happens in this negotiation, you need to know the underlying facts. Briefly, the case involves the sale of "cottonburger."

Cottonburger is a pseudonym for actual technology developed by a European scientist—a high-protein meat substitute made from cotton seed, which was very cheap at the time. It was developed by a scientist we have named Dr. Schwartz, of Switzerland. His goal is to make cottonburger available on a nonprofit basis in the protein-deficient developing nations—a very humanitarian goal. He plans to start in India and Nigeria (which at the time were the countries of greatest need). To do this, he needs to generate some income. His only sales to date have been in Europe, to elementary-level schools at 3 cents a pound. There is no prospect of other sales in Europe. The salespeople have beaten the pavement and no one seems to be interested. He has 100,000 pounds on hand in warehouses in Europe that need to be sold or they will have to be destroyed.

Because he is not making money in Europe, the U.S. market really becomes the key to his being able to carry his plan forward. The profits in the U.S. market are crucial. He does not have the know-how to produce it or market it himself in the United States, so he must find a good U.S. producer and distributor. He has found the right person, he believes, in a Mr. Jones of Chicago. As reflected in their correspondence to date and his instructions to his attorney, Mr. Schwartz is willing to offer the following terms and conditions: to grant an exclusive distributorship as an inducement to the distributor; to receive 12 cents a pound; to include protective provisions in the contract to protect the enzyme formula from being stolen; to come to the United States for 3 months or so to help set up production; to work half-time on his own product, which is a kind of ice cream (and he wants access to a good laboratory to work on that); and finally, to have three lab assistants available to help him. It turns out that an aggressive negotiator is representing him. Schwartz knows that Jones has very conservative political views, but this is not a problem for him and he deems it irrelevant.

Jones is a Chicago-based distributor of meat products. As reflected in Jones's correspondence with Schwartz and instructions to his attorney, these are the particulars: He wants to test-market cottonburger in the United States; he needs 50,000 pounds of cottonburger to run the test; he is offering 5 cents a pound, which is 2 cents over break-even for Schwartz, and he will pay the shipping costs; he wants Dr. Schwartz to come to the United States to help set up production of cottonburger (he feels Schwartz should stay 8 to 10 months); he is offering to pay $1,500 per month, plus travel expenses; and he (Jones) must have exclusive rights to distribute cottonburger in the United States (and he and Schwartz have already agreed to that).

There is a complicating factor, however. Jones would like to "steal" the formula and go into production independent of Schwartz. Although it might sound artificial, we built this complication into the facts to see how an experienced negotiator would deal with it. Of course, if Jones had this intention, he would not reveal it to counsel, so we put the information in the file as if by mistake. Then, we tried to give Jones a persona that would somewhat excuse his low standards in this matter.

As fate would have it, the person assigned to represent Jones is a true cooperative negotiator, and as you might suppose, cooperatives do not like to leave ethical dilemmas unresolved. His first duty, of course, would be to work this problem through with his client. But since this was a simulation and there was no actual client, what could he do? As is seen on the videotape, his solution is simply to inform the lawyer on the other side that Jones wants to learn to make the formula. His opponent, who is a tough-minded aggressive, hears the warning and proceeds to protect his client by building clauses into the proposed contract in order to prevent discovery of the formula and to prevent any unauthorized sales of cottonburger if the formula were discovered.

All that remains for these attorneys to do is work out the details of the issues given to them in their instructions. They both have general authority to resolve the issues anywhere within the parameters given there. We gave the negotiators absolutely no instructions about how to negotiate; we merely asked them to negotiate just as they would if they represented these two parties on these facts.

When you watch the *Cottonburger* videotape, you can observe how literally the behavior of the two negotiators is also anticipated by our research findings about cooperative and aggressive patterns. Compare the factual assertions of both negotiators with the facts they were given by their clients. This will give you a feeling for what it means when we say that cooperative negotiators are willing to share information, and that aggressive negotiators reveal information only gradually and are willing to stretch the facts.

In the videotape, viewers notice how, in this initial encounter between two skilled negotiators, they both made inaccurate initial assumptions about the other, and neither of them is able, under the pressure of a one-time negotiation on videotape, to diagnose and confront the problem. If this can happen to negotiators as experienced and highly regarded as these two, then no one is immune. It can happen to us all.

In my opinion, when negotiating against our opposite pattern, we also tend to make unfounded assumptions about the other that undercut our effectiveness with the negotiation process. A major challenge for negotiators of both types is to become much more conscious of their own patterns and assumptions, to be consistently more attentive to discerning their opponents' patterns, and to develop the ability to make continuous, appropriate adjustments to correct for these factors.

CONCLUSION

I will conclude with two final observations. In my opinion, the most important single statement by

the aggressive negotiator in *Cottonburger* is this:

> Let me indicate what I think are the essential items of any contract we're going to reach, without saying that if you reject all of them, or any one of them, that we can't continue to search this. I want to put this into a context of the kind of an arrangement that Jones can live with and still protect Schwartz's interest.

What is the aggressive negotiator saying here? Recall from the empirical data reported in Figure 11.3 that cooperative negotiators want to be fair. There is an internal, personal sense that I want to get a good outcome for my client, but within the limits of what would be fair to the other side as well. Cooperative negotiators are self monitors; they feel a responsibility to keep their demands within the limits of fairness or good faith.

By contrast, as the aggressive's statement clearly implies, aggressive negotiators have a completely different attitude. If I am an aggressive negotiator, I do not know all of the other side's facts, and since the other side is represented by able counsel, why should I try to impose limits? My task is to push the other side as far as it will go; it is up to them to stop me if I go too far. So aggressive negotiators are not self monitors; their strategy is to go as far as they can, and to shift the responsibility onto the other side to stop them when it hurts too much. In his statement, the aggressive feels he has adequately warned his opponent that he's playing by aggressive rules. But, in my opinion, the cooperative opponent fails to hear this warning, and continues to rely on the assumption that his opponent is monitoring his demands and keeping them within good faith limits of fairness. Otherwise, he would respond in a very different way to the escalating demands of his aggressive opponent.

The most important statement by the cooperative attorney came somewhat later in the negotiation, when the aggressive negotiator had laid out virtually all of his demands. There was a pause, and after a few seconds, the cooperative looked up at him and said, "Does that pretty well cover your points?"

This phrase offers a valuable insight into the cooperative's perception of the negotiation to this point. When he asks, "Does that pretty well cover your points?" he seems to be assuming that the escalating points or demands by the aggressive attorney are made in good faith, and that they would have come out the same way regardless of how he, the cooperative, reacted as he heard them. He does not see that his failure to react to the increasingly extreme demands creates an almost irresistible invitation to the aggressive attorney to continue escalating them. The cooperative attorney interprets his task relatively passively up to this point, receiving information about the good faith interests and needs of the other side. Unfortunately, his opponent interprets this as weakness and an opportunity to get a better deal for his client by escalating his demands to extreme proportions.

There is a temptation to say "It couldn't happen to me" rather than to grapple with the implications of these two inconsistent patterns. In my experience, no one is immune from the tensions created by the conflicting motives and strategies of these two dominant negotiating patterns, and we will all become more effective in proportion to our ability to appropriately respond to them.[5]

NOTES

1. For a description of the Q-Analysis, see Williams (1983, pp. 138–139).

2. There is a good reason for this. Actually, in each category, the Q-Analysis produced five or six distinct groups of negotiators, but only the first two groups had significant numbers of attorneys, so for convenience in discussing the results, I have been presenting the information as if Groups 3, 4, 5, and 6 were a single "third" group.

3. *Cottonburger,* made by Williams, is a videotaped negotiation session involving an aggressive negotiator and a cooperative negotiator, and is approximately one-half hour long. It can be purchased through the Program of Negotiation's Case Clearinghouse (see Appendix 11). There are also teaching notes available and accompanying text for classroom use. If you are using this chapter in a course, the students can be instructed to see the video and read the chapter afterward.

4. Axelrod (1984).

5. My current research suggests that cooperative and aggressive patterns are components or subcategories of two larger roles or functions in society, and that we must look to those larger functions for a more complete understanding of the significance of these strategies and their appropriate use on behalf of clients.

TODAY'S NEGOTIATOR

Ira G. Asherman and Sandy Asherman

INTRODUCTION

Few of us have the absolute power necessary to force others to do what we want. Therefore, we must negotiate with our co-workers, project team members, and representatives of government agencies, as well as with family and friends. We negotiate over roles and responsibilities; car and home purchases, job assignments, family chores, and government requirements.

The successful negotiation is one that reaches the *best* agreement—not just any agreement. It ensures that both parties have met their objectives and will live up to their commitments. Negotiation is a vehicle for problem-solving—nothing more and nothing less.

NEGOTIATION SUCCESS

Negotiation does not take place in a vacuum, but within the context of a relationship. What happened between us yesterday will affect what happens today, and what happens today will impact tomorrow. It is not necessary that we like each other, but rather that we trust each other. When people trust each other, the communication is likely to be more open, and the parties more willing to take risks with each other. In low-trust rela-

tionships, the parties are likely to be much more circumspect in what they say and do—they are risk-averse. There are many factors at play in the successful negotiation, but none as important as the degree of trust between the parties. As Dale Zand pointed out in a 1972 article on managerial problem-solving:

" . . . in low-trust groups, interpersonal relationships interfere with and distort perspectives of the problem. Energy and creativity are diverted from finding comprehensive realistic solutions. By contrast, in high-trust groups there is less socially-generated uncertainty, and problems are solved more effectively."

The remainder of this article looks at what negotiators must do to ensure success prior to the negotiation and during negotiation, and after it ends.

PRIOR TO THE NEGOTIATION

Most people just walk into a negotiation and fire away . . . However, it is crucial that you do your homework. "The trick is to acquire all the information concerning the issues involved, even ones [issues] you may not deem important at first glance," Bob Woolf wrote about his life as a negotiator.[2]

Preparation:

We suggest you start your planning by asking the following questions:

- What are your objectives?
- Are some objectives more important than others?
- What is your ideal settlement?
- What are your needs and interests?
- What will you accept if you can't achieve your primary objectives?
- Is there a point at which you'll decide it's not worth doing the deal?
- What concessions are you prepared to make?

The same questions should be asked of the other party. Walk in his or her shoes for a while:

- What do you think the other person needs to be able to say yes?
- What are the other person's needs and interests?
- What do you think will be influencing the other person?
- What do you believe is the other person's ideal settlement?
- Is there a point beyond which you think the other person will not go?

Several additional items should be included as part of the planning process:

Team negotiations

If you are negotiating as part of a team, it is critical to review how you plan to work together. Everyone on the team should have a role: e.g., observer, note-taker, spokesperson. You should also decide how to signal each other if things are not going well, or if you think something has been missed.

Cross-cultural issues

Americans tend to be insensitive to other cultures. If you are going to another country, it is critical that you understand the people and cultures. Not everyone sees the world through the unique American perspective. When negotiating with colleagues in other parts of the world, many Americans fail to consider the effect of culture and language differences. Although many of our international associates speak and write English, few can do it at the pace and tempo with which we are comfortable. Nor are they familiar with our idioms and colloquial expressions. This leads to a great deal of misunderstanding and confusion.

Clarifying authority

You must clarify the amount of authority you have in reaching an agreement. It is hard, if not impossible, to be effective at the bargaining table if your status as a negotiator has not been previously clarified with your significant other—be it spouse, boss, or co-worker. There is nothing more embarrassing than returning home or to the office and being told that the deal you worked so hard to achieve is not acceptable.

Put it in writing

Write down your plan's key points and take that summary with you to the negotiation.

DURING THE NEGOTIATION

Once negotiations begin, successful negotiators follow a rational process:

Climate-setting

Many people think climate-setting, where the process of building trust begins, means spending a few minutes on small talk—"how's the family" type of questions. Instead, climate-setting is where you and the other party set the tone for the entire negotiation, be it friendly or serious.

The physical aspects of climate-setting can be as important as what you say. Where you negotiate and how you greet the other person send a strong message. The objective is to set an atmosphere that says, "I'm someone you can trust. We're in this together; this is something we'll handle successfully." Climate-setting is particularly important in new relationships.

Clarifying issues

The next important step is identifying the issues and outlining the problems to be solved. All too frequently, people neglect to identify the issues and rush from small talk directly to bargaining. Clarifying issues sets the agenda for the meeting and provides a strong anchor for the negotiation —it gives the negotiation a center.

The following guidelines will assist you in defining the issues under discussion:

- Encourage the other party to share his or her issues.

- Listen and don't interrupt.

- Be prepared to discuss your own issues, needs, and interests.

- Summarize all the issues before you move into the bargaining stage.

You set the framework for a more open, rational process when the issues are clearly identified and both parties work to build a joint agenda. The temptation to begin bargaining as soon as an issue is listed is strong. You should resist this temptation and continue to list issues. Once all the issues are listed, there will be more room to find answers both parties can be comfortable with. When time is of the essence or the issues are particularly complex, issue identification can be enhanced through the use of e-mail or faxes before the parties meet.

Finding a solution

The primary objective of any negotiation is to achieve a mutually satisfactory solution both parties can support. However, many negotiators are so focused on what they want that they don't take the time to ask questions so they can understand the issues, interests, and needs of the other party. Instead, both parties try to sell each other on their respective points of view. They argue about whose position is right, rather than exploring the problem and trying to understand where the other party is coming from. It is important to remember that the other side believes they, too, are right. The goal is to determine why they believe they are right, and see if a new definition of "right" can be found. Throughout the problem-solving phase, successful negotiators work hard to avoid position bargaining and are willing to share their needs and interests—and to understand those of the other party.

We have found that good negotiators:

1. Clarify. To make sure they fully understand what is being said (both the words and feelings), negotiators clarify to ensure that there will be no misunderstandings.

2. Summarize. Good negotiators frequently summarize important points to make sure there is mutual understanding and agreement throughout the negotiation.

3. Propose and seek solutions. Once the nature of the issue is clearly understood, good negotiators are willing to take some risks and offer suggestions or solutions to solve the problem. Conversely, these negotiators encourage the other party to offer potential solutions. If the trust level is high enough, this can be an extremely rich process.

4. Ask questions. In an effort to clarify the issues and understand the needs and interests of the other party, good negotiators are active interviewers. In a very subtle way, they are able to control the negotiation through their questioning.

5. Actively listen. Good negotiators listen carefully to ensure that what is being said is fully understood, and they rarely interrupt.

Put it in writing

At the end of the negotiation, it is very important to take the time to reiterate what each side has agreed to accomplish. Failure to summarize the agreement and put it into writing frequently leads to confusion and disagreement during the implementation phase. We suggest you include in this summation the action steps both sides will complete when they leave the room.

AFTER THE NEGOTIATION

In this phase, successful negotiators work hard to meet their commitments, and make sure the other party is informed of any problems that arise. As a result, there are no surprises, and the relationship is reinforced.

SUMMARY

Becoming a good negotiator does not happen as if by magic. It is a procedure that takes time, effort, and practice. However, we believe you can radically improve your skills by attending to each of the steps outlined above. Following these steps will increase the potential that you will achieve a solution both parties can support.

NOTES

1. Zand, Dale E. Trust and managerial problem-solving. *Adminstrative Science Quarterly* 7 (June 1972): 238.

2. Woolf, Bob. *Friendly persuasion: My life as a negotiator.* New York: Putnam, 1990, page 63.

Ira and **Sandy Asherman** are management consultants who specialize in the issues and problems of the pharmaceutical industry, most typically working with the clinical research, project management, and regulatory affairs functions.

THE ART OF NEGOTIATION: AN ESSENTIAL MANAGEMENT SKILL

David Kuechle

The art of negotiation may be the most important skill possessed by today's successful executive. Each year businesses are confronted with more and more situations where negotiating skills are needed, and these involve executives at all levels of an organization. Now, with the proliferation of social legislation and accompanying regulatory agencies, there is increased need to deal with bureaucrats, politicians, lobbyists, citizen groups, community leaders, other business executives, field investigators, mediators, arbitrators, fact finders, and members of the judiciary. Traditional forms for resolving conflicts such as courts and legislatures and union-management grievance procedures are often too cumbersome or ill-equipped to deal with today's conflicts: Many cut across traditional jurisdictional lines and involve a great number of parties, with and without official statutes. Conflicts are rarely resolved by decree these days. In our judicial system, for example, over 90 percent of all cases are resolved by negotiation. Most disputes involving businesses and governmental and regulatory agencies are resolved through negotiation.

From *Business Quarterly*, Summer 1980. Reprinted with permission. All rights reserved.

We now know that in some settings a lack of negotiating skills is responsible for disputes that threaten the survival of an organization or even an industry. The U.S. coal industry provides an example: Coal is the cheapest and most immediate source of alternate energy in the U.S., but the industry is in the throes of creeping paralysis because of a staggering number of work stoppages brought about by wildcat strikes. Most of these stem from grievances that have festered too long without resolution. During one contract period between the United Mineworkers and the U.S. bituminous coal companies, approximately 2,700 grievances per year were arbitrated. There were 160,000 miners working under the contract, so this meant that 1.69 cases were arbitrated per 100 miners yearly.[1] By contrast, the arbitration rate was 1.5 cases per year per 10,000 employees under the General Motors 1950–1958 contracts with the United Auto Workers.[2] The cost of arbitration to the mineworkers' union and industry between September, 1975 and August, 1977 was estimated to be $4 million, split equally between the two. The average time elapsing between filing a grievance and ultimate determination by an arbitrator ranged from 138 days to 204 days.

Similarly disturbing statistics have shown up in other forums for dispute resolution. The Equal Employment Opportunities Commission (EEOC), which is charged in the United States with dispute-settling responsibilities under the Civil Rights Act, has a backlog exceeding 200,000 cases, some dating back as far as 1970. The U.S. court system is similarly bogged down. A recent case involving Yeshiva University in New York City was decided by the U.S. Supreme Court on February 20, 1980. This had been in the court system since October 17, 1977, following hearings and various appeals before the National Labor Relations Board that started in May of 1974. Judges in courts, labor arbitrators, and heads of governmental agencies agree, without dissent, that most cases they hear might have been settled much earlier at a lower step in the dispute-settling procedure if meaningful negotiation had taken place.

Considerable attention has been devoted in recent years to processes by which outsiders such as mediators and arbitrators help parties reach agreement. In addition, more attention is being paid to applying game theory to practical problems in order to aid settlement. In one example, game theory applied by a mediator helped resolve a dispute between five communities regarding the location of a nuclear power plant. All five communities wanted to receive the benefits of lower-cost electricity, which had been promised upon completion of the plant. None, however, wanted the plant to be located near them. A mutually-selected mediator proposed that all five communities submit sealed bids to pay for construction of the plant. It was understood in advance that the plant would be awarded to the community making the second-lowest bid at the price of the lowest bid—the cost to be shared by the four communities where the plant would not be located. Presumably, this idea would be satisfactory to all. The plant would be built at the lowest cost that any community was willing to spend, and it would be built in a place

where resistance, as reflected by the bids, was relatively low, but at no cost to that community.

The plan seemed to provide an attractive solution, but its success depended on all parties to the exercise becoming gamblers willing to take certain risks in hopes of maximizing their personal rewards. If any party had been risk-averse (not a gambler) this might have ruined the plan. Structural devices such as this and outside agents such as mediators and arbitrators might help resolve a dispute, but they do not generally help develop negotiation skills and, for the most part, it is negotiation skills that are likely to bring about resolution of conflicts without the need for outside assistance. Few attempts have been made to study the negotiating *process*—to identify strategies and skills that are most likely to produce settlements satisfactory to the parties, with minimal expenditure of time, money, and risk of warfare. This article attempts to do that.

Three case studies are presented, two from industry and one from international relations. The latter, involving the Iranian crisis, had not been resolved when this article was written. The other two had been resolved, and all parties expressed satisfaction with the results. In studying the two examples of successful negotiations, we will identify the ingredients of success and judge whether these ingredients have transfer value to other settings. Do they, for example, offer a way to understand as well as settle hostage disputes such as the one in Iran?

DEFINITION OF THE TERM "NEGOTIATION"

For our purposes, the term "negotiation" is defined as follows: *Negotiation is the art of securing agreement between two or more parties, each of whom usually wants to get more than she/he has and to yield less than the other party would like.* Its essence is the reluctant exchange of commitments by those who have less than 100 percent trust in one another. It is at the same time an exercise in conflict and compromise, and it depends for its success on parties who believe they can gain more by working together than by remaining apart.

Meaningful negotiation almost always involves parties who are either relating to each other in the context of a continuing relationship or are conducting an initial transaction that is likely to mark the beginning of a longer term relationship. It is not our purpose here to deal with negotiations of a single-transaction nature such as purchasing a rug in a Middle Eastern market, here both parties walk away from the bartering encounter with little prospect of seeing each other again.

Case Number 1:
Commonwealth Paper Company*

Commonwealth Paper Company is an integrated paper products firm with operations throughout Canada, ranging from New Brunswick to British Columbia. Near St. Stephen, New Brunswick, across the border from Calais, Maine, the company has a medium-sized mill wherein various grades of paper are produced. These range from fancy rag-content bonds to newsprint. In 1977, the company decided to purchase five new paper-making machines, one each year starting in 1979, and each worth over $2.5 million. These machines would be highly automated, with sophisticated computer-programmed control mechanisms. One person, highly trained in the technology involved in operating the machines, would replace all five people required to operate an existing machine. Once installed, the machines would allow for a three-fold increase in paper-making capacity.

Workers in the St. Stephen mill were represented by the United Papermakers Union, and when the decision to buy the new machines was made in 1977, the union and management negotiated provisions in their collective agreement to deal

* The company's name is disguised.

with the changes. One such provision called for employees selected to operate the machines to undergo an exacting training program. They would be taught some basic electronics circuitry, and they would learn something of computer programming during their training. They would also be taught how to make adjustments and repairs if the sophisticated control apparatus failed. Upon satisfactory completion of the program, they would qualify to operate the large, new machines.

Under the new labor agreement, operators of the new machines would be called paper machine operators A. Their pay rate would be 20 percent higher than paper machine operators B, who would act as lead hands for the old machines until all were replaced. The parties also agreed that there would be two other lower paid operator classifications, C and D. Persons classified as C or D would be helpers on the old machines. All the B, C, and D positions would eventually be eliminated.

In setting up the new operator classifications, the company and union negotiators agreed that workers should generally move from Class D to C, B, and A classifications. The union wanted movement to be automatic, based on years of service. The company insisted that those who graduated into the B and A categories should pass competency tests and, in the case of the A category, these would be especially rigorous. Eventually the parties reached an agreement that provided that operators would move from one classification to another after one year of experience in each, provided they could meet certain competency requirements for the next grade. These requirements would be jointly agreed upon by the company and union. Employees could grieve if they felt the requirements were not applied fairly. The parties also agreed that failure to move from one classification to the next would result in reassignment to another job in the mill, if it were available, or dis-

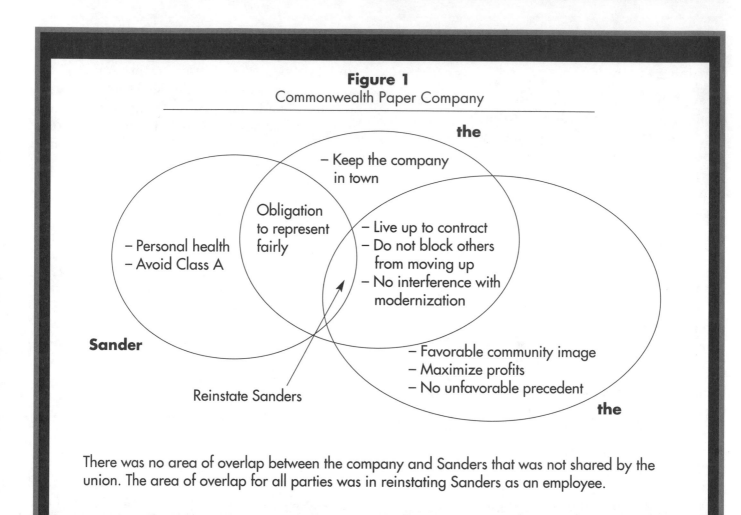

Figure 1
Commonwealth Paper Company

There was no area of overlap between the company and Sanders that was not shared by the union. The area of overlap for all parties was in reinstating Sanders as an employee.

missal if it were not. No one could elect to stay in a certain class, and no one could regress to a lower class upon failure to pass the competency test. These features were designed to ensure that the bottom ranks of the operator classifications would not become clogged with people who didn't have the desire or ability to move up—thus blocking others from these opportunities and thwarting or delaying the company's modernization program.

In 1979, following installation of the first new machine, the union filed a grievance. It seems that one of their members—John Sanders, a paper-machine operator B—had become eligible for assignment to the A classification. He had undergone training and passed the competency test, but he had refused the A classification when the company assigned him to the new machine. He said he was afraid of the machine and did not want the responsibility for dealing with a piece of equipment where one mistake on his part could cause millions of dollars worth of damage. He wanted to stay on as a Class B operator. Sanders' foreman sought to find other work in the mill for him, without success. There were no openings, and there was no opportunity for him to bump into another classification of work. According to the union-management contract, Sanders could not stay in his old classification. So he was given notice of discharge, and filed a grievance.

The grievance went through all steps of the contract's procedures and was eventually heard by the Industrial Relations Director. Company representatives acknowledged that Sanders was an excellent employee with an unblemished work record. They also shared with the union a concern that if Sanders was discharged, there would be adverse reactions in the community. St. Stephen is not a large town, and opportunities for alternative employment are scant. Nevertheless, company representatives argued that the contract was clear, and if they made an exception for Sanders, they would set a precedent which, in a few years, *could* result in the possession of five new paper machines and no one to operate them. For these reasons, the Industrial Relations Director rejected the grievance—upholding Sanders' discharge. The union appealed to arbitration, and the case was heard on April 26, 1977, in St. Stephen. The issue, agreed upon by the parties, was the following:

Was John Sanders discharged for just cause?
If not, what remedy shall apply?

During opening statements by each of the two parties, it became apparent that the facts were not in dispute. It also was apparent that the company did not want to discharge Sanders—that they were uncomfortable in circumstances that they did not anticipate.

During its opening statement, the union introduced a letter signed by a psychiatrist in Calais, Maine that indicated that John Sanders had visited that psychiatrist a week earlier. According to the letter, Sanders should not be required to operate the new paper-making machine; the doctor indicated that this increased responsibility would raise anxieties in Sanders that could cause serious medical complications for him.

On hearing this, the company's Industrial Relations director said: "If we had known *that*, we might have made other arrangements." The arbitrator thereupon called the Industrial Relations Director and the union's representative aside and asked if the parties wanted to try settling the matter in some other way. The Industrial Relations director said he would be willing to explore negotiation, but that he was skeptical. He said he had no knowledge of the psychiatrist who had written the letter. Nor was there evidence that the psychiatrist had ever seen the inside of a paper mill. The letter indicated that the psychiatrist had made a judgment based solely on what Sanders had told him, and the company representative said this was not sufficient to warrant an exception to the contract language. The union representative then asked whether the company would be willing to reconsider its position if a competent medical authority agreeable to all parties certified in writing (after looking at the operation and examining Sanders further) that assignment to the job could cause serious medical damage. The Industrial Relations director said he would talk to the mill superintendent and report back. About two hours later he returned and said he might consider making an exception under certain circumstances.

For the rest of the day, the arbitrator acted as mediator—going from one party to the other trying to forge a settlement. He accompanied the union's spokesman back to the hearing room, where union representatives and Sanders waited. The mediator assured them that the company did not want to fire Sanders, but said that the company representatives wanted to be sure they did not set a precedent wherein the new machines might not be manned by qualified operators. He also related the company's reservations about the psychiatrist's letter, which was dated April 20—only six days before: If there was a medical problem, why hadn't they known about it earlier? Sanders, in response to that question, said he should have gone to the doctor earlier, because he was aware for a long time that he got very nervous thinking about the new job, that it caused him to lose sleep, and that he couldn't hold food in his stomach. He said his wife had finally forced him to get medical attention when he was notified of discharge. Before that, he had hoped for another form of settlement.

The mediator related this information back to company representatives, and after several hours the parties finally reached an agreement: Sanders would be reinstated temporarily as a machine operator B. Meanwhile, competent medical counsel, agreeable to all parties, would be asked to visit the workplace. In addition, Sanders would be examined by the doctor and if, in the doctor's opinion, physical or mental harm would be likely upon assignment to the machine, the doctor would be asked to indicate that in writing. The same person who had examined Sanders earlier could be employed, provided that he was a member of the American Psychiatric Association, was affiliated with a recognized hospital and/or university, and was approved by the parties.

The company would make an exception for Sanders under these conditions. He could stay on as a machine operator B as long as his seniority allowed and as long as he did not block the upward movement of others. But the Industrial Relations director wanted written assurance from the union that this was an exception and that it would not be used as a precedent for future situations where people might not wish to operate one of the new machines. The union representatives happily signed the agreement. All parties left that day expressing satisfaction. No one won; no one lost. They had worked out their own settlement.

Case Number 2: Pegasus Chemical Company*

Pegasus Chemical Company is located in southwestern Ontario. During the 1970s many chem-

* The company's name, names of people in the company, and dates are disguised.

ical companies in Canada and the United States were under attack from environmentalists, citizen groups, the media, and politicians for allegedly pumping pollutants into nearby lakes and streams, for emitting noxious gases into the atmosphere, and for burying caustic chemical wastes in surrounding land areas. As of 1976, Pegasus, one of the smaller companies in the industry, had largely escaped criticism, but its president, Frank Spitzer, knew that his company's time was coming—that government regulations would force installation of pollution-control equipment, and that penalties for failure to comply could be serious. Of at least equal concern to Spitzer was the possibility that the company's image would worsen—that adverse publicity would cost it millions of dollars worth of harassment and, possibly, lost sales. At the outside, they might be forced to close operations.

One of Pegasus' bright young engineers, John Hoffer, had been hired three years earlier by Mr. Spitzer to work as a staff assistant in the line organization. Hoffer had an inventive mind, and this, coupled with high social consciousness, caused him to spend considerable time developing a process whereby electro-chemical reactors would treat waste liquids before they were dumped into a nearby lake, eliminating virtually all of their noxious properties. The idea was radical, but if it worked on a large scale, it could essentially stop all pollution by Pegasus through liquid wastes. Hoffer had developed and demonstrated the process on a small scale and, but for a few bugs that could be expected on any new process, it seemed to work well. The idea might even have commercial value for sale to others.

Hoffer was staff assistant to Charles Bednarek, the Vice-President of Production for the company's Industrial Chemicals Division. Bednarek encouraged Hoffer in his work and even tapped the budget for $50,000 to pay for the demonstration project. Hoffer worked closely with Robert Davidson, the local plant manager, in the project's design and construction. Then, after a

FIGURE 2
Pegasus Chemical Company

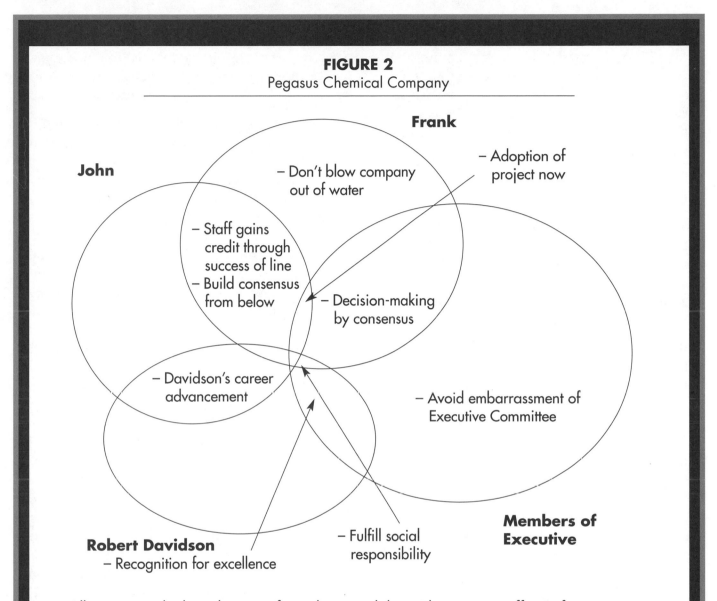

– All parties touched on objective of social responsibilities. This was not sufficient for agreement.

– All *essential* parties to settlement eventually agreed on adoption of the project. Davidson was not a participant in the final settlement.

series of successful experiments, he proposed that the company construct a full-scale treatment plant. The estimated cost was $3.5 million. Bednarek resisted. He pointed out that the process was not needed yet, that no pressure had been put on the company to control these wastes, and that other larger companies were depositing far more pollution-causing chemicals into the lake than Pegasus. Bednarek expressed doubt that environmental regulations would ever require the high level of control that Hoffer's process provided. "When and if environmental regulations come down on us," said Bednarek, "we will have sufficient time to install all the necessary equipment. Meanwhile, we can use the $3.5 million for other things that are more important."

Hoffer, an impatient young man, was angry. He believed the company should adopt the process immediately—that they had a social responsibility to stop polluting their surroundings and that it did not matter what others were doing or whether government regulations were imminent. He knew from his earlier associations with the division's general manager that a corporate decision to spend as much as $3.5 million had to be approved by the company's Executive Committee. This committee, consisting of the four divisional vice-presidents and seven general managers, made recommendations to the president. The president, in turn, would approve such a project if at least two of the vice-presidents and the relevant general manager were in favor, and if he could answer "no" to the following two questions:

1. Could the proposal "blow the company out of the water" or cause bankruptcy or destruction?

2. Does the proposal represent a change in corporate strategy?

If more than one division would be involved, the president had one additional question:

Have all who would be affected approved?

If the answer to this question was "yes," the president would give the go ahead, and the appropriate people would be directed to implement it. The Hoffer proposal would affect two divisions: Industrial Chemicals and Fertilizers.

Knowing that Bednarek opposed spending the money and knowing that the president would not give approval unless Bednarek, Paul Oliviera (the vice-president of the Fertilizer Division), and the general manager of the plan were in favor, Hoffer set out to gain the backing of all three men. He conferred with President Spitzer first and learned that Spitzer himself favored the project, but that he would not say so publicly. Spitzer then directed Hoffer to go out and negotiate with the relevant Executive Committee members, cautioning him that any mention of his having already conferred on the subject with the president—thus attempting to apply downward organizational pressure—would destroy prospects for the project and would result in Hoffer's own dismissal from the company. While he was interested in the project, Spitzer said he was more interested in Hoffer's own ability to fit in with the company's system of management. "I don't believe in rule by fiat," said Spitzer. "Consequently, your job is to build consensus among members of the organization so they will apply appropriate pressure on me, the president." He told Hoffer than an essential element for getting ahead in the organization was to develop competence in "managing your boss."

The situation was resolved in the following manner: Hoffer contacted Robert Davidson, the plant manager, who had worked with Hoffer on the experimental project. Davidson shared Hoffer's belief that the project should be converted into a full-fledged company commitment, and he was convinced by Hoffer that a written document from him (Davidson) to the general manager, his immediate superior, and Charles Bednarek, the relevant vice-president, reporting on the success of the experiment would be useful to his own career, inside or outside of Pegasus. Hoffer, as a staff assistant, would help Davidson develop the report—augmenting it with scientific data and including material on legal responsibilities and possible penalties against the company if they delayed implementing the project.

Subsequently, Hoffer approached Paul Oliviera, vice-president of the Fertilizer Division, and shared economic data that showed how the project would serve the needs of both his and the Industrial Chemicals Division. He also showed him projections of figures from possible sales of the process to others. Hoffer had learned from Oliviera's subordinates that he would generally support a project if he believed there would be no adverse consequences to himself personally. To be the only Executive Committee member in favor of something would be embarrassing to Oliviera. Likewise, it would be embarrassing to Oliviera if a matter concerning two divisions was raised in the Executive Committee and the vice-presidents involved were not in agreement— either for or against the project.

Hoffer told Oliviera about Bednarek's objections to spending the $3.5 million, but he also told him about Davidson's report, which would be forthcoming. The report would deal with each of Bednarek's objections—not labeling them as such—and, according to Hoffer, would give overwhelming factual data to overcome the objections. Oliviera, knowing about Hoffer's favorable reputation as a careful and astute scientist (and aware of the fact that the president had hired Hoffer), expressed enthusiasm.

Hoffer did not approach Bednarek on the subject again. Rather, he encouraged Davidson to deliver the report, when completed, to both Bednarek and Oliviera—then to make appointments to see them in order to answer their questions about it. Meanwhile, Hoffer would work on David Hannigan, the general manager of Opera-

tions, who was likely to be supportive. He would also continue to operate as Davidson's consultant, but would remain in the background, allowing Davidson to take full credit for the proposal. Hoffer's satisfaction would come when Davidson received praise from his superior, from Bednarek, and, possibly, from Oliviera. Hoffer hoped that Bednarek would receive a call directly from Oliviera, who would at least convince Bednarek with enthusiasm that the report should be submitted to the Executive Committee for its consideration, suggesting that the initial $3.5 million outlay would be cheap compared to the inflated costs that would almost certainly be encountered later.

There was no time deadline put on any part of this campaign. Hoffer maintained a low profile throughout—creating conditions so that others could identify and focus on shared objectives— then work toward them. Bednarek, after hearing from Davidson and Oliviera, wrote a guarded memorandum to the president, stating that while he supported the plan, he viewed with alarm the consequences of spending $3.5 million now when the money might be used for other worthy purposes. Davidson's report then went to Spitzer, along with Bednarek's memorandum. Spitzer praised it and, in a letter prepared by Hoffer (carbon copy to Bednarek), wrote to Davidson complimenting him on an expert research job. The anti-pollution project was approved without dissent at the next Executive Committee meeting.

Case Number 3: the Iranian Crisis

When this case was written, 50 Americans were being held hostage in the United States Embassy in Teheran by a group of Iranian militants who professed loyalty to the Ayatollah Khomeini. The militants took over the U.S. Embassy on November 4, 1979, following information that the deposed Shah of Iran, who had been living in exile in Mexico, was admitted to a New York hospital for treatment of cancer. The militants felt that they had been betrayed by the United States. Earlier, following the Iranian revolution and the return of Khomeini as leader of the revolutionaries, the U.S. had publicly expressed support for the Ayatollah. When the U.S. admitted the Shah to the country on Nov. 4, militant Iranians came to believe that the United States supported *him* and might help him regain the throne.

The Shah was despised by supporters of the revolution. During his regime he had encouraged development of Iran's oil-producing capacity until the country was exporting 6 million barrels a day. The resulting income was more than Iran needed, so over $30 million went to the Imperial Court for the "glory of the monarchy."[3] Those who opposed the Shah for his extravagance, among other reasons, suffered. His was said to be one of the most violent regimes in the history of mankind. The Shah and his followers engaged in terrorism, alleged violations of human rights, and cruelty to his own people that had few parallels. And during his days of power, he was supported by the U.S.

Immediately following the takeover of the U.S. Embassy, many Americans expressed outrage toward the militants and toward Khomeini, who publicly backed them. Americans, by and large, saw no connection between the Shah's admission to a New York hospital and the militants' action. The militants demanded return of the Shah to Iran for trial. U.S. officials said that this was impossible. Then both Iran and the U.S. resorted to judicial and international forums to develop support for their positions. The government of Iran filed suit in New York State Supreme Court seeking an accounting from the Shah of funds in his possession. The suit also sought a temporary injunction to prevent movement of those funds. The U.S., on the other hand, sought assistance from the United Nations Security Council and the International Court of

Justice. On December 4, the Security Council unanimously adopted a resolution "urgently" demanding that Iran immediately release the American hostages. Then, on December 15, the International Court in The Hague—also in a unanimous opinion—ordered that Iran immediately release all American hostages.

In spite of these actions, the hostages stayed behind embassy walls in Iran, and the Shah stayed in New York. When the Shah finally left the U.S. for Panama on December 15, the hostages were not released. A spokesman for the militants, upon hearing about the Shah's departure, said that "spy trials" for the 50 hostages would be held.

Having been unsuccessful in the United Nations and the International Court of Justice in securing release of the hostages, the United States moved to seek economic sanctions among U.N. members against Iran. In addition, President Carter dispatched naval forces to the Indian Ocean in a show of military strength, and he ordered deportation of all Iranians in the United States who did not have valid visas. Meanwhile, U.N. Secretary General Kurt Waldheim asked the U.S. to delay any economic or military action while he sought to mediate the dispute, and the United States agreed.

On January 24, 1980, the 81st day of captivity for the hostages, Abolhassin Bani-Sadr, formerly the Foreign Minister and Minister of Finance and Economy for Iran, was elected president. Bani-Sadr, a supporter of the Ayatollah, was supported in the election by 70 percent of the voters. The day after the election, the Ayatollah suffered a mild heart attack, so Bani-Sadr acquired some unexpected interim power. Then, in early February, Bani-Sadr was given control over Iran's military forces. He seemed to represent a moderating force, calling the militants a group of children who represented an intolerable "government within the government."

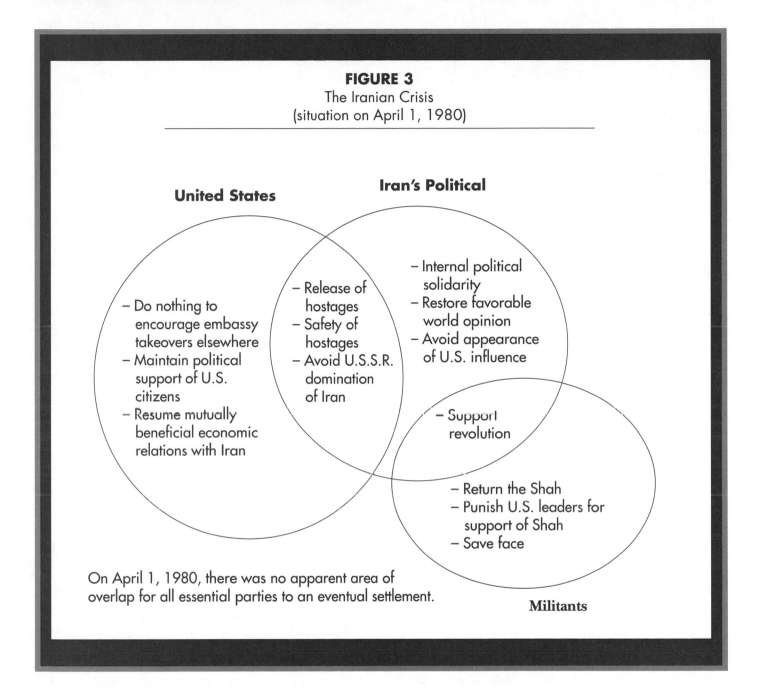

FIGURE 3
The Iranian Crisis
(situation on April 1, 1980)

United States

Iran's Political

- Do nothing to encourage embassy takeovers elsewhere
- Maintain political support of U.S. citizens
- Resume mutually beneficial economic relations with Iran

- Release of hostages
- Safety of hostages
- Avoid U.S.S.R. domination of Iran

- Internal political solidarity
- Restore favorable world opinion
- Avoid appearance of U.S. influence

- Support revolution

- Return the Shah
- Punish U.S. leaders for support of Shah
- Save face

On April 1, 1980, there was no apparent area of overlap for all essential parties to an eventual settlement.

Militants

Waldheim, working behind scenes, had been able to talk to Iran's policy-making Revolutionary Council in early January, but was unable to arrange a meeting with the Ayatollah. However, he had better luck with Bani-Sadr. On February 19, following meetings between Bani-Sadr and Waldheim, a U.N. panel was established and approved by Bani-Sadr to inquire into the activities of the deposed Shah. Bani-Sadr had apparently given his word that the hostages would be released in return. The panel began its work on February 25, and there was apparent agreement between Bani-Sadr (backed by Khomeini) and Waldheim that the hostages would be transferred to the custody of the Revolutionary Council. However, on March 9 the militants refused to turn them over to Foreign Minister Sadegh Ghotbzadeh. Subsequently, they refused to let the U.N. panel members meet with the hostages. So the panel members departed from the country, and the situation was still unresolved, with little prospect of solution until the election of a new parliament, scheduled to take place over the next two months.

On March 24, the Shah left Panama on a chartered jet for Egypt, where he would undergo a second operation for cancer. He would most probably remain in that country indefinitely. This move frustrated efforts by Iranian officials to serve him with extradition papers and served to complicate matters still further.

As of April 1, the hostages were still being held. Americans, becoming more agitated, were urged by Secretary-General Waldheim to remain patient. The negotiation process was extremely delicate, and a wrong move could be disastrous. From the viewpoint of the U.S., there was a desire to obtain safe release of the hostages without giving the impression to the world that they gave in to pressure—lest they stimulate embassy takeovers elsewhere. For the Iranian leaders, it was a matter of restoring world-wide favor, which had turned so severely against them, and, at the same time, to avoid confrontation with the militants—who expressed resolve not to give up the hostages unless the Shah was returned. The militants were apparently looking for a way to save face, but it was not clear when, or under what circumstances, the hostages would be released.

ANALYSIS

When this article was written, the Iranian crisis had not been resolved. President Bani-Sadr, apparently speaking for a significant faction in Iran that wanted to end the ugly episode and restore the country's international standing,

expressed frustration. He said the militants had been manipulated by Communists working to isolate Iran from the world community, and he accused his own Revolutionary Council of "weakness" and "indecision." As elections for parliament were proceeding, militant clergy-supported candidates seemed to be getting the most votes, signaling that Bani-Sadr's power might be waning.

The two other cases cited here—one involving John Sanders of Commonwealth Paper Company and the other involving John Hoffer of Pegasus Chemical Company—were resolved satisfactorily. Are there elements of success in the Commonwealth and Pegasus cases that have transfer value to Iran and other settings? What can we learn from these cases about the art of negotiation?

Certain elements are common to all three instances. Most important among these are the following:

- More than two parties were involved in each.

- All parties had reason to want to continue their relationships.

- There were no deadlines imposed.

- Primary objectives of the principal parties were different.

- Some objectives held by the principal parties overlapped.

- Settlements were obtained when all parties shared some objectives.

The three situations can be illustrated graphically by using partially overlapping ovals—each illustrating the principal objectives of the parties. (See Figure 1, 2, and 3.) The areas of overlap are those that contain objectives shared by more than one party or group. Areas outside the overlap contain objectives held only by the party or group described. The areas where all ovals overlap are those that provided a focal point toward which settlement efforts were aimed. By April 1,

1980, there was no overlap of ovals representing the major parties to the Iranian crisis, and this helps explain why that situation was still unsolved.

The diagrams demonstrate that settlement of complex disputes requires negotiators who work toward creating areas of overlap for all the principal parties. There are three essential steps in this process:

1. *Identify all of the major objectives of each party.* Most often the parties will be able to state some of these, but the effective negotiator moves beyond the obvious to identify objectives that might be unstated, and to clarify those that are not clear.

2. *Place the objectives in categories:* Those that are essential for settlement and not subject to compromise, and those that are desirable but subject to compromise, or, possibly, to being dropped.

3. *Identify those objectives that are shared by more than one party, and those that are not.* The figures indicate shared objectives in areas of overlap.

Following these exercises, the effective negotiator, recognizing that the process itself is dynamic, must be alert to changing objectives. The mere passage of time will likely bring about some changes, both anticipated and not anticipated. A classic example of changing objectives with passage of time occurred in Russia during the winter of 1811–1812. There the Russian Army's Commander-in-Chief, Mihail Larionovich Kutuzov, waited—even led his armies in retreat. He went so far as to abandon Moscow, until the cold got so severe and the supply lines stretched so far that Napoleon's armies could not sustain themselves. Napoleon's objectives changed, and his armies fled the country in disarray.

Negotiators in the Iranian crisis have played a waiting game, and conditions have changed. The Russian invasion of Afghanistan was not generally anticipated, but Soviet presence on Iran's borders developed a new jointly-shared objective between leaders of Iran and the United States— moving *their* ovals toward greater overlap. That same presence might have moved the oval representing the militants farther away from the others, if Bani-Sadr was correct in his belief that they have been influenced by Communists.

In the three cases cited here, the main objectives of each of the principal parties are indicated in the chart on the following page, in order of apparent importance.

Working with lists of objectives such as these, the effective negotiator has two important tasks:

1. To eliminate or compromise incompatible or unattainable objectives.

2. To increase areas of overlap.

In the Commonwealth case, union leaders had seemingly incompatible objectives at the start. On one hand they sought to obtain Sanders' reinstatement; on the other hand they wanted to avoid blocking advancement opportunities for other members. Some members of the union wanted to prevent installation of more new paper-making machines by the company, because each machine represented eventual elimination of a substantial number of jobs. The arbitrator (later mediator) identified these objectives, pointed out their incompatibility, and sought compromise within the union. The company was not party to this effort. Eventually, it became clear that objectives were changing; that Sanders' job was most important to everyone, and preservation of the company's competitive standing was of almost-equal importance. Inside the union's caucus it soon became apparent that most of the members believed that installation of the new machines was essential to survival of the company in St. Stephen: that the dismissal of some workers might be necessary in order to assure work for the majority. So they rationalized their opposition to a decline in the work force, pointing out to each other that most of the decline

Three Cases: The Objectives of Each Principal, in Priority Order

Commonwealth

John Sanders
- Personal health
- Reinstatement
- Avoidance of Class A assignment

Union Leaders
- Fulfill legal obligation of fair representation
- Reinstate Sanders to employment
- Do not block opportunities to advance for other Union members
- Live up to contract
- Do not interfere with modernization
- Keep company in town

Company Representatives
- Modernize to remain competitive
- Make certain that new machines have qualified operators
- Keep channels for advancement open
- Maintain and build favorable community image
- Keep Sanders as an employee

Pegasus

John Hoffer
- Fulfill social responsibilities
- Obtain approval of project
- Gain satisfaction through success of others
- Personal advancement

Bednarek, V.P. Industrial Chemicals
- Avoid embarrassment
- Do not spend money unless necessary
- Maintain company's competitive advantages
- Do not lose Davidson or Hoffer
- Be socially responsible

Oliviera, V.P. Fertilizers
- Avoid adverse personal consequences
- Gain favor of President
- Be socially responsible

Hannigan, General Manager
- Support programs with apparent merit
- Don't lose Davidson
- Social responsibility

Spitzer, President
- Decision-making by consensus
- No rule by fiat
- Staff persons help line persons perform better
- Social responsibility

Davidson, Plant Manager
- Enhance his own career
- Social responsibility

Iran

U.S.
- Do not encourage embassy takeovers elsewhere
- Safe return of hostages
- Media coverage

Revolutionary Government
- Do not foment internal strife
- Restore world favor
- Avoid physical harm to hostages
- Avoid U.S. influence
- Do not let militants dictate policy

Militants
- Strong self-image
- Return of Shah
- Punish U.S. leaders for support of the Shah
- Media coverage

would be accomplished through attrition. Then the negotiators were able to think about a compromise, wherein Sanders could remain as a Class B operator, but certain controls would be instituted to be sure that the decision did not set a precedent that would block others from training in Class A work. Once this was accomplished, and once the company was assured by the union that if Sanders remained as a Class B operator this instance would not, in itself, prevent their long-range plans from going ahead, they were ready to forge an agreement.

In the Pegasus case, John Hoffer played a similar role to the arbitrator-mediator in Commonwealth. He worked constantly to increase the areas of overlapping objectives among the principal parties. He did this by focusing on broad objectives—beyond those that were initially acknowledged. All parties professed interest in social responsibility and all agreed that Pegasus, as a socially responsible company, ought to cease polluting the waterways. There was general agreement among all principals that the Hoffer-Davidson proposal represented a high probability of success in accomplishing these objectives. However, they did not agree on whether the project was worthy of a $3.5 million expenditure *now*.

Hoffer attempted to associate each person's personal objectives to the broader objectives of social responsibility and then to demonstrate how support of the project at the Executive Committee level could accomplish both. He focused attention away from the dollar cost and the timing issues. For Davidson, there was the desire for recognition; for Oliviera and Bednarek, there was the desire not to be embarrassed in the Executive Committee; for Spitzer, there was the desire to reinforce his management style. All of them eventually saw a chance to achieve these, their most important objectives, through support of the broader objectives. This, then, gave Hoffer the wedge he needed to demonstrate how sup-

port of the project *now* was in everyone's best interest.

In Iran by April 1 there was no focal point wherein the objectives of all parties could achieve overlap. There the militants had an apparently unattainable objective: the return of the Shah. In absence of an extradition treaty between Egypt, U.S., and Iran, it was not within legal authority of Iran or its leaders to require this. After the Shah's departure for Panama, and, later Egypt, the possibility of his physical return was essentially beyond control of the U.S.

Therefore, the negotiators, assisted by Secretary-General Waldheim, sought a compromise—a redefinition of the militants' objectives. Their job was to help the militants change their minds, but not to weaken their self-image in the process. The U.N. panel seemed to provide a method for doing this. The militants expressed hope that the panel would expose misdeeds of the Shah and possibly the U.S. for the world to see. If sufficient publicity were given to his alleged misdeeds, the militants might be satisfied to the point where they would release the hostages. They could then say that by taking the hostages they effected a world-wide exposé. By April 1, however, the panel had disbanded, at least temporarily, while leaders in Iran tried to resolve differences between themselves and the militants.

Throughout the process, there were skeptics among all the principal groups involved who believed that the willingness of the U.S. to listen to and cooperate in solving of Iran's grievances would last only as long as the hostages were being held, so there was incentive on the part of some Iranians to prolong the crisis as long as possible. Through passage of time, the focal point for settlement in Iran would, most likely, emerge. However, the Iranians and Americans look at time in a different way: Iranians, by and large, saw no urgency to the matter. After all, the Ayatollah himself was in exile for 26 years! Americans are not so patient; there was fear on all sides that their impatience could lead to establishment of deadlines, possibly accompanied by the use of military force. However, there was little confidence that deadlines or force would cause the Iranian government officials or the militants to change their objectives.

The route to success in the Iranian situation seemed no different than the route followed in the Commonwealth and Pegasus cases. It involved constantly working toward elimination of incompatible objectives and toward increasing areas of overlap. Imposition of deadlines or threats had no place in this process.

SUMMARY

The art of effective negotiation can be learned. It is an art that can be applied to many settings: from international relations and labor relations to interpersonal relations within an organization.

The need for negotiation skills among executives at all levels is apparent. Business organizations are forced to deal with more and more parties, ranging from governmental regulatory agencies to the judiciary; there is less opportunity to make decisions by fiat and more need to hammer out agreements through negotiation. Traditional forums for dispute resolution, like courts of law, are too cumbersome and too time-consuming to effectively deal with the vast majority of today's conflicts.

Effective negotiators often turn to outside agents such as mediators and arbitrators to assist in the process. On occasion they search for structural devices, such as those proposed by game theorists. All this can be helpful, but such devices are not a substitute for assumption of responsibility by the negotiator himself: responsibility to identify the principal parties who are involved, to define the objectives held by each, and then to work to eliminate unattainable and incompatible objectives by focusing on broad goals with which none of the parties can disagree. The process of effective negotiation involves identification of overlapping objectives— a process that is often difficult and time consuming, but the patient and skillful application of which can yield agreeable results.

NOTES

1. Jean Brett and Stephen Goldberg, Wildcat strikes in bituminous coal mining. *Industrial and Labor Relations Review.* 32; 465, 466(1979).

2. Ross, Distressed grievance procedures and their rehabilitation. In *Proceedings, 16th Annual Meeting, National Academy of Arbitrators.* 104; 110–111, 125–126 (1963).

3. William H. Forbis. *Fall of the peacock throne: The story.* New York: Harper and Row. January, 1980.

ACHIEVING INTEGRATIVE AGREEMENTS

Dean G. Pruitt

Integrative agreements in bargaining are those that reconcile (i.e., integrate) the parties' interests and hence yield high joint benefit. They can be contrasted with compromises, which are reached when the parties concede along an obvious dimension to some middle ground, and which usually produce lower joint benefit (Follett, 1940). Consider, for example, the story of two sisters who quarreled over an orange (Fisher and Ury, 1981). A compromise agreement was reached to split the fruit in half, whereupon one sister squeezed her portion for juice while the other used the peel from her portion in a cake. For whatever reasons, they overlooked the integrative agreement of giving the first sister all the juice and the second all the peel.

Integrative agreements sometimes make use of known alternatives, whose joint value becomes apparent during the controversy. But more often they involve the development of novel alternatives. Hence it is proper to say that they usually emerge from creative problem-solving. Integrative alternatives (those that form the basis for

integrative agreements) can be devised by either party acting separately, by the two of them in joint session, or by a third party such as a mediator.

In the story of the sisters, the situation had unusually high *integrative potential* in the sense of allowing the development of an agreement that totally satisfied both parties' aspirations. Not all situations are so hopeful. For example, in negotiating the price of a car, both dealer and customer usually must reduce their aspirations in order to reach agreement.

However, most situations have more integrative potential than is commonly assumed. For example, car dealers can often sweeten the deal by throwing in a radio or other accessory that costs them little but benefits their customer a lot. Hence problem-solving is often richly rewarded.

There are four main reasons for bargainers (or the mediators assisting them) to seek integrative agreements rather than compromises (Pruitt, 1981);

1. If aspirations are high and both sides are resistant to conceding, it might not be possible to resolve the conflict unless a way can be found to reconcile the two parties' interests.

2. Integrative agreements are likely to be more stable. Compromises are often unsat-

isfactory to one or both parties, causing the issue to come up again at a later time.

3. Because they are mutually rewarding, integrative agreements tend to strengthen the relationship between the parties. This has a number of benefits, including facilitating problem-solving in later conflicts.

4. Integrative agreements ordinarily contribute to the welfare of the broader community of which the two parties are members. For example, a firm will usually benefit as a whole if its departments are able to reconcile their differences creatively.

METHODS FOR ACHIEVING INTEGRATIVE AGREEMENTS

Five methods for achieving integrative agreements will now be described. These are means by which the parties' initially opposing demands can be transformed into alternatives that reconcile their interests. They can be used by one party, by both parties working together, or by a third party such as a mediator. Each method involves a different way of refocusing the issues under dispute. Hence potentially useful refocusing questions will be provided under each heading. Information that is useful for implementing each method will also be mentioned, and the methods will be listed in order of increasing difficulty of getting this information.

The methods will be illustrated by a running example concerning a husband and wife who are trying to decide where to go on a two-week vacation. The husband wants to go to the mountains, his wife to the seashore. They have considered the compromise of spending one week in each location, but are hoping for something better. What approach should they take?

1. Expanding the Pie

Some conflicts hinge on a resource shortage. For example, time, money, space, and automobiles are in short supply but long demand. In such circumstances, integrative agreements can be devised by increasing the available resources. This is called *expanding the pie*. For example, our married couple might solve their problems by persuading their employers to give them four weeks of vacation so that they can take two in the mountains and two at the seashore. Another example (cited by Follett, 1940) is that of two milk companies vying to be first to unload cans on a platform. The controversy was resolved when somebody thought of widening the platform.

Expanding the pie is a useful formula when the parties reject one another's demands because of opportunity costs, such as if the husband rejects the seashore because it keeps him away from the mountains and the wife rejects the mountains because this would deny her the pleasure of the seashore. But it is by no means a universal remedy. Expanding the pie might yield strikingly poor benefits if there are inherent costs in the other's proposal—if, for example, the husband cannot stand the seashore or the wife the mountains. Other methods are better in such cases.

Expanding the pie requires no analysis of the interests underlying the parties' demands. Hence its information requirements are slim. However, this does not mean that a solution by this method is always easy to find. There might not be a resource shortage, or the shortage might not be easy to identify or to remedy.

Some refocusing questions that can be useful in seeking a solution through pie-expansion include: How can both parties get what they want? Does the conflict hinge on a resource shortage? How can the critical resource be expanded?

2. Nonspecific Compensation

In *nonspecific compensation*, one party gets what he or she wants and the other is repaid in some unrelated coin. Compensation is nonspecific if it does not deal with the precise costs incurred by the other party. For example, the wife in our example might agree to go to the mountains, even though she finds them boring, if her husband promises to buy her an expensive coat. Another example would be giving an employee a bonus for working through dinner.

Compensation usually comes from the party whose demands are granted. But it can also originate with a third party, or even with the party who is compensated. An example of the latter would be an employee who pampers him- or herself by finding a nice office to work in while working through the dinner hour.

Two kinds of information are useful for devising a solution by nonspecific compensation: (a) information about what is valuable to the other party (knowledge that he or she values love, or attention, or money, for example); (b) information about how badly the other party is hurting by making concessions. This is useful for devising adequate compensation for these concessions. If such information is not available, it might be possible to conduct an "auction" for the other party's acquiescence, changing the sort of benefit offered or raising one's offer, in trial-and-error fashion, until an acceptable formula is found.

Refocusing questions that can help locate a means of compensation include: How much is the other party hurting in conceding to me? What does the other party value that I can supply? How valuable is this to the other party?

3. Logrolling

Logrolling is possible in complex agendas where several issues are under consideration and the parties have differing priorities among these issues. Each party concedes on low priority issues in exchange for concessions on issues of higher priority to them. Each party gets the part of the demands that it finds most important. For example, suppose that in addition to disagreeing

about where to go on vacation, the wife in our example wants to go to a first-class hotel while her husband prefers a bed and breakfast. If accommodations are a high priority issue for the wife and location is the issue for the husband, they can reach a fairly integrative solution by agreeing to go to a first-class hotel in the mountains. Logrolling can be viewed as a variant of nonspecific compensation, in which both parties instead of one are compensated for making concessions desired by the other.

To develop solutions by logrolling, it is useful to have information about the two parties' priorities so that exchangeable concessions can be identified. But it is not necessary to have information about the interests (e.g., the aspirations, values) underlying these priorities. Solutions by logrolling can also be developed by a process of trial and error in which one party moves systematically through a series of possible packages, keeping his or her own outcomes as high as possible, until an alternative is found that is acceptable to the other party (Kelley and Schenitzki, 1972; Pruitt and Carnevale, 1982).

Refocusing questions that can be useful for developing solutions by logrolling include: Which issues are of higher and lower priority to myself? Which issues are of higher and lower priority to the other party? Are some of my high-priority issues of low priority to the other party, and vice versa?

4. Cost-Cutting

In solutions achieved through *cost-cutting*, one party gets what he or she wants and the other's costs are reduced or eliminated. The result is high joint benefit, not because the first party has changed his or her demands, but because the second party suffers less. For instance, suppose that the husband in our example dislikes the beach because of the hustle and bustle. He might be quite willing to go there on vacation if his costs are cut by renting a house with a quiet inner courtyard, where he can read while his wife goes out among the crowds.

Cost-cutting often takes the form of specific compensation in which the party who concedes receives something in return that satisfies the precise values frustrated. For example, the employee who must work through dinnertime can be specifically compensated by having dinner brought in. Specific compensation differs from nonspecific compensation in that it deals with the precise costs incurred, rather than repayment in an unrelated coin. The costs are actually canceled out, rather than overbalanced by benefits experienced in some other realm.

Information about the nature of one of the parties' costs is, of course, helpful for developing solutions by cost-cutting. This is a deeper kind of information than knowledge of that party's priorities. It involves knowing something about the interests—the values, aspirations, and standards—underlying that party's overt position.

Refocusing questions for developing solutions by cost-cutting include: What costs are posed for the other party by our proposal? How can these costs be mitigated or eliminated?

5. Bridging

In *bridging*, neither party achieves its initial demands, but a new option is devised that satisfies the most important interests underlying these demands. For example, suppose that the husband in our vacation example is mainly interested in fishing and hunting and the wife in swimming and sunbathing. There interests might be bridged by finding an inland resort with a lake and a beach that is close to woods and streams. Follett (1940) gives another domestic example of two women reading in a library room. One wanted to open the window for ventilation, while the other wanted to keep it closed so as not to catch cold. The ultimate solution involved opening a window in the next room,

which satisfied both the need for fresh air and the need to avoid a draft.

Bridging typically involves a reformulation of the issue(s) based on an analysis of the underlying interests on both sides. For example, a critical turning point in our vacation example is likely to come when the initial formulation, "Shall we go to the mountains, or to the seashore?" is replaced by "Where can we find fishing, hunting, swimming, and sunbathing?" This new formulation becomes the basis for a search model (Simon, 1957), which is employed in an effort to locate a novel alternative. The process of reformulation can be done by either or both parties, or by a third party who is trying to help.

People who seek to develop solutions by bridging need information about the nature of the two parties' interests and their priorities among these interests. Priority information is useful because it is rare to find a solution, like opening the window in the next room of the library, that bridges all of the two parties' interests. More often, higher-priority interests are served while lower-priority interests are discarded. For example, the wife who agrees to go to an inland lake might be willing to do without the lesser value of smelling the sea air and the husband might willingly give up his goal of having spectacular mountain vistas.

In the initial phase of a search for a solution by bridging, the search model can include all of the interests on both sides. But if this does not generate a mutually acceptable alternative, some of the lower-priority interests must be discarded from the model and the search begun anew. The result will not be an ideal solution, but perhaps one that is mutually acceptable. Dropping low-priority interests in the development of a solution by bridging is similar to dropping low-priority demands in the search for a solution by logrolling. However, the latter is in the realm of concrete proposals, while the former is in the realm of the interests underlying these proposals.

• • • • •

Refocusing questions that can be raised in search of a solution by bridging include: What are the two parties' basic interests? What are their priorities among these interests? How can the two sets of high-priority interests be reconciled?

THE ANALYSIS OF INTERESTS

To devise integrative solutions involving cost-cutting or bridging, it is usually necessary to know something about the interests underlying one or both parties' proposals. The only other possible approach is one of trial and error, which is usually inferior.

Interests are commonly organized into hierarchical trees, with more basic interests underpinning more superficial ones. Hence it is often useful to go deeper than the interests immediately underlying a party's proposals to the interests underlying these interests, or even to the interests underlying the interests underlying the interests. If one goes far enough down the tree, an interest might be located that can be easily reconciled with the opposing party's interests.

An example of an interest tree can be seen in the left column of Figure 1. It belongs to a hypothetical boy who is trying to persuade his father to allow him to buy a motorcycle. At the top right are the father's interests that conflict with the son's. At the top of the tree is the boy's initial proposal (buy a motorcycle), which is hopelessly opposed to his father's proposal (no motorcycle). Analysis of the boy's proposal yields a first-level underlying interest: to make noise in the neighborhood. This is opposed to his dad's interests of maintaining peace and quiet. Further analysis of the boy's position reveals a second-level interest underlying the first level: to gain attention from the neighbors. But again this conflicts with one of his father's basic interests: to live unobtrusively. The controversy is only resolved when someone (the father, the boy, the boy's mother) discovers an even more basic interest underlying the desire for a motorcycle—the boy's desire to impress important people. This discovery is helpful, because there are ways of making such an impression that do not contradict the father's interests—trying out for the high school soccer team, for example. At the bot-

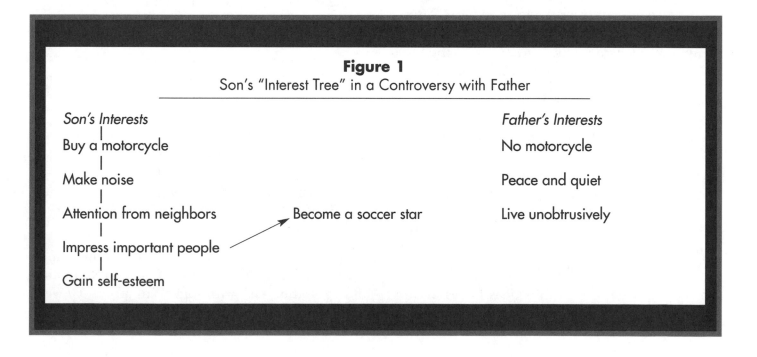

Figure 1
Son's "Interest Tree" in a Controversy with Father

Son's Interests

Buy a motorcycle

Make noise

Attention from neighbors → Become a soccer star

Impress important people

Gain self-esteem

Father's Interests

No motorcycle

Peace and quiet

Live unobtrusively

◆ ◆ ◆ ◆ ◆

tom of the boy's tree is a fourth-level interest: self-esteem. But it is unnecessary to go down this far, because the controversy can be resolved at the third level.

Analysis of the interests underlying divergent positions often reveals that the initial area of disagreement had different meanings to the two parties. While there appeared to be disagreement, there was no fundamental opposition in what they were really asking. For example, one party might be more concerned with substance while the other cares more for appearances; one might be seeking an immediate settlement, while the other is seeking a long-term solution, and so on. Fisher and Ury (1981, p. 77) list nine other dimensions of this kind.

THE NATURE OF PROBLEM-SOLVING

Bargainers are sometimes able to "luck into" a highly integrative agreement as, for example, when prior creative activity has produced a good standard solution. But more often a bargainer or some third party working with them must engage in problem-solving; that is, they must seek a new option that better satisfies both parties' interests than those currently available. The more vigorous is this problem-solving, the more integrative is the final agreement likely to be, up to the limits imposed by the integrative potential.

Problem-solving takes a variety of forms. For example, one can raise refocusing questions of the kind described earlier, or seek and provide information about priorities and interests. (When both parties provide such information, it is called *information exchange.*) An important part of problem-solving is being open to new alternatives— being willing to seek our alternatives and seriously consider any alternatives proposed by the opponent or some third party.

In seeking new alternatives, it is necessary to adopt a policy of *firm flexibility*.[1] One must be *firm* with respect to one's *ends* (i.e., one's interests),

giving them up only if they are clearly unobtainable. Otherwise the solution will be one-sided in favor of the other party rather than represent a true integration of the two parties' needs. Yet one must also be *flexible* with respect to the *means* to these ends, continually seeking new alternatives until a mutually acceptable one can be found.

An example of firm flexibility can be seen in actions taken by President John F. Kennedy in 1961 during the second Berlin crisis. The Russians, led by Premier Nikita Khrushchev, had been trying to end American occupation of West Berlin by threatening to sign a separate peace treaty with East Germany and buzzing planes in the Berlin Corridor. Recognizing that some concessions had to be made, Kennedy "decided to be firm on essentials but negotiate on nonessentials" (Snyder and Diesing, 1977, p. 566). In a speech on July 25, 1961, he announced three fundamental principles that ensured the integrity and continued American occupation of West Berlin. The firmness of these principles was underscored by a pledge to defend them by force, and a concomitant military buildup (Pruitt and Holland, 1972). Yet Kennedy also indicated flexibility and a concern for Russian priorities by calling for negotiations to remove "actual irritants" to the Soviet Union and its allies. Two results were achieved: the building of the Berlin Wall (which can be viewed as a bridging solution that solved the problem of population loss from East Germany without disturbing American rights in West Berlin) and eventual negotiations that put these rights clearly in writing.

CONDITIONS ENCOURAGING THE DEVELOPMENT OF INTEGRATIVE SOLUTIONS

In three recent studies, the antecedents of integrative agreements by means of a simulated negotiation task with logrolling potential were explored. The subjects, playing the roles of buyer or seller in a wholesale appliance market, were expected to reach agreement on prices for television sets, vacuum cleaners, and typewriters. Profit schedules were arranged so that the buyer's highest profits were achieved on television sets and the seller's on typewriters. Hence the best agreement for both parties involved a low price for television sets and a high price for typewriters. (This method is described in more detail in Kimmel, Pruitt, Magenau, Konar-Goldband, and Carnevale 1980 and Pruitt and Lewis 1975.)

Theoretical guidance was derived from a *dual concern model* based on the writings of Blake and Mouton (1979), Filley (1975), and Thomas (1976). This postulates that problem-solving and hence (when there is integrative potential) high joint benefit will arise to the extent that bargainers are concerned about both their own and the other party's outcomes. If they are mainly concerned about their own outcomes, they will engage instead in contentious behavior designed to elicit concessions from the other party. As a result, they will be inflexible with respect to means and thus achieve low joint benefit. If they are concerned primarily about the other party's outcomes, they will be overly flexible with respect to ends, also leading to low joint benefit.

All three studies employed 2×2 factorial designs involving various interpretations of concern about own and other's outcomes. All variables were manipulated bilaterally in the sense that both bargainers received identical instructions and experiences.

In the first two studies, concern about own outcomes was interpreted as resistance to reducing one's aspirations (i.e., forsaking one's interests). High resistance was produced by sending the bargainers private communications from their companies instructing them to reach an agreement involving a total profit of $4600 or more. (This figure was chosen because past experience had shown that it was a moderately difficult goal.) Low resistance was produced by saying

nothing about a lower limit on profit. In Study 1 (Ben Yoav and Pruitt, 1982), concern about the other party's outcomes was encouraged by inducing a concern about the relationship with the other party. We told the bargainers that they would have to work together toward a common goal on a task following the negotiation. In the contrasting condition, they were told that they would be working alone on a subsequent task. In Study 2 (Nachajsky, Carnevale, Van Slyck, and Pruitt, 1982), high concern about the other party's outcomes was encouraged by putting the bargainers in a good mood. Shortly before the beginning of negotiation, each bargainer received a gift from a confederate of the experimenter. Earlier research (Isen and Levin, 1972) suggests that gifts induce a good mood that encourages a desire to help others. There was no gift in the low-concern condition.

The results of both studies supported the predictions from the dual-concern model. High resistance to reducing aspirations in conjunction with either a concern about the relationship or a good mood encouraged the development of agreements involving high joint benefit. A content analysis of verbalizations showed that the bargainers in these conditions tended to exchange information about their profit schedules, a form of problem-solving. However, the separate elements of this combination led to low joint benefit. Resistance to reducing aspirations alone encouraged contentious behavior, often leading to failure to reach agreement. Concern about the relationship and a good mood produced the worst joint outcomes of all, presumably by encouraging efforts to seek a simple compromise.

These results lead to interesting conclusions about conditions that foster a desire to be cooperative or helpful. When people are also motivated to hold fast to their basic aspirations, such conditions encourage creative problem-solving and hence high joint benefit. But when aspirations are free to vary, such conditions encourage quick concessions and hence result in low joint benefit. It follows that conditions that foster cooperativeness must be balanced by conditions that support aspirations if they are to produce creative problem solving in interpersonal and intergroup relations.

In Study 3 (Ben Yoav and Pruitt, 1983), concern about own outcomes was produced by making the bargainers highly accountable to constituents. Two confederates served as constituents. Under high accountability, the constituents were able to divide the money earned in the negotiation and to write an evaluation of the outcome achieved by their negotiators. Under low accountability, the bargainers divided the money earned and no evaluations were written. Concern about the other's outcomes was produced as in Study 1 by the expectation of cooperative future interaction.

Again, the winning combination involved a combination of both concerns. Highly accountable representatives who were concerned about their relationship with the other party achieved unusually high joint benefit. But accountability alone or concern about the relationship alone had no such effect.

Both conditions produced low joint benefit, the former in conjunction with heavy contentious behavior.

These last findings have interesting implications for bargaining efforts between group representatives. Accountability is shown to be a double-edged sword. Under normal conditions, it encourages contentious behavior and low joint benefit. But in association with good relations between the opposing representatives, it fosters problem-solving and high joint benefit. Good relations between opposing representatives are also shown to be a double-edged sword. When coupled with high accountability, they foster creative problem-solving, leading to a productive resolution of intergroup controversy. But when account-

ability is low, they encourage "cozy" arrangements in which the representatives lose track of their constituent's interests and end up with simple, unimaginative compromise agreements.

These findings also relate to the impact of role conflict. The combination of high accountability and concern about the relationship places bargainers in a conflict between constituent expectations and a desire to please the other bargainer. Our research suggests that such role conflict can, under some circumstances, encourage a creative synthesis of the two sets of demands, rather than the sort of debilitating psychological reaction found by Kahn, Wolfe, Quinn, Snoek, and Rosenthal (1964).

THE ROLE OF CONTENTIOUS BEHAVIOR

Contentious behavior[2] consists of all those actions that are designed to elicit concessions from the other party. Examples include persuasive arguments, threats, and positional commitments.

Contentious behavior has traditionally been assumed to militate against the development of integrative agreements (Blake and Mouton, 1979; Deutsch, 1973; Walton and McKersie, 1965), and there is solid research evidence supporting this assumption (Pruitt and Carnevale, 1982), including some reported just above. There are four reasons why this should be true:

1. Contentious behavior ordinarily involves standing firm on a particular proposal that one seeks to foist on the other party. This is incompatible with the flexibility about means that is an important element of successful problem-solving.

2. Contentious behavior encourages hostility toward the other party by a principle of psychological consistency. This diminishes one's willingness to contribute to the other's welfare and hence one's willingness to devise or accept jointly beneficial alternatives.

3. Contentious behavior encourages the other party to feel hostile and to engage in contentious behavior in return. A conflict spiral can ensue in which both parties become increasingly rigid and progressively more reluctant to take any actions that benefit the other.

4. Contentious behavior signals to the other party that one has a win/lose orientation, calling into question the possibility of achieving a jointly beneficial agreement. In other words, it tends to reduce the integrative potential perceived by the other party.

However, the indictment against contentious behavior has been clearly overdrawn. Under some circumstances, this behavior can actually make problem-solving more likely, or contribute to the effectiveness of problem-solving. This can occur in two ways:

1. *It encourages the other party to face the controversy when he or she benefits from the status quo.*

If present circumstances favor the other party, it is often necessary to employ threats to force his or her attention to one's concerns. Such threats run the risk of eliciting contentious behavior in return and starting a conflict spiral. But they can encourage problem-solving behavior by the other party (Pruitt and Gleason, 1978).

Consider the Berlin situation we referred to earlier. At the beginning of the second Berlin crisis, Russian Premier Nikita Khrushchev threatened to sign a separate peace treaty with East Germany if the status of West Berlin were not settled to his liking. At the same time, he proposed negotiation. Had he not made this threat, which was tantamount to a proposal to give East Germany control of the access routes to West Berlin, it is doubtful that the West would have accepted his offer of negotiation.

2. *It underlines one's areas of firmness.*

Threats and other contentious actions are a kind of communication. They can be used to empha-

size the rigidity of one's high priority interests, making it doubly clear that certain elements of one's position are non-negotiable. An example would be the Kennedy speech mentioned earlier, in which he threatened to use force to defend the integrity of and American access to West Berlin. Concomitant troop movements added emphasis to his message. Such a message can contribute to the development of an integrative solution in two ways:

a. It makes the other party less likely to try to dislodge the other from his areas of firmness. Instead, the other is motivated to try to devise a way to live within these constraints—perhaps even to engage in problem-solving.

b. It makes one more likely to take problem-solving actions, since there is less need to fear that the other side will misinterpret them as signs of weakness. Thus shielded from being misinterpreted by his own threats, Kennedy was able to call for negotiations to remove "actual irritants" to the Soviet Union.

In short, contentious behavior can contribute to and militate against the development of integrative agreements.

How can the advantages of this kind of behavior be achieved while avoiding the pitfalls? Four tentative answers to this question are proposed:

1. Send signals of flexibility and a concern about the other party's interests in conjunction with contentious displays. Khrushchev did this by coupling his threat with hints of a willingness to make concessions; Kennedy did the same thing by offering to negotiate about "actual irritants." Such maneuvers are designed to make the integrative potential seem large enough to the other party that problem-solving seems warranted.

2. Insulate contentious behavior from problem-solving behavior so that neither undermines the other. The most common form of insulation is the "black-hat/white-hat" routine, in which contentious behavior is assigned to one team member (the black hat) and problem-solving behavior to another (the white hat). In the context of the black hat's threats, the white hat's offer of cooperation is more likely to be reciprocated by the target. In the context of the white hat's blandishments, the black hat's escalation is less likely to be reciprocated by the target.

3. Use contentious tactics to defend basic interests rather than a particular solution to the controversy. It is possible for the other party to cope with such rigidities.

4. Employ deterrent rather than compellent threats. Deterrent threats indicate that a particular action or solution favored by the other is intolerable but does not judge the adequacy of other solutions. They involve saying "no" to the other party without demanding that the other say "yes."

NOTES

1. Called "flexible rigidity" in a prior publication (Pruitt, 1981).

2. The term "contentious" is used in preference to "competitive" because the latter carries the excess meaning of trying to do better than the other party; it is used in preference to "distributive" to avoid confusion with distributive justice.

REFERENCES

Ben Yoav, O., and Pruitt, D.G. *Level of aspiration and expectation of future interaction in negotiation.* Paper presented at the annual convention of the American Psychological Association. Washington D.C.: August, 1982.

Ben Yoav, O., and Pruitt, D.G. *Accountability, a two-edged sword: Friend and foe of integrative agreements.* Paper presented at the annual convention of the Eastern Academy of Management. Pittsburgh: May, 1983.

Blake, R. R., and Mouton, J. S. Intergroup problem-solving organization: From theory to practice. In W. G. Austin and S. Wormhole (eds.), *The social psychology of inter-group relations.* Monterey, Calif.: Brook/Cole, 1979.

Chapter Seven

PLANNING AND PREPARATION

BEFORE YOU NEGOTIATE: GET YOUR ACT TOGETHER

Gary G. Whitney

Negotiation is a pervasive activity. Sometimes it is easy to recognize—for example, when one is bargaining the terms of a union contract, a merger between two companies, or a sole-source procurement contract. On the other hand, one occasionally faces subtle situations that are difficult to recognize as negotiations—such as setting the conditions for new employment, assigning jobs within an organization, or handling an audit by the Internal Revenue Service (IRS). These are negotiations nonetheless, and should be treated accordingly.

It is important to recognize a negotiation situation for what it is—an attempt by two parties to change the terms and conditions of their relationship in a situation in which it is to their mutual benefit to do so, or in which it is impossible to quit the relationship (for example, a company's relationship with the IRS). Most negotiations involve a variety of issues that must be settled.

GENERAL RULES OF THE GAME

As in warfare, a negotiator should never get caught by surprise. If you unexpectedly find yourself in a negotiation situation for which you are not prepared, the best tactic is to stall: Ask for time to prepare; say you need to call your boss; say you need some backup material that you don't have with you; or do anything else that will enable you to back out of the situation until you are ready. Preparation is essential. Without thorough preparation, you have little chance of reaching a truly successful conclusion.

Success in negotiation is defined by three criteria: (1) reaching a favorable solution, (2) concluding the process in a reasonable amount of time, and (3) ensuring that the psychological relationship between the negotiating parties ends up in the desired state when the process is completed. (The third criterion, a constraint on the other two, is too frequently ignored.)

PREPARATION FOR NEGOTIATION

Negotiating is stressful because it is complex and generally occurs at a fast clip, and the negotiators get their egos involved in the process and the outcome. This leads to a paradox: Stress limits creativity and reduces behavioral repertoires, but successful negotiation requires intellectual creativity and flexible behavior. Thorough preparation is the antidote to this dilemma.

Reprinted by permission of publisher, from *Personnel*, July/August 1982. Copyright © 1982, American Management Association, New York. All rights reserved.

Pre-Negotiation Worksheet

Step 1a: Analyze the issues.

1. Assess relative power: rate your own and opponent's power on the following scale:

I depend on opponent for things that are vital to my future. There is no alternative source.	__10	10__	Opponent depends on me for things that are vital to his or her future. There are no alternative sources.
	9	9	
	8	8	
	7	7	
	6	6	
I need opponent for things that are important to my future. There are some alternative sources.	__ 5	5 __	Opponent needs me to provide things important to his or her future. There are some alternative sources.
	4	4	
	3	3	
	3	3	
	2	2	
I want opponent to provide things that are desirable. There are many alternative sources.	__ 1	1 __	Opponent wants me to provide things that are desirable to his or her future. There are no alternative sources.

2. Assess future desired relationship between the parties. Check off the level of relationship you wish to have with opponent after completing the negotiations. Note the implications for tactics.

Relationship	*Implication*
– No interdependence.	Minimal restrictions on tactics.
– Continued interaction.	Restricted from most offensive tactics.
– Vital interdependence.	Trust and fairness essential.

Preparation focuses attention on creativity before the stress of actual negotiation. Such preparation includes generating creative concessions, role playing the opponent's responses, reformulating the issues, and so forth. Preparation broadens the negotiator's behavioral repertoire by anticipating effective behaviors (for example, demanding, conceding, bluffing, being candid, being secretive) and, if necessary, practicing those behaviors. In addition, preparation increases confidence, which reduces stress and its attendant inhibitions on behavior.

An effective preparatory approach includes the following steps:

Worksheet *(continued)*

Steps 1b and 2: Analyze the issues and set goals.

Major Issues to Settle	Elements after Fractionating	Issue Type (Win/win win/lose or mixed)	Opponent's		My	
			Aspiration	Minimum	Aspiration	Minimum
1. _____	_____	_____	_____	_____	_____	_____
	_____	_____	_____	_____	_____	_____
	_____	_____	_____	_____	_____	_____
	_____	_____	_____	_____	_____	_____
	_____	_____	_____	_____	_____	_____
2. _____	_____	_____	_____	_____	_____	_____
	_____	_____	_____	_____	_____	_____
	_____	_____	_____	_____	_____	_____
	_____	_____	_____	_____	_____	_____
3. _____	_____	_____	_____	_____	_____	_____
	_____	_____	_____	_____	_____	_____
	_____	_____	_____	_____	_____	_____

Step 3: Set the stage.
Consider the following questions:

Agenda—Are the issues in advantageous order?
Physical setting—Is the setting advantageous or neutral?
Agent—Might an agent be in a better position to negotiate for me?
Audience—Will an audience be helpful or detrimental?

---

(1) Analyze the issues. (2) Set your goals. (3) Set the stage. (4) Tactically plan your moves.

Step 1. ANALYZE THE ISSUES

The first step in an effective preparation is to identify all the issues to be settled during the negotiation. On a worksheet (see pages 78, 79, and 80) list all the terms and conditions that need to be settled to reach a conclusion to your negotiation. If, for example, you are representing a large corporation that is buying a small owner-managed proprietorship, the first and most obvious issue is the total price to be paid for the company—but there are many other issues that would also have to be settled before

Worksheet *(continued)*

Step 4: Tactically Plan Your Moves.

1. For each issue, determine your initial demand. (Remember, this establishes the opponent's perception of your aspiration level.) Determine what concessions you can make and how important each concession is.

Issue	Initial Demand	Concessions	Importance (0 = throwaway to 10 = vital)
_____	_____	_____	_____
_____	_____	_____	_____
_____	_____	_____	_____

2. List specific things you can do to make the opponent feel good during the negotiation.

_____	_____	_____	_____
_____	_____	_____	_____
_____	_____	_____	_____

3. List ways to break an impasse.
   We should take a recess because _____

   A useful joke is the one about the _____

4. List issues that are likely to cause an impasse, and then list a repackaged version of the same issues.

Original Issue	Repackaged Version
_____	_____
_____	_____
_____	_____
_____	_____

the sale can be completed. Some of these, for example, might include the following:

- How will the payment be made—cash, notes, or stock?

- Will there be management continuity?

- How will the operations of this acquisition be integrated into the acquiring company?

- How will the reputation of both companies be affected by the acquisition?

Fractionate the Issues

Once all major issues have been identified, the next step is to subdivide each issue into its smallest possible components. By fractionating, you create flexibility that can be used later in the negotiation process. Continuing with the acquisition example, the issue of management continuity can be subdivided into the following components:

■ Will the seller be paid a salary after the company is acquired?

■ Will the seller retain a title, such as president?

■ Will the seller have an office and the status associated with it?

■ Will the seller be consulted on issues that arise after the sale?

■ Will the seller have influence on the issues?

■ Will the seller retain the personal loyalty of the employees?

Classify Issues

Each issue component should be classified as either a win-win issue, a win-lose issue, or a mixed issue. A win-lose issue is one in which a gain to one party comes at the direct expense of the other. Negotiations over price are usually of this type. A win-win issue is one in which a good agreement can benefit both parties—but not necessarily equally. In other words, both parties are winners. A mixed issue contains elements of both win-win and win-lose. In a mixed issue there is motivation for both parties to reach a solution that benefits both. However, there are some aspects of the issue that motivate one party to attempt to make a gain that can come only at greater expense to the opponent. (The term "opponent" is used throughout this article to designate the other party in a negotiation.) Thus, there is a mixed motivation. There is motivation to cooperate to reach a beneficial solution, but there is still motivation to gain a slight advantage.

In the acquisition example, the price of acquiring the company is a win-lose issue. Assume that you, as the buyer, can afford to spend $100,000 to buy the proprietorship. (Although $100,000 is, of course, much less than the probable price for any going business, we use that figure to simplify the illustration.) Naturally, you would like to spend as little as possible. Realistically, you know that you will have to pay a price in the $80,000 or $90,000 range. The seller naturally would like to get as much of your $100,000 as possible. As the price paid for the company increases, obviously the money left to the buyer decreases an equivalent amount. This is a perfect win-lose situation.

Let us assume that in acquiring this company you do not want the owner to continue as manager because he or she is no longer effective; on the other hand, he or she wants to remain. On the face of it, this appears to be a win-lose issue. The buyer will win if the manager (seller) leaves, but the seller will lose. The reverse is true if the manager stays; thus management continuity looks like a win-lose issue.

However, when this issue is subdivided into its component parts instead of remaining as one all-inclusive win-lose issue, there are six smaller issues. Each of these is classified according to type because the type of issue determines the appropriate tactic. Whether to pay the seller a salary after the acquisition is a win-lose issue because everything the seller receives is a cost to the buyer. Whether the seller retains a title is a potential win-win issue. It costs virtually nothing to bestow a title, but that action might be greatly appreciated. Whether the seller should be given an office after the sale is a mixed issue. It will cost very little to provide that office, but he or she might place a great value on having access to an office and the status associated with it. Whether to consult the seller on issues arising after the sale is also a mixed issue. There might be some value to the buyer in doing so—for example, taking advantage of the seller's knowledge of the market—and the value to the seller might be extremely high—retaining prestige in the industry, for example. Whether the seller will directly influence decisions is a win-lose issue. As stated earlier, the buyer does not want the seller to exert any influence because he or she is no longer an effective manager, but the seller wants this power. Retaining the employees' personal loyalty after the sale is a potential win-win issue also. The buyer benefits if the employees maintain good feelings toward the company, and the seller benefits if the employees don't resent the sale.

By splitting up this issue of management continuity, one win-lose issue has been converted into two win-lose issues, two mixed issues, and two win-win issues. Similar splitting should be done for every issue identified.

Identify Opponent's Needs

Identifying your opponent's needs is the next step in the analysis. The opponent has two types of needs: issue needs, and psychological needs. Issue needs are each party's goals and aspirations for all the issues to be settled during the negotiation. Psychological needs are those internal feelings aroused by the negotiation process.

Psychological needs are not directly negotiable—you cannot concede $6,000 for 12 ego points. However, it is important to identify these needs before beginning the negotiation because then you can anticipate them and manipulate them to your advantage. The best way to accomplish this is to evaluate the negotiation from the opponent's viewpoint. Do not assume that the opponent perceives the negotiations in the same way that you do or in the way you hope he or she perceives them. Maintaining a good self-image is probably each party's strongest psychological need—and therefore the most highly motivating need—during any negotiation. Negotiators want to look good to their opponents and their constituents; they want to save face when making concessions, and they want to be able to give themselves high marks—that is, a positive evaluation.

Determine Aspiration Levels

Each party's aspiration level and minimum acceptable level on each issue should also be identified and, when possible, they should be quantified for one's self and one's opponent. The aspiration level is the highest goal that the party will attempt to achieve; the minimum acceptable level is the least he or she will accept before withdrawing from the negotiation. Keep in mind that even on dollar-quantified issues, the personal value of a particular payoff for an individual is not necessarily linearly related to dollars. Our first dollar is worth far more to us than our millionth dollar. Also, money has great symbolic value for some people and, therefore, they attach greater value to it than simply economic buying power.

Because of the differing utility of money and its symbolic value, you can never assume that your opponent's minimum and aspiration levels are consistent with what you believe them to be. One way to identify your opponent's probable needs in a negotiation is to ask a co-worker to play the opponent's role and have him or her prepare a negotiating position for the opponent. Then sit down and run a mock negotiation with that person. Afterwards, you can ask about the various goals that were set, the methods by which the goals were established, his or her feelings when making concessions, and the particular psychological needs that were aroused during the mock negotiations.

Determine the Personal Relationship Desired

The last step in the analysis phase of preparation is to categorize what you want the personal relationship between the parties to be after the negotiations are completed. These are the three possible post-negotiation relationships:

1. No interdependence.
2. Continued interaction with weak interdependence.
3. Vital interdependence.

Examples of the no-interdependence situation would be a negotiated settlement with a bankrupt vendor, or a termination agreement with a departing executive. In situations of no interdependence, there are minimal restrictions on the kinds of tactics that can be used because you are not concerned about offending the other party and you're not seeking a reasonable and just settlement of the issues. Your only concern is achieving your own goal.

When negotiations will culminate in continued interaction but weak interdependence, you are restricted from using the most offensive tactics. In those situations in which you will have continuous, important, vital interdependence after the negotiations are completed—for example, after settling the terms of a union-management contract or an individual employment contract— a natural feeling of trust and goodwill after reaching final agreement is essential.

The dilemma once faced by those involved in the New York City newspaper business is a prime example of what can happen when the parties fail to consider their interdependence. During the late 1960s, Bertram Powers, as the head of the Printers Union (International Typographical Union, Local 6), was a very powerful and hard bargainer. He bargained for high wages and succeeded in obtaining clauses in the newspaper contracts that prevented the newspapers from automating their composing processes. The printers won that battle, but lost the war; the newspapers were subsequently forced into an uneconomical situation and at least three of the major newspapers ultimately went out of business, leaving several thousand newspaper people without jobs. Because he didn't consider the continuous and important interdependence between the printers and newspapers, Powers negotiated as though there was no interdependence at all.

STEP 2. SET YOUR GOALS

Unless you know where you are going, you are unlikely to get there. This truism is particularly true in negotiations. You must know exactly what you want before you reach the negotiating table. On quantifiable win-lose issues, you need to establish your aspiration level and your minimum acceptable level. These are identified for our example in Figure 1 as the buyer's aspiration level ($80,000) and the buyer's highest possible offering price ($93,000). Because the seller's lowest acceptable price is $85,000, which is less than $93,000 (the highest price the buyer can offer), there is a possibility of reaching an agreement. The range between $85,000 and $93,000 is the settlement range.

After they are split up, many issues will no longer be quantifiable on a continuous scale; they will be discrete issues. The response to them will be either "yes" or "no." Each of the discrete issues should be rated as "vital," "desirable," or "don't care." Referring back to the management continuity issue in our example, it might be desirable not to pay the seller a salary after the sale is consummated. Or we might plan to offset any salary that is paid in the original purchase price. The retention of a title for the seller is a "don't care." Giving him or her an office and associated status is "desirable to avoid" because it does cost money but it might also have value far in excess of cost to the seller. It is also desirable to avoid consulting the seller on the issues after the sale because this can be bothersome and his or her advice would have little value; on the other hand, it might be relatively cheaper to do so, and this might have great value for the seller.

One vital issue among the fractionated issues is influence. The seller ought not to have influence over the company after it is sold. And finally, it is desirable that the employees become personally loyal to the buyer after the company is sold.

The goal-setting process is not complete until there is a specific goal for every component of every issue, and the importance of each goal is determined. Failure to establish goals for every item makes a negotiator vulnerable to manipulation by the opponent during negotiations; the opponent will find it

Figure 1
Aspiration Levels and Acceptable Price

much easier to change their aspiration levels if you haven't established goals and committed yourself to those goals by recording them.

STEP 3. SET THE STAGE

There are four aspects of negotiations that are manipulable: the agenda, the physical arrangements, the use of negotiating agents, and the audience.

The Agenda

Prepare your own agenda for the negotiation. Do not accept the opponent's agenda without careful scrutiny to make sure that it is neutral or to your advantage. By preparing your own agenda you have the advantage of determining which issues will be discussed, defining those issues, and setting the order of the items to be discussed. Perhaps more important, you can omit issues you do not want to discuss. Here is a recommended order for the agenda:

1. *Define terms and clarify any assumptions necessary to make the negotiation successful.* This is best done early in the negotiation before tempers flare and feelings rise. Failure to clarify terms and assumptions before the

negotiations get heated can cause unnecessary problems later on.

2. *Discuss issues requiring creative solutions.* Again, these are items that should be handled while the mood is calm and things are under control. It becomes very difficult to be creative when you are digging in your heels during a particularly heated negotiation session.

3. *Discuss win-win issues.*

4. *Negotiate the easy or the less important win-lose issues.*

5. *Settle the difficult win-lose issues.* The difficult win-lose issues are usually settled last because they are the most difficult, and most negotiators intuitively avoid them until very near the end of a negotiation.

In laying out the agenda, set the time limits to your own advantage. As the time limit approaches in the negotiation process, aspirations tend to fall, and concessions tend to be made very quickly.

During negotiations, do not be rigid about the agenda. Use log-rolling techniques. When you encounter difficulty on one issue, switch to a different issue; when that one gets difficult, switch back again.

♦　♦　♦　♦　♦

The Physical Arrangements

Negotiate at your own facility if possible. If not, negotiate at a neutral site. Do not negotiate at the opponent's site because that puts you in a subordinate position. The party that hosts a negotiation controls such amenities as coffee and can control the time schedule; most important, the host has the advantage of having his or her information and other resources conveniently at hand.

Other aspects of the arrangement can be manipulated in ways that I don't recommend. For example, you can put bright lights behind your head so they shine into the opponent's eyes during a negotiation and put your face in a shadow. You can provide chairs that are uncomfortable for the opponent. You can turn the temperature up or down so that it will make the opponent uncomfortable while you dress appropriately. Most opponents, however, will see right through these maneuvers and will demand a change. Furthermore, you will probably alienate the opponent and lose the advantage. You might find such tactics useful, however, when you expect to have no continuing interdependence with the opponent, or when upsetting the opponent is a deliberate tactic.

Use of Agents

A general rule you should keep in mind: Never negotiate with your *opponent's* agent. There are advantages, however, to using your own agent. An agent can be sent into a negotiation with limited authority to make commitments. If an agent makes a concession that you find untenable, it is easier to withdraw that concession than if you made it yourself. If your agent negotiates to an impasse, it is easy for you, as the principal, to order him or her to make a new concession to break the impasse.

The biggest advantage in using agents is that they are less psychologically involved in the process and have less ego at stake. Because they are not representing their own interests, they are less likely to let emotions interfere with their cool and rational approach to negotiation. Agents can be psychologically detached from negotiations; therefore, they suffer less from "loss of face" when they make concessions, and their egos don't interfere with the use of the appropriate tactic. In some instances agents have an added advantage; they can put more time into preparation than a busy executive can. They might also have a better background knowledge of the specific subject areas under negotiation, and that makes them more effective negotiators. Experienced negotiating agents can be particularly valuable because they are familiar with negotiating tactics and are likely to have a wider repertoire of negotiating behaviors. In addition, familiarity and confidence that reduce stress also broaden their behavioral repertoire.

Audience Effects

Negotiators, like most people, want positive rather than negative reactions to their behavior. This is particularly the case with negotiators because their egos are involved in the negotiations and because negotiations are competitive. Because of this need to earn favorable marks, negotiators tend to advocate what they believe to be their audience's position. If only two negotiators are present in a room, the negotiators tend to seek positive evaluation from each other. If, however, a negotiator has a partisan audience, he or she will more strongly adhere to the position that he or she conceives of as that of the audience.

From this, we can deduce two decision-making rules about the presence of an audience during negotiations: (1) For maximum flexibility in creative solutions, no audience should be present. Negotiators can then speak tentatively, make compromises, and propose rather unusual solutions that would probably be initially unacceptable to the audience. (2) For tough win-lose negotiations, your negotiator should have an audience. This will compel your negotiator to adhere to your position and prevent him or her from making concessions too easily or being too concerned with a positive evaluation by the opponent. It is also advantageous to isolate the opponent from his or her audience while your negotiator negotiates with a partisan audience present. This is difficult to arrange but it can be done, especially if the negotiation takes place at your facility.

STEP 4. TACTICALLY PLAN YOUR MOVES

You should enter negotiations with tactical plans for your opening demands, your concession pattern, ways to make the opponent look good (that is, to help him or her save face), and ways to break impasses. You should have them recorded on planning sheets so that you have them readily available at negotiations.

The Opening Demand

The initial demands do more to influence the outcome than any other single tactic in the entire negotiation because the opening demands have a major effect on the parties' aspiration levels. Two rules apply to the opening demand. The first is get your opponent to state his or her position first so that you can gain information from the opponent and find out what his or her aspiration level is.

The second rule is make your opening demand extreme but plausible. Again, the purpose is to change your opponent's aspiration level. An extreme demand on your part will tend to reduce the opponent's aspiration level and deliver minimum information about your actual aspiration level. If the *opponent* sets an extreme opening demand and you set a moderate opening demand, the tendency to split the difference puts you at a disadvantage. If both parties open

with moderate demands and the negotiators split the difference, the result does not favor either party. Obviously, it is to your advantage to set an extreme opening demand, have the *opponent* set a moderate opening demand, and then split the difference.

CONCESSION PATTERN

Before the negotiations, you should make a list of concessions that you are willing to make. This list should be complete, containing three things: small concessions on the large issues; as many concessions on the less important issues as you can devise; and some "throw away" items that look like concessions but cost you nothing at all. There are two advantages to having such a list prepared before the negotiations:

1. You won't feel as if you're losing face when you give up something that you had planned to give up anyway.

2. Negotiations are stressful situations. You will have a list to refer to so you do not concede anything you didn't plan to.

During the negotiation remember these important points about concessions.

1. Many small concessions are better than fewer large ones.

2. Always extract a concession from your opponent for each concession that you make.

3. Use throw-away concessions to get substantive concessions from your opponent.

If you have carefully fractionated all of the negotiation issues, you can advantageously repackage the concessions. Packaging is the opposite of fractionating. You put several concessions together into one package and make one concession that appears to be substantial. The advantage is that you can package concessions in ways that benefit your negotiating position.

The final rule in concession planning: Never rush into making them.

Breaking Impasses

Coming to an impasse during a negotiation creates extreme tension. For this reason, it is particularly important to prepare methods of trying to break impasses well before the negotiation meeting. Of course, one way to break an impasse is to make concessions, but you should have a list of ways to break impasses without making any concessions of substance.

Calling a recess is the most frequently used method to break an impasse. You don't need any other reason to call for a recess—but it might be a good idea to be prepared with a few such excuses as "It's time for lunch" or "I have to talk with my experts." Impasses are fraught with tension; having a joke ready to tell is an effective way to break that tension. Because it is difficult to remember jokes in times of extreme tension, it helps to have one written in your notes.

If you happen to be negotiating with an agent representing the opponent, this is clearly the time to ask to negotiate directly with the principals. The impasse might have occurred because the agent reached the limit of his authority. Demand to negotiate with someone who has the authority to make binding decisions.

Granting a throw-away concession is another way to break an impasse. If the concession has some value for the opponent, your action will certainly get the negotiations moving again. But even if it has no value and the opponent recognizes it for what it is, your action can possibly get discussion started again—even if only to discuss why the concession has no particular value. The important thing in breaking an impasse is to keep the communication flowing.

An alternative version of the throw-away concession is repackaging the issues—that is, saying the same thing in different ways. Let's take the example discussed earlier. In the merger under negotiation, a company was being acquired at an offering price of $85,000 with no additional salary to be paid to the company's seller. To repackage the issues, you could offer to pay $80,000 for the company and include a consulting contract to the seller paying $500 a day for ten days. Even though your actual cost is still $85,000, the value to the seller might be greater if he or she values being called a "consultant" after the sale is consummated. Again, even if the opponent doesn't think that repackaging has any value, it will get the discussion moving while he or she explains more about his or her position; in the process, some useful information might be divulged.

Make the Opposing Negotiator Feel Good

Negotiators who make concessions frequently feel that they have lost some pride. The more strongly the negotiator is committed to a particular position, the more deflating it is to deviate from that position. Therefore, one tactic that can make the opponent feel good is to prevent him or her from becoming overly committed to a particular position. For example, if the opposing negotiator says "I must have a price of $90,000" or "I demand an irrevocable contract," you can rephrase the statement so that it becomes a desire instead of a demand. For example, "I understand that you would like to get a price of at least $90,000" or "You think that it is in your best interest to have an irrevocable contract." The object is to maintain your opponent's flexibility.

It is gratifying to be understood. One way to make opponents feel good is to simply let them know you understand their position. To do this you can paraphrase the position accurately. That way, they know that you understand the objective even if you don't necessarily agree with it. If the only thing opponents hear is your counterdemand, they are likely to feel frustrated because they will probably conclude that you do not understand the basic objective.

The most effective way to make the opponent feel good is to praise him or her publicly, especially to his or her constituents. A comment to the audience such as "Charlie drives a hard bargain and represents your interests very effectively" is a potent ego-booster and might lead him or her to make a concession later, knowing that the constituents appreciate that their interests are being handled effectively.

SUMMARY

Negotiating is extremely complex interpersonal behavior. Many variables are at play simultaneously, and in the heat of the confrontation no one negotiator can remember or deal effectively with them all. For this reason, it is mandatory to prepare for negotiations. Preparation will broaden the negotiator's flexibility and tactical repertoire; having planned the tactics well ahead of time, the negotiator will not be operating solely on momentary emotions.

TEAMWORK

Bill Scott

In this chapter, we focus on negotiating-team issues: choosing and organizing the negotiating team; choosing the team leader; deciding how the team will operate; and keeping the colleagues who remain at home involved.

TEAM SELECTION AND ORGANIZATION

How big should a negotiating team be?

In one sense, the size of a team should conform to the old adage about the size of a committee—"The best number of people to have on a committee is one." The problems of ensuring collaboration, ensuring communication between team members, ensuring that each member has a satisfying element in the negotiation—all these problems of satisfying the team members can exceed the problems of negotiating with the Other Party. In the words of one highly experienced negotiator: "When we were in Mexico, we had a lot of trouble negotiating with the Mexicans. But that was nothing compare to the trouble I had with my own colleagues."

But there is often need to have more information and more expertise available than any one

person can contribute—business knowledge, financial knowledge, transport information, international experts. A case can be made for a dozen or twenty people, each having a contribution to make within some major international negotiation, but if we take a dozen and the Other Party takes a dozen, that is a total of twenty-four. Obviously, twenty-four is not a comfortable number to be negotiating.

What, then, is a commendable size for a negotiating team?

I suggest that the number is probably four. The main reasons for this number are:

1. Size of group.
2. Control of team.
3. Range of expertise.
4. Changing membership.

Size of the group

There is a maximum size for work-groups such as committees, if that work-group is to be productive and full of ideas with everybody contributing. You don't want the work-group to grow too big for everybody to be involved, or too diffuse in the range of interests and ideas conveyed. The maximum is about eight people. In negoti-

From Scott, Bill. *The Skills of Negotiating* (1993). Gower Publishing: Gower House, Croft Road, Aldershot, Hampshire GU 11 34R England. Reprinted by permission.

ation, two teams of four people each will probably work out well.

Control of team

For team-control reasons, four is also a convenient number. Management principles suggest that the span of control for any manager operating in such dramatic and changing circumstances as the conduct of a negotiation is about three or four people. If the team leader is required to oversee the negotiations and the co-ordination of a team with as many as six or seven people responsible to him, the team leader will have difficulty comfortably controlling the team.

Range of expertise

The expertise required in a protracted negotiation that lasts over several months might well need to include a dozen or a score of different perspectives from each team. But within the scope of any one negotiating meeting, it will not be possible to take more than three or four different perspectives.

There might be need for more detailed discussion than can be handled by the leader and three or four members. For example, a production member might not have sufficient detailed information on production plans, material supplies, technical feasibilities, etc. and might need the support of specialists from those fields. When this happens, it is normally possible to arrange a sub-negotiation: a separate work-group consisting of the production member from each team, together with three or four specialists assisting each, who would meet as a separate group, independently of the main negotiation. The respective specialist members would report back to the main negotiation.

Changing membership

There is no need to keep the same team throughout. As negotiations develop, the need for particular forms of expertise changes. For example, production and technical expertise might be invaluable in exploratory and creative phases, but redundant when it comes to the legal embodiment of settlement. Equally, the presence of lawyers who should be concerned with details of drafting is an encumbrance at the creative phase of a negotiation. It is not necessary for the team membership to remain constant—the production member might well be present for the first three or four meetings in a series, leaving a seat vacant for the next couple of meetings. A lawyer can be brought in for the final two sessions.

In this respect, four should be regarded as a maximum size for a negotiating team. If there is need for more people to be present at a negotiation—for example, if further experts are needed—they should be there in the role of advisers to the members who are negotiating, and not as full members of the team. They should, literally and metaphorically, sit behind the members.

In making this assertion that four is an effective number, we are considering genuine patterns of negotiation. We must distinguish nominal patterns in which groups of possibly a dozen people are required to act as a team. Such patterns are found, for example, within the jurisdiction of some governments. Where such governments are involved in commercial negotiations, the apparent formalities are conducted within the forum of teams of twelve, but in these circumstances real patterns of negotiation tend to take place outside the formal negotiating room.

Key people are needed at the negotiating table. In the selection of negotiating teams, there is always likely to be conflict between this need for key people to be involved in the negotiation and the need for the same key people to keep things going back home. This is a managerial problem, and priorities need to be set by the bosses of the negotiating team.

However, the case for key people being included in negotiating teams does not rest solely on the contribution that they will make at the negotiating table. It rests also on the degree of commitment that these key people will have for the results of the negotiation. Commitment to implementation is highest when such key executives have been involved in the negotiations and feel a sense of ownership of the results.

Specialists and experts, however brilliant in their own field, are often strangers to the world of negotiation. If they are to be effective supports (and especially if they are to participate as negotiating members of the team), they need training to cover:

1. The presentation of information.

2. Negotiating tactics.

3. Teamwork—both role-handling and support of colleagues.

4. Rehearsals, which should include exposure to tough opposition if that is the style the Other Party is expected to adopt.

Always, the individuals selected for any particular negotiation should be welded into a team before meeting with the Other Party. This requires some discipline in terms of preparation, as well as a good understanding among team members.

To summarize:

1. The size of a negotiating team should be limited to a maximum of four members.

2. If more experts and specialists are needed, they should attend as observers and advisers to full members of the team. They should not have speaking roles.

3. Key people might have to be taken away from their other duties within the enterprise, and brought in not only to carry weight at the negotiating table, but also to give them ownership of decisions and of subsequent implementation.

4. Experts and specialists need training just as much as negotiators.

THE TEAM LEADER

Who is the ideal leader of a negotiating team?

The hierarchical status of the team leader is important. He or she must be seen to be on the same level as the team leader of Other Party. Without this equal status and authorization to deal on the same level as the other side, our Party will soon become subjugated by the Other Party, leading to defensiveness, counter-aggression, and the risk of being over-powered.

But beyond that question of status, there is no single style of leader who is, in all circumstances, to be preferred to any other style. What is important is that the team works together effectively, and team-effectiveness depends upon the members being able to operate in a style to which they are accustomed. If they are in an enterprise where all information is fed to one boss who then makes all the management decisions, then the negotiating team will need a similar type of leader: one who will bear the brunt of the discussion during the negotiation, turning to his team members only for advice about situations and possibilities within their areas of expertise which he will then pass on. If, on the other hand, the enterprise is one with a style that includes much delegation, the team leader needs to be someone who will control the negotiating process with a loose rein, encouraging his team members to make major contributions.

The style of the team leader needs to reflect the style of the enterprise from which the team comes, and there is no one style that is always "right." Nor is there any particular discipline that is the ideal background for a team leader. A good team leader might be found among production people, marketing people, or financial people. It is most likely to be found amongst people with business experience and less likely to be found in those with technical expertise. As a rough generalization, experienced negotiators seem most often to come from those who have spent their formative years in the hustle and bustle of the business world, rather than in academia.

TEAM SUPPORT

Team members should support one another both verbally and non-verbally.

The way the team leader introduces his colleagues at the very start of the negotiation will influence the way the team is perceived by the Other Party.

> One team leader introduced his teammate this way: "Our accountant, Norman Kellett." At another negotiation, the leader introduced him like this: "Norman Kellett, who has fifteen years' experience in handling the financing and the financial control of projects up to £15 million . . "
>
> Norman Kellett was noticeably more influential in one negotiation than in the other.

Throughout the negotiations, you must make sure that each person's statements are reinforced by his colleagues.

Some helpful verbal reinforcements: "absolutely correct" and "Yes, that is right." You can verbally reinforce by these statements with a few from your own perception.

> The production man's comment about delivery problems—"I am afraid that all machines are fully booked up for the next three months"—can be reinforced by the marketing man: "Yes, and I am also afraid that the order book is continuously full. Even three months will be terribly difficult."

However obvious such support might seem, it is neglected in far too many negotiations.

> **Principal:** "Well, if you really expect us to pay that much for a pump, we will just do without one."

> **His technical adviser,** privately commenting to him: "But we have got to have one."

It is not only verbal support that is important between team members: Non-verbal support is also critical.

When Tom and Harry go out regularly to conduct negotiations together, Harry becomes used to what Tom says every time. Good old Tom—he goes on for ten minutes talking about the technical qualities of our nuts and bolts. It is always the same story, and Harry is a bit bored by it. He concentrates his eyes on the paper in front of him and his thoughts on yesterday's golf. It is natural for Harry to do so, and it is natural that the Other Party picks up on it: Harry treats Tom's views as if they were completely worthless.

Then there comes the day when Tom conducts a negotiation with Jack, instead of Harry. Tom makes exactly the same series of statements, but as he does so, Jack shifts his chair a couple of inches so that he faces more toward Tom. He watches Tom intently, and nods his head approvingly at some of the statements. He looks across at the Other Party to make sure that they are giving their full attention to Tom and are recognizing that these are the words of a man of great experience and wisdom.

Tom is more influential with Jack than when he's paired up with Harry.

THE BACK-HOME TEAM

The negotiating team will need the support of the people back home. These will in part include bosses, as well as peers, secretaries, and subordinates.

The negotiating team might well need to negotiate with this back-home team before setting off.

They will need to check on the extent to which they can commit the organization and their colleagues informally as well as formally. They need to communicate and involve the back-home members so that they can expect support while they are away.

You must also be aware of the probability that there will be conflict between an away-team and the back-home team. This type of conflict has been systematically researched. It will inevitably grow between the home and away teams unless positive steps are taken to prevent it. The only steps that have been shown to work require eyeball-to-eyeball contact between the two teams— the away and the back-home. Perhaps the negotiating team can return to base for progress discussions with colleagues; emissaries from either the negotiating team or the home-team can visit on a regular basis. Video conferencing can be set up on a regular basis, as well; this would be especially helpful to keep the away-team abreast of any new information that might affect negotiations.

SUMMARY

1. Teamwork depends on the size and selection of the original team.

2. The team leader must be chosen on the basis of appropriate status, as well as skills, and operate in ways that are familiar to team members.

3. Members of the team should support one another, both verbally and non-verbally.

4. Liaison with the back-home team requires face-to-face contact both before and during the negotiations.

Chapter Eight

NEGOTIATION FAILURE

WHY NEGOTIATIONS GO WRONG

Max H. Bazerman

On the eve of the Revolutionary War, English political philosopher Edmund Burke eloquently exhorted members of the House of Commons to head off the coming conflict by negotiating with the upstart colonials: "All government—indeed, every human benefit and enjoyment, every virtue, and every prudent act—is founded on compromise and barter."

His observation is at least as accurate today, when negotiation is woven into the daily fabric of our lives. On the personal level, we buy and sell houses and cars, jointly decide where to eat dinner, and bargain over salaries. On a larger scale, unions and management negotiate contracts, and nations arrange treaties and trade agreements. Failed negotiations can produce anything from minor inconveniences to nuclear holocaust.

In studying why negotiations fail, I have built on what other researchers have learned about decision-making in general, concentrating on the biases that can undermine negotiations. I will describe five common cognitive mistakes negotiators make, and suggest some strategies for avoiding them.

EXPANDING THE FIXED PIE

Two sisters have a single orange to share. One wants to make orange juice. The other wants the peel to make a cake. After much discussion, they agree to a distributive compromise. They each take half the orange and end up with a very small glass of juice for one sister and a very small cake for the other.

In this example, first presented by Mary Follett many years ago, the sisters overlooked an integrative solution to their problem: One sister takes all the juice and the other takes all the peel. This way, each gets exactly what she wants and twice as much as she actually received. Such integrative solutions reconcile the parties' interests and yield a higher joint benefit than is possible through simple compromise. Unfortunately, too many negotiators have the same "fixed-pie" bias that kept the sisters fighting over the orange: They assume that there is only a fixed amount of profit or gain in what is being negotiated, and that in order for them to win something, the other party must necessarily lose it.

This is true in some negotiations, of course, but too often we assume it is true without trying to think integratively. I believe this comes from our highly competitive society. We experience so many real win-lose situations—in athletics, in admission to college, in job promotion—that we apply the lessons learned indiscriminately. Faced with negotiations that require both competition and cooperation, as most do, we think only of the competitive aspects. This orientation produces a distributive rather than an integrative approach to bargaining.

Psychologists Dean Pruitt and Jeffrey Rubin describe the Camp David talks this way in their book *Social Conflict:* "When Egypt and Israel sat down to negotiate at Camp David in October 1978, it appeared that they had before them an intractable conflict. Egypt demanded the immediate return of the entire Sinai Peninsula; Israel, which had occupied the Sinai since the 1967 Middle East War, refused to return an inch of this land. Efforts to reach agreement, including the proposal of a compromise in which each nation would retain half of the Sinai, proved completely unacceptable to both sides."

As long as the dispute was defined in terms of what percentage of the land each side would control, no agreement could be reached. However, once both realized that what Israel really cared about was the security that the land offered while Egypt was primarily interested in sovereignty over it, the stalemate was broken. The two countries were then able to reach an integrative solution: Israel would return the Sinai to Egypt in exchange for assurances of a demilitarized zone and Israeli air bases in the Sinai.

The fixed-pie assumption reduces our ability to negotiate matters of day-to-day existence as well as those of international politics. Consider a Friday evening dinner and a movie. You and your date like each other's company, but you have different tastes in restaurants and movies. Instead of haggling about each issue separately, see if one of you cares more about the restaurant and the other more about the movie. If you do, you can work out an integrative trade-off—one picks the restaurant and the other the movie—in which you both get what is most important to you.

Similarly, while purchasing goods is usually thought of in win-lose terms, another approach is sometimes possible. For example, a retailer might be willing to cut the price if payment is made in cash—especially, in some cases, if you don't ask for a receipt or other documentation the IRS might find of interest.

DE-HEXING THE WINNER'S CURSE

While on vacation in a foreign country, you spot a very attractive ruby in a jewelry store window. You know something about rubies, but you are far from being an expert. After some preliminary discussion, you make the merchant an offer that you think is on the low side. He quickly accepts and the sale is made. How do you feel as you walk out the door?

If you are like most people in this situation, you find yourself suffering from "the winner's curse," a sinking feeling that you've been taken. Why else would the merchant have accepted your offer so quickly?

My research with economist William Samuelson suggests that a key factor in the winner's curse is that one side has much better information than the other. A good negotiator must consider the knowledge and likely strategy of the other side, but this is hard to do when our opponents know something we don't and can use the information to selectively accept or reject our offer. This quandary was expressed humorously by Groucho Marx when he said he didn't care to belong to any club that would accept him as a member. Its willingness to take him—to accept his offer—suggested that its standards were so low that the club wasn't worth joining. Although we are all familiar with the saying "Let the buyer beware," we seem to have difficulty putting it into practice. We consistently undervalue the importance of looking at a situation from the opponent's standpoint and getting comparable information before we complete a transaction: a good mechanic's evaluation of a used car, an inspector's assessment of a house we are considering buying, a jeweler's assessment of a coveted gem. To protect yourself in negotiations of any sort, you need to develop or borrow the expertise to balance the quality of information. If you can't get such information before making an offer, ask yourself, "Will I be happy if the offer is accepted quickly?" If not, reconsider your offer.

DE-ESCALATING CONFLICT

The Professional Air Traffic Controllers Organization (PATCO) strikes to obtain a set of concessions from the government. When the government refuses to meet the demands, PATCO has two options: to back off and return to work under the old conditions, or to continue the strike, despite the threat of dismissal.

Shortly after the strike started, it became clear to objective observers that, faced with an unyielding administration, PATCO had a weak negotiating position. Rational analysis would have led its leaders to end the strike or at least reduce their demands before its members were fired. Instead, PATCO acted just as individuals, organizations, and countries so often do in this situation: It increased its commitment to the strike to justify the earlier decision to proceed with it.

In negotiations, both sides often start with extreme demands, expecting to compromise somewhere in the middle. But they get caught up in the struggle, feel they have too much time, money, and ego invested to back off, and take a hard line instead of adopting a conciliatory or problem-solving approach.

Why does this happen, when rational outsiders realize that continuing or escalating the conflict is a mistake? There are at least four complementary reasons. First, once negotiators make an initial commitment to a position, they are more likely to notice information that supports their initial evaluation of the situation. Second, their judgment is biased to interpret what they see and hear in a way that justifies their initial position. Third, negotiators often increase their demands or hold out too long to save face with their constituency. They might even act against their constituents' best interest to "look strong" to them.

Finally, the competitive context of the negotiation adds to the likelihood of escalation. Unilaterally giving up or even reducing demands seems like defeat, while escalating commitment leaves the future uncertain. It is easy for negotiators to see this uncertain future as more desirable than the certain loss of concession. After all, the other side might be ready to cave in.

This last point is illustrated by a game known as the Dollar Auction (see "'Psychological Traps," *Psychology Today*, March 1981). Someone offers to auction off a dollar bill to the highest bidder. The highest bidder will get the dollar, but the second highest must also pay what he or she bid and receive nothing.

The bidding typically starts out fast and furious until it reaches the *50-to-75* cent range, at which point everyone except the two highest bidders normally drops out of the auction. What usually follows is an escalating pattern in which both end up bidding far more than a dollar, since neither is willing to quit and accept a loss. People escalate their commitment to justify their earlier bids and to prevent the financial and ego loss of coming in second.

No specific bid is clearly wrong, since it is rational to bid "just another 10 cents," if the other party is about to quit bidding. But when both parties think this way, an escalatory spiral emerges that is very reminiscent of the Vietnam War and other international and industrial failures in which both competitors get trapped by their previous commitments. To prevent this kind of escalation, negotiators must be aware of their tendency to justify past actions and must constantly evaluate the costs and benefits of continuing along the same lines. Being aware of the tendency to escalate can also be very helpful in anticipating how opponents are likely to think and act. People usually hold out when they have too much invested in their position psychologically to give in. This suggests that a negotiator should avoid pushing opponents into a corner, getting them angry, or otherwise making them feel that they can't afford to give up the struggle.

UNDERCUTTING OVERCONFIDENCE

After a baseball player is in the major leagues for three years, he can choose arbitration if he and his team are unable to agree on a contract. Under the system of final-offer arbitration, the two sides submit offers and the arbitrator must accept one or the other, not a compromise. The challenge for each side is to come just a little closer than the opposition to what the arbitrator thinks is appropriate.

Let's say the player's agent estimates that the team owner will offer $400,000 per year. The agent believes his player is worth twice that, but estimates that the arbitrator will think $600,000 is right. What amount should the agent propose?

A naive analysis would suggest an offer of, say, $775,000—a bit closer to $600,000 than the expected $400,000 offer from the team. This reasoning illustrates a fourth common negotiator error. Individuals are consistently overconfident of the reasonableness of their position and of the likelihood that an objective third party will agree with them. In this case, if the arbitrator's assessment of the appropriate wage turns out to be $550,000 rather than $600,000, the agent's overconfident offer of $775,000 will cost the client hundreds of thousands of dollars when the arbitrator accepts the team's offer because it is closer to his estimate.

Colleague Margaret Neale and I demonstrated this error in several experiments in which negotiator overconfidence showed itself in two areas. In simple two-party negotiations, negotiators

consistently expected the other side to concede more than objective analysis would suggest; and under final-offer arbitration, negotiators overestimated the likelihood that their final offer would be accepted.

For example, while obviously only half of all final offers can be accepted in final-offer arbitration, the people in our experiments estimated, on the average, a 65 to 68 percent probability that their offer would win out. This overconfidence reduces the incentive to compromise, while a less optimistic assessment makes a negotiator more uncertain and thus more likely to compromise further. In our studies, negotiators who were simply appropriately confident were consistently more willing to compromise and more successful in negotiations than their overconfident fellows.

Negotiators seem to follow the intuitive rule, "When in doubt, be overconfident." To avoid this, negotiators should try to obtain objective assessments from outside experts to temper overconfidence and overestimation.

REFRAMING NEGOTIATIONS

You bought your house in 1982 for $60,000. It is now on the market for $109,000, with a real target of $100,000, which you estimate is the true market value. You receive an offer of $90,000. Does this represent a $30,000 gain (compared to the original price), or a $10,000 loss (compared to your target price)?

Both answers are correct. But which way you think of the situation strongly affects your attitude toward the offer. Research by psychologists Daniel Kahneman and Amos Tversky suggests that there are important differences in how people respond to problems, depending on whether they are framed in terms of losses or gains. In a series of experiments covering situations as diverse as risking lives and risking money, they demonstrated that if a situation is presented in terms that make it seem like a choice between a small sure gain and a risky larger gain, most will take the sure thing. But if exactly the same situation is presented in a way that makes it seem like a choice between a sure smaller loss and a possible larger loss, most prefer to gamble.

Neale and I extended this finding to the area of negotiations when we analyzed this hypothetical situation:

> The union claims it needs to raise pay scales to $12 an hour and that, considering inflation, anything less would represent a loss to its members. Management argues that the company can't remain competitive if it pays more than $10 an hour; anything more would be an unacceptable loss. What will happen if both sides have to choose between settling for $11 an hour (a certain settlement) or going to binding arbitration (a risky settlement, since both sides must agree to abide by whatever figure the arbitrator decides on)? If both labor and management continue to view the matter in terms of what they have to lose, they are likely to choose the risky road of arbitration. But if each side reframes the situation positively—the union seeing anything above $10 an hour as a gain, and management seeing anything under $12 an hour as a gain—then caution will rule and a negotiated settlement of $11 is more likely.

Neale, Thomas Magliozzi, and I confirmed the finding that people who frame the outcomes of negotiation in terms of gains or profit are more willing to make concessions to obtain the sure outcome available in a negotiated settlement. In contrast, negotiators who think in terms of losses or costs are more likely to take the risk-seeking action of holding out and possibly losing all in an attempt to force further concessions from their opponent.

Negotiators need to be aware of how framing affects the decision process. If you are evaluating a negotiation in terms of what you can lose, make sure you also consider what you can gain, and vice versa. Otherwise, your behavior might reflect the distortion of framing rather than your actual preference for a particular action.

The framing effect also suggests that a negotiator should try to present information in a way that leads the opposition to see what they have to gain from a risk-free settlement. Finally, when third parties are trying to get others to compromise, they should strive to frame suggestions in ways that show what both sides will gain from a settlement.

I have presented these common negotiator errors as separate problems, but clearly they overlap. To mention just a few examples, negotiators who don't start out with a fixed-pie bias find it easier to avoid escalating demands and to reframe their thinking and proposals in a positive way. Negotiators who try to understand an opponent's thinking are less likely to feel overconfident in their judgment or to escalate demands needlessly. Negotiators who are aware of the tendency to be overconfident in their judgment are more likely to consider what opponents are thinking and to reframe their perceptions in positive terms.

HOW TO AVOID THE EIGHT BIGGEST NEGOTIATING TRAPS

Bob Busch and Phil Faris

Negotiating is a challenging process for even the best salesperson. Budgets, and sometime careers, are made and lost as a result of one's negotiating skills. Although there are no "quick fixes" or instant formulas for negotiation success, there are predictable mistakes or "traps" that our research has been able to identify. Knowing these traps in advance and taking the action that top performing salespeople take to avoid them can go a long way toward improving your negotiation effectiveness.

This article identifies the Eight Most Common Negotiation Traps and outlines several approaches aimed at minimizing or eliminating their impact on the negotiation outcome.

1. Failure to plan.

2. Setting low aspiration levels.

3. Negotiating price before the value of the product is established.

4. Not being prepared to walk away.

5. Focusing on demands, not needs.

6. Making unnecessary concessions.

7. Letting emotions influence negotiating strategy

Published by Sales Management Resources, Barrington, Illinois. Reprinted by permission.

8. Failing to create a positive negotiating climate.

1. FAILURE TO PLAN

People don't plan to fail in a negotiation, but they often fail to plan. Many salespeople walk into a negotiation virtually blindfolded. They have only a vague idea of what they want and an even vaguer idea of what the other party wants or needs.

Don't go into a negotiation blindfolded!

Solution: Know where you're going and how you're going to get there before you start. Before each negotiation:

- Schedule planning time.

- Identify the following things for yourself, the buyer (or buyers) and the competition:

- Needs (must have)

- Wants (like to have)

- Currencies (things of value to the other party in the negotiation)

- Your best-case proposal

- Options (listing alternative solutions that would be acceptable to both sides, and what to do if no agreement is reached)

▌ Anticipate resistance, objections, and tactics.

▌ Identify internal obstacles and solutions.

▌ Visualize success.

2. SETTING LOW ASPIRATION LEVELS

Most salespeople take one of two approaches when setting their initial aspirations for a negotiation. Some salespeople lower their expectations *in anticipation* of buyer resistance. Others have unrealistically high expectations that aren't defensible, which often leads to large concessions or unnecessary lost sales.

Don't set your sights too low!

Solution: You get what you expect, so expect what you deserve. Higher aspiration levels are generally a result of confidence, and a great confidence builder is preparation. Good preparation can help salespeople discover a higher price that is realistic and defendable.

A good technique for increasing your aspiration level is to add five to ten percent to every proposal and then defend your price to someone

(e.g., manager, another salesperson). If you can defend your price, you increase the chances of getting some, if not all, of the five- to ten-percent increase. If you can't defend your price, you'll need to do some more homework.

When a buyer says, "How much?" (especially early in the negotiation), don't flinch. Confidently state the highest yet defendable price by framing it with a reference like, "Many advertisers spend up to $10,000 per month based on their needs and budget," or "Our rate card is $100 per spot." Then ask, "What were you considering?"

This approach establishes the upper limits of your price, but gives you the flexibility to adjust it based on the buyer's response and needs. Remember, it's much easier to negotiate down than to negotiate up.

Another way to comfortably ask for higher rates or greater share is to know the buyer's budget. Some salespeople feel uncomfortable asking for a $2,000 monthly cable budget until they learn the buyer is spending $30,000 per month for newspaper advertising. Although many buyers won't tell you their budgets, you can develop a fairly reliable estimate based on your knowledge of the buyer's current advertising practices (e.g., two full-page ads in the newspaper) and the basic rates of competing advertising media.

3. NEGOTIATING THE PRICE BEFORE THE VALUE OF THE PRODUCT IS ESTABLISHED

Discussing the price before you've established the value of your product greatly reduces the options available to create a win/win agreement. Talking price up-front usually results in a "single currency negotiation." These negotiations are generally not in the salesperson's best interest because the only thing to negotiate is price. The options facing salespeople in this situation is to either meet the price demand or lose the sale.

"Who cares what it does?
At $19.95, it's a great deal!"

Solution: Sell the value of your product before you negotiate price. Before you discuss price, review and gain agreement on the buyer's needs and buying criteria. Simply say, "Before I discuss the price, I'd like to review my understanding of your needs. To begin with, you're interested in X, Y, and Z?" Be sure to get the buyer's agreement on his/her needs before you move on to the presentation and price. This can even be accomplished if you don't get an opportunity to discuss your proposal with the buyer; start your proposal with a review of the client's needs, and then present your solutions to the needs.

When you present your proposal, link your features and benefits to the buyer's stated needs. To ensure buyer involvement, try using the "feature, feedback, benefit" technique. This approach involves presenting a feature and then asking the buyer to describe how it will be of benefit. For example, you can say, "The package I just showed you reaches the buyers you said you want but aren't getting with your current advertising. How would reaching that audience impact your business?"

Then listen to the buyer's response. The buyer will usually respond in one of three ways:

■ Describe a benefit you've identified. If this is the case, reinforce the buyer's desire for that benefit.

■ Describe a benefit you weren't expecting. If this happens, it's an added plus that you can build on.

■ The buyer can't describe or doesn't see a specific benefit when compared to your competition. In this case, you point out the benefits and confirm the buyer's understanding and acceptance of the benefits.

4. NOT BEING PREPARED TO WALK AWAY

If you feel you "need to make a deal at all costs," that's usually what you'll do. Not being prepared to walk away from a win/lose negotiation is like surrendering unconditionally to the enemy. Your plight is left to the compassion of the buyer, and most of the time sets a bad precedent for future negotiation.

Sometimes we need to know
when it's time to walk away!

Solution: Don't negotiate if you're not prepared to walk away. Before you negotiate, determine your walk-away price. This is the price or set of terms and conditions that absolutely must be met in order for your needs to be met. If your needs aren't met, it can't be a win/win negotiation. To give yourself confidence and prevent yourself from being painted in a no-win corner, have a viable option to a negotiated agreement. In your own mind, decide what's your best alternative to making this deal. If you have a good alternative, (e.g., selling to another account, making up the lost revenue next week) it's easier to walk away from a bad deal.

If you've tried a number of options and still feel the proposed solution will not work for you, simply agree to disagree. One possible ending is to say, "Thanks, but I can't make this work for us." Then give your rationale and keep the door open for future negotiations, as well as last minute concessions by the other party. Remember, when you walk, the pressure to make the deal falls back on the buyer. This pressure often leads to the buyer altering their demands and creating opportunities for a win/win solution.

5. FOCUSING ON DEMANDS, NOT NEEDS

When buyers say, "You'll have to cut your price," many salespeople respond by either saying, "How much?" or "I can't." Both responses contribute little to the resolution of a successful negotiation. What salespeople should do is explore the buyer's reasons for making the demand. To craft a solution, salespeople must get beyond the surface of a demand and understand the underlying needs that drive it.

"I guess this means we aren't getting the room with a view, king-size beds, and color TV we asked for."

Solution: Seek understanding before proposing a solution. If the buyer makes a demand by saying, "I need you to cut your price 10 percent," respond by agreeing with the buyer and saying, "We *could* do that, but help me understand why that's a concern for you." Once you understand the underlying need (i.e., "get more for my budget") you can offer alternatives to meet those interests (e.g., changing the offering mix, extending the contract, or reducing the number of spots/pages).

To stay focused on needs is to be clear and firm on your own needs, but be flexible on your demands. High performers are firm on meeting both parties' needs, but they are extremely receptive and flexible on exactly how those needs are met. To help you do this, develop several options that can successfully meet your needs. The more options you have, the more flexible you can be in getting both parties' needs met.

Another key point to remember is that buyers are people who have product, business, and personal needs. They are looking to get all these needs satisfied during the negotiation. An unmet need often derails a potentially successful negotiation. Therefore, be sure you've uncovered and addressed all the buyer's needs at several levels.

6. MAKING UNNECESSARY CONCESSIONS

Fear of losing the sale can be a powerful motivator to make unnecessary concessions. Buyers are often adept at using tactics that put pressure on account executives to make price concessions or to provide costly value-added services (e.g., production, bonus spots, merchandising) that are often undervalued by the customer.

Solution: Yield to principle, not pressure. When pressed to make concessions, do so reluctantly and with careful consideration. Make sure both you and the buyer are fully aware of the value of what you concede.

"If that's out of your price range, how about
$200 . . . and we'll pay to have
it delivered . . . and insure it . . . ?

Instead of making outright concessions, try to make contingent concessions. This is where you give something in exchange for getting something. For example, "I can cut the cost ten percent if you'll extend the contract for six months." *This establishes your desire to help meet the buyer's needs, and asserts your needs as well.*

Four other techniques you can use to maximize the value of the concessions you make:

- Avoid making predictable concessions (i.e., always dropping the price in five- or ten-percent increments). Consider making three percent instead of five percent, and seven percent instead of ten percent. This allows you to retain more value if you must make concessions.

- If you must concede, start with concessions that are easy for you to make and important to the buyer.

- Make your concessions in small increments. Each one should be deliberated and made only after careful thought.

- Have a plan for making concessions. Know what you're willing to give and what you want in return.

7. LETTING EMOTIONS INFLUENCE NEGOTIATING STRATEGY

Emotions are a big part of negotiations. Fear of failure, fear of competition, and discomfort with conflict, coupled with personal chemistry, all influence how you prepare and conduct a negotiation. When left unmanaged, emotions can cause you to take actions that can have a negative impact on negotiation outcomes.

When you lose your emotions,
you lose control!

Solution: Separate people from the problem. Be supportive of people and tough on problems. To do this, you must first be aware of your own emotions (e.g., giving in too easily, taking demands personally) and how they influence you. Second, you must channel your emotional energies into listening to and understanding the buyer's needs, and staying focused on your needs.

If your emotions get the better of you, ask for a "time out." Move away from the negotiation, regain your focus and perspective, and then return to the process.

8. FAILING TO CREATE A POSITIVE NEGOTIATION CLIMATE

By its nature, negotiation involves conflict. However, conflict isn't always bad. The process of *how* conflicts are resolved often influences people's satisfaction level as much or more than the final outcome.

◆ ◆ ◆ ◆ ◆

If you don't invest the time to create a favorable climate, the negotiation often deteriorates into adversarial haggling—a situation where it is difficult, if not impossible, to arrive at a win/win solution.

> "Please have a seat and
> make yourself at home."

Solution: Establish a "me and you against the problem" climate. The time to establish the climate is before the negotiation begins. Be sure you've invested the necessary time to create the climate you feel is most conducive to win/win. Here are a few techniques that can help:

- Agree on the negotiation process. Simply state your intention to play win/win. Then ask the other party to make the same commitment. Establish mutual expectations and ground rules.

- Build trust by being trustworthy.

- Create openness by being open.

- Reward trust and openness in others.

- Assert your needs without attacking the person.

SUMMARY

As we said earlier, "There is no shortcut to negotiation success." However, you can improve your effectiveness by doing what top performers do to avoid the eight biggest negotiating traps.

Phil Faris is president of Phil Faris Associates, a consulting firm specializing in customized sales and management programs designed to produce measurable results.

Bob Busch is vice president of business development for Sterling Institute, McLean, Virginia.

Section IV

Gender Issues in Negotiation

Chapter Nine   *Women at the Bargaining Table*

Chapter Nine

WOMEN AT THE BARGAINING TABLE

OUR GAME, YOUR RULES: DEVELOPING EFFECTIVE NEGOTIATING APPROACHES

Leonard Greenhaigh and Roderick W. Gilkey

Consider the following scenario: A female manager is having a discussion with a male counterpart. They are trying to reach agreement on some issue in dispute. The woman takes a flexible, friendly stance; the man is argumentative and holds firmly to his position. They have made little progress toward agreement. After some time, the woman makes concessions, telling the man she will give in on this issue and that he can make it up to her next time. Some time after the negotiation is over, she learns that he did not disclose all the information he must have had, and that he even made some claims that subsequently proved to be untrue. But she gave him the benefit of the doubt on both these points; she figured he must have become a little confused while arguing for his position.

A couple of weeks later, they meet again to try to reach agreement on another issue in dispute. The woman politely reminds the man that she was generous on the last issue and therefore it is *his* turn to show some flexibility. He dismisses this reminder out of hand and proceeds to take a

firm stand on the current issue. The woman, feeling angry and betrayed, now blames herself for being too unassertive.

The scenario is a familiar one. Assertiveness training, however, is not the answer to this woman's problem. Her poor short-term performance in this negotiation will show little improvement if all she learns are firmer ways of expressing herself. Instead, she needs to understand that there tends to be a fundamental difference in the way men and women view such interactions.

Women in organizations need to understand this difference because the ability to negotiate is a crucial skill in male-dominated organizational life. In theory, business decisions are rational conclusions drawn when problems are considered in the abstract. In practice, however, most significant decisions in organizations emerge from a process of negotiation; that is, reaching the decision involves reconciling the conflicting interests of the people who have some say in the matter. Making an organizational decision that is acceptable and can be implemented might require negotiating with a host of people—peers, subordinates, superiors, people in staff or control roles, customers, suppliers, regulators, news media representatives, perhaps even family members and others who could be indirectly affected by the decision. Most of the time, these people are not conscious of the fact that they are negotiating. Nevertheless, negotiation is such a basic process in organizations that development of people's negotiating skills is as important as any other area of professional development.

During the seven years we have been teaching negotiating skills to managers, executives, and MBAs in training for careers in organizations, we have noticed a difference in the way men and women approach negotiation. We analyzed videotapes of simulated negotiation and found some of the differences reported in the popular press. For example, we saw that women are more likely to use powerless speech: Instead of saying, "Your price is too high based on what your competitors are charging," they tend to say something like, "I don't suppose you'd consider a slightly lower price." Such hesitant, unassuming ways of making a point invite an uncooperative response if the other person is looking for a short-term gain. Women tended to demand less and concede more.

We weren't satisfied, however, that we really understood the nature and full implications of this difference in approach. We studied the relevant literature in social, personality, and developmental psychology, and saw a link between early developmental experiences, adult personality, and the negotiating behavior of young professionals. We then conducted a study to investigate the relationships we expected to find. As a result, we now have a better-informed idea of how to train men and women to reach agreements.

In this chapter, we will talk about what we have learned from our research and how this information is useful in developing women's skills as negotiators.

BACKGROUND

One of the most important factors affecting your approach to negotiation is your time perspective. If you view a negotiation as a single event, you will tend to focus on your immediate gain and probably will not make sacrifices in order to preserve and improve your relationship with the other person. This is known as an *episodic orientation:* you see the negotiation as a single episode whereby the history and future of your relationship with the other person are largely irrelevant. The contrasting time perspective is known as a *continuous orientation*. With such a perspective, you pay attention to the long-term relationship between you and the other person. The present negotiation is one event in a stream of interactions. Therefore, the history and future of the relationship are important—perhaps more important than immediate gain. Thus it is natural to expect that differences in time perspective will lead to differences in negotiating behavior. An episodic orientation should be associated with a competitive approach ("I need to come out ahead in this deal, and it's going to be at your expense"), whereas a continuous orientation should be associated with a more cooperative approach ("Let's find a way to meet both our needs").

Negotiators' different personalities are likely to affect whether they tend to perceive a bargaining situation as more episodic or more continuous. In particular, such differences in time perspective seem to result from a more fundamental difference in men's and women's orientations toward interpersonal relationships. This difference has been noted in a number of studies that have concluded that women tend to be concerned with their need to get along with others, cooperativeness, and fairness to both parties; men, by contrast, are concerned with their own interests, with competing, and with avoiding being controlled or dominated by others.[1]

One researcher attributes these contrasting orientations to differences in early developmental experiences.[2] Females develop their sex-role identity from an interaction *with* the mother that emphasizes interdependence, whereas males establish their sex-role identity through separation and individuation *from* their mothers. These differing experiences produce fundamental sex differences later in life that lead women to define themselves *in relation* to others and men *in contrast* to others.

A related factor is the difference in the way boys and girls approach games. Boys are brought up to play competitive games, in which the objective is to beat the opponent. It is acceptable to gloat about victory and deride the loser. Girls play games that focus less on winning and losing. In fact, if their games are progressing in such a way that someone is going to feel bad, girls are likely to stop the game or change the rules: girls don't sacrifice relationships in order to win games.

Carol Gilligan, in her now-classic book *In a Different Voice*, examines the consequences of such basic differences when those individuals become older children. She notes that the greater emphasis on interdependence and mutuality in women's development accounts for the difference between the sexes in their perspective on moral dilemmas: women tend to emphasize their long-term responsibilities and men their immediate rights.

Gilligan cites as an example the case of two eleven-year-old children, a boy and a girl, who respond to questions about a moral dilemma. The boy, Jake, uses deductive logic to deal with what he sees as a conflict over rights and principles among three people, and he describes the solution that would quickly resolve the issues. The response of the girl, Amy, seems less clear and more equivocal. It is tempting to view Amy's response as being logically inferior to and less morally mature than Jake's, but on closer examination it becomes clear that she is viewing the conflict in very different terms. For her, the problem is one of trying to resolve a human-relations issue through ongoing personal communication. Jake, by contrast, views it as a conflict over rights that can be resolved through a morally informed legal system (the set of rules by which the "game" is played). Amy's response is actually based on a

relatively sophisticated analysis of interpersonal dynamics. Her response calls for an ongoing series of interactions concerned more with preserving the relationships between conflicting parties than with deciding the parties' rights in the immediate situation.

Support for Gilligan's point of view can be found in studies that investigate the motivation of individuals to determine how they relate to other people. For example, some researchers have found a difference between boys and girls in the kinds of achievement toward which they aspire. Boys primarily strive to achieve success and therefore are more task-oriented; girls strive primarily to achieve praise and therefore are more relationship-oriented. Other studies have shown a tendency for males to be more competitive and women more cooperative in their interpersonal interactions.[3] Still other studies have examined whether males and females want different things from their jobs.[4] Those studies examine the view that women tend to be more concerned with interpersonal relationships in the work environment, whereas men appear to be more concerned with such factors as the opportunity for advancement (winning) and greater responsibility and influence (dominance).

One difficulty in conducting these studies is that women react to the experimental situation itself. A group of studies suggests that females appear to be more sensitive than males to a number of interpersonal cues that can influence their responses to the experiments. Such cues include the sex of the experimenter, whether communication is controlled or free in the experiment, and whether fairness issues are involved in the conflict.[5] These factors tend to affect women more than men and indeed explain some of why research findings have been inconsistent.

Thus, some of the traits that tend to characterize women make it difficult for researchers to identify male-female differences accurately.

Taken as a whole, the diverse studies of gender differences show some general tendencies but are inconsistent in their specific conclusions. The inconsistencies are understandable when one takes into account that the behavior of adult negotiators is a function not only of biological sex but also of the effects of developmental experiences. The different childhood socialization experiences of males and females can result in different sex-role orientations, ranging from strongly masculine to strongly feminine. A strongly masculine person is concerned with power and prefers to dominate others rather than be dominated by them; a strongly feminine person is less concerned with dominance and more concerned with nurturance. Masculinity-femininity, however, does not correspond exactly to biological sex. Some boys are raised to have predominantly feminine orientations, and some girls are raised to have predominantly masculine orientations. All people fall on a continuum between these two extremes. Because sex role is expected to have greater effect on negotiating behavior, sex role rather than biological sex is used in the research reported here and in the discussion that follows.

THE STUDY

Having come this far in researching the literature, we were confident that there were masculine-feminine differences in negotiating approaches. As social scientists, however, we realized that our past observations could simply be hunches, that the studies we had read reported some inconsistencies, and that no one had yet directly studied masculine-feminine differences of adult negotiators. The burden of proof was on us to show that such differences really exist.

We decided to study masculine-feminine differences in a controlled, laboratory setting. Instead of observing everyday negotiations, we simulated the situations under controlled conditions and had young professionals role-play the negotia-

tions. There was enough flexibility in the role instructions to allow masculine-feminine differences to emerge as expected. The use of a laboratory study had two advantages over observing naturally occurring negotiations: First, it allowed us to eliminate most extraneous factors that could contaminate the results; second, it would allow other researchers to replicate our study, thereby adding to its scientific value. (A description of the study can be found at the end of this chapter.)

The results of the study proved consistent with what we had hypothesized. Several differences between masculine and feminine negotiators emerged and are summarized in Table 1. The most basic finding was that feminine negotiators tend to visualize the long-term relationship between the people involved when they think about negotiations. Their masculine counterparts tend to visualize a sporting event in which the other person is an opponent who has to be beaten.

Consistent with this basic difference in orientation, feminine negotiators were likely to be more empathic: that is, they had a natural tendency to try to see the situation from the other person's point of view. This put them in a position to meet mutual needs, which is an ideal outcome of negotiations when there is an ongoing relationship. Furthermore, in the absence of an urgency to "win," feminine negotiators sought fairness and were willing to compromise to achieve a fair outcome.

Finally, the feminine negotiators' concern with the long-term relationship seems to lead them to avoid using tactics that might jeopardize that relationship. Thus we found that feminine negotiators were less likely to deceive the other person. Ironically, the stereotypical view of women's and men's relative trustworthiness is just the opposite. When social psychologists ask people whether women or men are more likely to use underhanded tactics, most people choose women

TABLE 1

Summary of the Different Tendencies of Masculine and Feminine Negotiators

Masculine Tendencies	*Feminine Tendencies*
▪ Visualize a one-shot deal	▪ Visualize the present transaction as one event in a long-term relationship.
▪ Seek a sports-type victory	▪ Seek mutual gain
▪ Emphasize rules-of-the-game, precedents, and power positions	▪ Emphasize fairness
▪ Explain logic of their position	▪ Inquire about the other's needs and make personal appeals
▪ Conceal or misrepresent their own needs	▪ Be up-front about their own needs
▪ Speak in a dominating or controlling manner	▪ Use "powerless" speech
▪ Be intransigent about their position, perhaps trying to conceal their rigid stance	▪ Be willing to compromise
▪ Interrupt and deceive the other party	▪ Avoid tactics that might jeopardize the long-term relationship

as the less trustworthy. Our research shows that, in fact, women are likely to be more trustworthy than men.

IMPLICATIONS FOR NEGOTIATION RESEARCH

The time horizon makes a big difference in how a person approaches a negotiation. If the person visualizes a one-shot deal, any tactic that will produce an advantage is considered because there is no need to worry about future consequences. If, on the other hand, the person's focus is on the longer-term relationship, then immediate gain is less important than maintaining good will.

Two things determine whether a negotiator takes an episodic or a continuous orientation toward a particular transaction. The first is the objective situation: some transactions *are* one-shot deals in which the negotiators have never interacted beforehand and will probably never deal with each other again. Examples of such transactions include buying an item in a bazaar in a foreign country, or selling an automobile through a newspaper advertisement. The second determinant is the negotiator's personality, which can create *tendencies* to perceive the time horizon to be long-term or short-term, regardless of what the objective situation really calls for. We have seen that a person's sex-role orientation, arising from developmental experiences, has such an effect.

The results of this research help explain some of the inconsistencies in the literature on sex differences in interpersonal relations. In many studies, sex is defined in terms of biological gender;

but that approach neglects the results of developmental experiences, which vary widely among individuals. If we are confident that sex-role orientation accurately measures the masculine-feminine perspective, it makes more sense to use this dimension rather than biological sex in our research.

This knowledge of masculine-feminine differences in negotiation approaches helps us understand the scenario we presented at the beginning of this chapter. The woman was willing to make concessions in the short term because she visualized a long-term relationship, in which present concessions would be reciprocated in the future. Her male counterpart had no such perspective. He was visualizing a one-shot deal in which the objective was to beat the other party. Because he saw the interaction as a game, any tactics were permissible—including withholding information and outright deception—as long as they did not violate the explicit rules of the game. The future was irrelevant once the game was over, and a victory in a past game did not obligate the man to try less hard in the next. Had the female negotiator realized that the man was approaching the interaction from this perspective, she could have imposed some rules on the game, or convinced the man not to think of it as a game and done a better job of emphasizing the long-term relationship between them.

IMPLICATIONS FOR DEVELOPMENT OF NEGOTIATING SKILL

Differences in socialization are among the many factors that explain personality differences among negotiators. There is no one best way to negotiate that is suitable for all personalities; rather, each person must develop an approach that capitalizes on unique strengths and compensates for weaknesses. Thus the development of individuals' negotiating approaches must be a highly individualized process that ideally begins with personality assessment.

Personality assessment, however, is not a process that can be taken lightly. The adage that "a little knowledge is a dangerous thing" can be particularly true in the case of understanding one's psychological makeup. Thus the personality assessment phase of our approach to training negotiators is a comprehensive process, involving standardized self-report personality measures, projective tests, psychological histories, observation of negotiating behavior, and an in-depth interview conducted by a clinical psychologist. Only when we have a good understanding of the individual do we feed back the insights thus gained to the person to improve his or her self-understanding. This process also sensitizes the person both to improve his or her self-understanding and to start thinking about how others might be different, so that negotiating tactics can be somewhat tailored to the type of individual being dealt with. This aspect of our program for developing negotiators is very effective, but we caution individuals undertaking their own self-development, as well as those seeking to develop others, to be sure that properly qualified people are involved in the assessment and that the analysis is comprehensive enough so that it does more good than harm.

Our next step is to help people evaluate their effectiveness as negotiators, given their uniqueness as individuals. The best way to do this is to help people become good self-critics. They learn to assess the effectiveness of their negotiating approaches by analyzing a videotape of their own negotiation performance. We have found that people tend to downplay their mistakes and overlook important factors in a negotiation, such as tone of voice, gestures, and body language. The videotape preserves such evidence for the purpose of constructive feedback.

Videotape feedback supervised by the instructor is extremely time-consuming, however. Therefore, it needs to be supplemented with supervised self-observation. A good way to accomplish this is to have students keep a journal of their negotiations inside and outside the classroom. They are encouraged to experiment with different approaches, and in the journal they analyze what tactics work well or poorly for them. After keeping a journal for a term, our trainees acquire the habit of constantly analyzing and critiquing their own performance in interactions. Finally, we expose them to a wide variety of negotiating situations—buying and selling, dealing with bosses and subordinates, negotiating and implementing a real estate contract, a corporate acquisition, collective bargaining, settling grievances, and various types of negotiations within and between groups.

Tailoring the learning experience to the unique needs of individuals provides the opportunity to address the special needs of women preparing for professional careers in organizations. For instance, the tendency for women to adopt a continuous time arrangement can be a considerable asset in some bargaining situations and a liability in others. It is an asset when relationship-oriented, cooperative, and empathic behavior elicits similar behavior from the other party and leads to mutual accommodation. The liability of this time perspective is that it can make the negotiator vulnerable to exploitation by someone who seeks only short-term gain. In short, the woman who is too nice can be ripped off by an unscrupulous opponent.

The need to adapt to different approaches of the other party requires women to develop flexibility in their negotiating approaches. In practice this means that we encourage women to begin with a positive approach but to be ready to fight fire with fire if they encounter an exploitative, unyielding stance. Specifically, we hope to develop the woman's skill at expressing her commitment to a longer-term relationship and persuading the other person of the advantages of this predisposition. If this gentle persuasion doesn't work, she might interrupt the flow of the negotiation to comment on what is going on between the two people. She might approach

this by trying to reflect back the position and assumptions of the other person. ("Let me see if I understand where you're coming from. You need to show your boss that you've gotten a good deal, and if you do that, I'm going to look bad to my boss. So why don't we brainstorm some ideas for how we can both look good?") If this positive approach does not work, the woman needs to have a more hard-line approach available as a deterrent to the tactics of a chronically episodic-oriented opponent.

Another example of the ways in which women can constructively adapt their instinctive approaches to negotiation situations is to capitalize on their natural tendency to be empathic—that is, to be able to understand the perspective of the other party. Empathic tendencies give rise to empathy ("I'd like to learn what you would like to achieve by means of this agreement"), which can elicit a wealth of information about the interests of the other party. An empathic appeal is one of the most effective tactics that can be used to exert influence in a negotiation: It involves simply pointing out how settlements that are of benefit to oneself meet the other party's needs ("If we agree to what I suggested earlier, here's how *you'll* benefit").

We realize we are perhaps coming close to suggesting ways to manipulate other people when we explain how to devise empathic appeals. Although it is true that information gained through empathic inquiries *could* be used exploitatively, such information also can be used in a way that ensures that both parties' needs are met and that both people feel good about the deal. The tendency of women to approach interactions from a continuous time perspective makes the manipulative use of information less likely.

The other feature of our development program that is worth mentioning attempts to undo some of the damage done during male socialization. Briefly, our mission is to help stamp out sports metaphors. This mission is as important to males whose thinking is distorted by these metaphors as it is to women who must suffer the effects.

Males become familiar with competitive games at an early age. When they encounter unfamiliar situations later on, they try to understand them in terms of what is familiar. As a result, many types of relationships are described in sports terms, from "making a big hit" in a business presentation to "scoring" on a date. Unfortunately, such metaphors shape the way males think about relationships in unhelpful ways. Sports contests are episodic by nature; they are either won or lost, so meeting mutual needs is inappropriate; any tactics that do not violate explicit rules are permissible; and the other person is defined as an opponent rather than a potential ally in solving a mutual problem.

It is very difficult to stamp out sports metaphors among negotiators. Because they so permeate the vocabulary of both men and women, they become invisible to those who are affected by them. Even some experts on negotiation cannot escape their effects. For example, some describe meeting mutual needs as a *win-win* solution, which stretches the metaphor beyond its logical limits: if there is a winner, someone else must be a loser; *both* people cannot win. Thus win-win imagery at best makes no sense and at worst perpetuates a view of the situation that fosters conflict rather than accommodation.

SUMMARY

Our professional development programs have been considerably enriched by the research we have conducted on masculine-feminine differences in negotiating. Improvement of negotiating skills, properly guided by research findings, is vital as women endeavor to become more influential in settings traditionally dominated by their male counterparts. Negotiation skills also are vital as organizations take new forms, such as matrix management, increasingly complex structures, team-centered work forces, and Japanese-

style management. All these innovations emphasize agreement and coordination between people, which in turn call for effective negotiation skills. Thus, individuals should be strongly concerned with this aspect of their professional development, as should their higher-level managers.

A NOTE ON THE STUDY

The specific hypotheses we tested were based on our review of the literature and our experience in observing and training negotiators. We expected that individuals who are primarily feminine in their sex-role orientation would (1) tend to conceptualize interactions as continuous rather than episodic and (2) use negotiating tactics that strengthen the interpersonal relationship between the parties.

Our study used two different simulated business negotiations—an automobile purchase and a television advertising contract negotiation. Both were videotaped. The participants in the study (our experimental subjects) were 64 MBA students, all with previous business experience. Both men and women participated in the study, but the important variable was their sex-role orientation. As mentioned earlier, there is nothing in males' and females' genes or hormones that makes them negotiate differently; masculine-feminine differences arise from childhood socialization.

We measured sex-role orientation by means of a questionnaire.[6] Other personality characteristics were investigated in depth by a clinical psychologist, who used multiple measures to be sure to achieve a comprehensive assessment of each subject. Special instructions in the second simulation (the television-advertising contract negotiation) informed subjects that they were in an episodic *situation*. Specifically, they were instructed that this was truly a one-shot deal; in fact, this was the last time they would be negotiating in this position for the company, and they would not be dealing with the other person again. This situation provided an opportunity to observe which subjects chose to respond to the situation by adopting an episodic *orientation* to their role and which subjects tried to maintain a continuous one.

The videotapes of the subjects' negotiating performance were analyzed by a trained observer, who was kept unaware of our hypotheses so that we could avoid possible biases to the analysis.

One of the clinical psychologist's specific tasks was to assess each subject's characteristic *tendency* to assume an episodic or a continuous orientation. In the one-hour, in-depth interview, he asked each subject to describe various interactions they were having *outside* the laboratory study. From the patterns in the behavior they described, the psychologist was able to identify *general* tendencies to see situations as one-shot deals or as events within a long-term relationship.

In summary, then, we recruited 64 young professionals to participate in the study. Then we used a questionnaire to determine whether they had acquired a masculine or feminine sex-role orientation during their childhood socialization. Setting this information aside, we then asked the clinical psychologist to determine whether each person had a natural tendency to see negotiations as one-shot deals or as events in a long-term relationship. Then we asked the participants to role-play two simulated negotiations, each with a different (randomly assigned) partner. Videotapes of the negotiations were then analyzed to

see what tactics were used. Finally, we put all the data together to see if, as we had hypothesized, the feminine negotiators had different time perspectives and used different tactics than their masculine counterparts.

NOTES

1. See, for example, the following studies: M. S. Homer, Toward an understanding of achievement-related conflicts in women, *Journal of Social Issues* 28(1972): 157–75; N. Chodorow, Family structure and feminine personality, in M. Z. Rosaldo and L. Lamphere (eds.), *Women, Culture and Society* (Stanford: Stanford University Press, 1974); J. B. Miller, *Toward a new psychology of women* (Boston: Beacon Press, 1976); C. Gilligan, *In a different voice* (Cambridge, Mass.: Harvard University Press, 1982).

2. See Chodorow, *Family structure.*

3. See E. E. Maccoby and C. N. Jacklin, *The psychology of sex differences* (Stanford: Stanford University Press, 1974).

4. See K. M. Bartol and D. A. Butterfield, Sex effects in evaluating leaders, *Journal of Applied Psychology* 61 (1976):446–54.

5. See J. Z. Rubin and B. R. Brown, *The social psychology of bargaining and negotiation* (New York: Academic Press, 1975).

6. The questionnaire was the Bem Sex-Role Inventory. For details of this measure, see S. L. Bem, The measurement of psychological androgyny, *Journal of Consulting and Clinical Psychology* 42 (1974): 155–62.

THE POWER OF TALK: WHO GETS HEARD AND WHY

Deborah Tannen

The head of a large division of a multinational corporation was running a meeting devoted to performance assessment. Each senior manager stood up, reviewed the individuals in his group, and evaluated them for promotion. Although there were women in every group, not one of them made the cut. One after another, each manager declared, in effect, that every woman in his group lacked the self-confidence needed to be promoted. The division head began to doubt his ears. How could it be that all the talented women in the division suffered from a lack of self-confidence?

In all likelihood, they didn't. Consider the many women who have left large corporations to start their own businesses, obviously exhibiting enough confidence to succeed on their own. Judgments about confidence can be inferred only from the way people present themselves, and much of that presentation is in the form of talk.

The CEO of a major corporation told me that he often has to make decisions in five minutes about matters on which others may have worked

five months. He said he uses this rule: If the person making the proposal seems confident, the CEO approves it. If not, he says no. This might seem like a reasonable approach. But my field of research, socio-linguistics, suggests otherwise. The CEO obviously thinks he knows what a confident person sounds like. But his judgment, which may be dead right for some people, may be dead wrong for others.

Communication isn't as simple as saying what you mean. How you say what you mean is crucial, and differs from one person to the next, because using language is learned social behavior: How we talk and listen are deeply influenced by cultural experience. Although we might think that our ways of saying what we mean are natural, we can run into trouble if we interpret and evaluate others as if they necessarily felt the same way we'd feel if we spoke the way they did.

Since 1974, I have been researching the influence of linguistic style on conversations and human relationships. In the past four years, I have extended that research to the workplace, where I have observed how ways of speaking learned in childhood affect judgments of competence and confidence, as well as who gets heard, who gets credit, and what gets done.

The division head who was dumbfounded to hear that all the talented women in his organization lacked confidence was probably right to be skeptical. The senior managers were judging the women in their groups by their own linguistic norms, but women—like people who have grown up in a different culture—have often learned different styles of speaking than men, which can make them seem less competent and self-assured than they are.

What Is Linguistic Style?

Everything that is said must be said in a certain way—in a certain tone of voice, at a certain rate of speed, and with a certain degree of loudness. Whereas often we consciously consider what to say before speaking, we rarely think about how to say it, unless the situation is obviously loaded —for example, a job interview or a tricky performance review. *Linguistic style* refers to a person's characteristic speaking pattern. It includes such features as directness or indirectness, pacing and pausing, word choice, and the use of such elements as jokes, figures of speech, stories, questions, and apologies. In other words, linguistic style is a set of culturally learned signals by which we not only communicate what we mean, but also interpret others' meaning and evaluate one another as people.

Consider turn-taking, one element of linguistic style. Conversation is an enterprise in which people take turns: One person speaks, then the other responds. However, this apparently simple exchange requires a subtle negotiation of signals so that you know when the other person is finished and it's your turn to begin. Cultural factors such as country or region of origin and ethnic background influence how long a pause seems natural. When Bob, who is from Detroit, has a conversation with his colleague Joe, from New York City, it's hard for him to get a word in edgewise because he expects a slightly longer pause between turns than Joe does. A pause of that length never comes because, before it has a chance to, Joe senses an uncomfortable silence, which he fills with more talk of his own.

Both men fail to realize that differences in conversational style are getting in their way. Bob thinks that Joe is pushy and uninterested in what he has to say, and Joe thinks that Bob doesn't have much to contribute. Similarly, when Sally relocated from Texas to Washington, D.C., she kept searching for the right time to break in during staff meetings—and never found it. Although in Texas she was considered outgoing and confident, in Washington she was perceived as shy and retiring. Her boss even suggested that she take an assertiveness training course. Thus slight differences in conversational style—in these cases, a few seconds of pause—can have a surprising impact on who gets heard and on the judgments, including psychological ones, that are made about people and their abilities.

Every utterance functions on two levels. We're all familiar with the first one: Language communicates ideas. The second level is mostly invisible to us, but it plays a powerful role in communication. As a form of social behavior, language also negotiates relationships. Through ways of speaking, we signal—and create—the relative status of speakers and their level of rapport. If you say, "Sit down!" you are signaling that you have higher status than the person you are addressing, that you are so close to each other that you can drop all pleasantries, or that you are angry. If you say, "I would be honored if you would sit down," you are signaling great respect—or great sarcasm, depending on your tone of voice, the situation, and what you both know about how close you really are. If you say, "You must be so tired— why don't you sit down," you are communicating either closeness and concern or condescension. Each of these ways of saying "the same thing"— telling someone to sit down—can have a vastly different meaning.

In every community known to linguists, the patterns that constitute linguistic style are relatively different for men and women. What's "natural" for most men speaking a given language is, in some cases, different from what's "natural" for most women. That is because we learn ways of speaking as children growing up, especially from peers, and children tend to play with other children of the same sex. The research of sociologists, anthropologists, and psychologists observing American children at play has shown that, although both girls and boys find ways of creating rapport and negotiating status, girls tend to learn conversational rituals that focus on the rapport dimension of relationships whereas boys tend to learn rituals that focus on the status dimension.

Girls tend to play with a single best friend or in small groups, and they spend a lot of time talking. They use language to negotiate how close they are; for example, the girl you tell your secrets to becomes your best friend. Girls learn to downplay ways in which one is better than the others and to emphasize ways in which they are all the same. From childhood, most girls learn that sounding too sure of themselves will make them unpopular with their peers—although nobody really takes such modesty literally. A group of girls will ostracize a girl who calls attention to her own superiority and criticize her by saying, "She thinks she's something"; a girl who tells others what to do is called "bossy." Thus girls learn to talk in ways that balance their own needs with those of others—to save face for one another in the broadest sense of the term.

Boys tend to play very differently. They usually play in larger groups in which more boys can be included, but not everyone is treated as an equal. Boys with high status in their group are expected to emphasize rather than downplay their status, and usually one or several boys will be seen as the leader or leaders. Boys generally don't accuse one another of being bossy, because the leader is expected to tell lower-status boys what to do. Boys learn to use language to negotiate their status in the group by displaying their abilities and knowledge, and by challenging others and resisting challenges. Giving orders is one way of getting and keeping the high-status role. Another is taking center stage by telling stories or jokes.

This is not to say that all boys and girls grow up this way or feel comfortable in these groups or are equally successful at negotiating within these norms. But, for the most part, these childhood play groups are where boys and girls learn their conversational styles. In this sense, they grow up in different worlds. The result is that women and men tend to have different habitual ways of saying what they mean, and conversations between them can be like cross-cultural communication: You can't assume that the other person means what you would mean if you said the same thing in the same way.

My research in companies across the United States shows that the lessons learned in childhood carry over into the workplace. Consider the following example: A focus group was organized at a major multinational company to evaluate a recently implemented flextime policy. The participants sat in a circle and discussed the new system. The group concluded that it was excellent, but they also agreed on ways to improve it. The meeting went well and was deemed a success by all, according to my own observations and everyone's comments to me. But the next day, I was in for a surprise.

I had left the meeting with the impression that Phil had been responsible for most of the suggestions adopted by the group. But as I typed up my notes, I noticed that Cheryl had made almost all those suggestions. I had thought that the key ideas came from Phil because he had picked up Cheryl's points and supported them, speaking at greater length in doing so than she had in raising them.

It would be easy to regard Phil as having stolen Cheryl's ideas—and her thunder. But that would be inaccurate. Phil never claimed Cheryl's ideas as his own. Cheryl herself told me later that she left the meeting confident that she had contributed significantly, and that she appreciated Phil's support. She volunteered, with a laugh, "It was not one of those times when a woman says something and it's ignored, then a man says it and it's picked up." In other words, Cheryl and Phil worked well as a team, the group fulfilled its charge, and the company got what it needed. So what was the problem?

I went back and asked all the participants who they thought had been the most influential group member, the one most responsible for the ideas that had been adopted. The pattern of answers was revealing. The two other women in the group named Cheryl. Two of the three men named Phil. Of the men, only Phil named Cheryl. In other words, in this instance, the women evaluated the contribution of another woman more accurately than the men did.

Meetings like this take place daily in companies around the country. Unless managers are unusually good at listening closely to how people say what they mean, the talents of someone like Cheryl may well be undervalued and underutilized.

One-Up, One-Down

Individual speakers vary in how sensitive they are to the social dynamics of language—in other words, to the subtle nuances of what others say to them. Men tend to be sensitive to the power dynamics of interaction, speaking in ways that position themselves as one-up and resisting being put in a one-down position by others. Women tend to react more strongly to the rapport dynamic, speaking in ways that save face for others and buffering statements that could be seen as putting others in a one-down position. These linguistic patterns are pervasive; you can hear

them in hundreds of exchanges in the workplace every day. And, as in the case of Cheryl and Phil, they affect who gets heard and who gets credit.

Getting Credit

Even so small a linguistic strategy as the choice of pronoun can affect who gets credit. In my research in the workplace, I heard men say "I" in situations where I heard women say "we." For example, one publishing company executive said, "I'm hiring a new manager. I'm going to put him in charge of my marketing division," as if he owned the corporation. In stark contrast, I recorded women saying "we" when referring to work they alone had done. One woman explained that it would sound too self-promoting to claim credit in an obvious way by saying, "I did this." Yet she expected—sometimes vainly—that others would know it was her work and would give her the credit she did not claim for herself.

Managers might leap to the conclusion that women who do not take credit for what they've done should be taught to do so. But that solution is problematic because we associate ways of speaking with moral qualities: The way we speak is who we are and who we want to be.

Veronica, a senior researcher in a high-tech company, had an observant boss. He noticed that many of the ideas coming out of the group were hers but that often someone else trumpeted them around the office and got credit for them. He advised her to "own" her ideas and make sure she got the credit. But Veronica found out that she simply didn't enjoy her work if she had to approach it as if it was an unattractive and unappealing "grabbing game." It was her dislike of such behavior that had led her to avoid it in the first place.

Whatever the motivation, women are less likely than men to have learned to blow their own horn. And they are more likely than men to believe that if they do so, they won't be liked.

◆ ◆ ◆ ◆ ◆

Many have argued that the growing trend of assigning work to teams might be especially congenial to women, but it may also create complications for performance evaluation. When ideas are generated and work is accomplished in the privacy of the team, the outcome of the team's effort might become associated with the person most vocal about reporting results. There are many women and men—but probably relatively more women—who are reluctant to put themselves forward in this way and who consequently risk not getting credit for their contributions.

Confidence and Boasting

The CEO who based his decisions on the confidence level of speakers was articulating a value that is widely shared in U.S. businesses: One way to judge confidence is by an individual's behavior, especially verbal behavior. Here again, many women are at a disadvantage.

Studies show that women are more likely to downplay their certainty and men are more likely to minimize their doubts. Psychologist Laurie Heatherington and her colleagues devised an ingenious experiment, which they reported in the journal *Sex Roles* (Volume 29, 1993). They asked hundreds of incoming college students to predict what grades they would get in their first year. Some subjects were asked to make their predictions privately by writing them down and placing them in an envelope; others were asked to make their predictions publicly, in the presence of a researcher. The results showed that more women than men predicted lower grades for themselves if they made their predictions publicly. If they made their predictions privately, the predictions were the same as those of the men—and the same as their actual grades. This study provides evidence that what comes across as lack of confidence— predicting lower grades for oneself—might reflect not one's actual level of confidence, but the desire not to seem boastful.

These habits with regard to appearing humble or confident result from the socialization of boys and girls by their peers in childhood play. As adults, both women and men find these behaviors reinforced by the positive responses they get from friends and relatives who share the same norms. But the norms of behavior in the U.S. business world are based on the style of interaction that is more common among men—at least, among American men.

Asking Questions

Although asking the right questions is one of the hallmarks of a good manager, how and when questions are asked can send unintended signals about competence and power. In a group, if only one person asks questions, he or she risks being seen as the only ignorant one. Furthermore, we judge others not only by how they speak but also by how they are spoken to. The person who asks questions might end up being lectured to and looking like a novice under a schoolmaster's tutelage. The way boys are socialized makes them more likely to be aware of the underlying power dynamic by which a question asker can be seen in a one-down position.

One practicing physician learned the hard way that any exchange of information can become the basis for judgments—or misjudgments— about competence. During her training, she received a negative evaluation that she thought was unfair, so she asked her supervising physician for an explanation. He said that she knew less than her peers. Amazed at his answer, she asked how he had reached that conclusion. He said, "You ask more questions."

Along with cultural influences and individual personality, gender seems to play a role in whether and when people ask questions. For example, of all the observations I've made in lectures and books, the one that sparks the most enthusiastic flash of recognition is that men are less likely than women to stop and ask for directions when they are lost. I explain that men often resist asking for directions because they are aware that it puts them in a one-down position and because they value the independence that comes with finding their way by themselves. Asking for directions while driving is only one instance—along with many others that researchers have examined—in which men seem less likely than women to ask questions. I believe this is because they are more attuned than women to the potential face-losing aspect of asking questions. And men who believe that asking questions might reflect negatively on them might, in turn, be likely to form a negative opinion of others who ask questions in situations where they would not.

Conversational Rituals

Conversation is fundamentally ritual in the sense that we speak in ways our culture has conventionalized, and expect certain types of responses. Take greetings, for example. I have heard visitors to the United States complain that Americans are hypocritical because they ask how you are but aren't interested in the answer. To Americans, *How are you?* is obviously a ritualized way to start a conversation rather than a literal request for information. In other parts of the world, including the Philippines, people ask each other, *"Where are you going?"* when they meet. The question seems intrusive to Americans, who do not realize that it, too, is a ritual query to which the only expected reply is a vague "Over there."

It's easy and entertaining to observe different rituals in foreign countries. But we don't expect differences, and are far less likely to recognize the ritualized nature of our conversations, when we are with our compatriots at work. Our differing rituals can be even more problematic when we think we're all speaking the same language.

Apologies

Consider the simple phrase *I'm sorry.*

Catherine: How did that big presentation go?

Bob: Oh, not very well. I got a lot of flak from the VP for Finance, and I didn't have the numbers at my fingertips.

Catherine: Oh, I'm sorry. I know how hard you worked on that.

In this case, *I'm sorry* probably means "I'm sorry that happened," not "I apologize," unless it was Catherine's responsibility to supply Bob with the numbers for the presentation. Women tend to say *I'm sorry* more frequently than men, and often they intend it in this way—as a ritualized means of expressing concern. It's one of many learned elements of conversational style that girls often use to establish rapport. Ritual apologies—like other conversational rituals—work well when both parties share the same assumptions about their use. But people who utter frequent ritual apologies might end up appearing weaker, less confident, and literally more blameworthy than people who don't.

Apologies tend to be regarded differently by men, who are more likely to focus on the status implications of exchanges. Many men avoid apologies because they see them as putting the speaker in a one-down position. I observed with some amazement an encounter among several lawyers engaged in a negotiation over a speakerphone. At one point, the lawyer in whose office I was sitting accidentally elbowed the telephone and cut off the call. When his secretary got the parties back on again, I expected him to say what I would have said: "Sorry about that. I knocked the phone with my elbow." Instead, he said, "Hey, what happened? One minute you were there; the next minute you were gone!" This lawyer seemed to have an automatic impulse not to admit fault if he didn't have to. For me, it was one of those pivotal moments when you realize that the world you live in is not the one everyone lives in, and that the way *you* assume is the way to talk is really only one of many.

◆   ◆   ◆   ◆   ◆

Those who caution managers not to undermine their authority by apologizing are approaching interaction from the perspective of the power dynamic. In many cases, this strategy is effective. On the other hand, when I asked people what frustrated them in their jobs, one frequently voiced complaint was working with or for someone who refuses to apologize or admit fault. In other words, accepting responsibility for errors and admitting mistakes might be an equally effective or superior strategy in some settings.

Feedback

Styles of giving feedback contain a ritual element that often is the cause for misunderstanding. Consider the following exchange: A manager had to tell her marketing director to rewrite a report. She began this potentially awkward task by citing the report's strengths, and then moved to the main point: the weaknesses that needed to be remedied. The marketing director seemed to understand and accept his supervisor's comments, but his revision contained only minor changes and failed to address the major weaknesses. When the manager told him of her dissatisfaction, he accused her of misleading him: "You told me it was fine."

The impasse resulted from different linguistic styles. To the manager, it was natural to buffer the criticism by beginning with praise. Telling her subordinate that his report is inadequate and has to be rewritten puts him in a one-down position. Praising him for the parts that are good is a ritualized way of saving face for him. But the marketing director did not share his supervisor's assumption about how feedback should be given. Instead, he assumed that what she mentioned first was the main point and that what she brought up later was an afterthought.

Those who expect feedback to come in the way the manager presented it would appreciate her tact and would regard a more blunt approach as unnecessarily callous. But those who share the marketing director's assumptions would regard the blunt approach as honest and no-nonsense, and the manager's as obfuscating. Because each one's assumptions seemed self-evident, each blamed the other: The manager thought the marketing director was not listening, and he thought she had not communicated clearly or had changed her mind. This is significant because it illustrates that incidents labeled vaguely as "poor communication" might be the result of differing linguistic styles.

Compliments

Exchanging compliments is a common ritual, especially among women. A mismatch in expectations about this ritual left Susan, a manager in the human resources field, in a one-down position. She and her colleague Bill had both given presentations at a national conference. On the airplane home, Susan told Bill, "That was a great talk!" "Thank you," he said. Then she asked, "What did you think of mine?" He responded with a lengthy and detailed critique, as she listened uncomfortably. An unpleasant feeling of having been put down came over her. Somehow she had been positioned as the novice in need of his expert advice. Even worse, she had only herself to blame, since she had, after all, asked Bill what he thought of her talk.

But had Susan asked for the response she received? When she asked Bill what he thought about her talk, she expected to hear not a critique but a compliment. In fact, her question had been an attempt to repair a ritual gone awry. Susan's initial compliment to Bill was the kind of automatic recognition she felt was more or less required after a colleague gives a presentation , and she expected Bill to respond with a matching compliment. She was just talking automatically, but he either sincerely misunderstood the ritual or simply took the opportunity to bask in the one-up position of critic. Whatever his motivation, it was Susan's attempt to spark an exchange of compliments that gave him the opening.

Although this exchange could have occurred between two men, it does not seem coincidental that it happened between a man and a woman. Linguist Janet Holmes discovered that women pay more compliments than men (*Anthropological Linguistics*, Volume 28, 1986). And, as I have observed, fewer men are likely to ask, "What did you think of my talk?" precisely because the question might invite an unwanted critique.

In the social structure of the peer groups in which they grow up, boys are indeed looking for opportunities to put others down and take the one-up position for themselves. In contrast, one of the rituals girls learn is taking the one-down position but assuming that the other person will recognize the ritual nature of the self-denigration and pull them back up.

The exchange between Susan and Bill also suggests how women's and men's characteristic styles can put women at a disadvantage in the workplace. If one person is trying to minimize status differences, maintain an appearance that everyone is equal, and save face for the other, while another person is trying to maintain the one-up position and avoid being positioned as one down, the person seeking the one-up position is likely to get it. At the same time, the person who has not been expending any effort to avoid the one-down position is likely to end up in it. Because women are more likely to take (or accept) the role of advice-seeker, men are more inclined to interpret a ritual question from a woman as a request for advice.

Ritual Opposition

Apologizing, mitigating criticism with praise, and exchanging compliments are rituals common among women that men often take literally. A ritual common among men that women often take literally is ritual opposition.

A woman in communications told me she watched with distaste and distress as her office mate argued heatedly with another colleague about whose division should suffer budget cuts. She was even more surprised, however, that a short time later they were as friendly as ever. "How can you pretend that fight never happened?" she asked. "Who's pretending it never happened?" he responded, as puzzled by her question as she had been by his behavior. "It happened," he said, "and it's over." What she took as literal fighting to him was a routine part of daily negotiation: a ritual fight.

Many Americans expect the discussion of ideas to be a ritual fight—that is, an exploration through verbal opposition. They present their own ideas in the most certain and absolute form they can, and wait to see if they are challenged. Being forced to defend an idea provides an opportunity to test it. In the same spirit, they play devil's advocate in challenging their colleagues' ideas—trying to poke holes and find weaknesses—as a way of helping them explore and test their ideas.

This style can work well if everyone shares it, but those unaccustomed to it are likely to miss its ritual nature. They might give up an idea that is challenged, taking the objections as an indication that the idea was a poor one. Worse, they can take the opposition as a personal attack and find it impossible to do their best in a contentious environment. People unaccustomed to this style might hedge when stating their ideas, in order to fend off potential attacks. Ironically, this posture makes their arguments appear weak and is more likely to invite attack from pugnacious colleagues than to fend it off.

Ritual opposition can even play a role in who gets hired. Some consulting firms that recruit graduates from the top business schools use a confrontational interviewing technique. They challenge the candidate to "crack a case" in real time. A partner at one firm told me, "Women tend to do less well in this kind of interaction, and it certainly affects who gets hired. But, in fact, many women who don't 'test well' turn out to be good consultants. They're often smarter than some of the men who looked like analytic powerhouses under pressure."

The level of verbal opposition varies from one company's culture to the next, but I saw instances of it in all the organizations I studied. Anyone who is uncomfortable with this linguistic style—and that includes some men as well as many women—risks appearing insecure about his or her ideas.

Negotiating Authority

In organizations, formal authority comes from the position one holds. But actual authority has to be negotiated day to day. The effectiveness of individual managers depends in part on their skill in negotiating authority and on whether others reinforce, or undercut, their efforts. The way linguistic style reflects status plays a subtle role in placing individuals within a hierarchy.

Managing Up and Down

In all the companies I researched, I heard from women who knew they were doing a superior job and knew that their co-workers (and sometimes their immediate bosses) knew it as well, but believed that the higher-ups did not. They frequently told me that something outside themselves was holding them back and found it frustrating because they thought that all that should be necessary for success was to do a great job, that superior performance should be recognized and rewarded. In contrast, men often told me that if women weren't promoted, it was because they simply weren't up to snuff. Looking around, however, I saw evidence that men more often than women behaved in ways likely to get them recognized by those with the power to determine their advancement.

In all the companies I visited, I observed what happened at lunchtime. I saw young men who regularly ate lunch with their boss, and senior men who ate with the big boss. I noticed far fewer women who sought out the highest-level person they could eat with. But one is more likely to get recognition for work done if one talks about it to those higher up, and it is easier to do so if the lines of communication are already open. Furthermore, given the opportunity for a conversation with superiors, men and women are likely to have different ways of talking about their accomplishments because of the different ways in which they were socialized as children. Boys are rewarded by their peers if they talk up their achievements, whereas girls are rewarded if they play theirs down. Linguistic styles common among men might tend to give them some advantages when it comes to managing up.

All speakers are aware of the status of the person they are talking to, and adjust accordingly. Everyone speaks differently when talking to a boss than when talking to a subordinate. But, surprisingly, the ways in which they adjust their talk are different and thus might project different images of themselves.

Communications researchers Karen Tracy and Eric Eisenberg studied how relative status affects the way people give criticism. They devised a business letter that contained some errors and asked 13 male and 11 female college students to role-play delivering criticism under two scenarios. In the first, the speaker was a boss talking to a subordinate; in the second, the speaker was a subordinate talking to his or her boss. The researchers measured how hard the speakers tried to avoid hurting the feelings of the person they were criticizing.

One might expect people to be more careful about how they deliver criticism when they are in a subordinate position. Tracy and Eisenberg found that hypothesis to be true for the men in their study but not for the women. As they reported in *Research on Language and Social Interaction* (Volume 24, 1990/1991), the women showed more concern about the other person's feelings when they were playing the role of superior. In other words, the women were more careful to save face for the other person when they were managing down than when they were managing up. This pattern recalls the way girls are socialized: Those who are in some way superior are expected to downplay rather than flaunt their superiority.

In my own recordings of workplace communication, I observed women talking in similar ways. For example, when a manager had to correct a mistake made by her secretary, she did so by acknowledging that there were mitigating circumstances. She said, laughing, "You know, it's hard to do things around here, isn't it, with all these people coming in!" The manager was saving face for her subordinate, just like the female students role-playing in the Tracy and Eisenberg study.

Is this an effective way to communicate? One must ask, effective for what? The manager in question established a positive environment in her group, and the work was done effectively. On the other hand, numerous women in many different fields told me that their bosses say they don't project the proper authority.

Indirectness

Another linguistic signal that varies with power and status is indirectness—the tendency to say what we mean without spelling it out in so many words. Despite the widespread belief in the United States that it's always best to say exactly what we mean, indirectness is a fundamental and pervasive element in human communication. It also is one of the elements that varies most from one culture to another, and it can cause enormous misunderstanding when speakers have different habits and expectations about how it is used. It's often said that American women are more indirect than American men, but in fact everyone tends to be indirect in some

situations and in different ways. Allowing for cultural, ethnic, regional, and individual differences, women are especially likely to be indirect when it comes to telling others what to do, which is not surprising, considering girls' readiness to brand other girls as bossy. On the other hand, men are especially likely to be indirect when it comes to admitting fault or weakness, which also is not surprising, considering boys' readiness to push around boys who assume the one-down position.

At first glance, it would seem that only the powerful can get away with bald commands such as, "Have that report on my desk by noon." But power in an organization also can lead to requests so indirect that they don't sound like requests at all. A boss who says, "Do we have the sales data by product line for each region?" would be surprised and frustrated if a subordinate responded, "We probably do" rather than "I'll get it for you."

Examples such as these notwithstanding, many researchers have claimed that those in subordinate positions are more likely to speak indirectly, and that is surely accurate in some situations. For example, linguist Charlotte Linde, in a study published in *Language in Society* (Volume 17, 1988), examined the black-box conversations that took place between pilots and co-pilots before airplane crashes. In one particularly tragic instance, an Air Florida plane crashed into the Potomac River immediately after attempting takeoff from National Airport in Washington, D.C., killing all but 5 of the 74 people on board. The pilot, it turned out, had little experience flying in icy weather. The co-pilot had a bit more, and it became heartbreakingly clear on analysis that he had tried to warn the pilot but had done so indirectly. Alerted by Linde's observation, I examined the transcript of the conversations and found evidence of her hypothesis. The co-pilot repeatedly called attention to the bad weather and to ice buildup on other planes:

Co-Pilot: Look how the ice is just hanging on his, ah, back, back there, see that? See all those icicles on the back there and everything?

Pilot: Yeah.

(The co-pilot also expressed concern about the long waiting time since de-icing.)

Co-Pilot: Boy, this is a, this is a losing battle here on trying to de-ice those things; it (gives) you a false feeling of security, that's all that does.

(Just before they took off, the co-pilot expressed another concern—about abnormal instrument readings—but again he didn't press the matter when it wasn't picked up by the pilot.)

Co-Pilot: That don't seem right, does it? (3-second pause). Ah, that's not right. Well—

Pilot: Yes it is, there's 80.

Co-Pilot: Naw, I don't think that's right. (7-second pause) Ah, maybe it is.

Shortly thereafter, the plane took off, with tragic results. In other instances as well as this one, Linde observed that co-pilots, who are second in command, are more likely to express themselves indirectly or otherwise mitigate, or soften, their communication when they are suggesting courses of action to the pilot. In an effort to avert similar disasters, some airlines now offer training for co-pilots to express themselves in more assertive ways.

This solution seems self-evidently appropriate to most Americans. But when I assigned Linde's article in a graduate seminar I taught, a Japanese student pointed out that it would be just as effective to train pilots to pick up on hints. This approach reflects assumptions about communication that typify Japanese culture, which places great value on the ability of people to understand one another without putting everything into words. Either directness or indirectness can be a successful means of communication as long as the linguistic style is understood by the participants.

In the world of work, however, there is more at stake than whether the communication is understood. People in powerful positions are likely to reward styles similar to their own, because we all tend to take as self-evident the logic of our own styles. Accordingly, there is evidence that in the U.S. workplace, where instructions from a superior are expected to be voiced in a relatively direct manner, those who tend to be indirect when telling subordinates what to do might be perceived as lacking in confidence.

Consider the case of the manager at a national magazine who was responsible for giving assignments to reporters. She tended to phrase her assignments as questions. For example, she asked, "How would you like to do the X project with Y?" or said, "I was thinking of putting you on the X project. Is that okay?" This worked extremely well with her staff; they liked working for her, and the work got done in an efficient and orderly manner. But when she had her mid-year evaluation with her own boss, he criticized her for not assuming the proper demeanor with her staff.

In any work environment, the higher-ranking person has the power to enforce his or her view of appropriate demeanor, created in part by linguistic style. In most U.S. contexts, that view is likely to assume that the person in authority has the right to be relatively direct rather than to mitigate orders. There also are cases, however, in which the higher-ranking person assumes a more indirect style. The owner of a retail operation told her subordinate, a store manager, to do something. He said he would do it, but a week later he still hadn't. They were able to trace the difficulty to the following conversation: She had said, "The bookkeeper needs help with the billing. How would you feel about helping her out?" He had said, "Fine." This conversation had seemed to be clear and flawless at the time, but it turned out that they had interpreted this simple exchange in very different ways. She thought he meant, "Fine, I'll help the bookkeeper out." He thought he meant, "Fine, I'll think about how I would feel about helping the bookkeeper out." He did think about it and came to the conclusion that he had more important things to do and couldn't spare the time.

To the owner, "How would you feel about helping the bookkeeper out?" was an obviously appropriate way to give the order "Help the bookkeeper out with the billing." Those who expect orders to be given as bald imperatives might find such locutions annoying or even misleading. But those for whom this style is natural do not think they are being indirect. They believe they are being clear in a polite or respectful way.

What is atypical in this example is that the person with the more indirect style was the boss, so the store manager was motivated to adapt to her style. She still gives orders the same way, but the store manager now understands how she means what she says. It's more common in U.S. business contexts for the highest-ranking people to take a more direct style, with the result that many women in authority risk being judged by their superiors as lacking the appropriate demeanor—and, consequently, lacking confidence.

What to Do?

I am often asked, *What is the best way to give criticism?* or *What is the best way to give orders?*—in other words, what is the best way to communicate? The answer is that there is no one best way. The results of a given way of speaking will vary depending on the situation, the culture of the company, the relative rank of speakers, their linguistic styles, and how those styles interact with one another. Because of all those influences, any way of speaking could be perfect for communicating with one person in one situation and disastrous with someone else in another. The critical skill for managers is to become aware of the workings and power of linguistic style, to

make sure that people with something valuable to contribute get heard.

It might seem, for example, that running a meeting in an unstructured way gives equal opportunity to all. But awareness of the differences in conversational style makes it easy to see the potential for unequal access. Those who are comfortable speaking up in groups, who need little or no silence before raising their hands, or who speak out easily without waiting to be recognized are far more likely to get heard at meetings. Those who refrain from talking until it's clear that the previous speaker is finished, who wait to be recognized, and who are inclined to link their comments to those of others will do fine at a meeting where everyone else is following the same rules, but will have a hard time getting heard in a meeting with people whose styles are more like the first pattern. Given the socialization typical of boys and girls, men are more likely to have learned the first style and women the second, making meetings more congenial for men than for women. It's common to observe women who participate actively in one-on-one discussions or in all female groups but who are seldom heard in meetings with a large proportion of men. On the other hand, there are women who share the style more common among men, and they run a different risk—of being seen as too aggressive.

A manager aware of those dynamics might devise any number of ways of ensuring that everyone's ideas are heard and credited. Although no single solution will fit all contexts, managers who understand the dynamics of linguistic style can develop more adaptive and flexible approaches to running or participating in meetings, mentoring or advancing the careers of others, evaluating performance, and so on. Talk is the lifeblood of managerial work, and understanding that different people have different ways of saying what they mean will make it possible to take advantage of the talents of people with a broad range of linguistic styles. As the workplace becomes more culturally diverse and business becomes more global, managers will need to become even better at reading interactions and more flexible in adjusting their own styles to the people with whom they interact.

Deborah Tannen is University Professor and a professor of linguistics at Georgetown University in Washington, D.C. She is the author of 15 books, including *You Just Don't Understand: Women and Men in Conversation* (William Morrow, 1990), which introduced to the general public the idea of female and male styles of communication. The material in this article is drawn from *Talking from 9 to 5* (Avon Books. 1995).

HER PLACE AT THE TABLE: A CONSIDERATION OF GENDER ISSUES IN NEGOTIATION

Deborah M. Kolb and Gloria G. Coolidge

A central agenda of recent feminist studies across the social sciences has been to heed the often "unheard" voices of women. Rather than treat women's experience as a typically inferior variant of a dominant male model (whether of personality, organizations, or research), recent scholarship has tried to right the record and include women.[1] In history and anthropology, this has meant documenting the experiences of women in their spheres of activity that are usually private (Collier, 1974; Lerner, 1974); in sociology, some of the attention has shifted from considering women in male-dominated organizations or activities to female-dominated structures (Kanter, 1977; Krieger, 1987; Keller, 1985). These structures, created by women for women, tend to be organized in webs or networks and run along different conceptions of management (Krieger, 1987; Menkel-Meadow, 1985). Several works associated with this feminist approach are those that document how traditional developmental theory excludes women's experience (Gilligan, 1982; Chodorow, 1978; Miller, 1976). What emerges from inquiry across these domains is a conception of an alternative way of making sense of the world and acting within it.

Published in *The Program on Negotiation*. Cambridge, Massachusetts: Harvard Law School, 1993. Reprinted by permission.

The alternative voice[2] starts with the notion that women's social development occurs in the context of relationships (Gilligan, 1982; Chodorow, 1978; Miller, 1984), and that this fact affects significant aspects of their social lives. Oriented toward nurturance and affiliation, women make meaning through a screen of interconnections. Never having to repudiate identification with a caretaking mother to define her own sexual identity in adolescence, the developing woman need not rupture connection for her own growth (Chodorow, 1978). Instead of separation and individuation as a primary motive for action, women conceive of action within the context of affiliation and relatedness to others. What this means in the area of moral reasoning, for example, is that dilemmas can be resolved with reference either to abstract principles of justice or guided by grounded considerations of the ways decisions affect the people involved (Gilligan, 1982). While mature adults manifest both considerations in their decision-making, there is a noticeable proclivity for one dimension to become prominent and this orientation tends to be associated with gender.

Our purpose here is to explore the ramifications of feminist theories of development and social organization to the exercise of power and the resolution of conflict in negotiated settings.

Based on a review of some of the leading works, we suggest that there are four themes that are most relevant to an understanding of some of the ways that women frame and conduct negotiations. These are:

■ a relational view of others;

■ an embedded view of agency;

■ an understanding of control through empowerment; and

■ problem-solving through dialogue.

While these themes suggest some of the ways women define their place in negotiated settings, we do not mean to suggest that all women would necessarily view themselves in this way. Clearly variations in class, race, culture, family constellation, and social setting affect the meaning ascribed to gender differences, and color the ways in which they are enacted (Krieger, 1987). Existing research and our own experience suggest that this voice, or the multiple voices of women, while real and distinct, is often hushed in formal negotiation. What might be occurring is that formal negotiation, conceived as a context in which conflict and competition are important, might perhaps not be a comfortable place for many women. In coping with what they might experience as an unnatural place, some women might try to emulate a culturally dominant style (and do so quite successfully), while others find their accustomed strengths and skills impaired when placed in conflictual situations. What we try to do in the second part of this article, therefore, is to explore the ways in which women experience conflict and how this can impact their behavior and the perceptions others have of them in negotiation. In examining these themes, we draw both on anecdotal data from novice women negotiators and on existing research in negotiations and related fields.

HER VOICE IN NEGOTIATION

There is a certain irony about trying to articulate a woman's voice in negotiation. Negotiation is often put forth as an alternative to violence and adversarial proceedings; it is an alternative that some argue reflects a feminine view of interaction. That is, it is better to talk than fight, and to consider everybody's needs rather than pitting one party against the other in a win-lose contest (Menkel-Meadow, 1983; Northrup, 1987; Rothchild, 1988; Silbey and Sarat, 1988). Further, advocates of negotiation and alternative forms of dispute resolution often espouse a model of negotiation that is based on problem-solving principles presumably designed to create outcomes that meet the interests and needs of all those involved, again a presumed feminine principle (Fisher and Ury, 1981; Menkel-Meadow, 1983; Susskind and Cruiksank, 1987; Fisher and Brown, 1988). If this is so, why should we care about articulating another voice? Presumably, if these authors are correct, that voice is already being heard and dominates much of the current prescriptive thinking about negotiation.

There are at least three reasons why the subject of an alternative voice in negotiation is not closed. First, our experience and those of others suggest that there are significant differences in the ways men and women are likely to approach negotiation and the styles they use in a search for agreement.

Although the research often yields contradictory conclusions (Rubin and Brown, 1975; Deux, 1984; Eagly, 1987; Linn, 1986), in every training situation in which we have been engaged, women come up and ask us to talk about the gender issues. The inference we draw from these interactions is that at least some women experience their gender as a factor in negotiation. The fact that research might not capture this experience perhaps derives from the settings of research (usually the laboratory) and the questions the research poses (which are usually aggregate behavioral indicators).[4] Secondly, there is evidence that in real negotiations (as opposed to simulations), women do not fare that well. In divorce mediation, for example, the settlements women received are inferior economically to those awarded in adjudication (Rifkin, 1984; Pearson and Thoennes, 1988). In queries about salary negotiations, men report higher raises than women (Womack, 1987). If negotiation is a woman's place, we would expect women to excel, not be disadvantaged. There is a third reason why we need to focus on a woman's voice in negotiation: The prescriptions to get to win-win outcomes in negotiation offer ambiguous advice to the negotiator, whether male or female.[5] The advice to focus on interests, not positions, and invent options for mutual gain (Fisher and Ury, 1981) emphasizes the relational dimension of negotiation. There are indications, however, that this advice is quite difficult for many to heed because it runs counter to prevailing cultural norms about the competitive and gaming aspect of negotiation (McCarthy, 1985).

On the other hand, advice to separate people from problems and to focus on objective criteria gives a rationalized and objective cast to negotiation that might be quite different from the subjective and embedded forms of feminine understanding. Further, in the press to provide prescription, it is the technical and rationalized analysis that increasingly dominates. Integrative bargaining or joint-gain negotiation, while acknowledging the importance of empathetic relationships, suggests that the critical skills necessary to implement win-win outcomes are primarily technical and analytic. Negotiators are advised to become more rational in their thinking and analysis (Bazerman, 1983). Even analysis of interests, presumably the ability to empathize with the other party, has become in the language of modern negotiation theory a technical problem:

> Identify the interests that may be at stake. For each interest, imagine the possible packages that serve it best and worst; for example imagine the range of precedents that might follow from the negotiation. This

roughly defines the increment of value associated with each interest. . .the importance of each interest depends on the relative importance of its increment compared to those of the other interest; for example, how does the gain from the worst to the best possible precedent compare with the gain from the worst to the best possible monetary outcome? (Lax and Sebenius, 1986: 184–85)

Articulating an alternative voice (or voices) becomes increasingly important in an emerging field in which the driving force is toward prescription. These popular theories of negotiation imply that all conflicts are susceptible to similar formulations and that all parties, despite differences in experience and status, can become equally proficient at and achieve the same results in its application (Northrup and Segall, 1988). The prescriptive voice of principled or joint gain negotiation, while there is much to applaud in its perspective, has a tendency to drown out alternative ways of seeing and doing things. We need to consider the structures and contexts in more nuanced ways. From our perspective we begin with gender and the themes that might comprise an alternative voice.[6]

Relational View of Others

Research pioneered by Miller (1976), Chodorow (1978), and Gilligan (1982) suggests that girls differ from boys in that they come to define themselves through their relationships. When asked to describe their resolution of moral dilemmas, girls' narratives consistently show a sensitivity to others' needs and an inclusion of others' points of view in their judgments (Gilligan, 1982). Keller (1986) describes women as living "in a domain between one and two" where self and other are not cast in opposition but rather in terms of mutual aid and support. In interactions, this translates for women into an interest in and attention to the other as a grounding for emotional connection, an expectation of a process of empathy and shared experiences, and an expectation of mutual sensitivity and responsibility (Surrey, 1985). In this two-way interactional model, to understand is as important as to be understood, empowering as important as being empowered.

There seem to be two major ways that a relational view of self is potentially manifest in negotiation. The first is the conception a woman has of herself as a negotiating party. She conceives of her interests within a constellation of responsibilities and commitments already made. That is, she is always aware of how her actions in one context impact on other parts of her life and on other people significant to her. Constraints from greater personal responsibilities for day-to-day management of private life and the impact those obligations have in limiting a woman's flexibility within working roles make it difficult to consider and separate interests in any single negotiation from the life context of which it is a part.

The second implication is that relational ordering in negotiation can be a prerequisite for interaction. Relational ordering means creating a climate in which people can come to know each other, share (or do not share) values, and learn of each other's modes of interacting. Expressions of emotion and feeling and learning how the other experiences the situation are as important, if not more important, than the substance of the discourse (Hochshild, 1983; Northrup and Seagall, 1988). In other words, separating the people from the problem *is* the problem. Negotiation conducted in a woman's voice would, we predict, start from a different point and run a different course than either a purely principled or purely positional model.

Embedded View of Agency

Women understand events contextually, both in terms of their impact on important ongoing relationships and as passing frames in evolving situations that grow out of a past and are still to be shaped in the future. The male imagination stereotypically focuses on individual achievement and is sparked by opportunities for distinctive activity that are bounded by task and structure. This exemplifies a self-contained concept of agency (Bakan, 1966; Sampson, 1988). An embedded form of agency emphasizes the fluidity between the boundaries of self and other (Sampson, 1988). Thus, women are energized by their connections and so interpret and locate activities in a spatial and temporal context in which boundaries between self and others and between the task and its surroundings are overlapping and blurred (Keller, 1985; Sampson, 1988).

If one operates from an embedded view of agency, any negotiation must be understood against the background from which it emerges.[7] That means that there is the expectation that people in negotiation will act in a way that is consistent with their past and future behavior in other contexts. Negotiation is not, therefore, experienced as a separate game with its own set of rules but as part of the extended organization context in which it occurs (Greenhaigh and Gilkey, 1985). Further, in order to appreciate negotiating positions or the interests that underlie them, we need to understand their context and their historical evolution. Indeed, several of our students have commented that they rarely separated negotiation from other facets of their work. One student, for instance, noted:

> I worked in real estate. I remember an occasion where I had given a listing to an associate without a prior agreement as to the split arrangement. I trusted my associate. We had worked together for a long time and I assumed that he would realize my previous input and include me in the split. He did not and I had to go to management to get my share.

Operating from an embedded sense of agency, it is possible that women are slow to recognize that negotiations are occurring unless they are specifically demarcated from the background against which they occur. At the same time, background understandings are likely to be imported into the negotiated setting and to shape what happens there. In a prisoner's dilemma-type game that we ran with our students (all women in a woman's organization), the relationships the women had with each other spilled over into the game such that cooperative outcomes marked the behavior of all the groups.

Control through Empowerment

Power is often conceived as the exertion of control over others through the use of strength, authority, or expertise. It is usually defined as the ability to exert influence in order to obtain an outcome on one's own terms (Emerson, 1962). Conceiving of power in this way leads to a dichotomous division between those who are powerful and those who are powerless (Miller, 1982).[8] A model in which power is accrued for oneself at the expense of others may feel alien to some women and/or be seen by others as somehow incongruent with female roles. Anticipating that assertiveness might lead away from connection, women tend to emphasize the needs of the other person so as to allow that other person to feel powerful. Her behavior appears to be passive, inactive, or depressed.

Instead of accepting the notion of power as dominion, mastery, or "power over," feminist researchers propose an alternative model of interaction stressing "power with" or "power from emerging interaction" (Surrey, 1987). Through mutual empowerment rather than competition, a context is created and sustained that increases understanding and moves participants to joint action. This model overrides the active/passive dichotomy and calls for interaction among all participants in the relationship to build connection and enhance everyone's power.

There is a continuing debate about the place of power in negotiation. Some (e.g., Fisher, 1983)

argue that it is possible to mobilize power in ways that contribute to better outcomes, while others suggest that such a view denies the economic and political context in which negotiation occurs (McCarthy, 1985; Bazerman, 1987). An empowerment view that allows all parties to speak their interests and incorporates these into agreements that transcend the individualized and personalized notion of acquiring, using, and benefiting from the exercise of power is often dismissed as hopelessly naive. However, it is clear that there are situations (particularly those that involve ongoing and valued relationships) in which mutual empowerment is a much-desired end.

Problem Solving through Dialogue

Dialogue is central to a woman's model of problem-solving. It is through communication and interaction with others that problems are framed, considered, and resolved. This kind of communication has specific characteristics that differentiate it from persuasion, argument, and debate. According to Surrey (1985), women seek to engage the other in a joint exploration of ideas, whereby understanding is progressively clarified through interaction. There is the expectation that the other will play active listener and contribute to the developing movement of ideas. Women come to distinguish between "really talking" (which requires careful listening and shared interactions so that emergent ideas can grow as both participants draw deeply from their experiences and analytic abilities) and "didactic talk" where people hold forth without sharing ideas (Belenky et al., 1986). Studies of women in management roles suggest that women reveal more about their attitudes, beliefs, and concerns than men in similar positions and that this contributes to productive dialogue in certain situations (Baird and Bradley, 1979).

Women perceive problem-solving to be an interactive process. Just as conflicts build up over time as individuals or groups struggle for future resources or valued positions, women see conflict resolution as evolutionary and collaborative. While it is possible to plan and strategize about one's role prior to an interaction, a woman's strength might well be in her ability to adapt and grow as she learns more about situations from involvement (Warren, 1988; Rosaldo, 1974). Women's well-honed problem-solving skills, which create interactive engagement and foster growth in the private sphere, are often not given free expression in public dispute resolution (Collier, 1974).

Problem solving through dialogue in negotiation suggests a special kind of joining and openness in negotiation. In place of a strategic planning model of negotiation in which considerable effort is devoted to analyzing and second-guessing the possible interests and positions of the other, problem-solving through dialogue involves the weaving of collective narratives that reflect newly-emerging understanding. There exists through this kind of interaction the potential for transformed understanding and outcomes.[9] It is a stance of learning about the problem together, built on the premise that you have a high regard for the other's interest and she has a high regard for yours. Such a framework suggests a rather different structure of negotiation than the "dance" of positions (Raiffa, 1982).

It also suggests a different process from that which is often described as the essence of joint gain negotiation (Fisher and Ury, 1981; Raiffa, 1982; Lax and Sebenius, 1986; Susskind and Cruikshank, 1987). The essence of negotiating for joint gains involves a search for those sets of agreements that satisfy interests that the parties are seen to value differently. The tactics entail the logical identification of these differences and the creative exploration of options that will satisfy them. Implied in this model is a view that goals and interests are relatively fixed and potentially known by the parties. The secret to making agreement lies in designing a process where goals and interests can be discovered and incorporated into an

agreement. In problem-solving through dialogue, the process is less structured and becomes the vehicle through which goals can emerge from mutual inquiry. The stance of those involved is one of flexibility and adaptiveness (distinguished from control) in response to potential uncertainty (Marshall, 1984). This kind of sensing can lead to transformed understandings of problems and possible solutions.

HER PLACE AT THE TABLE

We rarely hear the woman's voice in formal, public negotiation. When it is there, it tends to be muted and easily overwhelmed. This might occur because the formal negotiating table may be an alien place for a woman.[10] Negotiations are settings for conflict resolution and conflict itself is uncomfortable for some women, because it locates them in opposition to others and is hostile to their qualities and values (Marshall, 1984; Keller, 1985). Conflict is associated with aggressiveness, a stereotypical masculine attribute (Northrup and Segall, 1988). When women or girls act aggressively, their behavior is interpreted differently from aggressive actions of boys or men (Van Wagner and Swanson, 1979; Hennig and Jardim, 1976). Attitude studies consistently show that women are more peaceful and rejecting of violence than men (Northrup, 1987). Women are socialized to believe that conflict with men or others in authority is wrong, and feel vulnerable in the face of it (Miller, 1984; Northrup and Segall, 1988). In their private sphere of influence, conflict more often takes on personal and emotional overtones that are quite different from the structured disputing in public settings (Collier, 1974). In common with others who are subordinate, women's conflict is traditionally suppressed, and so they perhaps lack experience in dealing openly with it (MacKinnon, 1982; Miller, 1984).

For all these reasons, many women experience conflict situations as ones in which they have few options and limited ability to affect outcomes. It is not surprising, therefore, that in bargaining situations many women find that natural problem-solving skills they might bring to the table are mitigated by their feelings about place.[11] These feelings may be expressed in a variety of ways. Some, fearing possible hostility or acrimonious relations, emphasize harmony over other interests, including their own. Others, anxious about the situation, find their presentation style and their ability to communicate impaired. Women whose socialization and professional experience lead them to cultivate a style that is congruent with dominant modes of negotiating often find that conventional stereotypes and perceptions of them undermine their behavior and performance.

Preserving Harmony

In a recent class, one of the female students raised her hand and described herself as "incorrigibly integrative." Upon further discussion, it turned out that her definition of integrative, in contrast to others' (see Raiffa, 1982; Lax and Sebenius, 1986), was one in which all parties were happy even when she downplayed her own interests. Studies of negotiation suggest that this preference for harmony can dominate other possible interests. Watson and Kasten (1988) observed experimentally that female negotiating pairs can avoid discussing the main point of a conflict and yet still believe they have negotiated effectively if their interaction with the other party has been pleasant. In studies of managers, it is clear that women, relative to men, have lower tolerance for antagonistic situations and do what they can to smooth over differences, even when it means they are the ones to do the sacrificing (Hennig and Jardim, 1976; Champion, 1979; Loden, 1985).

There is evidence that empathy, considered to be a particular strength of women, leads them to behavior that promotes harmony (Ford, 1982). Empathy should be an advantage in ferreting out

a negotiating partner's interests and intentions, and research has generally supported the assumption that women are more empathetic than males (Ford, 1982). Studies of empathy (Jordan, 1984) suggest that, while males and females tend to be equal in their cognitive awareness or ability to recognize and label other people's feelings, women generally are more personally responsive on an affective level and know how it feels.

However, there is some indication that when they get into negotiating situations, women find their ability to empathize impaired (Womack, 1986). There are several possible explanations why women may not be as empathetic in negotiation and as able to take the role of the other, as we might predict. One is that empathy can lead to exploitation. In negotiation, learning of another's interests is motivated by a desire to enhance one's own position—sometimes (although not always) at the expense of the other. If women are highly responsive to how their actions can impact their relationships, they might be more reluctant to exploit what information they might acquire.

Secondly, since a negotiating table is not a "natural" place for a woman, the natural tendency to empathize might be suppressed. We have some evidence from our students (all of whom are women) that in bilateral negotiating situations where the structure of the game is such that parties are pitted against each other they had difficulty placing themselves in the role of the other. In other classroom contexts where the situations involved group decision-making, women distinguished themselves in listening to, understanding, and responding to each other. Yet when active listening was required for successful performance in the bilateral negotiation role plays, the students said that anxiety interfered with their ability to listen. Concern over their own next response led them to miss clues revealing unexplored issues of importance to their opponents. They experienced difficulty in eliciting information as they were reluctant to probe, persuade, influence, or uncover alternatives. They assessed their opponents' interests based only on the information that was volunteered.

Third, it has been suggested that, in empathizing with others, women sometimes undervalue their own interests and do not develop self-empathy (Surrey, 1985; Greenhalgh and Gilkey, 1985). Studies suggest that in a variety of group settings, women listen more and speak less, perhaps limiting their opportunities to satisfy their own interests (Robb, 1988). The dilemma for women is to resolve the conflict between compassion for others and their own autonomy (Gilligan, 1982), and to overcome a tendency to be responsive only. Comments from our students support these findings; typical are the remarks of the following student:

> In real life I find it easier to negotiate for others. While supervising two editors this fall, I fought tooth and nail for reasonable schedules, appropriate workloads, and fair performance evaluations. Interestingly enough, I fared better when I represented their interests than when I represented my own!

The ability to take the role of the other in negotiation and to ascertain interests and needs is an important skill in negotiation (Bazerman, 1983). What the research suggests, however, is that it can be a double-edged sword for women.

Styles of Talk

The essence of negotiation is strategic communication. Parties want to learn about the alternatives available and the priority of interests of the other. At the same time, they want to communicate in ways that further their own aims, whether it is to elucidate their interests or obfuscate them, depending on strategy (Lax and Sebenius, 1986). Research on gender in communications suggests that women's distinctive communication style, which serves them well in other contexts, can be a liability in negotiation (Smeltzer and Watson, 1986).

Women speak differently. Their assertions are qualified through the use of tag questions and modifiers (Lakoff, 1975; Nadler and Nadler, 1984; Womack, 1986). Krieger (1987) notes that the female pattern of communication involves deference, relational thinking in argument, and indirection. The male pattern typically involves linear or legalistic argument, depersonalization, and a more directional style. While women speak with many qualifiers to show flexibility and an opportunity for discussion, men use confident, self-enhancing terms. In negotiation, these forms of communication can be read as weakness or lack of clarity, and thus might get in the way of focusing on the real issues in conflict (Watson and Kasten, 1988). Indeed, the women in our class had difficulty putting their wants into words and tended instead to wait for information that was volunteered.

Similarly, women's modes of discourse do not signal influence. Women's speech is more conforming and less powerful (Rosaldo, 1974; Lakoff, 1975; Eagly, 1987). Women talk less and are easily interrupted while they, in turn, are less likely to interrupt (Zimmerman and West, 1979). In mixed groups, they adopt a deferential posture and are less likely to openly advocate their positions (Krieger, 1987). At the same time, there is a proclivity to be too revealing—to talk too much about their attitudes, beliefs, and concerns (Baird and Bradley, 1979). One of our students described her deferential efforts to negotiate with the mayor of her community for AIDS resources:

> My strategy was to seek incremental progress to ensure that appropriate steps were taken to address the educational and service needs presented by the AIDS epidemic, and to eliminate discrimination against gay people. Given the environment of the Mayor's Office, I believe now that I weakened my position by being too reasonable for too long. My strategy initially had been to

demonstrate that I would not waste the mayor's time with trivialities, thereby establishing the understanding that when I pressured him, he should understand that it was a serious issue. I look back now on how polite, calm, and respectful I was with him in communicating the urgency of the AIDS epidemic and in pushing funding and program proposals. It is a horrible and laughable memory, for I failed to make him uncomfortable enough to warrant his attention. My subtlety was a liability when it came to "persuading" the mayor to take action where he was resistant.

My negotiation style didn't change, even though I watched the mayor for two years and seldom saw him take action on anything unless he was pinned to the wall. I should have been far less deferential. . . I made it too easy for him to dismiss me. I was liked and relatively well respected, but as a negotiator these qualities don't go far. To risk being more of a kick-ass would have served me better, and the mayor as well, by getting things attended to *before* they reached crisis proportions.

Given that the process of negotiation as it is customarily enacted calls for parties to be clear and communicate directly and authoritatively about their goals, feelings, interests, and problems, a deferential, self-effacing, and qualified style can be a significant detriment. It is also possible that such a stance can also be an asset in projecting a caring and understanding posture (Nadler and Nadler, 1984). The choice for women is to learn to become more conversant with negotiation skills, but also to be more adept in an alternative style of communication at the negotiating table, one that is more congruent with the task.

Expectations at the Table

When men and women come to the table to negotiate, they bring with them expectations and

ways of seeing the other that shape how each is seen and the credibility and legitimacy accorded their actions. When women come to the table to negotiate, they often evoke certain stereotypes about feminine behavior that can affect how they are seen by their negotiating partners. The stereotypes are familiar: Women are expected to act passive, compliant, nonaggressive, noncompetitive, and accommodating, and attend to the socioemotional needs of those present (Eisenstein, 1984). If a woman displays these characteristics through her behavior, then she reinforces some of these stereotypes and, as suggested above, might find her efficacy impaired. However (and this is often the situation with professional women), she can also act in ways that contradict these stereotypes. That is, she can be aggressive and competitive in pursuing her interests; indeed, she can be quite distributive in the tactics she uses. The question is, can she pull it off?

Existing research is not encouraging. Evidence from research on women in organizations, particularly in management, suggests that it is not so easy for women to act forcefully and competitively without inviting criticism and questions about both her femininity and her ability, and by threatening something of the accustomed social order (Kanter, 1977; Bradley, 1981; Harlan and Weiss, 1982; Marshall, 1984). When performance in decision-making and negotiating tasks is judged equivalent by objective measures, men and women are rated differently by those involved, to the detriment of women (Deux, 1987). They are seen as less influential and receive less credit for what influence they may have exerted (Devanna, 1987; Harmon et al. 1988; Hoffman and Day, 1988). As mediators they are judged less effective, even when the outcomes they achieved are superior (Burrell, 1988).

At the same time, women are expected to do the emotional work in a group (Hochschild, 1983). In negotiation contexts, they often carry the burden for attending to relationships and the emotional needs of those involved. While such a burden might be consistent with a voice she might like to speak in, a woman who has trained herself to negotiate from a different premise might find that these expectations frequently constrain her ability to maneuver for herself or those she represents. Learning how to use their strengths and manage the dual impressions of femininity and strategic resolve are important aspects of negotiating tactics for women.

CONCLUSIONS

We have tried to develop in this article two themes that in some respects stand in contradiction to each other. The first, arguing from existing feminist literature, describes what a woman's voice in negotiation might sound like. Here we are suggesting that women, if given the opportunity and setting, might create an alternative structure and process in public negotiation. We do not mean to imply that women would always speak in such a voice. Variations in class, race, culture, and social setting certainly affect the meaning ascribed to negotiated situations and so color the ways in which the process and women's roles within it are enacted. It would be more accurate, perhaps, to speak of alternative voices. However, an alternative voice, to the degree it exists in relatively coherent form, opens up possibilities in certain kinds of negotiations, not just to change the kinds of strategies we employ, but to transform our understanding of process. In situations where trust, openness, and long-term relationships are critical, this voice is likely to be heard and be influential. There are many other situations (indeed, the prototypical negotiated scene), in which the voice is not only hushed but might even put its speaker in a situation in which she is open to compromise or exploitation. This is the theme we speak to in the second part of this article.

Gender has been a variable in hundreds of negotiating experiments and yields a picture that is contradictory at best (Rubin and Brown, 1976).

A focus on central behavioral tendencies of either the cooperative, competitive, or enlightened self-interest sort can obscure some of the interesting ways that gender is important in negotiation. How an individual acts in a setting has to do with her sense of place and how she defines the situation in which she finds herself (McHugh, 1968). To the degree that negotiation signals conflict and competing interests, a situation often at odds with the voice in which they speak, women sometimes experience anxiety and a sense of fraudulence in that place. These feelings compounded by her demeanor and style of communication can impact and sometimes impair her efficacy at the bargaining table. From experienced and professional women, we learn about the specific tactics and strategies they use to manage *place* at the table.

Our dual focus on voice and place suggests some new ways to pursue the "gender issue" in negotiation as a topic of research and training. First, there is the matter of voice. We speculate that an alternative voice, one based on a relational view of others, an embedded view of agency, a focus on empowerment, and problem-solving through dialogue, can be deciphered. How can we document this? Comparative study of homogenous gender groups do not always provide a reliable context. First, study suggests that in the laboratory women can be especially susceptible to cues in the experimental situation (Greenhaigh and Gilkey, 1985). Further, most comparisons would take place in a cultural context (professional schools, business and legal negotiations) where the voice dominates. What is required is a context in which another voice can be potentially heard, such as all-female law firms and consulting practices (Krieger, 1987). We need to learn more about how negotiation in these settings is conducted.

Inquiry about her place at the table, however, is a facet of understanding that we can study in more traditional settings. What we are after here are not simple descriptions of behavior, but rather interpretive understandings about how men and women experience the process of negotiation. We want to know not just what they do, but how they think and feel about what they do; how this is related to outcomes; and how those involved think about and feel about the outcomes and the process they used to get there. Inquiry of this sort will enhance our understanding about the phenomenon of place at the table that will form the basis for studying variations among men and women (Bailyn, 1988).

Education and training are quite complicated. On the one hand, we believe that it is important to know and articulate the voice women tend to bring to negotiation. It is part of the interpretive lens through which we understand what will happen at the table. What it is and how it is likely to be heard should become part of any analysis we carry out in preparation for negotiation. It is obviously important to realize that speaking in that voice has its time and place. We need to help people become better at recognizing it and planning with such contingencies in mind. At the same time, we must be realistic about expectations that are placed on us as women at the table and develop ways to anticipate and manage these expectations. Appreciating some of the ways our style might impede our success, we need to experiment with a variety of presentation modes. There is much we can learn from experience and from each woman who has successfully managed to find a place at the table and come to speak with a voice that is her own.

NOTES

An earlier version of this article was presented at a symposium on Gender, Power, and Conflict at the Annual Meeting of the Academy of Management, Anaheim, California on August 8, 1988.

1. Some argue that this distinction is more apparent than real. If women are evaluated relative to men either as deviating from a male standard or representing a different perspective entirely, the comparison with the dominant male model still grounds the observations (Marcus et al., 1984).

2. Significant works in the field of psychology describe moral, cognitive, and affective development as the evolution of identity through a process of separation and differentiation. Self-reliant adults grow beyond the dependence of childhood to define their individual goals, to enter contractual relationships for the achievement of their ends, to apply laws justly in the settlement of their disputes, and, when mature, to join with partners in mutually beneficial relationships and in procreation. The claim is made that each of these thinkers derives his theory primarily from the study of male subjects and that these chronicles of growth might not capture women's experience.

3. In recent studies of adolescents and young adults, Gilligan and her colleagues found that "there is an overwhelming tendency in men to focus on justice and only minimally to represent caring. Only three men from a total of 60 demonstrated a care focus." Sixty percent of a sample of 140 women focused on care (Marcus et al., 1984: 48).

4. Gender is one of the most studied variables in negotiation simulations in the laboratory, in part because of the ease of measurement. Despite these prolific efforts, the question of how gender might matter in negotiations is still very much a matter of debate. There are several reasons why these matters are still unsettled.

   The first relates to the conception of gender that informs much of the laboratory study. Gender is usually conceived as a stable set of behavioral attributes, the result of biology, sociology, and social role (Eagly, 1987; Hanisch and Carnevale, 1988). Aggregate comparisons of men and women in negotiation situations emphasize gender-based differences along the following:

   a. dimensions of cooperative-competitive moves (Maccoby and Jacklin, 1974; Amidjaja and Vinacke, 1965; Bond and Vinacke, 1961;

Fisher and Smith, 1969; Grant and Sermat, 1969; Greenhaigh and Gilkey, 1984; Miller and Pyke, 1973; Rubin and Brown, 1975; Rapoport and Chammah, 1965; Sampson and Kardush, 1965; Nadler and Nadler, 1984; Wall and Virtue, 1976; Putnam and Jones, 1982; Loden, 1985);

b. assertive v. expressive styles of negotiation (Kimmel et al., 1980; Yamada et al., 1983; Hanisch and Carnevale, 1988; Harmon et al. , 1988); and

c. forms of communication (Nadler and Nadler, 1984; Womack, 1986; Greenhaigh and Gilkey, 1984; Kimmel et al., 1980; Semltzer, and Watson, 1986).

The findings of these studies are equivocal. Although we have not counted directly, at least as many studies conclude that men are cooperative as find that it is women who are so (Greenhaigh and Gilkey, 1984). Whether a man or women adopts an assertive or expressive style is also highly variable and seems to depend on such factors as the sex of the negotiating partner, the role the subject is called upon to play, experience with the process, time horizon, and goals to achieve (Putnam and Jones, 1982; Womack, 1986; Greenhaigh and Gilkey, 1984; Rubin and Brown, 1976; Wall and Virtue, 1976; Krieger, 1987). Communication styles that are predicted to detract from a woman's efficacy, the use of apology, equivocal language, and reluctance to press for information (Lakoff, 1973) are not uniformly supported in more recent studies (Nadler and Nadler, 1984; Womack, 1986).

One problem with much of this research is its very conception of gender as a stable set of characteristics that describe all women (or men) in negotiation situations. The characteristics describe central tendencies and tell us very little about variation within each gender group (Bailyn, 1988). It is clear that context matters in terms of the degree to which gender-related characteristics are observed (Deux, 1984). For example, there is evidence that

when women negotiate with other women, they tend to be more cooperative and use different forms of argument than they do in mixed groups (Wall and Virtue, 1976; Putnam and Jones, 1982). Our own experience of women in a women's organization reinforces these perceptions (see Krieger, 1987).

Another issue is the focus on behavior. Negotiation tactics are likely to be highly variable, and depend on a host of individual and situational factors. To trace behavior back to gender is to ignore the multiple influences on tactical choice (Neale and Northeraft, 1988). However, there is some evidence that the way negotiators interpret and experience negotiation contexts has some basis in gender. For example, Rubin and Brown (1976) conclude that women are perhaps more responsive to interpersonal and situational cues and so conceive their strategic choices differently. Similarly, Greenhaigh and Gilkey (1984) demonstrate that women apply a longer time frame to negotiation and so interpret isolated negotiation events in the context of longer-term relationships. Research must attend more to the ways that different groups experience negotiation situations and see what aspects of these differences can be traced to gender and variations within groups.

5. Some suggest that a woman's voice resembles the kinds of tactics associated with integrative (as opposed to distributive) bargaining. The difficulty with this formulation is that it equates voice with behavior. Voice refers not just to what people do, but to how they understand what they are doing. It is a way that individuals define situations so that they can act in them. The particular tactics, whether they are distributive or integrative, are likely to be quite variable as individual negotiators respond to the particular situations they face.

6. While gender has cultural and psychological dimensions like other social variables, gender identity has its roots in biology. Research on parent-infant interaction shows that, from

birth, girls are handled with less horseplay and their cries are interpreted to signal different needs and evoke different parental responses than the cries of male infants. By the age of three, most children identify themselves as male or female (Marcus et al., 1984), and that dimension of identity remains constant until death for all but a very few. Perceptions of appropriate action for "a young lady" or the admonition for boys not to "act like a girl" or praise for a professional woman's ability to "think like a man" color each person's understanding of how to act in the world. Particularly in this time of re-examination of the roles women and men ought to play in both public and private spheres, the implications of gender merit careful study. At the same time it is quite clear that it would be a mistake to lump all women into one category and men into another. A focus on women provides the source of ideas about alternative voices. These then become the bases for studies of how these characteristics of voice vary among both men and women (see Bailyn, 1988).

7. Obviously, considerations of ongoing relationships are not relevant to all negotiated settings. In short-term, distributive bargaining situations like automobile or real estate purchases, negotiators bring no common background or relational history to their dealings. Women's reported discomfort with such transactions might be attributable to their lack of familiarity with the snapshot nature of such an interaction (Greenhaigh and Gilkey, 1985).

8. Radical feminists take the position that in legal, political, economic, and private spheres, in fact, women are a subordinate group. MacKinnon (Marcus et al., 1984: 27) asserts, "Dominance and submission made into sex, made into the gender difference, constitute the suppressed social content of the gender definitions of men and women." The "feminine" voice is actually the voice of the victim, they argue, and speaks in the only way differential status allows it to be heard by a dominant group bent on suppress-

ing conflicts that challenge the established male-dominated hierarchy.

Our culture socializes men and women into different roles as a result of their status differences, some theorists argue (Northrup, 1987; Miller, 1976). While men are brought up to be achievers and winners in highly-valued, public roles, women are primarily trained to be caretakers and nurturers with responsibility for maintenance and support activities. When women are dependent on men both economically and psychologically, they find initiating open conflict practically impossible (Collier, 1974). In situations of inequality, women lose conflicts. Urging values of care makes sense for women, MacKinnon argues, because that is what women have been valued for and because they have been given little choice to be valued for anything else (Marcus et al., 1984).

9. Gilligan (Marcus et al., 1984: 45) relates the interaction of a pair of four-year-olds who were playing together as an example of reaching an inclusive solution through transformational thinking. The girl suggested that they play next-door neighbors. The boy wanted to play pirates instead. "Okay," said the girl, "then you can be the pirate who lives next door." Rather than coming to a fair solution where each child would have an equal turn to play a favored game, in her inclusive solution, both the pirate and neighbor game changed into a combined pirate-neighbor game that neither child had separately imagined. This new game arose because a dialogue was established about what to play.

10. Research and experience in training situations demonstrate that mastery of negotiating skills and their practiced application will diminish women's sense of alienation. As women become more used to negotiating, their outcomes improve (Raiffa, 1982; Schenkel, 1984). However, some evidence suggests that women for whom considerations of relationship guide moral reasoning will continue to experience a sense of alienation even from their own words

and actions as they reason from principles of justice at the negotiating table. Gilligan illustrates this tension with a girl named Amy, to whom she twice poses the Heinz dilemma, a moral reasoning problem about whether a husband should steal a drug he cannot afford in order to save his wife's life. At age 15, Amy gives the "right" answer that he should steal the drug because life comes before property. She explains, though, that she "really thinks" just as she did at age 11 that "It all depends. What if the husband got caught? It would not help his wife. And anyway, from everything I know about cancer, it cannot be cured in a single treatment . . ." (Marcus et al., 1984: 41) By 15, Amy has learned not to voice her contextual and relationship-based frame for judgment.

This feeling of being out of place was also confirmed by Isabel Marcus, Associate Professor of Law at the State University of New York at Buffalo, who responded to a lecture by Gilligan with the insight, "Now I understand at a new level why I felt so uncomfortable in law school" (Marcus et al., 1984: 11).

11. McIntosh (1985) has found feelings of fraudulence to be especially severe in women and to arise in acute forms in particular situations. Training experiences indicate that negotiation settings trigger feelings of fraudulence in inexperienced women. McIntosh describes fraudulence as feeling illegitimate in doing or appearing as something unfamiliar; as feeling anxious, uncomfortable, incompetent, undeserving, tenuous, and guilty. She contends that women are taught to feel like frauds and that the teaching is no accident but is designed to perpetuate existing hierarchies.

REFERENCES

Amidjaja, I. R. and Vinacke, W. E. (1965). Achievement, nurturance, and competition in male and female triads. *Journal of Personality and Social Psychology* 2: 447–451.

Bailyn, L. (1988). Issues of gender in technical work. Paper presented at the Tokyo Symposium on Women, August 25–27.

Baird, J. E. and Bradley, P. H. (1979). Styles of management and communication: A comparative study of men and women. *Communications Monographs* 46: 101–111.

Bakan, D. (1966). *The duality of human existence.* Chicago: Rand McNally.

Bazerman, M. H. (1987). *Getting to YES* six years later. *Dispute Resolution Forum*, Washington, D.C.: National Institute for Dispute Resolution. May, 1987.

Bazerman, M. H.(1983). Negotiator judgment: A critical look at the rationality assumption. *American Behavioral Scientist* 27: 211–228.

Belenky, M. F., Clinchy, B. M., Goldberger, N. R. and Tarule, J. M. (1986). *Women's ways of knowing: The development of self voice and mind.* New York: Basic Books.

Bond, J. R. and Vinacke, W. E. (1961). Coalitions in mixed-sex triads. *Sociometry* 24: 61–75.

Bradley, P. (1981). The folk linguistics of women's sphere: An empirical examination. *Communication Monographs* 48: 73–90.

Burrell, N. (1988). Training mediators as interests mergers: The impact of gender stereotype on roommate disputes. *Communication Research.*

Champion, D. L. (1979) A comparison of men and women managers on preference for organizational conflict management. *DBA,* Florida State University.

Chodorow, N. (1978). *The reproduction of mothering.* Berkeley: University of California Press.

Collier, J. F. (1974). Women in politics. In *Women, culture and society*, edited by M. Z. Rosaldo and L. Lamphere. Stanford: Stanford University Press.

Conrath, D. W. (1960). Sex roles and 'cooperation' in the game of chicken. *Journal of Conflict Resolution* 60: 265–277.

Devanna, M. A. (1987). Women in management: Progress and promise. *Human Resource Management* 26 (4): 469–481.

Deux, K. K. (1984). From individual differences to social categories: Analysis of a decade's research on gender. *American Psychologist* 39: 105–116.

Eagly, A. (1987). *Sex differences in social behavior: A social-role interpretation.* Hillsdale, N.J.: Lawrence Erlbaum.

Eisenstein, H. (1984). *Contemporary feminist thought.* London: Unwin Paperbacks.

Emerson, R. A. (1962). Power-dependence relations. *American Sociological Review* 27: 31–40.

Fisher, R. (1983). Negotiating power. *American Behavioral Scientist* 27: 149–166.

Fisher, R. and Brown, S. (1988). *Getting together: Building a relationship that gets to YES.* Boston: Houghton Mifflin Company.

Fisher, R. and Ury, W. (1981). *Getting to YES: Negotiating agreement without giving in.* Boston: Houghton Mifflin Company.

Fisher, R. and Smith, W. P. (1969). Conflict of interest and attraction in the development of cooperation. *Psychonomic Science* 14: 154–155.

Ford, M. E. (1982). Social cognition and social competence in adolescence. *Developmental Psychology* 18 (3): 323–340.

Gilligan, C. (1982). *In a different voice: Psychological theory and women's development.* Cambridge, Mass.: Harvard University Press.

Grant, M. J. and Sermat, V. (1969). Status and sex of other as determinants of behavior in a mixed-motive game. *Journal of Personality and Social Psychology* 12: 151–157.

Greenhaigh, L. and Gilkey, R. W. (1985). Our game, your rules: Developing effective negotiating approaches. In *Not as far as you think,* edited by L. Moore. Lexington, Mass.: Lexington Books.

Greenhalgh, L. and Gilkey, R. W. (1984). *Effects of sex-role differences on approaches to interpersonal and interorganizational negotiations.* Paper presented at the Academy of Management Annual Meeting, Boston, Mass., August.

Hanisch, K. A. and Carnevale, P. (1988). Gender differences in mediation and negotiation: General effects and situation-specific effects. Unpublished paper.

Harlan, A. and Weiss, C. (1982). Sex differences in factors affecting managerial career advancement. In *Women in the Workplace,* edited by P. Wallace. Boston: Arbor House.

Harmon, J., Schneer, J. A., and Hoffman, L. R. (1988). *Power, influence, and conflict-handling behavior in established groups: Gender differences and medium of communication.* Paper presented at the Academy of Management, Anaheim, Calif. August, 1988.

Hennig, M. and Jardim, A. (1976). *The managerial woman.* Garden City, New York: Anchor Press/ Doubleday.

Hochschild, A. (1983). *The managed heart.* Berkeley: University of California Press.

Hoffman, L. R. and Day, A. (1988). Gender and influence in the problem-solving process in groups. Paper presented at the Academy of Management, Anaheim, Calif., August 8.

Jordan, J. V. (1984). Empathy and self boundaries. *Work in Progress* No. 84–05. Wellesley, Mass.: Stone Center Working Paper Series.

Kanter, R. M. (1977). *Men and women of the corporation.* New York: Basic Books.

Keller, E. F. (1986). How gender matters, or, why it's so hard for us to count past two. *New Ideas in Psychology.*

Keller, E. F. (1985). *Reflections on gender and science.* New Haven: Yale University Press.

Kimmel, M. J., Pruitt, D. G., Magenau, J. M, Konar-Goldband, E., and Carnevale, P. J. (1980). Effects of trust, aspiration, and gender on negotiation tactics. *Journal of Personality and Social Psychology* 38: 9–22.

Krieger, S. (1987). "Organizational theory: Implications of recent feminist research (ways women organize)." Talk presented at the Organizational Behavior and Industrial Relations Colloquium. School of Business Administration, University of California, Berkeley, 29 October 1987.

Lakoff, R. (1975). *Language and women's place.* New York: Harper and Colophon.

Lax, D. A. and Sebenius, J. K. (1986). Interests: The measure of negotiation. *Negotiation Journal* 2: 73–92.

Lerner, G. (1979). *The majority finds its past: Placing women in history.* New York: Oxford University Press.

Linn, M. (1986). Meta-analysis of studies of gender differences: Implications and future directions. *The Psychology of gender, advances through meta -analysis.* London: Johns Hopkins University Press.

Loden, M. (1985). *Feminine leadership, or how to succeed in business without being one of the boys.* New York: Time Books.

Maccoby, E. E. and Jacklin, C. N. (1974). *The psychology of sex differences.* Stanford: Stanford University Press.

MacKinnon, C. (1982). Feminism, Marxism, method and the state: An agenda for theory. *Signs* 7: 515–544.

Marcus, I., Spiegelman, P. J., DuBois, E. C., Dunlap, M. C., Gilligan, C. J., MacKinnon, C. A., and Menkel-Meadow, C. J. (1985). Feminist discourse, moral values, and the law—A conversation. Edited transcript of the 1984 James McCormick Mitchell Lecture at the Law School of the State University of New York at Buffalo. *Buffalo Law Review* 35: 11–87.

Marshall, J. (1984). *Women managers: Travelling in a male world.* Chichester, England: Wiley.

McCarthy, W. (1985). The role of power and politics in Getting to YES. *Negotiation Journal* 1: 59–66.

McHugh, P. (1968). *Defining the situation: The organization of meaning in social interaction.* New York: Bobbs-Merrill.

McIntosh, P. (1985). Feeling like a fraud. *Work in Progress* No. 18. Wellesley, Mass.: Stone Center Working Paper Series.

Menkel-Meadow, C. (1985). Portia in a different voice: Speculating on a women's lawyering process. *Berkeley Women's Law Journal* 1: 39–63.

Miller, G. H. and Pyke, S. G. (1973). Sex, matrix variations, and perceived personality effects in mixed-motive games. *Journal of Conflict Resolution* 17: 335–349.

Miller, J. B. (1984). The development of women's sense of self. *Work in Progress* no. 84–01. Wellesley, Mass.: Stone Center Working Paper Series.

Miller, J. B. (1982). Women and power: Some psychological dimensions. *Work in Progress* no. 82–01. Wellesley, Mass.: Stone Center Working Paper Series.

Miller, J. B. (1976). *Toward a new psychology of women.* Boston: Beacon Press.

Nadler, L. B. and Nadler, M. K. (1984). Communication, gender, and negotiation: Theory and findings. Eastern Communication Association Convention, Philadelphia, 9 March 1984.

Neale, M. and Northcraft, G. (1988). Experience, expertise and decision bias in negotiation. In *Research in Bargaining and Negotiating in Organizations*, vol. II. edited by B. Sheppard, M. H. Bazerman, and R. Lewicki. Greenwich, Conn.: JAI Press, in press.

Northrup, T. A. and Segall, M. H. (1988). Subjective vulnerability: The role of disempowerment in the utilization of mediation services by women. Proposal submitted to The Fund for Research on Dispute Resolution, June.

Northrup, T. A. (1987). Women's and men's conceptualizations of war, peace, and security: Two realities. Working Paper No. 3. Syracuse, N.Y.: Maxwell School of Citizenship and Public Affairs.

Pearson, J. and Thoennes, N. (1988). An empirical study of child support mediation. Unpublished paper.

Putnam, L. L. and Jones, T. S. (1982). Reciprocity in negotiations: An analysis of bargaining interaction. *Communication Monographs* 49: 171–191.

Raiffa, H. (1982). *The art and science of negotiation.* Cambridge, Mass.: Harvard University Press.

Rapoport, A. and Chammah, A.M. (1965). Sex differences in factors contributing to the level of cooperation in the prisoner's dilemma game. *Journal of Personality and Social Psychology* 2: 831–838.

Rifkin, J. (1984). Mediation from a feminist perspective: Problems and promise. *Law and Inequality*, 21: 2.

Robb, C. (1988). What did you say? *The Boston Globe Magazine*, 30 March 1988.

Rothschild, J. (1988). *The feminization of conflict resolution: The influence of gender on the ideology, language, and practice of mediation.* Paper presented at the Annual Meeting of the Law and Society Association, Chicago, Ill., June, 1988.

Rosaldo, M. Z. (1974). Women, culture, and society: A theoretical overview. In *Women, culture and society*, edited by M. Z. Rosaldo and L. Lamphere. Stanford: Stanford University Press.

Rubin, J. Z. and Brown, B. R. (1975). *The psychology of bargaining and negotiation.* New York: Academic Press.

Sampson, E. E. and Kardush, M. (1965). Age, sex, class, and race differences in response to a two person non-zero sum game. *Journal of Conflict Resolution* 9: 212–220.

Sampson, E. E. (1988). The debate on individualism: Indigenous psychologies of the individual and their role in personal and societal functioning. *American Psychologist*, January.

Schenkel, S. (1984). *Giving away success: Why women get stuck and what to do about it.* New York: McGraw-Hill.

Segall, M. (1988). Psychocultural antecedents of male aggression: Some implications involving gender, parenting, and adolescence. In *Psychological implications for health and human development*, edited by M. Sartorium, P. Dasen, and J. W. Berry. Newbury Park: Sage.

Silbey, S. and Sarat, A. (1988). *Dispute processing in law and legal scholarship.* Paper prepared for the Institute for Legal Studies, University of Wisconsin School of Law.

Smeltzer, L. and Watson, K. W. (1986). Gender differences in verbal communication during negotiations. *Communication Research Reports* 3: 74–79.

Surrey, J. L. (1987). Relationship and empowerment. *Work in Progress* No. 30. Wellesley, Mass.: Stone Center Working Paper Series.

Surrey, J. L. (1985). Self-in-relation: A theory of women's development. *Work in Progress* no. 13. Wellesley, Mass.: Stone Center Working Paper Series.

Susskind, L. and Cruikshank, J. (1987). *Breaking the impasse: Consensual approaches to resolving public disputes.* New York: Basic Books.

Van Wagner, K. and Swanson, C. (1979). From Machiavelli to Ms: Differences in male-female power styles. *Public Administration Review* 39: 66–72.

Wall, J. A. and Virtue, R. (1976). Women as negotiators. *Business Horizons* 19: 67–68.

Warren, C. A. B. (1988). *Gender issues in field research.* Beverly Hills: Sage.

Watson, C. and Kasten, B. (1988). Separate strengths? How women and men negotiate. Newark, N.J.: Center for Negotiation and Conflict Resolution at Rutgers University.

Womack, D. E (1987). Implications for women in organizational negotiations. Presented at the Speech Communication Association Convention.

Yamada, E. M., Tjosvold, D., and Draguns, J. G. (1983). Effects of sex-linked situations and sex composition on cooperation and style of interaction. *Sex Roles* 9: 541–553.

Zimmerman, D. and West, C. (1979). Sex roles, interruptions, and silence in conversations. In *Language and sex*, edited by B. Thorne and N. Henley. Rowley, Mass.: Newbury House.

Deborah M. Kolb is Professor of Management at the Simmons College Graduate School of Management, and Executive Director of the Program on Negotiation at Harvard Law School.

Gloria G. Coolidge is Planning Coordinator for the Boston Children's Service Association, and is a Research Associate at the Simmons College Graduate School of Management.

Section V

Cross-Cultural Negotiation

Chapter Ten   *International Negotiations*

Chapter Eleven   *Negotiating with Americans*

Chapter Ten

INTERNATIONAL NEGOTIATIONS

THE NUANCES OF NEGOTIATING OVERSEAS

David N. Burt

American industry spends billions of dollars to purchase supplies and capital equipment from foreign sources. Virtually all of these purchases are the result of negotiations. The success of each of these negotiations is influenced, in part, by the American negotiator's ability to understand the needs and the ways of thinking and acting of the representatives of these foreign firms.

Negotiating is a process that is greatly enhanced when negotiators understand their counterparts—the wants, needs, and frame of reference of those at the other side of the table. This type of understanding helps all negotiators reach a satisfactory agreement. U.S. negotiators perform more effectively in these negotiations if they understand the cultural and business heritage of their counterparts and the effect of this heritage on the opposite side's negotiation strategies and tactics.

The United States Air Force has sponsored research on this important issue. A majority of the individuals contacted in conjunction with this research reported their firm belief that most

From *The Journal of Purchasing and Materials Management,* Winter 1984. Reprinted by permission of the National Association of Purchasing Management. All rights reserved.

American negotiators need this information to assist them in their work.

Intercultural communication can be difficult. Even when one overcomes language differences, one can still fail to understand or be understood. When one is unaware of the significant role culture plays in communication, one tends to place the blame for communication failure on the other person. It might be obvious that there are language differences between cultural groups, but many busy American executives believe that a competent interpreter is all that is necessary to overcome these differences. The use of interpreters, while allowing communication to take place, does not obviate the need for an understanding of the non-American's culture.

During the research, it became clear that the ability to understand a non-American's cultural background is of great practical advantage. It puts the non-American off his guard. He expects most Americans to be clumsy and able to do business only in the American way. The American heritage of team sports appears to result in what can best be described as good team players. This is not the case in Europe. The Europeans tend not to be as well prepared nor as coordinated as their American counterparts. The teamwork and team play commonly present on the American side was usually absent on the European side. The Japanese, on the other hand, are excellent team players.

PREPARATION

All the individuals interviewed in conjunction with this particular research project emphasized the need for extensive preparation for the face-to-face phase of the negotiation. They also stressed the importance of the conventional preparation for any negotiation and the need for extensive study of the culture(s). This should include reading about the history and customs of the country in question, and discussions with others who have had experience dealing with citizens of the foreign country. The focus of these preparations should be on the culture, not the language.

A second aspect of the "cultural" preparation process emerged as the research progressed. This second step apparently became important in cases where there was a strong likelihood of continuing relations, such as one or more transactions that would require a year or so for completion. Under such circumstances, the non-Americans (accompanied by their wives) normally would visit the United States firm. The American hosts went to considerable lengths to become acquainted with their counterparts (and their wives) on a social basis. The Americans hosted the visitors in their homes (a rarity in Europe and Japan). The Americans and their wives developed good relations with their counterparts. This bank of goodwill, while not a means of co-opting the opposition, provided a desire and willingness to *understand*, which frequently proved to be invaluable during subsequent transactions.

Some of the firms took a different approach, but one that yielded the same result. They stationed a well-qualified person in the foreign country for a period long enough to allow him or her to become culturally adroit.

At least one other aspect of the preparatory process requires attention: it takes much longer to negotiate with Europeans and the Japanese than with Americans. This is especially true if the foreign firm has not had extensive exposure to U.S. business practices and specifications. The organization of most European and Japanese businesses and their mode of operation usually require considerably more time to negotiate than is the case in American firms. In the case of European firms, it usually takes at least twice as much time; Japanese firms require up to six times the time. The American negotiator must be aware of the requirement for additional time—and plan accordingly. He or she must be patient and thick-skinned when progress is slow.

GENERAL CONSIDERATIONS IN EUROPE

Pricing. The European concept of a fair and reasonable price is tied directly to the marketplace. "Whatever the market will bear" is often the sole basis for a European firm's pricing policy. The Europeans tend to be unprepared to support their price proposals. Understanding this tendency should cause the American negotiator to (1) conduct a detailed and realistic cost analysis before entering negotiations, and (2) be prepared to deal with an "opposite" who might not know his firm's true costs.

The Europeans tend to be sensitive to discussions that might show that their productivity is lower than that of their U.S. counterparts. Focusing has been found to be more effective. As one interviewee said, "Don't push for details on productivity. It gets their pride up and can disrupt the negotiation."

Many European firms are closely held by financial institutions, and return on investment and dividend payments tend to be lower than in the United States. Therefore, it frequently is possible to negotiate a lower target profit figure in Europe than in the United States.

Many European firms tend to have cash flow problems. Frequently, it is possible to gain a significant price concession if advance or progress payments are incorporated in the resulting agreement. However, this approach must not be treated in isolation. European financing rates are often lower than American ones. Thus, it might be less costly to have the European supplier assign his contract payments to a local financial institution in order to obtain low cost temporary financing.

It also helps to be familiar with the tax laws in the European supplier's country, which might also allow you to negotiate significant price reductions.

The negotiator must be guided by his firm's comptroller about the likely costs or advantages of using a particular currency. Then the negotiator should be free to negotiate the exchange rate as he would any other term or condition.

Tactics

At this point, consider several tactical issues. Hold frequent caucuses during negotiations with foreigners to help relieve the tensions introduced by different cultural and business practices.

The winner of a negotiation in some countries is the one who gains the most concessions, regardless of the value of the concessions. When a negotiator treats all concessions as if they are of equal importance, his counterpart should make certain that many issues are introduced, and take care in properly sequencing them.

Usually the "package approach" is more productive than the sequential one. Using the package approach, each issue is addressed in turn. If agreement is possible, it is so noted. If agreement is not possible, the issue is deferred and finally included as part of a final package proposal. One negotiator was quite successful with what he called the "bucket approach." He would refer to his package proposal as a bucket, pointing out that if something were to be added,

something else would have to be taken out and vice versa.

Cancellation

Cancellation procedures are especially difficult to negotiate with European suppliers because they are unable to manipulate the size of their labor force. In some instances, representatives of a firm have concluded that rather than prolong negotiations on this issue, it is better not to include cancellation procedures in the resulting contract. The issue is addressed only if cancellation later becomes necessary. In Europe, disputes over such issues as cancellation costs are resolved through arbitration or jurisprudence. In such cases the decision goes beyond the terms of the contract in an effort to arrive at what is considered an equitable decision.

Negotiating Table Language

Several approaches were encountered in deciding what language to use at the negotiating table. In the 1950s and 1960s, it was common to employ negotiators who were native to the foreign country. Negotiations thus were conducted in the appropriate foreign language. On relatively small non-critical negotiations, a senior American official would be present and the foreign employee would function as an "intelligent interpreter"—one who conveyed the meaning, nuances, and intent, not merely a literal translation. Several American firms still use this approach.

An alternative approach, which seemed to be equally successful, requires all discussions to be in English. Many foreign business officials have an excellent command of English. The American negotiators who require all discussions to be in English contend that this produces a freer discussion, and a better, quicker understanding.

The Recorder. Several of the interviewees stressed the importance of appointing a member of their own team as the official recorder. This is a powerful position—especially in dealings with foreigners.

Authority

Many European firms like to start low-level negotiations with emissaries who obtain information and then scurry back to their superiors. This approach can be a frustrating waste of time. It can be avoided by insisting that the key decision-maker be present.

Openness

It is quite common in the U.S. culture to be open and frank in negotiations. This is especially true if one negotiator tends to be in a superior position to the other. For example, such a negotiator might indicate the target cost for a project to an unsophisticated supplier in order to convey the scope of the work. Many Europeans, however, do not react well to this approach. In fact, such an approach often appears to be very dysfunctional.

A Few Words of Caution

Most Europeans have a sense of humor, but their humor often is extremely localized. The typical American approach to joviality does not come off well in Europe. In fact, such joking can be dangerous.

Care should be taken in the selection of American negotiators in order to avoid the "Ugly American" syndrome. The American negotiator should not be loud, should not be a carouser, and should not be in any way disrespectful to the local culture.

Europeans tend to be very title-conscious. Some American firms have found it desirable to "promote" their personnel while they are conducting business overseas.

For some years after the end of World War II, many European firms derived a unique satisfaction from dealing with American customers.

These days, however, are long gone—the romance is over. It is now business as usual.

With these general observations as background, consider now some of the individual nuances of negotiating in three European countries.

THE UNITED KINGDOM

One of the first causes of problems that arise in dealing with the British is the tendency to assume that "they" are just like "us." Don't fall prey to that tendency. We might have a common heritage and language, but there are many differences between Americans and the British. Second, do not assume that when they are "down" they are "out." The British typically respond well to adversity, as demonstrated admirably in World War II. Third, one is not dealing with a homogenous population. The United Kingdom is a virtual polyglot of ancient cultural influences, peppered with recent immigrants from commonwealth nations. Fourth, respect the contributions of British technology. Radar, jet engines, electronics, optics, and other areas all show the impact of British ingenuity.

While an Englishman will appear to be polite, reserved, and friendly, he can be tough and ruthless when required.

Hard work and toil are less common with the British worker than with his American counterpart. And, interestingly, most Englishmen are not as motivated by money as are their American cousins. They value free time and the status and convention of the workplace. Many Englishmen, in fact, still view profit as a dirty word, and seem to be less concerned about any productivity gap when compared with Americans or the Japanese.

One of the biggest frustrations in dealing with the British is that top quality people frequently avoid careers in industry. Consequently, relatively speaking, a larger number of individuals who enter top management tend to be poor managers. Firms frequently are overstaffed, retarding the decision-making process significantly.

British negotiators tend to be deliberate and often less prepared than their counterparts, yet open and forthright. They generally do not "play games," but they do appear to be very risk-averse and often nit-pick on details, especially the terms and conditions of the transaction. Some of them still view Americans as the lost colonials, and at times find it difficult to "lower" themselves to the American level. They are, nevertheless, impressed by education and degrees.

Experienced negotiators have found it important to develop a rapport with their British opposites. The British, they say, are receptive to genuine compliments about their country. British middle management as a rule is reputed to be quite reasonable and easy to work with, but upper management, especially those in finance, often tend to assume superior attitudes, are difficult to work with, and appear to relish debate for its own sake.

After extended discussions, American negotiators sometimes find it necessary to develop a final package proposal that is advanced on a "take it or leave it" basis. Such packages do not necessarily represent instances of bluffing or unreasonably hard bargaining. In the research study, they were packages with which the American firms felt they could live, but which they were unwilling to improve. In a majority of the instances, the package was accepted—in others, it was not.

The British appear to be very sensitive, in comparison to the Germans. Although this is an emotional area, occasionally it has been used successfully to force concessions otherwise unobtainable from British firms.

THE FEDERAL REPUBLIC OF GERMANY

Some eighty percent or more of Germany's top management people have attended universities, with an estimated fifty percent holding doctor-

ates at the time of the study. The title "Dr." commands instant respect whether or not the particular area of expertise is relevant when defending a position at the negotiating table. A Ph.D. "expert" will probably be a great deal more persuasive than a functional expert who might have many years' experience in working with the item under discussion.

The vast majority of German managers have experience in more than one firm, although they tend to become specialists within the same industry. German managers are more like American managers than most other Europeans (except, possibly, for the Dutch). While it is true that German managers have a greater entrepreneurial spirit than other Europeans, they tend to be more risk-averse than their American counterparts. This cautious and conservative behavior makes them more willing to seek compromise than to shoulder the risk of confrontation or controversy.

The Germans are slow to reach a decision because of the way most firms are organized. Decisions are made by committee, and most firms require two signatures on everything. Many negotiations are with technical people, not businessmen, who tend to be deliberate and extremely cautious. The U.S. negotiator must be well prepared on all technical aspects of the item under discussion.

German negotiators frequently suffer from an extreme case of the "not invented here" syndrome. They tend not to be receptive to technical suggestions and are sensitive to unfavorable comparisons with the French and the British. This sensitivity can be used as a tactic during negotiations if alternative sources are available in either country.

The Germans are men of their word. A handshake is as good as a written contract. Although the German negotiator always has a goal in mind, he can be obtuse in letting the American know what the goal is. But once it is out, negotiations proceed quickly. The Germans *do* accommodate to logic and thoroughness; in fact, they are very concerned with the precision of the written word. They are very "face conscious," too, so you should avoid open disagreements when staff people are present.

With the exception of regional jokes and puns, German humor is hard to find. Very little levity is experienced at the negotiating table. To a German, the quick-flash American smile is considered to be an insincere gesture.

A good negotiator will be sensitive to emotional issues, such as Germany's technical excellence and approaches that will require changes in the level of employment. The negotiator should be polite to all of the many staff people, but focus on the one or two key players. The Germans (in contrast with the French) do not play at negotiating; they are serious and honest.

U.S. negotiators who are fluent in German hold an advantage over those who are not. Even when the Germans are aware that an American understands German, they seem powerless to break their habit of caucusing in German in the negotiating room. Tactics are frequently discussed at these caucuses.

Breaks in the negotiations might be needed to allow the German team to gain approval of some proposal. But before such a break, an agreement must be reached on the duration of the break and the topic to be discussed immediately following the break. Otherwise, negotiations might become protracted.

A short working lunch is an effective means of getting a German's attention, since such a lunch is not consistent with the routinely heavy noon meal. The period just after lunch is a good time to introduce important issues. Friday afternoons also are extremely productive times, since the Germans typically want to clear things up before leaving for their weekend.

FRANCE

The French are the least-like Americans of the three European cultures in the study. The average Frenchman is not greatly influenced by competition. In a 1978 New Year's Eve television speech, former President Giscard d'Estaing tried to motivate his countrymen by saying that the economic welfare of the French people depends on how competitive French goods are in the international marketplace. M. d'Estaing tried to awaken the French to the notion of competition, so that they would motivate themselves to work harder and be more productive. The general impression is that the former president did not succeed in this endeavor.

The French are friendly, humorous, and sardonic. Unlike most Americans, they show no need to be liked. They are more likely to be interested in a person who disagrees with them than one who agrees. The French are very hard to impress, and are impatient with those who try too hard to do so. The French frequently gain recognition and develop their identity by thinking and acting against others. They are "inner" oriented, and base their behavior on feelings, preferences, and expectations.

French workers do not respect the work ethic as much as most Americans do. They are not motivated by competition; they frown on working overtime; and they are said to have the longest vacations in the world. However, they usually work hard in their allotted working time. Many Frenchmen take pride in work that is done well because traditionally they have not been employed in huge, impersonal industrial concerns. They often have a direct stake in the work they are doing, and usually are concerned with quality as a matter of personal pride.

Decision-making is more centralized in French companies than in American firms; hence, it tends to take longer for decisions to be reached and applied. Status consciousness runs very high with the French. Most of the U.S. negotiators interviewed in the research study discussed in this chapter found the French to be insistent that the French negotiator have the same organizational status as his American counterpart. Thus, an American negotiator might want to determine a French negotiator's position and adjust his or her own titles accordingly.

Many Americans do not like conflict, especially interpersonal conflict. They feel uncomfortable, and are concerned about what others think when they are involved in conflict. Because most Americans tend to be pragmatic, they think of conflict as a hindrance to the achievement of goals. The French, however, partly because they live in a more closed society with relatively little social mobility, are used to conflict. They are aware that some positions are irreconcilable and that people must live with these irreconcilable opinions. They do not mind conflict, and sometimes even enjoy it. They even respect others who carry it off with style and get results. The French are also less concerned about negative reactions from those with whom they are in conflict.

The French are extremely difficult to negotiate with. Often they will not accept facts, no matter how convincing they may be. Although they might consider themselves to be experts at negotiating, at times they tend to be amateurish and inadequately prepared. They are quite secretive about their position during negotiations; it is difficult to obtain data from them, even in support of one of their positions. Emotionalism and theatrics are rather common tactics employed by the French. The U.S. negotiator should not panic in such a situation; the passage of time will restore the situation to a manageable level. When one experienced negotiator was asked, "How do you deal with an excitable Latin?" he responded, "Don't get excited with him. Stop the meeting for a cooling off period. Don't play their game. They are masters at it. Their apparent emotionalism can be real, or a game, or a tactic!"

The French seem to enjoy negotiating for its own sake. When they are in this mood—sometimes for several days—little real progress is made. Sooner or later, though, they tire of the game and want to reach closure. A careful count of the numbers of cigarettes consumed per hour serves as an indication of the restlessness and the willingness to make concessions in order to reach closure. Leisure time and the desire for the "good life" are key motivators. An awareness of these motivators can be useful in reaching agreement, as is indicated in the following dialogue:

American: "We need to reach agreement, since I've booked us at (the Frenchman's favorite restaurant). But we can't go until we reach agreement on these remaining issues."

Frenchman: "I agree. Let's go!"

JAPAN

The Japanese are a source of wonderment and confusion. Their culture is vastly different from those of the United States and the European countries covered in the study. Breakdowns in communication based on cultural differences are common. But the effort to develop sound, mutually satisfying relations is an investment that usually yields an excellent return. Japanese firms typically are dependable and loyal suppliers.

The Japanese are diligent, loyal employees of their respective firms. They are an especially polite people. They are much more concerned about the well being of their firms and their country than they are of themselves as individuals. While Americans are far better team players than their European counterparts, the Japanese out-play the Americans. They are more concerned with saving face and achieving harmony than with achieving higher sales and profits. They are also extremely cautious: If a proposed transaction requires recruitment of many new employees, the Japanese might refuse the deal if there is not a reasonable assurance of steady employment for the new personnel.

The Japanese should never be placed in a position in which they must admit failure or impotency. They resist pressure for deadlines and delivery dates, but once an agreement is reached, they treat their customers as valuable members of their "family." While a great deal of time is required to reach a decision, the time required to implement the decision is far less than in America. The total time required for both the agreement and its implementation is not too different from the U.S. wherein both sides are American companies.

The Japanese possess great emotional sensitivity, but they go to considerable lengths to conceal their emotions. They are uncomfortable when others lose control and show anger or impatience. Most are ill at ease in the presence of egotistical, abrasive, or harsh individuals, and they might even break off negotiations to avoid dealing with such people.

The Japanese appear to have trouble saying no. Many American business representatives who have presented their ideas and requirements and then assumed that an agreement had been reached have learned later that the apparent agreement was based on the Japanese counterpart's desire to be polite, and not on reality! The Asian custom of telling people what they want to hear rather than the hard facts can be extremely frustrating. When a Japanese says yes but then draws breath through his teeth or when he says "It is very difficult," he is probably saying no.

As in Europe, good personal relations are a great asset. An effort to speak a little Japanese is greatly appreciated. Entertainment is an important part of the process of developing the personal relations and goodwill that are prerequisites to a good agreement. Gift-giving is a common and accepted factor in Japanese business transactions. Usually, the gift is not of great monetary value. The most enhancing gifts are those that are selected with a knowledge of the recipient's preferences and a desire to bring happiness and pleasure.

Negotiating in Japan is a wondrous experience. When negotiating, it is necessary to convince the whole group whose activities will be influenced by the proposed transaction. Begin the discussions at as high a level as possible, since the first person contacted will be involved through the conclusion of the discussions. The Japanese negotiator typically asks what seems to be an endless list of questions—frequently far afield of issues bearing on the proposed transaction. He has learned that his colleagues will want such information, and he must be prepared.

The Japanese place great emphasis on decision by consensus. This consensus frequently is achieved through the "Ringi" process. With "Ringi," a proposal is developed between buyer and seller. The pertinent facts and a recommendation then are circulated to all concerned members of the Japanese firm. Each recipient is expected to review the proposal and affix his seal to the accompanying routing slip. Questions and disagreements are then resolved at conferences until a consensus evolves.

Americans who are about to negotiate with a member of a Japanese firm are well advised to develop personal relations away from the negotiating room. The usual intense and rather dry American approach to doing business must be supplemented with a social relationship. The Japanese are accustomed to the use of entertainment as a means of becoming better acquainted and of developing goodwill. The feeling a Japanese has about his counterpart can have as much impact on the outcome of a transaction as do the cold facts. Honesty and sincerity are essential traits for the American negotiator.

Once the right degree of rapport has been established, it is possible to get on with the details of

◆ ◆ ◆ ◆ ◆

the negotiation. In these discussions, it is important for the American negotiator to realize that growth, steady employment, and superiority over competitors are far more important to the Japanese than are profits.

Americans tend to be uncomfortable with extended silences. The Japanese are not. They feel no compulsion to break a silence. American impatience or desire to hammer out an agreement often results in a breaking of the silences, which in turn can mean yielding or compromising on the point being discussed. Again, such silences are culturally inspired and are not ploys. A good negotiator will recognize that such silences indicate doubt or uncertainty, and will be content to allow the silence to run its course.

During complex and protracted negotiations, a crisis might develop. In contrast with some negotiations in France, this is not a ploy: rather, one or more members of the Japanese firm have likely voiced disagreement or concern over the proposal. The crisis might continue for several days or weeks, so it will be important for the American to keep communication channels open during this period, even if there are no formal meetings. When a crisis is protracted, the American should maintain discreet contact with those who favor the transaction and seek advice on how to get the negotiations back on track.

When final agreement appears to have been reached, it is essential to prepare a written contract. Many apparently minor points might have been put aside in the interest of reaching a general agreement. Compromise might even be necessary to reach a final agreement on all points. While the Japanese are excellent conciliators, one must remember how important "face" is: They do not like the appearance of having made forced concessions. The American approach of "splitting the difference" results in an obvious compromise. A mutually acceptable agreement based on the facts—even if somewhat bent—should be the goal.

CONCLUDING SUGGESTIONS

When negotiating with non-Americans, the following summary of key points should be helpful.

1. Be sensitive to the culture of the supplier's negotiator(s). Read about his culture during the preparation phase. Ask questions of others who have had experience negotiating with individuals from that culture. Obtain information on local circumstances in the country.

2. Be well prepared on all issues, especially technical ones.

3. If continuing relations are likely, attempt to develop a personal rapport, a base of understanding, and a bank of goodwill.

4. Find out who the supplier's negotiator is, who his family is, and what his education is, as well as his approximate income level and what makes him tick.

5. In Europe, be prepared for negotiations to take two or three times as long as in the United States. In Japan, negotiations can take six times as long as in America.

6. Conduct extensive cost and price analysis before the formal negotiation meeting. Do *not* expect the supplier's negotiator to have a well developed cost breakdown.

7. Do nothing that might put the opposing negotiator in a face-saving position over the issue of productivity. Focus on rates, not man-hours.

8. Attempt to establish a lower profit objective than would normally be done in the United States.

9. Become familiar with local tax laws.

10. Obtain guidance from experienced international finance people on the issue of exchange rates and the likely costs or advantages of using a particular currency. Then negotiate the exchange rate just as any other issue.

◆   ◆   ◆   ◆   ◆

11. Arrange issues in such a manner that the opposing negotiator can win his share of the issues.

12. Use the package approach of discussing each issue in turn, reaching agreement when possible, and finally developing an acceptable package containing all issues.

13. The recorder occupies an important position; he should be selected from the American team when possible.

14. If possible, make sure that the head of the non-American team has the authority to reach agreement on behalf of his firm. In Japan, however, such an approach cannot be used; therefore, time must be allowed for the consensus process to function.

15. Be extremely cautious about being frank and open during discussions. Non-Americans are not accustomed to such an approach. It can be misunderstood and may be disruptive.

POSTLUDE

This article quite obviously is written from the American point of view, which is not entirely unbiased. In the interests of fair play and improved intercultural relations, foreign readers are invited to forward their thoughts and observations on the nuances of dealing with American negotiators.

HOFSTEDE'S DIMENSIONS: A HIGH-LEVEL ANALYTICAL TOOL FOR WORKING INTERNATIONALLY

John W. Bing

BACKGROUND

One of the success stories in the always tentative relationship between academic scholarship and business and industry is to be found in the area of cross-cultural business training. In the early 1980s, company training for international staff was rare, and employees were often sent to the far ends of the earth with little information as to what they would find there, much less how to successfully conduct business.

What training there was was often anecdotal, with returned employees or others dominating programs with "war stories" and personal experiences suffered or enjoyed at the far corners of the world. Such programs not only lacked depth, they seldom gave an accurate picture of the places and people under review.

Times have changed, Corporations are eager to expand internationally and need such training to do so. The largest global companies have by and large determined that the cost of *not* training transferred employees is too great in terms of early returnees and low productivity; the pro-

grams themselves have changed, increasingly relying on research rather than anecdotes as fundamental learning blocks.

PROGRAM TYPES AND LEVELS

The programs offered to employees of international businesses today can be categorized according to content, or in terms of the tools used in the program.

Level I

These programs offer the "Do's and Don'ts" of international business, often mixing information about etiquette with advice on what types of business gifts to give and how to best form business relationships in other countries. They also provide specific information about travel, banking, embassies, etc., and seem to be the most useful to employees with little or no international business experience. In the words of the old fable, these programs provide people with fish, rather than teaching them how to fish. At the end of these programs, participants have a good idea of how to conduct specific business transactions, but little idea how to transfer those lessons to other situations.

ITAP International (1998). Princeton, New York. Reprinted by permission.

Level II

Level II programs teach participants how to fish; that is, they provide analytic tools that can be used to understand the relationship between culture and business. They do this by providing models of cultures based on research in the field of comparative sociology or anthropology. Participants learn to understand social and business transactions by applying these analytic tools, and are often tested through the use of critical incidents or case studies. At the end of these programs, participants are able to analyze general culture-based business transactions to determine how, in a specific culture, the business transaction might be different from the transaction in their own cultures.

Level III

At this level, specific level I-type information and analytic tools common to level II are used to address:

1. Specific business problems or opportunities in, say, sales or marketing, or mergers and acquisitions within the area of these employees' professional scope.

2. How to assist employees who must relocate to other countries.

3. Decision-making at upper levels (e.g., where to locate a new plant in a region).

At the end of these sessions, participants are able to apply the analytic tools and specific country, regional, and culture-based information to business problems in their areas of expertise.

THE HOFSTEDE DIMENSIONS

Geert Hofstede is Professor Emeritus of Management at the University of Limburg at Maastricht in the Netherlands, and the founder and first director there of the Institute for Research on Intercultural Cooperation (IRIC). His work *Culture's Consequences*, a pioneering work in sociology, is the first attempt to use survey research to provide quantitative comparisons of over fifty countries concerning the influence of culture in the workplace.

The four Hofstede Dimensions to be described in this chapter have been used in Level II and Level III programs and represent the highest levels of scholarship; that is, their relationship to real cultural variables has been established through research and testing. They represent a kind of cultural map of the world. A fifth dimension was added later: "LongTerm vs. Short-Term Orientation," which focuses on the differences between East Asian countries and the rest of the world. These dimensions have been researched by means of questionnaires filled out by IBM employees and the results yield numeric values by dimension, making it possible to compare by country. That research was used to develop didactic tools, including a questionnaire that helps individuals understand their own cultural profiles. Knowing our own cultural profile helps us understand others and understand how business transactions differ according to the four dimensions.

Hofstede's four dimensions are described and interpreted in the Culture in the Workplace Questionnaire system, a didactic tool used in instructional programs. The dimensions include:

- Individualism: The degree of individual or group orientation

- Power Distance: The level of preference for equality or inequality within groups

- Certainty: The preference for risk vs. structure

- Achievement: The relative degrees of relationship vs. task orientation. This dimension also tracks the relative masculine and feminine influences in the workplace.

These dimensions, then, along with the research-based quantitative data and the questionnaire, are useful for Level II and III programs as a tested, analytic tool to provide participants with important skills for conducting international business.

Individualism

This dimension is a way of measuring the degree to which action is taken in a particular culture for the benefit of the individual or the group. An *individualistic* society is a culture of the "self" where individuals are supposed to take care of themselves and have a flexible-independent relationship with social groups. A *group* society gives preference to belonging to the "we," where individuals contribute to the wealth of their parents, clan, or organization in exchange for group support.

GROUP STYLE	*INDIVIDUAL STYLE*
"We" consciousness	"I" consciousness
Relatives and those in group take care of the individual in exchange for loyalty	Individual takes care of self and immediate family
Interests of the group prevail over individual ones	Self-interests come before those of the group
Emotional dependence of the individual on the organization	Personal life and professional life are separated
Cooperation and harmony	Competition between individuals
Loyalty prevails over efficiency	Efficiency prevails over loyalty

Example:

Mr. Yakashima was reporting to Mr. Cannon, his American manager, on the difficulties he had with the negotiation he recently conducted with an outside American client. Mr. Yakashima noted that Mr. Roberts, who represented the American side, seemed tired and frustrated at the last meeting. Yakashima stated that he didn't understand why, since *he* had been finding the meetings very informative. Yakashima admitted, however, that he was getting annoyed at Roberts' continuing insistence on decisions and answers to questions that Yakashima knew we would have to consult with his group about. "It was uncomfortable for me to always say that I had no answer now to his questions," Yakashima said to Cannon. "But it was even more difficult for me when Roberts finally said, 'O.K., I am willing to lower my price by $5000, but only if your company would make a decision on this price right here and now at the table. No more stalling, please.'" "What did you do?" Cannon asked. "Nothing," Yakashima answered. "I couldn't make that decision alone."

Power Distance

Power distance is a way of measuring the degree to which inequality or distance between those in charge and the less powerful (subordinates) is accepted in a culture. A society with an autocratic style leans toward a tight hierarchical structure where each individual knows their place and the limit of their role. A society with a participative style seeks status equality and interdependence between different layers of power.

PARTICIPATIVE STYLE	HIERARCHICAL STYLE
Participative, consultative approach	Hierarchical, or "top-down" approach
Informality	Formality (reserve)
All should have equal rights to privileges	Power-holders are entitled
Pragmatic organization centered on tasks	Pyramidal structure
Independence, initiative	Dependency, obedience
Latent harmony between the powerful and the powerless accepted	Latent conflict between the powerful and powerless is accepted

Example:

Although she held merely a clerical position, Ms. Marku always approached her work with diligence and responsibility. Since arriving in the U. S. nine months ago, Marku had proved herself to be an extremely capable worker. Ms. Smith, the American manager, began to offer Marku more responsibility, with the hope of developing her into her assistant. Smith gave Marku more and more challenges: projects that required independent problem-solving, and opportunities that demanded individual initiative. How disappointing it was, then, for Smith to find Marku apparently avoiding new responsibilities, tasks, and challenges. It seemed that Marku always offered a reason, an excuse, or an explanation for not being able to branch off on her own. Whatever relationship they had before Smith began her plan was now being threatened by Marku's apparent resistance. Smith was very concerned.

Certainty

This dimension measures the extent to which people of different cultures prefer unstructured, risky, ambiguous, or unpredicatble situations. It also assesses the preferences of those who would rather live by rules, regulations, and controls. Organizations in societies that are structure-oriented have a preference for strong codes of behaviors and management practices, and tolerate less deviation from them; they tend to support their employees. Organizations that are risk-oriented encourage individuals to take initiatives and risks; they tend to give their employees less structure and support.

RISK-ORIENTED	STRUCTURE-ORIENTED
Flexibility. Rules should fit situations, and may be broken	Rules and procedures specified and should not be broken
Pragmatism, practical principles	Philosophical, normative rules
Risk-taking	Conservative
Relatively tolerant vis-a-vis different or marginal people	Relatively intolerant vis-a-vis original or marginal people
Information to share is power	Information held is power

Example:

Ms. Nicole Francois, director of training for the French headquarters of a major French firm, was becoming increasingly exasperated with her counterpart, Ms. Janet Stevens, U. S. director of training. Ms. Francois believed that Stevens had been relentless in her pursuit of information on the training needs of the Paris office. (Stevens was doing a global study.)

In the most recent discussion, Stevens stated that she had hoped to receive information from Ms. Francois two weeks ago; Ms. Francois answered that the time available had been insufficient to gather the information. Furthermore, Ms. Francois repeated that it was going to take longer to get the report ready because it would be based on information that Ms. Francois would need to obtain from her superiors. She insisted that she was doing her best to follow Stevens' requests, but could not continue to do so if she were harrassed. It would have helped, she told Stevens, if the original request had gone through channels.

What follows are descriptions of each of the four dimensions.

◆ ◆ ◆ ◆ ◆

Achievement

This dimension measures the degree to which cultures value tasks and work or relationships, and quality of life.

RELATIONSHIP-ORIENTED	TASK-ORIENTED
Quality of life has priority over goal achievement	Goal achievement has priority over quality of life
Modesty, solidarity, and helping others are virtues	Assertiveness, competitiveness, and ambition are virtues
Small and slow are beautiful	Big and fast are beautiful
Sympathy for the underdog	Admiration for the strong
Sex roles overlap, with men taking caring roles. Strong ambitions are unusual among men as well as women. Women accepted at work without having to dress and behave like men.	At home, biological differences mean different roles for the sexes: Men are expected to achieve, women to care. In some cultures, women accepted at work if they imitate masculine roles.

Example:

John Williams, Manager of Personnel Programs for the Chicago-based XYZ Corporation, walked into the office of Peter Van Dam, the personnel manager of XYZ's Dutch subsidiary in Amsterdam, on a Friday afternoon at 3 p.m. Williams' plane from Chicago was due in at 10 a.m., and he had announced his visit for 11:30, asking Van Dam to keep the rest of the day free. However, the plane was four hours late.

"You must be almost dead with fatigue, flying against the clock and with this delay," Van Dam said. "Shouldn't we postpone our meeting until Monday?" Williams said he felt just fine, and started discussing business right away. At 5 p.m., Van Dam showed some unease. He asked to be excused for a moment and grabbed the telephone, chatting in Dutch. "I called home to say I will be somewhat late," he explained. "I got permission until six. I have to make dinner for the children."

At five minutes to six, Peter Van Dam started to pack his briefcase and put on his coat. "Shall I drop you off at your hotel?" he said. In the car, Williams proposed to continue the discussion on Saturday morning. "So sorry, " Van Dam said, "but I promised to take the kids to the zoo. Would you like to join us? My wife has a meeting tomorrow—she is in politics." Williams muttered something about a presentation to the General Manager he still want to prepare, and the two men parted rather painfully at the hotel.

NEGOTIATING ACROSS CULTURES

Gary P. Ferraro

In a very general sense, the process of negotiating is absolutely fundamental to human communication and interaction. If we stop to consider it, we are negotiating all the time. We negotiate with our spouses, children, co-workers, friends, bosses, landlords, customers, bankers, neighbors, and clients. Because negotiating is such an integral part of our everyday lives, it becomes largely an unconscious process, for we do not spend a lot of time thinking about how we do it. As with so many other aspects of our behavior, the way we negotiate is colored by our cultural assumptions. Whether we are effective negotiators or not, our culturally conditioned negotiating styles are largely operating at an unconscious level.

When negotiating within our own culture, it is possible to operate effectively at the intuitive or unconscious level. However, when we leave our familiar cultural context and enter into international negotiations, the scene changes dramatically. There are no longer shared values, interests, goals, ethical principles, or cultural assumptions between the negotiating parties. Different cultures have different values, attitudes, morals, behaviors, and linguistic styles, all of which can

greatly affect the process and outcome of our negotiations. Thus, we cannot negotiate across cultural lines without being conscious of the negotiation process. This chapter is aimed at analyzing the cross-cultural negotiation process, for by heightening our awareness of some of the potential pitfalls, we become more effective international negotiators.

THE NATURE OF CROSS-CULTURAL NEGOTIATION

Because the act of negotiating is so central to our lives, we forget to define it. Those who write about the process of negotiation, on the other hand, do define it—sometimes in excruciating detail—but not everyone agrees on a common definition. Moran and Stripp (1991:71–72) remind us that the common theme running through all of the definitions, however, is that two or more parties with common as well as conflicting interests interact with one another for the purpose of reaching a mutually beneficial agreement.

Effective negotiation does not involve bludgeoning the other side into submission. Rather, it involves the more subtle art of *persuasion*, whereby all parties feel as though they have benefited. There is no simple formula for success. Each situation must be assessed within its own

Taken from Ferraro, Gary P. *The Cultural Dimension of International Business.* (1998). Englewood Cliffs, New Jersey: Prentice Hall. Reprinted with permission.

unique set of circumstances. The successful negotiator must choose the appropriate strategy, project the correct personal and organizational images, do the right type of homework, ask the most relevant questions, and offer and request the appropriate types of concessions at the right time. Negotiating within one's own culture is difficult enough, but negotiating in the international/intercultural arena is significantly more challenging.

Being a skilled negotiator in any context entails being an intelligent, well-prepared, creative, flexible, and patient problem-solver. International negotiators, however, face an additional set of problems/obstacles not ordinarily encountered by domestic negotiators. One very important obstacle to international negotiations is culture. Because culture involves everything that a people have, think, and do, it goes without saying that it will influence or color the negotiation process. One party in a negotiation usually travels to the country of the other party; this alone establishes a foreign negotiating setting for at least one party, and it is this "strangeness" that acts as a formidable barrier to communication, understanding, and agreement.

There are other barriers as well. For example, international negotiation entails working within the confines of two different and sometimes conflicting legal structures. Unless the negotiating parties are able to both understand and cope with the differing legal requirements, a joint international contract might be governed by two or more legal systems. Another barrier might be the extent to which government bureaucracies in other countries exert their influence on the negotiation process, a problem not always understood by Westerners whose governments are relatively unobtrusive in business negotiations.

And, finally, an additional obstacle that goes beyond cultural differences is the sometimes-volatile (or at least unpredictable) geopolitical realities of the two countries of the negotiating

parties. Sudden changes in governments, the enactment of new legislation, or even natural disasters can disrupt international business negotiations either temporarily or permanently. The disintegration of the Soviet Union, Iraq's invasion of Kuwait, or an earthquake in Mexico all had far-reaching implications for Western businesspeople who were in the process of negotiating business deals in those parts of the world when those events took place.

While we recognize the importance to international negotiations of these non-cultural obstacles (different legal structures, interference by government bureaucracies, and geopolitical instability), our discussion of international business negotiation will focus on the cultural dimension.

It should be apparent by now that success in negotiating international business contracts requires a deep understanding of the culture of those on the other side of the table. This cultural awareness, however, is not important because it might bring the other side to its knees—to make them do what we want them to do. Nor is it intended to accommodate the other side by giving up some of our own strongly adhered-to principles. Rather, an appreciation of the important cultural elements of the other side is essential if one is to get on with the business at hand *so that all parties concerned can feel as though they are better off after the negotiations than before.* Moreover, it is equally the responsibility of both sides in the negotiating process to understand the cultural realities of their negotiation partners. Intercultural communication, in other words, is a two-way street, with both sides sharing the burden and responsibility of cultural awareness.

WHERE TO NEGOTIATE

Earlier we defined negotiation as a process between people who share some common interests—people who stand to benefit from bringing the process to a successful conclusion. Both sides have a stake in the outcome, so it stands to reason that the place of negotiations might be on the home turf of either party or in a neutral environment. The selection of a site for the negotiations is of critical importance because there are a number of advantages to negotiating in your own backyard. In the world of international diplomatic negotiations, the question of where a summit meeting will occur is taken very seriously because it is assumed that the location will very likely affect the nature and the outcome of the negotiations. The business negotiator who travels abroad is confronted with an appreciable number of problems and challenges not faced by those who negotiate at home. Let us consider some of the difficulties encountered when negotiating abroad.

First, and perhaps most important, the negotiator abroad must adjust to an unfamiliar environment during the days, weeks, or even months of the negotiations. This involves getting used to differences in language, foods, pace of life, and other aspects of culture. The negotiator who is well prepared will make a relatively smooth and quick adjustment, yet not without moments of discomfort, awkwardness, and general psychological disorientation. Time and effort must be spent learning about the new environment, such as how to make a telephone call, where to find a fax machine, or simply how to locate the rest room. For those who are less well prepared, the adjustment process can be so difficult that there is little energy left for the important work of negotiating.

Second, the business negotiator cannot avoid the deleterious effects of jet lag. Even for those international travelers who heed all of the conventional wisdom concerning minimizing jet lag (avoid alcohol and eat certain foods), an intercontinental flight will nevertheless take its toll on one's physical condition. Thus, the traveling negotiator is likely not to be as rested or alert as his or her counterpart who doesn't have to cope with jet lag.

Third, the negotiator has little or no control over the setting in which the discussions take place. The size of the conference room, the seating arrangements, and the scheduling of times for both negotiating and socializing are decisions made by the host negotiating team. The side that controls these various details of the process can use them to their own advantage.

Fourth, the negotiator working in a foreign country is further hampered by being physically separated from his or her business organization and its various support personnel. Frequently, before negotiators can agree to certain conditions of a contract, they must obtain additional information from the manufacturing, shipping, or financial department of their home office. Those negotiating at home have a marked advantage over the traveling negotiator because it is always easier to get a question answered by a colleague down the hall than by relying on transcontinental telephones or fax messages.

Finally, negotiators working on foreign soil are under pressure to conclude the negotiations as soon as possible, a type of pressure not experienced by those negotiating at home. The longer negotiations drag on, the longer the negotiator will be away from the other operations of the office that need attention, the longer his or her family and social life will be disrupted, and the more it will cost the firm in terms of travel-related expenses. Given these very real pressures, negotiators working abroad are more likely to make certain concessions than they might if they were negotiating at home.

It would appear that negotiating abroad has a number of distinct disadvantages as compared to negotiating at home, including the hassle of an unfamiliar cultural setting, uncertain lines of communication with the home office, lack of control over the negotiating setting, and considerable expenditure of both time and travel funds. There is little doubt that, given the choice, most Western businesspeople would opt to conduct their negotiations at home. Yet, more often than not, Westerners are attempting to sell their products and ideas abroad. And if the potential international customers are to learn about the products or services, it is essential that the Westerners go to them. Moreover, in many parts of the world, particularly in developing areas, potential customers from both the private and public sectors have very limited resources for traveling. Thus, in many cases, if Westerners desire to remain competitive in the international marketplace, they will have no other choice than to do their negotiating on foreign soil.

EFFECTIVE STRATEGIES FOR INTERNATIONAL NEGOTIATORS

This chapter does not attempt to list all of the do's and don't's of negotiating in all of the cultures of the world. Such an approach—given the vast number of features found in each culture—would be well beyond the scope of the present book and certainly beyond any single individual's capacity to comprehend. Whereas some books on the subject of negotiating have taken a country-by-country approach to international negotiating (Kennedy, 1985; Moran and Stripp, 1991), here we will focus on certain general principles of cross-cultural negotiating that can be applied to most, if not all, international situations. This chapter will not provide a cookbook-style guide for avoiding negotiating *faux pas* in all of the major cultures of the world, but it will draw upon some of the most positive experiences of successful intercultural negotiators.

1. Concentrate on long-term relationships, not short-term contracts.

If there is one central theme running through the literature on international business negotiations, it is that the single most important piece of advice is to build relationships over the long run rather than focus on a single contract. At times, U.S. businesspeople have been criticized

for their short-term view of doing business. Some feel that they should not waste time; they should get in there and get the contract signed and get on to other business. If the other side fails to meet their contractual obligations, the lawyers can sue. Frequently this approach carries with it the implicit analogy of a sports contest. Negotiating across cultures is like a football game, the purpose of which is to outmaneuver, outmanipulate, outsmart, and generally overpower the other side, which is seen as the opponent. And the wider the margin of victory, the better. But conventional wisdom, coupled with the experience of successful negotiators, strongly suggests that international business negotiating is not about winning big, humiliating the opposition, making a killing, and gaining all of the advantages. Rather, successful international business negotiating is conducted in a cooperative climate in which the needs of both sides are met and in which both sides can emerge as winners.

To be certain, there exists considerable variation throughout the world in terms of why people enter into business negotiation in the first place. In some societies, such as our own, businesspeople enter into negotiations for the sake of obtaining the signed contract; other societies, however, view the negotiations as primarily aimed at creating a long-standing relationship and only secondarily for the purpose of signing a short-term contract. As Salacuse (1991:60) reminds us, for many Americans a signed contract represents *closing* a deal, whereas to a Japanese, signing a contract is seen as *opening* a relationship. With those cultures that tend to emphasize the relationship over the contract, it is likely that there will be no contract unless a relationship of trust and mutual respect has been established. And even though relationship-building does not always conform to the typical American's time frame, the inescapable truth is that, because relationships are so important in the international arena, negotiations are unlikely to succeed without them.

Building relationships requires that negotiators take the time to get to know one another. Frequently this involves activities—eating, drinking, visiting national monuments, playing golf—that strike the typical North American as being outside the realm of business and consequently a waste of time. But this type of ritual socializing is vital because it represents an honest effort to understand, as fully as possible, the needs, goals, values, interests, and opinions of the negotiators on the other side. It is not necessary for the two sides to have similar needs, goals, and values in order to have a good relationship, for it is possible to disagree in a number of areas and still have a good working relationship. However, both parties need to be willing to identify their shared interests while at the same time work at reconciling their conflicting interests in a spirit of cooperation and mutual respect. And this twofold task, which is never easy to accomplish, has the very best chance of succeeding if a relationship built on trust and mutual respect has been established between the negotiating parties.

2. Focus on the interests behind the positions.

After the parties in a negotiation have developed a relationship, the discussion of positions can begin. This stage of negotiating involves both sides setting forth what they want to achieve from the negotiations. From a seller's perspective, it might involve selling a certain number of sewing machines at X dollars per unit. From the perspective of the purchaser, it might involve receiving a certain number of sewing machines within a month's time at X minus $30 per unit. Once the positions have been clearly stated, the effective international negotiator will then look behind those positions for the underlying needs of the other party. The stated position is usually one way of satisfying needs. But often the position of one side is in direct opposition to the position of the other side. If the negotiators focus just on the positions, it is unlikely that they will resolve or reconcile their differences. But by looking beyond the position to the basic needs that gave rise to those positions in the first place, it is likely that creative solutions can be found that will satisfy both parties.

The need to distinguish between a *position* and the *needs underlying the position* has been effectively illustrated by Foster (1992:286–87). The representative of a U.S. telecommunications firm had been negotiating with the communications representative from the Chinese government. After months of relationship-building and discussing terms, the finalization of the agreement appeared to be in sight. But at the eleventh hour the Chinese representative raised an additional condition that took the American by surprise. The Chinese representative argued that since they were about to embark on a long-term business relationship between friends, the U.S. firm should give its Chinese friends a special reduced price that it would not give to other customers. The problem with this request was that the U.S. firm had a strict policy of uniform pricing for all countries with which it did business.

If we look at this situation solely in terms of the positions of the two parties, it would appear to be an impasse. For anything to be resolved, one party would have to get what it wanted while the other would have to abandon its position. But, by understanding the basic needs behind the positions, both sides will have more room to maneuver so that a win-win situation can result.

Let us consider the needs behind the positions. The Chinese position was based on two essential needs: to get a lower price (thus saving money), and to receive a special favor as a sign of the American's friendship and commitment to the relationship. The position of the U.S. firm was based on its need to adhere to the principle of uniform pricing. By looking at the situation from the perspective of underlying needs rather than positions, it now became possible to suggest some alternative solutions. In fact, the U.S.

negotiator offered another proposal: to sell the Chinese some new additional equipment at a very favorable price in exchange for sticking with the original pricing agreement. Such an arrangement met all of the needs of both parties. The Chinese were saving money on the new equipment *and* they were receiving a special favor of friendship from the U.S. firm. At the same time, the U.S. company did not have to violate its own policy of uniform pricing. In this example, a win-win solution was possible because the negotiators were able to concentrate on the needs behind the positions, rather than on the positions themselves. Once the negotiators were willing to look beyond a prepackaged, non-negotiable, unilateral position for having their own needs met, they were ready to explore new and creative ways of satisfying each other's needs.

3. Do not rely on cultural generalizations.

Success in any aspect of international business is directly related to one's knowledge of the cultural environment in which one is operating. Simply put, the more knowledge a person has of the culture of his or her international business partners, the less likely he or she will misinterpret what is being said or done, and the more likely one's business objectives will be met. Communication patterns—both linguistic and nonverbal—need to be mastered as well as the myriad of other culture-specific details that can get in the way of effective intercultural business communication. But just as it would be imprudent to place too little emphasis on cultural information, it is equally inadvisable to be overly dependent on such knowledge.

As was pointed out in Chapter 2, cultural "facts" are generalizations based on a sample of human behavior, and as such can only point out *tendencies* at the negotiating table. Not all Middle Easterners engage in verbal overkill, and not all Japanese are reluctant to give a direct answer. If we tend to interpret cultural generalizations too

rigidly, we run the risk of turning the generalizations into cultural stereotypes. We might chuckle when we hear heaven defined as the place where the police are British, the cooks all French, the mechanics all German, and the lovers Italian, and it's all organized by the Swiss. Conversely, hell is defined as the place where the cooks are British, the mechanics all French, the lovers all Swiss, and the police all German, and it's all organized by Italians. Such cultural stereotypes can be offensive to those being lumped together uncritically, but they can be particularly harmful in the process of international business negotiations because they can be wrong. Sometimes negotiators on the other side of the table do not act the way the generalization would predict.

To be certain, negotiating behavior is influenced by their culture, but there are other factors at work as well. How a person behaves might be conditioned by such variables as education, biology, or experience. To illustrate, a Mexican business negotiator who has an MBA from the Wharton School might not object to discussing business at lunch, while most other Mexicans might. We should not automatically assume that all Mexicans will act in a stereotypical way. Owing to this particular Mexican's education and experience, he has learned how to behave within the U.S. frame of reference. It is, therefore, important that we move beyond cultural stereotyping and get to know the negotiators on the other side not only as members of a particular cultural group, but also as individuals with their own unique set of personality traits and experiences.

4. Be sensitive to timing.

Timing is not everything, but in international negotiations it certainly can make a difference between success and failure. Different cultures have different rhythms and different concepts of time. In cultures like our own, with tight schedules and a precise reckoning of time, we expect business to be conducted without wasting time.

But in many parts of the world, it is not realistic to expect to arrive one day and consummate a deal the next before jetting off to another client in another country. The more likely scenario involves spending what might seem like inordinately long periods on insignificant details, frustrating delays, and unanticipated postponements. Bringing the U.S. notion of time into an international negotiation will invariably result in either frustration or the eventual alienation of those with whom one is negotiating.

As a general rule, international negotiations, for a number of reasons, take longer than domestic negotiations. We should keep in mind that McDonald's engaged in negotiations for nearly a decade before it began selling hamburgers in Moscow. In another situation, a high-level salesperson for a U.S. modular office furniture company spent months negotiating a deal in Saudi Arabia. He made frequent courtesy calls, engaged in long discussions on a large number of topics other than office furniture, and drank enough coffee to float a small ship. But the months of patience paid off. His personal commission (not his company's profit) was in excess of $2 million dollars! The lesson here is clear. An international negotiator must first understand the local rhythm of time, and if it is slower than at home, exercise the good sense to be patient.

Another important dimension of time that must be understood is that some times of the year are better than others for negotiating internationally. All cultures have certain times of the year when people are preoccupied with social or religious concerns, or when everything having to do with business simply shuts down. Before negotiating abroad, one should become familiar with the national calendar. To illustrate, one should not plan to do any global deal-making with the Taiwanese on October 10, their national day of independence; or with the Japanese during "Golden Week," when most people take a vacation; or anywhere in the Islamic world during Ramadan, when Muslim businessmen are more concerned with fasting than with negotiating. Any attempt to conduct negotiations on these holidays, traditional vacation times, or times of religious observance will generally meet with as much success as a non-American might have trying to conduct business negotiations in the United States during the week between Christmas and New Year's.

Still another consideration of time has to do with the different time zones between one's home office and the country in which the negotiations are taking place. Because of these different time zones, an American negotiating in Manila cannot fax the home office in New York and expect an answer within minutes, as might be expected if the negotiations were taking place in Boston. If at 4:00 p.m. Manila-time a question is raised in the negotiations that requires clearance or clarification from the home office, it is not likely that an answer will be received until the next day because in New York it is 3:00 a.m. Thus, attempting to operate between two distant time zones can be frustrating for most Americans because it tends to slow down the pace of the negotiations.

5. Remain flexible.

The Western negotiator, despite the best preparation, will always have an imperfect command of how things work in international negotiations. In such an environment, some of the best laid plans frequently go unexecuted: Schedules change unexpectedly; government bureaucrats become more recalcitrant than predicted; people don't follow through with what they promise. When things don't go as expected, it is important to be able to readjust quickly and efficiently. To be flexible does not mean to be weak; rather, it means being capable of responding to changing situations. Flexibility, in other words, means avoiding the all-too-common malady known as "hardening of the categories."

The importance of remaining open and flexible has been well illustrated by Foster (1992:254–55), who tells of a U.S. businessman trying to sell data-processing equipment to a high-level government official in India. After preparing himself thoroughly, the American was escorted into the official's office for their initial meeting. But much to the American's surprise, seated on a nearby sofa was another gentleman who was never introduced. For the entire meeting, the host government official acted as if the third man were not there. The American became increasingly uncomfortable with the presence of this mystery man who was sitting in on the negotiations, particularly as they discussed specific details. After a while, the American began having paranoid delusions. Who was this man listening in on these private discussions? He even imagined that the man might be one of his competitors. The American negotiator became so uncomfortable with this situation that he lost his capacity to concentrate on the negotiations and eventually lost the potential contract. Here was a perfect example of a negotiator who was unsuccessful because he could not adjust to an unfamiliar situation. In India, as in some other parts of the world as well, it is not unusual for a third party to be present at negotiations. They might be friends, relatives, or advisors of the host negotiator invited to listen in to provide advice—and perhaps a different perspective. Unaware of this customary practice in India, this U.S. negotiator began to imagine the worst until it had irreparably destroyed his capacity to focus on the negotiations at hand.

We can see how flexibility is important in order to most effectively adapt to unfamiliar cultural situations that are bound to emerge when negotiating internationally. But remaining flexible has another advantage as well: Flexibility creates an environment in which creative solutions to negotiating problems can emerge. We have said earlier that negotiations should be win-win situations, whereby both sides can communicate their basic needs and interests, rather than just their positions, and then proceed to brainstorm on how best to meet the needs of both sides. A win-win type of negotiation is most likely to occur when both sides remain flexible and open to exploring nontraditional solutions.

6. Prepare carefully.

It is hard to imagine any undertaking—be it in business, government, education, or athletics—where advanced preparation would not be an asset. Nowhere is this more true than in the arena of international negotiating, where the variables are so complex. There is a straightforward and direct relationship between the amount of preparation and the chances for success when engaging in global deal-making. Those who take the rather cavalier attitude of "Let's go over and see what the Japanese have to say" are bound to be disappointed. Rather, what is needed is a substantial amount of advance preparation, starting, of course, with as full an understanding as possible of the local cultural realities. But in addition, the would-be negotiator needs to seek answers to important questions concerning his or her own objectives, the bottom-line position, the types of information needed as the negotiations progress, an agenda, and the accessibility of support services, to mention a few. These and many other questions need to be answered *prior* to getting on the plane. Failure to prepare adequately will have at least two negative consequences. First, it will communicate to the other side that you don't consider the negotiations sufficiently important to have done your homework. And second, ill-prepared negotiators frequently are forced into making certain concessions that they might later regret.

We often hear the old adage "knowledge is power." Although most North Americans would agree, we are a society that tends to downplay, at least in principle, status distinctions based on power. Our democratic philosophy, coupled with our insistence on universal education, encourages people from all parts of the society to get as much education (and information) as possible. Even the recent computer revolution in the United States now puts vast quantities of information into virtually anyone's hands. Consequently, Americans usually do not equate high status or power with the possession of information. In some other cultures, however, there is a very close association between knowledge and power. Unless Americans negotiating in such cultures have as much information as possible, they are likely to be seen as weak and, by implication, ineffectual negotiators.

A basic part of preparing for negotiations is self-knowledge. How well do you understand yourself, the assumptions of your own culture, and your own goals and objectives for this particular negotiation? If you are part of a negotiating team, a number of questions must be answered: Who are the team members? How have they been selected? Is there general consensus on what the team hopes to accomplish? Is there a proper balance between functional skills, cross-cultural experience, and negotiating expertise? Has a rational division of labor been agreed upon in terms of such tasks as note taking, serving as a spokesperson, or making local arrangements? Has there been sufficient time for team building, including discussions of strategies and counterstrategies?

A particularly important area of preparation has to do with getting to know the negotiators on the other side of the table. At the outset, it must be determined whether or not the organization is the appropriate one to be negotiating with in the first place. Once that has been decided, it is important to know whether their negotiators have the authority and responsibility to make decisions. Having this information *prior* to the negotiations can eliminate the possibility of long delays stemming from the last-minute disclosure that the negotiators on the other side really can-

not make final contractual decisions. But once involved in the negotiating process, it is important, as a general rule, to get to know the other team's negotiators as people, rather than simply as members of a particular culture.

7. Learn to listen, not just speak.

The style of oral discourse in the United States is essentially a very assertive one. Imbued with a high sense of competition, most North Americans want to make certain that their views and positions are presented as clearly and as powerfully as possible. As a consequence, they tend to concentrate far more on sending messages than on receiving them. Many Westerners treat a discussion as a debate, the objective of which is to win by convincing the other party of the superiority of their position. Operating under such an assumption, many Americans concentrate more on their own response than on what the other party is actually saying. They seem to have a stronger desire to be heard than to hear. Although public speaking courses are quite common in our high schools and colleges, courses on how to listen are virtually nonexistent. Because effective listening is a vital component of the negotiating process, Westerners in general, and Americans in particular, are at a marked disadvantage when they appear at the negotiating table.

If the best negotiator is the well-informed negotiator, as we have tried to suggest throughout this chapter, then active listening is absolutely essential in order to understand the other side's positions and interests. The understanding that comes from your active listening can have a positive persuasive effect on your negotiating partners in at least two important ways. First, the knowledge gleaned through listening can convince your negotiating partners that you are knowledgeable and, thus, worthy of a long-term business relationship. And second, the very fact that you made the effort to really hear what they were saying will, in almost every case, enhance the rapport and trust between the two parties.

Developing good listening skills is easier said than done. Nevertheless, there are some general guidelines that, if followed, can help us receive oral messages more effectively.

1. Be aware of the phenomenon that psychologists call *cognitive dissonance*, the tendency to discount, or simply not hear, any message that is inconsistent with what we already believe or want to believe. In other words, if the message does not conform to our preconceived way of thinking, we subconsciously tend to dismiss its importance. It is important to give yourself permission to actively hear all messages—those that you agree with and those that you don't. It is not necessary that you agree with everything that is being said, but it is important to hear the message so that you will then be in a position to seek creative ways of resolving whatever differences exist.

2. Listen to the whole message before offering a response. Focus on understanding rather than interrupting the message, so that you can give a rebuttal/response. Because no one likes to be cut off before he or she is finished speaking, it is vital for the effective negotiator to practice allowing other people to finish their ideas and sentences.

3. Concentrate on the message rather than the style of the presentation. It is easy to get distracted from what is being said by focusing instead on how it is presented. No matter how inarticulate, disorganized, or inept the speaker might be, try to look beyond those stylistic features and concentrate on the content of the message.

4. Learn to ask open-ended questions which are designed to allow the speaker to elaborate on a particular point.

5. Be conscious of staying in the present. All people bring into a negotiation session a wide variety of baggage from the past. It is tempting to start thinking about yesterday's racquetball game, this morning's intense conversation with your boss, or the argument you had with your spouse at breakfast, but to do so will distract you from actively hearing what is being said.

6. Consider the possibility of having a friend or close associate serve as an official listener whose job it is to listen to the other side with another set of ears. Such a person can provide a valuable new perspective on what is being said and can also serve as a check on your own perceptions.

7. In almost all situations, it will help to take notes if you want to become a more effective listener. Provided you don't attempt to record every word, selective note-taking can help to highlight what is being said. Not only will note-taking help to document the messages, but when the speaker notices that you are taking notes, he or she will in all likelihood make a special effort to be clear and accurate.

THE USE OF INTERPRETERS

We must stress the importance of knowing as much as possible about the language and culture of the people with whom one is doing business. Being able to speak the language of your business partner will give you an enormous advantage; it enhances rapport, and allows you to understand more fully the thought patterns of your business partners. However, when deciding on which language to use in the negotiation, you should not be guided by the principle that a little knowledge is better than none at all. In other words, unless you are extremely well versed in a foreign language, you should not try to negotiate in that language directly, but rather rely on the services of a competent interpreter. But even if the negotiator has a relatively good command of the language, it might be helpful to work through an interpreter because it will give you more time to formulate your response. On the other hand, there are certain disadvantages: it will increase the number of people involved, increase the costs of the negotiations, and serve as a barrier to the two sides really getting to know one another.

If you are considering the use of a linguistic intermediary in cross-cultural negotiations, it is important that you first make the distinction between a translator and an interpreter. Although both responsibilities involve turning the words of one language into the words of another language, the translator usually works with documents, whereas the interpreter works with the spoken word in a face-to-face situation. Translators have the luxury of using dictionaries, and generally are not under any great time constraints. Interpreters, on the other hand, must listen to what is being said and then instantaneously translate those words into the other language. Interpreting is a demanding job, for it requires constant translating, evaluating, and weighing the meaning of specific words within the specific social context. A good interpreter not only will need to be aware of the usual meaning of the words in the two languages, but must also consider the intent of the words and the meanings of the nonverbal gestures as well. Because of these special demands, language interpretation is more exhausting—and consequently, less accurate—than language translation.

When selecting an interpreter, it is important for that person to be intimately knowledgeable of the two languages, and have a technical expertise in the area being negotiated. For example, while an American university professor of Spanish literature might have an excellent command of the language, he or she might not be particularly effective at translating scientific terms or highly technical data on weaving equipment. It is this type of shortcoming that could lead an interpreter to translate the term "hydraulic ram" into the term "wet sheep."

Because the use of an interpreter involves placing an additional person between the two primary negotiators, one should take a number of precautions to ensure that the interpreter clarifies communication rather than obscures it. First, the negotiator and the interpreter should allow sufficient time before the negotiators begin to get to know one another. Only when the interpreter understands your goals and expectations can he or she represent your interests to the other side and be on the lookout for the type of information that you need. Second, help the interpreter by speaking slowly and in complete sentences. By pausing momentarily between sentences, you are actually providing a little more time for the interpreter to do his or her job. Third, because interpreting is an exhausting job that requires intense concentration, interpreters should be given breaks periodically to recharge their intellectual batteries. Fourth, plan your words carefully so as to avoid ambiguities, slang, or other forms of the language that do not translate well. And finally, it is imperative that interpreters be treated with respect and acknowledged as the highly qualified professionals that they are. The purposeful development of cordial relations with your interpreter can only help to facilitate the process of communication at the negotiating table.

THE GLOBAL NEGOTIATOR

We have examined, in a very general way, some of the problems and challenges of negotiating abroad. This chapter is not intended to be a cookbook for the would-be international negotiator. Rather, it is offered as a set of general guidelines for those who find themselves negotiating across cultures. We should bear in mind that there are never any two negotiating situations that are exactly alike. But most of the strategies suggested here are applicable to whatever type of cross-cultural negotiating session one can imagine. We have suggested that international negotiators should: (a) concentrate on building long-term relationships rather than short-term contracts, (b) focus on the interests that lay behind the positions, (c) avoid overdependence on cultural generalizations, (d) develop a sensitivity to timing, (e) remain flexible, (f) prepare carefully ahead of time, (g) learn to listen effectively, and (h) know when to use interpreters.

One critical principle appears throughout the contemporary literature on negotiation: Because negotiating across cultures involves mutual interdependence between the parties, it must be conducted in an atmosphere of mutual trust and cooperation. It is important to maintain a high degree of personal respect for those on the other side of the table, regardless of your personal position on the issues that are being negotiated. Even though it is very likely that the negotiators on the other side of the table view the world very differently than you do, they should always be approached with respect and with a willingness to learn. You should not try to reform those from another culture at the negotiating table in hopes that they will eventually be more like yourself, for the simple reason that it will not work. On the other hand, you should not go overboard in the other direction by "going native." Most people tend to be suspicious of anyone imitating their gestures or behaviors. The soundest advice is to learn to understand and respect cultural differences while retaining one's own. This spirit of mutual respect and cooperation has been cogently expressed by Salacuse (1991:164):

> At times the two sides at the negotiating table are like two persons in a canoe who must combine their skills and strength if they are to make headway against powerful currents, through dangerous rapids, around hidden rocks, and over rough portages. Alone they can make no progress and will probably lose control. Unless they cooperate, they risk wrecking or overturning the canoe on the obstacles in the river. Similarly, unless global deal makers find ways of working together, their negotiations will founder on the many barriers encountered in putting together an international business transaction.

Respect, mutual trust, cooperation, and a willingness to learn—important factors in every successful cross-cultural negotiation.

THE BASICS OF INTERCULTURAL COMMUNICATION

The American Society for Training and Development

"Diversity competence" in tomorrow's supervisors and managers will mean the capacity to effectively monitor and motivate differences across race, gender, age, social attitudes, and lifestyles.

Badi G. Foster, Gerald Jackson, William E. Cross, Bailey Jackson, and Rita Hardiman, *Training and Development Journal*

■ A training specialist gives instructions to a worker about an exercise that needs to be completed. The worker smiles agreeably and nods. When the trainer checks back with the worker later, she discovers that the worker has not completed the exercise, and she becomes upset that the instruction has not been carried out.

■ A human resource specialist interviews a job applicant whose resumé contains exactly the qualifications and experience required for an opening in the company. But when the applicant refuses to elaborate or give details about his accomplishments, however, the HR specialist decides that the resume is "padded."

From *Info-line*, published by the American Society for Training and Development, 1630 Duke St., Alexandria, Virginia 22313 (703-683-8100). Reprinted by permission.

■ A female executive is sent overseas to present a new sales contract to a major purchaser. The client keeps her waiting and then interrupts the meeting to take numerous telephone calls and to handle in-person interruptions. The woman leaves, feeling that she's somehow mishandled the assignment.

Each of these interactions contains the seeds of misunderstanding and conflict. Each can have an impact on a person's livelihood, and can leave all parties bewildered and defensive. And, in each case, the basis of the difficulty is a simple miscommunication based on differing cultural backgrounds. Scenarios such as these will become more and more common as international trade barriers fall and as the American workforce becomes increasingly diverse. Close to 80 percent of the American workforce is made up of women, minorities, and persons from other countries: Despite this, many supervisors still communicate as though their workers are "mainstream" white American males.

This chapter will discuss the major stumbling blocks to communicating with people from diverse cultural backgrounds, and explain how to become more sensitive to cultural differences.

CULTURE SHOCK

Culture refers to an individual's patterned ways of thinking, feeling, and reacting, but it also means the social legacy an individual acquires from his group. Misunderstandings occur when members of one culture are unable to understand cultural differences in communication practices, traditions, and thought processes within their own country, or abroad. We sometimes refer to this as "culture shock."

Symptoms of culture shock include disorientation, changes in eating and sleeping habits, anxiety, depression, and identity issues.

Communicating "across" cultures is never easy. One researcher likens the difficulties involved in cross-cultural communication to light passing through a stained glass window. "To understand how people from another culture perceive the message sent to them," write Doris Borisoff and David Victor, "it is first necessary to understand to what extent their culture has tinted the window of communication." That window also is tinted by our own perceptions.

Many conflicts result when one or more parties to the communication cling to an ethnocentric view of the world. Borisoff and Victor define ethnocentricism as the "unconscious tendency to interpret or judge all other groups and situations according to the categories and values of our own culture." Unfortunately, ethnocentrism can be manifested by the judgment that differences in communication techniques are wrong, rather than merely different.

In order to reduce intercultural communication problems, trainers and supervisors need to be aware of their own culturally imbued ways of viewing the world. To be effective, the trainer or supervisor must understand how the perception of a given message changes, depending on the cultural viewpoint of those communicating. This is true whether the communication is verbal or non-verbal.

INFLUENCING FACTORS

Several factors influence intercultural communication. These factors include language, place, thought processing, and non-verbal communication.

Language

Even when both parties speak the same language, differences and misunderstandings can occur. Among the most often cited difficulties with intercultural communication in terms of language:

▪ **Accent.** Accents are the way an individual pronounces, enunciates, and articulates words. Trainers and managers should understand what an accent does or does not indicate about an individual's education, degree of assimilation into the host culture, and ability to understand the language.

Even after years in this country, some immigrants still have heavy accents. Their trainers or supervisors need to remember that accent doesn't reflect the speaker's ability to understand what is said or what is written, or the speaker's knowledge of English grammar and vocabulary.

Variations in accent are also tied to geography and social class. These differences are compounded by dialectical differences in word meanings. Within the United States, for example, Americans might judge a slow-speaking Southerner as being less educated than a faster-speaking New Yorker, when the reality might be far different.

- **Linguistics.** Some linguistic experts believe that language shapes the way the culture uses it, basically influencing the way its speakers think. "Since language shapes thought, those speaking different languages understand the world around them —including the message they communicate —in a way which is essentially linked to the language used," Borisoff and Victor state. "For anyone not using the language, the message received will, by nature, be only approximate."

In addition to problems of language and linguistics, translation itself presents difficulties. These difficulties include:

- **Gross translation errors.** Gross translation errors are relatively frequent, but they are also usually the easiest to detect and correct. Many errors are simply ridiculous or silly. The GM slogan "Body by Fisher," for example, was once translated into "Corpse by Fisher." The possibility of conflict arises when one party assumes that the person makes the error because he or she does not respect the other culture.

- **Nuance errors.** When both parties do not have similar command of a language, mild distinctions between meanings can lead to misunderstandings. The nuances between "misunderstand" and "misinterpret," for example, can produce some uncomfortable moments.

PLACE

"Place" in the intercultural sense can mean more than one thing, but generally refers to the existing technological level of the culture and the physical environment. "Many place-related differences," Borisoff and Victor state, "are

based primarily on a lack of *knowledge* rather than on culturally intrinsic *values*." Place differences manifest themselves in many ways, such as the realm of personal space and of technology.

- **Personal space.** The way individuals use space varies greatly from culture to culture and is often steeped with cultural associations. Germans, for example, generally use space to reinforce social distance, and favor soundproofing and heavy curtains as ways to create it.

American businessmen may view German behavior as intentionally cold, isolating, and stand-offish. While a German manager might place great emphasis on the physical separation of his or her office, a Japanese manager usually has no separate office. Instead, the Japanese manager's status is indicated by the position of his or her desk in a large open area filled with other desks. The manager's desk usually is farthest from the door, near a window, and placed so that the entire work area is visible. Danger lies in the possibility that the German or American entering a Japanese environment might misread the Japanese's highly structured seating arrangement as being egalitarian.

- **Technology.** Technological advances in a specific culture directly reflect the value the culture places on technology. Technology, in turn, is the use a culture makes of its available resources. Never assume that a low level of technological use results from an inherently inferior culture, however. A low level of technological sophistication might well be the deliberate choice of a particular country. Westerners need to recognize their biased attitude that technological advancement is beneficial, because this bias often leads to a belief that cultures that do not have an equally sophisticated level of technology *want* to acquire it, but simply lack the access to it or the ability to achieve it.

Iran's leaders, for example, rapidly introduced changes based on high technology because they viewed the new ways as "advances." Unfortunately, the Iranian people tend to view the changes as attacks on traditional Iranian values.

THOUGHT PROCESSING

Thought processing—the way people view the world around them—also is culturally based. Four variables have an impact on how members of a culture think and express themselves.

- **Social Organization.** Social organization is defined as the individuals and groups in a society and the relationship between these individuals and groups. Those relationships that affect communication are familial, religious, economic, and political, as well as age, sex, and ethnic group. These social differences can be subtle and reflect an unstated meaning that everyone is supposed to know. Intercultural conflicts often arise when an individual's views of the social organization in which he or she operates are seen as universal.

   Reactions to praise and motivation, for example, are socially determined: Something that is motivating and persuading in one culture might not be in another. Eastern collectivistic cultures place much emphasis on maintaining harmony among the group, whereas the individual comes first in the United States. An American supervisor who singles out an employee for praise is being consistent with his or her cultural training, but this same action is likely to seem disruptive to Asian subordinates because the supervisor has drawn attention to the achievement of an individual, rather than the group.

Managers operating in different cultural environments—whether in foreign nations or in domestic situations—must remain nonjudgmental when their own cultural patterns clash with those with whom they're communicating. This sensitivity extends to hiring practices. If the applicant in our operation scenario at the beginning of this chapter was Asian, his reticence would probably be based on a cultural tradition to let individual accomplishments speak for themselves.

- **Contexting.** Contexting is the way in which one communicates and the circumstances surrounding the communication. The more information a receiver and sender share, the higher the context of the communication and the less necessary it is for the two to communicate in words or gestures. In a highly contexted situation, much of what the sender doesn't articulate is necessary if one is to understand what is said. Highly contexted societies determine meaning from how a message is delivered and under what circumstances. Low-context societies are more literal—that is, more dependent on what is said or written. The United States is a low-context society, while many Eastern societies are high context.

- **Authority.** The ability or inclination of an individual to act on his or her own initiative also is culturally determined. The level of respect for authority varies greatly. In some Eastern cultures, for example, supervisors view a subordinate's suggestion to try a new procedure as questioning the supervisor's authority; in the egalitarian U.S., such a suggestion would normally be welcomed.

   Another aspect of the authority issue is the extent to which a culture accepts the fact that power is distributed unequally. Societies with strong hierarchies, such as Japan, tend to have centralized flows of information. The emphasis of a communication is likely to be placed on a person's position in the hierarchy, rather than the person.

■ **Concept of time.** A cultural concept of time refers to the importance a culture places on time and its philosophy toward the past, present, and future. In intercultural communication, a person's concept of time influences communication behavior.

Most North Americans and Northern Europeans see time as a tool—something to be divided, used, or wasted. Throughout Latin America, Central Africa, and the Arab states, time is viewed as fluid. These people put personal involvement and completion of projects above schedules. The woman in the second opening scenario viewed her wait and the interruptions as a waste of time and an insult. If she was meeting with an Nigerian official, however, he would have paid her the compliment of completing the transaction, no matter how long that transaction took.

NON-VERBAL BEHAVIOR

"One of the most markedly varying dimensions of intercultural communication is non-verbal behavior," note Borisoff and Victor. This area can cause extreme difficulty, since as much as 65 percent of a message's meaning is conveyed through non-verbal behavior.

Non-verbal behavior runs the gamut from giggling and nodding through eye contact, but not all non-auditory communication is nonverbal: sign language used by the deaf, for example, is verbal.

There are five types of non-verbal, non-auditory behaviors:

■ **Appearance.** Contrary to the popular saying that you can't judge a book by its cover,

some research has shown that first impressions are often quite accurate. First impressions give information about gender, age, profession, relative economic position, race, and culture. Appearance "clues" fall into two categories:

■ *Artifacts* are those items of appearance over which an individual has control, such as jewelry, clothing, and eye wear. Artifacts also provide information on status or trade. These include cameras, cars, briefcases, and tool kits.

■ *Physical traits* are those characteristics over which one has little or no control. These traits, including skin color, sex, physical signs of age, body size, bone structure, baldness, and shape of face, can be used rightly or wrongly to predict behavior.

On the other hand, judgments based on appearance can be misleading. For example, two professionally dressed people, a man and a woman, are approached by an older client, who assumes that the man is the professional and the woman is part of his support staff. (This is not happening as frequently these days.) Similarly, a woman in a typical Western business suit might be judged as immoral by an Arab or Malaysian.

■ **Body Language.** Differences in how people walk, talk, bow, stand, or sit occur not only between cultures, but also between genders and subgroups within a culture. The purposes of body language fall into five discrete categories:

■ *Emblems* are the non-verbal signals that can be translated directly into words. The American "okay" sign (making a ring with the forefinger and thumb while holding the remaining three fingers up and with the palm facing away from the body), for example, is an obscene gesture in Greece! The danger in using such signs lies in assuming that they have universal meanings and unambiguous direct translations into words.

- *Illustrators* are movements that complement verbal communication by describing, accenting, or reinforcing what the speaker says. Illustrators generally are more universal than emblems. The frequency of illustrators increases when the speaker is excited or senses a lack of understanding.

- *Affect displays* carry emotional meanings —hate, love, disdain, fear, or anger. In North America, for example, smiling signifies pleasure or happiness. Orientals, on the other hand, might smile to save face.

- *Regulators* also seem to have more universality across cultures than emblems. Regulators are used to control conversation, although the communicators might not be consciously aware of them. Nodding to indicate understanding, for example, is a regulatory behavior.

- *Adaptors* are movements used to fulfill a personal need, such as twisting paper clips or scratching. People with whom the person interacts often are more aware of the movement than the user is.

Body language seems to be inseparable from language. A study of Fiorello LaGuardia, the trilingual mayor of New York, showed that his body language changed depending on whether he was speaking English, Italian, or Yiddish.

Miscommunication occurs when a person from one culture expects someone from another to understand the non-verbal behavior, or when the person receiving the messages doesn't respond in the way the sender expects. For example, Nikita Khrushchev, on a state visit to the U.S.,

clasped his hands and raised them over his shoulder when he was met at the airport. Khrushchev's gesture reminded most Americans of a victorious boxer; for Russians, the gesture represents hands clasped in friendship.

- **Touching.** Touching communicates intimacy. The more affectionate people are, the more they touch. In mainstream America, touching usually follows a progressive pattern: functional, social, friendship, love, and sexual. Each of these steps delineated are by cultural norms.

  In addition to communicating intimacy, touching can also mean dominance. Studies have shown than people in power are more apt to touch their subordinates than be touched by their subordinates. In some status situations, men tended to touch women more than women touched men.

- **Eye contact.** Eyes can convey a number of meanings, also varying from culture to culture. Among English-speaking Americans, four patterns have been defined:

  - *Cognitive* eye movements are associated with thinking. By looking away from a speaker, for example, a receiver indicates that no new information is being processed.

  - *Monitoring* eye movements are also associated with understanding. The speaker, in this case, monitors the degree of eye contact provided by the listener.

  - *Regulatory* eye movements are associated with the willingness of a communicator to respond to what is being said. The speaker regulates the communication flow by making eye contact and allowing the receiver to indicate whether he or she is open to further communication.

  - *Expressive* eye movements are associated with the emotional responses of the people communicating. Eyes and the

> Cultural background is an issue only when there are poor communications, for it is in the communication process that cultural issues surface immediately.
>
> Frederic William Sierczek, *Training and Development Journal*

surrounding facial area can express disgust, anger, happiness, and sadness, among others things.

- **Space.** The way people use space also communicates. "Spatial changes give a tone to communication, accent it, and at times even override the spoken word," Edward Hall writes. He identifies four categories of personal space:

  - *Intimate space* is the space around the body that is reserved for those with whom one is intimate. In the U.S., this space is about 18 inches.

  - *Casual-personal space* is for friends. In the U.S., this ranges from 18 inches to 4 feet.

  - *Social-consultative space* is used for most day-to-day interactions. In the U.S., this space is from 4 feet to 12 feet.

  - *Public space* lies outside 12 feet.

Americans might encounter difficulties with the space issue when communicating with people from other cultures. The American "arm's length" approach might be uncomfortable in those societies where friendly or serious conversations are conducted close enough to feel the other's breath on one's face, Borisoft and Victor note.

THE FOUR As

Intercultural communication can be enhanced by paying attention to four areas:

- **Assessment.** When communicating with someone of another culture, both parties have to assess the importance of the respective cultures in the communication. This includes what assumptions are common in the culture, as well as gestures and language used.

- **Acknowledgement.** The communicators must recognize not only the cultural biases of the other party, but also their own.

- **Attitude.** Flexibility is required when dealing with individuals from other cultures. Some adjustment in the individual's assumptions or approach might be necessary to develop an atmosphere conducive to conflict-free communications.

- **Action.** The communicator can take several steps to ensure better communications. These include—

  1. *Establish credibility.* Rather than approaching communication with a list of cultural do's and don'ts, be curious. Ask questions about differences in language, environment, technology, thought processing, and gesture.

  2. *Gain trust.* Recognize and act on the principles that convey trust in the specific cultures involved.

  3. *Maintain accurate communications.* Recognize that the "what you heard isn't what I meant" adage is apt when dealing across languages. Slang and jargon often do not translate into foreign tongues.

  4. *Anticipate reactions.* Acquire as much knowledge as possible about the culture from which the other comes. This acquisition is ongoing—learn as much as possible before and during the meeting.

  5. *Give feedback.* Providing and getting feedback about communication techniques implies an interest in and concern for the other party, as well as allowing the communicator to collect more data about the other culture, its

> It is crucial that international players know how to do business in the target countries or with people of the target cultures.
>
> Jean McEnery and Gaston DesHarnais
> Training and Development Journal

way of thinking, and whether it is low or high context.

6. *Remain flexible.* The ability to adapt to or understand the other's culture is mandatory. Flexibility and remaining non-judgmental are the fundamentals of open communication.

STEPS TO EFFECTIVE COMMUNICATION

Encouraging open communication between persons of diverse backgrounds will often require careful use of the communicator's preferred style. Donald Weiss suggests the following techniques to establish and maintain open communications:

- **Gatekeepers.** These are the ways to get a person to begin or continue talking. A gatekeeper can be an open-ended question, or a simple nodding of the head. Remember to be sensitive to those gatekeepers that may have different meanings across cultures.

- **Open-ended questions.** These questions require more than a yes or no answer, and encourage the speaker to talk freely. They often are used to gather general information. These questions usually begin with who, what, where, why, when, and how.

- **Closed-ended questions.** These questions are used to confirm specific information or facts. They can be answered with yes or no.

- **Pregnant pause.** This is the deliberate silence after a question that encourages the listener to answer. Americans are not used to silence, and find it very uncomfortable.

- Feedback. Feedback comes in two forms, and both are useful.

  - *Informational* feedback is used to show that the listener understands what is being conveyed. The listener must restate in his or her own words what the speaker has said.

  - *Behavioral* feedback explains how someone's behavior affects you.

  - *Mirroring* feedback demonstrates what emotional messages are being conveyed.

  - *Process check* feedback is used to ensure that everyone in the group has the same understanding of what's occurring.

Chapter Eleven

NEGOTIATING WITH AMERICANS

WELCOME TO AMERICA: WATCH OUT FOR CULTURE SHOCK

David Stamps

Working in the land of cubicles and cowboy individualism takes some getting used to. Foreign visitors wonder why we put up with e-mail, meetings, and 50-hour work weeks.

"Those who live in the midst of democratic fluctuations have always before their eyes the image of chance; and they end by liking all undertakings in which chance plays a part. They are therefore led to engage in commerce, not only for the sake of the profit it holds out to them, but for the love of the constant excitement occasioned by that pursuit."

Alexis De Tocqueville, *Democracy in America*

The Japanese management team that came to Flat Rock, Michigan, to launch the first Mazda manufacturing plant on U.S. soil had been warned that working with American autoworkers would be different than managing their counterparts back in Japan. In the mid-1980s the rumor circulating among the Japanese expatriate community was that Americans lacked dedicated work habits.

The Mazda managers might have been better served had they been instructed to worry less about the American work ethic and more about the opening week of deer season.

From *Training*, November, 1996. Reprinted by permission.

By fall of 1987 the plant was closing in on its targeted first-year production numbers, the Americans having proved able workers and the start-up having gone as well as could be expected. Then November rolled around and production slowed to a crawl, as half the plant's line workers and supervisors requested time off to go deer hunting.

That Americans hunt was hardly new information to the Japanese. The realization that Americans thought nothing of sacrificing the operation of an automobile assembly plant to opening day of deer season was the sort of blaze-orange reality jolt that hits foreign managers with a thud. Huddled behind closed doors, the Japanese pilgrims

"In America, there's a great pretense that the normal social dynamic between the sexes doesn't exist. In France, women dress to kill, and wouldn't be caught dead wearing sneakers. If a boss doesn't compliment a woman, she'll think something's wrong. That sort of interaction between the sexes is a natural part of life. It's fun when there is electricity in the air. French people working here don't understand why Americans want to put rubber shoes on everyone and take the electricity away."

—Helene Potter, a native of France now working as Senior Project Editor for Macmillan Reference USA in New York.

whispered grave misgivings about their American experiment.

Welcome to America, land of the bottom line, bastion of unbridled opportunity, home of empowerment, the Seven Habits, light beer, bullet points, management by objectives, and the Whopper. And, as Mazda's managers discovered, rude surprises.

To thousands of foreign nationals who arrive here each year to spend a couple of years working in this country, America is considered a plum assignment—a chance to learn how the capitalist leader of the world does things, an opportunity to add some polish to an ascendant resumé. But it's also a place of baffling contradictions that can leave newcomers reeling with culture shock.

"How's that?" you say. Culture shock in America?

Granted, with roughly six square miles of retail shopping space for every woman, man, child, and household pet in the nation, America is not what most people would consider a hardship post. To many visitors our abundance—or excess —is what makes this nation hugely appealing.

(Despite the trouble they get into here, Japanese businessmen still prefer the United States over other foreign assignments if for no other reason than the unlimited chance to golf. One Japanese executive on assignment at a Tennessee auto-parts manufacturer reportedly played 200 times in a single season.) So maybe we should just ignore those complaints from cantankerous Europeans who make sour faces and ask, *Where in the land of 4 million supermarkets and 40 million all-night minimarts can a person find a bakery that sells decent bread?*

Another way in which we deny the fact that people from other nations sometimes find themselves unhinged by our country is by embracing the media-spawned belief that We are the World —or that American culture is rapidly becoming the culture of the world. How can foreign visitors be shocked by what they find here, when we've packaged so much of ourselves and shipped it abroad for overseas consumption, such as Mickey Mouse, Madonna, and "Murphy Brown" reruns?

But stop to consider that the most popular American television show worldwide is "Baywatch." Then imagine the mixed message *that* sends to a Japanese businessman who, upon arrival in Babe Land, is shunted into a sexual-harassment seminar and told he'll be slapped with a lawsuit if he so much as glances at a woman's breasts.

Finally, Americans cherish an abiding belief in our own brand of slap-on-the-back friendliness. Why, if someone is having problems, we will lend a neighborly hand. Of course we will. . . unless we're under deadline pressure and don't have time right this second. "Can I get back to you on that? I'll send an e-mail."

SINK OR SWIM

"It *is* true that Americans are just about the friendliest people in the world," says John Bing, a man who earns his living explaining American ways to foreign visitors. It's also true that we are the most "I-centered," individualistic nation ever to hoist a flag, notes Bing, whose company International Training Associates of Princeton, New Jersey, specializes in cultural training for expatriate workers both here and abroad.

Individuality is not simply an American trait, he explains. It is our *most* distinctive cultural trait. "The idea ingrained into each of us is that, when all is said and done, you're on your own."

And it is that tough nugget of individualism that prevents visitors from more collective cultures like Latin America or Japan or Scandinavia from seeing the friendly aspect of Yankee helpfulness that we think we project. Bing says that many visitors, in fact, feel that they get very little support when they come to this country. "For the first three days, people smile and say 'Let us know what we can do.' Then, suddenly, [the visitor] is dropped, in the great American sink-or-swim tradition."

Our I-centered ways are a national trait that sets us apart from others and this is something that many Americans simply don't stop to think about. Those same traits can be emotionally jarring to visitors—especially in our fast-paced work environment. This is one of the principal themes of a message that Bing and a handful of cross-cultural training specialists scattered across the country are trying to convey to the business community these days.

For employers willing to entertain ideas about ways to ease the adjustment pangs of foreign workers, culture shock therapists are full of practical advice—much of it learned from having been called in to mop up after most of the bloodletting has occurred. Among their suggestions:

Meetings

Rethink them. American workers already loathe meetings, but at least *they* have a vague notion of the purpose behind these notorious time-wasters.

Foreign workers will have entirely different preconceptions about how time is supposed to be wasted in a meeting.

Workaholic Schedules

Foreign workers can toil long hours with the best of us, but don't expect them to embrace overtime with the same feigned alacrity displayed by job-nervous Americans. Europeans have a hard enough time fathoming how we survive on a paltry two- or three-week vacation a year; they're used to five or six. In other words, you'd better have an awfully good reason for asking a German or a Scandinavian to come to work on a weekend. Japanese, of course, are the exception to this rule.

E-mail

This may come as a shocker, but the rest of the world simply does not share our fascination with e-mail and voice mail. Whatever the message, most foreign workers would rather hear it face to face.

MBAs

An object of veneration in this country, the 27-year-old *wunder*-manager will likely be a source of bewilderment or irritation to foreign workers. Other work cultures, especially Germany and Japan, still place a premium on experience; managers in those countries are expected to actually know something about the inner workings of the products that a company makes or uses.

> "The idea that everything can be reduced to a half-day seminar or a computerized support system with pop-up answer screens strikes Germans as the height of absurdity."
>
> —Lynn Hawley-Wildmoser

"In Sweden, we are consensus-oriented. Americans are more likely to think on their own and act on their own. But American individualism is a doubled-edged sword, and Americans face a dilemma that Swedes don't. If you share an idea with others, will someone else try to take credit for it? If it turns out to be a bad idea, will there be repercussions? With the job security we enjoy in Sweden, a bad idea won't get you fired."

—Peder Moller, Director of Human Resources for Ericsson Messaging Systems in Woodbury, New York.

Feedback

Should you find yourself working for a boss from another country, don't expect the steady stream of compliments that American managers have been taught to dole out like jelly beans. That style of management-by-positive-feedback simply doesn't exist elsewhere. The need for up-to-the-minute reassurances that we know what the hell we are doing seems to be a phenomenon unique to late-20th-century America.

HELLO, CRUEL WORLD

With many companies exporting *and* importing workers in record numbers these days, one might assume that this sort of practical advice commands an eager audience. To the contrary, cross-cultural trainers will be the first to complain that they are swimming against a high tide of global opportunism.

"American companies, if they think at all about training for expatriate workers, may provide it for those going overseas, but seldom for inbound workers," observes Noel Kreicker, president of International Orientation Resources in Northbrook, Illinois, a firm that specializes in expat training and orientation services.

Not that Americans are the only pigheaded ones on this point: the Japanese are notorious for believing their technical prowess and analytical skills will see them through any situation. Such legendary shortsightedness has led some companies to misinterpret just how clueless Japanese managers can be in this country, right up to the point of finding themselves in big trouble. Witness the sexual-harassment lawsuits filed against Mitsubishi Motor Manufacturing of America Inc. this past year by female workers at the company's Normal, Illinois, plant and by the Equal Opportunity Employment Commission. (While Japanese managers weren't personally named as harassers, some female plaintiffs claimed that management's insensitivity to the issue allowed the creation of a hostile environment)

Top managers at most European companies are just as blind to the need for cross-cultural training for expatriates. The assumption on "the continent" is that any manager who's risen high enough to qualify for a foreign assignment will have attained sufficient language skills and *savoir faire* to charm the socks off Americans and most other foreigners, says Marian Stoltz-Loike, vice president with Windham International, a cultural-training firm in New York.

The upshot is this: In the headlong rush to turn the world into one big free-spending, 'multi-culti,' global market, companies are dispatching workers to all parts of the planet with little or no thought about how these displaced souls will cope in new social and work environments. Or what damage they might do to their employer's reputation before they eventually figure out how to behave like Romans—or Koreans, or Tuvans, or Texans.

"There are a lot of companies that are globally active, but very few that are interculturally sensitive." says Lynn Hawley-Wildmoser, manager of employee development and intercultural programs for Siemens Rolin Communications Inc. of Santa Clara, California.

◆　◆　◆　◆　◆

WHEN CULTURES COLLIDE

Hawley-Wildmoser earned her reputation as an authority on culture shock in the workplace the old-fashioned way. She experienced it firsthand . . . twice. The first jolt came in the early '70s when, armed with a college degree in German, she left the United States to teach in Germany. The second cultural wallop, far more sobering than the first, came 18 years later when she returned to America on a two-year assignment after having worked 16 years for Siemens. "I'd thought of Germany for all those years as my adopted country, and America as my native country," she says. "It was debilitating to come back here and find how strange everything seemed."

At that time, Siemens had just purchased Rolm Communications, a telephone manufacturer, from IBM and faced the daunting prospect of melding U.S. and German business cultures. Moreover, with the Rolm acquisition, Siemens was inheriting the unhappy hybrid of two irreconcilable U.S. business styles: There still remained traces of the original Rolm, with Silicon Valley's trademark laxity; superimposed over that was a heavy dose of IBM officialdom.

In hindsight, it looks like a no-brainer for Siemens to have recognized a need to provide cultural training before shipping boatloads of German managers and technicians to California, but the decision to do so was—and still is—a significant departure for the German company. Today, Siemens Communications provides cultural training not only for its U.S.-bound workers, but for all expatriates. But the communications unit is the only one of 14 separate Siemens companies that provides such training to expat workers, though all the other Siemens companies ship workers abroad in large numbers. One possible reason behind the decision to provide cultural training in this particular case, surmises Hawley-Wildmoser, is that a top Siemens executive involved in the Rolm acquisition was, himself,

a veteran of two previous overseas assignments—each time with no cultural training whatsoever.

To help ease the transition for the California-bound Germans, Hawley-Wildmoser helped Siemens put together an extensive program that begins with orientation and screening in Germany. Candidates are interviewed by supervisors and by cultural trainers to determine if they have the right language skills and work skills for the assignment. More important, do the candidate and his or her spouse possess the emotional wherewithal to survive a foreign posting? American assignments can be especially tough on families: Children might find themselves plunked down in an education system unlike anything they've ever known; and under U.S. immigration rules, spouses are seldom allowed to take jobs in this country.

Among the handful of companies that provide cross-cultural training for expatriate workers, most start with some type of pre-travel orientation. A few companies will send expatriate candidates on a trial visit to America before posting them here. When Mercedes-Benz was preparing to ship German workers to its new factory in Tuscaloosa, Alabama, it packed each candidate and his family off to Alabama, where American host families had been signed up to help show the German visitors the ropes. Mercedes also imported a team of American experts to explain what the expat candidates could expect from local schools, banks, and health care services in the region. While few companies carry orientations to that extreme, most will at least draw on the experiences of returned expatriates, who relate their first-person adventures of life in the United States.

As vitally important as these preliminary orientation sessions are, they actually do very little, warn cultural trainers, to convey the shock that typically sets in after a few weeks or months in a new country. Any real hope of bridging cultural

Welcome to Dilbert's World

Even without cultural coaching, foreign workers will figure out the obvious idiosyncrasies of the American workplace. Take, for instance, the seemingly innocent "How are you?"—a phrase uttered millions of times each day.

To a Swede or a New Zealander, people who take to heart even the most casual invitation to friendship, such an utterance dropped in the hallway by a passing co-worker who never breaks stride seems more than a little odd. But eventually they'll realize it's *not* an invitation to follow the speaker back to his cubicle and air one's views on everything from American food to our odd method of electing national leaders.

The cubicle itself, on the other hand, is another matter altogether, and much tougher to comprehend. "Cubicles are something I don't understand and don't think any Swede will ever understand," says Guy Grindborg, an employee of Stockholm-based Ericsson Inc. who has worked at the company's Richardson, Texas plant seven of the past 10 years.

To Swedes, accustomed to offices with open spaces and windows that let in fresh air and natural light, cubicles are part of an artificial, hermetically sealed environment that Americans have carried to a point of absurdity. "In America, we put a cubicle wall in front of a window so you can't see out, says Grindborg. "I guess if the cubicle had a window, that would make it too much like a real office. How Dilbert-like. In Sweden, you'd never do that."

Germans, likewise accustomed to fresh air and open-space work environments, also dislike cubes. But even more hateful is the windowless meeting room. *Ein schwarzes Loch*, the black hole, they call it.

To the Japanese, accustomed to working in open offices packed with a crowd of busy co-workers, cubicles are more than something to get used to. They are a hindrance to effective communication.

In Japan, communication was constant, if sometimes chaotic, says Atsushi Yanagida, who was moved from Mitsubishi Chemical in Japan two years ago to head up a research team at Saradyne, the company's Indianapolis subsidiary. "It was noisy but help was always close at hand when you had a question or a problem," laments Yanagida. With American team members tucked away in their separate cubicles, communication is less frequent. Yanagida says that he occasionally discovers team members are duplicating work because they fail to keep each other posted about what they are working on.

The French, on the other hand, prefer closed offices to cubicles. And they don't understand the semiprivate equivalent of the cubicle: the not-so private bathroom stall.—D.S.

gaps rests on follow-up meetings, anywhere from three to six months after the expatriate has landed in the States. Ideally, these sessions will be conducted with American co-workers present, so that all parties can dissect the nature of the misunderstandings that will almost certainly have occurred by that time.

"Back in Germany, we can talk all we want and it doesn't mean much," says Hawley-Wildmoser. "After people have been in this country a while, after they have a few scars, then they are ready to listen."

JUST THE FACTS, MA'AM

Hawley-Wildmoser remembers vividly her own discomfort upon returning to America after 18 years away. The first thing she noticed was the pace of activity. "Everything seemed so hectic, so manic. There was no time for conversation. I felt

"Americans tend to live to work. We put in long hours. We think we are sending the message that we are very dedicated. In fact, we send a very different message. Scandinavians ask me, 'What's the matter? Why can't we get the job done without working overtime?'"

—Gary Johnson, President of Inserv, a Dallas consultancy specializing in cross-cultural training for expatriate workers.

like I was going 40 miles per hour on the freeway while everyone else was going 80," she says.

And yet, the frenetic pace didn't mean that tasks actually got done any more quickly than they had back in Germany. To the contrary, things could be infuriatingly slow. Before her return to America, Hawley-Wildmoser accepted the stereotyped notion that Germans are deliberative while Americans are action-oriented. Now in America and working for a telephone company, she found herself waiting four weeks to get a telephone on her desk as the paperwork worked its tedious way through the formerly-IBM bureaucracy.

Hair-tearing moments of exasperation occurred over what she perceived as Americans' lack of commitment when promised supplies or reports failed to show up. "After I'd been here a while, I came to realize that it's not that Americans are flaky. It's because we have too few resources to do our jobs," she says. "You promise 20 'yeses' in a four-hour span, but by the end of the day, you find you just haven't had time to get to all of them."

But the most difficult thing to adjust to was Americans' approach to learning job skills, which she describes as a "let's get it over with quick and be done with it" attitude.

Once Siemens had made its decision to provide cultural training, it resolved in typical German

fashion to do more than offer a series of half-day seminars. Cross-cultural training was to become an ongoing part of the company's overseas business strategy. To Hawley-Wildmoser, that implied license to develop extensive training sessions in which Americans and Germans would actually learn about one another—instead of a series of shotgun seminars that laid out, in bullet points, the six things Americans needed to know to get by in Germany and vice versa.

She quickly discovered the German approach to learning doesn't fly in this country.

"Everything Americans do is guided by the idea that time is money," says Hawley-Wildmoser. "If I proposed a four-day training session, people would ask if it couldn't be restructured to cover the same material in two. If I proposed a two-day session, they'd ask why it couldn't be done in a half day."

Back in Germany, Hawley-Wildmoser had become accustomed to what she calls an "expert culture," which values knowing *about* things. "The idea that everything can be reduced to a half-day seminar or to a computerized support system with pop-up answer screens strikes Germans as the height of absurdity," she says.

Germans are not the only ones who have been surprised by Americans' task-oriented approach

"We are formula-driven. We want the latest miracle cure. The Japanese, the Germans, and many others are relationship-driven.

They look at our formulas, our mission statements, and our value statements, and wonder why we need these badges on our shoulders when those things should be implicit in a company's culture."

—Noel Kreicker, President of International Orientation Resources, a cross-cultural training firm in Northbrook, Illinois.

to their jobs. "We had to change our technical training to fit it with American expectations when we came to this country," says Guy Grindborg, a technical trainer for Ericsson Inc., a Swedish firm that's operated a manufacturing plant in Richardson, Texas since the mid-1980s. "The Swedish approach is more the engineering approach: 'Tell me why and how this thing works.' The American approach is much more direct: 'Don't teach me to be an expert; just tell me what I need to know to do my job.'"

To be sure, structural as well as cultural differences contribute to such divergent attitudes. In Europe, where it's difficult to fire people or to lay them off, workers enjoy a job security unknown in America. Given an environment in which both employer and employee assume that the worker will remain at the job for 20 years, employers think nothing of sending a worker to a four- or six-month class to acquire specialized job skills. That's no longer the case in this country, if it ever was.

But there are cultural differences beyond what can be explained by job stability, says Hawley-Wildmoser. "It's the difference between an investment vs. a fix-it culture. Americans see training and workshops as a way to fix something. Conflict-resolution seminars are a perfect example. Why do we think we need always to resolve conflict? Maybe conflict is a sign that we need to learn more *about* an issue. It's the difference between being solution-oriented and knowledge-oriented."

Hawley-Wildmoser is gratified to see that more companies, including more American companies, are starting to provide cultural training for expatriate workers. But she worries that few companies will give these programs the scope and follow-through they deserve, opting instead for the half-day seminar, the six bullet points.

Working for a German company, she appreciates the luxury of taking a longer, knowledge-ori-

ented approach. She describes Siemens' first cultural training program as embryonic. "We're still learning about how to bridge cultural gaps in the workplace," she says.

NON-MEETINGS OF THE MIND

Like Siemens, Rhone-Poulenc Rorer (RPR) was forced into the business of providing cultural training as the result of a merger between two incongruous corporate cultures. Six years ago Rhone-Poulenc, a French firm with a history as a nationalized chemical company, combined its pharmaceutical business with Rorer, an American pharmaceutical firm with an entrepreneurial background.

At the time of the merger, Paul Orleman, now RPR's director of global training and development, was working in Rorer's human resources department. He also happened to be finishing up a graduate degree from the University of Pennsylvania about that time; serendipitously, the melding of two companies with distinctly different national and corporate cultures turned into a master's thesis subject, dropped right into his lap.

Over a two-year span, Orleman interviewed more than 65 RPR workers from numerous countries —individuals who were expatriates or who were working closely with colleagues from other countries. His straightforward methodology was to ask a single question: "What's different?" He often got heartfelt answers that rambled on for an hour or more.

> "Americans are abrasive, shallow, and over-confident in their own abilities, but as an investment banker, I'm used to that sort of behavior, so it doesn't really bother me."
>
> —Michael Falconer, a New Zealander working for CS First Boston in New York.

"Obviously, a lot of things were different, but what was really interesting was that people seldom recognized those differences as *cultural* differences," says Orleman. "It's very easy to misinterpret things through the filter of your own culture."

Since his initial plunge into the subject, Orleman has had ample opportunity to observe how cultural differences play themselves out in the Franco-American workplace. Earlier this year, he returned to RPR's U.S. headquarters in Collegeville, Pennsylvania, after a three-year assignment at its Paris headquarters. (The firm maintains headquarters in both countries.)

From the beginning, Orleman noticed that meetings were a common source of misunderstanding. To Americans, a meeting is a place where decisions get made. Yes. We waste a lot of time in meetings, but we preserve the illusion of efficiency. We have an agenda; we follow the clock; we tick off the action items.

All of which absolutely baffles the French, says Orleman. "The point of meeting is not to get through an agenda," one French worker told him. "It's not the place to make decisions." To the French, a meeting is an opportunity to find out what others are thinking. After the meeting, those with the power to make decisions gather in private, review their newly acquired information, and . . . make a decision. "But of course that just infuriates Americans working in Paris, who sometimes feel that things that had been agreed upon in a meeting are being reversed afterward," says Orleman.

French workers in America are put off a little by the pace of American business, which is faster than they are accustomed to. But what absolutely mystifies the French is not the pace of American business; rather, it's what they perceive as the American obsession with deadlines, and our need always to be moving in the direction of a deadline or a decision. "Americans value moving, whether they are moving in the right direction or not," a French expat once confided to Orleman.

"There are different ways of doing business, and each way works in the context of its own culture," says Orleman. The challenge for any organization trying to be a global company is to figure out which model to adopt. Do you conduct meetings using the French model? The American model? The German model? The answer, of course, is none of the above. "You must invent your own culture, and that means you might end up with something that everyone is a little bit uncomfortable with at first," says Orleman. "Everyone has to adjust."

Six years after the merger, the need to understand others and to adjust to other ways of doing things is a message that RPR continues to emphasize. The company offers classes aimed at workers ("Working Cross-Culturally") and managers ("Managing Cross-Culturally"). It also has incorporated elements of those cross-cultural training classes into all of its management and leadership programs.

"The goal is not to eliminate culture shock," says Orleman. "You can't. But you can help people understand where it comes from and help them get past that initial gut reaction, when the natural tendency is to throw up your hands and ask, 'My god, why do they do it that way?'"

NEGOTIATORS ABROAD: DON'T SHOOT FROM THE HIP!

John L. Graham and Roy A. Herberger, Jr.

Picture if you will the closing scenes of John Wayne's Academy Award-winning performance in *True Grit*. Sheriff Rooster Cogburn is sitting astride his chestnut mare, a Colt .45 in one hand, a Winchester .73 in the other, whiskey on his breath, reins in his teeth, stampeding across the Arkansas prairie straight into the sights and range of the villains' guns. A face-to-face shootout with four very bad men erupts. How often has this scene been played out before our eyes? And, sure enough, the John Wayne character comes through again.

Great entertainment, yes! We *know* it's all fantasy and that in real life Sheriff Rooster Cogburn would have ended up face-down in the blood and dust, alongside his dead horse. But it's more fun to see it the other way.

There's just one problem. Such scenes from movies, television, and books influence our everyday behavior—in subtle, but powerful ways. Many of us model our behavior after such John Wayne figures. And when everyone else plays the

same game, often the bluff and bravado work. We need only look to Washington, D.C., to see examples.

A problem arises when we sit face-to-face across the negotiating table with business executives from other lands. Our minds play out the same Western scene again. Here, instead of six-guns and bowie knives, our weapons are words, questions, threats and promises, laughter and confrontation. And we anticipate the taste of victory, despite the odds—four against one is no problem. But, unfortunately, this time it's real life. At stake are the profits of our companies, not to mention our own compensation and reputation. But, like the "real life" Rooster, we lose.

Such scenes repeat themselves with increasing frequency as U.S. enterprise becomes more global. The John Wayne bargaining style that might have served us well in conference rooms across the country does us a great disservice in conference rooms across the sea. That this style might be hurting us is not a new idea. Back in the 1930s Will Rogers quipped, "America has never lost a war, and never won a conference." Twenty-three years ago in another Harvard Business Review article, anthropologist Edward T. Hall warned: "When the American executive travels abroad to do business, he is frequently shocked to discover to what extent the many variables of foreign behavior and custom complicate his efforts."[1]

Former chairman of the Senate Foreign Relations Committee J. William Fulbright once said, "Our linguistic and cultural myopia is losing us friends, business, and respect in the world."[2] The notion that our negotiating style doesn't work well overseas is not new, but it needs new emphasis in light of our growing interdependence with foreign trading partners.

SHOOT FIRST; ASK QUESTIONS LATER

Probably no single statement better summarizes the American negotiating style than "shoot first; ask questions later." Though the approach is right out of a Saturday afternoon Western, the roots go much deeper. Some basic aspects of our cultural background, in particular our immigrant heritage, our frontier history, and finally much of the training in our business and law schools, all contribute to the American negotiating style.

Throughout its history, the United States has been, and still is today, influenced by its immigrants. Certainly this continuous mixing of ideas and perspectives has enriched all our experiences. And every newcomer has had to work hard to succeed—thus the powerful work ethic of America. Another quality of our immigrant forefathers was a fierce independence—a characteristic necessary for survival in the wide open spaces. This latter quality is a disadvantage, however, at the negotiating table. Negotiation is by definition a situation of interdependence, a situation Americans have never handled well.

Our frontier history has encouraged this immigration-for-independence mentality. "Don't try to work things out—move out West where you don't have to see your neighbors so often, where there's elbow room." So runs one strain of the conventional wisdom of the first 150 years of our nation's existence. For Americans, there was always somewhere else to go if conflicts couldn't be resolved.

And the long distances between people allowed a social system to develop not only with fewer negotiations but also with shorter negotiations. A day-long horseback ride to the general store or stockyard didn't favor long-drawn-out bargaining. "Tell me yes, or tell me no—but give me a straight answer." Candor, "laying your cards on the table," was highly valued and expected in the Old West. It still is today in our boardrooms and classrooms.

What goes on in the classrooms in our business and law schools strongly influences our negotiating style. Throughout the American educational system, we are taught to compete—both academically and in sports. Adversary relationships and winning are essential themes of the American male's socialization process. But nowhere in the U.S. educational system are competition and winning more important than in a case discussion in our law and business school classrooms. The student who makes the best arguments, marshals the best evidence, or demolishes the opponents' arguments wins the respect of classmates and receives high marks. Such skills will be important at the negotiating table.

But neither business nor law schools emphasize the most important bargaining skills. We don't teach our students how to ask questions, how to get information, how to listen, or how to use questioning as a powerful persuasive tactic. Yet these latter skills are critical at the international negotiation table. Few of us realize that in most places in the world, the one who asks the questions controls the process of negotiation and thereby accomplishes more in bargaining situations.

Thus it becomes clear that by nature and training, Americans will have difficulty at the international bargaining table. We are inherently competitive, argumentative, and impatient—a bad combination indeed when the negotiation game is being played in a boardroom in Rio or in a Ginza night club, and when the other side is playing the game by Brazilian or Japanese rules.

Before we discuss specific aspects of the negotiating style that get us into trouble in international business negotiations, we must make a disclaimer. So far, we hope it is obvious that we are talking about the average or dominant behavior of American negotiators; we recognize that not every American executive is impatient or a poor listener. Nor is every American manager argumentative. Most of us do have trouble, however, in international negotiations when compared with business people from other countries.

THE JOHN WAYNE STYLE

A combination of attitudes, expectations, and habitual behavior comprises our negotiating style. We call it the "John Wayne" style for short, but it reflects the influences of immigrants and educational philosophies. Though we discuss each characteristic separately, each factor interacts with others to form the complex foundation for a series of negotiation strategies and tactics that are typically American.

1. I can go it alone.

Most U.S. executives are convinced they can handle any negotiating situation by themselves. "Four Japanese versus one American is no problem. I don't need any help. I can think and talk fast enough to get what I want and what the company needs." So goes the rationalization. And there's an economic justification: "Why take more people than I need?" There is also a more subtle reason: "How can I get the credit if I've brought along a gang of others to help? They'll just confuse things." So, most often the American side is outnumbered when it begins.

Being outnumbered or being alone (worse) is a terrible disadvantage in most negotiating situations. Several activities go on at once—talking, listening, thinking up arguments and making explanations, and formulating questions, as well as seeking an agreement. Greater numbers help in obvious ways with most of these. Indeed, on a Japanese negotiation team one member often has the sole duty of listening. Consider how carefully you might listen to a speaker if you didn't have to think up a response.

But perhaps the most important reason for having greater, or at least equal, numbers on your side is the subtle yet powerful influence of nodding heads and positive facial expressions. Negotiation is very much a social activity, and the approval and agreement of others (friend *and* foe) can determine the outcome. Also, numbers can be an indicator of the seriousness and the commitment of both parties to a successful outcome.

2. Just call me John.

Americans, more than any other national group, value informality and equality in human relations. The emphasis on first names is only the beginning. We go out of our way to make our clients feel comfortable by playing down status distinctions such as titles and by eliminating "unnecessary" formalities such as lengthy introductions. All too often, however, we succeed only in making ourselves feel comfortable while our clients become uneasy or even annoyed.

For example, in Japanese society, interpersonal relationships are vertical; in almost all two-person relationships a difference in status exists. The basis for this distinction can be any one of several factors: age, sex, university attended, position in an organization, and even one's particular firm or company. For example, the president of the "number 1" company in an industry holds a higher status position than the president of the "number 2" company in the same industry.

Each Japanese individual is very much aware of

his or her position relative to others with whom he or she deals. There are good reasons behind these distinctions. In Japan, knowledge of one's status dictates how one will act in interpersonal relations. Thus, it is easy to understand the importance of exchanging business cards—such a ritual clearly establishes the status relationships and lets each person know which role to play.

The roles of the higher status position and the lower status position are quite different, even to the extent that the Japanese use different words to express the same idea, depending on which person makes the statement. For example, a buyer would say *otaku* (your company), while a seller would say *on sha* (your great company). Status relations dictate not only *what is* said but also *how* it is said. Americans have a great deal of difficulty in understanding such conventions. In the United States we can perhaps get by with our informal, egalitarian style when we are dealing with foreigners. However, U.S. executives only make things difficult for themselves and their companies by saying to executives in Tokyo, Paris, or London, "Just call me John [or Mary]."

3. Pardon my French.

Americans aren't much good at speaking foreign languages, and often we don't even apologize about it. We correctly argue that English is the international language, particularly when it comes to technology and science, and everywhere we go, we expect to find someone who speaks English. But sometimes we don't, and we find ourselves at the mercy of third-party translators or middlemen.

Even when the other side (our clients or suppliers) does speak English, we are at a big disadvantage at the negotiating table, for three reasons. *First,* the use of interpreters gives the other side some great advantages. For example, we have observed the following pattern of interaction between U.S. managers and business people from several other countries. Often high-level

foreign executives use interpreters even when they have a good understanding of English. In one case, a Chinese executive asked questions in Mandarin. An interpreter then translated the questions for the American executive.

While the interpreter spoke, the American turned his attention to the interpreter. The Chinese executive, however, gazed at the American so that he could unobtrusively observe the American's non-verbal responses (facial expressions, et cetera). When the American spoke, the Chinese executive had twice the response time. Because he understood English, he could formulate his response during the translation process.

Bargaining in English puts a *second,* powerful negotiating tool in the hands of our opponents. On the surface, bargaining in our first language appears to be an advantage—we can more quickly formulate and articulate powerful arguments. But even the best argument fizzles when the other side responds, "Sorry, I'm not sure I understand. Can you repeat that, please?" Bargainers listening to a second language can use the tactic of selective understanding. It also works when they speak. Previous commitments are more easily dissolved with the excuse, "Well, that isn't exactly what I meant."

A *third* disadvantage has to do with our assumptions about those who speak English well. Facing a group of foreign executives, we naturally assume that the one who speaks English best is also the smartest and most influential person in the group, and therefore we direct our persuasive efforts to that member. But this is seldom the case in foreign business negotiations, so our argument suffers.

4. Check with the home office.

American bargainers get very upset when halfway through a negotiation the other side says, "I'll have to check with the home office"—the decision-makers also are not even at the bargaining table.

The Americans feel they have wasted time or have even been misled.

Limited authority among negotiators is common overseas, however, and can be a very useful bargaining tactic. In reality, the foreign executive is saying, "To get me to compromise, you not only have to convince me; you've also got to convince my boss, who is 5,000 miles away." Your arguments must be most persuasive indeed. Additionally, this tactic lets the home office make the final decision.

This tactic goes against the grain of the American bargaining style. Indeed, Americans pride themselves on having full authority to make a deal. John Wayne never had to check with the home office.

5. Get to the point.

As we mentioned earlier, Americans don't like to beat around the bush; they want to get to the heart of the matter quickly. Unfortunately, what is considered the heart of the matter in a business negotiation varies across cultures. In every country, we have found that business negotiations proceed in the following four stages: (1) non-task sounding, (2) task-related exchange of information, (3) persuasion, and (4) concessions and agreement.

The first stage, non-task sounding, includes all the activities that establish rapport, but it does not include information related to the "business" of the meeting. The information exchanged in the second stage of business negotiations concerns the parties' needs and preferences. The third stage, persuasion, involves negotiators' attempts to modify one another's views through various persuasive tactics. The final stage involves the consummation of an agreement that often is the result of a series of concessions or smaller agreements.

From the American point of view, the "heart of the matter" is the third stage—persuasion. We have a natural tendency to go through the first two stages quickly. We might talk about golf or the weather or the family, but we spend little time on these subjects relative to other cultures. We do say what our needs and preferences are and what we want and don't want, and we're quick about that too. We tend to be more interested in logical arguments than the people we're negotiating with.

But in many other countries, the heart of the matter or the point of the negotiation is not so much information and persuasion as it is to get to know the people involved. In Brazil, much time is spent in developing a strong relationship of trust before business can begin. Brazilians cannot depend on a legal system to iron out conflicts, so they depend on personal relationships. Americans new to the Brazilian way of doing business are particularly susceptible to the "wristwatch syndrome." In the United States, looking at your watch most always gets things moving along. However, in Brazil, impatience causes apprehension, thus necessitating even longer periods of non-task sounding.

American impatience causes problems in the second stage of negotiations also. Like no other cultural group, Americans tend to start bargaining at a price pretty close to what they want and expect to achieve—what they consider a fair price. Almost everywhere else in the world bargainers leave themselves room to maneuver. A Chinese or Brazilian bargainer expects to spend time negotiating and expects to make concessions. Americans do not have the same expectations and are often surprised and upset by the other side's "unreasonable" demands. But the demands are unreasonable only from the perspective of the American's slam-bang, "Old West" bargaining style. To the Oriental or Latin American it makes perfect sense to ask for a lot initially.

6. Lay your cards on the table.

Americans expect honest information at the bargaining table. When we don't get it, negotiations often end abruptly. We also understand that, like dollars, information must be traded. "You tell me what you want, and I'll tell you what I want." Sounds logical, doesn't it?

The problem is that in other countries, people have different attitudes and values about "honest" information. For example, in Brazil, being tricky is a less serious transgression of negotiation ethics. It's even expected if a strong personal relationship between negotiators does not exist. Brazilian executives explain that such attitudes and values are changing, but the tradition is strong.

In Japan, it can be difficult to get a straight answer for two reasons: first, the Japanese team often has not decided what it wants out of the deal, so a representative cannot give a definite yes or no. His group must be consulted, and he cannot yet speak for the group. If the answer is no, the Japanese side is unlikely to use that specific word. Even if the American representative demands, "Tell me yes or tell me no," the Japanese will sidestep, beat around the bush, or even remain silent. It is the Japanese style to avoid conflict and embarrassment, and to save face at all costs.

We misread and often feel misled by the subtle negative responses characteristic of the Japanese bargaining style. Japanese executives, particularly the younger ones (educated after World War II) with international experience, say they are learning to value directness, but here too the tradition is long-standing and has a powerful influence on behavior at the negotiation table.

7. Don't just sit there, speak up.

Americans don't deal well with silence during negotiations. It seems a minor point, but often we have seen Americans getting themselves into trouble (particularly in Japan) by filling silent periods with words.

The Japanese style of conversation includes occasional long periods of silence—particularly in response to an impasse. The American style consists of few long silent periods (that is, of ten seconds or more). We have found that American negotiators react to Japanese silence in one of two ways: either they make some kind of a concession, or they fill the space in the conversation with a persuasive appeal. The latter tactic has counterproductive results: the American does most of the talking, and he learns little about the Japanese point of view.

It should be noted that while handling silent periods is a problem for American negotiators, for Brazilians it is even worse. American conversational style is orderly and efficient—that is, each speaker takes his or her turn, with few silent periods. In Brazilian conversational style, particularly during the persuasion stages of negotiations, bargainers often speak simultaneously, fighting for the floor. To the American eye, Brazilians appear to be poor listeners and rather rude. Seldom indeed would an American bargaining with a Brazilian executive have to say: "Don't just sit there, speak up."

8. Don't take no for an answer.

Persistence is highly valued by Americans and is part of the deeply ingrained competitive spirit that manifests itself in every aspect of American life, particularly every aspect of the American male's life. We are taught from the earliest age never to give up. On the playing field, in the classroom, or in the boardroom, we learn to be aggressive, to win; thus, we view a negotiating session as something you *win*. Like a game, the negotiation should have a definite conclusion—a signed contract. We are dissatisfied and distressed if negotiations do not end with the biggest piece of pie going to our side. But even worse than losing a negotiation is not concluding it. We can take a loss ("We'll do better next time"), but not the ambiguity of no decision.

Our foreign clients and vendors do not necessarily share this competitive, adversarial, persistence-pays view of negotiation. Many countries see negotiations as a means of establishing long-term commercial relations that have no definite conclusion. They see negotiations more as a cooperative effort where interdependence is manifest, where each side tries to add to the pie.

When these two views (cooperative and competitive) meet across the table, difficulties naturally crop up. Americans tend to use tactics such as threats and warnings—pushing too far even when the other side is clearly signaling no. One can imagine what happens when a Japanese client, for instance, gives a subtle negative response. The Americans do not back off. They expect minds to be changed at the negotiation table, when in many situations attitudes and positions can change only with time. In some circumstances Americans might do better to take no for an answer, while preserving the all-important relationships among people and companies.

9. One thing at a time.

Americans usually attack a complex negotiation task sequentially—that is, they separate the issues and settle them one at a time. For example, we have heard U.S. bargainers say, "Let's settle the quantity first and then discuss price." Thus, in an American negotiation, the final agreement is a sum of the several concessions made on individual issues, and progress can be measured easily: "We're halfway done when we're through half the issues." In other countries, particularly Far Eastern cultures, however, concessions might come only at the end of a negotiation. All issues are discussed with a holistic approach—settling nothing until the end.

Because the other side never seems to commit itself to anything, U.S. executives invariably think

that they are making little progress during cross-cultural negotiations. Agreements might come as a surprise, and they often follow unnecessary concessions by impatient American bargainers.

10. A deal is a deal.

When Americans make an agreement and give their word, they expect to honor the agreement no matter what the circumstances. But agreements are viewed differently in different parts of the world. W.H. Newman describes this problem:

> In some parts of the world it is impolite to refuse openly to do something that has been requested by another person. What a Westerner takes as a commitment may be little more than a friendly conversation. In some societies, it is understood that today's commitment may be superseded by a conflicting request received tomorrow, especially if that request comes from a highly influential person. In still other situations, agreements merely signify intention and have little relation to capacity to perform; as long as the person tries to perform, he feels no pangs of conscience and he makes no special effort if he is unable to fulfill the agreement. Obviously, such circumstances make business dealings much more uncertain, especially for new undertakings.[3]

11. I am what I am.

Few Americans take pride in changing their minds, even in difficult circumstances. Certainly John Wayne's character and behavior were constant and predictable. He treated everyone and every situation with his action-oriented, forthright style. He could never be accused of being a chameleon.

Many American bargainers take the same attitude with them to the negotiation table, but during international business negotiations, inflexibility can be a fatal flaw. There simply is no single strategy or tactic that always works; different countries and different personalities require different approaches.

HOW TO NEGOTIATE IN OTHER COUNTRIES

Now let us map out an action strategy to deal with such problems. Americans must adjust their negotiation behaviors to fit the style of the host country executives. The following prescriptions correspond to each element of the bargaining style we have discussed.

1. I can go it alone.

Use team assistance wisely. Don't hesitate to include extra members on your team, such as financial or technical experts. The extra expense might be an excellent investment. Also, observation of negotiations can be a valuable training experience for younger members of the organization. Even if they add little to the discussion, their presence can make a difference.

2. Just call me John.

The way to make foreign clients more comfortable is to follow *their* traditions and customs. American informality and egalitarian views are simply out of place in most countries in the world. Status relations and business procedures must be carefully considered with the aid and advice of your local representatives.

3. Pardon my French.

Ideally, U.S. negotiators should speak the local language, although in practice this is seldom possible. Americans usually travel overseas for short trips, and the investment in executive time for extensive language training appears unwarranted. However, American representatives should recognize the conversational disadvantages when foreign executives use an interpreter, even though they understand English. Even a rudimentary

knowledge of key foreign terms or numbers can aid the American.

4. Check with the home office.

An important part of the preparations for any negotiation is the determination of authority limits—both theirs and yours. Americans should weigh the disadvantages of having full authority against the expenses of communication with the home office. Not having the final say might be a useful strategy for maintaining the proper interpersonal relationship and harmony, particularly in international negotiations.

5. Get to the point.

We Americans depend on tightly written contracts and corporate lawyers for protection against the unscrupulous. Since in many places in the world legal systems are not as dependable, foreign executives invest much time in establishing personal relationships. Americans bargaining in foreign countries must be patient and plan to spend more time in non-task sounding. Let the other side bring up business, and put your wristwatch in your coat pocket.

Moreover, remarks such as "We will need to get our legal staff to review this proposal" can quickly sour international deals. Other countries see us as a nation of lawyers in a world where law is used to handle business agreements that are in trouble, not at the beginning of the discussions. Be careful of open references to "legal review." To the foreigner, it can be a signal that the business relationship will be short-lived.

6. Lay your cards on the table.

Foreign executives seldom lay their cards on the table. They are more likely to hold an ace or two in reserve. Often, initial demands will be irritatingly high from the American point of view. Most foreign executives expect to spend more time negotiating and expect to make concessions. You should adjust your initial offer accordingly and anticipate having to ask the same questions in several ways to get what we would call straight answers.

7. Don't just sit there, speak up.

Recognize that silence can be a much more powerful negotiating tool than good arguments. Consider its uses, but in particular be aware of its use against you. Look at your notes, fiddle with your pen—anything, but let *them* break the silence.

8. Don't take no for an answer.

The correct strategy for Americans negotiating with Japanese or other foreign clients is a Japanese strategy: ask questions. When you think you understand, ask more questions. Carefully feel for pressure points. If an impasse is reached, don't pressure. Suggest a recess or another meeting. Large concessions by the Japanese side at the negotiation table are unlikely. They see negotiations as a ritual where harmony is foremost. In Japan, minds are changed behind the scenes.

9. One thing at a time.

Avoid making concessions on any issue until the group has fully discussed all issues. This is also good advice for bargaining with American clients. And do not measure progress by the number of issues that have been settled; in other countries, different signals may be much more important.

10. A deal is a deal.

Recognize differences in what an agreement means across cultures. A signed contract does not mean the same thing in Tokyo, Rio, or Riyadh as it means in New York.

11. I am what I am.

Flexibility is critical in cross-cultural negotiations. Americans must adapt to the circumstances of world economic interdependence. Our power at the international negotiation table will continue to erode as our trading partners develop industrially. We must change our negotiating style accordingly.

Training Implications

The American negotiating style is part of a larger problem—our entire approach to export trade. With the dramatic growth in international business activity during the last ten years, U.S. industry has slowly adjusted business approaches to foreign markets. Early on, U.S. companies sent their executives to live overseas and deal directly with foreign clients. The point of contact for the two cultures was often between an American sales representative and foreign client personnel. Thus, Americans had to operate in a new environment and had to promote communication and understanding not only between cultures but also between organizations—a demanding task. This strategy has proved unsuccessful.

In response to these difficulties and others (such as unfavorable tax laws) American corporations are increasingly hiring foreign nationals to represent their interests overseas. This moves the point of cross-cultural contact into the company where it can be more effectively managed. Consequently, the trend is for American executives (managers and technical experts) to take only short trips to other countries.

Such a strategy for marketing our products and services overseas neatly avoids the serious problem of training executives to live in other cultures, but we must now focus our attention on teaching executives how to negotiate with people from other countries.

Such training is not easy—for two reasons. First, knowledge and experience in another culture do not necessarily help in understanding still others. Various writers have tried to generalize about doing business in "similar" cultures, but their contributions are limited.[4] Second, executives' time has practical limitations. Often management or technical people must participate in sales negotiations in other countries on short notice. The focus is on commercial and technical issues, not on how to communicate effectively with foreigners.

Given these two constraints—the need for knowledge of several cultures, and various time limitations—what can be done to better prepare our representatives? Both short- and long-term actions can help American companies solve such problems.

Our lack of knowledge about other cultures is losing us business overseas. Ideally, a prerequisite for work in international operations would be participation in an experiential training program involving cross-cultural interactions in a low-risk environment. Feedback from foreign participants and videotaped sessions would aid in building awareness of one's own negotiation behavior and values, as well as those of foreigners.

If experiential training is not practical, videotape as a training medium is the next best thing. Most large companies with international clients have a few people with knowledge and experience in individual cultures who have learned to overcome the natural tendencies of the American negotiating style. The cost of sitting these people down in front of a videotape camera and an expert on cross-cultural communication to lead a discussion on important aspects of negotiation (language, nonverbal behavior, values, and decision processes), say, in Saudi Arabia, is minimal. Larger companies might develop a library of such training tapes for management and technical people embarking on short notice and short-term foreign assignments.

The long-run solutions to the cultural myopia of our business community are more challenging. If we are to take advantage of our technology, creativity, and other natural resources, we must invest in the education and training of our potential business leaders. This training must start early, for true understanding of another culture comes from total immersion in it. Ideally, training for U.S. multinational executives of the future would begin in high school.

During their freshman and sophomore years they would learn a foreign language (the language of one of our major trading partners). They would spend their junior year living with a family in a foreign country where the language they have studied is spoken, as part of the exchange programs now available. Students would continue their language training in college and again spend one year in a university in the country of focus. Finally, initial assignments in the multinational corporation would include a tour of duty in the foreign country. Through such a program, American executives of the future would gain an understanding of our foreign trading partners and their environment, a bicultural competence that would open the many doors that foreigners frequently shut in our faces.

Such a long-term plan sounds idealistic; however, the leaders of our large corporations are beginning to recognize our weaknesses in the world marketplace. These same executives must make the commitment to invest in high school and college foreign exchange programs and language training programs that look forward to the growth of international trade rather than back to a part of our own cultural heritage.

NOTES

1. Edward T. Hall. The silent language in overseas business. *Harvard Business Review*, May-June 1960, p. 87.

2. We're tongue-tied. *Newsweek*, July 30, 1979, p. 15.

3. Cultural assumptions underlying U.S. management concepts. In *Management in International Context*, ed. James L. Massie, Jan Luytjons, and

N. William Hazen. (New York: Harper & Row, 1972), p. 75.

4. Edward T. Hall and others suggested classifying cultures into two categories—high context and low context. Such a concept is useful, but does not hold for negotiation style. For more detail see Warren J. Keegan, *Multinational Marketing Management* (Englewood Cliffs, N.J.: Prentice-Hall, 1980), p. 86.

◆ ◆ ◆ ◆ ◆

AMERICAN VALUES AND ASSUMPTIONS

Gary Althen

As people grow, they learn certain values and assumptions from their parents and other relatives, their teachers, their books, newspapers, and television programs. "Values" are ideas about what is right and wrong, desirable and undesirable, normal and abnormal, proper and improper. In some cultures, for example, people are taught that men and women should inhabit separate social worlds, with some activities clearly in the men's domain and others clearly in the women's. In other cultures that value is not taught, or at least not widely. Men and women are considered to have more or less equal access to most roles in the society.

"Assumptions," as the term is used here, are the postulates, the unquestioned givens, about people, life, and "the way things are." (Scholars debate about the definition of such terms as "values," "assumptions," and others that appear here. But the information here is not for scholars. It is for foreign visitors who want some basic understanding of America.) People in some societies assume, for example, that education takes place most efficiently when respectful young people absorb all they can of what older, wiser

From Gary Althen, *American Ways: A Guide to Foreigners in the United States,* 1981. Yarmouth, Maine: Intercultural Press, Inc. Reprinted with permission.

people already know. The young people do not challenge or even discuss what they are taught. The assumption is that learners are seeking *wisdom,* which comes with age. Young and inexperienced people are not wise enough to know what is worth discussing.

People in other societies assume that education requires learners to question and challenge the older "expert" when the expert's ideas disagree with the learner's. The assumption is that learners are seeking *knowledge,* which a person can obtain regardless of age or social standing.

People who grow up in a particular culture share certain values and assumptions. That does not mean they all share exactly the same values to exactly the same extent; it does mean that most of them, most of the time, agree with each others' ideas about what is right and wrong, desirable and undesirable, and so on. They also mostly agree with each other's assumptions about human nature, social relationships, and so on.

Any list of values and assumptions is arbitrary. Depending on how one defines and categorizes things, one could make a three-item list of a country's major values and assumptions or a 30-item one. The list offered below has eight entries, each covering a set of closely related ideas.

Notice that these values and assumptions overlap with and support each other. In general, they agree with each other. They fit together. A culture can be viewed as a collection of values and assumptions that go together to shape the way a group of people perceive and relate to the world around them.

INDIVIDUALISM AND PRIVACY

The most important thing to understand about Americans is probably their devotion to "individualism." They have been trained since very early in their lives to consider themselves as separate individuals who are responsible for their own situations in life and their own destinies. They have not been trained to see themselves as members of a close-knit, tightly interdependent family, religious group, tribe, nation, or other collectivity.

You can see it in the way Americans treat their children. Even very young children are given opportunities to make their own choices and express their opinions. A parent will ask a one-year-old child what color balloon she wants, which candy bar she would prefer, or whether she wants to sit next to mommy or daddy. The child's preference will normally be accommodated.

Through this process, Americans come to see themselves as separate human beings who have their own opinions and who are responsible for their own decisions.

Indeed, American child-rearing manuals (such as Dr. Benjamin Spock's famous *Baby and Child Care*) state that the parents' objective in raising a child is to create a responsible, self-reliant individual who, by the age of 18 or so, is ready to move out of the parents' house and make his or her own way in life. Americans take this advice very seriously, so much so that a person beyond the age of about 20 who is still living at home with his or her parents may be thought to be "immature," "tied to the mother's apron strings,"

or otherwise unable to lead a normal, independent life.

Margaret Wohlenberg was the only American student among about 900 Malays enrolled at Indiana University's branch campus in Shah Alam, Malaysia, in 1986. She took Psychology 101, an introductory psychology course from the Indiana University curriculum, and earned a grade of A +. The other students' grades were lower. After the experience she reported:

> I do not think that Psych 101 is considered a very difficult course for the average freshman on the Bloomington campus (Indiana University's main location) but it is a great challenge to these (Malay) kids who have very little, if any, exposure to the concepts of Western psychology. . . . The American (while growing up) is surrounded, maybe even bombarded, by the propaganda of self-fulfillment and self-identity. Self-improvement and self-help—doing my own thing—seem at the core of American ideology.

But these are quite unfamiliar ideas to the Malay students, Ms. Wohlenberg says. The Malay students' upbringing emphasizes the importance of family relationships and individual subservience to the family and the community.

Americans are trained to think of themselves as separate individuals, and they assume everyone else in the world is, too. When they encounter a person from abroad who seems to them excessively concerned with the opinions of parents, with following traditions, or with fulfilling obligations to others, they assume that the person feels trapped or is weak, indecisive, or "overly dependent." They assume that all people must resent being in situations where they are not "free to make up their own minds." They assume, furthermore, that after living for a time in the United States, people will come to feel liberated from constraints arising outside themselves and will be grateful for the opportunity to "do their own thing" and "have it their own way."

It is this concept of themselves as individual decision-makers that blinds at least some Americans to the fact that they share a culture with each other. They have the idea, as mentioned above, that they have independently made up their own minds about the values and assumptions they hold. The notion that social factors outside themselves have made them "just like everyone else" in important ways offends their sense of dignity.

Americans, then, consider the ideal person to be an individualistic, self-reliant, independent person. They assume, incorrectly, that people from elsewhere share this value and this self-concept. In the degree to which they glorify "the individual" who stands alone and makes his or her own decisions, Americans are quite distinctive.

The individual that Americans idealize prefers an atmosphere of *freedom*, where neither the government nor any other external force or agency dictates what the individual does. For Americans, the idea of individual freedom has strong, positive connotations.

By contrast, people from many other cultures regard some of the behavior Americans legitimize by the label "individual freedom" to be self-centered and lacking in consideration for others. Mr. Wilson and his mother are good American individualists, living their own lives and interfering as little as possible with others. Mohammad Abdullah found their behavior almost immoral.

Foreigners who understand the degree to which Americans are imbued with the notion that the free, self-reliant individual is the ideal kind of human being will be able to understand many aspects of American behavior and thought that otherwise might not make sense. A very few of the many possible examples:

Americans see as heroes those individuals who stand out from the crowd by doing something first, longest, most often, or otherwise "best." Examples are aviators Charles Lindbergh and Amelia Earhart.

Americans admire people who overcame adverse circumstances (for example, poverty or a physical handicap) and "succeeded" in life. Black educator Booker T. Washington was one example; the blind and deaf author and lecturer Helen Keller was another.

Many Americans do not display the degree of respect for their parents that people in more traditional or family-oriented societies commonly display. They have the conception that it was a sort of historical or biological accident that put them in the hands of particular parents, that the parents fulfilled their responsibilities to the children while the children were young, and now that the children have reached "the age of independence" the close child-parent tie is loosened, if not broken.

It is not unusual for Americans who are beyond the age of about 22 and who are still living with their parents to pay their parents for room and board. Elderly parents living with their grown children can do likewise. Paying for room and board is a way of showing independence, self-reliance, and responsibility for oneself.

Certain phrases one commonly hears among Americans capture their devotion to individualism: "Do your own thing." "I did it my way." "You'll have to decide that for yourself." "You made your bed, now lie in it." "If you don't look out for yourself, no one else will." "Look out for number one."

Closely associated with the value they place on individualism is the importance Americans assign to *privacy*. Americans assume that people "need some time to themselves" or "some time alone" to think about things or recover their spent psychological energy. Americans have great difficulty understanding foreigners who always want to be with another person, who dislike being alone.

If the parents can afford it, each child will have his or her own bedroom. Having one's own bedroom, even as an infant, inculcates in a person the notion that she is entitled to a place of her own where she can be by herself and—notice—keep her possessions. She will have *her* clothes, her toys, her books, and so on. These things will be hers and no one else's.

Americans assume that people have their "private thoughts" that might never be shared with anyone. Doctors, lawyers, psychiatrists, and others have rules governing "confidentiality" that are intended to prevent information about their clients' personal situations from becoming known to others.

Americans' attitudes about privacy can be difficult for foreigners to understand. Americans' houses, yards, and even their offices can seem open and inviting, yet in the Americans' minds, there are boundaries that other people are simply not supposed to cross. When the boundaries are crossed, an American's body will visibly stiffen and his or her manner will become cool and aloof.

EQUALITY

Americans are also distinctive in the degree to which they believe in the ideal, as stated in their Declaration of Independence, that "all men are created equal." Although they sometimes violate the ideal in their daily lives, particularly in matters of interracial relationships, Americans have a deep faith that in some fundamental way all people (at least all American people) are of equal value, that no one is born superior to anyone else. "One man, one vote," they say, conveying the idea that any person's opinion is as valid and worthy of attention as any other person's opinion.

Americans are generally quite uncomfortable when someone treats them with obvious deference. They dislike being the subjects of open displays of respect—being bowed to, being deferred to, being treated as though they could do no wrong or make no unreasonable requests.

It is not just males who are created equal, in the American conception, but females too. While Americans often violate the idea in practice, they do generally assume that women are the equal of men, deserving of the same level of respect. Women, according to the viewpoint of the feminists who since the 1970s have been struggling to get what they consider a "fair shake" for females in the society, might be different from men, but are in no way inferior to them.

This is not to say that Americans make no distinctions among themselves as a result of such factors as sex, age, wealth, or social position. They do. But the distinctions are acknowledged in subtle ways. Tone of voice, order of speaking, choice of words, seating arrangements—such are the means by which Americans acknowledge status differences among themselves. People of higher status are more likely to speak first, louder, and longer. They sit at the head of the table, or in the most comfortable chair. They feel free to interrupt other speakers more than others feel free to interrupt them. The higher status person can put a hand on the shoulder of the lower status person; if there is touching between the people involved, the higher status person will touch first.

Foreigners who are accustomed to more obvious displays of respect (such as bowing, averting eyes from the face of the higher-status person, or using honorific titles) often overlook the ways in which Americans show respect for people of higher status. They think, incorrectly, that Americans are generally unaware of status differences and are disrespectful of other people. What is distinctive about the American outlook on the matter of equality are the underlying assumptions that no matter what his or her initial station in life, any individual has the potential to achieve high standing and everyone, no matter how unfortunate, deserves some basic level of respectful treatment.

INFORMALITY

Their notions of equality lead Americans to be quite *informal* in their general behavior and in their relationships with other people. Store clerks and waiters, for example, may introduce themselves by their first (given) names and treat customers in a casual, friendly manner. American clerks, like other Americans, have been trained to believe that they are as valuable as any other people, even if they happen to be engaged at a given time in an occupation that others might consider lowly. This informal behavior can outrage foreign visitors who hold high stations in countries where it is not assumed that "all men are created equal."

People from societies where general behavior is more formal than it is in America are struck by the informality of American speech, dress, and postures. Idiomatic speech (commonly called "slang") is heavily used on most occasions, with formal speech reserved for public events and fairly formal situations. People of almost any station in life can be seen in public wearing jeans, sandals, or other informal attire. People slouch down in chairs or lean on walls or furniture when they talk, rather than maintain an erect bearing.

A brochure advertising a highly-regarded liberal-arts college contains a photograph showing the college's president, dressed in shorts and an old T-shirt, jogging past one of the classroom buildings on his campus. Americans are likely to find the photograph appealing: "Here is a college president who's just like anyone else. He doesn't think he's too good for us."

The superficial *friendliness* for which Americans are so well known is related to their informal, egalitarian approach to other people. "Hi!" they will say to just about anyone. "Howya' doin?" (That is, "How are you doing?" or "How are you?") This behavior reflects less a special interest in the person addressed than a subconscious concern for showing that one is a "regular guy,"

part of a group of normal, pleasant people —like the college president.

More ideas about American notions of friendship will be discussed later.

THE FUTURE: CHANGE AND PROGRESS

Americans are generally less concerned about history and traditions than are people from older societies. "History doesn't matter," many of them will say. "It's the future that counts." They look ahead. They have the idea that what happens in the future is within their control, or at least subject to their influence. They believe that the mature, sensible person sets goals for the future and works systematically toward them. They believe that people, as individuals or working cooperatively together, can change most aspects of the physical and social environment if they decide to do so, make appropriate plans, and get to work. Changes will presumably produce improvements. New things are better than old ones.

The long-time slogans of two major American corporations capture the Americans' assumptions about the future and about change. A maker of electrical appliances ended its radio and television commercials with the slogan, "Progress is our most important product." A huge chemical company that manufactured, among many other things, various plastics and synthetic fabrics, had this slogan: "Better things for better living through chemistry."

Closely associated with their assumption that they can bring about desirable changes in the future is the Americans' assumption that their physical and social environments are subject to human domination or control. Early Americans cleared forests, drained swamps, and altered the course of rivers in order to "build" the country. Contemporary Americans have gone to the moon in part just to prove they could do so.

This fundamental American belief in progress and a better future contrasts sharply with the fatalistic (Americans are likely to use that term with a negative or critical connotation) attitude that characterizes people from many other cultures, notably Latin, Asian, and Arab, where there is a pronounced reverence for the past. In those cultures the future is considered to be in the hands of "fate," "God," or at least the few powerful people or families that dominate the society. The idea that they could somehow shape their own futures seems naive or even arrogant.

Americans are generally impatient with people they see as passively accepting conditions that are less than desirable. "Why don't they do something about it?" Americans will ask. Americans don't realize that a large portion of the world's population sees the world around them as something they cannot change, but rather as something to which they must submit, or at least something with which they must seek to live in harmony.

GOODNESS OF HUMANITY

The future cannot be better if people in general are not fundamentally good and improvable. Americans assume that human nature is basically good, not basically evil. Foreign visitors will see them doing many things that are based on the assumption that people are good and can make themselves better. Some examples:

Getting More Education or Training

Formal education is not just for young people, but for everyone. Educational institutions offer "extension classes," night classes, correspondence courses, and television courses so that people who have full-time jobs or who live far from a college or university have the opportunity to get more education. Many post-secondary students are adults who seek to "improve themselves" by learning more.

"Non-formal" educational opportunities in the form of workshops, seminars, or training programs are widely available. Through them people can learn about a huge array of topics, from being a better parent to investing money more wisely to behaving more assertively.

Rehabilitation

Except in extreme cases where it would clearly be futile, efforts are made to rehabilitate people who have lost some physical capacity as a result of injury or illness. A person who "learned to walk again" after a debilitating accident is widely admired.

Rehabilitation is not just for the physically infirm, but for those who have failed socially as well. Jails, prisons, and detention centers are intended as much to train inmates to be socially useful as they are to punish them. A widespread (but not universally-held) assumption is that people who violate the law do so more because of adverse environmental conditions such as poverty than because they themselves are evil individuals.

Belief in Democratic Government

We have already discussed some of the assumptions that underlie the American belief that a democratic form of government is best—assumptions about individualism, freedom, and equality. Another assumption is that people can make life better for themselves and others through the actions of governments they choose.

Volunteerism

It is not just through the actions of government or other formal bodies that life can be improved, but through the actions of citizen volunteers as well. Many foreign visitors are awed by the array of activities Americans support on a voluntary basis: parent-teacher organizations in elementary and secondary schools, community "service clubs" that raise money for worthy causes, organizations of families that play host to foreign students, "clean-up, paint-up, fix-up" campaigns to beautify communities, organizations working to preserve wilderness areas, and on and on.

Educational Campaigns

When Americans perceive a social problem, they are likely (often on a voluntary basis) to establish an "educational campaign" to "make the public aware" of the dangers of something and induce people to take preventative or corrective action. Thus there are campaigns concerning smoking, drugs, alcohol, child abuse, and many specific diseases.

Self-Improvement

Americans assume themselves to be improvable. We have already mentioned their participation in various educational and training programs. Mention should also be made of the array of "how-to" books Americans buy, and the number of group activities they join in order to make themselves "better." Through things they read or groups they join, Americans can stop smoking, stop using alcohol, lose weight, get into better physical condition, manage their time more effectively, manage their money more effectively, become better at their jobs, and improve themselves in countless other ways.

"Where there's a will, there's a way," the Americans say. People who want to make things better can do so if only they have a strong enough motivation.

TIME

For Americans, time is a resource that, like water or coal, can be used well or poorly. "Time is money," they say. "You only get so much time in this life; you'd best use it wisely." The future will not be better than the past or the present, as Americans are trained to see things, unless people use their time for constructive, future-oriented activities. Thus, Americans admire a "well-organized" person, one who has a written list of things to do and a schedule for doing them. The ideal person is punctual and arrives at the scheduled time for a meeting or event, and is considerate of other people's time rather than wasting people's time with conversation or other activity that has no visible, beneficial outcome.

The American attitude toward time is not necessarily shared by others—especially non-Europeans, who are more likely to conceive of time as something that is simply there around them, not something they can "use." One of the more difficult things many foreign businessmen and students must adjust to in the States is the notion that time must be saved whenever possible and used wisely every day.

In their efforts to use their time wisely, Americans are sometimes seen by foreign visitors as automatons, unhuman creatures who are so tied to their clocks and their schedules that they cannot participate in or enjoy the human interactions that are the truly important things in life. "They are like little machines running around," one foreign visitor said.

The premium Americans place on *efficiency is* closely related to their concepts of the future, change, and time. To do something efficiently is to do it in the way that is quickest and requires the smallest expenditure of resources. American businesses sometimes hire "efficiency experts" to review their operations and suggest ways in which they could accomplish more than they are currently accomplishing with the resources they are investing. Popular periodicals carry suggestions for more efficient ways to shop, cook, clean house, do errands, raise children, tend the yard, and on and on.

In this context, the "fast-food industry" can be seen as a clear example of an American cultural product. McDonald's, Kentucky Fried Chicken, Pizza Hut, and other fast-food establishments prosper in a country where many people want to minimize the amount of time they spend preparing and eating meals. The millions of Americans who take their meals at fast-food restaurants cannot have much interest in lingering over their food while conversing with friends, as millions of Europeans do. McDonald's restaurants have popped up all around the world, and they are viewed as symbols of American society and culture, bringing not just hamburgers but an emphasis on speed, efficiency, and shiny cleanliness. The typical American food, some observers argue, is fast food.

ACHIEVEMENT, ACTION, WORK, AND MATERIALISM

"He's a hard worker, " one American might say in praise of another, or "She gets the job done." These expressions convey the typical American's admiration for a person who approaches a task conscientiously and persistently, seeing it through to a successful conclusion. More than that, these expressions convey an admiration for *achievers*, people whose lives are centered around efforts to accomplish some physical, measurable thing. Social psychologists use the term "achievement motivation" to describe what appears to be the intention underlying Americans' behavior. "Affiliation" is another kind of motivation, shown by people whose main intent seems to be to establish and retain a set of relationships with other people. The achievement motivation predominates in America.

Foreign visitors commonly remark that Americans work harder than they expected them to. Perhaps these visitors have been excessively influenced by American movies and television programs, which are less likely to show people working than to show them driving around in fast cars or pursuing members of the opposite sex. While the so-called "Protestant work ethic" has lost some of its hold on some Americans, there is still a strong belief that the ideal person is a "hard worker." A hard worker is one who gets right to work on a task without delay, works efficiently, and then completes the task in a way that meets reasonably high standards of quality.

Hard workers are admired not just on the job, but in other aspects of life as well. Housewives, students, and people volunteering their services to charitable organizations can also be hard workers who make significant achievements.

More generally, Americans like *action*. They do indeed believe it is important to devote significant energy to their jobs or to other daily responsibilities. Beyond that, they tend to believe they should be *doing* something most of the time. They are usually not content, as people from many countries are, to sit for hours and talk with other people. They get restless and impatient. They believe they should be doing something, or at least making plans and arrangements for doing something later.

People without the American action orientation often see Americans as frenzied, always on the go, never satisfied, compulsively active. They sometimes evaluate Americans negatively for being unable to relax and enjoy life's pleasures. Even recreation, for Americans, is often a matter of acquiring lavish equipment, making elaborate plans, and then going somewhere to *do* something.

Americans tend to define people by the jobs they have. ("Who is he?" "He's the vice president in charge of personal loans at the bank.") Their family backgrounds, educational attainments, and other characteristics are considered less important in identifying people than the jobs they have.

There is usually a close relationship between the job a person has and the level of the person's income. Americans tend to measure a person's success in life by referring to the amount of money he has acquired. Being a bank vice president is quite respectable, but being a bank president is more so. The president gets a higher salary, so the president can buy more things—a bigger house and car, a boat, more neckties and shoes, and so on.

Americans are often criticized for being materialistic and too concerned with acquiring possessions. For Americans, though, this materialism is natural and proper. They have been taught that it is a good thing to achieve—to work hard, acquire more material badges of their success, and in the process assure a better future for themselves and their immediate families. And, like people from elsewhere, they do what they are taught.

DIRECTNESS AND ASSERTIVENESS

Americans, as has been said before, generally consider themselves to be frank, open, and direct in their dealings with other people. "Let's lay our cards on the table," they say, or "Let's stop playing games and get to the point." These and many other common phrases convey the American notion that people should explicitly state what they think and what they want from other people.

Americans tend to assume that conflicts or disagreements are best settled by means of forthright discussions among the people involved. If I dislike something you are doing, I should tell you about it directly so you will know, clearly and from me personally, how I feel about it. Bringing in other people to mediate a dispute is considered somewhat cowardly—the act of a person without enough courage to speak directly to someone.

The word "assertive" is the adjective Americans commonly use to describe the person who plainly and directly expresses feelings and requests. People who are inadequately assertive can take "assertiveness-training classes."

Americans will often speak openly and directly to others about things they dislike. They will try to do so in a manner they call "constructive," which the other person will not find offensive or unacceptable. If they do not speak openly about what is on their minds, they will often convey their reactions in nonverbal ways (without words, but through facial expressions, body positions, and gestures). Americans are not

taught, as people in many Asian countries are, that they should mask their emotional responses. Their words, the tone of their voices, or their facial expressions will usually reveal when they are feeling angry, unhappy, and confused, or happy and content. They do not think it improper to display these feelings, at least within limits. Many Asians feel embarrassed around Americans who are exhibiting a strong emotional response to something. On the other hand, Latins and Arabs are generally inclined to display their emotions more openly than Americans do, and to view Americans as unemotional and "cold."

But Americans are often less direct and open than they realize. There are, in fact, many restrictions on their willingness to discuss things openly. It is difficult to categorize those restrictions, and the restrictions are often not "logical" in the sense of being consistent with each other. Generally, though, Americans are reluctant to speak openly:

- when the topic is in an area they consider excessively personal, such as unpleasant body or mouth odors, sexual function, or personal inadequacies;

- when they want to say "no" to a request that has been made of them but do not want to offend or hurt the feelings of the person who made the request;

- when they are not well enough acquainted with the other person to be confident that direct discussion will be accepted in the constructive way that is intended;

- and, paradoxically, when they know the other person very well (it might be a spouse or close friend) and they do not wish to risk giving offense and creating negative feelings by talking about some delicate problem.

A Chinese student invited an American couple to his apartment to share a dinner he had prepared. They complimented him warmly about the quality of his meal. "Several Americans have told me they like my cooking," he replied, "but I cannot tell whether they are sincere or just being polite. Do you think they really like it?"

All of this is to say that even though Americans see themselves as properly assertive and even though they often behave in open and direct ways, they put limits on their openness. It is not unusual for them to try to avoid direct confrontations with other people when they are not confident that the confrontation with other people can be carried out in a constructive way that will result in an acceptable compromise.

Foreigners often find themselves in situations where they are unsure of or even unaware of what the Americans around them are thinking or feeling, and are unable to find out because the Americans will not tell them directly what they have in mind. Two examples:

Sometimes a person from another country will smell bad to Americans because the individual does not follow the same hygienic practices (daily bathing and use of deodorants) that Americans tend to think are necessary. But Americans will rarely tell a person (foreign or otherwise) that he has "body odor" because that topic is considered too sensitive.

A foreigner (or another American, for that matter) may ask a "favor" that an American considers inappropriate. She might ask to borrow a car, for example, or ask for help with an undertaking that will require more time than the American

thinks she has available. The American will want to decline the request, but will fear saying "no" directly.

Americans might feel especially reluctant to say "no" directly to a foreigner, for fear of making the person feel unwelcome or discriminated against. They will often try to convey the "no" indirectly, by saying such things as "it's not convenient now" or by repeatedly postponing an agreed-upon time for doing something.

Despite these limitations, Americans are generally more direct and open than people from many other countries. They will not try to mask their emotions, as Scandinavians tend to do. They are much less concerned with "face" (avoiding embarrassment to themselves or others) than most Asians are. To them, being "honest" is usually more important than preserving harmony in interpersonal relationships.

Americans use the words "pushy" or "aggressive" to describe a person who is excessively assertive in expressing opinions or making requests. The line between acceptable assertiveness and unacceptable aggressiveness is difficult to draw. Iranians and people from other countries where forceful arguing and negotiating are common forms of interaction risk being seen as aggressive or pushy when they treat Americans in the way they treat people at home.

This explanation of American values, ideas, assumptions, and behavior should help anyone involved in cross-cultural negotiations, but reveals a great deal to Americans themselves about why they are easily misunderstood abroad.

Section VI

Individual Differences

Chapter Twelve   *Dealing with Difficult People*

Chapter Thirteen   *Dealing with Stakeholders*

Chapter Twelve

DEALING WITH DIFFICULT PEOPLE

WHEN THE BOSS IS A BULLY

Hara Estroff Marano

They verbally abuse you and humiliate you in front of others. Maybe it's because power hovers in the air, but offices tend to bring out the bully in people. Here are some strategies for handling bad bosses.

If the schoolyard is the stomping ground of bully boys and bully girls, then the office is the playground of adult bullies. Perhaps because power is the chief perk in most companies, especially those with tight hierarchies, offices tend to bring out the bully in some people.

Everyone has a war story. There's the boss who calls at 2 a.m. from Paris—just because he's there. The boss who asks for your evaluation of a problem and then proceeds to denigrate you and your opinion in front of the whole staff as you seethe with what you hope is hidden rage. "It's a demonstration of power. It's demeaning," contends Harry Levinson, Ph.D., dean of organizational psychologists and head of the Levinson Institute in Waltham, Massachusetts.

"I haven't studied office bullying systematically," he says. In fact, no one has. Despite common perceptions of its prevalence, it's essentially vir-

gin turf for organizational psychology. Trouble is, organizational psychologists are often called in at the highest level of management; nowadays, most bullies are weeded out before they get to the top.

Nevertheless, says Levinson, 40 years of consulting have given him some idea of what they do and why. They over-control, micro-manage, and display contempt for others, usually by repeated verbal abuse and sheer exploitation. They constantly put others down with snide remarks or harsh, repetitive, and unfair criticism. They don't just differ with you, they differ with you contemptuously; they question your adequacy and your commitment. They humiliate you in front of others.

There are two kinds of bullies, observes organizational psychologist Laurence Stybel, Ph.D., a principal of Boston's Stybel Peabody Lincolnshire and Associates: "Successful ones and unsuccessful ones. The latter don't last long in organizations. The successful bullies create problems, but they are competent."

Often they are very bright workers. And therein lies the problem. They make a significant contribution to the company as workers. They get promoted because of their technical expertise. Then they wind up supervising others, and spew on support staff, on competitors, perhaps even on their own bosses.

Competent bullies are especially rampant in high-tech companies, engineering firms, and financial organizations—a stock fund manager doing an incredible job with investments, for example. "The typical successful bully thinks, 'They won't do anything to me—I'm the best they've got,'" Stybel says. But sooner or later, it's too costly to tolerate their behavior.

It's getting too costly much sooner in most companies. Stybel cites the example of a large New England hospital where the bully there was a brilliant physician who was the director of radiology for 11 years. The bullying was an issue over the years—in the exit interviews of departing technical staff.

Why did the hospital finally decide to do something? The administrator told Stybel: "We can't tolerate the high turnover anymore. It's too costly in the face of managed care."

Occasionally, bullies do get to the very top. Levinson points to Harold Geneen, the legendary head of ITT, and coach Vince Lombardi. And then there's the issue of *Fortune* magazine devoted every couple of years to America's "toughest" bosses. Take the female CEO who reportedly yelled at the executives of a division she felt was underperforming: "You're eunuchs! How can your wives stand you? You've got nothing between your legs!"

At least in large corporations, bullying is not as blatant as it once was. "The John Wayne image of a leader doesn't go over so well in the '90s," notes Pat Alexander of the Center for Creative Leadership in Greensboro, North Carolina. "It

affects the efficiency of the entire organization." Intimidation tends now to be more polished.

While it's no longer cool to throw around your authority, counterforces are leading to greater tolerance of negative behavior. Stybel points to a growing 'What can you do for me now?' attitude. "There's a new generation of CEOs who expect to be in place four years and move on. This fosters emotional distancing from employees and an excessive focus on transactions; it does not foster a positive relationship mode. Companies are growing increasingly performance-oriented; do they care how anyone feels about an executive's behavior?

"Where I have been retained, it's not because they don't like bullies," notes Stybel. "Only the underlying economics make it a dysfunctional behavior."

While bullies inhabit the middle ranks of large concerns, they are positively thriving at small companies. "There are lots of bad bosses out there," says Atlanta-based management consultant Neil Lewis, Ph.D. "In smaller companies, the quality of management is not as good as at large companies. They're not professional managers."

Stybel warns workers not to focus on where bullying comes from. "When observers see a boss behave as a bully, they attribute it to trait characteristics. That may not be the case. It's almost always a product of individual history and make-up—and the company atmosphere. But who cares? The most important thing is the behavior."

Bullies do a lot of damage in organizations. They make subordinates run scared. They put people in a protective mode, which interferes with the company's ability to generate innovation. They don't build in perpetuation of the organization, says Levinson. "It keeps you in a state of psychological emergency. And add to it the rage you feel towards the bully and a sense of self-rage for putting up with such behavior." These are hardly prime conditions for doing your best work—any work.

As with kids, bully bosses have blind spots. They don't see themselves accurately. They see themselves as better than others—which only acts to justify their bullying behavior, a feeling reinforced by promotion. Another big blind spot: sensitivity to others' feelings. Often, says Levinson, this arises in competitive settings, where "you learn to focus on your own behavior. It breeds a kind of psychological ignorance."

Stybel has developed a psychological karate chop to "unfreeze" executives' attitudes—a customized letter of probation. It essentially tells an executive that, due to changes in market conditions or some other external factor, his weaknesses now outweigh the strengths he has long displayed. "It spells out desired behavioral changes in a positive way—not 'people are complaining that you are a bully' but 'if you make these changes, you'll have a reputation as someone who is considerate.'" It gives honchos 90 days to shape up—or else.

It's never easy to make headway with an office bully, observers agree. The first step is to recognize when it's happening. Repetitive verbal abuse. Micromanagement. Exploitation. Any activity that repeatedly demeans you or is discourteous. "Whenever you're dissed, you're dealing with a bully," says Levinson. "Sometimes it's inadvertent. We all get caught up in that—once. You apologize and it's over. But bullies don't recognize their impoliteness and they don't apologize."

TACTICS FROM THE PROS

Here are tactics from seasoned organizational consultants:

- Confront the bully: "I'm sorry you feel you have to do that, but I will not put up with that kind of behavior. It has no place here." It can be startlingly effective. "Bullies lack boundaries on their own behavior. Some external controls may force them to back off," says Levinson. "A bully can't bully if you don't let yourself be bullied."

- Conduct the confrontation in private—behind closed doors far from the bully's office, or at lunch away from the office. The bully won't back down in front of an audience.

- Specify the behavior that's unworkable: "You can't just fire from the hip and demean me in front of my staff or others."

- Don't play armchair psychologist. Restrict the discussion to specific behaviors, not theories of motivation.

- Make your boss aware by showing him or her the consequences of his behavior on others. "I've been noticing how Jim seems so demoralized lately. I think one of the contributing factors may be last week's meeting when you ridiculed him for producing an inadequate sales report." Many executives have no information on how their leadership style impacts others, says Alexander. "Peers don't tell them—they are in competition. Why feed information that may make your competitor more effective?"

- Awareness is not enough; help your boss figure out what to do. Specify the behavioral change you want. "Your boss is likely to brush off criticism with, 'That's just my style,'" observes Marquand. "Furnish your boss with an example of desirable behavior—from his or her own repertoire of actions. Jump in with 'But I can recall a month ago when you were . . . lavish in your praise of that new assistant,' or whatever."

- Point out how the boss's behavior is seen by others. "You embarrass me when you publicly humiliate me in a meeting, but you also embarrass yourself. You're demonstrating your weakness." Comparing self-perceptions and the perceptions of others is often a "grabber," finds Alexander. "The fact of difference gets people's attention."

■ Try humor. If you point out to your boss that she or he is acting like a caricature, that may be enough to make them aware.

■ Recruit an ally or allies. Standing up for yourself can stop a bully by earning his/her respect. But it could also cost your job. The higher your boss is in the organization, says Lewis, the more you need allies. "It pays to check out with other workers whether the behavior you are experiencing is generalized or idiosyncatic," says Levinson. "If it's generalized, it's easier for two or three people to confront a boss than one alone."

■ If the company you work for is large enough to have one, talk to the human resources department. Unfortunately, says Levinson, companies often don't learn about bullying experiences until an exit interview. But the larger the company you work for, the more mechanisms there are in place to deal with bullies. Unfortunately, the corollary is that in a smaller organization, you may have little choice except to leave.

■ If you are important to the organization, you might accomplish your goal by going to your boss's boss. But that's always a chancy move; you'll have to live with your boss in the morning.

TAKING THE BULL OUT OF THE BULLY

Len Leritz

Negotiating would be easy if we didn't have to deal with problem people—if everyone were reasonable and saw things our way. The reality, however, is that much of the time we are dealing with problem people. Much of the time we are negotiating with people who look like adults on the outside but think like kids on the inside.

Enforcer Types: Bullies, Avoiders, Withdrawers, Highrollers, and Wad-Shooters

1. *Bullies*—Bullies will verbally or physically attack, use threats, demand, or otherwise attempt to intimidate and push others around. Their basic approach is to use force. You hear them say things like:

"That's a stupid thing to say!"
"Do you expect me to respond to that?"
"If you don't, I will . . .!"
"I want it, and I want it now!"
"Move it!"
"You can't do that!"
"You better shape up!"

We read newspaper accounts of Bully behavior every day, like those that appeared under these headlines:

- Bus Drivers Walk Out
- Tutu's Son Jailed for Insulting Police
- Nigerian Leader Overthrown
- TWA Airliner Highjacked
- Corporation Dismembered after Hostile Takeover

And we don't have to read the newspapers to find Bullies. They have a way of popping up in our own lives. A few years ago, one of my boys had a soccer coach who had a high need to win. He assumed that the best way to improve athletic performance was by berating kids. He also assumed that no one had a right to question his style of coaching. I did. . . he showed up at my front door, using the same bully behaviors. He wasn't able to hear me when I talked in a normal tone of voice. It required the filing of a formal complaint against him with the soccer board to get his attention.

On another occasion, I was representing a client in the dissolution of a business partnership. My client was tired of fighting and wanted to retire. His partner knew that and used it as a leverage to renege on an earlier agreement, and to demand an additional $100,000.

In Response: The first rule in negotiating with Bullies is that you have to get their attention. You have to draw a boundary of consequence. They need to believe that if they proceed on their present course, you will create negative consequences that will outweigh the benefits they hope to gain. You have to draw a boundary and you have to mean it.

Sometimes our tone of voice is enough of a boundary. When I say to you, "I will not tolerate your attempt to take advantage of me," and mean it, my words and voice tone might be enough to get your attention. Other times, tone of voice is not enough and we will need to use stronger measures to get their attention.

In the previous example, my client and I did a little research and found two important leverages. The first was that we found two prospective buyers for the business.

When we met with my client's partner again, we offered to buy him out based on the same formula he was requesting. At first, he refused. We then hauled out our second lever, which was that the three key employees who made the business work had agreed to quit if he refused a reasonable settlement, and that they intended to set up a competing business financed by my client. At that point, the partner committed to our earlier agreement. We had succeeded in getting his attention. This example also points out the importance of creating as many options as possible. *Your power is in direct proportion to how many options you have.*

2. *Avoiders*—Avoiders will physically avoid or procrastinate, hide out, or refuse to negotiate out of fear of losing. You'll hear them say things like:

"I'll do it tomorrow."

"We don't have anything to talk about."
"I don't have time."

"That's not my problem. "

In Response: In negotiating with Avoiders, you must identify what their fear is and find a way to make it safe enough for them to stop running away.

My friend Rob had an office manager he needed to fire. After procrastinating for four months, he brought the issue up over breakfast one morning, saying that he had several major contracts coming up and a new person would not be able to cover all the bases quickly enough.

I invited him to do two things. One was to make a detailed list of all his performance requirements, and to find out from an employment agency how hard it would be to find a replacement. The second was to estimate what his manager's mistakes had cost him over the last six months.

Rob then came up with another concern. His manager had formed friendships with several of his key clients. He was afraid that it might damage him if he fired her. My response: check it out.

Rob did all three assignments and had a new person in place functioning at 30 percent better productivity within three weeks. So much for our fears.

3. *Withdrawers*—Withdrawers will emotionally withdraw, get confused, go dumb and numb, or become paralyzed with fear. You'll hear them say things like:

"I don't understand."
"That doesn't make sense."
"I don't know."

In Response: The appropriate response toward someone who is withdrawing is much the same as with someone who is avoiding. Your task is to make it safe enough so the person does not have to withdraw or become confused. You need to ask yourself what it is that you might be doing that is contributing to the other person's fear.

You may be closing the person down by your tone of voice, your persistent questions, your position in the organization, your threats, or your silence.

Some possible verbal responses might be:

"What is it that is confusing you?"
"What don't you know?"
"What do you need to be clearer about this?"

4. *High Rollers*—High Rollers will attempt to shock and intimidate their opposition by making extreme demands.

"You have until five o'clock to comply."
"I want $50,000 for my car."
"I want it all done by noon."

In Response: When responding to High Rollers, insist on fair principles or invite them to explain how they arrived at their position. Both of these strategies are explained in the next section of this chapter.

"Can you tell me your criteria for that price?"

"I want to respond to your request, but I will need to do it in a manner that is also reasonable for me."

5. *Wad-Shooters*—Wad-Shooters assume an all-or-nothing, take-it-or-leave-it stance.

"That's my bottom line."

"If you don't want it, forget it."

"Either you agree to all five points or I'm leaving now."

"Take it or leave it."

In Response: Your possible responses are to ignore their statements, take a break, use silence, or insist on fair principles. All of these are described below.

What to Do With Them

Enforcer behaviors tend to be uncomplicated and obvious. Consequently, certain responses tend to work effectively with most Enforcer behaviors. As we move into describing the upper or more sophisticated levels of thinking, we'll see that more individualized responses are needed.

The above examples of responses were brief. The following is a more developed list of useful responses for countering the various types of Enforcer behavior just described. These strategies will be carried out most effectively if you are operating from the Generative style of thinking.

1. Get their attention.

The first step in dealing with Enforcers is to get their attention. Until you get their attention, you are wasting your time. Nothing constructive will happen until you do.

When you recall the limited emotional capacities enforcers have for empathy, you'll understand why it is essential to first get their attention. At this stage, you are not a flesh and blood person to them. You are simply an object to be eliminated, beaten, or avoided. Enforcers, being egocentric, are prisoners within their own bodies. Who you are and what you need does not exist for them.

Enforcers have no capacity to understand the effects of their behavior on you. To be passive or aggressive with them is nonproductive. To respond to them with aggression will scare them more and further constrict their ability to think. They will become more aggressive or more withdrawn. To respond passively will not get the Avoider's attention and will encourage Enforcers to push on, since aggression appears to be working. To turn the other cheek to an Enforcer is suicidal.

Instead, you need to assertively get their attention. You need to shock them out of their self-centered stance and let them know that you mean business—that you intend to be taken seriously. You need to make them feel your presence.

You will get their attention by drawing a boundary. The intention in drawing a boundary is not to punish the other person. The purpose is simply to let them know what you will and will not tolerate. The purpose is to create a negative consequence that will outweigh whatever benefit they are deriving from their current behavior.

How you draw your boundary will differ in each situation. You need to ask yourself what it is that will get the other person's attention—what is important to them. You may do it by physical action, by shouting at them, by walking out, by filing for divorce, by initiating legal litigation, or by telling them in a quiet and firm voice what you will and won't accept.

The key to drawing a boundary is that you have to mean it. If you don't mean it, you're wasting your energy. The other person almost always knows whether you are serious in backing up your boundary. When you mean it, they know it. No one crosses your boundary when you mean it.

Here is an example of what I call the "Skillet Approach" to dealing with Enforcers. I once had a client who had been physically abused by her husband for years. On her part, she whined and nagged at him. When he couldn't stand it any longer, he'd let her have it. She had threatened to leave him for years, but he knew she didn't mean it.

One night she finally decided to mean it. He had pushed her around earlier in the evening. She waited until he went to sleep and then went to the kitchen and got her biggest cast-iron skillet. She woke him up while holding the skillet over his head. "If you ever hit me again, I'll kill you in your sleep," she told him.

This time she meant it and he believed her. Though he had trouble sleeping for a while, the abusive behavior stopped. The woman had gotten her husband's attention by creating a consequence (the skillet), and she meant it. She said it in a quiet, firm voice, not a whining nag.

Ask yourself what "skillet" you need to use—and mean it when you use it. When you don't mean it, you are reinforcing the behavior you don't want. If you don't mean it, don't draw the boundary. And remember, if you don't draw the boundary, nothing is likely to change.

2. Explicitly identify their behavior.

The second step after getting the other person's attention is to explicitly identify the behavior and invite him to do something more constructive. Explicitly identifying his behavior will help him become conscious of what he is doing and will often take the power out of it. This is especially true if others are involved and the Enforcer feels embarrassed. Suggesting other options at this point will help him save face and will keep the negotiations moving. For example:

> "Your repeated attacks are not getting us any closer to an agreement. I'd like to suggest that we each try to explain what we need, then work together to brainstorm some ways that we might both get what we need."

3. Help them feel safer.

Help Enforcers feel safer so their capacities expand and they can move into more cooperative behaviors. You can help them feel safer by not becoming defensive and by looking behind their behavior to their underlying needs and interests.

"Would you be more comfortable if we met in your office?"

Respond to the needs of their "inner child," not to their external behavior.

"I can see how you feel frustrated."

Actively listen to them so they feel understood.

"What I hear you saying is . . ."

Help them create safe conditions by asking them what they need.

"What do you need to be willing to stay here and talk this out?"

Meet on their territory. Be aware of their constituency and to whom they need to look good.

"I want you to be able to go back to your department and feel proud of what we accomplished."

Above all, do not attack in return. Remember, the more aggressive the bully, the more frightened the internal kid. Helping bullies feel safer is usually the last thing you think of doing. And that's precisely what you need to do to get them on your level.

4. Insist on fair principles.

Bullies, High Rollers, and Wad-Shooters will attempt to force you to accept unreasonable agreements. When this happens, refuse to negotiate except on the basis of fair principles. Refuse to be pressured. Instead, insist on fair criteria for both the process and the final settlement. In getting their attention, firmly make it clear that you will continue negotiating only on this basis.

> I refuse to be pressured into an agreement. I am only willing to continue the negotiation if we can agree to some fair procedures that we will both honor."

> "Let's check with some other suppliers and see what they are charging."

> "The bluebook price for my car is $400 higher. I want to trade cars, but I am not willing to accept an unfair price for my car."

5. Invite them to explain.

When the other person takes extreme stands and makes extreme demands, ask them to explain how they arrived at their position. Point out that you need to better understand their underlying needs. This strategy throws the ball back to them to justify themselves and allows them to be heard. Demands that cannot reasonably be justified lose their power.

> "In order to understand your demands, I need to hear more from you about how you arrived at those points."

> "Your price is a little higher than I expected. I want to pay you fairly for your work. Explain to me what you will need to do to complete the job."

6. Use silence.

Silence can be one of your most powerful strategies. When the other person is being aggressive or unreasonable, don't respond verbally. Just sit there and look at them calmly. Silence gives them nothing to push against. Calm silence communicates power. The other person will feel uncomfortable with the power of your silence and will probably begin to fill it in—often by backtracking and becoming more reasonable. You have nothing to lose by letting them do the talking at this point.

A variation of using silence is to walk away. "I'm willing to talk about this whenever you are willing to stop attacking me. Until then, we have nothing to talk about."

7. Sidestep/Ignore.

Sidestepping or ignoring can be an effective response to personal attacks, extreme demands, and take-it-or-leave-it challenges. Instead of responding directly, act as if you didn't hear them. Change the topic and/or refocus the discussion on the underlying problem or conflict at hand.

Corporate Attorney: "I can't believe they pay you a professional salary."

Opposing Attorney: "I think we still have four issues we have not settled. Let's look at them one at a time."

Film Supplier: "The price is $10,000 per segment. Take it or leave it."

Production Manager: "Your tone of voice sounds angry. Do you feel as if we have not been fair to you in the past?"

or "How many segments did you say you had?"

or "What do you think would be fair criteria for deciding what the price should be?"

8. Don't become defensive or invite criticism.

Becoming defensive and justifying your position or needs encourages the other party to step up their attack. If you become defensive, they know that they have you on the run. Invite their criticism and refocus it as an attack on the problem needing to be solved. Invite them to explain how their comments will help solve the problem or conflict.

> **Magazine Editor:** If you were committed to this magazine, you would have been here last week.
> **Art Director:** (defensive reply) I couldn't help it. I was burned out and needed the time off.
> (Non-defensive reply) I know you are under a lot of pressure and last week was frustrating. What do you think we need to do so we don't get caught in that kind of last-minute bind in the future?

9. Refuse to be punished.

Anyone has a right to be angry from time to time, but no one has the right to punish you. You do not deserve to be punished. You will know you are being punished when:

> The other person keeps repeating their attack.

> The other person vents their anger but refuses to tell you what they want from you behaviorally in response.

Refuse to be punished. Draw a boundary by asking the other person what they want from you. If their response is "I don't know," inform them that you are willing to continue the discussion when they do know. In the meantime, you're not willing to be punished.

10. Ask questions.

Making statements in which you take a stand will make the other person defensive. Instead, ask questions. Asking questions doesn't give them an object to attack and it invites them to justify their position or to vent their feelings. Asking questions gives you more information about the other party.

When asking your questions, ask "what" questions rather than "why" questions, "What" questions invite factual responses. "Why" questions are usually sneaky judgments that make the other party defensive. Listen to whether you want to make the other person feel guilty or whether you really want information. "What" questions will keep the negotiation moving. "Why" questions will tend to lead you to battle positions.

(Attacking) Why did you think you could do that?

(Information-seeking) What was your motivation for doing that?

(Attacking) Why did you do that?

(Information-seeking) What are the assumptions behind your actions?

11. Point out consequences.

When the other person refuses to agree to a reasonable settlement, point out the consequences for them if you fail to reach an agreement. Try to present it as a statement of "inevitable consequences" rather than as threat.

"The reality is, if our company shows a loss again in the fourth quarter due to the strike, we will have no choice but to lay off five hundred union workers."

Summary

In this chapter we have seen some common Enforcer behavior patterns and a number of options for responding to them. Keep in mind the importance of getting the Enforcer's attention before anything else contructive is likely to happen. And remember, the bigger the bully, the more frightened the internal kid. Don't let yourself be bullied. If they were really all that strong, they would be operating from a posture of quiet strength rather than trying to push you around.

HOW TO NEGOTIATE WITH REALLY TOUGH GUYS

An Interview with Bill Richardson

When the US. needs to negotiate with hostile governments for the release of political prisoners, the task often falls to Bill Richardson, Secretary of Energy in the Clinton administration who served seven terms as Democratic Congressman from New Mexico. The former pro-baseball prospect has played hardball with the likes of Saddam Hussein, Fidel Castro, and General Sani Abacha of Nigeria. In most cases, he walked away a winner: Richardson engineered the return of two American defense contractors who wandered across the Iraq-Kuwait border, prevailed upon the North Korean government to release a captured US. helicopter pilot and turn over the body of his co-pilot, and persuaded Castro to free three political prisoners. He also held a critical meeting with Raoul Cedras of Haiti to try to smooth Jean-Bertrand Aristide's return to power. Richardson spoke with FORTUNE'S Justin Martin about the art of negotiating.

What does it take to be a good negotiator?

You have to be a good listener. You have to respect the other side's point of view. You have

From *Fortune Magazine*, (interview by Justin Martin) May 27, 1996. Reprinted with permission.

to know what makes your adversary tick. Certainly you want to have a goal. You want to come out of a meeting with something, even if it's only a second meeting. And basically you have to use every single negotiating technique you know—bluster, reverence, humor.

How much leverage do you have when you're negotiating to release a hostage?

I can't really offer the other side any concessions. I have to be clear at the outset that we're not going to resolve differences between our countries. Just building in the minds of some of these dictators that they'll have somebody to talk to that they can trust is helpful. I let these governments, especially unfriendly ones, know I can pass messages. They know I'm going to end up talking to the White House. There's now the perception that the United States is the only superpower out there. Any entity associated with the U.S. government automatically has a leg up.

How do you prepare for a negotiation?

I talk to people who know the guy I'll be negotiating with. I talk to scholars, State Department experts, journalists. Before meeting with Saddam Hussein, I relied a lot on Iraq's ambassador to the U.N. He told me to be very honest with

Saddam—not to pull any punches. With Castro, I learned that he was always hungry for information about America. Sure enough, he was fascinated by Steve Forbes, fascinated with the Congressional budget impasse. He fancies himself an expert on U.S. politics. With Cedras of Haiti, I learned that he played good cop and that a top general, Philippe Biamby, played bad cop. So I was prepared. During our meeting, Biamby leaped up on the table and started screaming, "I don't like the U.S. government to call me a thug . . . Je ne *suis pas un thug*." I remember turning to Cedras as Biamby was doing this and saying, "I don't think he likes me very much." Cedras laughed and laughed. He said, "All right, Biamby, sit down."

What else can you do if negotiations get dicey?

Dictators often try to take advantage of you at the outset. They try to catch you off guard.

At the beginning of my meeting with Saddam Hussein, I crossed my legs and the soles of my feet were visible. He got up and left the room. I asked the interpreter, "What did I do?" He said, "The President was insulted that you crossed your legs. To an Arab that's a nasty insult, and you should apologize." I asked, "Is he coming back?" The interpreter said, "Yeah, he'll come back." When he did, I made the decision not to apologize. I wasn't going to grovel, say, "Hey, I'm real sorry I crossed my legs." I planted my feet and said, "Mr. President, let me resume." And I think he respected that, because the discussions got better. You try to show that you're a humble person, but at the same time you can't back down. You can't show weakness. You keep coming at them.

What other techniques do you use?

I try to appeal to the leader's advisers, the ones I've talked to in advance, to cut a deal. I did that

in Cuba. I said to Castro, "Look, I just talked to your assistant here, and I thought we had an agreement." I turned to Carlos Lage, a vice president, and said. "Come on, help me out, will you?" Finally he did. And so we kept the conversation alive.

A lot of these leaders are isolated. They're told only what they want to hear. So you bring them a dose of reality. If they think you're honest, sometimes they'll respond to that. With Castro, it was nearing midnight, and I said, "I came here to negotiate an agreement. I'm going to have to go back to the United States empty-handed. I'm going to have to say to the press when I leave that I got nothing. Is that the message you want?" I started making inroads after that.

When you finish a negotiation, can you tell right away whether you achieved your objectives?

You always know by the end, when you get either a pleasant or a perfunctory goodbye. With Saddam there was a grudging respect. There was definitely a rapport with Castro over baseball and Latin culture. I spoke with him in Spanish, and he gave me five cigars; he said they were the best —Cohiba.

You wound up smoking a cigar with Castro?

No, he doesn't smoke anymore.

Have you ever walked out of a negotiation?

Yes, in Nigeria four months ago. My objective was to secure the release of Moshood Abiola, who was imprisoned after he won the 1993 election. But General Abacha was taking such a hard line that I didn't even get to visit Abiola. Finally, I said, "Mr. President, I'm leaving the country. Let me know if you change your mind." You want to keep the channels open. They've sent messages, and I've coordinated with the State Department. I think eventually Abiola will be released.

Who are the toughest people you've ever negotiated with?

The North Koreans. They're the most relentless, the most dogmatic. They can't make any deci-sions on the spot. They always have to check with their superiors, but you don't know who the superiors are. Saddam Hussein is tough too. He starts out with a very menacing image. It sets you back a bit. I remember looking at my hands, and I was sweating. I was conscious that he knew what his reputation was. And he knew that I knew his reputation.

Chapter Thirteen

DEALING WITH STAKHOLDERS

STAKEHOLDER NEGOTIATIONS: BUILDING BRIDGES WITH CORPORATE CONSTITUENTS

Ram Charan and R. Edward Freeman

In addition to negotiating in the marketplace to improve economic performance, senior business executives must now increasingly negotiate with a growing number of external groups. These groups, conceptualized as "stakeholders," can include government agencies, environmentalists, consumer advocates, and other constituencies. They must be reckoned with because they can often influence an entire market or industry, and because failure to negotiate adequately with them might result in drastic changes in a company's objectives—or even its destiny.

Research at the Wharton Applied Research Center suggests that in all major businesses, senior executives must develop strategies for dealing with these external stakeholders. And to deal effectively with stakeholders, managers must learn how to negotiate with them.

The main difference between negotiations with stakeholders and other kinds of negotiations is that stakeholder negotiation is rarely a one-shot case. Consumer groups, state legislators, agency managers, competitors, shareholder groups, and others are not going to disappear at the end of

the negotiations, never to be heard from again. Some of the personalities in the groups might change, but the fundamental interests and motivations of these stakeholders are long-term and must be considered on that basis. Thus negotiating with stakeholders is fundamentally a matter of building cooperative bridges among the interested parties, and establishing on-going relationships that will enable executives to better manage the external environment while taking social responsibility.

Examples of Stakeholder Negotiations

During the controversy over selling infant formula in third world countries that erupted in the late 1970s, the infant formula industry was accused by critics of selling a product (using "hard sell" tactics) that harmed—even killed—babies. One U.S. company's response was to send executives out to listen to the critics, to formulate proposals based on what they heard as well as the company's objectives, and to establish effective liaisons between the company and its critics. In short, their response was to negotiate with their stakeholders.

The process was complicated and time-consuming because the company also had to negotiate with competitors and an industry association, all of whom maintained different positions in the controversy. By negotiating directly and changing its marketing practices, the company was able to differentiate itself from the industry, which continued to face hostile criticism.

Another case in point involved an international consumer goods company that began to think systematically about its stakeholders and to realize that the government plays as critical a role in determining the company's future as the consumers of its products. The company also realized that more than 90 percent of its available resources were spent on trying to influence the consumer. As a result, it instituted an ongoing process of negotiation with the government as a key stakeholder on a wide variety of issues. That process is relatively inexpensive, but extremely important to the company's survival.

In the 1950s, managers recognized the need to develop generalized negotiating skills, but stakeholders were fewer and usually less influential than they are today. The United States clearly dominated the world economic scene. Also, strong coalitions often developed among business and government and/or interest groups such as labor. Thus few executives felt the need to negotiate directly with stakeholders. In this environment, it was possible to delegate the management time needed to negotiate with stakeholders through a specialized department, such as industrial relations. Lower-level line personnel, such as foremen, were trained and encouraged to implement negotiated arrangements.

But the world has changed. The United States belongs to a global market that is challenging its dominance. In addition, specialized elements of society are asking a variety of hard questions about the goals and means of social institutions, including business. These groups are actively participating, or seeking to participate, in the *how* of decision-making. They question the legitimacy of power exercised by business that would exclude the participation of relevant stakeholders.

Today's manager has to learn not only WHAT the right decision is, but also the process of HOW it is to be decided. The HOW impacts on the WHAT and involves the participation of stakeholders and, therefore, the negotiating process.

The Framework for Negotiating

The central elements of our negotiating framework include:

- Doing your homework.
- Structuring the situation.
- Negotiating mutually beneficial outcomes.
- Communicating with your stakeholders.
- Managing the dynamics of the negotiation process by using personal, individual skills.
- Understanding the principles of Conflict Resolution.

Implicit in this framework is the realization that the need for negotiations with stakeholders doesn't appear suddenly. Rather, negotiating is fundamental to the philosophy of designing productive strategies for managing the external environment. Early warning signals usually indicate which stakeholders will be willing to negotiate on key strategic issues. Therefore, as we formulate our strategies, we must be able to anticipate who will be involved in their outcomes, even though at the outset an active group or individual might not have emerged.

The Elements

1. Do your homework.

Thorough preparation is necessary in any negotiation, but is especially important in stakeholder negotiations because managers simply don't have the same span of control with stakeholders as they have in internal situations. The advance preparations should be directed to three critical questions:

◆   ◆   ◆   ◆   ◆

■ What are your objectives? Crystallizing your own objectives is the most important element in preparing for stakeholder negotiations; otherwise you'll have to rely on luck and intuition. Determine early which points are negotiable and which are not. Managers tend to remain open about what their objectives really are, or they define them in terms of "motherhood and apple pie," thus permitting any outcome to be in keeping with their goals. Failing to zero in on concrete objectives because you believe the situation "will evolve" is a mistake; the situation can quickly "evolve" right out of control.

Objectives must be defined in terms of economic and political measures, and they must be developed in sequence. It is helpful to check yourself out on these points:

1. What is the best we can get out of these negotiations?

2. What is the worst?

3. What is the range of acceptable compromise, given the demands of our own organization?

■ What is the total situation? To assess it, you must distill the objectives of each stakeholder group. Try to determine the basic motives behind these objectives. Beware of basing your assessment of stakeholder behavior solely on what you perceive as the motivation of one or two key leaders of the stakeholder group. If these leaders do not represent the fundamental purposes of the group, your strategy will be off target. Obviously, all this analysis should be completed before the negotiations begin. It helps to have answers to the following questions:

1. Who are the key stakeholders involved in this issue?

2. Why are they involved and what are their objectives?

3. What is the relative power of each stakeholder? Vis-á-vis us? Vis-á-vis the other stakeholders?

4. Which are susceptible to influence from other stakeholders?

5. How can you stimulate stakeholder A to influence stakeholder B?

■ What is the range of overlap between our objectives and the stakeholders' objectives? This is the toughest assignment, and it is critical. Not only must you understand both your objectives and theirs, but you must also determine the range of response acceptable to each stakeholder group. Outside of that range, their unanticipated (and probably unpredictable) responses can quickly change the course of the negotiations.

For this reason, try to develop in advance a range within which your objectives and the stakeholders' objectives merge or overlap. Chances are that these goals do not always conflict. Certain precautions must be taken, however. Avoid being too comprehensive and too detailed; otherwise you can make it too difficult to find alternatives leading to a solution or resolution. The skill required here is the ability to identify those stakeholders who are in fact crucial to solving the problem. Each stakeholder probably has a dominant coalition within the group. It is up to the corporate manager to identify this decision-making unit and to analyze how individual egos, motives, and related factors bear upon the tactics of the negotiations.

The controversy in the late 1970s over the Firestone 500 radial tire provides a negative example. When problems with the product were first indicated, Firestone's response was to try to thwart investigation by the Traffic Safety Administration. Instead of negotiating, Firestone resorted to legal tactics, which backfired. As reported by *Fortune:* "People who had been unaware of the radial tire crisis learned about the court's action and began asking what the company had to hide." The company thus misread the objectives of customers and underestimated the range of their concern. Firestone also miscalculated in its dealings with government agencies, and the overall consequences of the company management's failure to deal adequately with stakeholders have been costly.

2. Structure the situation.

Since negotiations with stakeholders normally involve more than one contact or meeting, the manager must determine the timing and scope of the negotiations. What kind of cycles is the process likely to go through? Can the situation be structured in terms of who is present at the negotiation table? How should contacts between the organizations be sequenced? Remember that it is not unusual for negotiations to take place without the correct parties present; you might end up dealing with someone who lacks real authority to speak for his or her group, or who might not even be able to report back properly to other stakeholders. These details have to be carefully analyzed ahead of time.

If there is to be a formal meeting (not all negotiations require it), where should it take place? Home turf? Opponent's turf? Neutral ground? Each location has advantages and disadvantages.

Consider the agenda. Make certain you know in advance what issues are to be discussed. How is it to be decided whether the agenda will be formal or informal? Remember that there's no need to set an agenda of 100 items if there are only two or three key issues.

Time is also an important element. If a deadline is involved, it puts added pressure on the participants in the negotiations. You must decide in advance how the presence or absence of a deadline will affect the resolution of the tough issues.

How do you create a climate for positive cooperation? Do you take the most difficult issue first and perhaps run the risk of fragmentation? Or do you start with lesser issues on which there is some chance of cooperation that will help create a more favorable climate for the tough issues? More important, how do all of these structural elements fit together to create a cooperative win-win situation?

The plight of utilities in filing for basic rate increases illustrates the importance of structuring negotiations properly. The usual rate-setting method is to negotiate only when a person or group objects to the rate proposal. Such negotiations are normally quite formal and usually lead to hearings at which the state public utilities commission decides the issues.

The commission's decision might well be based on such factors as who represents the utility, who represents the stakeholders, the kind of day a commissioner is having, or even how tired the parties are.

Utilities would do well to negotiate with their stakeholders before a rate case is ever filed. One consumer-group leader believes that much can be accomplished by prior consultation: "When we get to the hearing room," he said, "we are adversaries. By negotiating ahead of time, you may find that would-be interveners won't even come to the hearing."

3. Negotiate mutually beneficial outcomes.

The most critical factor in successfully negotiating with stakeholders is to build a bridge among all the parties. The bridge need not be built in a day. It might be necessary to establish mutual trust through an ongoing relationship or series of negotiations. This means building in sequence —first one stakeholder, then another, and so on.

Bridge-building is most difficult at the start of the negotiations. If feelings are hostile, the job will be even more difficult. In the spirit of negotiating as a cooperative venture, the objective is not to outsmart the opponent, but to have both parties gain something that each didn't have before. This approach requires creativity and a conscious search for win-win positions. It requires not only that you know what you have and what you can get, but also that you know what the stakeholder has and can get. Above all, it requires looking at a broad picture rather than simply trying to outsmart each other. The durability of short-term, narrowly focused negotiations is dubious, and an unbalanced outcome might turn out to be self-destructive. The "best deal" might not be the best for either party in terms of long-run interests. Adversity has a way of exciting the underdog. Even if you "win" a particular point, if the other party feels injured, the "victory" will come back to haunt you. Utilities sometimes win rate increases in court only to see the power base of their opponents grow.

Negotiating cooperatively is an approach that is gaining attention nationwide; it has generated the establishment of "joint panels," which provide a vehicle for industry leaders and consumer advocates to negotiate on issues of mutual interest. One joint panel established by a local telephone company and a consumer group discussed issues arising from customer complaints about rate structure changes. The parties understood each other better and reached agreements more easily than if they had confronted each other in a hearing room.

4. Communicate with stakeholders.

Two aspects of communication must be considered: the content of the message, and the channel of communication.

On the question of content, it's important to see whether you can influence the perceptions of stakeholders. But suppose a stakeholder does not know enough about his own goals, or the consequences of his actions? What kind of message can you communicate regarding what his aspirations should be? Can this be accomplished in a nonthreatening and nonmanipulative manner?

As for how the message is sent, the choice must be made carefully. Do you write a letter, or make a phone call? Do you set up a meeting and prepare special memoranda and reports? Or do you try to communicate through a third party? Inside contacts and the media are other possibilities.

In his handling of the Cuban missile crisis, President John F. Kennedy's incisive ability to communicate illustrated the benefits of effective communications. Kennedy used both formal diplomatic channels and informal channels (such as sending his brother Robert to call on a Soviet official with whom he was friendly) to communicate with Khrushchev. He also used the media to convey the fact that he had good military intelligence on the missile activity in Cuba. The Russians also used various channels of communications, ultimately using their KGB agent in Washington, who turned to his contacts in the U.S. media.

5. Manage the dynamics of the negotiation process by using personal skills.

The critical personal skill for success in stakeholder negotiations is the ability to listen. This skill must be developed, and there are a number of techniques, such as starting your conversation by articulating the other person's position (to his satisfaction) before you reveal your own ideas. Listen for content, and try to pick up patterns of prejudice. The aim is to grasp your stakeholder's frame of reference. Everyone has a frame of reference; stakeholder behavior is rarely irrational, but is often misunderstood.

A story told about baseball star Pete Rose spotlights the vital frame-of-reference factor. During an argument with an umpire, Rose brought the exchange to a climax by calling him "the second best umpire I've ever seen." The umpire, who was about to toss Rose out of the game, cheered up at this point and asked, "Who's the best?" Rose replied, "All the others!"

The business community is finally showing signs that it is becoming aware of the need for developing the individual skills necessary for direct involvement with stockholders. The Business Roundtable is an organization of major-company CEOs, each of whom is directly involved in negotiations on issues affecting the business community. The Roundtable members have generally concentrated on negotiating with government agencies, Congress, and the White House on legislation, regulations, and other issues of national policy. A relationship is slowly being built that, it is hoped, will spread toward cooperative relationships with other stakeholders. It is time to realize that the fundamental guidelines by which business operates must emerge through stakeholder negotiations. As professor George Lodge has argued (in *The New American Ideology*), no one can dictate ideology any longer.

6. Understand the principles of Conflict Resolution.

As mentioned, managers must analyze in advance the range of objectives sought by both an organization and its stakeholders. Here are some other important principles:

- Negotiating with stakeholders is not a zero-sum game. Both shares of the pie can increase as a result of a cooperative approach to the issues. Win-win solutions are possible. Some companies have approached the problem of corporate social responsibility in this light. For example, one car manufacturer offered to plant a tree for every test drive by potential customers, as a gesture toward improving the environment.

- Power flows toward the vacuum. The downfall of the supersonic transport (SST)

in the United States illustrates this point. A single individual operating from his home in Cambridge had little to lose in trying to organize a coalition to oppose construction of the SST. This person succeeded in organizing the Coalition Against the Sonic Boom, which helped focus media, public, and Congressional attention on the issue, resulting in eventual abandonment of the SST program.

- Coalitions are stronger than individuals. The SST issue also illustrates this point, but an example closer to the interests of business in general is the Japanese coalition of government and business. Bolstered by *Japan Inc.*, as this combination is sometimes termed, Japanese competitors represent formidable forces in the U.S. and other markets where American business lacks comparable advantages.

- Stakeholders will not necessarily make mistakes. Assume that a stakeholder is as accurate as you are. A stakeholder can make mistakes, of course, but management must be careful not to take undue short-term advantage of these mistakes without assessing the long-term consequences.

- Threats against stakeholders shouldn't be made unless you are willing to execute them. Management must be certain that the stakeholder's response to a threat won't defeat both sides. The Cuban missile crisis in the 1960s in particular and the international political scene in general are examples of this potential outcome. "Every stick has two ends."

- Collecting and disseminating information is vital to understanding each stakeholder's position and making proper preparations for the negotiations. Without adequate information, fundamental misperceptions can drive strategies. The beverage industry fell victim to this error when it concluded that voters cared little about litter and a great deal about jobs and energy. On the basis of this conclusion, the industry's strategy with no-return cans was to emphasize the ill effects on jobs and energy of legislation restricting their use. When this tactic failed and anti-litter legislation was enacted in several states, the beverage industry initiated research that found litter to be the critical issue after all.

Practice Negotiating Skills

The only way managers can negotiate more effectively with stakeholders is through actual experience. Is there any way to make this learning process less costly to both the individual and the organization?

A major company worked with Wharton researchers to design a stakeholder negotiation game that would give its executives some simulated experience in understanding stakeholders and negotiating with them. Most of the executives were divided into stakeholder teams, each of which was concerned with the issue that became the game's theme. They had a company team, a customer team, a consumer group, a government agency team, and a media group. Real representatives from each faction were brought in from outside to work with the groups and help them take on the role of a particular stakeholder. For example, a reporter was brought in to work with the executives on the media team. Each group was charged with negotiating a win-win solution on the issue within 24 hours. The remaining executives acted as observers to play back the key learning points of the process.

Use of the stakeholder/management negotiation game has proved extremely helpful. When forced to take on stakeholder roles, executives begin to develop a genuine understanding of the need for cooperative stakeholder negotiations.

Negotiation is the only positive method for reconciling differences. If business is to survive, managers must learn to negotiate with their stakeholders. The more you practice, the better you will become.

· · · · ·

HOW TO NEGOTIATE WITH EMPLOYEE OBJECTORS

David W. Ewing

Few executives need to be told about the current proliferation of employees who criticize or resist management decisions. In one sense, the problem is an old one. Many types of recalcitrants have been with us for a long time—chronic complainers, malcontents, incompetents, and misfits. Perhaps they always will be. But other types of employee critics are relatively new to the business scene.

These are employees who, perceiving what appears to be wrongdoing, speak up against it; or who, believing a company action to be unwise or irresponsible, object to it; or who, convinced that a company practice or procedure is hazardous, resist it. Variously referred to as whistleblowers, dissenters, or dissidents, more often than not they are able and well-intentioned people. Not surprisingly, they stir the concern of many executives and fellow employees. To separate them from the traditional recalcitrants, I refer to them as *employee objectors*.

The increasing number of employee objectors is one reason for concern. While no quantitative studies of the trend have been made, increases in the frequency of lawsuits, complaints handled by employee assistance departments, executives' personal experiences, and other information suggest that employee objectors are at least ten times more numerous today than they were say, 10 or 15 years ago.

What is more, objectors are costly to an organization. One well-known Eastern company has spent many millions of dollars defending itself against the legal attacks of a single determined objector. An organization in Texas that tangled with an objector received the not-too-kindly attention of dozens of newspapers, an eminent scientific publication, and scores of speakers at professional meetings. One chief executive of a giant corporation had to make a long and painful court appearance in his company's defense to testify against a whistleblower. A struggle with dissidents in the construction of the San Francisco Bay Area's rapid transit (BART) system was the subject of a book written by a team of scholars.[1]

One could go on and on with such examples. Yet until only about a decade ago, around the time the famous case of Pentagon whistleblower A. Ernest Fitzgerald caught national attention, such examples were almost unknown. However, the trend is not unexpected. Some time ago, Peter McColough, chairman of Xerox, predicted that the 1980s would be the decade of employee rights. And Peter P. Drucker made similar predictions. As both men saw, the sources of the trend had been in the making for some time.

A few companies, including Bank of America, Donnelly Mirrors, IBM, Northwestern National Bank, Pitney-Bowes, Polaroid, and Puget Sound Plywood Company, have been testing organizational procedures for responding to objectors.[2] In government, the Nuclear Regulatory Commission established in 1981 a carefully devised system for meeting "professional criticism" from its employees. But, of course, systems alone are not enough. Indeed, they are not the most important thing. The most useful, valuable, and economical management response to employee objectors is the one that only superiors and supervisors can make: prompt and effective person-to-person handling of the problem when it arises.

How should managers deal with able, well-intentioned employees who begin to "make waves" about perceived wrongdoings? In principle, the wheel of this answer need not be reinvented, for it lies in techniques developed over the years by many negotiators and mediators. Some of the approaches have been written up in manuals on negotiation and conflict resolution. Of the many offerings, my own preference is the four-step sequence proposed by Roger Fisher and William Ury in their book, *Getting to Yes*, which considers negotiation in a wide range of government, business, and domestic settings (but not employee dissidence).[3] Here I will use that book's sequence, simplified and adapted to the employee–objector problem. For the sake of simplicity, I illustrate its various steps with three mini-cases described in the sidebars.

1. Draw out the objector's personal concerns.

While you may see the facts, arguments, and positions advanced by an employee objector as inaccurate or misconceived, you would be wise to treat the person's fears and worries as important facts. This is the first principle of conflict resolution in the Fisher-Ury scheme, and probably accounts for more successes with employee objectors than any other step. Get the objector's personal reactions into the open. Consider them respectfully, even if you find the person's arguments foolish and irritating. If the objector is wrought up, it is wise in the beginning to keep the focus on substantive ideas and positions taken.

Quick Descent to Disaster

Unfortunately, managers and supervisors repeatedly forget this simple first step when they confront a worried subordinate. Turning the case of the concerned airline pilot (see sidebar) into a hypothetical situation, here is the way the crucial opening discussion can go:

Manager: What's going on here, Mr. Pilot? It was bad enough when you complained about the "automatic hold" equipment to the vice president, but now you've gone and written the National Transportation Safety Board.

Pilot: But if a pilot accidentally presses the wheel control column, the "automatic hold" can disengage.

Manager: You had training in how to use this equipment, and your instructors showed you how to avoid that problem. The other pilots aren't complaining. I read your letters and I've listened to my engineers, and I'm convinced the equipment is safe. Are you disputing my judgment?

Pilot: I've flown the plane myself and—

Manager: I know, you told us all about that, and you told the Safety Board, too. Are you saying we don't know our job?

Protesting Airline Pilot

The senior pilot of an airline believed that a piece of eqiupment used in certain planes, an automatic control device ("automatic hold") to maintain a set altitude level, could become disengaged under certain circumstances without a warning to the pilot on the annunciator panels. After a plane crash that he thought might have been caused by such a failure, the pilot wrote a letter to three top executives of the airline, detailing why the automatic control device was defective.

When the operations vice president failed to investigate or correct the problem, the pilot sent a similar letter to the Airline Pilots Association, as well as the National Transportation Safety Board, which was conducting hearings on the crash. The Board called him to testify, which he did. After the Board decided that pilot error, not equipment failure, was the cause of the crash, the pilot continued to note possible failures in the equipment when he was flying. After writing a 12-page petition to the Board, with a copy to the operations vice president, he was demoted to co-pilot. He protested this demotion and was grounded. Victorious in a grievance proceeding, he resumed flying. Later he took the airline to court.

Pilot: No, sir, I'm saying no such thing, only—

Manager: Now listen, we're paying you to fly these planes in the best way you know how, and we're doing everything we can to make them as safe as possible. What kind of fools do you take us for? Do you think we're going to sit by while you go around writing letters to everybody, saying the equipment is unsafe? We won't have it. We'll speak with one voice on this issue. As of now, Mr. Pilot, you're grounded. Good day.

Openers like this one are likely to take you right into a thunderhead. Taking the objector's self-esteem on such a bumpy ride, dropping it in one air pocket after another, is a risky thing to do with motivated professionals and technical people. The bittersweet maxim attributed to a government autocrat—"First we drive them crazy, then we tell people not to listen to them because they're crazy"—is dangerous advice for today's manager.

In addition, objectors are not likely to be as impressed as you are with your understanding of the situation, nor are they likely to appreciate the value of your sources of information—your discussions with other managers, perhaps, or your knowledge of confidential company information, or possibly your familiarity with a new company plan that alters the situation.

A Better Approach

Far better to avoid any evaluations or judgments and make some such opening statement as this: "Mr. Pilot, you complained about the 'automatic hold' in a letter to the vice president, and you sent a copy of it to the National Transportation Safety Board. Naturally we're concerned." Then encourage him to tell his side of the story. Listen as attentively as you can. Avoid using words that prejudge his behavior, and ask open-ended questions that invite him to lay out in detail his fears and criticisms. Questions that begin with "what" or "how" and requests that begin with "tell me" or "would you describe" work best. Nod your head. From time to time, restate the objector's views in your words. "So what you're afraid of is that accidentally a pilot might push the wheel" or "In other words, you felt that the vice president wasn't paying any attention to your first letter. . . ."

The beauty of this approach, as Fisher and Ury point out, is that it keeps the objector's personality from becoming entangled with the issues. The accident that the pilot fears might not be real, but his fears *are* real. Demolishing the factual basis of the fears does not necessarily demolish the fears.

Just as you encourage the pilot to express his fears and concerns, so should you tell him your own: You're afraid of the bad publicity. You're afraid the criticism will lead to a chain reaction, igniting needless complaints from other employees. You're concerned your leadership will be questioned. And so on. This discussion should take place frankly and honestly, without either side blaming the other.

Though dissidents might be too emotional to talk this way at first, after a while they should react positively to your good example. The pilot confides, "Well, to tell the truth, Mr. Manager, there's this guy, Hottemper, in operations control. And you know, I went to him about this way back in March—a couple of us were worried about it then—and you know what he tells me? 'You goddamn pilots think you know everything, just because you get paid so much.' And before he got through, he was saying something about my ancestry, too."

Strive to avoid giving any impression that your response is a routine that you learned in some training program. Don't let your eyes suggest that you're listening just to make the person feel better. Interrupt occasionally to ask, "Do I understand correctly that you're saying that the vice president never answers those letters himself anyway?" or "Excuse me, but you just said some operations controllers were spies for management. How do you mean that?" Don't be concerned about how far off base you think the objector is. Put these questions or rephrasings in his or her own words.

And remember: listening sympathetically does not mean you agree with employee critics, only that you take them seriously. As A.W. Clausen, erstwhile head of Bank of America, said when I asked him how his organization handled "frivolous" employee complaints: "No employee complaint is frivolous. To the employee, that complaint is serious." But Clausen did not by any means agree with the *substance* of every complaint.

One well-known university administrator is unusually adept at defusing angry complainants and getting talks on a constructive basis. The reaction of one objector gives the secret: "I hardly ever saw eye to eye with him, but he always made me feel important."

Finally, Fisher and Ury offer this counsel: "In many negotiations, each side explains and condemns at great length the motivations and intentions of the other side. It is more persuasive, however, to describe a problem in terms of its impact on you than in terms of what they did or why: 'I feel let down' instead of 'You broke your word.' 'We feel discriminated against' rather than 'You're a racist.' . . . A statement about how you feel is difficult to challenge. You convey the same information without provoking a defensive reaction that will prevent them from taking it in."[4]

2. Find out what motivates the objector.

Even after drawing out the objector's fears and concerns, continue to avoid a head-to-head hassle over the merits of his or her argument. Don't get led into a debate. Instead, try to understand the person's purposes and interests in challenging management. Ask yourself what this person is trying to achieve and what gain he or she seeks. This is much more likely to help you progress than focusing only on the position taken.

The difference between positions and interests was brought out forcefully to me one time when I was talking with a hospital employee. As an objector, she argued that the hospital should set up a staff group to monitor the enforcement of a bill of rights published for patients. This was totally impractical; in no way could the hospital afford an extra staff group, nor could such a group hope to inspire most medics and patients

Novel-writing Chemist

A chemist with 16 years of service and promotion in a chemical plant believed that scientists and engineers deserved more rights, as well as the kind of protection of rights afforded production workers under the National Labor Relations Act. He and his wife collaborated on writing a novel, published by a local firm, that portrayed the disadvantaged situation of professionals. The novel did not name his employer or identify him with the employer company. Shortly after the novel came out, the chemist ran unsuccessfully in the state primary for the U.S. House of Representatives. During the campaign, he distributed several thousand copies of the book. Shortly after, he received a letter from his superior indicating that he was dismissed. When he went to the superior's office to protest, he got nowhere. After dismissal, he began a series of legal actions against the company.

to cooperate. But the objector's interests—her desire for better understanding of and respect for patients' rights—deserved (and later got) sympathetic management attention.

How can you ascertain an objector's true interests? The person might not oblige by candidly reporting them to you. You may have to figure them out by inference and deduction, paraphrase them for the objector, and see if they are acceptable.

Using this time the mini-case of the chemist (see sidebar), ask yourself why this chemist and his wife have gone to all the work of writing a novel criticizing the way management treats scientists and engineers. Is their motive to put public pressure on companies like yours to recognize the rights of professional people to bargain with top management? And if so, what kinds of management unfairness are they most concerned about?

Unequal pay? Unfair discharge? Arbitrary assignment and transfer? Is their motive to attract publicity and attention? Or perhaps to "get back" at the company for some wrong in the past? Perhaps as you're sitting there listening, it will become clear that one of these is their real interest.

If this approach does not yield a good answer, ask yourself (a) what the objector may think you want him or her to do; and (b) why the person chooses not to do it. For instance, suppose you believe Mr. Chemist realizes how much you want him to get that anti-business book off the market—to expunge it, if possible. If he sees that, why doesn't he oblige? Does he see this issue as one on which he has a right to speak out, just as a person has a constitutional right, say, to speak out against a governmental action?

"If I do what the company wants and take the book out of circulation," Mr. Chemist might be thinking, "I sell out to management. Professionals like me will look weak, our superiors will scoff at us for doing nothing. But if I refuse to comply with management's obvious wishes, I uphold the rights of professional people to speak out, I will be praised by my colleagues, others will be encouraged to do what I have done, we'll get publicity and public support, we'll gain more respect and recognition by executives. . . ."

Perhaps you cannot forgive Mr. Chemist for writing a book that is contemptuous of management. But, you realize, he is doing something that to him seems completely logical. He practically *has* to keep promoting it and subsidizing more printings in order to justify himself.

Usually, an employee dissident or a dissident group has more than one interest. The chemist, for instance, might be seeking not only a preferred status for professional employees as a class but also security and advancement for himself. He might also be after increased status and recognition from his colleagues, or perhaps from professional associations. Intending to run for

Congress again, he perhaps sees the book as a way to keep himself in the eyes of the voters:

Instead of just letting these thoughts pass idly through your mind, Fisher and Ury recommend that you write them down when you have a moment to yourself. In so doing, you will remember them better and perhaps hit on some good ideas for dealing with them. If possible, rank them in order of their probable significance to the employee.

Encouragement by Example

To encourage the objector to talk about his purposes and desires, be candid about your own. "You see, Mr. Chemist, what management is worried about is that a union will come in and organize the technical people. We don't want to get involved in the kind of bitter rivalry that Detroit suffers from." Or if management's right to manage is a salient concern: "Frankly, Mr. Chemist, some of the executives around there think that if this goes on, they won't be able to manage any more—keep high standards, get rid of nonproducers, that sort of thing. Now personally, I'm not concerned so much about what your book has done as about what it might start some of the others to writing."

Be as specific as you can in outlining your interests. Details make your view more convincing. "Just last month, for instance, we asked your colleague Nohelp to assist us in interviewing candidates for the agricultural chemicals department, and he refused. He said that was below his level, an administrator's job, not a professional's." Or: "Maybe you'll recall, Mr. Chemist, that we all got together at the beginning of the year and budgeted $200,000 for modifications of the equipment in YLab. Well, they used up that amount in three months and went right on spending as if the budget didn't mean a thing, never bothering to tell us. Can you blame management for getting uptight? Everybody can't go flying off in his own direction."

When the objector begins to discuss his interests, show that you have listened and understood. "What I hear you saying, Mr. Chemist, is that you want credit for what you're doing, and you don't think the company has been fair with you. Am I right? Is there more to it than that?"

The object, as in the first step, is to get the focus off positions, away from a pointless debate over who's right. Once interests become the subject of attention, you and the objector won't get trapped in recriminatory argument, with you asserting, "Mr. Chemist, you can't treat us like that; don't forget who's in charge," and him accusing, "The company wants to treat me like a blue-collar worker and I'm not going to let them!"

3. Think up mutually beneficial options.

Having gotten the discussion away from "I'm right and reasonable and you're wrong and ridiculous" to "Now you know what I'm really interested in, and I think I know what you're really interested in," you can begin the payoff stage: devising options and alternatives that will leave you both better off. What might be an exercise in futility if you were trying to reconcile conflicting positions can become a productive negotiation because each side understands the other's motives and desires.

For an example, let us take the story about dissident engineers working on San Francisco's BART system (see sidebar). Your interests as a manager would be speedy and efficient construction of a safe transit system, with favorable publicity in the media. You don't want leaks to the press about problems. You don't want anonymous memoranda about perceived mistakes circulating among engineers. On the other hand, Hjortsvang, Bruder, and Blankenzee, the employee objectors, would be fearful of being made the scapegoats for operating failures, worried about management's perceived obsession with speed at the expense of safety, and inter-

Dissident Engineers

Holger Hjortsvang, Max Blankenzee, and Robert Bruder, three engineers working on the construction of the San Francisco Bay Area Rapid Transit system, became concerned about faults in the design of the control equipment. They reported their worries to their supervisors but got little response. Convinced that going to top management would be an equal waste of time, they wrote an unsigned memorandum spelling out their concerns and left copies of it on the desks of many engineers, middle managers, and senior managers. Then they met confidentially with a member of the board, laying out all their concerns to him and explaining their fears that to continue to object openly, as they had at first, would lead to their being branded as troublemakers and being penalized.

After the director gave the facts to an outside consulting engineer, the consultant produced a highly critical report of BART's technical planning. A newspaper learned about the report and ran a story on it. Incensed, BART's top management learned the identities of the three engineers and fired them. The action precipitated spates of hostile newspaper articles, resolutions of support for the engineers from professional societies, criticism from legislators, and a legal action by the engineers (settled before the case came to trial).

months and go all-out on the present program, if management would agree to hire an impartial outside consulting team to evaluate progress at the end of the period and, if necessary, recommend major changes in approach. If the engineers pooh-pooh budget restrictions that management regards as very important, they might agree to respect a new budget for a period of six months, at the end of which time meetings will be called to consider changes in the amounts budgeted.

If management wants harmony and unison in the ranks but the engineers feel more comfortable in an atmosphere that permits disagreement and encourages individual opinion, management's interest in the organization's image might be preserved by a code of strict confidentiality, while the engineers' interest might be served by regularly scheduled rap sessions. If the engineers are more interested in job security than management is, both sides' interests might be served by management's agreement to a policy of no layoffs except for reasons approved by an impartial panel of arbiters.

Throughout this stage, avoid trying to influence the three objectors by warnings; instead, emphasize the beneficial consequences of adopting your proposal. For instance, a ten-month moratorium on resistance followed by a critical review would give management an opportunity to prove its belief in the current program without delaying too long the engineers' desire to see a thorough critique carried out—and the critique should serve the interests of both sides. Again, your layoff proposal is not going to hurt capable people like Hjortsvang, Bruder, or Blankenzee; it will, however, enable BART to deal with incompetents and misfits who are a pain to everybody.

Try to keep in mind the politics of the other side's agreement with your proposed solution. In advance of the meeting, jot down on the back of an envelope how your proposal for a moratorium might be seen by the engineers' peers. Will it be

ested in gaining credit for contributing to a successful, innovative venture. For the sake of the job prospects and reputations with their peers, they want the BART project to succeed in engineering terms (whatever the cost).

With such divergent interests, what kinds of solutions might you propose? Perhaps the engineers would agree to put aside their objections for ten criticized as a sell-out? Would it be more agreeable if the technical review panel were named in advance? Suppose one of the three dissidents decided to seek a job elsewhere in the months ahead. How might your proposal affect the track record he can claim for his work at BART?

Keep referring to the goals that both you and the objectors are interested in. "We want these trains to work. . . . We don't want to disappoint the public. . . . We want the best technical thinking we can get. . . . We don't want any last-minute surprises. . . . If the budget isn't right, we need to know enough in advance so we can get it revised. . . . We don't want to scare away good people. . . ."

The late Eli Goldston, chief executive of Eastern Gas & Fuel Associates, told of his troubles with efforts to reduce lung disease in coal mines owned by the company. After equipping miners with face masks, management found out that-workers often didn't wear the devices. Although efforts were made to increase use of the masks, many miners obstinately laid them aside, claiming that they interfered with visibility or "didn't work right." After some talks, Goldston and others realized that the balky miners indeed had a strong interest in protecting their lungs—only they didn't want to admit it because they wanted to smoke while working. So the company set up work breaks during which smokers were allowed to light up away from the areas of heavy air pollution. At all other times, they would wear the masks.

4. Propose objective tests to determine outcomes.

In seeking a resolution of a conflict with employee objectors, don't let the outcome depend on willpower or staying power. And don't settle for a solution that is a compromise between your interests and the employees' interests and in effect won't satisfy anyone. If experience teaches anything, such compromises are not a solid answer. If you and the objectors can-

not agree on a solution that meets both of your needs, as described in the third step, try to devise objective tests or criteria, agreeable to both sides, that can be used to decide on an outcome.

For example, in your negotiations with the BART engineers, a stumbling block might be differences of opinion over what constitutes reasonable and adequate safety from collisions due to faulty switching. You might take this tack:

"We're both interested in safety, right? But management also is interested in keeping operations going at a profit and in minimizing downtime, and in the long run, that's in your interest too. So what would be a fair way to decide on the proper safety level? If an arbiter from the Institute of Electrical Engineers won't do, what about one from the Cal Tech faculty? Or what about a list of nominations from you engineers and a list of nominations from management, so we can draw up a panel of arbiters using both lists?"

Remember: As management's representative, you generally have an important advantage in these discussions. For instance, as a top executive of BART, you're known to the business and government communities, whereas the engineers have no public identities. The visibility and authority of your office enable you to communicate to many more people—and faster—than the engineers can. As a manager of the chemical company, you have instant access to support and resources that are beyond the reach of the chemist. As an executive of the airline company, you have similar advantages.

"Look," you can say to Mr. Chemist, "you don't think your campaigning is prejudicial to the company, but I think it is. Now, isn't there some way we can find out what other people think? What about an independent outside survey? Depending on the outcome of that, we'll decide on a rule for clearing future publications and speeches." Or, to Mr. Pilot, "All right, now, we both want safe planes, but we disagree on this altimeter equipment. How about agreeing that nothing more will be said about it until we can get a good outside opinion? What about asking the National Transportation Safety Board to recommend an expert to look into it and render an opinion?" So long as your proposal is reasonable, your advantage as a member of management makes it difficult for the objector to reject your suggestion.

Values and Variations

In essence, this was the successful approach worked out by one chief executive of an industrial manufacturer when confronted with complaints from foundry workers who thought the air was unfit for breathing. He suggested that they get the air quality measurements of a well-known rival foundry and use them as a benchmark. They agreed, and the dispute was resolved. In another situation, the head of Sentry Insurance Company was challenged by several employees who felt that the company's tests for job applicants were an invasion of privacy. He suggested that the next employee opinion survey include a question on what other employees thought. In the first case, after the results were in, management decided it had better make some improvements in a few areas; in the second, the dissidents learned that few others agreed with them, so they dropped their complaint.

An interesting wrinkle in this approach is to ask the other side to put in writing the most reasonable proposal he or she can make; you do the same for your side. Then give the two "most reasonable" proposals to an arbitrator to choose between. The idea is that such a procedure puts pressure on both sides to make their proposals as fair as possible. In professional baseball and in states where the procedure is compulsory in certain types of public sector disputes, this approach reportedly has produced more settlements than have conventional types of arbitration.

If you and the subordinate agree on a criterion or procedure for resolving the dispute, ask the subordinate to summarize the discussion and agreed-on solution and send you a memorandum. Write a memo on the talk for your own records too, and if there is much divergence between the two, get in touch again with the dissident.

Parting Observations

In most organizations in most states, managers are not legally compelled to negotiate with employee objectors who are not union members. Managers can throw the objectors out of the company, if they want to. As a practical matter, however, it is becoming less desirable to do so. Especially with employees who have served the company for a while and whose capabilities are proved, it pays to seek a mutually advantageous solution.

Still, even the most adept managers do not always find employee objectors responsive to negotiation. What should be done then? If the objector seems to be more interested in being a gadfly or rabblerouser than in being cooperative and helpful, then if you have done your best to negotiate and assuming you comply with any company policies on the subject, it might be time to fire the person.

If anyone questions you, offer your notes on the discussions. If one or two others joined you at some stage, they can attest to your efforts. If company policy or government regulations require you to submit to a hearing procedure, your duly noted discussions should serve as documentation for your decision. To broaden your understanding of procedures at this stage, consult one of the good professional books available.[5]

The guiding principle is simple: Aim to keep the conflict from becoming an "I win, you lose" affair. Instead, approach it as a "we both can win" situation. Don't make the mistake of the superior who, feeling that his or her managerial prerogatives are threatened, refuses to negotiate with the objector because of "principle." The approach you take can be judged by the three criteria proposed by Fisher and Ury: "It should produce a wise agreement if agreement is possible. It should be efficient. And it should improve or at least not damage the relationship between the parties."

NOTES

1   Robert M. Anderson, Robert Perrucci, Dan E. Schendel, and Leon F. Trachtman, *Divided loyalties* (West Lafayette, Ind.: Purdue University, 1980).

2   See my article, Due process: Will business default? *Harvard Business Review*, November-December, 1982, p. 114.

3   Roger Fisher and William Ury, *Getting to YES* (Boston: Houghton Mifflin, 1981).

4   *Ibid., p. 37.*

5. See, for example, Robert Coulson, *The termination handbook* (New York: Free Press, 1981), or *Employee termination handbook* (New York: Executive Enterprises Publications, 1981).

Section VII

Team-Based Negotiation

Chapter Fourteen   *Negotiating in Groups*

Chapter Fourteen

NEGOTIATING IN GROUPS

NEGOTIATING GROUP DECISIONS

Jeanne M. Brett

Organizations frequently create special task forces and provisional groups to manage projects that are under tight time constraints or that are too large, too complex, or too political to be managed by an individual. Examples of situations necessiating such groups include the following:

- The CEO of a hospital supplies company wants ideas on the design of a new management information system that meets the needs of the sales, marketing, sales administration, and systems development divisions. She therefore appoints the vice presidents of each division to a special task force charged with designing a new system.

- An investment bank forms a group to design and syndicate a multi-billion-dollar bank credit facility. The group includes the borrower's chief financial officer, investment advisers, and legal counsel, in addition to representatives of the bank.

- A consumer products company establishes a team consisting of the managers for marketing, sales, finance, production,

Jeanne M. Brett, "Negotiating group decision", *The Negotiation Journal*, July 1991. Reprinted by permission.

and production engineering to oversee the development of a new product.

While groups such as these provide resource expertise and communication links that will be needed to manage such projects, they also present their own significant management problems. Conflict among members with differing technical backgrounds and political agendas is likely. Stalemates occur. And decisions that do get made can be of poor quality. The challenge in managing groups such as these comes in finding a way to use conflict to produce high quality group decisions.

This article draws on recent negotiation research and theory to prescribe techniques for transforming conflict within organizational groups into high quality group decisions. Negotiation theory is all about decision-making between two or more parties in conflict. It applies to groups with two limiting conditions: first, the group's task must require that the group make one or more decisions; and second, group members must have conflicting opinions as to what the group's decisions should be.

In the first section of this article, I use negotiation concepts to develop criteria for determining when a group has reached a high quality decision. The research reviewed in this section indicates that making such decisions under conditions of conflict requires integrating diverse information and perspectives, but groups often do not do this very well. (Individuals seldom do, either.) Group members frequently fail to question assumptions or seek out information from diverse sources, and often do not welcome perspectives very different from their own. When groups do consider diverse opinions, they often have difficulty integrating this diversity into a high quality decision.

In the second section, I offer a number of suggestions on how to improve the process of group decision-making under conflict—improvements that should lead to higher quality decisions. The first step is to make sure that the information and the opinions are sufficiently diverse to match the complexity of the group's task, and that they are available to the group. The second step is to make certain that the group considers the diverse information and opinions available to it. The last step is to integrate this diversity into a high-quality group decision.

Knowing When the Group Has Reached a High-Quality Decision

Easier than knowing when the group has reached a high-quality decision is knowing when a group's decision is of poor quality and thus knowing that the group should continue to deliberate. To help make this determination, group members can use two concepts from negotiation theory as standards against which to evaluate any potential group decision: the no-agreement alternative, and the second agreement.[2]

The No-Agreement Alternative

The no-agreement alternative is what happens if the group fails to reach an agreement. It is important as a standard for evaluating potential agreements as well as for analyzing the power relations within the group.

If the new product team in the third example outlined at the start of this article fails to agree, for instance, about how many models of the new product to produce, top management will step in and decide.[3] In evaluating alternatives—one model, three models, eight models—team members should weigh how well the alternative being considered meets their interests, as compared to the uncertain outcome of the no-agreement alternative. In doing so, they should not only consider the likelihood of top management's supporting their point of view, but also other potentially negative ramifications of top management's involvement, both for the team as a whole and themselves individually.

Group members with the better no-agreement alternative are more powerful because they are less dependent on the group's making a decision. They should be able to take advantage of that power to tip the group's decision toward their position. If, in our example, new product team members agree that top management is slightly more likely to select multiple models, marketing and sales members who are pressing for more models are more powerful. Their power stems from their lesser dependency (and production and production engineering's greater dependency) on the group's making a decision favorable to their interests. To avoid the uncertain, but potentially negative, decision of top management, production and production engineering should be willing to agree to at least some models, though perhaps not as many as the others want.

Often there can differences of opinion within the group concerning which group members are the more powerful. For example, marketing and sales members of the new product team might think that their multiple-model position will be supported by top management, while production and production engineering might think that top management, if involved, would support them. These differences of opinion are due to the uncertainty of information on which judgments are based—no one knows for sure how top management would decide. Differences of opinion can also be exacerbated by the self-serving bias.

The self-serving bias enters into the judgment of the no-agreement alternative because of the pervasive tendency to perceive one's self as better than others, to exaggerate personal control, and to be unrealistically optimistic (Taylor and Brown, 1988). These illusions lead individuals to be less sensitive to their own faults and more sensitive to the faults of others. When it comes to evaluating the quality of a no-agreement alternative, a group member might perceive his own no-agreement alternative as more positive and other members' alternatives as more negative than they are, according to some objective assessment.

The questions in Table 1 direct group members to consider their no-agreement alternative. Doing so, however, does not ensure that the group can resolve its conflict. Differences of opinion among group members regarding the quality of the no-agreement alternative can actually contribute to the level of conflict.

Nevertheless, groups making decisions with the no-agreement standard in mind should reach higher quality decisions. The no-agreement alternative certainly has this effect on one-on-one negotiators. While negotiators do not all agree on the value of the no-agreement alternative to each other, they reach better quality agreements when they negotiate with a no-agreement alternative in mind (Pinkley, Neale, and Beggs, 1990). The no-agreement alternative is a hurdle that motivates negotiators to try harder and to be more creative in constructing superior agreements (Pinkley, Neale, and Beggs, 1990).

While acting as a hurdle, the no-agreement alternative does not have all the characteristics of a goal. It does not motivate negotiators to select the best possible alternative, but merely encour-

---

Table 1

Questions for Assessing the No-Agreement Alternative

1. What will occur if the group does not reach an agreement?

2. Is the no-agreement alternative the same for all group members, or different? Which group members have the better no-agreement alternative?

3. Are group members likely to agree about the quality of their own and other group members' no-agreement alternatives, or are there likely to be differences in perceptions? Which members are most likely to have different perceptions?

---

ages them to improve upon the no-agreement alternative. Second agreements actually help negotiators and groups make higher quality decisions.

The Second Agreement

Second agreements are decisions that are superior to a group's first agreement, according to some standard or norm (Mater and Hoffman, 1960; Nemeth, 1986), or that meet all members' interests as well as or better than the group's first agreement (Raiffa, 1982). If a group continues to deliberate after it has reached a preliminary decision, it might be able to improve upon that decision.

There are many examples of inferior group decisions that might have been improved had a second agreement been considered: President Kennedy and the National Security Council's decision to go ahead with the ill-fated Bay of Pigs invasion in Cuba (Janis, 1972); the vote of the board of Lehman Brothers to redistribute a large percentage of the firm's equity, leading to the depletion of the firm's resources and its sale (Auletta, 1986); Simplicity Pattern's leveraged buyout, characterized by the September 2, 1989 *New York Times* as a "mutual seduction" between management and Wesray, leaving a formerly profitable company struggling to stay out of bankruptcy court.

First agreements frequently reflect the views of the majority of group members, the position of a powerful group member, or an established norm (Nemeth, 1986, 1989). When the group's task is large, complex, political, or under tight time constraints and group members have divergent interests, these approaches to group decision-making might not be appropriate to the task.

In contrast, dissent and minority views can foster the kinds of attention and thought processes that raise the quality of the decision, even when the dissenting views are wrong (Nemeth, 1986: 28). Dissent stimulates consideration not just of the minority's views, but of a host of alternatives.

Majorities and powerful individuals, however, are often intolerant of dissent. After all, why should they risk losing control over the group decision by providing an opportunity for dissent? A second agreement resolves this dilemma. It preserves the control of the powerful party—if no better agreement is forthcoming, the first agreement will stand. A second agreement also protects the interests of both the majority and the minority, letting them reveal strategic information about their weaknesses and hidden agendas without fear that the group will use the information against them. At their best, second agreement deliberations encourage the sharing of minority points of view, the questioning of assumptions, the discussion of decision ramifi-

cations, the search for superior alternatives, and the testing of consensus.

The MIS task force in the introductory example used second agreements very successfully. This group had a difficult start. For six months, meetings were acrimonious and unproductive as members argued that their divisions' interests should take priority. Finally, in desperation, the group developed a strategy for decision-making. They agreed that they would brainstorm ideas, and then each group member would prepare a cost/benefit analysis, evaluating how each alternative would affect his department. They agreed that they would select the alternative that minimized the costs and maximized the opportunities for the line departments—because they were the income producing component of the company—but not before the group had fully discussed and tried to resolve the problems that that alternative would generate for other departments. This final provision acted in the same way as a second agreement: increasing the quality of the decision for some members without diminishing its benefits to others.

Second agreements are not without their own problems. While second agreements are by definition superior to first agreements, group members, frustrated by the difficulties of reaching a first agreement, might not be very motivated to continue to deliberate. The checklist in Table 2 should help a group search systematically for superior agreements, but it will take time to go through and it is no guarantee that the group will find a second agreement. At some point, a balance must be struck between spending more time on a decision and moving on.

There are several ways to help groups strike this balance. One is to give groups decision-making training so that they learn for themselves about the superiority of second decisions. Another way is to wait until a group appears to be hopelessly stalled, like the MIS task force mentioned above,

> **Table 2**
> Checklist for Assessing
> First Agreements and Developing
> Second Agreements
>
> 1. What problems does the first agreement raise for group members? Why?
>
> 2. Are there ramifications of the first agreement that may have a negative effect on individuals, groups, or organizations not represented in the group?
>
> 3. What assumptions does the first agreement make, for instance, about market conditions and implementation? Are these assumptions justified?
>
> 4. Is there an alternative that better meets the interests of at least some members of the group without hurting the interests of others?

and introduce second agreements as part of a negotiated approach to decision-making. A third way is to help groups improve the process by which they make first decisions. This third approach is the focus of the remaining sections of this article.

Improving the Process of Group Decision-Making

There are three interrelated aspects to the task of improving the process of group decision-making: 1) ensuring that a diversity of information adequate to match the complexity of the decision is available to the group, 2) ensuring that available information is considered by the group, and 3) providing mechanisms to help the group integrate diverse and conflicting information into a high quality decision.

Ensuring Diversity of Information and Perspective

Whether or not adequately diverse information is available to the group depends on members' task-specific skills and their facility in managing external relations. Group members can be selected on the basis of their knowledge and skills or, in the case of external relations, perhaps trained.

The specific skills needed in a group depend on the nature of the task. A task with political connotations, such as the MIS task force's, needs a group whose members represent the warring political factions. A task such as the one faced by the new product team, for which success turns on implementation, requires a group whose members represent the areas that will need to be coordinated during implementation. In selecting group members, it is also useful to keep in mind three general skills that are relevant to all tasks: intelligence, creativity, and practicality.

High-performing groups also manage their external relations with their constituencies and other groups particularly well. Frequency of external communications distinguishes successful and less successful research and development laboratory groups (Allen, 1984; Katz and Tushman, 1981; Tushman, 1977, 1979.) Members of high performing product-development teams both initiate communications with and react to communications from others more frequently than members of poorly performing teams (Ancona and Caldwell, 1988). Successful negotiating groups communicate the minimum amount of information needed for their constituencies to maintain confidence in their negotiating behavior. Too much information communicated to the constituency early in the negotiation reduced the negotiating teams' flexibility; too little information communicated late in the simulation precluded the constituencies' acceptance of a negotiated agreement (Winham and Bovis, 1978).

One of the reasons the MIS task force in our example had so much initial difficulty was that they were not managing their external relations particularly well. Group members were providing too much information to their constituencies early in the group's deliberations. After each meeting, members would brief their bosses, who would then veto any progress that had been made. When the group met to work out their decision-making arrangement, they also agreed to change their handling of external relations. They sought the protection and support of a vice president senior to their bosses, who also very much wanted the MIS project done. This vice president agreed to announce all the group's decisions. The group agreed among themselves to stop keeping minutes and to stop briefing their bosses. They recognized that removing their bosses from the information loop was risky, but coupled with their arrangement for second agreements, they were willing to take the risk in order to make some progress.

Ancona and Caldwell (1989), after studying numerous product development teams, concluded that group members need the skills to play four distinct external roles: scout, ambassador, coordinator, and guard. *Scouts* constitute the main source of external information about markets, technology, and competition. *Ambassadors* handle the information channel between the group and upper management. They take on the joint responsibilities of acquiring resources for the group and buffering the group from organizational politics. *Coordinators* handle the group's lateral communications with constituencies and other groups with which the group is interdependent. *Guard* activities differ from the others' in that they are designed to keep information and resources inside the group. These roles could provide a focal point in training groups to handle external relations.

Ensuring That Available Information Is Considered by the Group

Two aspects of a group's process can increase or decrease the likelihood that available information and perspectives are considered by the group. These are "discussion norms" and "decision rules." Both affect not just how much gets said, but how well what is said is listened to.

Groups quickly develop norms—standards for what is and is not appropriate behavior—and operating procedures such as decision rules (Bettenhausen and Murnighan, 1985). Often, neither is discussed explicitly, but both emerge out of group interaction. Norms about discussion develop as group members are positively or negatively reinforced by others for what they say. For instance, group members can quickly stifle the creative exchange of ideas by pointing out their negative aspects (McGrath, 1984). Sometimes a decision rule, such as consensus, is assumed by group members to be in effect and is never explicitly agreed to. Other groups end up discussing a decision rule—for example majority rule—only after it becomes clear that consensus cannot be achieved.

There is no reason why groups cannot agree to discussion norms and decision rules prior to beginning deliberations on the substantive aspects of the group task—it is just that they do not seem to do so naturally. In order to ensure that available information and perspectives are considered, groups need to adapt particular discussion norms and decision rules.

Perhaps the most important norm for a group to develop is tolerance for conflicting points of view. Many techniques to enact this norm are available. The MIS task force in our example used several different ones. They agreed that members could make no negative comments about ideas during the presentation and brainstorming stages of group decision-making. They gave their facilitator the responsibilities of eliciting participation from all members, enforcing the no-negative-comments rule, recording all ideas, and making sure that as the group organized and refined ideas, none was lost. Janis (1972) suggests other techniques for ensuring an exchange of ideas, including assigning the same problem to multiple groups or splitting the group in half, assigning a group member to play the role of devil's advocate, and inviting outside experts to challenge group members' assumptions.

One of the biggest problems in fostering an open exchange of ideas is that interpersonal relations become emotionally charged, especially when a group is working under a tight deadline. Members become frustrated and tempers flare. If this situation persists, both creativity and motivation to complete the task will suffer (Taylor and Brown, 1988). To counteract emotional tension, groups need to provide members with ways to vent emotion without creating emotional escalation throughout the group.

The bank credit group in our example confronted just such a situation. They were working under an extremely tight deadline. The borrower wanted to use the credit facility for an acquisition, and the acquisition candidate's price was being bid up on rumors of a takeover. As group members began to realize how far apart their positions actually were—covenant restrictions that the bank members believed they could not live without, company members believed they could not live with—morale started to fade, and frustration set in. Tempers were short, and emotional tension was fast becoming an obstacle to meeting the deadline. The group enacted a rule that became known as the "morning rule" (the idea was thought up sometime after midnight). The rule was that anyone who needed to blow off some steam could do so without running the risk of offending another if he cited the "morning rule" as his reason. Simply making the "morning rule" explicit reduced the group's need for it.

Too often, group members tear out of their offices to attend a group meeting with preparation limited to reading the agenda on the elevator. If they have considered anything in preparation for the meeting, they may have thought about their own positions on the issues to be resolved. The result is likely to be a conflict-filled meeting about as effective as the early ones of the MIS task force in our example. Thorough preparation for a group meeting involves knowing your own and estimating the other group members' positions, interests, and priorities on the issues. These are terms commonly used in negotiations (see Fisher and Ury, 1981; Lax and Sebenius, 1986). "Positions" are what group members want; "interests" are the reasons why. One way to think about interests is to consider what assumptions underlie a group member's position or what that person's hidden agenda might be. "Priorities" are the makings of the issues on a group's agenda in terms of importance.

A technique for managing all this information is to make an issue-by-group member matrix, fill in interests associated with each issue, and then rank order the issues for yourself and the other members of the group. A rule of thumb negotiators use is that if they cannot fill out the matrix, they do not know enough about the others attending the meeting and should postpone the meeting (or at least decision-making) until they do.

Preparing for a meeting as though it were a negotiation is useful on a number of dimensions. First, it provides a structure for the group's discussion. Positions must be backed up with explanations that reveal interests and priorities. Once interests are revealed, creative solutions can sometimes be identified. Alternatively, solutions can be developed that mesh different members' priorities. Second, it encourages listening. Since all columns of the matrix but one are estimates, group discussion provides a good opportunity to test assumptions and update the matrix. The updated matrix might reveal new alternatives. Third, it helps group members develop a strategic plan for revealing their own interests and priorities. This third point requires a bit of explanation, since how much information to reveal about interests and priorities poses a major dilemma to the group member.

A group member's interests and priorities are his vulnerabilities. Once the group knows a member's interests and priorities, it can design an agreement that gives that member the very least that is acceptable to him—an agreement just a little better for him than the no-agreement alternative. There is no guarantee that the full sharing of interests associated with discussion leading to a second agreement will improve this member's situation. In contrast, when a group member's interests and priorities are not well known to the group, it is harder to design the first agreement at the edge of what is minimally acceptable. And, when the first agreement is very beneficial to a member, the second agreement must preserve that benefit. The dilemma is how much information to reveal and how quickly to reveal it. When trying to construct an agreement, it is always better to ask questions and learn more about others' interests and priorities than to reveal information about one's own. On the other hand, group members may expect reciprocal information-sharing and tend to be intolerant of those who do not participate. A matrix of issues, positions, interests, and priorities might help a group member plan a strategy for revealing information about himself contingent on the information being revealed by other group members.

The decision rule used by the group affects how many members' interests must be considered by the group before it can make a decision. The larger the number of members needed to make a decision, the longer will be the group's deliberations, the greater will be the number of alternatives that the group considers, and the higher will be the quality of the group's decision (Hastie, 1985; and Thompson, Mannix, and Bazerman, 1988). Among the decision rules a group might use are dictatorship (one person decides), oligarchy (a few powerful people decide), simple majority (one more than half of the group), two-thirds majority, consensus (about a two-thirds majority, with the minority withdrawing their dissent), and unanimity (all group members decide).

The new product team example is a good lesson in how a decision rule affects the quality of the group's decision. This five-person group used a simple majority decision rule. The marketing and sales members met with the member representing finance before the group meeting and convinced her that the profits to be made by introducing multiple models would far outstrip the costs of producing them. Marketing and sales representatives dominated the group discussion with their profit projections, and ultimately controlled the group decision. They could not, however, control its implementation. While sales and marketing went ahead with an advertising campaign, production and production engineering began struggling to transform a production process designed to produce prototypes into one that could produce volume. At the time the advertising campaign was aired, dealers had limited inventory of a few models. As projected, initial demand was high, but customers were unwilling to wait for delivery and turned to other manufacturers. The product never gained significant market share, and all models were withdrawn 18 months later.

This example illustrates how the decision rule influences the approach taken to decision-making and the role and the power of dissent. Majority rules imply that the decision will be dominated by faction or coalition formation and that the views of the majority coalition will dominate group discussion. Consensus and unanimity rules imply that the decision will be made by joint problem-solving and that the interests of all members will be considered. Put simply, the power of dissenters increases with the number of people necessary to make a decision.

If the new product team had used even a two-thirds majority decision rule, the simple majority would have had to recruit one more member. In doing so, it is possible that information that would have increased the quality of the decision would have surfaced. There are two somewhat different approaches to building a coalition. The core members of the coalition might try to recruit others by arguing that their point of view is correct and the others' points of view are wrong. This approach can be successful if new information surfaces. Alternatively, the majority can determine the others' interests and provide for them in the decision. Marketing and sales used the latter approach to recruit the finance member.

The discussion norms and decision rules advocated here and summarized in Table 3 are what many people consider to be fair, so they are readily acceptable to most. Note that the MIS task force members agreed to a process of group deliberations that treated each of them equally, recognizing that their ultimate decisions would not necessarily treat each member equally.[4]

However, there are situations in which a powerful party—either a majority, a strong individual, or group leader—realizes that it will be much more difficult to control the group's decisions with these norms and rules in place. It is always interesting to see whether such a party objects when discussion norms and decision rules are suggested. Many in this position will realize that the group's performance of its task is jeopardized when at least some members believe the group's process is unfair and consequently will not object to egalitarian processes.

Methods of Integrating Diverse Points of View

Group decision-making should be a process of generation of alternatives followed by integration around one, but which one? How can a group, once it has generated so much information and so many perspectives, then integrate them? There are three fundamentally different approaches, depending on how information is manipulated or, in negotiator's argot, what tactics are employed. These approaches are mutual gain, coalition gain, and individual gain. The *mutual gain approach* focuses on maximizing joint gain—identifying the best possible alternative for all members; the *coalition approach* is oriented toward maximizing gain for a subgroup and their constituencies; the *individual approach* attempts to maximize gain for an individual group member and his constituency. Group members, in addition to using the tactics appropriate to the approach they have chosen, might also try to influence the group's decision rule, its goal orientation, and the use of decision aids. These factors affect the three approaches to information integration differently. Table 4 summarizes the prescriptions regarding tactics, decision rules, goal orientations, and decision aids as they relate to the mutual, coalition, and individual approaches to group decision-making.

Table 3
Effective Discussion Norms and Decision Rules

Discussion Norms
- Tolerance for the Conflict of Ideas
- Means of Diffusing Emotional Tension
- Preparation

Decision Rules
- Two-Thirds Majority
- Consensus
- Unanimity

TABLE 4

Tactics, Decision Rules, Goal Orientations, and Decision Aids for Mutual, Coalition, and Individual Gain

Mutual	Coalition	Individual
Tactics		
1. Share own and elicit others' interests.	1. Seek similar others and construct an alternative that meets your interests.	1. Open with a high, but not outrageously high, demand.
2. Consider many alternatives; be creative; look for ways to use available resources.	2. Recruit just enough members to control the group's decision.	2. Argue the merits of your alternative; do not reveal your interests.
3. Don't just compromise; make trade-offs.	3. Encourage interpersonal obligations among coalition members.	3. Appear unable or unwilling to concede.
4. Encourage positive relations.		4. Encourage positive relations.
		5. Use threats, time deadlines, and promises, if necessary.
Decision Rules		
Consensus	Oligarchy	Dictator
Unanimity	Majority	
Goal Orientation		
Cooperative	Cooperative or Individual	Individual
Decision Aids		
Packaging	Packaging	
Search models	Search models	

Tactics for Mutual Gain

Negotiation tactics for mutual gain, many of which may be used in the group setting, are discussed in Fisher and Ury (1981). (See also Walton and McKersie, 1965.) There is substantial research in the negotiations literature that shows that these tactics are indeed linked to high mutual gain outcomes (Pruitt, 1981).

Share own and elicit others' interests. Mutual gain agreements are those that take all group members' interests into consideration. Information about interests is the raw material from which mutual gain agreements are constructed.

Consider many alternatives; be creative; look for ways to use available resources. Mutual gain solutions in negotiations often use resources creatively. Sometimes resources are added so that there is no longer any conflict over the lack of them. For instance, the MIS task force might have been able to add enough programmers so that the system would be available to all group members

◆　◆　◆　◆　◆

simultaneously. Another example of the creative use of resources is the cost cutting engaged in by the MIS task force. One of the problems that the MIS task force had to deal with once they assigned priorities was how to continue to do long-range market forecasting in the interim between the conversion to the new system of current sales data (high priority) and market forecasting (low priority). The cost-cutting solution was for systems development to provide a temporary interface.

Don't just compromise; make tradeoffs. When a group must make a number of interrelated decisions, no mutual gain will be realized by reaching issue-by-issue compromises. In a multi-party, multi-issue negotiation, mutual gain comes from dovetailing interests. This means that the group needs to consider multi-issue alternatives that incorporate all parties' high-priority interests (Mannix, Thompson, and Bazerman, 1989; Beggs, Brett, and Weingart, 1989). The result is a decision in which group members receive as much as possible on issues of highest priority to them and make substantial concessions on low-priority issues. The new product team in our example, in deciding how many models to produce, really had a two-issue problem: number of models and amount of inventory. Their final decision should have reflected a trade-off between these two issues.

Encourage positive relations. Books on group performance (e.g., Dyer, 1977; Zander, 1987) as well as those on negotiations (Fisher and Ury, 1981; Pruitt, 1981) advise encouraging positive interpersonal relations among group members. Their advice is not without a psychological basis. People do tend to help those whom they like (Pruitt, 1981:80). Positive feelings do increase individuals' capacity for creative, productive work by facilitating intellectual functioning and motivation (Taylor and Brown, 1988: 197–199). A positive group atmosphere should facilitate groups grappling with complex decision-making tasks.

A word of caution is in order, however. Studies of groups do not support this prescription. In a series of recent studies of sales teams (Gladstein, 1984), consulting teams (Ancona, 1989), and new product teams (Ancona and Caldwell, 1989), the quality of *external* but not *internal* relations was related to group performance. The development of positive interpersonal relations is not the primary task of the group. It should not distract the group from working on its task or reduce group members' tolerance for the conflict of ideas.

Tactics for Coalition Gain

A coalition is a subset of a group that unites to determine the group decision (Murnighan and Brass, 1989). The effect of coalition formation is a group decision that benefits coalition members more than others (Thompson et al., 1988).

Seek others who are similar in some way and construct an alternative that meets your interests. Coalitions form around individuals who suggest an alternative that is attractive both to themselves and to others. When the number of decision alternatives is few, a sizable subgroup might prefer the same alternative before the group ever meets. Even with numerous alternatives, a little informal, pre-meeting polling might uncover a nascent coalition.

Recruit just enough members to control the group's decision. When the coalition's initial core of members is not sufficiently powerful to determine the group's decision, additional members must be recruited. Recruiting costs the core members of the coalition. Either the coalition's alternative must be adjusted (diluted) to incorporate the new members' interests, or some kind of side deal, usually a creative use of resources, is made.

Encourage interpersonal obligations among coalition members. Coalitions are instrumental relationships; members quickly switch allegiance to the highest bidder, unless somehow the costs of leaving one coalition for another offset the promised gains. Interpersonal ties that increase the costs of leaving a coalition increase coalitional stability, according to some researchers (Thompson et al., 1988).

Tactics for Individual Gain

Negotiation tactics for individual gain that can be used in the group setting are described in several books on negotiation, such as those by Walton and McKersie (1965) and Pruitt (1981). Pruitt (1981) also surveys the research linking these tactics to individual gain.

Begin with a high, but not outrageously high, demand. The first rule of negotiations is: "What you don't ask for, you don't get." Especially in the group setting, where support for an alternative can build quickly, it is important to introduce your preferred alternative early. While you might occasionally be in a situation (based on an analysis of your no-agreement alternative) of having the group choose your alternative or forcing the group to impasse, more frequently an opening demand is a position from which you expect to make concessions. It is for this reason that the opening demand should be everything you want plus more—you need to give yourself negotiating latitude or room to make concessions. But, since outrageously high demands often are not taken seriously, the opening demand needs to be carefully positioned between the outrageous and the generous.

Argue the merits of your alternative as persuasively as possible. Do not reveal your own interests. Research on group decision-making has shown that group discussion reflects the distribution of preferences prior to the group meeting (Poole, McPhee, and Seibold, 1982) and that selection of an alternative is related to the relative number of positive to negative comments it receives. In several studies, groups eventually selected the first alternative to receive 15 more positive than negative comments (Hoffman, 1983). In short, sitting passively while the group's deliberations range across numerous alternatives is unlikely to promote yours.

What should you say about your alternative? Experts suggest framing your arguments in the other party's interests. For instance, production and production engineering members of the new product team in our example might frame their argument for a single model in marketing and sales interests as follows: "If we have to produce multiple models, we think there will be long delivery delays. On the other hand, if we produce only one model, we can assure you of inventory when your advertising campaign is aired." This communication provides new information, and is directed toward marketing and sales' interests.

Why say as little as possible about your interests? They are, after all, your reasons for making your demand. The more others know about your interests, the more vulnerable you are to their overtures for trading off aspects of your proposal that are less important, but nonetheless, desirable to you.

Appear unable or unwilling to concede. If concessions are necessary, concede slowly, in small steps, and demand reciprocal concessions. Often, winning in negotiation—and that, after all, is what the individual gain approach is all about—is due to being steadfast. Your demand, while undesirable to the other party(ies), is considered to be better than their no-agreement alternative. Their time and patience wear thin, and they concede.

Conceding, albeit slowly, invites concessions from the other party while preserving your own negotiating latitude. In order to build in reciprocal concessions, it is useful to ask for a concession from the others contingent on your own concession. For example, production and production engineering might make the following contingent concession: "We'll produce multiple models, if you will let us phase them in over a one year period."

◆ ◆ ◆ ◆ ◆

Encourage positive relations. While it is extraordinarily manipulative (since in the individual gain situation you do not care at all for others' interests, being what Fisher and Ury call "soft on the people"), trying to enhance their liking and dependence on you as a person might encourage them to make concessions.

Use threats, time deadlines, and promises, if necessary. A threat is an intent to punish, if a concession is not forthcoming. A promise is an offer of a reward for conceding. Both threats and promises entail costs. The cost of the promise depends on exactly what was promised. The cost of a threat that must be acted upon is the loss of the relationship. Paradoxically, threats, promises, and time deadlines are often viewed as manipulative, while ingratiation is not. As a result, they can interfere with attempts to encourage positive interpersonal relations.

Decision Rules and the Integration of Information

Decision rules—dictatorship, oligarchy, majority, two-thirds majority, consensus, unanimity—vary with respect to how many group members must be involved in the final decision. Decision rules map onto information integration approaches as follows: individual gain—dictator; coalition gain—oligarchy or majority; mutual gain—consensus or unanimity. The correspondence between decision rules and approaches to information integration is not one-to-one. It is certainly possible, though it might be difficult, to take an individual approach when the decision rule calls for unanimity. Likewise, when the group's leader is ultimately going to make the decision, it might be a waste of time to take a mutual gain approach to information integration.

Goal Orientation and the Integration of Information

Goal orientation, a term taken from the negotiations literature, can be cooperative, where the focus is on maximizing one's own and other's gain; competitive, where negotiators try to maximize the difference between their own and the other party's gains; or individualistic, where only one's own gains are important. An individual goal orientation motivates the individual gain approach. A cooperative goal orientation facilitates the mutual gain approach (Pruitt, 1981). The coalition approach can be looked at as a pragmatic middle ground and therefore motivated by either orientation. Negotiators' goal orientations affect the content and pattern of their tactics (Pruitt, 1981).

What happens when negotiators have different goal orientations—a situation that is surely likely in groups? Communications researchers (Putnam, 1985) have found that regardless of negotiators' initial orientations, their communications tend to fall into a pattern. In general, cooperative patterns develop when cooperative communications/tactics are reciprocated, such as when one negotiator shares information about her interests, and the other responds by sharing information about his interests. When cooperative tactics are not reciprocated, negotiators switch to a competitive/individualistic pattern, making demands and counterdemands, even when one of them prefers cooperation. (See Putnam, 1985:228–229, for a summary of this research). It seems likely that patterns of communication will develop similarly in groups, where initial communications are consistent with members' goal orientations and later ones are more dependent on the pattern of communication that has developed.

Decision Aids and the Integration of Information

Decision aids are formalized approaches to information handling. Two decision aids found to be effective in generating high quality negotiated agreements are the simultaneous consideration of issues, or packaging, and search models (Pruitt, 1981).

TABLE 5
Ideas for Managing High Quality Group Decisions

Step 1: Tasks for management forming the group

1. Define the mission of the group. What is it supposed to do?

2. Define the scope of the group's decision-making authority. Is the group to make recommendations to senior management, or does it have the authority to set organizational policy?

3. What skills are needed? Consider technical and political expertise; intelligence, creativity, and practicality; and external relations and group process skills.

4. How motivated are group members likely to be? Is time devoted to the group going to be a problem? Should something be changed about the task, the scope of decision-making authority, the relationship between the group and the organization, or the intended membership to increase members' motivation?

5. Who is to be the leader? Should a leader be appointed, or should the leadership question be left up to the group? If a leader is named, what should be the scope of the leader's decision-making authority? What should be the leader's responsibilities?

Step 2: Tasks for the group leader or members, as the group begins to meet

1. Provide opportunities, perhaps informal ones, for group members to learn about each other's expertise and preferences.

2. Develop ground rules for communication within the group, with constituencies, and with top management.

3. Encourage a cooperative goal orientation, perhaps by discussing a superordinate goal that all members have in common.

4. Agree on a decision rule.

Step 3: Tasks for the group leader or members, as the group begins to integrate diverse information

1. Compare potential agreements to group members' no-agreement alternatives.

2. Use decision aids such as packaging and search models.

3. Reciprocate cooperative tactics and respond to competitive tactics with counterbalancing responses, such as questions that probe interests, rather than counterdemands that risk escalation.

4. Use resources and trade-offs creatively.

5. Integrate other group members' interests in multi-issue proposals.

6. Probe group members' concerns about agreements made by majority coalitions.

7. Search for a second agreement.

• • • • •

When multiple issues must be decided, the natural approach is to develop an agenda and consider each issue sequentially. However, mutual gain is higher when groups are instructed to consider issues simultaneously in a package (Pruitt, 1981; Mannix et al., 1989; Beggs, Brett, and Weingart, 1989). A package incorporates all the issues. Packaging facilitates mutual gain because it systematizes trade-offs. Those making multi-issue proposals try to incorporate something for everyone in the group.

A search model is a set of criteria that a decision-maker can use to screen alternatives (Simon, 1957). If negotiators can agree on the criteria that their joint decision must meet, they can then engage in a joint search. This is what happened in the MIS task force where the agreed-upon decision criteria were to give line departments' interests priority, but to minimize the resulting costs to staff departments. These criteria allowed the MIS task force to evaluate all alternatives in terms of opportunities versus costs. Like packaging, search models (which typically involve a set of criteria) help decision-makers set priorities and consider multiple issues simultaneously.

Packaging and search models can be effective decision aids for coalitions. A package or set of search criteria can be constructed that maximize the coalition's interests to the detriment of the interests of the other group members. Because both decision aids facilitate the simultaneous consideration of issues, both should encourage coalition stability.

Neither decision aid is likely to facilitate individual gain. Effective packaging turns on prioritization of issues and trade-offs, which those seeking individual gain do not wish to do. When the standards for a search model are sufficiently high to satisfy a group member seeking to maximize individual gain, there might be only a few alternatives (if any) that exceed the search model's criteria. A relaxation of the search model's stan-

dards, the normal course of action in this situation, is not in the interest of those seeking to maximize individual gain.

When to Use Which Approach?

The choice of approaches is necessarily dictated by circumstances: the quality of the no-agreement alternative to each group member or previous interactions with the members of the group, for example. Furthermore, circumstances can change and require a change in tactics. Yet, with these qualifications, a few rules of thumb do exist.

Starting out with a combined mutual gain/individual gain approach might be the most effective for most group decision-making situations. Groups focusing uniquely on mutual gain risk accepting a satisfactory, but low-quality, alternative. Second agreements are intended to minimize this risk, but as previously discussed, they too have their limitations. Group members with a mix of individual and cooperative goals might be able to motivate the group to maximize mutual gain, while at the same time maximizing their own individual gain.

Another reason for combining the individual/mutual gain approaches in practice is that frequently many different agreements meet the no-agreement and second-agreement criteria. These agreements differ in terms of how much they maximize individual group members' gain. When mutual gain is equal, and perhaps even when it is not, it is entirely reasonable that a group member would prefer the alternative that maximizes his individual gain, as well as the mutual gain, as opposed to the alternative that maximizes mutual gain and some other group member's individual gain.

How can these seemingly mutually exclusive approaches be combined? Negotiators do so regularly, switching back and forth between competitive and cooperative tactics as they search for a compatible approach and an acceptable agreement (Putnam, 1985).

Reserve the individual approach for situations where the no-agreement alternative is attractive compared with alternatives offered to other group members. The individual approach seems somewhat risky in a group setting, riskier than in a one-on-one negotiation. If everyone in the group takes the individual approach, as was true initially in the MIS task force, a stalemate is likely. If only one member takes an individual approach, that member risks being isolated by the others in the group. The group will choose an alternative that maximizes their joint outcomes, minus the obstinate member. Thus, in considering a pure individual gain approach, it is wise to assess both your control over the group's decision rule and the quality of your no-agreement alternative.

Use the coalition approach as a fallback position from the other approaches. The coalition approach poses two risks. First, decisions made by coalitions are often of poor quality because they are not based on an assessment of all group members' underlying interests or needs, but rather on the power of the coalition (Mannix, 1989; Nemeth, 1986). Second, coalitions are so unstable that it can be difficult to sustain the coalition long enough to implement the decision.

Coalitions are unstable because the only bond holding members together is their preference for a common decision alternative. The interests underlying that preference and the expectations for it are often very different. Discussing the alternative in depth or finding out too much about the other coalition partners can threaten the existence of the coalition. And, to make matters even more difficult, members of other coalitions are always trying to recruit new members from existing coalitions.

Despite these limitations of the coalition approach, it is sometimes the only way to avoid an impasse, when either the mutual or individual approaches have failed. Provisions for second agreements help to minimize the risks of poor decisions made by coalitions.

Conclusion

The research on negotiations, coalition formation, and group decision-making suggests numerous ways to improve the quality of group decisions, ranging from selection and training of group members, development of norms to maximize the amount of relevant information considered by the group, and the selection of an approach to integrate that information. In thinking about managing the process, it is useful to consider what can be done at the time a task force or team is formed, what needs to be done prior to decision-making, and what might be done to integrate information and preferences to make high quality decisions. Table 5 organizes the ideas discussed in this article by stages.

An interesting question is how overtly a group leader or member can act in managing this process. Groups themselves do not seem to engage in much deliberate planning. They often jump into their tasks, only to back off and plan when they find themselves hopelessly frustrated, such as in the MIS task force in our example. Most groups do not have the luxury of "team-building" training—learning techniques to reach high quality group decisions in a simulated environment. So, it is often up to individual group members to direct the group to use processes that will produce high quality decisions.

NOTES

1. The MIS task force case study was provided by Michael B. McIntosh, Kellogg Graduate School of Management Executive Masters Program, based on his experience as a member of the task force. It is used with his permission. The investment bank case study was provided by Kerry N. Kearney, Kellogg Graduate School of Management, Executive Masters Program, based on his experience as a member of the group. It is used with his permission. Finally, the consumer products company case study is a variant of a case originally written for class-

room use by Roy Lewicki, Associate Dean in the Graduate Business Programs at Ohio State University.

2. In negotiations theory, the no-alternative agreement concept is called BATNA, or Best Alternative to a Negotiated Agreement (Fisher and Ury, 1981; Lax and Sebenius, 1986). The second-agreement concept is called "post-settlement" by Raiffa (1982), a negotiation theorist. Maier and Hoffman (1960), social psychologists studying groups, call these "second solutions."

3. No-agreement alternatives need not be the same for all group members. In our example of the group putting together the credit facility, lender and borrower each have separate no-agreement alternatives: the lender has alternative opportunities for investment; and the borrower has alternative lenders.

4. There is much literature on procedural and distributive justice (perceived fairness of the process by which decisions get made and perceived fairness of the decision itself) that is relevant to the observations made here. Fair procedures are important to parties involved in decision-making. Parties are more satisfied with negative decisions when they perceive the process to have been fair than when they perceive the process to have been unfair (Lied and Tyler, 1988).

REFERENCES

Allen, T. J. (1984). *Managing the flow of technology: Technology transfer and the dissemination of technological information within the RD organization.* Cambridge, Mass.: M.I.T. Press.

Ancona, D. G. (1989). "Outward bound: Strategies for team survival in the organization." M.I.T. Working Paper 3006-89–BPS.

Ancona, D. G. and Caldwell, D. F. (1988). Beyond task and maintenance: External roles in groups. *Group and Organization Studies* 13: 468–494.

Ancona, D. G. and Caldwell, D. F. (1989). *"Improving the performance of new product teams."* M.I.T. Working Paper 2114-88.

Auletta, K. (1986). *Greed and glory on Wall Street: The fall of the House of Lehman.* New York: Warner.

Beggs R., Brett, J. M., and Weingart, L. R. (1989). *"The effect of decision aids and goal orientations on group negotiations."* Dispute Resolution Research Center, Northwestern University Working Paper #48.

Bettenhausen, K. and Murnighan, J. K. (1985). The emergence of norms in competitive decision-making groups. *Administrative Science Quarterly* 30: 350–372.

Dyer, W. G. (1977). *Team building: Issues and alternatives.* Reading, Mass.: Addison-Wesley.

Emerson, R. M. (1962). Power dependence relations. *American Sociological Review* 27: 31–34.

Fisher, R. and Ury, W. L. (1981). *Getting to YES.* Boston: Houghton Mifflin.

Gladstein, D. L. (1984). Groups in context: A model of task group effectiveness. *Administrative Science Quarterly* 29: 499–517.

Hastie, R. (1985). *"Jury decision-making."* Northwestern University working paper.

Hoffman, L. R. (1983). The hierarchial model of problem-solving groups. In *Small groups and social interaction,* edited by H.H. Blumberg, A. Paul Hare, Valerie Kent, and Martin F. Davies. New York: Wiley.

Janis, I. (1972). *Victims of group-think.* Boston: Houghton Mifflin.

Katz, R. and Tushman, M. (1981). An investigation into the managerial roles and career paths of gatekeepers and project supervisors in a major R & D facility. *R & D Management* 11: 103–110.

Lax, D. A. and Sebenius, J. K. (1986). *The manager as negotiator.* New York: The Free Press.

Lind, E. A. and Tyler, T. R. (1988). *The social psychology of procedural justice.* New York: Plenum.

Maier, N. R. F., and Hoffman, L. R. (1960). Quality of first and second solutions in group problem solving. *Journal of Applied Psychology* 44: 278–283.

Mannix, E. A. (1989). *"Resource dilemmas and discounts in organizational decision-making groups."* Dispute Resolution Research Center, Northwestern University Working Paper #47.

Mannix, E. A., Thompson, L. L., and Bazerman, M. H. (1989). Negotiation in small groups. *Journal of Applied Psychology* 74: 508–517.

McGrath, J. E. (1984). *Groups: Interaction and performance.* Englewood Cliffs, NJ.: Prentice Hall.

Murnighan, J. K. and Brass, D.J. (1991). Intra-organizational coalitions. In *Research on Negotiation in Organizations*, edited by M. Bazerman, R. Lewicki, and B. Sheppard. Greenwich, Conn.: JAI Press.

Nemeth, C. J. (1986). Differential contributions of majority and minority influence. *Psychological Review* 93: 23–32.

Nemeth, C. J. (1989). "The stimulating properties of dissent." Paper presented at the first annual Conference on Group Processes and Productivity, Texas A & M University.

Pinkley, R., Neale, M., and Beggs, R. (1990). *"Alternatives, reservation prices, and outcomes."* Dispute Resolution Research Center, Northwestern University, Working Paper #54 (to be revised and resubmitted).

Poole, M. S., McPhee, R. D., and Seibold, D. R. (1982). A comparison of normative and interactional explanations of group decision-making: Social decision schemes versus valence distributions. *Communication Monographs* 49: 1–19.

Pruitt, D. (1981). *Negotiation behavior.* New York: Academic Press.

Putnam, L. L. (1985). Bargaining as task and process: Multiple functions of interaction sequences. In *Sequence and pattern in communicative behavior*, edited by R.L. Street Jr. and J.N. Capealla. London: Edward Arnold.

Raiffa. H. (1982). *The art and science of negotiation.* Cambridge, Mass.: Harvard University Press.

Simon, H. (1957). *Models of man: Social and rational.* New York: Wiley.

Taylor, S. E. and Brown, J. D. (1988). Illusion and well-being: A social psychological perspective on mental health. *Psychological Bulletin* 103: 193–210.

Thompson, L. L., Mannix, E. A., and Bazerman, M. H. (1988). Group negotiation: Effects of decision rule, agenda, and aspiration. *Journal of Personality and Social Psychology* 54: 86–95.

Tushman, M. (1977). Special boundary roles in the innovation process. *Administrative Science Quarterly* 22: 587–605.

Tushman, M. (1979). Work characteristics and subunit communication structure: A contingency analysis. *Administrative Science Quarterly* 29: 82–98.

Walton, R. E. and McKersie, R. B. (1965). *A behavioral theory of labor negotiations: An analysis of a social interaction system.* New York: McGraw-Hill.

Winham, G. R. and Bovis, H. E. (1978). Agreement and breakdown in negotiation: Report on a State Department training simulation. *Journal of Peace Research* 15: 285–303.

Zander, A. (1987). *Groups at work.* San Francisco: Jossey Bass.

Jeanne M. Brett is the DeWitt W. Buchanan, Jr. Professor of Dispute Resolution and Organizations at the J.L. Kellogg Graduate School of Management, Northwestern University, Evenston, Illinois.

THE GROUP AND WHAT HAPPENS ON THE WAY TO "YES"

Deborah G. Ancona
Raymond A. Friedman
Deborah M. Kolb

While the negotiation archetype is of two individuals haggling with each other, more typically negotiation takes place within and between groups. In labor relations, union and management bargainers meet in committees; in community disputes (e.g., the siting of a waste disposal facility), groups of government officials, neighborhood residents, and environmental advocates face one another; and in international diplomacy, groups of political leaders, diplomats, military and economic advisers, and others are commonly involved. Since negotiation takes place in groups, group dynamics play an important part in how bargainers come to agreement.

Curiously, analysts have only rarely considered group phenomena as an integral part of negotiation theory in either the descriptive or prescriptive literature (for exceptions, see Pruitt and Lewis, 1977; Friedman and Gal, 1990). A substantial body of work delineates both win-lose and win-win strategies and tactics that individual negotiators can pursue (Walton and McKersie, 1965; Pruitt, 1981; Fisher and Ury, 1981). Other researchers focus on the individual cognitive limitations and barriers that can impede a negotiator's ability to achieve beneficial outcomes

(Raiffa, 1982; Bazerman and Neale, 1983; Lax and Sebenius, 1986). Finally, there is considerable work documenting the interactive dynamics of competition, cooperation, and the perils of escalating conflict (Deutsch, 1973; Axelrod, 1984; Pruitt and Rubin, 1986).

The neglect of group dynamics is particularly problematic since new bargaining models encourage a problem-solving process that differs significantly from more traditional, linear concessionary models.[1] Groups have their own dynamics that arise from the collective enterprise, and these can support or detract from a problem-solving process in negotiated contexts. Our purpose here is to draw from scholarship on group dynamics, particularly recent work on task forces and new product teams, and explore the implications for mutual-gains bargaining. To clarify our argument and to allow greater specificity, we will examine one particular bargaining situation: contract negotiations between labor and management. A similar analysis could be done for other negotiating contexts.

Groups in Traditional and Mutual Gains Bargaining

A group is a collection of individuals who interact, who are interdependent at least to some degree, and who influence or can be influenced

Deborah Ancora, R. Friedman & D. M. Kolb, "The group and what happens on the way to 'yes'", *The Negotiation Journal*, July 1991. Reprinted by permission.

by each other (Cartwright and Zander, 1968; Shaw, 1981). In most negotiations, there are three sets of group relationships.

First, each side is usually represented by a bargaining team. Each team is charged to negotiate an agreement acceptable to its respective constituency. We call these groups the *primary* negotiating teams. Each primary negotiating team needs to develop a group identity and a set of norms that will allow it to coalesce effectively. It needs to develop internal mechanisms for structuring work and for making decisions. In labor negotiations, labor and management each has a primary team.

While the primary teams need to coordinate internally, they also need to coordinate with the other primary team: they need to work with the opponent. We label this larger group, which includes primary negotiating teams from both sides, the *integrated* team. In most negotiations, including labor negotiations, the primary teams function at arm's-length and only occasionally cohere into an integrated team.

Finally, each primary team (and the integrated team) has a relationship it must manage with its "second table," the constituents who have ultimate authority over the terms of an agreement. The exact nature of that authority varies a great deal. In traditional collective bargaining, the authority relationship between management-primary teams and their constituent groups is based primarily on hierarchy, while the authority relationship between union-primary teams and their constituents is based primarily on politics. These arrangements affect the ways in which constituent groups are involved and consulted.

Mutual gains bargaining (MGB) introduces a new set of ideas and processes into this pattern of relations. MGB suggests a focus on interests and not on positions, on inventing options for mutual gain rather than haggling over a fixed amount of resources, and on judging these options according to objective criteria instead of

relying heavily on bargaining power to influence outcomes. In other words, negotiators are urged to engage in a process of joint problem solving in order to fashion agreements that maximize gains for both parties.

Normative models of mutual-gains bargaining describe a set of steps for carrying out this type of negotiation. Typically, parties are advised to establish an agenda that begins with mutual sharing of interests, followed by collective "brainstorming" to identify creative ways of satisfying these interests and of establishing criteria by which possible ideas can be evaluated. This process is intended to result in agreements that meet the interests of the various parties (Fisher and Ury, 1981; Susskind and Cruikshank, 1987).

But MGB does not just introduce new concepts and steps; it creates and depends on a pattern of group dynamics that is different from traditional bargaining. In order for MGB to be successful, group norms within primary teams must change to allow for broader participation. In addition, the integrated team must develop dynamics that are less cautious, becoming a place where interests are shared, and where the collective enterprise replaces some of the activities that had occurred in the primary team. This change, in turn, has an impact on how primary teams work. And, as more new ideas are generated, the nature and intensity of relations between primary teams and constituent groups need to be changed; the teams are under increased pressure to bring their constituents along in a process that is really being designed *as* it occurs.

The elements of the MGB process, while well defined in theory, provide little guidance once the parties actually begin negotiating. It is at this point that individual bargainers move into a group context, within their own team and across the table, and that the group dynamics can contribute to—or detract from—the problem-solving. From a group perspective, the model should address the following:

1. the underlying individual and organizing dynamics that mark the early phases of group activity, specifically the development of group norms, that impact how the group does its work (Bettenhausen and Murnighan, 1985; Schein, 1988);

2. the importance of the middle stages of a group's life as an occasion for change in its normative and task structure (Gersick, 1989); and

3. the tension between developing the internal processes of the team and managing the relationships between external groups that will influence the group's product (Ancona, 1990).

Mutual Gains Bargaining differs significantly from traditional collective bargaining in terms of the demands it makes on the relationships within the primary negotiating teams, the integrated team, and constituent groups. We explore these differences and the challenges they pose in the context of the three group perspectives, using data from ongoing field experiments in mutual gains bargaining. Drawing from the study of groups in other contexts, we conclude by suggesting ways in which principles of group process can be used to resolve these dilemmas.

Data and Methodology

The data used in this analysis is drawn from observations of three negotiations that took place in the United States in the late 1980s (the names have been changed to preserve confidentiality). In each case, negotiators attempted to implement mutual-gains bargaining. We will not try to present a comprehensive analysis of these cases; instead we will draw from them to illustrate the ways in which group dynamics in negotiations affect, and are affected by, a mutual-gains approach to bargaining.

In the first case, which we will call Northwest, Inc., mutual-gains bargaining was effectively implemented, albeit in the face of great resis-

tance from some constituents, and an agreement was reached by the appointed deadline. Mutual-gains bargaining was initiated after extensive meetings between constituents months before negotiations began. The pre-bargaining training program included one phase attended by constituents and another for negotiators alone; most of the negotiators said they supported the mutual-gains approach to bargaining. The actual negotiations, as in the other cases, lasted for several months. There was a great deal of open discussion during negotiations, as well as plenty of frustration and conflict. Most people on both sides strongly supported the final agreement and the MGB process. We observed this negotiation from beginning to end.

In the second case, Southwest, Inc., the mutual-gains approach worked well during the first half of negotiations, but was effectively abandoned at that point. In the end, the parties reached an impasse, and the union struck for three weeks. The mutual-gains process at Southwest was introduced more than a year before actual negotiations began, and included three separate training sessions. The first included negotiators and constituents; the others were for negotiators only. Both during training and in negotiations, many constituents were ambivalent about the MGB process. A major influence in these negotiations was resistance from the company's corporate headquarters, and from the union's national leadership. In this case, we observed the training, and interviewed the negotiators during and after negotiations.

In the third case, Eastern, Inc., MGB was not effectively implemented at any time during negotiations. Instead, the negotiators reverted to traditional negotiations almost immediately. However, the effort did take some of the "edge" from the negotiations, and the parties did reach an agreement and did feel that the *relationships* had not been damaged by negotiations. Training for this company began several months before negotiations, but it did not include constituents, and there was great controversy within the union about attending the training. In the last week before negotiations began, a new person was assigned to lead negotiations for the union. We were able to observe most of these negotiations from beginning to end.

In all three cases, the training occurred at off-site meetings. It included general presentations of the core ideas of Mutual Gains Bargaining, negotiating simulations designed to illustrate those ideas, and, for the actual negotiators, an all-day bargaining simulation that gave people a chance to practice the MGB ideas that they were learning. The training also included explicit discussions about the merits of MGB compared with traditional negotiations, and some actual negotiations over the process they would use to negotiate.

Getting Started: Norm Development in Groups

For primary teams, integrated teams, and constituents, as for other kinds of groups, getting started is a particularly difficult yet influential part of a group's evolution. Team members are often anxious about how they will fit in and establish themselves in this new social arena. Norms, or expectations about how members should behave, are formed early (sometimes in the first few minutes of the first meeting), and set the stage for future interaction. For example, if the leader sets the agenda, leads the meetings, and criticizes anyone who disagrees with her, then the group members soon learn to nod their heads and follow her lead. Understanding this early stage of a group's life is particularly important in mutual-gains bargaining, where teams must embark on new ways of interacting.

Schein (1988) suggests that issues of individual identity, control, and acceptance must be resolved before members can fully engage in the task of the group. Identity is established as individuals figure out the roles they will play on the team—whether they will be outspoken or quiet,

aggressive or humorous, a leader or a follower. As members concentrate on these issues and work through the possibilities, their ability to listen and participate is often curtailed. Concerns about control (authority and influence) also affect behavior in the early stages of a group. Members attend to the early dynamics in order to determine who will be in a controlling position and who will be influenced by others. As a result, early stages are often marked by testing of oneself and others—sometimes through conflicts over seemingly inconsequential things—to see where authority and influence lie. Finally, members are always concerned about whether they will be accepted by the group. Members often test their level of acceptance by participating heavily for a period of time, then shifting to a quiet "wait and see" attitude, while they observe how their input is received. In this respect also, group progress can follow the rhythms of member comfort rather than task work.

In addition to the individual problems of identity, control, and acceptance, groups also face the collective problem of establishing norms. Norms evolve from the experiences of individual members combined with the experience the group develops as a whole. Team members bring familiar "scripts" from other group experiences to a new group situation, and these scripts give members a sequence of activity to follow in new and uncertain situations (Abelson, 1976; Taylor et al., 1978). In other words, a group's process is never a *tabula rasa*; its foundation is built on the existing scripts of the group members.

Early anxiety to make some progress pushes team members to follow existing scripts and to begin work quickly by assigning roles and responsibilities. This "solution mindedness" (Hoffman and Maier, 1964) often pushes members toward solutions before they fully consider whether their assumptions are shared or accurate, what the assumptions are, and whether the structure they create will lead to the outcomes they seek.

While such progress can be comforting to the group, early norm development can be problematic over the long haul. Hackman et al (1975) show that when groups try new or complex tasks, such as mutual-gains bargaining, previous modes of operating are often not congruent with the new task. They suggest that, before automatically following implicit patterns, members explicitly discuss "performance strategies—how they will work together. Bettenhausen and Murnighan (1985) illustrate another problem with early, untested norm formation. In their zest to move the team along, members often ignore or don't realize that members bring different scripts and assumptions to the table. Thus, while task progress can be made quickly under an assumed consensus, conflict is often just postponed until the differing assumptions become clear. When this happens, it forces the group to backtrack and openly negotiate about the norms under which they will operate.

Norm formation and individual adjustment to the group occur not only in formal group meetings, but in other arenas as well. Informal dinners and parties, subgroup meetings, and one-on-one communications are all arenas in which identity, control, and acceptance issues are worked out and expectations and work rules are set. Such activities can be designed to facilitate this early development process.

Finally, norm formation is not solely a function of implicit scripts and explicit planning. Key events in the group's life can shape the rules by which the group functions. For example, a team that is penalized by top management for leaking key information is likely to develop strict norms about secrecy. Thus, a team's early formation process involves individual experiences, group meetings, informal contacts, and key events. All are important to the development of group norms.

Getting Started in Traditional Labor Negotiations

At their first meeting, all groups experience anxiety about what norms of behavior and social order will emerge. In traditional labor negotiations, this concern is heightened by the high stakes involved in the bargaining and because, for many team members, bargaining is not part of their regular job or experience. Collective bargaining is carried out, therefore, in a highly charged atmosphere marked by pressure, uncertainty and complexity.

Some clarity can be provided by the existence of broadly understood scripts for negotiating that are reinforced by leaders and individuals who have previously been through negotiations (Friedman, 1989).

Elements of the established script include:

- Each side begins with a "laundry list" of demands, and then lets some issues "fall off the table" at the appropriate time.

- Chief negotiators are aggressive at the public bargaining table and more conciliatory and open in private "sidebar meetings."

- Chief negotiators exert control over their primary groups in order to channel communication across the table.

These norms help people know how to act, what to say, and what to expect. Further, traditional patterns of behavior are strategically important in that they help to keep negotiators' goals, constraints, and desires hidden from the other side, while impressing constituents with the negotiators' strength and fervor. If these norms were not taught by old hands, they would be invented anew.

What supports these norms is a social order that structures relationships within and between groups in negotiations (Friedman and Gal, 1990). There is strict hierarchical control within the primary team, and opposition between primary teams (the integrated team is not legitimate);

members of the primary team are agents representing (and under the control of) constituents. This social order maintains control over the information and impressions that are the core of traditional bargaining. It also provides a clear notion of who is in control, who sets the norms, and whom to trust.

Getting Started in Mutual-Gains Bargaining

Development of norms in mutual-gains bargaining is complicated for two reasons. First, the desired norms of interaction are different. Members of the integrated team need to reveal and explain their underlying interests and discuss options for addressing those interests. Second, existing scripts and power structures based on traditional norms will drive behavior, unless there are explicit efforts to shape norms in an alternative direction. This tendency results from lack of experience with a new process and the need to reduce ambiguity; because of these factors, negotiators return to more familiar and comfortable scripts.

In order for the MGB approach to work, a new set of norms needs to emerge, and emerge early. It is in the earliest stages of bargaining that the negotiations path is determined. This is when groups struggle not only with the concepts of mutual-gains bargaining, but also over the implications of MGB for their own behavior and control needs. These struggles occur during training and continue into the early stages of bargaining. The norms, whether they support mutual-gains bargaining or not, emerge from these dynamics.

Joint training is the usual method used to introduce labor and management to mutual-gains bargaining. Such training brings both sides together off-site to learn MGB principles, to discuss how they will negotiate, and to practice by using bargaining simulations (often switching roles). In addition to being a time when members learn new skills, such training also marks the first time the differences between the traditional and the mutual gains bargaining scripts are played out. Thus as the groups go through training, they confront issues of dominance, control, and habit, and they develop—either implicitly or explicitly—the guidelines that will characterize their negotiations.

During training, negotiators first consider the implications that mutual-gains bargaining might have for their power and control. At Southwest, Inc., for example, one lead negotiator was worried when he realized that mutual-gains bargaining involved direct participation by all members of the bargaining team. He was reluctant to allow control to be so diffuse, and developed careful instructions for his team, detailing precisely what they could do or say during the simulations. The Southwest lead negotiator was worried not only that team members would subtly "give away" the company's positions, but also that they would become accustomed to acting independently. Throughout the simulations and subsequent negotiations, when this negotiator was present, members of his team continued to defer to him and so limited their own contributions.

There is also a tendency in these early training sessions to reproduce old patterns. "Old hands"—people who have been through bargaining before—can inadvertently "train" newcomers in the traditional approach. During the initial moments of the bargaining simulation at Northwest, Inc., for example, the union's most experienced negotiator explained the procedure to newcomers: If they wanted to have an idea conveyed, they should send a note to him. Based on what they had learned in the training, some of the newcomers argued that this stance was inconsistent with mutual-gains bargaining, which led to an explicit discussion about process. In contrast with the situation at Southwest, this discussion helped set the norm of open participation, which continued well into the bargaining.

More generally, training allows both the primary teams and the integrated teams to discuss consciously what norms should be established for negotiations. During the training, they have the opportunity to explain why the traditional process made sense, express fears about the new process, and negotiate over the very process of negotiating. As the result of the training sessions at both Northwest and Southwest, negotiators developed lists of rules that they believed should govern negotiations.

The training phase is also critical because impressions made and formed there can last throughout negotiations. At Northwest, for example, two simulations were run concurrently (each included negotiators from both sides). One group fell into old patterns of negotiating, while the other used the mutual gains bargaining approach quite well. During the debriefing, everyone learned which group had "failed" and which had "succeeded." Over the next months, individuals from the first group would occasionally be reminded, jokingly, that they were from the "remedial group."

When negotiations actually begin, group norms are still being formed. Because lines of authority are challenged by the mutual-gains bargaining training, people are often not sure how to act: No one quite knows how to start, and there are many long, awkward pauses. People ask each other: Can we disagree, or do we have to be "nice"? Can everyone talk? Will we have caucuses? Indeed, some of the first conflicts were over the mutual-gains bargaining process itself. At Northwest, for example, one side was convinced that mutual-gains bargaining meant meeting together all the time so that everyone could share ideas. The other side was equally sure that mutual-gains bargaining meant meeting in subcommittees so that members could develop individual areas of expertise and the integrated group would not have to depend on outside staff support. This was a confusing time for the integrated team; each side dealt with the confusion by accusing the other of not doing mutual-gains

bargaining "right." Further, at the individual level, negotiators at Northwest corrected each other when any clearly understood aspect of mutual-gains bargaining was violated (e.g., referring to an "interest" as a "position"). Some even corrected themselves, stopping and apologizing when they recognized that they had made an inappropriate statement.

At Eastern, Inc., mutual-gains bargaining was essentially abandoned during this early stage. The lead union negotiator, who had not attended the training program, insisted on maintaining the traditional process with which he was familiar. He established a pattern in the first days of negotiations that continued throughout the rest of the meetings. At the first meeting, the negotiators who had been through joint training hesitated to sit down, not knowing if they should be interspersed with the other side or with their team. The lead union negotiator settled the issue by seating himself in the middle chair on one side of the table, instructing his team to sit next to him. At this point, the two primary teams sat facing each other across the table in traditional fashion, a signal that the lead negotiator was in control of his team and that the two sides would not be working together. This pattern persisted throughout the negotiations.

Establishing norms that support mutual-gains bargaining might mean re-labeling the steps in the negotiating process. At Southwest, for example, negotiators called the initial meetings "pre-bargaining" sessions so that they would not preclude using traditional bargaining later. At Northwest, the initial phases were labeled "pre-negotiations," in order to align actual bargaining with the steps outlined in training. This labeling led to the question that some negotiators asked each other later in negotiations: "Are we 'negotiating' yet?"

In all three cases, relationships stabilized in different ways. Negotiators at Northwest and Southwest eventually settled into a pattern of open discussion as an integrated team. At Northwest, the integrated team included all negotiators, while at Southwest there were several integrated teams operating in specialized subcommittees. At Eastern, the traditional approach prevailed.

The Midpoint in a Group's Life

Collective bargaining passes through decision-making stages where parties establish a bargaining range, explore it, and ultimately make decisions about settlement (Douglas, 1962: Gulliver, 1979). Studies of groups operating on a variety of tasks with set time limits suggest that the midpoint in a group's existence is a second critical juncture.[2] It is at this point that groups engaged in negotiations have the opportunity to shift their work patterns.

Gersick (1988, 1989) provides some understanding of the midpoint's pivotal role. In contexts as diverse as student projects and task forces at a bank and a hospital, she found that teams develop basic approaches to work, to relationships among members, and to their environment early, often during the first meeting. These early patterns dominate team functioning until the midpoint, which serves as a time to reevaluate the group's efforts. Team members often realize that progress has not been as fast as desired (or that the product does not look as if it will meet the group's objectives), and that there is a limited amount of time to get all the work done.

While the first half of a team's life is spent making incremental or evolutionary changes, the midpoint can be a period of revolution. Group members are suddenly open to assessing how well they have done and what needs to be changed. If at first members were closed to outside feedback, now they seek it out. If a team was preoccupied with generating ideas, now they start evaluating those ideas. During this time of reassessment, team members reshape the way they approach their task, each other, and their

environment. Thus, during the early and midpoint stages of a group, members are most open to suggestion and facilitation. Following the midpoint revolution, teams go back to incremental adjustments along the lines set by the midpoint change.

Teams sometimes fail to carry out a midpoint change because of their organizational contexts (Ancona 1990; Hackman, 1990). Teams often get labeled by management based on early indicators of performance. Once a team is labeled as either a high or low-potential performer, that reputation becomes a self-fulfilling prophecy from which the team cannot escape. Even if the team changes its mode of operation, the change might not be acknowledged in the surrounding environment. Alternatively, the revolution might be inhibited because group members feel constrained by their reputation. As with early formation processes, the midpoint and labeling phenomena can be managed to facilitate mutual gains bargaining.

The Midpoint in Traditional Negotiations

The first phase of negotiations in traditional bargaining is a "feeling out" process: each side presents its demands, hears the other side's problems and concerns, and works out some preliminary agreement on nonfinancial issues. However, negotiations often do not get "serious" until many weeks later. There has been no research explicitly on the midpoint in negotiations, but the notion that at some point the style, tone, and topic of negotiations go through a major shift conforms to observations of traditional bargaining (Douglas, 1962). This switch tends to mark the point when the "show" ends and "real bargaining" begins. At this point, many of the trivial issues quickly "fall off the table," the lead bargainers tighten control over negotiations, more happens in sidebar discussions, financial elements of the contract become more prominent, and each side begins to seriously assess the impact of a strike.

The Midpoint in Mutual-Gains Bargaining

In mutual-gains bargaining as well, the midpoint seems to be a major point of transition. As in traditional bargaining, deadlines become salient and the volume of work seems daunting. Further, the mutual-gains bargaining process adds its own pressures. There tend to be more outstanding issues, more suspicion from constituent groups, and a required shift in process from generating ideas to actually deciding what the ultimate package will be. Many of the problems experienced in the initial phases are reintroduced at the midpoint; there are questions about authority, confusion about what to do, and debates about what is "right" according to mutual gains bargaining. Thus the midpoint constitutes a significant point of risk.

In the two cases where mutual gains bargaining was actually used, the experiences were quite different. At Northwest, about halfway through negotiations, bargainers began to worry about whether they would be able to finish by the deadline. During the first month of negotiations, norms supported open discussions, sharing ideas, and avoiding premature criticism of options. But nothing had been *decided*. Because mutual-gains bargaining was taken seriously, more issues were raised and more ideas (including radical ones) were generated than would be the case in traditional bargaining; in addition, negotiators tried to judge these ideas by using objective criteria. All of these factors created more work for negotiators, stretching their capacity to collect relevant data. When negotiators began to realize this, panic set in.

At this point, the issue that had dominated the first days of negotiations reemerged: How do we do mutual-gains bargaining? The negotiators agreed they had reached a different phase. While they had learned how to discuss interests and generate options, they had not yet experienced *packaging* and *deciding*. Each primary team had different ideas on how to deal with this problem.

In the face of this pressure, the integrated team at Northwest asked the MGB trainer for assistance. He supported one side's proposal that they break up into subcommittees that would specialize in different issues. This would allow for more efficient use of time, and allow for the development of expertise in certain areas (health insurance provisions, for example, were complicated and required time to master). At this point, small groups worked intensively to eliminate unrealistic options, decide on concrete numbers, and make relevant trade-offs. The midpoint shift was productive.

In contrast, at Southwest, the teams reverted to the traditional script at the midpoint. About halfway through negotiations, "pre-bargaining" ended and "bargaining" began. During pre-bargaining, integrated teams worked in subcommittees exploring problems and generating options. Constituents and the lead bargainers permitted this activity as long as "real bargaining" was not occurring.

But once actual decisions had to be made, lead bargainers, under pressure from constituents, again took control. "Real bargaining" occurred at the main table, where the lead bargainers controlled what was said. As in traditional approaches, much of the final bargaining was carried out among the top negotiators in sidebar meetings. The bargainers who had formed integrated teams in subcommittees felt isolated and angry that the lead bargainers (who had not participated in pre-bargaining and therefore did not gain experience in the mutual-gains bargaining approach) took control of negotiations.

At the midpoint, the MGB process can be scuttled. If there were doubts about the process from the beginning, they are likely to come to the fore when negotiators realize that time is running out. In addition, constituent groups and others increase their monitoring of the integrated team's activities and might try to pressure the team to behave in more accustomed ways. Mutual-gains bargaining is thus especially vulnerable at the midpoint.

Ironically, however, teams following a traditional approach can shift to using elements of mutual-gains bargaining at the midpoint. In one case not in our study, the union backed out of scheduled joint training in mutual-gains bargaining prior to bargaining, while management attended the training. As a result, negotiators initially used the traditional approach. However, in one subcommittee where progress was stymied, a management negotiator suggested that they try using some elements of mutual-gains bargaining. The integrated team agreed and spent several days brainstorming for innovative ways to solve a sales commission formula problem. This process helped, but members of the integrated team said that too little was done too late. A switch to mutual-gains bargaining can occur at the midpoint, but it is more likely that external pressures, time constraints, and a focus on financial issues will drive out mutual-gains bargaining at this point.

Balancing Internal and External Group Processes

When parties engage in mutual-gains bargaining, the relationships between the primary, integrated, and constituent groups are more complicated than they are in traditional bargaining. Each team must not only manage its own internal dynamics, but also the interactions with the other groups. Research on other types of teams (new product teams, consulting teams, and top management teams) suggests that the management of these external relationships is a better predictor of team performance than is its internal dynamics (Ancona, 1990; Ancona and Caldwell, 1989; Pennings, 1980; Pfeffer, 1986).

Teams charged with the same task balance their attention to internal and external dynamics in different ways. Groups use three major strategies to define their initiatives toward outside groups (Ancona, 1990):

> *Informing* teams remain relatively isolated from their environment, prefer that mem-

bers concentrate on internal processes, use existing member knowledge to carry out their task, and later inform other groups about what they have decided.

Parading teams have more interaction with other groups and top management, but the interaction is passive—they observe and scan what these other groups are doing.

Probing teams, on the other hand, actively engage outsiders in all phases of their work. They continually gather information and revise their knowledge through contact with others in the organization. Probing team members also ask for feedback on their work, test out new ideas with outsiders, and promote their team's achievements throughout the organization.

For teams whose success depends on outsider support or acceptance (such as the ratification requirement of collective bargaining), a probing strategy seems to result in the highest performance. Internally-oriented informing teams are most likely to fail because their work is insulated from critical constituencies. They can develop an outstanding product or process, but it will never be accepted or implemented because of resistance among constituent groups. Probing teams, however, do pay a price for their success. In the short term, members of these teams experience confusion, unclear goals, and dissatisfaction with the work of the group. Because these team members are actively engaged in trying to understand external views, they bring diverse opinions and perspectives into the team, which in turn exacerbates the conflict and confusion attending any group effort. However, as teams learn to work with this ambiguity and develop ways of dealing with conflict, they eventually become the higher performers (Ancona, 1990).

Teams can use a probing strategy to handle interdependence and coordination with other groups. For example, representatives of these other groups can be invited to present their views. Or a team can negotiate with other groups about the parameters within which it will work and then remain within those limits. A third alternative is to introduce a parallel structure whereby other members of management and the union participate with the integrated group in certain phases of training and negotiation. Periodic sharing of ideas between the parallel groups can improve the understanding and acceptance of the final products. A probing strategy might be superfluous if top management sponsorship is strong right from the start. Groups do not have to work on gaining support, since it is provided by the sponsor at pivotal times and places.

Constituent Relations in Traditional Negotiations

Relationships with constituents (or "intra-organizational" bargaining) in traditional bargaining situations is always problematic (Walton and McKersie, 1965). Adams (1976) describes it as a "cycle of distrust": If negotiators get too close to opponents, constituents become suspicious, monitor the negotiators, and thereby reduce their flexibility to act and produce a good agreement. When the agreement is not what is expected, this reinforces the distrust that began the monitoring. Given the requirements for ratification, managing constituents is a critical element in labor negotiations.

In traditional bargaining, constituent relations are often managed with some drama—public shows of anger that mask the private, unobserved arenas of "real" negotiations (Friedman, forthcoming). Constituents observe the shows directly or hear about them indirectly from members of the bargaining team. Either way, constituent groups need to be convinced that their representatives are working hard on their behalf. Whatever private deals are reached must then be "sold" to constituents as the best that could be achieved. This is a careful blend of the isolated "informing" approach and the more active "probing" approach. This pattern is not well suited to mutual-gains bargaining.

Constituent Relations in Mutual-Gains Bargaining

Constituent relations seem to be more of a problem in mutual-gains bargaining. Typically, constituents are not centrally involved in the decision to use the MGB approach. Their exposure to the process is limited because they do not receive extensive training; and, even if they were to participate more fully, learning about mutual-gains bargaining comes more from the doing than the training. Further, the process itself is likely to lead to innovations and ideas that were not foreseen or preapproved by constituents. Finally, distrust builds as constituent groups see their representatives working together in an integrated fashion. For these reasons, mutual-gains bargaining presents the primary teams with significant environmental management challenges.

In all three cases, negotiators faced pressures from constituents even before negotiations began. At Northwest, constituents allowed negotiators to commit to training only after they agreed to set an early deadline for negotiations so that, if the MGB process did not work, they would still have time to negotiate in the traditional manner. At Southwest, initial constituent worries were deflected when the negotiators said that the MGB approach would only be used during "pre-bargaining." The group would then revert to traditional bargaining when real negotiations began. In both cases, negotiators had to convince constituents that traditional bargaining was not precluded by trying mutual-gains bargaining.

When negotiations began, constituent expectations and misunderstanding of mutual-gains bargaining continued to constrain negotiators. Before the MGB approach was completely scuttled at Eastern, union constituents insisted that their demands be presented to management.

The primary union team understood that these demands were traditional "positions," not a list of "interests" (the beginning point for mutual-gains bargaining discussions), but they felt compelled to make the presentation anyway. They tried to skirt the problem by claiming, "We are just doing this for our members, then we can do mutual-gains bargaining." However, it was hard to develop an MGB approach once the stage had been set by these demands. A similar problem occurred at Northwest. Even though a broad range of constituents from both sides attended the first day of training, they failed to understand the distinction between interests and positions. As a result, the list of "interests" presented by the union to management were seen as inappropriate by management negotiators and an indication of the union's inability to do mutual-gains bargaining.

Constituents also resisted mutual-gains bargaining because it generated innovative options that they had not foreseen or approved. Once bargainers understood brainstorming, they became excited about the process and generated new ideas. Inevitably they found themselves too far ahead of their constituents. They discussed ideas that were not "approved" by constituents and, when word got out that new, "dangerous" proposals were being negotiated, constituent monitoring intensified. At Northwest, the lead union bargainer faced an angry constituent-advisory group member, who complained that the advisory group was not needed if the primary team could launch into new areas without its approval. On the management side, the president and other members of the senior management team often rejected new ideas. Similarly, at Southwest, when top managers and union leaders heard that some temporary agreements were being reached in subcommittee meetings, they quickly rejected the agreements.

In mutual-gains bargaining, negotiators are caught between constituent expectations that they will be kept informed on every aspect of negotiations, and the need for open, innovative discussions. Constituents could be informed of every new idea, but this would greatly restrict the brainstorming phase and tie negotiators up in constant meetings with constituents. Yet, if negotiators eventually bring back ideas to constituents that are too radical or too difficult to understand without bringing them along gradually, the new ideas will not be accepted. And since radically new ideas are apt to be generated in mutual gains bargaining, constituent management problems are heightened considerably Moreover, these problems are likely to accumulate as the midpoint of negotiations approaches, so constituent pressures are likely to push the midpoint switching process in the direction of traditional bargaining.

Some basic tenets of traditional constituent management are violated in mutual-gains bargaining: the primary teams become an integrated team, raising constituent suspicion; radical rather than incremental changes are discussed; and information flows freely, to constituents as well as to opponents, so that it is more difficult to manage constituent impressions of the content and process of negotiations. In traditional bargaining, the negotiating group has a process for managing its relationships across boundaries. Those who use the MGB approach will need to create a new way to balance the tension between informing and probing.

Conclusions

Theory in mutual-gains bargaining generally presumes that negotiators act as unitary actors. Group dynamics is a relatively understudied and undertheorized dimension of negotiation. As a result, the prescriptive advice that comes from theory and practice tends to focus on the individual levels. Based on this exploration of group process, it is possible to supplement existing normative theory with recommendations aimed at the group level. Many of these recommendations presume either that an outside interventionist is present, or that an insider takes the lead in introducing changes.

Assistance in Getting Started

Getting started requires that you pay attention to individual members' concerns about their position, authority, and acceptance. These concerns are likely to be most pronounced among leaders and others who will perceive that mutual-gains bargaining erodes their power and influence. Assistance in getting started must ensure the development of norms that support the MGB approach, not traditional models.

It is clear that the individual concerns of members regarding identity, acceptance, and authority need to be addressed if the primary and integrated groups are to function effectively. Members need to get to know each other, to test one another, and to find their place in the group process. Until they do so, they will be unlikely to map out a reasonable approach to negotiations, create a realistic agenda, or share the kinds of information required for mutual-gains bargaining.

These concerns can be addressed in a variety of ways. *Any* occasion that provides opportunities for members to interact and get to know each other will ease some of the concerns and anxieties experienced in the early stages. Preliminary meetings held to plan upcoming negotiations or to share information also give members an opportunity to test and get to know each other. For example, in a new labor-management relationship, the Harvard University administration and Harvard support staff allocated 60 days to meet, exchange information about the university and the union, and get to know each other before they went into formal bargaining. Training that precedes mutual-gains bargaining can have the same effect, especially if there is sufficient time for participants to learn the skills and become comfortable with the process.

While formal meetings are important, some of these issues can be worked out in informal get-togethers away from the immediate demands of the moment. Dinners, drinks, and volleyball games give people an opportunity to step out of role and get to know each other on a more personal basis (Friedman and Gal, 1990; Kolb and Coolidge, 1988). Indeed, meeting away from the table is an oft-mentioned characteristic of negotiations in other cultures.

There are people whose roles and positions will always change dramatically when negotiations shift to a mutual-gains approach. In collective bargaining, these are the chief negotiators for both management and labor. Under traditional methods, they exert considerable control and authority, which must change if the more participative mutual-gains model is to be implemented. Thus, to be successful, an MGB intervention should pay attention to the leadership. First, it is important to recognize these stakeholders as the ones most likely to resist the MGB approach. Second, any intervention must include some separate time with leaders so that their special concerns can be addressed. Generally, any discussions of this sort should be handled in private, over drinks or dinner, so that the leader is not embarrassed or humiliated in front of the group. Observations about their behavior and the subtle ways in which they might be undercutting the process can be discussed in a casual way. Indeed, what we know about successful change efforts suggests that unless the leader is solidly on board, significant change is unlikely to result. Thus, these meetings become a test of commitment. It is important to realize, however, that special attention to leaders can reinforce their position rather than assist them to give up some control and authority.

Norms form and solidify early in a group's life. Groups new to mutual-gains bargaining need to attend to the norm-development process and be on the lookout for existing scripts that threaten to drive out new behaviors. This is as important a part of training as learning the actual skills themselves.

• • • • •

Indeed, a key norm to develop is to confront explicitly traditional ways of doing things when they creep in. There are several ways that this can be accomplished:

First, traditional and mutual gains approaches can be formally debated by having people act as "devil's advocates" for the old approach (Mitroff and Mason, 1981). Or the group can agree to comment when people are not behaving according to the mutual gains model. Thus, like the groups at Northwest, they can humorously label traditional behaviors as "remedial." Generally doing things in new ways can break up old patterns. These new things might include sitting in different positions, exchanging roles in simulations, or trying exercises that loosen up existing scripts (such as creativity-generating games). All of these are attempts by the group to break down barriers that impede the development of norms that support mutual-gains bargaining.

Assistance at the Midpoint

The negotiations midpoint presents both special challenges and special opportunities for mutual-gains bargaining negotiators. In order for the MGB process to continue beyond the midpoint, it is necessary to anticipate the changes that will occur. It is discouraging, even for the most committed negotiators, to discover that they are far from agreement despite their best efforts, and to begin to wonder if this new process actually works.

Negotiators need to be reassured that the transition they face at the midpoint is a natural one, and that their efforts thus far were not for nothing. An apt analogy is to a building that is under construction. One can go by the building lot for months and months and see no visible progress. It appears that nothing is getting done. Then suddenly the building frame goes up in a few days and it seems like a miraculous accomplish-

ment. Yet the frame could not have been put up so quickly and easily if months had not been spent putting in a foundation underground. After the frame goes up, progress slows again as the work changes to that of putting up walls and interiors. Because the initial period of this transition process can be so frustrating, support and intervention can be very helpful.

Midpoint intervention can include analysis, brainstorming, relearning negotiation skills, and restructuring. As a first step, negotiators should be encouraged to look at what they have accomplished, what is left to accomplish, and what changes in the bargaining process are needed to complete negotiations. Negotiators can use the very process they applied in the first half of negotiations—that is, they can brainstorm about ways to proceed that are neither the traditional ones nor the ones used during the inventing stage.

Thinking in terms of opposites can facilitate brainstorming:

If groups worked in subcommittee before, maybe working at the main table would be better now; if they focused on the internal process before, maybe they should focus on external relations now. Once they have analyzed what needs to be accomplished and developed new ideas for approaching those needs, the groups will have to renegotiate the structure and process that they will use in the final stages of bargaining.

The midpoint can be a time when the group feels overwhelmed. Although it might appear counterproductive, this is a a good time for the group to take some time out from their work. Sessions where group members can vent frustration or where additional training occurs help the group to deal explicitly with its midpoint issues. Some group members will resist such a break when they already feel short of time. However, directly confronting some of these issues will help the group to deal less emotionally with the time problem. It might be appropriate for the consultant to assist in running these kinds of sessions.

The midpoint is also an opportune time to restructure the group. This can include a change of personnel or a change in the patterns of group work. For example, this could be a time to bring in a constituent or someone with a particular expertise that the group now needs. Similarly a group that was meeting two times a week for two hours might now need to meet more often or for a longer duration.

Vigilance is particularly important at the midpoint. Negotiators need to keep a sharp eye on behavior, as old habits and safe, traditional routines can easily reemerge under the increased pressures of the second half of negotiations. At the same time, it is also important for the groups to commend themselves. They need to celebrate the progress that they have made thus far and use that as a basis for continuing to the final stages.

Assistance in Managing Internal/External Relationships

Balancing internal and external demands is among the most difficult tasks facing the team engaged in mutual-gains bargaining. Whatever strategy is chosen involves tradeoffs between internal cohesion and external acceptance, between creating an innovative product and seeing that product implemented. Several kinds of interventions can facilitate this delicate balancing act, including: training external constituents more thoroughly; encouraging explicit probing activity; making brainstorming an intergroup rather than an intragroup activity, and obtaining sponsorship early in the process.

External constituents often feel like "second-class" citizens when mutual-gains bargaining is introduced. The prospects for better support often lie in the ways constituents are treated during the early stages. Training these "outsiders" in the elements of mutual-gains bargaining is a

start, but it is not enough. External constituents also need to be prepared for the new roles that they will play over the course of the negotiating process. They will be called upon to provide information, suggestions, feedback, and support throughout the negotiations. They will be asked to comment on only partially formed ideas, ideas that might be very different from those formulated in traditional bargaining. Consultants and members of the primary group need to forewarn constituents that such ideas will perhaps seem useless or even bizarre, but that additional time and thought will improve them. Thus, constituencies need to understand—and perhaps contribute to—the inventing process that is an integral element of the MGB approach.

Because buy-in from external groups is a key requirement of success, a probing strategy promises to be an effective tool in mutual-gains bargaining. Therefore teams, as part of their training, need to be instructed about the elements of a probing strategy. First, primary and integrating team members need to think strategically about the change to mutual-gains bargaining. Such a change will result in stakeholders who are allies, and others who may attempt to block the effort. Once supporters are identified, they need to be "courted", and convinced to bring constituent groups along with them. Likewise, resisters need to be contained and diffused. Perhaps they can be given inducements to support the negotiated settlement, or at least to keep silent so that they do not mobilize a blocking coalition. This political aspect of probing requires proactive behavior. It is not enough for the team to deal with management and labor representatives who happen to show up at meetings. Both allies and resisters have to be managed (with or without the help of a facilitator).

A second aspect of probing is testing, in which the team tests its ideas out on various constituent groups. Questions such as, "If we did this, what would your reaction be?" and "Does this satisfy your need for an easy-to-implement compensation package?" are examples of testing procedures. Testing should be an ongoing process; it should also be started early, before blocking groups have an opportunity to mobilize against an option. Many teams generate excellent ideas only to be criticized—or even disowned—by constituent groups when those ideas are presented. Those external groups need to get used to the new ideas and to feel as if they had a part in shaping them. In the short term, testing might demoralize some team members, as many of their ideas will likely be derided or actually vetoed. To avoid constituent testing, however, is to pay a high price later in the negotiations.

Inventing options through brainstorming is typically seen as a task that occupies the integrated group or subcommittee of its members. For probing teams, however, brainstorming becomes an activity for both the integrated and the constituent groups. Both sets of groups can produce, criticize, and evaluate ideas and options. It is a well-known phenomenon that ideas are more easily accepted when people feel that they have participated in their production. Therefore, bringing a wider range of stakeholders into the brainstorming process increases the probability that those ideas will eventually be implemented. Again, there are costs to this strategy. It takes time to contact outsiders, and the group may already have more ideas than it can handle. Further, the group might will feel pressured to accept the external input it solicited. Nonetheless, these potential costs are a small price to pay for acceptance of the settlement in the final stages.

Finally, it should be clear that managing all these external activities will be much easier if there is clear, public support from a well-placed sponsor at the outset. Support from the top of the labor and management organizations provides legitimacy for the integrated group. With blessings from on high, it becomes easier to garner additional backing from other stakeholders. Generally,

probing is facilitated when the teams do not have to fight to schedule meetings, and when an influential sponsor has already done some of the marketing. The probability of success is improved enormously when the project begins with top-level support and when that support is given in both public and private domains.

This exploration of group process and its implications for mutual gains bargaining has focused exclusively on labor and management negotiations. However, the concepts developed and the recommendations offered have implications for negotiations conducted in other settings as well. From a fuller appreciation of the demands mutual gains bargaining makes on group process, we can all enhance our chances of Getting to Yes.

NOTES

The authors are listed in alphabetical order; each contributed equally to the paper.

1. This new approach to negotiations is sometimes referred to as "principled" or "interest-based" negotiations (Fisher and Ury, 1981); "integrative bargaining" (Walton and McKersie, 1965; Pruitt, 1981) or "mutual gains bargaining" (Raiffa, 1983; Lax and Sebenius, 1986; Susskind and Cruikshank, 1987). While these labels have slightly different meanings, the core of the processes are similar. We use these terms interchangeably to refer to a form of negotiation in which parties focus on interests, look for ways to expand resources, and focus on tactics other than power to find agreements that provide gain for all parties.

2. The concept of the midpoint revolution was "discovered" in a study of eight temporary task forces, all of which faced explicit deadlines (Gersick 1988). Although many teams do not have similarly definitive timelines, they do have milestones and subtasks with defined timeframes. So a team can go through this pattern of evolutionary change punctuated by revolution during a particular portion of its work or development.

REFERENCES

Abelson, R. P. (1976). Script processing in attitude formation and decision-making. In *Cognition and social behavior*, edited by J. S. Carroll and J. W. Payne. Hillside, N. J.: Lawrence Erlbaum Associates.

Adams, J. S. (1976). The structure and dynamics of behavior in organizational boundary-roles. In *Handbook of industrial and organizational psychology*, edited by M. Dunnette. Chicago: Rand McNally.

Ancona, D. G. (1990). Outward bound: Strategies for team survival in the organization. *Academy of Management Journal* 33 (2): 334–365.

Ancona, D. G. and Caldwell, D. F. (1989). Information technology and work groups: The case of new product teams. In *Intellectual teamwork: Social and technological bases of cooperative work*, edited by J. Galegher, R. E. Kraut and C. Egido. Hillside, N.J.: Lawrence Erlbaum Associates, Inc.

Axelrod, R. (1984). *The evolution of cooperation.* New York: Basic Books.

Bazerman, M. and Neale, M. (1983). Heuristics in negotiation. In *Negotiating in organizations*, edited by M. Bazerman and R. J. Lewicki. Newbury Park, Calif.: Sage.

Bettenhausen, K. and Murnighan, J. K. (1985). The emergence of norms in competitive decision-making groups. *Administrative Science Quarterly* 30: 350–372.

Cartwright, D. and Zander, A. (eds.), 1968. *Group dynamics: Research and theory.* (3rd ed.) New York: Harper and Row.

Deutsch, M. (1973). *The resolution of conflict.* New Haven: Yale University Press.

Douglas, A. (1962). *Industrial peacemaking.* New York: Columbia University Press.

Fisher, R., and Ury, W. L. (1981). *Getting to YES.* Boston: Houghton Mifflin.

Friedman, R. A. (forthcoming). Cultures of mediation: Private understanding in the context of public conflict. In *Conflict in the crevices: New perspectives in the study of conflict in organizations*, edited by D. Kolb and J. Bartunek. Beverly Hills: Sage.

Friedman, R. A. (1989). Interaction norms as carriers of organizational culture: A study of labor negotiations at International Harvester. *Journal of Contemporary Ethnography* 18 (1): 3–29.

Friedman, R. A. and Gal, S. (1990). "Managing around roles: Building groups in labor negotiations," Harvard Business School Working Paper 91–001.

Gersick, C. J. C. (1988). Time and transition in work teams: Toward a new model of group development. *Academy of Management Journal* 31: 9–41.

Gersick, C. J. C. (1989). Marking time: Predictable transitions in task groups. *Academy of Management Journal* 32 (2): 274–309.

Gulliver, P. H. (1979). *Disputes and negotiations: A cross-cultural perspective.* New York: Academic Press.

Hackman, J. R. (ed.) (1990). *Groups that work (and those that don't).* San Francisco: Jossey-Bass.

Hackman, J. R. , Brousseau, K. R., and Weiss, J. A. (1975). The interaction of task design and group performance strategies in determining group effectiveness. *Organizational Behavior and Human Performance* 16: 350–365.

Hoffman, L. R. and Maier, M. R. F. (1964). Valence in the adoption of solutions by problem-solving groups: Concept, method, and results. *Journal of Abnormal and Social Psychology* 69: 264–271.

Kolb, D. M. and Coolidge, G. (1988). "Her place at the table: A consideration of gender issues in negotiation." Working paper 88–5, Program on Negotiation at Harvard Law School.

Lax, D. A. and Sebenius, J. K. (1986). *The manager as negotiator.* New York: The Free Press.

Mitroff, I. I. and Mason, R. O. (1981). *Creating a dialectical social science.* Dordrecht, Holland: Dr. Reidel Publishing.

Pennings, J. M. (1980). *Interlocking directorates.* San Francisco: Jossey-Bass.

Pfeffer, J. (1986). A resource dependence perspective on intercorporate relations. In *Structural Analysis of Business,* edited by M. S. Mizruchi and M. Schwartz. New York: Academic Press.

Pruitt, D. (1981). *Negotiation behavior.* New York: Academic Press.

Pruitt, D. and Lewis, S. A. (1977). The psychology of integrative bargaining. In *Negotiations: A social psychological perspective,* edited by D. Druckman. Beverly-Hills: Sage.

Pruitt, D. and Rubin, J. Z. (1986). *Social conflict: Escalation, stalemate, and settlement.* New York: Random House.

Raiffa, H. (1982). *The art and science of negotiation.* Cambridge, Mass.: Harvard University Press.

Schein, E. (1988). *Process consultation: Its role in organization development* (vol. 1). Reading, Mass.: Addison Wesley.

Shaw, M. E. (1981). *Group dynamics: The psychology of small-group behavior.* New York: McGraw-Hill.

Susskind, L. and Cruikshank, J. (1987). *Breaking the impasse.* New York: Basic Books.

Taylor, S. E., Crocker, J. and D'Agostino, J. (1978). Schematic bases of social problem solving. *Personality and Social Psychology Bulletin* 4: 447–45 l.

Walton, R. E. and McKersie, R. B. (1965). *A behavioral theory of labor negotiations.* New York: McGraw-Hill.

Deborah G. Ancona is Associate Professor of Organization Studies at the Sloan School of Management, Massachusetts Institute of Technology, 50 Memorial Drive Cambridge, Mass. 02139.

Raymond A. Friedman is Assistant Professor of Business Administration at the Harvard Business School, Soldiers Field, Boston, Mass. 02163.

Deborah M. Kolb is Professor of Management at the Simmons College Graduate School of Management in Boston and Executive Director of the Program on Negotiation at Harvard Law School.

Section VIII

Individual Negotiations

Chapter Fifteen   *Career Negotiations*

Chapter Sixteen   *Personal Negotiations*

Chapter Fifteen

CAREER NEGOTIATIONS

HOW TO ASK FOR A RAISE

Jeff B. Copeland and Peter McKillop

At Scrooge Industries, as at so many companies, this is the time of year when employees get up their courage and ask for a raise. Bob Cratchit, a mid-level paper rearranger, is in the office of president E. Scrooge IV.

"I wouldn't even ask for more money, sir, except that Tiny Tim hurt his legs again when his dirt bike flipped and . . ."

"You think you've got problems? Humbug! Sales are flat and I had to raise $500 million to fight off Carl Icahn. And you have the nerve to want more?"

Asking for a raise is just about the hardest thing any of us do for our living. Senior management is often happy to spare employees the confrontation and give all the authority to itself through formulaic "compensation reviews." The lower echelons, unless they are represented by a union, often have a lot more individual bargaining power than they think. But fear, pride, and intimidating notions about negotiation keep these people from speaking up—or result in failure when they try.

The trick is to learn how to put your emotions aside and bargain rationally. Cratchit has just made a common mistake. "So many people will put it totally through the employee's needs but what really matters to the corporation is how important you are to it," says Nella Barkley, a New York career planner. Bob ought to speak about ways he saved the company money.

Scrooge makes the classic boss's response that the corporation's needs are monumentally larger. If Bob had researched company finances, he might have responded that an upcoming contract will boost sales. Let's listen as he blunders on:

"I deserve it because I worked hard at everything you told me to do."

Touchingly naive, Bob. "If you want a raise you have to do extra work," advises Adele Scheele, a Los Angeles career counselor. Learn what more the boss needs done and suggest an expansion of your job responsibilities to do it, she says.

"I was only looking for an extra 3 percent."

Wrong again, Bob. Most people tend to undervalue themselves. Scheele has clients practice demanding large salary figures. The point is not to ask for something ridiculously big just as a ploy. It's wise to find out what comparable jobs pay elsewhere by checking with business friends, trade journals, or employment agencies.

"And I heard they're paying paper rearrangers a lot more over at Pickwick Industries. I think I'll pay them a visit."

Dangerous move, Bob. Even if the threat works, "from that moment on, you're not a secure employee" to management, says Gerard I. Nierenberg, a negotiation expert. Have a firm job offer, because your bluff may be called. Even now, Scrooge IV propels Bob from his office toward Pickwick.

But holiday-season stories ought to have a happy ending. Let's give Bob a second chance to do it the right way. Months earlier, Bob suggests a raise at the end of the year and tells Scrooge IV about work goals he set and met. He studies his boss's personality and needs so that his pitch will be made in terms of mutual satisfaction.

Cratchit rehearses the meeting ahead to help overcome fear and resentment. After all, says Barkley, "you are not being measured as a person, you are being measured for your output." And remember, "No only means no for now," says Herb Cohen, author of "You Can Negotiate Anything" (Bantam). This time the meeting goes differently.

"As you can see by this chart, sir, through my efforts, paper rearranging productivity is up 46 percent for a savings to the company of $83,000. If I train and supervise the rest of the department in my techniques, you and I could improve that achievement even more.

What would you think would be a fair level of compensation for my extra effort and our extra savings?"

Scrooge IV is so awed he hands the presidency over to Cratchit and goes off to distribute turkeys to the poor.

"God bless us every one!" says Tiny Tim. "Now, how about raising my allowance?"

HOW TO NEGOTIATE
A JOB TRANSFER

William C. Banks

For Gary Schindler, 40, a marketing manager at AT&T, the shortest route to promotion has been a 6,000-mile zigzagging trail of transfers. Starting in 1975 in Oakland, Calif., where he was a sales representative for Pacific Telephone, he has moved with his wife and two children to AT&T's marketing headquarters in New Jersey, and from there to Denver. This month, the Schindlers will move again, to Los Angeles, where Gary will head AT&T's Southern California marketing division. "Each transfer has meant a great new opportunity for me," he says. "But I realize now there's a lot more to a transfer than just waiting for the moving van to arrive."

For example, Gary found that when his company offered to buy his house in New Jersey, its appraisal and subsequent bid was, at best, conservative. In two weeks he sold it for $10,000 more than the company price. He also convinced AT&T to cover 90 days of temporary living expenses in Denver, instead of the customary 60. Says Gary: "Mine was basically the company's standard moving deal, but I know that sometimes there is a little flexibility."

Reprinted from *Money Magazine*, June 1984. Reprinted with permission. All rights reserved.

For decades, many U.S. corporations have routinely shunted promising employees around the country and abroad, reasoning that experience at several outposts is valuable for top-management candidates. But in the early 1980s, quite a few firms cut back on such seasoning in an effort to contain costs. Now transfers are increasing again. Once more, tens of thousands of employees must weigh the promise of career advancement against the trauma of uprooting their families. And for two-income couples, a transfer for one may mean unemployment for the other. Nearly half a million employees will be moved by their companies this year, according to the Employee Relocation Council, a Washington, D.C., research organization. IBM alone transferred some 6,600 people last year—reaffirming the old saw that the company's initials really mean "I've Been Moved."

Most large companies have standard moving policies that leave little room for negotiation. But no matter how rigid the company position seems, transfer veterans report that employers are sometimes willing to make adjustments. In fact, relocation counselors advise asking for additional allowances to offset a variety of hidden costs that can add up quickly during any move. If you know what to ask for, you can save yourself some unpleasant financial surprises in an already stressful situation.

Many small firms also have formal guidelines for transfers, but it is by no means uncommon to find companies with few or no established provisions for helping employees move. If your firm has no transfer policy, knowing the benefits that are standard at large corporations can provide you with a starting point for your negotiations.

MOBILITY ON DEMAND

"The smoother the transfer, the better for all," says Thomas Peiffer, vice president of marketing at Runzheimer & Co., a management consulting firm based in Rochester, Wisconsin. "Corporations demand mobility where and when they want it, so they tend to offer attractive deals to their workers," he explains. To this end, a company can easily spend the equivalent of the employee's yearly salary on a transfer. The bill for moving a family typically comes to about $40,000—$20,000 for the physical move and $20,000 in additional financial subsidies such as temporary living costs.

The standard transfer-benefits package offered by big companies that frequently move employees begins with an agreement to pay the costs of transporting your household goods. Typically, the company will arrange for the purchase of your house at a price established by two or more local appraisers. In addition, the package should include reimbursement for the following:

- A loan for the down payment on a new house based on your equity in your old residence.

- Brokerage fees if you should decide to use your own real estate agent to sell the house.

- Any prepayment penalty on your old mortgage.

- One or two house-hunting trips to the new location.

- Temporary living expenses for six weeks.

- Up to three points for mortgage origination fees.

- Normal closing costs on the purchase of a new house, including loan application fees, other bank administrative charges, and your attorney's fees.

- The difference between the interest rate of your old fixed-rate mortgage and the interest on part or all of a new fixed-rate loan over a period of three years. Many companies have similar benefits for adjustable-rate mortgages.

Also standard is a tax allowance. Most moving costs are tax deductible, but reimbursements for nondeductible expenses, such as private school tuition should you not like the public schools at the new location, are taxed at the federal, state, and local level as ordinary income. Most companies provide an extra stipend to offset your additional tax liability. Sometimes called "grossing up" your expenses, this bonus should be large enough to compensate not only for the taxes on the reimbursements for your nondeductible expenses, but also for the stipend itself, because that too is taxable. Before you break even, this benefit might have to add up to more than twice the amount of your nondeductible expenses.

The standard deal for renters also covers the cost of moving, but they usually get less money for resettlement. Most large companies pay apartment finder's fees as well as all moving and temporary living expenses. In addition, the company will often pay a lease-termination fee, but only rarely will it reimburse you for a lost security deposit.

As generous as those standard company terms seem, they often omit many expenses that can surface long after you move. Looking ahead and asking your employer to cover such costs is by no means a matter of avarice, says Dennis O'Neel, a partner in the Santa Monica-based executive search firm of Finnegan and White. "You have to remember that the transaction is a business deal. You should never be afraid to ask for what you are going to need to at least break even on the expenses you incur as the result of being transferred."

DELUXE BENEFITS

According to Ayse Kenmore, director of career planning and placement at Stanford's Graduate School of Business, the first thing to negotiate for when you are asked to accept a transfer is more time. "Don't let them rush you through the process. Ask for a month to think things over. Then make an appointment with your boss to talk about transfer terms." Ideally, Kenmore suggests, negotiations should move slowly, in small steps, so in the end you and your boss feel that you arrived at the solution together.

According to relocation counselors, a deluxe negotiating list might include the following:

- Provision for additional house-hunting trips, if needed.

- Cost of living compensation. If food, clothing, and entertainment are more expensive where you're bound, ask for a raise at least large enough to offset the higher cost of living.

- Home improvement money. Sometimes called a "funny fund," this allowance might range from $1,000 to $5,000 to cover the costs of carpets, drapes, and any other items you have to leave behind in your old house.

- An allowance for your children's private school, if your new location doesn't have good public schools.

- Initiation fees for organizations such as country clubs at the new locale. As cushy as this perk appears, it can be important. If you are already a member of a club where you are, the cost of the new membership is an expense you suffer because of the move.

- A company car. If you are moving to an area with poor public transportation, a second car might be a must. However, personal use of a company car is considered taxable compensation.

- Financial help in selling a vacation house. Ask for the same terms that apply to your residence, including a reimbursement for broker's fees and closing costs, and mortgage assistance on a comparable new second house.

- Help in finding a job for a salaried spouse. One growing area of concern is the steady rise in the number of two-income couples: When one spouse accepts a transfer, the other often faces a long job search in the new location. Try to get the company to hire a relocation firm to assist with resumes and to provide job counseling. Also ask for compensation for child-care costs while the spouse is job hunting. Only about one company in five will help a working spouse find employment. "A lot of companies are still in the Dark Ages about the problem of working spouses," says John Moore, Merrill Lynch Relocation Management Inc. executive vice president. "It's a subject that's constantly being discussed, but no one seems to know what to do about it." Asking for company assistance in this area is especially important if you're moving overseas to a country where non-citizens need work permits.

- Special overseas benefits. Ask for an annual visit to the U.S. for your family, and payment for the cost of private schools for your children. If you doubt the strength of the local currency, you can ask to be paid in dollars rather than in the coin of the realm. Don't sell your house in the States. Instead, request financial help with the costs of maintaining and renting out the house. This could include reimbursement for upkeep and for property management and broker fees. Especially plush benefits for overseas transfers include reimbursement for the difference between the carrying cost of the house and the rent—including months when the house is not occupied because no renters can be found.

You may not get any of the extras you ask for, but that shouldn't discourage you, says Peiffer of Runzheimer & Co. "Companies that have a lot of relocations every year often have little room for negotiations because they're afraid of setting costly precedents.

As important as they are, financial matters should be only one part of your overall transfer-negotiation strategy. Another crucial consideration is how the new job will affect your career path. "You don't want a job in the boondocks if it means you're going to disappear from the corporate map back at headquarters," advises Ayse Kenmore. One way to discover where the transfer might lead is to find out where the person you are replacing is going.

SOUR MOVES

Then there are personal costs to consider. No matter how vital the new job is to your career, the success of a transfer often depends heavily on your family's ability to adapt quickly to a new home. Most families weather the disruption of a transfer well. Moving goes sour for everyone in the family if the reward for the move doesn't justify the inevitable upheaval of family life.

According to Jeanne Brett, professor of organizational behavior at Northwestern University's Kellogg Graduate School of Management, if it's a lateral move without adequate financial support from the company, problems are more likely to crop up. Brett, who has studied 350 families that have accepted several transfers, has discovered a surprising bonus for the employee who negotiates a soft landing for his dependents: The transfer may well be good for everyone. "A lot of people say that mobility breaks up the nuclear family, but my study shows just the opposite: People who move a lot report that they enjoy a high degree of marital, family, and work satisfaction. Often the family is united by the move, and its members become closer as a result." So in the end, the best benefit might turn out to be the one you *didn't* bargain for.

DON'T JUST SIT THERE —NEGOTIATE

Nkiru Asika, Kevin J. Delaney, Brooke Deterline, and Vera Gibbons

Satyam Wadhwani, a California software engineer, asked his boss last summer to let him work just one day a week—at 50 percent of his previous salary, with full benefits, stock options, and a company-bought laptop computer—so he could start up his own firm. He got it.

Before taking his new job at a Los Angeles medical-supplies company, Gary Gibson asked for $20,000 more than the company's first offer, a promise that he'd travel in business class only (the company's policy was to fly coach) and an eight-month severance package (the company's policy was one-month). He got it.

Recruiter Ray Lilja has seen job candidates ask for it all. Cell phones. Flex time. Car allowances. Several months ago, when he found a job for a telecom executive in Chicago, the guy demanded a golf-club membership as part of his package. "I asked him, 'Do you play golf?'" Lilja recalls. "He said, 'No, but maybe I'd like to learn sometime.'"

Guess what. He got it.

These are the new rules of compensation: The employee, not the employer, is calling the shots

From *Smart Money Magazine*, June, 1998. Reprinted with permission of the publisher.

in many cases. With unemployment running at the lowest level in decades, the fact is that talented people are in seriously short supply. In some fields, such as information technology, it's thought that unemployment is virtually nil. Other sectors seeing double-digit gains in demand, according to a recent survey by the recruiting firm Korn/Ferry International, include financial services, manufacturing, health care and pharmaceuticals, and professional services. In an environment like this, companies simply can't *afford* to turn down their employees' requests for more money, more perks, more whatever they want.

Bonuses and stock options are probably the most asked-for types of compensation these days, followed by extra vacation time and flexible hours, according to headhunters and employers. "Family-life issues are really hot," explains Barbara Cohen, director of human resources and training at Brown Brothers Harriman, a Boston financial services company. Flex time, reduced hours—we're acquiescing and offering a lot more of this." (It helps that flex time and reduced hours are among the least expensive perks for a company to give its employees.

But sometimes it seems that nothing is out of the question. Virginia headhunter Killian Cousins

Your Net Worth

Where to learn what your peers earn.

Interviewing for a new job, Kempton Coady did his homework. The 50–year-old medical-devices executive pored over the literature his prospective employers sent him, reviewed each company's stock performance and financial analyst's reports, and read John Tarrant's classic treatise on contract negotiation, *Perks and Parachutes*. One of his best moves, though, was heading to the Internet, where he used the Securities and Exchange Commission's online database (*www.sec.gov*) to see what the other top executives in the companies were making. Armed with that information, he could easily choose a "target value" for his own services. "It's a very powerful thing to use," Coady says.

Even if you're not a top executive, you'll find the Web is home to all sorts of useful—and free—salary information these days. The best place to start is one of the omnibus job sites that link users to data organized by profession. The most up-to-date and easy-to-read is *The Wall Street Journal Interactive*'s career site (*careers.wsj.com*), which provides surveys from one of the Journal's sister publications, the *National Business Employment Weekly*. (Both are published by Dow Jones & Co., co-owner of SmartMoney.) The listings include median salaries for job categories ranging from advertising copywriters ($54,900 at a mid-size agency) to industrial engineers ($52,722 in the aerospace industry) to mutual fund managers ($136,200 for senior portfolio positions, plus an $82,800 bonus).

The California-based JobSmart site (www.jobsmart.org) offers links to similarly comprehensive national data. One warning: Some of the linked surveys are decidedly outdated. In this hot job market, the last thing you want to do is use salary data from 1994.

As you might suspect, the richest store of salary information on the Web relates to technology positions. But everyone from chief financial officers to supermarket meat buyers can find decent data. If the omnibus sites don't link you to it, Internet search engines such as Hotbot (www.hotbot.com) and AltaVista (www.altavista. digital. com) will usually turn up something. Try entering "salary survey" plus your job title.

You can also graze the classified ads online for your position to get a sense of what other companies are offering new hires. The Monster Board (www. monsterboard. com) and CareerPath.com (www.career-path. com) host two of the most comprehensive listings.

But since a dollar in Manhattan is not equal to a dollar in Topeka, Kansas, you should adjust the figures for the cost of living in your area. That takes just a few clicks with the help of the salary calculator at Home Fair (homefair.com).   —K. D.

has a client who insists that any employer pay for his fertility drugs if they're not covered by the company's health plan. One marketing executive recently had his employer replace his septic system—a $20,000 job—so he could sell his house when transferring from Boston to Philadelphia. "Management told me to keep it under my hat," he says.

And it's not just the uppermost executives who are getting this treatment, either. Though top managers' negotiating positions are as strong as ever—another Korn/Ferry survey puts worldwide demand for senior executives at a 27-year high—even the most junior-level people are asking for and getting perks that would have seemed extraordinary just a few years ago. When

Soft Money

What your compensation really costs.

If you'd be just as happy with $10,000 worth of stock options as a $10,000 bonus, why not ask for the one that's most palatable to your company? From the cheapest to the most expensive, here are some of the most popular things people are asking for now, and how they affect most companies.

Lifestyle accommodations Flex time, extra vacation time—these perks cost your company nothing out-of-pocket, so ask away. Though some companies still argue that time away from the office can't possibly be productive, lots have come to see things differently. "I do think people can be more productive at home," says Barbara Cone, head of human resources at Brown Brothers Harridan. "When our employees are more content, we're better off as a company."

Stock options They're "beautiful" in terms of cost-efficiency, says William Dunn, a CPA and compensation expert at Coopers and Lybrand. Not only do stock options motivate employees to get that stock price up, but they cost your company next to nothing to give away. Unlike your salary or a bonus, they don't reduce your company's earnings in the slightest. And when you exercise your options, the company gets to take a tax deduction on any appreciation in their value.

Restricted Stock These are shares in your company that you won't get to keep before a "vesting period" of three years or so. They're less attractive to companies than options because, like salary, they directly reduce earnings. But they're more attractive than a bonus because of the vesting: Rather than taking a onetime hit against earnings, your company can spread out the cost of giving you restricted stock over your vesting period.

Perks Upgraded business travel, laptop computers, car allowances, and job-related tuition are all examples of perks that companies can usually write off as a cost of doing business without their being considered compensation. This means the company doesn't pay Social Security or unemployment tax on them—which makes them considerably cheaper to give away.

Bonuses Handing you an extra check at year-end counts as compensation for tax purposes—but it's still got advantages over giving you a raise: It's a one-time event. It won't knock your company's salary ranges out of whack. And it probably won't affect your company's contribution to your retirement plan.

Raises To an employee, what's not to like about a raise? More money in every paycheck, a bigger retirement-plan contribution, a bigger base from which you'll get next year's raise, etc. The problem is, everything you like about a raise, your company doesn't. Flex time, anyone?   —B.D.

Stannie Holt was offered an entry-level editorial job at the trade magazine *InfoWorld*, for example, she asked her boss what he could do to "sweeten the deal." To her delight, he came up with a $2,000 signing bonus.

But there's more to this shift in power than just the tight labor market. Over the past few years, there's also been a fundamental change in the boss-employee relationship. The old ties linking people to their companies have eroded, stripped away by downsizing and restructuring. Fueling this change: the surging recruitment business, whose biggest firms reported 24.5 percent revenue gains last year, according to *Executive Recruiter News.* Once reserved for only the highest-level executives, there are at least 13,000 firms that recruit midlevel managers or below, says Paul Hawkinson, editor of *The Fordyce Letter.* "Middle managers and middle professionals are going through the roof right now."

Now, the average American will work for seven or eight companies over his or her lifetime, says John Challenger, executive vice president of the outplacement firm Challenger, Gray and Christmas. Fifteen years ago the number was more like two or three. When people start feeling less of a connection to their employers, they're more willing to play companies off each other, and their bosses are less likely to take offense. John Lloyd, chairman of the Association of Executive Search Consultants, recalls how one insurance executive recently went to hand in his resignation. He walked out with a raise and the presidency of the company.

It used to be a once-a-year ritual—the dreaded salary review. But now people are going in year-round and asking their bosses for more money or perks or promotions. And you know what? Their bosses actually expect them to. The fact is, management would rather have you come in and make the case that you're underpaid than, say, come in and submit your resignation, says Kiko Washington, vice president of human resources at the cable channel HBO.

Still, many of us would rather have dental surgery than ask our boss for more money. Why is that? Because we're chicken, says Belinda Plutz, owner of New York's Career Mentors consulting firm. "People are afraid they'll be forced into quitting or, if they're job hunting, that the company will withdraw the offer. But that doesn't happen. Most of the time people will either get the money or a very good explanation of why that's not an option."

There are two key things you need to know beforehand. First, how much are you contributing to the company's performance? "People think the toughest part of a raise is getting up the gumption to go to your manager and ask for

it," says Nick Corcodilos, host of a Web site called Ask the Headhunter. "That's nothing. The toughest thing is justifying it. It's like going to your customers and asking them to pay 20 percent more."

The other thing you must know: what other people in similar jobs are making. Some people will stop at nothing to figure that one out. At one Florida company, an employee got so desperate to find out everyone else's salaries, she tried to break into the company's computer system to rifle its personnel files—15 times. Bob Bache, a Long Island marketing manager, has never gone quite that far, but he has resorted to subterfuge. A few years ago, for instance, he got an offer from a company he knew little about, so he phoned the human-resources department. "I said I was doing research in the business-development area and was interested in salary ranges, Bache recalls. "We went through the departments, title by title."

Did he ever identify himself? Well, no. "But it wasn't a complete lie because I was doing research." He pauses to reflect on that. "I guess it was kind of a white lie." (In the end he decided not to pursue the job, since the top management wasn't making the kind of money he aspired to.)

You don't really need to be that sneaky to find out what you're worth. Today there are more tools and resources available to employees than ever before. Headhunters, for one, can be invaluable sources of information about who's making what. "Even when people aren't really interested in finding a new job, they'll call me up and say, 'I'm looking', just to see what others are making," says Debra Levine, a recruiter who specializes in the retail and apparel industries.

The Internet, too, has been an incredible boon. There are hundreds of Web sites listing salary surveys, so you can easily see how much other people in your industry are making—and more (see "Your Net Worth" sidebar).

That kind of data goes a long way with employers, as Mike Malone, chief operating officer of Stellcom Technologies, found out in his latest salary talks.

"I've always paid my people based on market data," Malone told his boss, passing a photocopied salary survey across the desk. "And that's what I expect."

Though the first offer fell short of Malone's expectations, he wouldn't budge. "Nope," Malone said. "That's not market."

He wound up with slightly less than the market average—but 15 percent more than the chief executive's initial offer, along with the promise that he'd be first in line for bonuses. And the negotiations could not have been faster or easier. That's because he had the facts on his side, Malone explains. "I really only had to put one stake in the ground and say, 'Pay me market'."

Mike Malone wasn't asking for anything fancy. He basically just wanted more money in his paycheck every month. But these days compensation often isn't that simple, what with more and more pay coming from hard-to-value bonuses, stock options, and even time off from work.

Out of that complexity, however, comes opportunity. Here's how you can successfully make the most of it.

Don't Take Any Old Bonus— Design One Yourself

Every company's looking for an edge these days, and increasingly, they get it by tying their employees' bonuses to performance. Though the most common area for bonuses is sales, where an employee's performance is easily quantified, many other types of workers are also getting them nowadays. At HBO, for example, some producers ask for bonuses tied to the number of awards they win, says Washington.

Running into a brick wall in your salary talks? Try getting around it with bonuses. Digital Equipment, for instance, got a new director of sales who took a 28 percent salary cut to join the company. He was coming from a flashier electronics company, and Digital's more modest salary scale just couldn't accommodate him. The solution: Digital let him work out a bonus schedule that actually put him 60 percent *ahead* of where he was before.

How'd he do it? Flying home from the job interview, he did some simple math on a notepad. "I was looking to make about $60,000 in bonuses for the first two quarters, to be on track to make my goal of $200,000 a year, including salary," he says. "So I divided $60,000 by the number of [accounts] I thought I could open and then asked for that amount of bonus per [account]. Basically, I backed into the numbers." Digital, he says, was happy to oblige—especially since, in selling it to management, "I focused on what the program would make for them—and not on what it would make for me."

How to Weigh the "Options" Option

We've all heard countless stories about Microsoft millionaires, employees made rich by the stock options the company spreads around. These days, of course, options are not purely a West Coast phenomenon. They're lining the pockets of people from coast to coast and everywhere in between. You'll find them among factory workers at Procter and Gamble, as well as among the makers of GoreTex fabric and the loan officers at First Tennessee Bank, where even part-time employees are offered stock options.

The allure of options is undeniable, and some people are even willing to take less salary—a lot less—when options are on the table. A good idea? Joseph Diefenbach sure hopes so. Until recently, he was earning $70,000 a year as a senior software developer. Though a competitor

Claudette Beyer: The Reluctant Trustee

When Claudette Beyer took the role of president and CEO of Heat Transfer Research, an engineering consortium in College Station, Texas, she knew there'd be plenty to learn. While Heat Transfer was a relatively small company (it currently has just 32 employees and assets of $5 million), it was a far cry from her last job as an academic research administrator. There, she had management responsibility for a mere eight subordinates, as well as no monthly overhead or marketing and business development to worry about. Still, one thing she never counted on was having to become an expert stock and fund picker.

That's what the representative of the local A. G. Edwards office seemed to be telling her, however, when she went to set up a new 401(k) account for her employees in 1992. Everyone's money would be kept in one account, for which she would serve as sole trustee. Translation: It was up to Beyer to choose the investments herself.

Soon, she found herself spending precious time studying Standard & Poor's reports, checking Morningstar evaluations, and scanning the papers for fund returns. After three years, she started squeezing in meetings with a financial planner for suggestions—but it was still up to Beyer to call the shots. And this wasn't chump change either: Last year the plan's total assets reached $1.7 million.

Although the plan's holdings have "mostly matched the broader market," she says, a number of her investment choices—typically she maintained a conservative portfolio of blue-chip equity, bond, and money-market funds—have led some employees to grumble. "I know at least one or two people who were not happy," agrees Stan Kistler, a chemical engineer who's been with the company for 25 years.

Beyer says that if she'd been trading only for her own account, she'd have chosen a more aggressive mix. But some of the older workers feared losing their secure—though smaller—returns. "It was never something I wanted to do," she says. "The responsibility should not have been mine. It just came with the job."

That's a sentiment shared by many small-business owners today, says David Wray of the Profit Sharing/401(k) Council of America, who notes that less than a fifth of small companies even offer retirement plans. Another obstacle is the often daunting expense ratios. With plan assets modest in size, small firms generally must pay fees 30 percent higher than those of their large-company counterparts.

But lower fees aren't the only reason Beyer switched the firm's s 401(k) to Vanguard this past winter. With the new plan, employees pick their own investments—leaving Beyer to concentrate on more important things, like keeping Heat Transfer Research profitable. "If there's no company," she says, "there's no pension plan." — Lisa Kalis

came along and offered a straight salary of $104,000 plus bonus, tuition reimbursement, and other benefits, he turned it down to join Sybarite Interactive, a New York-based Web software company, for a salary in the low $60s and a bundle of options.

He thinks he has a good idea of how much the company is worth, having seen other companies get taken over in the industry. "So even if we get bought out by another company, I could make $100,000 or more as a lump sum," he says. "That right there would make up [for the difference in base salary]." His best-case scenario is a lot rosier than that: "I could potentially be a millionaire."

If you're going to take a lower base salary for more options, compensation guru Graef Crystal suggests you consider *everything* you're giving up, not just the smaller paycheck. For instance, is the contribution to your retirement account based on your salary? The life insurance you're getting from the company? Your bonus? Crystal also advises sitting down and figuring out where your break-even point is. It's not hard. Just look at how much you're giving up in salary each year, when your options vest (that is, become available to you) and what price the stock would have to be for you to make up the lost salary and extras. Do you realistically think the stock is capable of reaching that price in that amount of time? Then it's a good deal.

FLEX TIME NEEDN'T SQUEEZE YOUR SALARY

How do you value a job that lets you work from home one day a week—or maybe even work just three days a week instead of five? Some recruiters insist that you'll have to give up some financial compensation for such "quality of life" improvements, if only because your boss might take you less seriously. But while that may be true in larger, more hide-bound companies, it's definitely not so in smaller outfits these days. When David Bishop left his job as an auditor at one of the Big Six accounting firms two years ago, his chief requirement was that the new firm would let him leave the office at 4:30 p.m. or 5:00 p.m. —so he could attend—not business school— culinary school.

Richard Ostroff, a recruiter in New York, knew of a law firm that "wasn't a sweatshop"—and thus would probably agree to his demands. Only when the firm said it wanted Bishop did Ostroff bring up the culinary school. No problem. "The company was offering mid-$40s and we got him $45,000," Ostroff says. "So the company didn't get him at a discount" just because he wanted to leave early.

First Offers Are for Suckers Only.

We know, it's not easy turning up your nose at a perfectly good offer. But look at it this way—if you don't, you're basically a chump. Why? Because nobody's first offer is as good as it's going to get, and everything is negotiable.

One way to make it easier on yourself: Go into your negotiations having already practiced saying no—or a more pleasant-sounding alternative. For Antoinette McKelvy, the magic phrase was a simple: "That's not what I expected to hear." She'd picked up the line from career consultant Bill Karlson, whom she'd met at a seminar on negotiating. When McKelvy's prospective boss suggested a salary, she whipped out the line and it worked like a charm. Next thing she knew, her employer came back with nearly 10 percent more.

"I'd use that line again in a heartbeat," says McKelvy.

THERE IS SUCH A THING AS TOO MUCH NEGOTIATING

Once you get a whiff of negotiation, it can be fairly intoxicating: "Well, all right! My boss is bending to *my* will for once!" But there's a thin line between pushing for what you deserve and pushing simply because you can.

Peter Batarseh finds himself pondering that line these days. Last spring, when he was made an offer to join an Internet provider as regional sales manager, he was on top of the world. Heading his 12-point checklist of demands: a laptop, a cell phone with a paging device, a car allowance, and tuition reimbursement of $1,000 a semester so he could finish his M.B.A. (He'd completed only 12 hours toward the degree at that point.) Those "tools" aside, he also asked for a 20 percent larger base salary and a 4 percent commission hike. He got it all, he says.

Just three months later, Batarseh says, he was promoted to sales manager. This time he asked for a 20 percent salary increase and a "restructuring" of his commissions so he'd benefit from his team's efforts rather than

Ramsey Tarazi: The Job-Hopper

As a boy, Ramsey Tarazi remembers asking his dad about the older guy they saw at church each week—the one who wore the same polyester suit every Sunday.

"That guy never had a retirement plan," Tarazi's father responded sternly. "He lived one day at a time, and now he's suffering for it." On the street, the younger Tarazi recalls, it was the same story. His dad would occasionally point to an acquaintance, out of the blue, and warn: "See Jack over there? He didn't really have any kind of plan. Now look, everyone in his family has to fend for himself."

While it's hard for anyone to escape panic about his or her retirement, for 32-year-old Ramsey Tarazi, that fear might be genetically encoded. To complicate matters, he has yet another—rather common—trait that makes financial planners and parents alike squirm:

Tarazi is a career-changer, having switched jobs three times in four years.

Only once, in fact, has he stayed anywhere long enough to qualify for an employer's 401(k) matching funds. That was at Comerica Bank, where Tarazi spent a rather respectable eight years in business development. In 1994, however, he traded away his job security and matching grants to buy the Last Laugh Comedy Club in downtown San Jose, California. Two years later, with the comedy business looking grim and profits no laughing matter, Tarazi sold the business and took a job as a sales manager with Karus Corp., a printed-label manufacturer, which he left after just 21 months. And of these he took a job as a marketing communications specialist for a semiconductor manufacturer.

So, with all that moving around, how much has he managed to save for retirement? Well, surprisingly, quite a bit. Tarazi has already socked away some $40,000, in fact—putting him squarely at the head of his generation. According to a 1997 survey conducted by the Employee Benefit Research Institute, 81 percent of people 33 years old and younger have saved $50,000 or less for retirement.

How'd he do it? By the time Tarazi left his bank job, he had about $14,000 in qualified savings. A strong start, certainly. But then he moved on to the comedy club, where he not only had to take a 50 percent cut in pay, down to $25,000 a year, but where he also had no company savings plan whatsoever. Still, by downsizing his living space from a three-bedroom house to a two-bedroom apartment, he says—and by slashing his entertainment spending to almost nothing—he was able to squeeze $1,500 a year into an IRA. At Karus he invested 10 percent of his salary in his 401(k) after the one-year waiting period. And he put that $4,800 into a large-cap fund, Investment Company of America, that returned 30 percent in 1997. Over time, thanks in part to smart investments, Tarazi's $21,800 in contributions has nearly doubled.

Despite his penchant for professional soul-searching, Tarazi says the itch to switch careers has been subdued. "My thinking has changed," he promises. "I'm staying put for a while. I want to get my (401(k)] match."

So, what if he got a phone call today offering him a new job and a 30 percent raise? Well, that's different. "More than likely I'd take it," Tarazi laughs. "I'd be able to maintain my lifestyle and still put money aside on my own." —*Michelle Andrews* from his individual accomplishments alone. He also wanted membership in the local golf club ($6,000, plus annual fees), computer and phone upgrades ($6,600 combined), and 3 percent ownership of the company.

He got it all, he says, except the 3 percent stake.

There's only one little problem. When new investors came on board in April, Batarseh was let go. No, he doesn't think it was because of all the things he asked for. "This was standard stuff based on my position," he says. "Having been in sales for 13 years, I knew what others in the industry were making." So why was he let go? Frankly, he's at a loss. "It's possible they thought I was greedy," Batarseh concedes.

"I'll tell you one thing," he adds. "I should have negotiated a severance package."

◆ ◆ ◆ ◆ ◆

Chapter Sixteen

PERSONAL NEGOTIATIONS

HOW MUCH WILL YOU PAY FOR THIS HOTEL ROOM? TOO MUCH

Everett Potter

Same room. Same night. Six different prices. Here's how to negotiate the best rate.

It doesn't take a seasoned traveler to know that the first air fare an airline quotes you is probably not its lowest. Most people realize that you've got to shop around, ask for specials, and use your frequent-flier miles like $100 chips in a high-stakes poker game to get the best deal.

When it comes to hotels, though, most of us drop our guard. We don't seek out a deal; we employ no special strategies. All too often we automatically accept the first rate that a hotel clerk or travel agent provides us. And if the word "special" is used, we accept that rate with a smile and hand over a credit card.

But chances are, that rate might not be so special after all.

It might, in fact, be more than the price you're quoted if you call back five minutes later, or the one you might be able to obtain if you prod the desk clerk for a bit more information.

From *Smart Money Magazine*, August, 1993. Reprinted with permission of the publisher.

The truth is, room pricing is one of the least logical and most confusing aspects of the hotel industry these days, and good luck to the traveler who stumbles upon it blindly.

Take, for example, our experience when we recently tried to book a room at the St. James Court Hotel, which is located just a short walk

WASHINGTON D. C.	
WASHINGTON VISTA HOTEL	
For the night of June 9, 1993	
Rack rate	$165.00
Corporate rate	158.00
Second corporate rate	130.00
Hotel's "special" rate	129.00
Hotel's discount rate	140.00
Discount program rate	92.50

First Rule of Thumb: Never rely on the hotel's 800 number.

These off-site reservation clerks have very little room to negotiate.

from Buckingham Palace in central London and is a member of the Taj Hotel Group.

Inquiring about a double room for a weekend about six weeks away, we were told by the hotel that the rack rate (regular rate) was 130 pounds per night (about $198, with sterling at $1.52). But the reservationist added that a weekend special of $172 was available. Great.

Then we called back a bit later and said we were members of the International Airline Passengers Association (IAPA), an organization that, for $99 a year, provides "preferred-rate discounts" for its members.

We were then told that the rack rate was 160 pounds ($243) but that, as IAPA members, we could get a deluxe room for $182. But we didn't need or want a deluxe room.

We decided to call the 800 number in the U.S. for Taj Hotels, despite the assurance of the reservationist at the St. James that one did not exist. Straight off. we were offered a rate of $160 a night.

"Normally it's 160 pounds, but we're doing a special [rate] of $1 to 1 pound, so the rate is $160," the reservationist explained.

That was better. Still, we weren't finished. We called the St. James once again to tell them that we were members of World Hotel Express, a half-price club that charges $49.95 a year and promises its members half-price rooms at selected hotels on a space-available basis. There was indeed a room available, and we were quoted a rate of $122, which we were told was half the normal rack rate.

Thus, after four quick calls, we had reduced the price of the room by $50 a night, enough for a theater ticket to a West End show and a pint of bitters afterward.

We decided to quit while we were ahead.

Booking a hotel room always carries with it an element of chance. The St. James Court is not unique among hotels in offering an array of different rates to the same customer. In fact, we tried the same thing at more than a dozen hotels and got similar contradictory results. The Doral Inn in New York, for instance, quoted us four different fares for a standard room—ranging from $125 to $190, with an even cheaper rate ($95) offered by Entertainment Publications, a discount program. The Mark Hopkins in San Francisco also provided us with four rates for the same standard room, the lowest a $129 rate that the front-desk clerk said was a "limited special"; the highest, $205, was quoted by the hotel's 800-number reservation service. "That's the best we can do for you," the reservations operator cheerfully but erroneously told us.

Similarly, a series of calls to the Plaza Hotel in New York yielded four rates (again for the same room), ranging from $155 to $235, and other calls to the Washington Vista Hotel in Washington, D.C., gave us the choice of spending either $92.50 or $165 (with four options between) on a double room for the night.

If you think that one hand doesn't know what the other is doing, you're right. There are so many rates on a given day at a given hotel that such confusion has become the norm. "I'd say there are about 15 rates per room at our properties, which is probably lower than the norm," states Geof Rochester, vice president of marketing for Radisson Hotels International. Carlos Tolosa, senior vice president of operations at Embassy Suites, which prides itself on having identical suites, says that "on a given day, there are between 10 and 20 different rates." Even a humble Comfort Inn typically has "six or more rates," according to Andrea Butler, a spokeswoman for Choice Hotels International, parent company of Comfort Inns.

The question is: What does all this mean for you?

Well, you should never again pay the first price quoted when trying to book a room. There are plenty of ways to negotiate the labyrinthine process of hotel pricing, and there are plenty of bargains to be had for those who know the tricks of the trade.

To understand why hotel rates are so fungible takes some knowledge of the hotel business itself. "A hotel room is a perishable product," explains Richard Hanks, vice president of revenue management for Marriott. If it's not sold, it dies every night. So the idea is to sell as many rooms at normal rates as possible. But that's only possible to a point. So hoteliers discount rooms in order to fill them and raise their occupancy levels. For a hotel to do this effectively, it has to segment customers and sell different rates to different people."

With U.S. hotel occupancy around 60 percent and holding, according to Smith Travel Research, selling rooms at full price is difficult at best. Some hotels even change their rates hourly, depending on how much traffic there is that day, and how likely the prospects of a full house look by midafternoon.

Typically, says John Keeling, director of PKF Consulting, the negotiating process begins with hotels quoting the highest rate they think they can get. Or, as Ed Perkins, editor of *Consumer Reports Travel Letter*, puts it, "A hotel will set a rack rate of $200 for anyone dumb enough to pay it."

The truth is, most people are.

"Hotels have discovered that 80 to 85 percent of people will accept the first rate. And of the 20 percent or so that don't take the first rate, 80

percent will accept the second rate," says Keeling. "So there's an incentive to give high rates."

The practice of squeezing the most revenue out of each unit is called *yield management*—and it's nothing new. The airlines have been doing it for years. It's the reason for that now-classic airborne moment when three side-by-side passengers alternately express shock, anger, and smugness when they discover that they've all paid different fares for the same flight.

Hotel pricing essentially works the same way, and it has produced the same confusion and resentment on the part of the consumer, who doesn't want to pay more than the next guy. But hotels have an added wrinkle—the customer who attempts to get a bargain at the front desk. This is a little like boarding an aircraft without a ticket, pointing to an empty seat, and asking the pilot what he wants for it. Airline pilots aren't empowered to do this; hoteliers are.

Increasingly, though, hoteliers are trying to rein in their most ardent negotiators. Executives at Radisson and Westin hotels say that both chains have streamlined their rates so there is less leeway when calling up to book a room. "We're trying to make sure that a travel agent, our 800

SAN FRANCISCO

MARK HOPKINS HOTEL
For the night of June 9, 1993

Rate offered through 800 number $205.00

Hotel's corporate rate 180.00

American Express's discount rate 155.00

Hotel's discount rate 149.00

Hotel's "special" discount rate 129.00

Quickbook's discount rate 120.00

reservations number and our front desk all have the same rates available when you call," says Radisson's Rochester.

Other chains are simplifying their rates as well. Taking their cue from American Airlines, Sheraton instituted three-tier SureSaver rates last year. They provide set discounts for business travelers, for those who reserve 14 days in advance, and for weekend travelers. American's idea didn't work; Sheraton's apparently has, setting what Ed Stahl, director of marketing and advertising, likes to call "a new pricing rationale."

Marriott has taken the concept a step further. Its Advance Purchase Rates require prepayment, unheard of in the industry when the policy was implemented in 1990. "We wanted to get away from the used car/rug bazaar mentality of haggling for a room," says Marriott's Flanks. "So you pay us 14 or 21 days in advance and we give you up to 50 percent, sometimes 60 percent, off. If you cancel, you lose your money."

But the fact remains that even when hotels do their best to simplify their rates, there are often ways of beating them. "The SureSaver program is a framework," admits Stahl of Sheraton. "Individual hotel pricing is the province of the property. We have to look to each hotel to be sensitive to their market."

It's the standard routine, one you follow by rote. You're planning a trip to Los Angeles next week and want to book a hotel room for a few nights. So you pick up the phone and start dialing the hotel's toll-free number. Might as well save on long-distance charges, you figure.

Take our advice: Hang up.

Despite the dollar or two it might cost you, you should always call the hotel's front desk directly. You can't rely on information from a chain's central reservation number, because it invariably connects you with someone who's not on-site, who doesn't have access to all of the rates at a

> Don't assume the first price quoted is the one you have to pay. "On a given day, there are between 10 and 20 different rates," concedes one hotel executive.

given property, and who has no authority to negotiate a price. Indeed, we found through our sample testing of major hotels in the U.S. and Europe that the 800-number reservation clerks consistently quoted us the highest rates.

When you call, inquire about weekend, seasonal, or holiday specials. (Weekends, with their slackening of business traffic, offer the most negotiating room.) "Call the hotel directly and say 'I understand you have a weekend rate,'" says Tom Parsons, editor of *Best Fares*, a magazine that tracks hotel and airline discounts. "Don't say, 'Do you have a weekend rate?' Never play the field with a question mark. Act as if you know. Then the clerk says to himself, 'This guy must know about our $49 rate.' So he tells you about it. You've got to be cagey."

When it comes to actual discounts, the corporate rate, typically 10 percent off the rack rate, is the easiest to get. This often requires no more evidence of corporate employment than showing a business card at the front desk, if that. But watch out. A corporate rate can be higher than the lowest rack rate in order to cover the cost of a superior room or other amenities. You'll also discover that corporate rates vary; the deal your company has cut might not be the best one the hotel has to offer. So if both spouses work, and you're traveling together, see which of your employers has wangled the best corporate rate.

Then, of course, there are upgrades. There is probably no sweeter term in the travel business—certainly not for the traveler who gets a deluxe room for the price of a standard. For a few dollars more—sometimes nothing at all, if the hotel is convinced that you are a frequent traveler worth cozying up to—you can often negotiate with the front desk (or, more likely, someone in the sales department for such amenities as a room on a concierge floor, a more panoramic view, or a late checkout. Mentioning your frequent-flier connections is also a good way to get an upgrade: there are often promotional tie-ins with various hotels.

Probably the best single way to get a deep cut on a hotel room rate is to join one of a number of discount programs that have sprung up in the past few years. These companies, such as Entertainment Publications, the Privilege Card, Quest International, and World Hotel Express, charge a fee ranging from $19.95 to $99.95 and promise 50 percent off rack rates at selected hotels. Most provide a hotel phone number that you call, identifying yourself as a program member, to request discounts.

It pays to check out the geographical strength of each company. Privilege and Quest have a number of Caribbean destinations, for example, while America at 50% Discount has resort condos. The one drawback to these programs, however, is that they are typically blacked out when the affiliated hotel is projecting an occupancy of 80 percent or more. (For more details, see accompanying sidebar.)

Naturally, one would expect a travel agent to be capable of weeding through the rates to get you the best deal, just as they are supposed to do with airline fares. But don't count on it. The American Society of Travel Agents (ASTA), which represents 16,000 agents, reports that while 80 percent of all air tickets are booked through travel agents, only 25 percent of all hotel rooms are.

"It's a love/hate relationship," says David Love, a spokesman for ASTA. "Hotels love to sell the rooms themselves so they don't have to pay the 10 percent commission that travel agents receive.

For a price, typically $35 to $99 a year, travelers can join a number of hotel discount clubs that offer savings of up to 50 percent off a room's standard rate. There are some restrictions, however. Discounts are subject to availability, and hotels don't have to offer the lower rate if they are already 80 percent full. Also, some hotels require that you identify yourself as a discount-club member the minute you call about a room. If not, you lose your chance at the special rate. One other thing: Don't expect palatial surroundings at bungalow prices. Hotels that are affiliated with discount clubs typically run in the budget to medium-price range.

America At 50% Discount

Phone 800-248-2783

Fees $49.95 first year; $24.95 per year after that.

Discount: 50 percent off the rack rate in a standard room.

Hotel Affiliations: 1,400 hotels in the U.S. and Canada.

Restrictions: Reservations must be made at least two days in advance.

Additional Perks: Car-rental discounts and an airline reservation service that offers a five percent rebate on selected air fares.

Comments: Affiliated hotels are similar to those offered by other discounters, but the directory provided to members at least has dollar symbols next to hotel names to indicate price range.

But the relationship between the two is getting better."

Yet some can't be bothered and others will do it only as part of an air/hotel package that promises them a higher commission, as we found out when we tried to use a travel agent to book a hotel room. One agent demanded a surcharge of $20.

Technology, or the lack of it, is at the heart of the problem. Typically, a travel agent who uses a cen-

Some discount programs offer great deals for travelers—but at a price. Do you really want to spend April in Paris at a Holiday Inn, even at $119 a night?

tral reservation system such as American Airlines SABRE Travel Information Network has access to about 27,000 hotel properties world-wide, each one theoretically having five to 20 rates on a given day. But unlike the airlines, who post all their fare changes daily, the SABRE system does not show all the hotel rates. This is because there are technical limitations with the system and because each hotel property lists only the rates that it wants to provide to the system—typically a rack rate and a corporate rate. A hotel is under no obligation, legal or otherwise, to post all of its rates on a central reservation system.

"The hotel says, 'Here's your chunk of information,' and that's that," explains Teresa Hanson, a spokeswoman for SABRE. "Don't forget, this system originated as an airline reservation system. It was not intended to be used as a hotel reservation system. But it's evolved into one."

Hanson admits that "the technology just hasn't been put into place yet" where the average travel agent can scan a screen and see every rate a hotel offers.

"We don't get every rate," confirms Joan Duran, a travel agent and owner of La Rochelle Travel in New Rochelle, N.Y. "There are no fare-search programs for the lowest rate as there are for airline tickets. We have to physically pick up the phone and call a hotel to see if there are any specials. So why go to us? Because we know what questions to ask. The consumer often doesn't."

What travel agents often do have access to, however, are preferred-rate discounts—discounts offered by a hotel because the travel agent sends it a large volume of business. Typically knocking

10 to 40 percent off the rack rate, these discounts are not as steep as some of the rates offered by half-price clubs (see sidebar), but they also are not subject to the 80 percent occupancy rule. If there's a room in the house, you get it. In fact, some hotels block rooms off for customers in these programs, so there might be times when you'll get a room when the hotel is telling other travelers that it's full.

The best-known preferred-rate programs are TravelGraphics and ABC Corporate Services, a division of Reed Travel Group. ABC Corporate Services is available through 2,000 travel agents and it promises an average discount of about 14 percent below the corporate rate (figure 25 percent below rack rate) at about 700 hotels. In addition, it promises corporate rates or better at 12,000 properties world-wide. TravelGraphics is affiliated with about 1,400 hotels, and its discounts are similar to those offered by ABC. (TravelGraphics is also available directly to the public through a pocket directory that it sells for $18, but a spot-check of one hotel listed in that directory—New York's Parker Meridien—raised some skepticism about its effectiveness for those who are not travel agents. The reservations clerk didn't recognize the name of the program and we didn't get a discount.)

Travel agents aren't the only ones, however, who can benefit from bulk discounts. It's possible to bypass the middleman altogether and take advantage of the special rates offered by discount reservation services. Such companies as Hotel Reservation Network, Central Reservations Service, and Quikbook act as brokers for big-city hotels, which employ them to keep their occupancy rates high. As a customer, you call an 800 number, say where you want to go and get a list of hotels offering a discount in return. Discounts typically range from 10 to 40 percent off the rack rate.

The main advantage of these services is that they come at no cost to the consumer, or at least no annual membership fee. But there are a couple of disadvantages. First, you might be steered to a particular hotel if the discounter is trying to fill it. Second, discounters work with just a handful of European properties—and not the most glamorous ones at that. Do you really want to spend April in Paris at a Holiday Inn, even at $119 a night including tax?

Choices for travelers range from discounter to discounter. For example, Hotel Reservations Network (800-96-HOTEL) is affiliated with 850 properties in the U.S. and 50 in Europe, including London and Paris, but typically has access to only 10 rooms a night in any one hotel. New York is its biggest market, with 20 properties, including the Royatron, the Sheraton Manhattan, Royalton and Holiday Inn Crowne Plaza. And while getting through can occasionally be difficult—we failed several times—HRN often delivers a good rate. It got us a standard room at the Westin St. Francis in San Francisco for $75, half the rack rate.

Travelers to Miami, New York, Orlando, or San Francisco should consider using Central Reservations Service (800-548-3311), which offers discounts of 10 percent to 40 percent on hotels in those four cities. Discounts of more than 40 percent often can be obtained through Quickbook (800-221-3531), but its 100-plus hotels tend to be in the medium-price range. New York's offerings are, for example, the Milford Plaza, the Gorham, and the Inn on 57th—rather than more luxurious sites. A more limited—but more upscale—selection is offered through Express Reservations (800-356-1123). Although its discounts, up to 35 percent off the rack rate, are limited to just 40 hotels in New York and Los Angeles, they are available at hotels that typically have no ties to other discounters. Among its offerings: $70 off a standard room at New York's Essex House, $20 lower than the hotel's own special rate.

Some bargains can also be found for travelers with international destinations in mind.

For instance, Travel Interlink (800-477-7172) and Vacationland's Hotemart (800-245-0050) specialize in heavily discounted rooms in Asia, where half-price programs have so far made few inroads. Travel Interlink offers discounts of 25 percent to 65 percent off the rack rate in more than 3,000 hotels in the Far East and Southeast Asia, India, Australia, and New Zealand. Hotemart has a much smaller pool of hotels to draw from—450 in the Far East and Southeast Asia—and slightly lower discounts, but among its offerings are two of the best hotels in the world: Hong Kong's Mandarin Oriental, and Peninsula. The drawback to both these bulk discounters: They require prepayment, they don't accept credit cards, and they have stiff cancellation penalties that can cost you your entire payment if you cancel at the last minute.

Then there are the plethora of "specials" being promoted by hotels anxious to keep their occupancy levels at a high rate by discounting their rooms anywhere from 10 percent to 50 percent. But these special rates can turn out to be quite ordinary.

"You'll often find that hotels have different specials with different names but with identical

NEW YORK CITY
DORAL INN
For the night of June 9, 1993
800 number $190.00
Front desk 135.00
Hotel's corporate rate 138.00
Hotel's "special" discount rate 125.00
Quikbook's discount rate 112.00
Entertainment's discount rate 95.00

rates," explains Edgar Garin, director of rooms and reservations for the Continental Companies, a hotel-management company that handles such properties as the Grand Bay in Miami and the Jerome in Aspen. "It's because there are so many distribution channels."

And that leads to perhaps the most direct way to get a discount. Call it the "chutzpah factor." All it takes is the nerve to walk into a hotel, ask to speak to the manager, and then negotiate a good rate on the spot. "There is some of that," con-cedes Radisson's Rochester. If you don't have the personality for that tack—and many of us don't—at the very least ask to see your room before agreeing to stay the night. If you don't like it, ask for another one.

"Look, the manager can do anything,'" says Parsons of *Best Fares*. "And there's no embarrass-ment in asking. There are too many hotels out there. If one doesn't want to offer me a deal, then I'm moving on."

DEALER TACTICS AND HOW TO COUNTER THEM

Burke Leon and Stephanie Leon

How did he do it? How did that last salesman twist your mind into a pretzel and convince you to buy that car, which wasn't the one you came in for? That car you bought only five years ago, that car you didn't need, that car you are trading in right now to avoid further hassles. He did it so skillfully, you weren't even aware of what was happening. Well, it is no great mystery. As I have said many times before, professional salespeople have the edge on their own turfs with an *uninformed* consumer. They learn tricks and techniques from the masters, spend years trying to apply them, and spend even longer discovering the type of person who is most susceptible to each technique.

Knowledge is power. If you know when a "technique" is being used on you, it becomes easier to ignore it and single-mindedly get on with your business: buying the car of your choice at the lowest possible price. You cannot be confused or bamboozled if you can dismiss anything that even remotely resembles a manipulative technique. Once you recognize the techniques, you might even want to learn to use them yourself. Some might come in handy if you try to sell your own car.

From Burke and Stephanie Leon, *The Insider's Guide to Buying a New or Used Car,* 1997. Cincinnati: Betterway Publications. Reprinted by permission.

The following is a list of some of the most common and most successful techniques used by professional salespeople.

TAKE IT OR LEAVE IT

Take it or leave it is the standard marketing policy all Americans have grown up with. You go to a restaurant or a furniture or clothing store and you take it or leave it at the price marked on the item. However, in the auto business, **you don't have to take it or leave it.** You can negotiate for it. You can, of course, leave it and later come back and take it. It is a good negotiating practice always to leave it before you take it. The tactic is usually a ploy to force you into an early decision, but eventually it might really be the way it is. You'll never know unless you test it.

MAKING YOU FEEL GUILTY

"I really need the sales" or "You're just wasting my time" or "Are you serious about buying this car?" or "I may lose my job if I don't make this sale" or "I consider you a friend" or "One more sale this week will win me a trip to Hawaii," pleads the salesperson, trying to make you feel guilty.

If any one of these attempts at playing on your emotions succeeds, you will be had. Remember, the problems of the dealership staff are their problems, not yours. Remember why you are there; you want to buy a car, and that's all. You are not there to make a friend or solve the world's social problems. Showing empathy will merely encourage further appeals. Hard as it might be, **try to keep a business-like distance between you and the salesperson**.

WRITE MAKES RIGHT

Somehow or other if things are written down, we are not as apt to question them. The written word has a certain power of legitimacy. Car dealers are armed with an array of written facts, figures, forms, and rules that they say are etched in stone. **You should always assume that anything written is negotiable, that prices are meant to be tested, and that any item can be adjusted.** If you do your homework, you will know what all items cost, and which costs are fixed and which are not. The fact that a dealer has something written down doesn't mean it is true. Question everything.

THE CALIFORNIA APPROACH

"What do I have to do to get you to buy a car today?" the salesperson queries, over and over again, each time more forcefully, until the buyer's objections are understood and countered one by one. Hopefully, the buyer will peacefully sign on the dotted line just to end the pressure.

The counter to this is to *know* **what a good deal is, to ask for it, and to demand that the salesperson stop pressuring you.** The broken record technique (explained later) works well as a deterrent to the California approach.

GOOD GUY/BAD GUY

In this scenario, the salesperson becomes your friend and helps escort you through a maze of roadblocks. His sales manager keeps bringing up problems, and your friendly salesperson helps you solve them—usually by having you give way on point after point. Your best tactic is

to **keep a formal distance between you and the salesperson,** and to indicate that the good guy/bad guy tactic is so old, you are surprised that anybody is still using it.

CONTROL THROUGH QUESTIONING

Since **the person who asks the questions and demands answers is in control of the situation,** it might as well be you. The salesperson does have a need to ask some qualifying questions to find out what it is you need, want, and can afford, but he has no right to demand answers or to answer each of your questions with a closing question. For instance:

> **You:** Can you get me that car in red?
> **Salesperson:** If I do, will you buy the car today?
> Note: *His response shows that he is asking you to make a decision about buying prematurely. Your reply should be:*
> **You:** I would like an answer to my question please. Can you get *me* that car in red? When I get my answer, I will be better able to determine if I am going to buy or not.

THE TEAM APPROACH

In some dealerships, there are layers of salespeople. Each layer has a different responsibility. One greets you, another takes you for the test-drive, another starts the sale, and yet another closes it. Sometimes several salespeople will gang up on you in sequence and work on you until you wear out. The best way to handle this is **not to allow more than one salesperson at a time to work with you**, and to arrive so late that there are very few salespeople around. Don't allow them to double-team you. Leave if you can't control this situation.

DELAY

Sales people can extend negotiations in several ways: by running in lots of other salespeople, by losing your keys, or by having you wait around so long that you get anxious or tired and just want to consummate the deal as quickly as possible. However, they will only do this if you have signaled that you are susceptible to this type of treatment. So when you are sitting and waiting for the salesperson to come back with a counter offer, make him uneasy. Get up, walk around, go outside. **The customer who can successfully control the pace of negotiations is more likely to have them go his way.** A typical delaying scenario can go something like this:

> **Salesperson:** Your credit report seems to be presenting some problems. It will take about sixty minutes for us to check with our bank. Why don't you have a cup of coffee in the reception area and we'll get back to you soon?
> **You:** My credit is fine, and I'm late for dinner. Why don't I just go home and have you call me tomorrow when you finish your investigation?
> **Salesperson** (panicking—he is afraid you will walk off): Wait just a minute. Let's see if I can speed this up.

GOING, GOING, GONE

Saying that the dealership only has one car left like the one you want is a great way to force you to make an immediate, perhaps premature, decision. By making you feel that your choice is the dealer's hottest car and that the supply is limited, a salesperson thinks he can force you into a commitment. If this tactic is tried, you should be willing to let your dream car go if everything else isn't exactly right.

Another version of going, going, gone is the line, "This deal is good for one day only—today!" The only response to this variation is to say, "Well then, I might miss it." A deal is good for as long as anybody wants it to be good. There is usually no reason for a time limit on any offer. **Call his bluff** by adhering to your own agenda. If you lose it, you lose it.

"Only the payments are important . . . Right?"

Wrong! Sometimes, the real cost of a car can be obscured when the salesperson says, "We both know that the only important thing is to get your monthly payments down as low as possible." Beware of this ploy. Before you know it, you will have a lower payment, a much longer payment time and a higher down payment. If you are not careful, you won't even know the price you actually paid for the new car. This tactic is usually used when the buyer stalls on a high price because of sticker shock. **Never worry about payments until you talk to the finance person.** Always know what you actually paid for the car, and always fight hard for the lowest car price.

"Only the difference in price is important . . . Right?"

Wrong again. Often the salesperson will try to convince you that all that really matters is the difference between the new car price and the trade-in price. Your salesperson is deliberately trying to confuse you. In actuality, the difference between the new car and trade-in prices *is* important. But it is even more important to know the *exact price* of each in order to avoid being confused. If you are not careful, every time you get the new car price to drop, somehow or other the agreed-upon price for the used car will suddenly drop also. Determine the price of each separately, and keep track of each separately. This will prevent you from becoming confused as the buying progresses. It will also prevent you from losing money on your trade-in.

It is also easy to be confused by allowances: "I will allow you $_____ toward the purchase of your new car at $_____." **Get fixed, firm prices for each item in the negotiation.** The price of your new car should not be dependent on the allowance for your trade-in. Allowances never work for you.

• • • • •

LOWBALLING

To enhance their profits, car dealers usually strongly lowball trade-ins. This is because their profits on the new cars are sometimes limited by the amount of money banks will lend toward new car transactions. Remember, there are several parts to a transaction, and even though you get a low price for the new car, you still must get a reasonable price for your used car. Lowballing is used when the salesperson determines that you are very concerned about new car price but are relatively unconcerned about what you get for your trade-in. He will try to focus your attention on a reasonable price for the new car and yet lowball you on the price of your trade-in. While your attention is focused on saving hundreds of dollars on the new car, you might forget to watch the trade-in sale and can easily lose thousands.

The reverse can also happen. If the salesperson feels you are adamant about getting a good price for your trade-in (for the down payment on a new car), he will give you an unbelievable price for your trade-in, charge you above-list for the new car, and tie both prices together as a package deal. To counter this, first **make the salesperson believe the only thing of importance is a good price for your trade-in.** *After* **you get it, make him realize that the only important thing is a low new car price—but don't give back the great trade-in price.** Having previously written down the agreed-upon trade-in price will be helpful, especially if you have had the salesperson acknowledge it at some point in the transaction.

BAIT AND SWITCH

If you are not careful, you can walk into a dealership to buy the car you have thoroughly researched, the one that suits your needs and price structure, and come out instead with one you just fell in love with. When you find yourself switched for any reason (perhaps away from a low-priced sale car), **leave until you can think your way through the new situation and do the necessary homework.**

VERBAL PROMISES

During your buy, a lot of things will be promised to you verbally. Every time something is offered, *write it down* and keep a list. Even better, have the salesperson or his boss initial the items agreed upon. **Save this list for the closing** when they will probably try to take back some of the items they have given you.

LIMITED AUTHORITY

Not having authority would seem to make a person's negotiating position weaker, but, in actuality, the best negotiating position is to have no authority at all. Then you can back off any agreement you have made by merely indicating that you aren't authorized to make it. Automobile salespeople operate effectively by relying on this lack of authority. This allows the salesperson to make an agreement with you and also say, "My boss might not go for this." You, however, are expected to be able to make and stick to all your agreements. Ask the salesperson at the onset of negotiations if he has the authority to make a deal. His usual response will be not to answer, to answer, to ask a different question, or to be evasive. At this point, indicate that if he has no authority, you want to deal with someone who has. **Do not let his lack of authority control you.**

GETTING YOU TO SAY "YES, YES, YES"

The theory is that if you say yes to a long line of questions, it will then become easier for you to say yes to accepting a less than adequate deal. When this happens, get obstinate and **say no** or "Maybe, if . . ." a few times. Other options are to change the subject or to get the salesperson to say yes to one of your demands.

NIBBLES

Car dealers are good at asking for small concession after small concession. Before you know it, you have given away the store. If this is happening, counter-nibble. **Don't give away anything without asking for something back.** For instance, if the salesperson wants you to agree to a higher price before he presents the offer to his boss, use it as an opportunity to ask for free air-conditioning and an upholstery upgrade. Who knows, he may just say yes. Never let a nibble go unanswered. Ask, ask, ask. No one will give you anything unless you ask for it.

TEMPORARY CONCESSIONS

Many times things that have been granted to you at earlier stages of negotiations disappear in financing—usually at about the time you start to feel good because you have almost bought a car. All those things you have fought so hard for sometimes get forgotten when you can smell the leather seats. To keep this from happening, *write down* **all the agreed upon items, and don't sign until you have everything you were promised**. Get really upset if promises don't materialize. Concessions tend to disappear when the salesperson has promised you the moon, and the person in financing knows nothing about it. Your best tactic here is to walk away quickly if one doesn't honor the other's commitments.

REFUSING TO NEGOTIATE

Some car companies, like the Saturn line or other car types that are in high demand, claim that they don't negotiate. While they might not be flexible on new car price, they can give you a much higher trade-in price, throw in extra accessories, or allow you a lower financing rate. Claiming not to negotiate is a great negotiating tactic or, at the very least, an interesting initial negotiating posture. **Don't take them at their word.** Even Saturn dealerships do sometimes negotiate on car price. In reality, a small percentage are sold below sticker price. My advice: Keep probing for other concessions that effectively lower the price of the car, or shop elsewhere for a better deal.

QUOTING AVERAGES AND STATISTICS

Do long lists of facts, figures, and averages confuse you? If so, then block them out. Another way of dealing with your confusion is to **profess complete ignorance, and then move the conversation to a more comfortable topic**. Here's an example:

> **Sales Manager** (for the third time): And as you can see, you don't have to worry about price when you lease a car, because the average cost of a Rule-of-78 lease is much lower than even a conventional declining loan balance.
> **You:** I still don't understand. What about color of upholstery? What choices do I have?

APPEALING TO YOUR SENSE OF FAIRNESS

Sellers are the only people who ever demand that you recognize their need to make money and get what they consider their due. It is Detroit's responsibility to price its cars correctly and to make profit for the dealerships and sales staff, not yours. **Don't get sucked into this** kind of debate. This is just a **variation on the guilt tactic**.

THE SILENT TREATMENT

When you notice that the salesperson has stopped talking and you begin to feel awkward, you are experiencing the silent treatment. This is your signal to start talking politics, baseball, or cooking. If that doesn't work, it is time to see how quiet he becomes when you walk out of the negotiating room and into the parking lot toward your car. **If silence makes you feel uneasy, don't stand for it.**

"I'm new here"

Any good salesperson will attempt to make you his friend and elicit your sympathy. If he is really new, and naive, you can be sure he has an experienced, strong, and competent sales manager

---

backing him up. But who is going to intercede for you if you make a costly mistake based on his false information? Now is the time to take him at his word and to **ask for someone more experienced**. It's as simple as that.

THE GOOD FAITH DEPOSIT

Giving a deposit is perhaps one of the strongest signs of commitment. Don't do it unless you are prepared to really go through with the deal. If the salesperson will not take an offer to his boss without a check or deposit, demand that he do. Let him know that **until a firm price is agreed on, you will not commit to the sale**. If he refuses, threaten to walk. I guarantee he will chase you into the parking lot.

TAKING YOUR KEYS AND REGISTRATION

It is everybody's nightmare to have the dealer "lose" the keys to the customer's car so that he has to stay and negotiate. Always bring an extra set of keys, and **don't negotiate until you get your keys and registration back**.

"If I can _____, will you_____?"

This is a great technique, and it is used all the time to get a buying commitment from the customer. This technique is designed to see if you are a real buyer, and perhaps to probe your limits. A typical example follows:

> **Salesperson:** If I can get the car in blue at your price, will you buy it right now?
>
> or
>
> **Salesperson:** If I can get my manager to buy your trade-in at your price, will you accept our price for the new car?

The best way to handle this tactic is to become a broken record. **Keep restating your terms**. If he gives you what you want, of course you will buy right then and there, if you want to. Later on, you can change your position if it suits you. After all, you can negotiate from limited authority as well as he can.

INTIMIDATION

At some point in the negotiations, usually an impasse, your salesperson will try to intimidate you by cheerfully inviting you to meet his manager. This is not like meeting the Queen of England. This is the real strong arm, and he looks like he probably eats pit bulls for lunch. He also is pretty busy, so the best way to handle him is to delay, waffle, and then stick to your demands without being intimidated. The manager's job is to spend as much time as it takes to close the sale, so be prepared with some "killer" tactics.

STONEWALLING

Stonewalling, a classic negotiating position, is the granting of concessions slowly and grudgingly. The average person quickly becomes impatient and discouraged, and compromises just to get the negotiations going. To beat this technique, you must **be willing to outwait the salesperson** or to come in at a time that is so inconvenient that all he wants to do is get the transaction over with. This is why starting the buy one to two hours before closing will work well for you.

UPCOMING PRICE INCREASE

This is a scare tactic designed to get you to move really quickly. Typically, the salesperson tries to speed you toward making a decision by indicating that there is going to be a large price increase soon. Therefore, you *must* buy this car now because the price will be 6.8 percent or 10.2 percent or $500 more by the weekend.

The way to handle this is to ask the salesperson to document, through a bulletin or some other printed document, that there is going to be price hike soon. Note the amount and the date it becomes effective, and see if the price rise applies to your chosen car. Make sure it does apply, because some price increases are not on all models.

If the salesperson can't produce documents, consider the statement as hot air and disregard it and go on negotiating at your own speed. If it does apply, note it, and **go on negotiating at your own speed.**

BARGAIN FOR THAT HOUSE LIKE A PRO

from Kiplinger/Changing Times,
Guide to Buying and Selling a Home

You've found the right house and you want to buy it. Starting now, every signal you send the seller, either directly or through an agent, is part of the bargaining process, so be careful what you say and do within earshot of either.

You know what you can afford to pay. Now decide what you are willing to pay for this particular home. There are several ways to go about it. Some methods are more realistic in slow markets when you have plenty of time to make a decision, but all require you to gather certain information.

One thing you can do quickly is get an analysis of comparable properties from your assisting agent. There should be several on the list. Obviously, no two can be exactly alike, but be sure that those being represented as comparable are similar enough to the property you intend to bid on to be useful in setting an offering price. Look at the date of sale for each case on the list. Under normal market conditions, it should be no more than six months old. Note the location. A similar property in a different neighborhood

may not really be comparable at all, and the same house on a prime lot in the same block may be worth more. Examine each property. Comparables should be roughly the same age and condition. The size of the lot, the number of rooms and total square feet should be close.

Finally, scrutinize the terms and conditions of the sale. A property sold with seller financing does not compare directly with one sold using standard financing. For example, if the seller took back a second mortgage at a below-market interest rate, that's the equivalent of a reduction of the sale price, so you should discount the price of the house when you use it for comparison.

If you already know the neighborhood, have obtained good comparables, and have an adequate sense of the seller's motivations, you may be prepared to make an offer without additional advice. But if you're not certain—and if time permits, which is not the case in a hot seller's market—consider paying for an appraisal to determine the value of the property.

An appraisal may cost you a few hundred dollars. Ask several prominent local mortgage lenders for recommendations from their list of appraisers they hire often. You will be required to pay for a lender's appraisal before your mortgage is approved, but if the appraiser you hire before making your offer is on the lender's approved list, you might not have to pay for a second, unnecessary appraisal later. (See "Nail Down What That House Is *Really* Worth," March 1986.)

Price is always important, but it may not be the most difficult part of the deal to agree on. Before you make your first offer, rank the elements of the deal according to your own wants and needs: price, financing, date of possession, extras. Put your priorities down on paper. They will be an important mental tool to employ in evaluating a counteroffer from the seller. Consider how you might accommodate the seller—at the right price.

For example, if the seller must remain in the house for a period after settlement, what would make that worthwhile to you? Do you need financing help from the seller? Would obtaining a price reduction of several hundred dollars, for example, assuage your sense of loss at not having the bedroom curtains included? You probably won't get everything you want, so try to decide in advance what you might be willing to give up in order to complete the purchase or what you might take in exchange for a feature or features both you and the seller really want to keep.

Good negotiating has more to do with knowing exactly what you want from a deal than it does with playing the role of tough bargainer. Whether you should make your highest bid right away or send up a trial balloon in the form of a lower offer depends on how fair you think the asking price is and how brisk the market is—particularly the market for the property you want.

Many asking prices have a good bit of padding built into the price to see whether someone will take the bait. Offer what you think the house is worth—both in broad market terms and to you in particular—based on your study of comparables or the appraisal. If the owner is offended by

a low bid, so be it. You'll find out in the counteroffer or lack of any response when the time limit expires. Conversely, sometimes a house is listed lower than market value, because of owner ignorance or a desire to sell very fast. If you're the only buyer who has spotted this bargain, offering the full asking price is fine, but it might be sold to someone else who offers more than the asking price.

If you decide to try for a lower figure first, don't let the seller's agent know that you are willing to go up. And remember that unless you specifically hired your own "buyer's agent," the agent who helped you find the house also works for the seller because he or she will be compensated out of the sales commission. If during the contract presentation the seller should ask directly whether you might go higher, either agent would be obliged to answer yes.

A SMART BUYER'S CONTRACT

Do all your negotiating in writing. Don't telegraph your strategy verbally, and don't make any verbal offers. A purchase offer in writing can become a binding agreement for both you and the seller. Whether it is called a contract to purchase, an offer, a binder, or an earnest-money agreement—and even if it spells out only the terms of the sale—you can be held to that offer once it is signed by the seller.

So be sure that your first contract submitted is all-inclusive, with everything of any importance written into it; if it's accepted by the seller and you've forgotten to put something you want in writing, it might be too late to add anything. A preprinted form is a good starting point, but you are free to amend or modify it in any way that meets your objectives. (If contingencies are typed onto the back of the preprinted form, they should be initialed by the buyer before the contract is submitted to the seller.) Feel free to have your own attorney draw up a contract or make it contingent on your attorney's review.

Everything of importance should be written into it, including the sales price, down payment, legal description of the property and any items being sold with the home; the way title is to be conveyed; the fees to be paid and who will pay them; the amount of deposit; the conditions under which the seller and buyer can void the contract; the settlement date; how financing will be arranged; and so on.

These are some of the major elements and contingencies to consider inserting in the contract.

- *Earnest-money deposit.* With the exception of court-ordered sales, no law requires buyers to make a deposit of a particular size, or any deposit at all. As a practical matter, however, a seller will look to the deposit as an indication of your serious intentions. If your offer is accepted but you fail to follow through on your commitments, the seller may be entitled to keep the money. The amount of deposit varies with local custom. In some areas it may run as much as 5% or 10% of the sales price. A seller might refuse to consider an offer that is not coupled with a reasonable deposit. Conversely, a large earnest-money check can help swing a deal in your favor.

  If the broker doesn't routinely deposit earnest money in an interest-bearing trust account or with a neutral third party, such as a title company, escrow service, or attorney acting as an escrow agent, insert that requirement in your contract. Also specify that any interest earned on your money will be credited to your side of the ledger at settlement. If your contract does not contain a clause requiring all money to be handled in escrow, insert one. Private individuals are not answerable to any regulatory authority on how they handle funds while a deal is pending. If it goes sour, you might have to sue to get your money back.

The check shouldn't be deposited until the contract has been accepted; write that into the contract. (On the other hand, if the seller has any qualms about your credit worthiness, you can suggest having the check deposited as proof that it's good.)

If your offer is accepted by the seller but the purchase falls apart later through no fault of yours, you should get your money back; a clause in your contract should specify return of the earnest money within a specified number of days if the contract collapses.

- *Settlement agent.* It's usually the buyer's privilege to select the attorney or title company that will perform the settlement services; write the name into the offer contract. If you don't have someone in mind at the time you submit your contract, specify that the settlement agent will be selected by you.

- *Settlement date and possession.* The date of settlement and the date when you will be entitled to take physical possession of your home are stated in the contract.

The settlement date is usually no sooner than the length of time required by the title search and mortgage approval—typically 45 days to 2 months. In a very busy market, such as during the refinancing boom of 1986, mortgage lenders get backed up, so make sure you allow yourself enough time before settlement. This is especially important if you are planning to sell your current house and need to take that equity to the settlement table on the next purchase. If the settlement is too soon, you'll have to seek an extension from the seller or get a bridge loan. If you're a first time buyer without a house to sell and the seller wants a fast settlement, you can oblige the seller and make your offer a little more attractive than that of another buyer who needs a long delay.

Possession usually occurs immediately after settlement. When a buyer needs to move in before settlement or a seller needs to remain after settlement, the preferred procedure is to arrange for a separate rental agreement between the parties. Rent can be set at any agreed-upon level; it's often set at a no-profit "wash" level, with the renter paying exactly the total monthly carrying costs on the house—principal, interest, taxes, utilities, and insurance.

■ *Loan conditions.* Unless you can swing the purchase without a mortgage loan, your contract should make the deal contingent on getting a written loan commitment within a specified time and at terms agreeable to you. The terms should state the maximum interest rate and number of discount points you are willing to pay. That way, should you fail to obtain the desired financing, you will be released from the contract and your deposit will be returned. If your contract is accepted, this clause temporarily takes the property off the market and enables you to shop for a mortgage.

If you went through a prequalifying process with a lender, you'll know what size loan and interest rate you will be eligible for, so use those figures on this section of the contract. Don't put down some unrealistic numbers—a below-market interest rate or bigger loan than you'll be able to manage. These might raise the seller's suspicions and make your offer unattractive compared with others.

Discount points, appraisal fees, and other items must be paid in order to get a loan. Your contract should state how these charges are to be apportioned between buyer and seller.

Just because an agent tells you it's customary for buyers to pay all points (one point equals 1% of the mortgage), that doesn't mean you must do so. In many areas it is common for the seller to help the buyer with financing by agreeing to pay a point or so, which is the same as reducing the sale price by that amount; an anxious seller in a slow market may agree to pay several points.

Finally, if you're proposing that the seller help you with financing, this is where the terms and interest rate must be spelled out.

■ *Sale of current residence.* You might be nervous about committing yourself to a purchase before you've sold your current home. You can add a clause in the purchase contract enabling you to back out of the deal if you don't get a viable contract on your current home within a specified period of time.

Sellers are justifiably leery of this kind of contingency, and a contract containing it will be far less desirable than one that doesn't. Avoid adding this clause unless there are compelling reasons for doing so, and be prepared for the seller to propose a so-called kick-out clause, which allows him to keep the home on the market and force you to remove the contingency or lose the contract if an offer comes along without such a contingency.

■ *Response time limit.* Your contract should require the seller to accept the offer *in writing* (not verbally) within a certain time—such as 48 hours—or the offer becomes void. How long depends on general market activity and buyer interest in that home. Failure to state a time limit invites having your contract "shopped." That means that the seller or agent may use your offer to stimulate slower-moving buyers to top your offer.

You are free to withdraw and cancel an offer at any time before the seller has accepted it. The phrase *time is of the essence* should be included to emphasize the time limit on the offer and the closing date. This does not prevent you or the seller from obtaining a mutually agreed-upon extension, but it precludes unilateral extensions on demand.

- *Home inspection.* This contingency clause should be inserted to give you the right to have the property inspected and to withdraw your offer if the inspection report isn't satisfactory for any reason. The clause might also contain language that will let you negotiate price adjustments to pay for any necessary repairs. Normally, you will not be granted a lot of time because sellers and brokers regard this as a gaping loophole. Buyers with second thoughts might use the report to get out of a deal, so don't be surprised if your seller insists that the inspection be done within a week by a recognized professional. The seller might also request a copy of the report, and that request should be granted.

The critical portion of a typical inspection clause reads: "This contract is contingent on a property inspection report, which, in the sole judgment of the purchaser, is deemed satisfactory." You can see that a contingency clause with that kind of wording leaves a loophole as big as the house itself.

If necessary, offset the negative impact of this clause with a larger earnest-money deposit or some other bargaining chip that will impress the seller with your interest in the property.

- *Termite inspection.* Many contracts today require the seller to order and pay for a termite inspection. The contract should set out the conditions that, if active termites are found, will permit the buyer to void the deal or negotiate with the seller for extermination and repairs.

- *What goes with the house.* It's customary for the seller to leave all major appliances and all built-in things that would normally be considered part of the property, such as lighting devices, wall-to-wall carpet, built-in bookcases, and landscaping. But custom varies from area to area, so you'd better be specific. The more things that are spelled out in the offering contract, the fewer the later misunderstandings.

- *Condition of house at settlement.* The contract should specify that everything in the house will be in demonstrable working order at the time of settlement, as verified during a walk-through of the premises a day or so before settlement. This means mechanical systems like heat, plumbing, and kitchen appliances. If there are any exceptions, they should be noted in the contract, with the notation that certain appliances are being conveyed "as is," with no guarantee made as to working order. It may be impossible to test the air-conditioning during the winter, so it should be noted that the test will be done as soon as temperature permits.

As for cleanliness, the contract should specify that the house will be empty of all stored objects and debris (including things in the attic, basement, and garage) and will be handed over in "broom-clean" condition.

- *Other conditions.* The list could go on and on, but every condition runs the risk of making your offer a little more complicated and a little less appealing than someone else's cleaner contract.

DOWN TO BRASS TACKS

At this point, your offer—signed and all clauses initialed—is presented to the seller, either by you, your attorney, the seller's agent, or the agent who has been assisting you.

You might also want to submit with the purchase offer a simple statement of your creditworthiness. Just as important as the terms of the contract—perhaps more so—is the buyer's ability to get a loan and get to settlement. The seller will be asked to take his property off the market while you arrange financing, so the seller's confidence in your financial strength will play a big role in whether the seller accepts your offer.

The financial statement needn't have a lot of detail, but it should include information about employment, current homeownership, and other assets. If you have already prequalified for a mortgage sufficient to swing this deal, that should be noted in the statement, with the name of the lender. Such information should be checkable by the seller or the seller's agent.

If the seller accepts everything in the contract, initials all clauses, and signs the contract within the acceptance date specified, the offer becomes binding on both parties, subject to removal of the contingencies. Rejection of even the smallest provision of the offer is a rejection of the entire thing. If, however, the seller wishes to negotiate, a counteroffer is made.

The counteroffer typically takes one of three forms: a fresh purchase contract identical to the buyer's offer except for the seller's changes; a counteroffer written on the back of the original or on a separate sheet of paper accepting the buyer's terms, with certain changes as stated; or the original offer marked up with the unacceptable items noted and substitutions proposed. A time limit to accept is added, and the seller signs and dates the counteroffer.

Then it comes to you. If it is acceptable, you sign and date it, and the deal is done. If not, you can allow the counteroffer to expire or you can make a second offer. At this point, you should have a new contract written out. Marking over and initialing extensively on a document can lead to confusion and mistakes.

Sometimes negotiating involves days of offer, counteroffer, offer, counteroffer. More commonly, an agreement is reached on the second or third offer.

If the seller has other contract offers besides yours, he will try to play one against the other, often with verbal messages. Sometimes a seller or seller's agent will not formally counter a contract in writing but will merely tell the prospective buyer that the offer is "too low" and if it's raised to some amount, it will be accepted. Do not raise your offer in response to such verbal signals; the seller has made no commitment to you, and you have no assurance that you'll get the house *even if* you raise your bid. The seller could change his mind again and keep trying to jack up your bid.

Instead, remind the seller that you have a formal offer on the table and you would appreciate a written counterproposal stating whatever higher price or other changes would make your offer acceptable. If the seller responds to your offer in writing, you're still in the ballgame; you can accept the seller's counteroffer and nail down the deal, counter again, or let the response time lapse. Your strategy should be to keep the seller involved with you alone until your negotiation has run its course. Remember that the seller can give a counteroffer to only one buyer at a time; otherwise, the seller would be offering to sell the same house to more than one party and would run the risk that both parties would accept.

How much you bend will depend on how much you want this particular house—which depends on whether you have to buy quickly, the state of the market, and how unusual the house is. If you have the luxury of time and houses similar to this one come on the market with some frequency, don't despair if negotiations break down.

Stick to your main objectives, whether price or some other point. If this house gets away, you might have a shot at a similar one later; it's not unheard of for a house hunter to put in unsuccessful contracts on two or three houses before finally buying. You might even have another chance to buy the first house later on—possibly at a lower price than you originally offered. By the time the seller wises up to the overpricing, the other interested buyers might have bought other houses, leaving you as the only bidder.

If it comes to that, you will have learned one of the most valuable lessons of successful negotiating: Patience pays off in the end.